ADAM SMITH

ADAM SMITH
HIS LIFE, THOUGHT, AND LEGACY

Edited by RYAN PATRICK HANLEY

PRINCETON UNIVERSITY PRESS

PRINCETON AND OXFORD

Published by Princeton University Press, 41 William Street, Princeton, New Jersey 08540

In the United Kingdom: Princeton University Press, 6 Oxford Street, Woodstock, Oxfordshire OX20 1TW

press.princeton.edu

Jacket art: Adam Smith (1723–1790), Scottish author and economics pioneer. Private collection/Bridgeman Images.

Library of Congress Cataloging-in-Publication Data
Adam Smith : his life, thought, and legacy / edited by Ryan Patrick Hanley.
pages cm
Includes bibliographical references and index.
ISBN 978-0-691-15405-3 (hardcover : alk. paper)
1. Smith, Adam, 1723–1790.   I. Hanley, Ryan Patrick, 1974–, editor.
B1545.Z7A63 2015
330.15´3092—dc23   2015014645

British Library Cataloging-in-Publication Data is available

This book has been composed in Sabon and Helvetica Neue by Integrated Publishing Solutions, Grand Rapids, Michigan.

Printed on acid-free paper. ∞

Printed in the United States of America

10 9 8 7 6 5 4 3 2 1

CONTENTS

III. SMITH AND ECONOMICS
• • • •

IV. SMITH BEYOND ECONOMICS
• • • •

V. SMITH BEYOND THE ACADEMY

• • • •

PREFACE

Ryan Patrick Hanley

Right now is the right time to rediscover Adam Smith. For generations Smith was known almost exclusively as capitalism's founding father. But now, around the world, readers are returning to Smith and rediscovering his relevance for our time, within the academy and beyond.

This relevance is in part political. Smith remains famous as one of the first champions of the free market, and his authority continues to be invoked in debates over regulation and deregulation. But now, and indeed more than ever before, the depth of Smith's engagement with several concerns prominent on our own political landscape—from global justice and poverty, to domestic inequality and freedoms, to the moral benefits and challenges inherent to life in a market society—is not only being appreciated, but indeed being appreciated as a valuable source of wisdom as we attempt to navigate these issues in our own right.

Concurrent with this rediscovery of Smith's practical relevance has been a similar rediscovery of Smith in the academy. A generation of excellent revisionist scholarship has put to rest the caricature of Smith as an apostle of selfishness, and in so doing has also reawakened appreciation of his intellectual contributions to fields beyond economics. Thanks to such scholarship, we now appreciate better than ever the depth of his engagements in and contributions to ethics and jurisprudence and rhetoric and the arts—engagements and contributions that are beginning to be explored at ever greater sophistication and depth by scholars in these and other fields.

The present project aims to further such explorations, and in so doing aspires to serve as a "guide" in the truest sense of the word. In particular, it aims to provide nonspecialist readers with introductions to his key ideas, and to provide advanced readers with suggestions as to how certain of these ideas might productively inform and contribute to current live debates in the contemporary academy as well as the contemporary public sphere. In so doing it aims to supplement without duplicating the excellent work gathered in recent volumes such as *The Cambridge Companion to Adam Smith* (2006), *The Elgar Companion to Adam Smith* (2009), and *The Oxford Handbook of Adam Smith* (2013). These volumes afford invaluable, comprehensive studies of key concepts in Smith, and are to be highly recommended to all students of Smith's thought. But the aim of the essays in this volume is somewhat different. Each contributor was asked to provide a short contribution—about one-third of the length of a standard academic essay. Our hope is that such contributions would not aspire to exhaust Smith's thoughts on a given concept or theme, but instead would open up the core elements of his thought on such issues in a manner that would be useful both to nonspecialist readers perhaps coming to Smith for the first time, as well as to more specialized or advanced scholars interested in the question of how engagement with Smith's thought might help to further debates in their own fields of research.

To these ends, the volume is organized into five sections. The first section offers overviews of the key themes of Smith's works as well as the essential details of his life and context. The second section surveys several of the core concepts out of which Smith constructed his vision of what Jerry Muller has called the "decent society"—including especially his concepts of virtue, equality, justice, sympathy, dignity, and freedom. The third section offers a series of reflections on the several lines of influence that Smith's thought exerted on various approaches to economics. The fourth section offers a series of reflections on the ways in which Smith's ideas have been recently taken up in several contemporary academic disciplines ranging well beyond economics—from literature and history and religion to philosophy and law and political science—and presents a series of suggestions as to how further engagement with Smith's thought might advance specific debates in these fields in productive ways. The volume's fifth and final section explores how Smith speaks to contemporary questions in the public sphere by presenting a series of reflections on the relevance of his insights for some of the most pressing questions of practical life today—from growth in the developing world and China, to the transformation of capitalism and the future of free trade, to the seemingly intractable divide between right and left especially evident in recent American politics.

For their efforts in helping to guide us in these inquiries, I am very grateful to our contributors—an outstanding international and interdisciplinary group that includes not only experts on Smith but also experts in fields beyond. I am especially grateful to our contributors for their willingness to take on the challenge of writing pieces that differ somewhat in format from conventional academic essays. I am also deeply indebted to a wonderful team of research assistants—Liliya Yakova, Alan Kellner, Shana Scogin, Brittany Hickman, and Darren Nah—whose collective labors were indispensable to helping to bring this project to press. Finally, I am deeply indebted to the Earhart Foundation for a fellowship instrumental to the completion of my editorial labors on this volume as well as the composition of my own chapter.

Travelers know that good guides offer something other than comprehensive surveys of their subjects. Done well, they afford introductions that entice readers to explore further and to make the most of their own visits. I hope this volume might do something of the same for those coming to Smith for the first time, as well as for those who may have visited with him already.

ABBREVIATIONS

Citations to Smith's works are to the Glasgow Edition as published in hardcover by Oxford University Press and in paperback by the Liberty Fund. Passages in Smith's texts are referenced using the Glasgow Edition's now-standard system of paragraph numbering. The exception is references to his correspondence, which are indicated by letter number. Individual texts take the following abbreviations:

CAS *Correspondence of Adam Smith*, ed. E. C. Mossner and I. S. Ross (1987).

CL "Considerations Concerning the First Formation of Languages," in LRBL.

EPS *Essays on Philosophical Subjects*, ed. W. P. D. Wightman and J. C. Bryce (1982).

HA "The Principles Which Lead and Direct Philosophical Enquiries; Illustrated by the History of Astronomy," in EPS.

HALM "The Principles Which Lead and Direct Philosophical Enquiries; Illustrated by the History of the Ancient Logic and Metaphysics," in EPS.

HAP "The Principles Which Lead and Direct Philosophical Enquiries; Illustrated by the History of the Ancient Physics," in EPS.

IA "Of the Nature of That Imitation Which Takes Places in What Are Called the Imitative Arts," in EPS.

LER "A Letter to the Authors of *Edinburgh Review*," in EPS.

LJ *Lectures on Jurisprudence*, ed. R. L. Meek, D. D. Raphael, and P. G. Stein (1982) [LJA = "Report of 1762–63" and LJB = "Report Dated 1766"].

LRBL *Lectures on Rhetoric and Belles Lettres*, ed. J. C. Bryce (1985).

Senses "Of the External Senses," in EPS.

Stewart "Account of the Life and Writings of Adam Smith," in EPS.

TMS   *The Theory of Moral Sentiments*, ed. D. D. Raphael and A. L. Macfie (1982).

WN   *An Inquiry into the Nature and Causes of the Wealth of Nations*, ed. R. H. Campbell, A. S. Skinner, and W. B. Todd (1981).

Fredrik Albritton Jonsson is Associate Professor of History at the University of Chicago. He is the author of *Enlightenment's Frontier: The Scottish Highlands and the Origins of Environmentalism* (Yale University Press, 2013). His other publications include "Rival Ecologies of Global Commerce: Adam Smith and the Natural Historians," *American Historical Review* 115 (December 2010); "The Industrial Revolution in the Anthropocene," *Journal of Modern History* 83 (2012); and "Adam Smith in the Forest," in *The Social Lives of the Forests*, ed. Susanna B. Hecht, Kathleen D. Morrison, and Christine Padoch (University of Chicago Press, 2013).

Elizabeth Anderson is John Dewey Distinguished University Professor and Arthur F. Thurnau Professor of Philosophy and Women's Studies at the University of Michigan, Ann Arbor. She is a Fellow of the American Academy of Arts and Sciences and author of *Value in Ethics and Economics* (Harvard University Press, 1993) and *The Imperative of Integration* (Princeton University Press, 2010). Much of her work focuses on egalitarianism, including "What Is the Point of Equality?," *Ethics* 109 (1999), pp. 287–337. She is currently working on a history of egalitarianism from the Levellers to the present.

Michaël Biziou is Professor of Philosophy at the University of Nice (France). He works on eighteenth-century British and French philosophy, and has a special interest in Adam Smith and classical liberalism. He has translated into French Smith's *Theory of Moral Sentiments* (Paris, 1999) and his essay on *The Imitative Arts* (Paris, 1997). He has published three books: *Le concept de système dans la tradition anglo-écossaise des sentiments moraux. De la métaphysique à l'économie politique (Shaftesbury, Hutcheson, Hume et Smith)* (Lille, 2000), *Adam Smith et l'origine du libéralisme* (Paris, 2003), and *Shaftesbury. Le sens moral* (Paris, 2005). He has also edited *Adam Smith et la Théorie des sentiments moraux*, a special issue of *Revue philosophique de la France et de l'étranger*, no. 4 (Paris, 2000), and *Adam Smith philosophe. De la morale à l'économie, ou philosophie du libéralisme*, coedited with Magali Bessone (Rennes, 2009).

John C. Bogle is a 1951 graduate of Princeton University, magna cum laude in economics, where he wrote his senior thesis—"The Economic Role of the Investment Company"—on the mutual fund industry. On the strength of that thesis, he entered the mutual fund industry in 1951 and remains an active participant to this day. In 1974, he founded The Vanguard Group of *mutual* (shareholder-owned) mutual funds; in 1975 he created the world's first index mutual fund. That combination led to Vanguard's becoming the world's largest mutual fund firm, with some $3 trillion in US mutual fund assets under management. He is the author of ten books, including *The Clash of the Cultures: Investment vs. Speculation* (Wiley, 2012), *Don't Count on It! Common Sense on Mutual Funds* (Wiley, 2010), and *Enough. True Measures of Money, Business, and Life* (Wiley, 2010), as well as twenty-one essays published in academic journals, primarily the *Journal of Portfolio Management* and the *Financial Analysts Journal*. He has received honorary degrees from fourteen colleges and universities, including Princeton University, Georgetown University, Villanova University, and the University of Delaware and is a fellow of the American Academy of Arts and Sciences.

Vivienne Brown is Emeritus Professor of Philosophy and Intellectual History at the Open University, UK. She is the founding editor of the *Adam Smith Review* (vols. 1–5) and the author of *Adam Smith's Discourse: Canonicity, Commerce and Conscience* (Routledge, 1994). She is interested in issues of methodology in intellectual history, rights, freedom, agency, and game theory; and as a longer-term project she is working toward a collection of essays on Adam Smith.

James Buchan is the author of a history of Edinburgh in the eighteenth century, *Capital of the Mind* (John Murray, 2003)/*Crowded with Genius* (Harper, 2003) and *Adam Smith and the Pursuit of*

Perfect Liberty (Profile, 2006)/*The Authentic Adam Smith* (Norton, 2006).

Remy Debes is Associate Professor of Philosophy at the University of Memphis. His research is in the areas of ethics and the history of ethics, with an emphasis on the Scottish Enlightenment, human dignity, moral psychology, empathy, and the philosophy of emotion. His published work includes "Humanity, Sympathy, and the Puzzle of Hume's Second Enquiry," *British Journal for the History of Philosophy* 15, no. 1 (2007), pp. 27–57; "Dignity's Gauntlet," *Philosophical Perspectives* 2, no. 1 (2009), pp. 45–78; "Adam Smith on Dignity and Equality," *British Journal for the History of Philosophy* 20, no. 1 (2012), pp. 109–40; and "Moral Rationalism and Moral Realism," in *The Routledge Companion to 18th Century Philosophy*, edited by Aaron Garrett (Routledge, 2014). He is currently editing *Dignity: History of a Concept* (forthcoming in the Oxford Philosophical Concepts series) and (with Karsten Stueber) *Ethical Sentimentalism* (forthcoming from Cambridge University Press).

Jerry Evensky is Professor of Economics and Meredith Professor for Teaching Excellence at Syracuse University. He has published a number of articles on Adam Smith in journals, including *History of Political Economy*, *Journal of the History of Economic Thought*, and *Journal of Economic Perspectives*. In 2005 he published *Adam Smith's Moral Philosophy* (Cambridge University Press). His most recent book is *Adam Smith's* Wealth of Nations: *A Reader's Guide* (Cambridge University Press, 2015).

Chad Flanders is Associate Professor of Law at Saint Louis University School of Law. Previously, he was a Fulbright lecturer at Nanjing University, China and a visiting professor of law at DePaul University School of Law. After law school, he clerked on the Alaska Supreme Court in Anchorage, Alaska and the Tenth Circuit Court of Appeals in Salt Lake City, Utah. He has authored over thirty articles and reviews on topics as diverse as election law, law and religion, the philosophy of punishment, as well as Adam Smith.

Samuel Fleischacker is a Professor of Philosophy at the University of Illinois–Chicago. He is the author, most recently, of *The Good and the Good Book* (Oxford, 2015). His prior publications include *A Short History of Distributive Justice* (Harvard University Press, 2004), *On Adam Smith's* Wealth of Nations: *A Philosophical Companion* (Princeton University Press, 2004), and *A Third Concept of Liberty: Judgment and Freedom in Kant and Adam Smith* (Princeton University Press, 1999). He coedited *The Philosophy of Adam Smith* (Routledge, 2010) with Vivienne Brown. From 2006 to 2010, he was President of the International Adam Smith Society.

Gordon Graham is Henry Luce III Professor of Philosophy and the Arts at Princeton Theological Seminary, where he also directs the Center for the Study of Scottish Philosophy and edits the *Journal of Scottish Philosophy*. A graduate of the University of St. Andrews, he was previously Regius Professor of Moral Philosophy at the University of Aberdeen. His most recent book is *Wittgenstein and Natural Religion* (Oxford University Press, 2014), and he is editor of *Scottish Philosophy in the 19th and 20th Centuries* (Oxford University Press, 2015).

Knud Haakonssen is Professor of Intellectual History, University of St. Andrews, and Fellow, Max Weber Center, Erfurt. He is a Fellow of the British Academy and of the Royal Society of Edinburgh. He works on moral, political, and legal thought, especially natural law, 1600–1800. His books include *The Science of a Legislator* (Cambridge University Press, 1981); *A Culture of Rights* (Cambridge University Press, 1991); *Natural Law and Moral Philosophy* (Cambridge University Press, 1996); *Enlightenment and Religion* (Cambridge University Press, 1996); *Cambridge Companion to Adam Smith* (2006); *Cambridge History of Eighteenth-Century Philosophy* (2006); *Northern Antiquities and National Identities* (Royal Danish Academy, 2008); and *Enlightenments and Religions* (Institute for Neohellenic Research, 2010). He is general editor of the *Edinburgh Edition of Thomas Reid* and of *Natural Law and Enlightenment Classics*.

Ryan Patrick Hanley holds the Mellon Distinguished Professorship in Political Science at Marquette University. He is the author of *Adam Smith and the Character of Virtue* (Cambridge University Press, 2009), editor of the Penguin Classics edition of *The Theory of Moral Sentiments* (Penguin, 2010), and past president of the International Adam Smith Society. His most recent book is *Love's Enlightenment: Rethinking Charity in Modernity* (Cambridge University Press, forthcoming).

Lisa Herzog works at the Institut für Sozialforschung and the research cluster Normative Orders at Goethe University, Frankfurt. In 2014–15 she held a postdoctoral fellowship at the Stanford Center for Ethics in Society. Her research focuses on the relation of economics and philosophy, currently focusing on normative dimensions of financial markets and on ethical agency in complex organizations. Her first monograph is *Inventing the Market: Smith, Hegel, and Political Theory* (Oxford University Press, 2013). Her recent articles include "Adam Smith's Account of Justice Between Naturalness and History" (Journal of the History of Philosophy, 2014) and "The Normative Stakes of Economic Growth, or: Why Adam Smith Does Not Rely on 'Trickle Down'" (Journal of Politics, forthcoming).

Lisa Hill is Professor of Politics at the University of Adelaide and previously was a Research Fellow in Political Science at the Australian National University. She is a political theorist and intellectual historian with an additional interest in electoral issues. Her key publications include *The Intellectual History of Political Corruption* (Palgrave Macmillan, 2014, with Bruce Buchan); *The Passionate Society*: *The Social, Political and Moral Thought of Adam Ferguson* (Springer, 2006); and *Compulsory Voting: For and Against* (Cambridge University Press, 2014, with Jason Brennan).

Douglas A. Irwin is Professor of Economics at Dartmouth College and a research associate of the National Bureau of Economic Research. He is author of *Trade Policy Disaster: Lessons from the 1930s* (MIT Press, 2012), *Peddling Protectionism: Smoot-Hawley and the Great Depression* (Princeton University Press, 2011),

Free Trade Under Fire (Princeton University Press, fourth edition 2015), and *Against the Tide: An Intellectual History of Free Trade* (Princeton University Press, 1996), and many articles on trade policy in books and professional journals.

Gavin Kennedy is Professor Emeritus, Edinburgh Business School, Heriot-Watt University, where he taught from 1986 to 2005, and from which he received in 2013 a doctor of letters for his academic research and publications on Adam Smith. His books include *Everything Is Negotiable* (Random House, 1982, five editions); *Pocket Negotiator* (The Economist, 1984, five editions); *New Negotiating Edge: A Behavioral Approach* (Brieley, 1998); *Adam Smith's Lost Legacy* (Palgrave, 2005); and *Adam Smith: A Moral Philosopher and Political Economist* (Palgrave, 2008; second edition, 2010). He is also the author of various chapters on Adam Smith in collections published by Oxford University Press and Palgrave, and articles in such journals as *Econ Journal Watch* (2010), *History of Economic Ideas* (2010), and *Journal of History of Economic Thought* (2012).

Stephen McKenna is Associate Professor of Media and Communication Studies at the Catholic University of America. He is the author of *Adam Smith: The Rhetoric of Propriety* (State University of New York Press, 2006), as well as articles and book chapters on Adam Smith, American presidential rhetoric, and the rhetoric of advertising.

Leonidas Montes is Professor of Economics at Universidad Adolfo Ibáñez, Santiago, Chile, and former Chairman of the Board of Television Nacional de Chile and Dean of the School of Government at Universidad Adolfo Ibáñez. He is the author of *Adam Smith in Context* (Palgrave Macmillan, 2004) and several articles on Adam Smith and the Scottish Enlightenment, and is coeditor, with Eric Schliesser, of *New Voices on Adam Smith* (Routledge, 2006). He is also a former member of the Executive Committee of the History of Economics Society (HES) and a current member of the Board of the International Adam Smith Society (IASS).

James R. Otteson is Thomas W. Smith Presidential Chair in Business Ethics at Wake Forest University. He is author of *Adam*

Smith's Marketplace of Life (Cambridge University Press, 2002), *Actual Ethics* (Cambridge University Press, 2006), *Adam Smith* (Bloomsbury, 2013), and *The End of Socialism* (Cambridge University Press, 2014).

Maria Pia Paganelli is an Associate Professor of Economics at Trinity University. She works on Adam Smith, David Hume, eighteenth-century monetary theories, and the links between the Scottish Enlightenment and behavioral economics. She is the book review editor for the *Journal of the History of Economic Thought* and coedited, with Christopher Berry and Craig Smith, *The Oxford Handbook of Adam Smith* (Oxford University Press, 2013).

Nicholas Phillipson was born in 1937, educated at Aberdeen and Cambridge, and taught history at Edinburgh University from 1965 to 2004. He has held visiting posts at Princeton, Yale, Tulsa, the Folger Shakespeare Library, and the Ludwig-Maximilians Universität, Munich. He was a founding editor of *Modern Intellectual History*. He has published widely on the history of the Scottish Enlightenment. His most recent books are *Adam Smith: An Enlightened Life* (London, 2010) and *David Hume: The Philosopher as Historian* (London, 2011). He is at present working on a history of the Scottish Enlightenment. He lives and works in Edinburgh.

Agnar Sandmo is Emeritus Professor of Economics at the Norwegian School of Economics (NHH) in Bergen. He has published in the areas of the economics of uncertainty, public finance, and the history of economic thought. His books include *The Public Economics of the Environment* (Oxford University Press, 2000) and *Economics Evolving* (Princeton University Press, 2011).

Eric Schliesser is Professor of Political Science at the University of Amsterdam and visiting professor, Philosophy & Moral Sciences, Ghent University, Belgium. He has published widely in early modern philosophy (including papers on Newton, Spinoza, Berkeley, Hume, Kant, Sophie de Grouchy, and Adam Smith) as well as recent philosophy of economics, especially on the so-called Chicago school. He has coedited *New Voices on Adam Smith* (Routledge, 2006, with Leonidas Montes), *Interpreting Newton* (Cambridge University Press, 2012, with Andrew Janiak), *Philosophy and Its*

History (Oxford University Press, 2013, with Mogens Laerke and Justin Smith), and *Newton and Empiricism* (Oxford University Press, 2014, with Zvi Biener). He is working on a monograph on Adam Smith.

David Schmidtz is Kendrick Professor at the University of Arizona. He is author of *Rational Choice and Moral Agency* (Princeton University Press, 1995), *Elements of Justice* (Cambridge University Press, 2006), and *Person, Polis, Planet* (Oxford University Press, 2008) and coauthor of *Social Welfare and Individual Responsibility* (Cambridge University Press, 1988, with Bob Goodin) plus *Brief History of Liberty* (Blackwell, 2010, with Jason Brennan). He currently is working on *Markets in Education* with Harry Brighouse for Oxford University Press. His articles have appeared in journals such as *Political Theory*, *Journal of Philosophy*, and *Ethics*.

Amartya Sen is Thomas W. Lamont University Professor, and Professor of Economics and Philosophy, at Harvard University and was until 2004 the Master of Trinity College, Cambridge. He is also Senior Fellow at the Harvard Society of Fellows, and has served as President of the Econometric Society, the American Economic Association, the Indian Economic Association, and the International Economic Association. His books have been translated into more than thirty languages, and include *Choice of Techniques* (1960), *Growth Economics* (1970), *Collective Choice and Social Welfare* (1970), *Choice, Welfare and Measurement* (1982), *Commodities and Capabilities* (1984), *The Standard of Living* (1987), *Development as Freedom* (1999), *Identity and Violence: The Illusion of Destiny* (2006), *The Idea of Justice* (2009), and (jointly with Jean Dreze) *An Uncertain Glory: India and Its Contradictions* (2013).

Craig Smith is the Adam Smith Lecturer in the Scottish Enlightenment at the University of Glasgow. He is the author of *Adam Smith's Political Philosophy: The Invisible Hand and Spontaneous Order* (Routledge, 2006) and is book review editor of the *Adam Smith Review*.

Vernon L. Smith is George L. Argyros Chair in Finance and Economics and Research Scholar in the Economic Science Institute at Chapman University. His books include *Rethinking Housing Bubbles* (Cambridge University Press, 2014, with S. Gjerstad), *Rationality in Economics: Constructivist and Ecological Forms* (Cambridge University Press, 2008), *Bargaining and Market Behavior: Essays in Experimental Economics* (Cambridge University Press, 2000), and *Papers in Experimental Economics* (Cambridge University Press, 1991).

Jacqueline Taylor is Professor of Philosophy at the University of San Francisco. Her book, *Reflecting Subjects: Passion, Sympathy and Society in Hume's Philosophy*, was published by Oxford University Press in 2015. She has an edited volume, *Reading Hume on the Principles of Morals*, also forthcoming from OUP. Her articles include "Hume on the Reality of Value," in *Feminist Interpretations of David Hume*, edited by Anne Jaap Jacobson (Pennsylvania State University Press, 2000), and "Humean Humanity vs. Hate," in *The Practice of Virtue*, edited by Jennifer Welchman (Hackett, 2006).

Karen Valihora teaches in the English Department at York University in Toronto. Her publications include *Austen's Oughts: Judgment after Locke and Shaftesbury* (Delaware, 2010), which connects the moral philosophy, aesthetics, and literature of the British eighteenth century, and several articles on related subjects, including "Impartial Spectator Meets Picturesque Tourist: The Framing of Mansfield Park," *Eighteenth-Century Fiction* 20 (2007); and "The Judgement of Judgement: Adam Smith's *Theory of Moral Sentiments*," *British Journal of Aesthetics* 41 (2001).

Luo Wei-Dong is Vice-President of Zhejiang University and Professor of Economics. He earned his bachelor's and master's degrees in economics at Hangzhou University, and his doctoral degree in foreign philosophy from Zhejiang University. His major research areas are political economy, development economics, and the history of economic thought, and he is the author of *Sentiments, Order, Virtue: The Ethics of Adam Smith* (published in Chinese by Chinese People's Press, 2006).

Nicholas Wolterstorff is Noah Porter Professor Emeritus of Philosophical Theology, Yale University, and Senior Fellow in the Institute for Advanced Studies in Culture, University of Virginia. He has been president of the American Philosophical Society (Central Division) and is a Fellow of the American Academy of Arts and Sciences. He is the author of, among other books, *John Locke and the Ethics of Belief* (Cambridge University Press, 1996), *Thomas Reid and the Story of Epistemology* (Cambridge University Press, 2004), *Justice: Rights and Wrongs* (Princeton University Press, 2008), and *Understanding Liberal Democracy: Essays in Political Philosophy* (Oxford University Press, 2012). His most recent books include *The Mighty and the Almighty* (Cambridge University Press, 2014), and two volumes of collected essays: *Inquiring About God* and *Practices of Belief* (Cambridge University Press, 2014).

PART I

Introduction: Texts and Context

THE BIOGRAPHY OF ADAM SMITH

James Buchan

The life of the philosopher Adam Smith offers small incident to the biographer. Smith passed much of his life in masculine institutions, such as Glasgow and Oxford Universities and the Scottish Customs Board. He came to London first in his late thirties, traveled abroad just once, to France and Geneva, and did not marry. His chief attachment was to his mother, whose death at a great age prostrated him. Yet this existence, which Smith once called "extremely uniform," has come to fascinate our age. A trickle of biographical studies began to flow at the beginning of the twentieth century and in the past fifty years has become a river.

Smith stands at the point where history changes direction. During his lifetime, between 1723 and 1790, the failed kingdom of drink, the Bible, and the dagger that was old Scotland became a pioneer of the new sciences. God was dismissed from the lecture hall and the drawing room. The old medieval departments of learning disintegrated. Psychology became a study not of the soul but of the passions. Political economy was separated out of moral philosophy and began its progress to respectability and then hegemony. Smith was at the heart of those changes.

Because Smith did his thinking before the French Revolution of 1789 and the division of the political house into left and right, he appeals to both sides: on the left, to Tom Paine, Karl Marx, and Mary Wollstonecraft, on the right to Margaret Thatcher and every business club from Boston to Shanghai. The left Smithians like their hero's devotion to the laboring poor and his contempt for colonialism, the right Smithians his scorn of big government. In the course of the twentieth century, as new biographical materials turned up in the attics of Scottish country houses, each side looked for ammunition to launch at their political rivals.

From this battle, the economists held themselves aloof. Because, in the words of J. S. Mill, modern political economy concerns itself not with the whole of human nature but "only such phenomena of the social state as take place in consequence of the pursuit of wealth," Smith's adventures and exploits were to most economists as uninteresting as the events of any other single life. Even J. M. Keynes, who had a taste for biography, showed little curiosity about Smith's life and times. The revolution in Smith's biography since the publication of his lectures on jurisprudence in 1896 has proceeded without troubling the great mass of economists.

Above all, Smith's life is intertwined with modern biography itself, as inaugurated by James Boswell in his *Life of Samuel Johnson, LL.D* (1791). Boswell had been Smith's pupil at Glasgow University and was entranced one day by a remark of Smith's in lecture that, in the life of a great man, even the smallest detail is of interest. Yet efforts by some authors (including this one) to Boswellize Smith have, for dearth of evidence, been unsuccessful.

These are the facts of Smith's life. Adam Smith was born in the early summer of 1723 in Kirkcaldy, a small port across the estuary or firth of the River Forth from Edinburgh, the ancient capital of Scotland. He was the son of Adam Smith, a commissioner of customs (who had died), and of Margaret Douglas. He was baptized on June 5, 1723. His birth date places him at the heart of a circle of Scotsmen known (since the early twentieth century) as the Scottish Enlightenment. A protégé of the philosophers Henry Home (b. 1696) and David Hume (1711), he was friend and colleague to the literary critic Hugh Blair (1718), the historian William Robertson (1721), the social philosopher Adam Ferguson (1723), and the natural scientists James Hutton (1726) and Joseph Black (1728).

Smith never knew his father, who had practiced as an attorney, supported the Union of the Scottish and English Parliaments in 1707, and was appointed comptroller of customs at Kirkcaldy in 1714. The family thus belonged to the "Whig" interest, supporters of the Protestant faith, a constitutional or limited monarchy under the House of Hanover, and political Union with England and

Wales. During Smith's lifetime, the Whigs triumphed over their principal rivals, the "Jacobites," adherents of the Roman Catholic House of Stuart and old notions of absolute or divine-right monarchy. Much of Scotland fell to a Jacobite insurrection in 1745 before the rebellion was broken up the following year.

From the age of seven, Adam attended the two-room Burgh School in the town (which survives as Kirkcaldy High School) and passed, in 1737, to the University of Glasgow as a stage on the way to Oxford. He was fourteen years old, an age then thought more than ripe for university. At that time, the merchants of Glasgow were beginning to prosper from trade with the British colonies across the Atlantic, including the tobacco states of Virginia and Maryland. At the college, Smith was exposed to several teachers of the first order, including the liberal philosopher Francis Hutcheson (1694–1746), the mathematician Robert Simson (1687–1768), and the natural scientist Robert Dick (d. 1751).

Oxford, in contrast, which Adam Smith attended from 1740 on a forty-pound exhibition or bursary at Balliol College, left no discernible impression. Adam stayed without interruption from July 7, 1740, to August 15, 1746. There is no sign that he made friends at Oxford, and he commemorates not a single of his professors. Years later, in his *Inquiry into the Nature and Causes of the Wealth of Nations*, Smith wrote of certain ancient universities as "sanctuaries in which exploded systems and obsolete prejudices found shelter and protection, after they had been hunted out of every other corner of the world" (WN V.i.f.34). That caused great offense among alumni of Oxford University, such as Dr. Samuel Johnson.

In August 1746, Smith rode back to Scotland. His bursary had destined him for the Episcopalian church, but according to his first biographer, the philosopher Dugald Stewart, Smith had no taste for the "ecclesiastical profession" for which he had been supported in his study. Scotland was still reverberating from the Jacobite rebellion of 1745. Edinburgh was under a cloud for surrendering to the rebels without firing a shot. Smith returned to Kirkcaldy and passes out of view.

He reappears in 1748, with his first published work, an unsigned preface to a collection of verses by a poet in Jacobite exile.

Later that year, under the patronage of the lawyer and philosopher Henry Home, he delivered a series of lectures on rhetoric and jurisprudence in the capital. The lectures, which brought him a hundred pounds (or as much as some college professors), he repeated over the next two winters. He made his most important friendship, with the philosopher David Hume. The popularity of the lectures ensured that when the chair of logic and rhetoric at Glasgow University fell vacant in late 1750, though he was but twenty-seven years old, Smith was elected. He then, in 1752, transferred to Francis Hutcheson's old chair of moral philosophy.

Smith was to spend thirteen years in Glasgow and later described those years "as by far the most useful, and therefore, as by far the happiest and most honourable period of my life" (Stewart V.10). At first, his mother kept house for him, and she was later helped by an unmarried cousin, Janet Douglas, of whom Smith became fond. He engaged himself in university business. In the intervals, he worked up his notes from his ethics course into the first of his two main philosophical works, *The Theory of Moral Sentiments*, which was printed in London in April 1759.

It was a success, praised by David Hume and Edmund Burke, among others, ran through six British editions and one Irish printing in his lifetime, and was translated into French and German. Though eclipsed by the *Wealth of Nations* in the eighteenth century, and neglected by the nineteenth century, the *Theory* has enjoyed a revival.

The *Theory* ended with a promise, which Smith could not keep but never abjured, that he would provide in a forthcoming work a historical "account of the general principles of law and government . . . not only in what concerns justice, but in what concerns police, revenue, and arms, and whatever else is the object of law" (TMS VII.iv.37).

One consequence of the *Theory*'s success was that Smith was asked to accompany as tutor a young nobleman, Henry, Duke of Buccleuch, on a tour of the European continent. The young man's family offered terms that few Scotsmen of that era would have refused: a salary of three hundred pounds per year, traveling expenses, and a pension of three hundred pounds for life. (For modern values, add two zeroes.) Though he was not required to do so,

Smith resigned his chair at Glasgow and set off for France with the seventeen-year-old duke in February 1764.

After a period of inaction in Toulouse, where Smith worked on his next book, they traveled to Geneva and met Voltaire, and then Paris where Smith proved an unlikely success in the salons. Armed with introductions from Hume, he met several philosophers interested in questions of commerce, banking, public credit, and agriculture, such as the tax farmer Claude-Adrien Helvétius, André Morellet, and Anne-Robert-Jacques Turgot, who was to become controller general of French finances in the 1770s. He also consorted with a sect of agricultural theorists, led by the royal physician François Quesnay, known as the *économistes* or, nowadays, *physiocrates*.

This pleasant and productive life came to an end in October 1766, when the duke's younger brother, Hew, who had joined them, fell ill. Quesnay could not save the young man. In great dejection, the party returned to England in November. Smith spent six months in London, reading commercial texts and supervising a third edition of the *Theory*, which also contained a fair copy of one of his rhetoric lectures, "A Dissertation on the Origin of Languages." Smith then returned to his mother and Miss Douglas in Kirkcaldy, where he worked on what was to become the *Wealth of Nations*.

Distracted by a banking crisis in western Scotland, which affected the Buccleuch interests, and tension with the colonists in North America (where Smith supported colonial taxation), progress was slow. His friends despaired that Smith would ever complete what Boswell called his "Jurisprudence." Yet on March 9, 1776, in the midst of the crisis in America, there appeared in London in two volumes quarto *An Inquiry into the Nature and Causes of the Wealth of Nations*, by Adam Smith, LL.D. and F.R.S. (Fellow of the Royal Society), Formerly Professor of Moral Philosophy in the University of Glasgow.

The work was a success. While some critics carped at the book's length and repetitions, or took issue with Smith's views on money and the corn trade, many recognized that Smith had broken new ground. Smith seemed to be laying foundations for a new style of government based not on force, the royal prerogative, religious enthusiasm, or sectional interest but on the impulse of all free men and women "to better their condition." The *Inquiry* was, as Burke put it, "a compleat analysis of society" in respect to not just arts and commerce, but finance, justice, police (public policy), "oeconomy of armies," and public education. The book went through five London editions in Smith's lifetime, and was also printed in Dublin and Philadelphia.

With his *Inquiry* out in the world, Smith could attend to his friend Hume, who was dying. Notorious for his skepticism in matters of religion, or "infidelity" as it was known, Hume died without recourse to clergy in August 1776. Even before his friend's death, Smith was preparing an account of Hume's last illness and of his calm and un-Christian demeanor in the face of extinction.

Smith's eulogy of his friend, written in the form of a letter to their publisher William Strahan and dated from Kirkcaldy on November 9, 1776, cast Hume as a sort of modern Socrates, "approaching as nearly to the idea of a perfectly wise and virtuous man, as perhaps the nature of human frailty will permit" (CAS 178). The letter infuriated the English Christians. Boswell, who under Dr. Johnson's influence had turned against his old teacher, suggested Johnson "knock Hume's and Smith's heads together, and make an ostentatious infidelity exceedingly ridiculous." Smith himself affected to be baffled that such a "very harmless Sheet of paper" had put the revolutionary message of the *Inquiry* in the shade (CAS 208).

Despite misgivings on the part of Smith, the *Letter* did not prevent his public employment. In 1777, death created a vacancy among the five commissioners of the Customs Board in Edinburgh, responsible for collecting duty on imported goods and suppressing smuggling in Scotland. Both the Treasury in London and the historian Edward Gibbon teased the philosopher for applying for so very modest a position. Now "affluent" if not rich on a salary of six hundred pounds per year, Smith tried to give up the Buccleuch annuity, but his pupil, who had more than absorbed *The Theory of Moral Sentiments*, refused. (The present duke once told me that Smith had shaped the history of his family, turning it away from the temptations of London and back toward Scotland.)

Smith moved his mother, Miss Douglas, and his boy cousin and heir, David Douglas, to Panmure House, an old-fashioned building (which survives, much damaged) in the Canongate of Edinburgh. In the next twelve years, Adam became an institution of the Scots capital. As he walked each morning up High Street to the Custom House (which still stands), he was sketched by the barber turned caricaturist John Kay. In one of the pictures that were engraved, Smith is dressed in a coat, wig, and hat, a posy of flowers in his left hand against the stench of the Edinburgh High Street, his cane like an infantry musket at the right shoulder.

Smith had, as he told a French correspondent in 1785, "two other great works upon the anvil; the one is a sort of Philosophical History of all the different branches of Literature, of Philosophy, Poetry and Eloquence; the other is a sort of theory and History of Law and Government. The materials of both are in a great measure collected, and some Part of both is put into tolerable good order. But the indolence of old age, tho' I struggle violently against it, I feel coming fast upon me, and whether I shall ever be able to finish either is extremely uncertain" (CAS 248).

What leisure remained him from his four days a week at the Scottish Customs Smith employed instead in producing a new and cheaper edition of the *Wealth of Nations*. It appeared with the printer Strahan in 1784 and included a new section attacking the trade monopoly and government of the British East India Company in the subcontinent. Smith traveled twice in this period to London, where at some point he sat for the portrait medallion by James Tassie that can be seen (in two states) in the Scottish National Portrait Gallery in Edinburgh. Later that year, he was appointed lord rector of his alma mater, the University of Glasgow. The deaths of his mother (May 23, 1784) and Janet Douglas (1788) left him desolate. His last work was a revision and expansion of *The Theory of Moral Sentiments*, which was printed in early 1790.

As his end approached, Smith despaired of his literary legacy. Looking back on his life's work, he found his masterpieces paltry. According to a visitor, he said, "I meant to have done more; and there are materials in my papers, of which I could have made a great deal. But that is now out of the question" (Stewart V.8n).

Some days before his death, probably Sunday, July 11, he asked one of his friends to burn most of his surviving papers, which was duly done in his presence. Smith died the Saturday following, July 17, 1790. His remains lie in the Canongate Kirkyard in Edinburgh.

The biography, as opposed to the life of Adam Smith, begins with a eulogy delivered by Dugald Stewart, the professor of moral philosophy at Edinburgh, to the Royal Society of Edinburgh on two evenings, January 21 and March 18, 1793. The eulogy was published the following year in the Society's *Transactions* and then, in 1795, in an edition of seven small works that Smith had spared from the flames and given to the scientists Hutton and Black, his literary executors: *Essays on Philosophical Subjects by the Late Adam Smith, LL.D.* Stewart's eulogy was somewhat expanded in a new edition of 1811 and later.

Stewart is a frustrating biographer. He is constrained by the air of repression and even panic that followed the execution of Louis XVI of France in January 1793; by respect for the men and women of Smith's circle still living; and by a reticence all of his own. In a manuscript note he added to his copy of the *Essays*, Stewart says that "in the early part of Mr. Smith's life it is well known to his friends that he was for several years attached to a young lady of great beauty and accomplishment," without giving her a name or address, except to say that he himself had known her in her eighties.

In summarizing the *Wealth of Nations*, Stewart felt stifled (he wrote later) by the political atmosphere of 1793 where "the doctrine of a Free Trade was itself represented as of a revolutionary tendency." Stewart makes a minimum of Smith's French influences. He goes to great pains to quote a manuscript note by Smith (now lost), in which the philosopher claimed that he had the "leading principles" of his political economy as early as 1751, long before he traveled to France. Stewart steers well clear of Smith's religion, or such as there was of it.

Smith comes across as an innocent fellow and political economy as a harmless, technical sort of subject. "He was certainly not fitted for the general commerce of the world, or for the business of active life," Stewart told his auditors (Stewart V.12). Stewart made much of Smith's absentmindedness in company, or what was then called "absence." Edinburgh itself had been transformed into a modern city in the years since the 1745 rebellion, and the memoirists of the new "polite" Edinburgh, such as Henry Mackenzie and Sir Walter Scott, portrayed Smith as a half barbarous relic of the Old Town. Yet even then, his former pupils Boswell and John Millar, the future prime minister Lord Shelburne, and some of the Parisians recollected a more suave and commanding figure.

Stewart also set several hares racing, which his successors have endeavored to run down, long after they had passed under the hedge. What did Smith do or think in those six years at Oxford in the 1740s? What happened to those elements of his "Jurisprudence" lectures that did not make it into the *Wealth of Nations*? And what, precisely, were the manuscripts burned that day in Smith's bedroom at Panmure House, except an "irreparable injury to letters" (Stewart V.8)?

For some time, little was added to Stewart's account. The French Revolution cast a long shadow. William Playfair, in his edition of 1805, condensed Stewart's biography and then digressed to absolve Smith from any influence from France. "There is no connection between Political Oeconomy," Playfair wrote, "and free thinking in matters of religion; and with respect to equality, the division of labour, the basis of wealth, is an eternal bar to it."

In the next three decades, free trade gained ground in Britain. The agitator Richard Cobden traveled "through the length and breadth of this country with Adam Smith in my hand to advocate the principles of free trade," and in 1846 the British Parliament permitted the free import of grain. Yet there was little biographical curiosity. In the new editions of the *Wealth of Nations*, the editors—J. R. McCulloch, the professor of political economy at the University of London (1828), the colonial promoter and scoundrel E. G. Wakefield (1836), and Cobden's disciple Thorold Rogers (1869)—printed Stewart's biography with trivial additions and subtractions. In the dearth of biographical knowledge, the idea that Smith underwent some change of mental course between *Theory* and *Inquiry* surfaced in Henry Buckle's *History of Civilisation* (London: 1861) and among political economists in Germany. The notion that Smith replaced fellow-feeling by self-interest as the basis of his social philosophy has proved impossible to eradicate.

Yet just as the last survivors of the eighteenth century went to their graves, the mid-Victorians began to admire the achievements of that century. Walter Bagehot, a country banker and the second editor of the *Economist* magazine, in an essay on Smith in the *Fortnightly Review* in 1876, took a new approach. He saw that the *Wealth of Nations*, whose centenary he was celebrating, was

> in the mind of its author only one of many books, or rather a single part of a great book, which he intended to write. A vast scheme floated before him, much like the dream of the late Mr. Buckle as to a "History of Civilisation," and he spent his life accordingly, in studying the origin and progress of the sciences, the laws, the politics, and all the other aids and forces which have raised man from the savage to the civilized state. He wanted to trace not only the progress of the race, but also of the individual; he wanted to show how each man being born (as he thought) with few faculties, came to attain to many and great faculties. He wanted to answer the question, how did man—race or individual—come to be what he is?

In a word, wrote Bagehot, unable to resist the gag, Smith wanted to demonstrate how "from being a savage, man rose to become a Scotchman."

Bagehot was followed in 1895 by John Rae with a full biography, *Life of Adam Smith*. This work, while not discussing Smith's writings, included many anecdotes of Smith, and much circumstantial information. Its fault, as W. R. Scott put it in the 1930s, was that Smith himself was somehow "absorbed in the background, so that there is, in reality, no adequate explanation of the essential qualities of heart and mind" that produced the *Wealth of Nations*.

That year occurred the revolution in Smith's biography, when Edwin Cannan, of the London School of Economics, received from his friend, the attorney Charles Maconochie, a manuscript set of lecture notes that Maconochie had found in 1876 in a garret of the family estate in West Lothian, Meadowbank House. Labeled on the front "Juris Prudence" and dated 1766, the notes appeared to Cannan to be a professional copyist's version of Smith's lectures of the winter of 1763–64.

Cannan set about reconstructing the rock or matrix from which the *Wealth of Nations* was cut. Noting that the lectures were delivered before Smith ever saw France, he judged that there was far more in the *Wealth of Nations* of Hutcheson than of Turgot. He also doubted whether the phantom third work on the principles of law and justice (mentioned at the end of the *Theory* and the 1785 letter) "ever consisted of very much more than those parts of the lectures on justice which were not incorporated in the *Wealth of Nations*." That judgment holds to this day.

The Maconochie lectures were just the first to turn up. A second set, found by John M. Lothian at the auction of the contents of an Aberdeenshire country house in 1958, appeared to cover lectures from the previous winter of 1762–63. A third set, consisting of partial notes of the jurisprudence lectures one year in the 1750s and preserved by Smith's Glasgow colleague John Anderson in his commonplace book, was published by R. L. Meek in 1976. In addition, notes of the lectures on rhetoric at Glasgow of 1762–63, bought by Lothian at the same Aberdeenshire country house sale in 1958, were published in 1963 as *Lectures on Rhetoric and Belles Lettres Delivered in the University of Glasgow by Adam Smith. Reported by a Student in 1762–63* (London: 1963). Truly, the Scots never throw anything away.

Meanwhile, a hoard of James Boswell's papers, first his letters to his friend William Temple in 1857 and then, in a flush after 1925, letters and journals from Malahide Castle, near Dublin, Ireland, and Fettercairn House, Kincardine, brought Smith's age and circle to life. In the 1920s, W. R. Scott examined the archives of Glasgow University to reveal Smith as a conscientious administrator and "business man." His book, *Adam Smith as Student and Professor*, appeared in a handsome edition in 1937 on the second centenary of Smith's matriculation at Glasgow. Scott also found in the

Buccleuch papers an early draft of the *Wealth of Nations*, copied out in Glasgow and therefore before 1764, and two fragments on the division of labor. Beginning in 1894, James Bonar and others reconstructed the library Smith had installed at Panmure House. The most important pieces of furniture from Panmure House were identified and located.

After World War II, and the vogue for nationalized industry and state welfare systems, Smith's reputation entered a sort of recession. Nonetheless, knowledge of eighteenth-century Scotland continued to expand, most notably through E. C. Mossner's biography of Hume and the work of North American scholars, such as Richard B. Sher, on the eighteenth-century book trade and the Scottish Presbyterian church or Kirk. The great revival in Smith's influence, evident in the House of Commons and the US Congress after 1979, was presaged by the publication of the bicentenary Glasgow Edition of all of Smith's works, his lectures and his letters, in 1976.

In the sheds and outbuildings of that great scholarly edifice, the editors Campbell and Skinner (London: 1982) and D. D. Raphael (Oxford: 1985) put their hands to biography. Raphael made a point that now seems obvious. Both *Theory* and *Inquiry* are littered with passages that show how much Smith went out into the world. He had watched greyhounds course a hare and people twist and turn their bodies in sympathy to keep aloft a dancer on a slack rope. The main biographical effort of the Glasgow editors was that of the Canadian scholar, I. S. Ross, *The Life of Adam Smith* (Oxford: 1995). In *Adam Smith and the Pursuit of Perfect Liberty* (2006: in the United States *The Authentic Adam Smith*), this author, drawing on fugitive passages in Smith's own writings and those of Boswell and other memoirists, emphasized Smith's despondency and found its source in his orphan condition. That approach has found small echo in the learned world.

That leaves the most recent biography to hand, Nicholas Phillipson's *Adam Smith: An Enlightened Life* (2010). Phillipson's chronology is distinctive. For Phillipson, Smith was reading Epictetus in the schoolhouse in Kirkcaldy at age thirteen and had the rudiments of the division of labor and commercial liberty by the late 1740s. Phillipson devotes a "conjectural" chapter to reconstructing lectures on jurisprudence that, on the evidence of the passage in Stewart quoted above, Smith seems to have delivered in Edinburgh in the winter of 1750–51. One effect of this chronology is that Phillipson's Smith has done all his important thinking by his thirties, leaving more leisure than many imagined for university business, the Scottish Customs, advice to ministers in London, and the management of the Buccleuch estates. From all we know of how lives unfolded in the eighteenth century, that sounds spot-on.

Phillipson's Smith is "tough-minded" and "ambitious." Far from being the unworldly chap of Stewart or an economist of modern character and habits, Phillipson's Smith passed a long life wrestling with a stupendous theory of everything. Phillipson calls this project the science of man, in which introspection in the manner pioneered by David Hume and a profound study of ancient and modern history lay bare the principles of social organization, the well-springs of the arts and sciences, and the ideal government and code of laws. Such an enterprise, ambitious even in antiquity, was in the wide world of the eighteenth century excessively so. No doubt that is why Smith felt that he had failed.

It is now accepted by all but the dyed-in-the-wool "Hidden Hand" ideologues that Smith's legacy is a vast ruin field of thought, a sort of Palmyra or Persepolis, in which two monumental columns survive erect and intact amid stones half achieved or half demolished. It is one of the sights of philosophy and, as the old Michelin tourist guides used to say, merits the detour.

It is hard to imagine that there is much to add to Phillipson, but that is also what the Victorians had to say about Stewart, and they were wrong. There may yet be, in some attic or linen press in one of the Buccleuch houses or some edition of Aristotle rattling around in the secondhand book trade, old notes or letters that might unblock a window onto the life of Adam Smith. We need to know more about the period in France. (An Edinburgh bookseller told W. R. Scott that he had sold a travel diary in Smith's hand, but had forgotten to whom, the ninny.) Phillipson calls for a redoubled effort: "There is still biographical work to be done."

BIBLIOGRAPHIC ESSAY

As detailed above, key biographical studies of Smith include Dugald Stewart, *Account of the Life and Writings of Adam Smith, LL.D* (1793), now republished in the Glasgow Edition volume of EPS; Walter Bagehot, "Adam Smith as a Person" (1876), available in vol. 7 of *The Works and Life of Walter Bagehot* (London: 1915); John Rae, *Life of Adam Smith* (London: 1895); Ian S. Ross, *The Life of Adam Smith*, 2nd ed. (Oxford: 2010); and Nicholas Phillipson, *Adam Smith: An Enlightened Life* (London: 2010).

2

THE *LECTURES ON RHETORIC AND BELLES LETTRES*

Vivienne Brown

1. SMITH'S LECTURES ON RHETORIC

The sociality of human life is fundamental for Adam Smith's writings. Human beings are social beings; any inquiry into ways of life, history, or morals must start from an understanding of this sociality rather than from any notion of an individual abstracted from social context. An important part of this sociality is given by language and discourse with others, whether this is everyday conversation, public speaking, learned writings, literature, or theater. It is perhaps not surprising then that Adam Smith's first lectures after his university studies (at Glasgow and then Oxford) were on rhetoric and belles lettres (polite learning).

These first lectures were delivered to a public audience in Edinburgh (1748–49) and were so successful that Smith was invited to repeat them in the following two years. Smith then lectured on rhetoric and belles lettres at the University of Glasgow (1751–63), where he was professor of logic and later of moral philosophy. Apart from Lecture 3, on the origin and development of language,[1] these lectures were unpublished. Although they were influential at the time, later scholars could only glimpse their content from other people's account of them until student notes of the Glasgow lectures, titled "Notes of Dr. Smith's Rhetorick Lectures," were discovered in 1958 at the sale of a manor house library in Scotland. These student notes were published in 1963 under the title *Lectures on Rhetoric and Belles Lettres* (LRBL). Smith's interest in literature and belles lettres continued into later life, but his projected volume on "a sort of Philosophical History of all the different branches of

Literature, of Philosophy, Poetry and Eloquence," as he put it in 1785 (CAS 248), was never completed. All we have now are the student notes of the 1762–63 lectures—almost complete but with Lecture 1 missing.

We do not know whether Smith changed his lectures on rhetoric during his time at Glasgow; nor do we know whether he was further developing his views on rhetoric and belles lettres after he left Glasgow. We do not know whether his later work in revising *The Theory of Moral Sentiments* or in writing (and later revising) the *Wealth of Nations* might have prompted some changes to his views, nor whether in planning his philosophical history of the subject he was developing it in new ways or simply putting the finishing touches to a system he had finalized many years earlier. Smith was a meticulous writer and had such anxiety about unpolished versions of his work reaching the public that, shortly before his death, he ordered all his working manuscripts to be burned. He also disliked the practice of note taking at lectures; the student notes that we have seem to have been written up after the lectures took place. We can be fairly certain, therefore, that Smith would be horrified to think that scholars would read the student notes of his lectures as if they were a finished statement of his mature views.

2. MODERNIZING RHETORIC

As a polymath with deep interests in philosophy, history, natural science, the history of language, and all forms of literature and writing, at home in the ancient classics as well as in English and French (and some Italian) literature, Smith was well placed to develop a modern conception of rhetoric. Furthermore, the time was ripe. Mid-eighteenth-century Scotland was experiencing the economic and political benefits of the 1707 Act of Union and was becoming more confident of its role within an English-speaking Britain. Its universities were modernizing the curriculum, and its political and social elites were ready to embrace improvement and modernization. The moment was thus propitious for forward-looking public intellectuals to help shape civil society; moreover, it did Smith no harm in the eyes of the Scottish literati that his six years of study at Oxford had more or less dissolved his Scottish accent.

Smith was well versed in the classical rhetoric of Aristotle and Cicero, but he was a proponent of what was then the modern approach to rhetoric. The coverage of rhetoric was being extended from public speaking or oratory, which was the core of classical rhetoric in the civic life of ancient Greece and Rome, to include learned and literary forms of discourse, including fine writing, polite learning, and the new scientific writing of the time. The modern aesthetic of writing and speaking valued plain language over what had come to be seen as "flowery eloquence," that is, an excessively ornamental form of language overladen with figures of speech and Latinate expressions that had become popular in Renaissance approaches to rhetoric in the sixteenth century. This plain language approach had been advocated by John Locke and members of the Royal Society of London in the seventeenth century, particularly for works of instruction such as the natural sciences and philosophy. Smith was thus involved in the process of reworking long-established rhetorical traditions.

Smith's lecture courses on rhetoric seem to have hit the right note at the right time. The lecture course at Glasgow might be thought of as a sort of writing and literary appreciation course for young gentlemen, ranging widely over ancient and modern authors, and including histories, essays, poetry, oratory, and works of instruction. It combines discussion of principles of good writing, modes of argumentation, and forms of intellectual inquiry, in the context of an overview of authors with which educated young men were expected to be familiar. The course also includes practical discussion of good writing and oratory, such as might be useful for students in their present studies as well as future duties in public life. In line with the modern view, Smith recommends a clear, plain, grammatically correct style. He also gives practical advice on writing, for example, on how to construct effective sentences (put what's important at the front).

In establishing principles of literary appreciation, the rhetoric course also provides guidelines for an appropriate decorum of expression for young men at the start of their careers, and Smith's analysis of the characters of the various authors and orators as disclosed in their writings also emphasizes the importance of good character. Smith's course on rhetoric was thus not only an academic analysis of different genres of writing and exposition, but also in part a practical and ethical education relating to linguistic communication for students growing up in an increasingly commercial, cosmopolitan, and scientifically informed world.

3. THE RHETORICAL THEORY OF LRBL

Presumably Smith used Lecture 1 to outline the distinctive features of his approach and indicate how the course was to be structured. Lecture 2 then opens with detailed remarks on clear writing, avoiding ambiguity and using native English words whenever possible.

Of the five traditional parts of classical rhetoric—style, invention, arrangement, memory, and delivery—Smith was most concerned with style (*elocutio*). Excellence of style had come to be associated with a highly ornate style with abundant use of the various figures of speech of which the rhetoric books at the time provided exhaustive lists and subdivisions. Smith dismisses this approach, saying that such books were generally "very silly" (LRBL i.v.59). Smith argues that plain style and propriety of language suited to the character of the author facilitate clear expression of the author's thoughts and sentiments: "When the sentiment of the speaker is expressed in a neat, clear, plain and clever manner, and the passion or affection he is possessed of and intends, *by sympathy*, to communicate to his hearer, is plainly and cleverly hit off, then and then only the expression has all the force and beauty that language can give it. It matters not the least whether the figures of speech are introduced or not" (LRBL i.v.56, emphasis original). Although Smith argues, against the rhetorical tradition, that figures of speech have no intrinsic value and add beauty only if they happen to be "just and naturall forms" of expressing the author's thoughts (i.v.56), he adheres to tradition in emphasizing the importance of an author's communication with his audience. Beauty of style also partly depends on its appropriateness, or propriety, in expressing an author's thoughts such that they are clear and pleasing to his audience. In explaining this Smith relies on the notion of "sympathy." This term is not explained in LRBL, although it is important in *The Theory of Moral Sentiments*, published a few years previous to the 1762–63 delivery of the course. Smith seems to be saying that it is by "empathy" with his audience that an author understands how to communicate his thoughts and feelings to them.[2]

Smith's rhetorical theory focuses on different forms of discourse with their distinctive styles. He identifies four main forms of discourse or styles of composition: poetic, narrative/historical, didactic, and rhetorical/oratorical.

Poetic discourse is aimed at providing amusement and entertainment. Smith expresses a preference for verse rather than prose because conciseness, harmony, and regular movement are beautiful and powerful in their effects. Here too the beauty of a plain style is noted, even for verse (see esp. Lectures 7 and 21, e.g., LRBL i.75).

Narrative discourse aims to narrate facts. This includes the genre of historical writing but also description generally and narration of facts in other genres. Smith argues that good writers explain causal relations between events, eliminating any "gaps" in the train of events they are recounting (LRBL ii.32, 36). Two sorts of facts are differentiated, "external facts," which are events that take place in the world, and "internal facts," which are thoughts and designs in people's minds. Smith recommends indirect description for portraying emotions. This involves describing the effects of emotions on the person concerned or on spectators at the time, rather than trying to describe the emotions themselves. Smith argues that this indirect method of description draws the reader to enter into the emotions and sympathize with the person concerned, thus experiencing the same emotions albeit at one remove, although the most extreme emotions can hardly be described at all, even indirectly. This sympathetic aspect of indirect description has instructional value for readers and has resonances with TMS, where spectators approve of others' emotions to the extent that they can enter into them (LRBL i.181–84, ii.5–8, 16–17, 28).[3]

Didactic and rhetorical discourses are the other two forms of discourse. They are similar insofar as they both aim to prove some proposition. Smith argues that didactic discourse fairly puts the arguments on both sides and tries to persuade no further than the arguments are convincing. Rhetorical (also called oratorical) discourse, by contrast, has persuasion as its main objective, and so it magnifies the arguments on the one side and excites the audience's emotions in its favor. Both discourses consist of two parts, the proposition that is laid down and the proof of that proposition, but in the case of didactic discourse the proof applies to "our reason and sound judgment," whereas in the case of rhetorical discourse the proof is designed to "affect our passions and by that means persuade us at any rate" (LRBL ii.14; also i.149–50, ii.13).

When the aim of the didactic writer is to deliver a system of knowledge, rather than to prove a single proposition, the structure of the argument becomes more complicated in involving "a long deduction of arguments." Two contrasting approaches are presented. One approach is to lay down just one or a few general principles by which the various rules and phenomena might all be explained in terms of a single chain of reasoning. This is the most satisfying and elegant approach, and its greatest exponent was Sir Isaac Newton, whose theory of gravity and planetary orbit was regarded as the most brilliant achievement of modern natural science. This accordingly is called the "Newtonian" method and is hailed as "undoubtedly the most Philosophical," on largely aesthetic grounds: "It gives us a pleasure to see the phaenomena which we reckoned the most unaccountable all deduced from some principle (commonly a well-known one) and all united in one chain" (LRBL ii.133–34).[4] This is contrasted with the "Aristotelian" method, which explains each phenomenon in terms of a separate principle. Smith is critical of the Aristotelian method because it lacks a unifying principle of explanation.

Smith's account of rhetorical discourse follows the ancient division of eloquence into demonstrative (panegyric), deliberative (legislative), and judicial (LRBL ii.97). In the case of deliberative eloquence there are two ways of proceeding (LRBL ii.135–37). If the audience is thought to be prejudiced against the orator, he should draw the audience gently over to his side, not telling them in advance what he is going to argue as that might turn them against him, but leading them along gradually. This is the "Socratic"

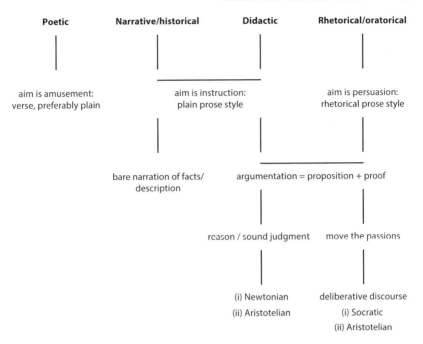

Figure 2.1. Four kinds of discourse/styles of composition.

method, the "smoothest and most engaging manner," although it does involve some deception in initially keeping from the audience what is to be argued. If, however, the audience is thought to be favorable to the orator's position, he should affirm at the outset what he is to prove and then proceed to adduce his arguments for it and controvert anything that goes against it. This, the "Aristotelian" method, is held out as "harsh and unmannerly."

These four kinds of discourse are summarized in figure 2.1, which illustrates that two different criteria are used to categorize the different discourses: style, which is determined by the aim of the discourse, and content, such as narration of facts or argumentation. On the criterion of style, narrative/historical and didactic discourses adopt a plain style as they both have the aim of instruction, whereas rhetorical/oratorical discourses have a rhetorical style as they aim at persuasion. On the criterion of content, didactic and rhetorical/oratorical discourses are similar in that both provide argumentation, although the different aims of these discourses determine the different ways in which they formulate their proofs.

Smith's discussion of style and kinds of discourse indicates that his rhetorical theory is based on a "communication" model of language, according to which language is used by an author (speaker or writer) to transmit his thoughts to an audience. Beauty of style is achieved when this communication from author to audience takes place without hindrance. Plain language is most admired because it provides a transparent medium through which the author's thoughts and feelings can be transmitted.

4. ISSUES FOR RHETORICAL THEORY

In spite of the modernity of Smith's approach to rhetoric, a number of long-standing issues about rhetoric are illustrated by Smith's arguments in LRBL.

One issue concerns the scope and bounds of "rhetoric." Classical rhetoric primarily concerned public speaking with its aim of persuading an audience. This focus can be understood in terms of the importance of effective public speaking, for example, in public debates and in the law courts, as part of the civic life of ancient Greece and Rome. Speeches can be written down, however, and it is in written form that ancient speeches, such as Cicero's, have come down to us. This implies a fluidity between oral and written forms, including genres as diverse as political and legal speeches, lectures, plays, poetry, storytelling, philosophical dialogues, and sermons. This fluidity in turn suggests that written discourses are also included within the concerns of rhetoric if they are directed at an audience. But this then raises a question of the boundaries of "rhetoric." In one sense, all written discourses are aimed at an audience, whether the aim is persuasion, entertainment, instruction, or a combination of these. Smith's rhetorical interest in fine writing and polite learning of all kinds, in addition to the traditional area of oratory, illustrates this expansion of rhetorical application. But the problem now is that, if all or even most human communication is deemed rhetorical, the term begins to lose its meaning. At least one twenty-first-century historian of rhetoric has argued that "[h]istorians of rhetoric must face the question of where the line between rhetoric and non-rhetoric ought to be drawn."[5]

Another issue concerns the intellectual and moral status of rhetoric. Since Plato, a strand of European intellectual culture has criticized "rhetoric" for pursuing persuasion at the cost of truth and arousing the passions of the audience instead of engaging their intellects. Plato's contrast of rhetoric with philosophy, for example, in *Gorgias* and *Phaedrus*, depicts rhetoric as the "other" of philosophy—as persuasion in contrast with the search for truth, as the manipulation of passion in contrast with the cultivation of reason. If we take the narrow-scope understanding of rhetoric, this criticism is localized to specific types of discourse. "Oh, that is just rhetoric," we might say of some flamboyant speech. Yet, if we accept that persuasion is an aspect of all discourse, the simple binary distinction between rhetoric and other forms of discourse begins to dissolve: philosophical works also seek to persuade, and the language of reason, or reasonable language, is not immune to emotive or figurative expressions.

On the other hand, even narrow-scope rhetoric has been valued for its contribution to making complicated arguments more orderly in presentation. Classical rhetoric also includes consideration of the ethics of public speaking, with a concern for propriety in address, good character in the author, and consideration of the audience—or, at least, with a concern for the appearance of such things. In view of this, defenders of rhetoric have argued that criticism of rhetoric's arts of persuasion is really criticism of the abuse of rhetoric rather than of rhetoric itself.

There is thus an ambiguity about both the scope and status of "rhetoric." Narrow-scope rhetoric applies to a restricted field of discourse where the arts of persuasion are particularly important, whereas wide-scope rhetoric applies across many if not all fields of discourse. The status of rhetoric is similarly ambiguous. Sometimes the term "rhetoric" is pejorative, dismissing a discourse as manipulative. Yet, in another sense, much of human discourse is "rhetorical" in that it is aimed at a particular audience, for a particular purpose, and follows (or adapts) the current conventions in doing so. This ambiguity is significant because it raises a question about the communication model of language. If much of human discourse is rhetorical in some sense, this suggests that language is not simply a transparent medium through which an author transmits his thoughts to others, but functions in a myriad of different ways to please, inform, persuade, amuse, deceive, and so forth.

5. APPLYING SMITH'S RHETORICAL THEORY TO LRBL

These long-standing ambiguities about rhetoric are also evident in LRBL. There is a double meaning of "rhetoric" in LRBL where it functions as the name of both a genus and a species. The LRBL refers to itself as "a system of Rhetorick," thus apparently endorsing a wide-scope sense of the term (LRBL i.v.59). This suggests that the study of rhetoric is akin to a combination of the cultivation of taste in literary matters and an intellectual appraisal of forms of argumentation. On the other hand, "rhetoric" is a derogated term applied to discourses that are dominated by the attempt to persuade at all costs. In the scheme of discourses/styles of composition, rhetorical discourse is contrasted with didactic discourse, and at these moments LRBL reproduces the binary distinctions between reason and passion, truth seeking and mere persuasion, that are frequently used against rhetoric.

Smith's distinction between didactic and rhetorical discourses, however, is not easy to maintain in practice. Didactic writers sometimes assume "an oratorical stile tho it may be questioned whether this be altogether so proper," and it turns out that the only writers who consistently adhere to the didactic style are Aristotle (who comes off worse in comparison with both the Newtonian and Socratic methods) and Machiavelli, with Cicero adopting a mixed style (LRBL i.84–85). It thus turns out that, in practice, didactic discourse finds it hard to do without elements of rhetorical discourse; and Aristotle, who does adhere to the didactic method, is compared unfavorably with others. This suggests that, in practice, an austerely didactic style, to the extent that it is possible, might not always be the most effective.

Smith's recommendation of plain style, even for poetry, rejects a traditional view that figures of speech are beautiful in their own right. Yet the distinction between plain style and rhetorical effect is not always easy to maintain in practice. Smith extols the plain style of Jonathan Swift, for example, whose writings "are so plain that one half asleep may carry the sense along with him" (LRBL i.10).[6] But Swift was one of the greatest prose satirists of the English language. Even a plain style may be used to rhetorical effect; for example, to take Swift's arguments in *A Modest Proposal* at face value would be to entirely misunderstand them.[7] Furthermore, Smith here recommends plain style using metaphor, that even "one half asleep may carry the sense along with him." This is in contrast with writing that is so burdened with figures of speech that it is hard to understand: "[s]tudying much to vary the expression leads one [the author] also frequently into a dungeon of metaphorical obscurity" (LRBL i.13). Here excessive metaphor is criticized using the metaphor of a dark dungeon. How are we to interpret LRBL at this point? Perhaps Smith was being ironic, or was parodying figurative usage in order to amuse his young students. Suggesting that "one half asleep may carry the sense along with him" might have been a jokey reference to the sleepy state of his students. Mention of a dark "dungeon" might also be thought to raise a smile among his young male audience. Or perhaps these figures of speech are just a "natural" form of expression for Smith in making vivid the advantages of plain speech.

On the other hand, these metaphors might be considered as linguistically complex. The expression "carry the sense along with him" might be thought to evoke the etymology of the word "metaphor," which derives from the Greek word, *metaphora*, meaning literally "carrying across," "transference." Smith's expression here might thus be interpreted as a metaphor that involves a wordplay on the notion of "metaphor." The second figure also involves a play on words, on the nonnative word "obscurity," which derives from the Latin *obscurus*, the literal meaning of which is "covered," and by extension "dark" or "unintelligible." The dungeon metaphor is also drawing on a classic metaphor that associates light with understanding and knowledge (as in the term "Enlightenment," now used to characterize Smith's own period) and darkness with ignorance (as in the epoch known as the Dark Ages). The success of both these metaphors might be thought to rely on Smith's knowledge that his students had sufficient Greek and Latin to pick up, even enjoy, the wordplay that they involve. Alternatively, perhaps "carry the sense" and "obscurity" should be regarded as dead metaphors, with no intended play on classical etymology.

It is thus difficult to know how these metaphors should be interpreted. Were they deliberate, a professor's attempt to amuse his audience of young students? Or were they perhaps unintentional, examples of the kind of spontaneous use of figures of speech that come so naturally. But, even the notion of "natural" in LRBL is not straightforward. Smith commends a "natural" way of speaking and writing, yet he also explains that the plain style is not itself "natural" as it is the modern style of the educated classes, those of "rank and breeding" (LRBL i.5–7). The plain style is not the way of speaking that comes "naturally" to all classes. Indeed, the "lowest and most vulgar conversation" is packed with figures of speech; as Smith puts it, referring to the fish market in London, the "Billingsgate language is full of it" (LRBL i.76). Restraint in speech and dress, by contrast, is particularly the way of the English educated classes (LRBL ii.249–50). The plain style, although held out as being natural, is thus as much of a rhetorical style—in the sense that it is designed to appeal to a specific, that is, an educated eighteenth-century British audience—as a highly ornate one. It was one of the aims of Smith's lecture course to inculcate this more refined way of speaking and writing among his students.

Interpreting Smith's lectures on rhetoric is thus not entirely straightforward. This section has considered the metatheoretical question of the "reflexivity" of Smith's lectures on rhetoric, that is, whether the lectures enact the rhetorical theory they present. Although the lectures are mostly written in plain style, ambiguities about the scope of rhetoric and issues of interpretation suggest some difficulties for the communication model of language they espouse.

6. APPLYING SMITH'S RHETORICAL THEORY
TO HIS PUBLISHED WORKS

The Theory of Moral Sentiments and the *Wealth of Nations* deal with different subject matter, but the rhetorical theory of LRBL suggests that they have it in common that they are both complex rhetorical works. As such they are candidates for rhetorical analysis.

One question is whether TMS and WN correspond to the forms of discourse in figure 2.1. Both TMS and WN are serious works of learning and instruction, written mainly in the plain style. As examples of didactic discourse, their style might be thought of as Newtonian in that each provides a detailed development of a single overarching principle. In the case of TMS, the notion of "sympathy" is introduced in the first chapter and forms the basis of the account of social and moral judgment; and in the case of WN, the "division of labor" is introduced in the first chapter and forms the basis of the analysis of markets, production, capital investment, and the system of natural liberty. It would be stretching the point, though, to say that these entire books are composed of a series of "deductions" from the principles introduced in the opening chapter.

In some other respects, these works do not satisfy all the characteristics of didactic discourse. Didactic discourse puts the arguments fairly on both sides (LRBL i.149). This is not really the case for TMS or WN. In TMS other systems of moral philosophy are not considered until the final Part VII of the book, and mostly the treatment there (apart from Stoicism) is cursory. The treatment of other systems (apart from Stoicism) is more or less to showcase what is distinctive about Smith's own theory and the extent to which the other systems correspond with his own. In the WN other systems (mercantilism and physiocracy) are not considered until the penultimate part (Book IV), which is directed to showing why they are both erroneous. In TMS and WN, therefore, the style of the comparison is to give pride of place to Smith's own system and then argue against other systems, or in the case of systems that are similar, acknowledge wherein they are correct. Furthermore, the style used in WN against mercantilism has elements of a "rhetorical" style in that mercantilism is denigrated and its supporters accused of "sophistry," thus echoing Plato's criticism of the sophists that they sacrifice truth for effect. TMS and WN are complex theoretical systems whose aim is to argue for a particular theory as against rival theories. In spite of their plain style and analytical seriousness, they are written to persuade; and the structure of the works and their style of composition contribute to that objective.

Furthermore, TMS and WN are not without significant figures of speech. In TMS Smith uses the metaphor of the "impartial spectator" to denote moral conscience. Ordinary everyday relations between people are presented in terms of a model where all are "spectators" to each other. This spectatorial model is extended to moral judgment about oneself, which is presented in terms of agents imagining themselves from the standpoint of an impartial spectator (TMS III.1.2). This metaphorical figure of the impartial spectator is central to Smith's moral theory and its interpretation has been much debated. Smith's metaphorical expression in WN about the "invisible hand" is widely known (WN IV.ii.9). It is also much disputed. It is often used to promote a view of Smith as an ardent supporter of laissez-faire, but many scholars dispute this interpretation, questioning the centrality of the metaphor for Smith's economic arguments (which are more nuanced than the invisible hand metaphor suggests) and even whether it refers to free market allocation as that is now understood in modern economics.

7. RHETORIC, COMMUNICATION, AND LANGUAGE

In LRBL a communication model of language explains Smith's preference for plain style over rhetorical style. As plain prose may have particular stylistic features and rhetorical effects, and didactic discourse may be rhetorically complex, this suggests that the communication model of language encounters some difficulties when it is applied in the context of rhetorical theory. An alternative model of language is that we think, speak, and write *within* language and its conventions. Although we might interpret the experience of reading an author's works as gaining access to the author's own thoughts, this itself is an artifact of language.[8]

Smith's model of communication suggests that a plain style should result in all readers having the same interpretation. In spite of Smith's recommendation of perspicuity and plain style, his own works are complex rhetorical products that have not resulted in agreed interpretations over the years. Is this an irony that Smith, as writer and connoisseur of fine writing, as rhetor and rhetorical theorist, would appreciate?

NOTES

1. An extended version of Lecture 3 was first published as "Considerations Concerning the First Formation of Languages, and the Different Genius of Original and Compounded Languages" in *The Philological Miscellany* (1761).

2. On the significance of the distinction between "empathy" and "sympathy" for TMS, see V. Brown, "Intersubjectivity and Moral Judgment in Adam Smith's *Theory of Moral Sentiments*," in *Intersubjectivity and Objectivity in Adam Smith and Edmund Husserl*, ed. C. Fricke and D. Føllesdal (Heusenstamm: 2012), pp. 243–72.

3. At LRBL ii.17–18 it is argued that only facts can have instructional value. This is not the view at TMS III.3.14.

4. A similar argument is made in "History of Astronomy" (HA II.7–9, IV.76).

5. D. L. Marshall, "Literature Survey Early Modern Rhetoric: Recent Research in German, Italian, French, and English," *Intellectual History Review* 17 (2007), pp. 75–93, at p. 76.

6. In a later lecture Smith advances the opposite opinion on Swift, that his style is "very close" so that "no word can be passed over without notice" (LRBL i.92).

7. *A Modest Proposal for Preventing the Children of Poor People in Ireland Being a Burthen on Their Parents or Country, and for Making Them Beneficial to the Publick* (1729) proposes that the young children of poor people in Ireland could be sold as tasty food for the rich.

8. For an application of this argument to theories of interpretation, see V. Brown, "Historical Interpretation, Intentionalism and Philosophy of Mind," *Journal of the Philosophy of History* 1 (2007), pp. 25–62.

BIBLIOGRAPHIC ESSAY

For a history and defense of rhetoric, see B. Vickers, *In Defence of Rhetoric* (Oxford: 1988). For histories of eighteenth-century British rhetoric, see W. S. Howell, *Eighteenth-Century British Logic and Rhetoric* (Princeton: 1971), and L. P. Agnew, *Outward, Visible Propriety: Stoic Philosophy and Eighteenth-Century British Rhetorics* (Columbia, SC: 2008).

For general discussion of LRBL, see W. S Howell, *Eighteenth-Century British Logic and Rhetoric* (Princeton: 1971), chap. 6.iv, pp. 536–76, earlier published as "Adam Smith's Lectures on Rhetoric: An Historical Assessment," *Speech Monographs* 36 (1969), pp. 393–418; and A. S. Skinner, *A System of Social Science: Papers Relating to Adam Smith*, 2nd ed. (Oxford: 1996), chap. 1, pp. 7–24.

On the significance of LRBL for understanding Smith's works as complex rhetorical products, see V. Brown, *Adam Smith's Discourse: Canonicity, Commerce and Conscience* (London: 1994), and "Dialogism, the Gaze and the Emergence of Economic Discourse," *New Literary History* 28 (1997), pp. 697–710; S. J. McKenna, *Adam Smith: The Rhetoric of Propriety* (Albany, NY: 2006); A. M. Endres, "Adam Smith's Rhetoric of Economics: An Illustration Using 'Smithian' Compositional Rules," *Scottish Journal of Political Economy* 38 (1991), pp. 76–95; B. Walraevens, "Adam Smith's Economics and the *Lectures on Rhetoric and Belles Lettres*: The Language of Commerce," *History of Economic Ideas* 18 (2010), pp. 11–32.

THE THEORY OF MORAL SENTIMENTS

Eric Schliesser

THE AIMS AND NATURE OF TMS

Adam Smith published TMS in 1759. At the time he was a professor of moral philosophy at Glasgow University, where he had worked since 1751. It was his first publication (if we except a few shorter, anonymous pieces). TMS is a contribution to understanding what Smith, echoing the title of Hume's second *Enquiry*, calls the "principles of morals" (TMS VII.i.2.2). Smith also states that TMS is intended to be read alongside his other works on the "general principles of law and government, and of the different revolutions which they had undergone in the different ages and periods of society" (TMS Advert.2; see also VII.iv.37). TMS, WN, and the intended but never completed "theory" or "history" of jurisprudence all belong to moral philosophy in Smith's sense.

Despite the immediate and ongoing success of TMS, Smith claims in the "Advertisement" of the (1790) sixth edition (the final one published during his lifetime) that he "always intended" to revise it "with care and attention" (TMS Advert.1). In the Advertisement, Smith calls his readers' attention to some of his "principal alterations" (TMS Advert.1). But the Advertisement does not mention "A Dissertation upon the Origin of Languages" (CL), which he had already added to the third edition of TMS (1767). TMS and CL could thus be seen as mutually enlightening. The editors of the standard Glasgow Edition however moved CL to LRBL, and thus in the Glasgow Edition TMS ends with a historical survey of moral theories (Part VII). This decision obscures Smith's final intent. TMS was meant to be read not only alongside WN and the never-completed history of jurisprudence, but *also* alongside

Smith's more theoretical (to use Hume's term) science of man, some parts of which appear in EPS.

The argument of TMS is thus connected to two, larger Smithian projects. One focuses on the moral and psychological requirements "sufficient for the harmony of society" (TMS I.i.4.7) in the context of a larger account of the origin and causes of flourishing of *civilized* law and government. This project is embedded in a second, more theoretical account that explains how from "savage" origins "remote from the societies of men" (CL 1) crucial features of human nature as found in civilization themselves *could* have developed over long expanses of time.[1]

With this in mind we can take a closer look at Smith's "principles of morals," which, according to Smith, aim to answer two, related questions:

> First, wherein does virtue consist? Or what is the tone of temper, and tenour of conduct, which constitutes the excellent and praiseworthy character, the character which is the natural object of esteem, honour, and approbation? And, secondly, by what power or faculty in the mind is it, that this character, whatever it be, is recommended to us? Or in other words, how and by what means does it come to pass, that the mind prefers one tenour of conduct to another, denominates the one right and the other wrong; considers the one as the object of approbation, honour, and reward, and the other of blame, censure, and punishment? (TMS VII.i.2)

Both questions imply that to be virtuous means having the right sort of character, that is, having a certain steady, "tenour of conduct" that can be judged to be virtuous by others. Much of TMS is taken up with the second question, and that's where the significance of the moral sentiments enter.

NATURAL VERSUS MORAL SENTIMENTS

The main focus of TMS is the moral sentiments. In TMS Smith does not define the meaning of "sentiment." Throughout his writings, Smith tends to use "sentiments," "feelings," "emotions," and "passions" interchangeably. What he has in mind with "moral sentiment" is perhaps best gleaned from the first sentence of TMS: "How selfish soever man may be supposed, there are evidently some principles in his nature, which interest him in the fortune of others, and render their happiness necessary to him, though he derives nothing from it except the pleasure of seeing it" (TMS I.i.1.1). As many previous commentators on TMS have noted, Hobbes and Mandeville are the unmistakable targets of this sentence. In order to refute them, Smith appeals to the fact that there are disinterested aspects of human nature that make the happiness of others an intrinsic part of our own happiness.[2] These "principles" are, in fact, other-regarding "emotions," such as "pity and compassion" (TMS I.i.1.1). But his main interest is in sympathy, which originally may have meant the same ("compassion" is the Latin translation of συμπάθεια, or fellow [συμ] feeling [πάθεια]), but "may now . . . without much impropriety, be made use of to denote our fellow-feeling with any passion whatever" (TMS I.i.1.5).[3]

As with "sentiment," Smith does not explicitly define "moral" in TMS. Yet his use of "moral" (as in "moral sentiments" and in "moral causes") conforms closely to our notion of the "social." For example, when Smith speaks of "irresistible moral causes" (WN V.i.e.26; WN V.iii.5), he is describing the effects of social circumstances.[4] The distinction between moral causation and physical causation is thus not primarily a contrast between the ethical and the natural, but rather a contrast between causation in the human sphere and causation among unthinking bodies. So, a "moral sentiment" is best rendered as a "social passion."

However, it turns out that a moral sentiment is also intrinsically normative because it is a cultivated feeling that in its content always includes reliable expectations about responses by others. As Smith explains through a revealing thought experiment, if we bring an individual into society, "his own passions will immediately become the causes of new passions," as "he will observe that mankind approve of some of them, and are disgusted by others" (TMS III.1.3). So, some passions are possible only in society; other people's responses to our passion-driven behavior generate new passions in us.

Once in society, passions quickly multiply. In particular, feelings are triggered by other people's responses of approval and disgust. These social passions can induce us to feel "elevated" or feel "cast down" (TMS III.1.3). Presumably this is accompanied by a certain valence (e.g., joy or increased power accompanying elevation, pain or impotence accompanying downfall).

So, moral sentiments are produced by social phenomena that make us view ourselves in terms of relative position toward others. The "position" is established by how we take others to judge us. Depending on our character we may interpret what we "observe" in distinct ways. So, the *content* of a moral sentiment includes three parts: (1) some desire (aversion, joy, etc.), (2) an idea of a social phenomenon that prompts the passion, (3) our (empowering/ impotent) sense of ourselves moving up or down in the estimation of an (internally) selected group of observers. While the presence of (2) makes any moral sentiment "social" in the modern sense, the presence of (3) makes any moral sentiment intrinsically normative.

It turns out, however, that not all emotions are other-regarding according to Smith. Throughout TMS Smith also treats of "original passions": these are the so-called natural sentiments. Even "a stranger to society" has such passions (TMS III.1.3). The content of natural sentiments is either desires or aversions, or joys or sorrows. Among natural sentiments, the relationship of "fit" is fairly simple: objects that are pleasing (or useful, tasty, etc.) excite a desire for or joy in that object. Such natural sentiments are not just caused by such objects, but also directed toward them. Thus, in Smith there is a distinction between the uncultivated feelings humans "naturally" possess, that is, natural sentiments, and the cultivated feelings humans acquire from local social institutions or practices that acculturate them, that is, moral sentiments.

SYMPATHY

The first chapter of TMS is dedicated to the concept of sympathy, which is arguably the central concept of the work as a whole. Leonidas Montes has helpfully distinguished two types of sympathy in

Smith: "sympathy as a process" and "sympathy as an outcome."[5] Smith himself indeed uses "sympathy" to refer to both the process by which mutual fellow-feeling is attained and the outcome of mutual fellow-feeling itself. He articulates the process of sympathy as follows:

> In order to produce this concord, as nature teaches the spectators to assume the circumstances of the person principally concerned, so she teaches this last in some measure to assume those of the spectators. As they are continually placing themselves in his situation, and thence conceiving emotions similar to what he feels; so he is as constantly placing himself in theirs, and thence conceiving some degree of that coolness about his own fortune, with which he is sensible that they will view it. As they are constantly considering what they themselves would feel, if they actually were the sufferers, so he is as constantly led to imagine in what manner he would be affected if he was only one of the spectators of his own situation. As their sympathy makes them look at it, in some measure, with his eyes, so his sympathy makes him look at it, in some measure, with theirs, especially when in their presence and acting under their observation: and as the reflected passion, which he thus conceives, is much weaker than the original one, it necessarily abates the violence of what he felt before he came into their presence, before he began to recollect in what manner they would be affected by it, and to view his situation in this candid and impartial light. (TMS I.i.4.8)

The outcome of a well-functioning sympathetic process is thus twofold: (1) the jointly occurring experience in two minds of a passion (whose intensity has been transformed during the sympathetic process) and (2) a further pleasure of sharing this sympathetic passion (e.g., TMS I.i.2.2).

If we just focus on the role of feelings in Smithian sympathy, the process and outcome of sympathy may seem to form a seamless whole.[6] There is evidence for this (e.g., TMS I.iii.1.5). But for Smith the process of sympathy also involves knowledge of (moral) causes that gave rise to the moral situation, as well as frequently counterfactual sympathetic mutual modulation in the imagination of the participant(s) (see TMS II.i.intro.2).[7]

Smith's concept of sympathy has often been read in the context of the influential account of sympathy given by his friend Hume in the *Treatise* (e.g., 3.3.2.2). In both Hume and Smith, the sympathetic process by way of the imagination transforms one's conceived feeling into a related kind of feeling. Even so, there are nontrivial differences between Hume and Smith on sympathy.[8] For example, in Hume relatively dull ideas are turned, as it were, back into vivacious impressions (that is, for Hume the sympathetic process is always vivifying); in Smith emotions are turned into reflected passions, and this is only sometimes vivifying (IA II.22; and TMS VI.ii.1.1).

Awareness of the very possibility of mutual sympathy creates an incentive to enter into the sympathetic process (see esp. TMS I.i.2.6). It's almost as if there is also a further, parasitic pleasure on the anticipation of the pleasure that mutual sympathy will produce. Rather than seeing this parasitic pleasure as a damaging, infinite regress, Smith regards it as the possible seeds of a virtuous cycle, where we draw each other into sympathy and delight in anticipating it. As Smith puts it in a passage crucial to his political philosophy, "Man, it has been said, has a natural love for society, and desires that the union of mankind should be preserved for its own sake, and though he himself was to derive no benefit from it. The orderly and flourishing state of society is agreeable to him, and he takes delight in contemplating it" (TMS II.ii.3.6).[9]

Here and elsewhere Smith thus suggests that we are naturally sociable and eager to enter into the sympathetic process. Yet Smith also knows that in the heat of the moment, it is often hard for us to imagine how we are being seen and evaluated. Our awareness of the existence of spectators can however help to create the circumstances by which we calm down and can start to adopt a more dispassionate perspective on ourselves—a process that Smith readily admits can take significant effort and, perhaps, even some proper acculturation, education, or cultivation. In addition, Smith discerns that when there is extreme inequality of power and fortune, we should not expect much moral sensitivity from others (WN IV.vii.c.80). As Smith puts it, "before we can feel much for others, we must in some measure be at ease ourselves" (TMS V.ii.9). So, the argument for commercial society is, in part, that it makes better moral functioning possible.[10]

THE IMPARTIAL SPECTATOR

Recall that all moral sentiments include three features: (1) some desire (aversion, joy), (2) an idea of a social object that prompts the
passion, (3) a sense of ourselves moving up or down in the estimation of an (internally) selected group of observers. It's the third,
other-regarding feature that renders our social passions capable of
becoming *moral* sentiments. For if our social passions incorporate
the standards of the right sort of observer, then they are properly
moral. Smith calls this right sort of observer the "impartial spectator,"
whose sympathetic feelings are the "precise and distinct measure"
of the "fitness and propriety" of our moral sentiments (TMS VII.ii.
1.49).

But who exactly is this "impartial spectator," and how does
he come to be? With this question in mind let us turn to Smith's
account of the origin of the impartial spectator. Smith offers
a thought experiment about "a human creature" who grows to
"manhood in some solitary place" (TMS III.1.3). It shows we learn
to judge (ourselves and others) morally and aesthetically from the
judgments of the people who surround us as we grow up. We then
develop the habit of seeing ourselves from without:

> In the same manner our first moral criticisms are exercised upon the
> characters and conduct of other people; and we are all very forward
> to observe how each of these affects us. But we soon learn, that
> other people are equally frank with regard to our own. We become
> anxious to know how far we deserve their censure or applause,
> and whether to them we must necessarily appear those agreeable or
> disagreeable creatures which they represent us. We begin, upon this
> account, to examine our own passions and conduct, and to consider
> how these must appear to them, by considering how they would
> appear to us if in their situation. We suppose ourselves the specta-
> tors of our own behaviour, and endeavour to imagine what effect it
> would, in this light, produce upon us. (TMS III.1.5)

So, in practice, as we grow up, we internalize the values and expectations of our community, and we learn to see ourselves in light
of their opinions. In effect, both our feelings (or derived passions)
and evaluations of these feelings refer to the estimations of others.

If these are in accord with each other we feel empowered, and if they are at odds we're ashamed (see also TMS IV.2.12).

Crucially, as we develop the habit of referring our feelings and actions to the judgments of *imagined* others, we already can, in principle, become independent of their actual praise or blame. At TMS III.1.5, Smith subtly implies that we are more likely to become independent of society's actual judgment if we are inclined to like how we see ourselves. So, a kind of inborn or properly cultivated self-satisfaction may, in fact, be necessary to become the right kind of judge who does not fall victim to fashion and social corruption—a judge who either correctly applies the general rules of morality latent in society or actually attains the right kind of distance on oneself. Presumably such self-satisfaction may lead to a form of socially useful pride. So we should not be surprised that for Smith the "divine virtues" can be practiced only by people who feel what he calls the "dignity, and superiority of our own characters" (TMS III.3.4).

Of course, there is a fine line here; in practice, we are likely to overvalue the way we see ourselves. Smith is especially adamant that in the heat of our "selfish passions" before and after we act, we are likely to see ourselves with a "very partial" view (TMS III.4.1–3). Smith has no doubt that "self-deceit, this fatal weakness of mankind, is the source of half the disorders of human life" (TMS III.4.6). Overcoming this, Smith explains, requires us to divide ourselves "as it were, into two persons" (TMS III.1.6). In general, the impartial spectator just is the internalized judgment of a properly impartial, properly indifferent (but not unfeeling), properly distant, well-informed person that we imagine within us, and "who" then engages "us" in the sympathetic process.

So far I have emphasized that the impartial spectator within (1) judges by way of the norms of society one has been socialized in, but (2) is capable of doing so in defiance of actual social judgments. Even so, this may be thought not sufficient for a morality worth having. After all, what if the norms of society are corrupt? Smith himself presents examples of whole societies having an erroneous judgment on a *particular* moral issues, as in the case of Aristotle's and Plato's views on infanticide (TMS V.2.15; see also WN IV.i.32;

WN III.iii.8). So, Smith clearly recognizes that local standards of good judgment do not always track all of what humanity demands from us.[11] So what resources within Smith's moral theory are available to properly cultivated impartial spectators who seek to stand against what is "commonly done"?

In a part that was added to the sixth edition of TMS, Smith writes of "two different standards to which we naturally compare them," namely the "idea of exact propriety and perfection, so far as we are each of us capable of comprehending that idea," and "the degree of approximation to this idea which is commonly attained in the world" (TMS VI.iii.23–25). According to Smith, the first standard can always inspire critical reflection. As long as a society has notions of exactitude and perfection in it, some critical distance toward prevailing norms can be generated immanently.[12] Smith thinks it clearly helps if within society there exists an "archetype of perfection" or an idea of a "divine artist" whose handiwork can be emulated (TMS VI.iii.25). Smith's claim that we sometimes judge our own and other people's efforts by a standard of exact propriety and perfection is not sufficiently appreciated by those who worry where in Smith's moral psychology or epistemology a critical stance can be developed. This is a very important issue to Smith, as he explained his letter to Sir Gilbert Elliot, when preparing revisions to be included in second edition of TMS: "that our judgments concerning our own conduct have always a reference to the sentiments of some other being, and to shew that, notwithstanding this, real magnanimity and conscious virtue can support itself under the disapprobation of all mankind" (CAS 40).[13]

Smith also argues that a very particular natural sentiment—namely the love of praiseworthiness—plays an important role in this process (see esp. TMS III.2.1–2; this was also added to the sixth edition of TMS). Smith goes on to insist that the love of praise and the love of praiseworthiness are distinct; in particular, he denies that the love of praiseworthiness is derived from or an extension of the love of praise, insisting instead that the love of praise is derived from the love of praiseworthiness (TMS III.2.3; also added in sixth edition). Smith is making a conceptual-developmental point;

in the right kind of circumstances, our experience of desiring to be praiseworthy activates our natural desire for praise.

In one sense Smith's theory is extremely promising; all humans start out as children, so we all are naturally in conditions that will make us desire praiseworthiness (even if we are orphans there will be surrogate parents of various sorts). Unfortunately, there is no guarantee that we will have proper objects of imitation. A reformist reader of Smith might well conclude that if we were exposed to institutions that were less likely to facilitate the disposition to worship the rich and powerful, there might well be less corruption of the moral sentiments. Yet Smith seems committed to the idea that nearly all of us encounter conditions that will prompt the desire for praiseworthiness.

So far I have not mentioned the role of conscience in Smith's system. One might think, perhaps, that in Smith's system, conscience simply is the moral sense. There is, in fact, a long tradition of reading Smith as a so-called moral sense theorist not unlike other eighteenth-century British moral philosophers. But Smith explicitly rejects this view: "The word conscience does not immediately denote any moral faculty by which we approve or disapprove," even if it "supposes . . . the existence of some such faculty" (TMS VII.iii.3.15).

Smithian conscience is thus not a moral faculty, but a form of self-awareness about us having acted properly according to and under the guidance of "some such faculty." The phrase "some such faculty" might lead one to believe that there is a moral sense that directs conscience (cf. TMS III.5.6). Smith attributes such a doctrine to his teacher, Francis Hutcheson (TMS VII.iii.3.6), but with delicious irony objects (TMS VII.iii.3.15; see also VII.iii.3.12).

Rather all Smith means at TMS VII.iii.3.15 is that conscience is guided by some passion(s). To a first approximation in Smith "conscience" and "the impartial spectator within" are synonymous (TMS III.3.4). Given that, as we have seen, the impartial spectator is formed in society and through interactions with society, we can say that Smith endorses what we might call the social formation of conscience.[14]

VIRTUE AND CHARACTER

Smith's concepts of sympathy and the impartial spectator form the core of his answer to the second of the two questions with which we began: "how and by what means does it come to pass, that the mind prefers one tenour of conduct to another, denominates the one right and the other wrong?" But for his answer to the first question—"wherein does virtue consist?"—we must turn to his theory of virtue itself. Sometimes Smith writes as if there is only one model of virtue, a monistic "idea of exact propriety and perfection" to which the "wise and virtuous" orient themselves (TMS VI.iii.25; see also TMS VII.ii.1.49). But what exactly distinguishes this "wise and virtuous" individual whom Smith holds up as an ideal? In part, the excellence of the wise and virtuous person is epistemic; as I have argued, her cultivated feelings involve epistemic judgments that rely on sophisticated (and sometimes subconscious) counterfactual reasoning, and Smith himself calls attention to these nontrivial epistemic contributions ("precise," "exact," "well informed").[15] The wise and virtuous individual is also distinguished by treating everybody equally. To be an excellent moral judge is an exacting skill, which requires keeping in mind that even the most outstanding person is, as "reason" teaches, "but one of the multitude" (TMS III.3.4). Related to this, wisdom and virtue also require practicing "humble modesty and equitable justice" (TMS I.iii.3.2). Smith does not comment much on the nature of such modesty. But in his addition to the final edition of TMS, Smith explains that the "whole mind" of "the wise and virtuous" is "deeply impressed, his whole behaviour and deportment are distinctly stamped with the character of real modesty; with that of a very moderate estimation of his own merit, and, at the same time, of a full sense of the merit of other people" (TMS VI.iii.25). Judgments of merit involve the proportionality among a sentiment of the heart, which leads to an action and its foreseeable effects, and, of course, the actual effects produced by it (e.g., TMS II.i.intro.2). "Real modesty" thus involves a proper estimation of the consequences of character in others and oneself.

As the invocation of "equitable justice" suggests, the wise and virtuous person also has an important political role. Elsewhere Smith writes that "the wise and virtuous man is at all times willing that his own private interest should be sacrificed to the public interest of his own particular order or society" (TMS VI.ii.3.3). Coupled with the fact that the wise and virtuous individual is a skilled judge of character, as we have seen, the willingness of the wise and virtuous person to sacrifice his private interest for the public interest suggests that he is of all candidates best entrusted with the maintenance of the legal order and the guardianship of our shared liberties. If this is right, then, one of Smith's most important moral exemplars is fundamentally committed to a moral understanding of political life. This implies that TMS is not just a book in moral psychology, but should be seen as contributing to political philosophy.

The wise and virtuous individual thus values the public interest over self-interest. But this is not to say that the wise and virtuous individual is simply disinterested. Not unlike the rich and great, the "wise and virtuous" also desires to earn and to claim "the respect and admiration of mankind." Smith's focus on these two specific categories of "admiration" and "respect" is important. Admiration is both an intellectual and aesthetic sentiment: we admire those things that are great and beautiful.[16] The wise and virtuous person pursues wisdom and virtue, in part, by "emulation" of other wise and virtuous individuals, whose character embodies an ideal "more correct and more exquisitely beautiful in its outline" (TMS I.iii.3.2).[17]

But what exactly does Smith mean by "respect" here? In context, Smith does not make clear what "respect" entails, and it is no help when later he calls the impartial spectator the "respectable judge" (TMS III.3.25). We seem trapped in some circle here (see also TMS VI.ii.1.16–18). Fortunately, Smith also connects the desire for respect to a sense of equality among one's recognized peers (TMS VI.1.3; see also VI.iii.39; and VI.iii.48). Stephen Darwall has offered a detailed account—centering on a second-person perspective that we adopt with each other in a moral community—of how recognition of such mutual equality is entailed by our justified resentment at injury (TMS II.iii.1.5).[18] The wise and virtuous person thus desires to be thought beautiful for her excellence as well as to receive in practice the recognition already properly due to being an equal member of a moral community. That is to say, she has a heightened sensitivity to her membership in a (to speak metaphorically) moral universe.

It's clear that the perfectly wise and virtuous is among the most highly valued by Smith (cf. TMS III.3.35). But it does not follow that there are no others excellent-in-virtue-of-character worth emulating and imitating. Throughout TMS Smith draws vivid vignettes of other such exemplars of characters exhibiting excellence in virtue (TMS VI.ii.intro.2; TMS VI.iii.28; TMS I.i.4.3; TMS VI.ii.2.14). All these characters have particular, cultivated virtues, practices, and, especially, mental dispositions associated with them. This further suggests that Smith is not simply a monist but a sort of moral pluralist who thinks society needs people with a variety of virtues.[19]

As Colin Heydt has emphasized, Smith's vivid drawings of exemplars do not function merely as descriptions, but are meant to be instructive.[20] An older generation of scholars tended to cite a passage from an extended footnote by Smith against the very idea of a normative dimension to TMS (TMS II.i.5.10). But in context, Smith is making a distinction between an inquiry into the "principles" upon which "a perfect being" would judge, and an inquiry into the principles by which "so weak and imperfect a creature as man" in fact judges. That is to say, he is claiming that for his enterprise a realistic human anthropology is required, rather than one beyond our reach. But he does so in order to establish what creatures like us ought to do.

NOTES

1. See Dugald Stewart's "Account of the Life and Writings of Adam Smith" in EPS; and Eric Schliesser, "Wonder in the Face of Scientific Revolutions: Adam Smith on Newton's 'Proof' of Copernicanism," *British Journal for the History of Philosophy* 13 (2006), pp. 697–732; and Schliesser, "Reading Adam Smith after Darwin: On the Evolution of Propensities, Institutions and Sentiments," *Journal of Economic Behavior and Organization* 77 (2011), pp. 14–22.

2. In addition to Hobbes and Mandeville, Rousseau is also one of the intended targets. In Smith's anonymous (1757) letter to the *Edinburgh Review*, he attributes to Rousseau (and Mandeville) the position that "that there is in man no powerful instinct which necessarily determines him to seek society for its own sake" (LER 11).

3. For Smith's relationships to ancient and early modern approaches to sympathy, see Eric Schliesser, ed., *Sympathy: The History of a Concept* (Oxford: 2015).

4. As Berry has emphasized, moral causes are also deterministic; see Christopher J. Berry, "Smith and Science," in *The Cambridge Companion to Adam Smith*, ed. Knud Haakonssen (Cambridge: 2006).

5. See Leonidas Montes, *Adam Smith in Context* (London: 2004).

6. See James Otteson, *Adam Smith's Marketplace of Life* (Cambridge: 2002).

7. For details, see E. Schliesser, "Counterfactual Causal Reasoning in Smithian Sympathy," *Revue internationale de philosophie* 269, no. 3 (2014), pp. 307–16.

8. Samuel Fleischacker, "Sympathy in Hume and Smith: A Contrast, Critique, and Reconstruction," in *Intersubjectivity and Objectivity in Adam Smith and Edmund Husserl*, ed. Christel Fricke and Dagfinn Føllesdal (Frankfurt: 2012).

9. See Ryan Hanley, "'The Wisdom of the State': Adam Smith on China and Tartary," *American Political Science Review* 108 (2014), pp. 371–82.

10. Lisa Herzog, *Inventing the Market: Smith, Hegel and Political Theory* (Oxford: 2013), p. 109; and Herzog, "Adam Smith's Account of Justice between Naturalness and Historicity," *Journal of the History of Philosophy* 52 (2014), pp. 703–26.

11. See the criticism of infanticide in China at WN I.viii.24. China is a wealthy society that suffers from imperfect institutions; for judicious analysis, see Hanley, "'Wisdom of the State.'"

12. See also Michael Frazer, *The Enlightenment of Sympathy* (Oxford: 2010), p. 105.

13. Lauren Brubaker, "Adam Smith and the Limits of Enlightenment" (doctoral diss., University of Chicago, 2002), and Andrew Corsa, "Modern Greatness of Soul in Hume and Smith," *Ergo, an Open Access Journal of Philosophy* 2 (2015), pp. 27–58, provide excellent discussion.

14. I thank a helpful referee. See Jerry Z. Muller, *Adam Smith in His Time and Ours: Designing the Decent Society* (Princeton: 1993), chap. 8.

15. See also Ryan Hanley, "Adam Smith and Virtue," in *The Oxford Handbook of Adam Smith*, ed. C. Berry, C. Smith, and M. P. Paganelli (Oxford: 2013), pp. 230–32.

16. HA intro.1; see also Karen Valihora, *Austen's Oughts: Judgment after Locke and Shaftesbury* (Newark: 2010), p. 141.

17. Charles Griswold, *Adam Smith and the Virtues of Enlightenment* (Cambridge: 1999), p. 331; and James Chandler, "Adam Smith as Critic," in Berry, Smith, and Paganelli, *Oxford Handbook of Adam Smith*; on emulation, see TMS III.2.3.

18. See Stephen Darwall, *The Second-Person Standpoint* (Cambridge, MA: 2006).

19. For an important article on how this links up to Smith's metaethics, see Michael Gill, "Moral Pluralism in Smith and His Contemporaries," *Revue internationale de philosophie* 68 (2014), pp. 275–306.

20. Colin Heydt, "'A Delicate and an Accurate Pencil': Adam Smith, Description, and Philosophy as Moral Education," *History of Philosophy Quarterly* 25 (2008), pp. 57–74.

BIBLIOGRAPHIC ESSAY

TMS long lived in the shadow of WN; until relatively recently, detailed studies of TMS were few. Among early works in English, especially important are Glenn R. Morrow, "Adam Smith: Moralist and Philosopher," *Journal of Political Economy* 35 (1927); Morrow, "The Significance of the Doctrine of Sympathy in Hume and Adam Smith," *Philosophical Review* 60–78 (1923); A. N. Prior, *Logic and the Basis of Ethics* (Oxford: 1949); Joseph Cropsey, *Polity and Economy* (The Hague: 1957); A. L. Macfie, *The Individual in Society* (London: 1967); and T. D. Campbell, *Adam Smith's Science of Morals* (London: 1971). A new stage in philosophical scholarship on TMS was inaugurated by the publication in the same year of Samuel Fleischacker's book *A Third Concept of Liberty* (Princeton: 1999) and Charles Griswold's book *Adam Smith and the Virtues of Enlightenment* (Cambridge: 1999), both of which offer indispensable comprehensive studies of Smith's project that include careful attention to the core concepts of TMS. More recently, a number of studies of various aspects of TMS have been published, including James Otteson, *Adam Smith's Marketplace of Life* (Cambridge: 2002); Leonidas Montes, *Adam Smith in Context* (London: 2004); D. D. Raphael, *The Impartial Spectator* (Oxford: 2007); Ryan Hanley, *Adam Smith and the Character of Virtue* (Cambridge: 2009); and Fonna Forman-Barzilai, *Adam Smith and the Circles of Sympathy* (Cambridge: 2010).

THE *LECTURES ON JURISPRUDENCE*

Knud Haakonssen

Adam Smith was professor of moral philosophy at the University
of Glasgow from 1752 to 1764.[1] He taught two classes, the "public
class" on moral philosophy and a more advanced class in which he
presented the new rhetoric and belles lettres (now LRBL) that he
had first taken up in a series of public lectures in Edinburgh prior
to his appointment in Glasgow. The former class encompassed
jurisprudence, a subject that Smith had likewise first presented
to the public in Edinburgh and that is the subject of the present
chapter. Smith did not write a work called "lectures on jurisprudence"; the works that have been published under this title are
transcriptions that derive from students' handwritten reports of
Smith's lectures. Three such reports have been found, one from the
early part of Smith's tenure in Glasgow, probably from the period
1753–55, one from 1762–63, and one virtually certainly from his
last year as professor, 1763–64. In addition, we have other much
shorter accounts of Smith's lectures, of which the most important
one will be mentioned below. These miscellaneous writings are the
main sources for the present overview of Smith's teaching of jurisprudence, and we shall begin with a brief characterization of each.

The earliest notes were found in a commonplace book of John
Anderson, who had been a student at Glasgow and later became
a professor.[2] It seems that Anderson made excerpts from a student's set of notes from Smith's lectures, and the result is a quite incomplete and in places somewhat confused record (of ten printed
pages). The Anderson Notes have mostly been ignored by Smith
scholars, but they are in fact important for several reasons. They
confirm that Smith from early on followed the general order of
presentation that he presumably maintained continuously until his

final year of teaching and that he had taken over this order from his teacher, Francis Hutcheson, to whose textbook he gives specific page references.[3] The notes also make it clear that Smith was already deeply interested in Montesquieu's recent *Spirit of Laws* (1748). Not least, Smith had formulated two principles that remained basic to his jurisprudence, and which seem to show the influence of David Hume.

The notes from 1762–63, now known as the "A" set of notes, form a large manuscript (nearly four hundred pages in print) that a student probably wrote up from shorthand notes taken in class.[4] On nearly all the topics covered, it is the most detailed record, but it has gaps and is incomplete, for no notes have been found from the final part of the lectures. Only discovered half a century ago and published in 1978, this set has played a major role in modern scholarship, as it seemed to provide significant information about the work on law and government that Smith maintained an ambition of publishing until the very end, when he had friends burn his papers as he lay dying.[5]

The "B" notes virtually certainly stem from 1763–64. In fact, Smith left in the middle of that academic year, but his assistant, Thomas Young, completed the course from Smith's lecture notes.[6] These notes were first discovered and published in the 1890s but had only a limited impact on the interpretation of Smith, until they were supplemented by the A notes. The former are dated 1766, when they presumably were professionally copied from a student's class notes. These notes are shorter (some 160 printed pages) and less detailed than the A notes, but they cover the whole of Smith's series of lectures on "Justice, Police, Revenue and Arms" (plus the law of nations). A remarkable thing about this set is that it records Smith as having made a drastic change in the order of his presentation for this final year of lecturing, a matter to be returned to below.

The three sets of notes mentioned so far are all concerned with jurisprudence, politics, economics, defense, and international relations. In Smith's course on moral philosophy there were, however, two preceding subjects, natural theology and "Ethics, strictly so called," as John Millar said. Millar, Smith's former student and later colleague and friend, gave an overview of the whole of Smith's course in a few paragraphs as part of information requested by Dugald Stewart, when the latter was preparing his memorial address for Smith to the Royal Society of Edinburgh. Only Stewart's quotations from Millar's letter have been preserved. About Smith's treatment of natural theology they say only that it dealt with the proofs of the existence and attributes of God and the principles on which the mind thinks about the divinity, that is, the standard topics of the discipline, presumably complemented by the psychology of projecting human characteristics to an image of divinity that he sketches in *The Theory of Moral Sentiments*. In contrast to the rest of Smith's course, the lectures on natural theology had no subsequent publication history, and we can infer from circumstantial evidence that they were brief. About the other parts of Smith's lectures Millar was more helpful. He confirmed that "Ethics" was largely published in *The Theory of Moral Sentiments*,[7] and he also explained that Smith's lectures on "the political institutions relating to commerce, to finances, to ecclesiastical and military establishments . . . contained the substance of the work he [Smith] afterwards published under the title of *An Inquiry into the Nature and Causes of the Wealth of Nations*."[8] This judgment has been confirmed in general terms by subsequent scholarship, which has discussed the development of Smith's views on the themes mentioned.[9] Apart from natural theology, which Smith evidently had no interest in pursuing, this leaves the lectures on justice without any published equivalent from his own hand. This is not, however, quite accurate, for these lectures were centrally concerned also with government and law, both of which are significant subjects in the *Wealth of Nations*, while the general theory of justice is developed in *The Theory of Moral Sentiments*. Still, it is in the justice section of the lectures on jurisprudence that we find the fullest systematic exposition of law and government, and the nexus of justice, law, and government will be the main subject for our analysis.

Smith began his lectures on jurisprudence nearly verbatim as he had concluded his *Theory of Moral Sentiments*: "Jurisprudence is that science which inquires into the general principles which ought to be the foundation of the laws of all nations" (LJB 1; cf.

TMS VIII.iv.37). What did he mean by "ought" and by "general principles"? Smith never formulated any fundamental law of nature, and in tune with this he never indicated any authoritative legislator. The divinity of revealed religion was never considered. He did acknowledge the providence of nature's God, but this was never a criterion for people's choice of behavior. The thought of acting in accordance with God's purpose could be an encouraging confirmation of our conscience, when, in hard cases, we imagined that we were acting morally right. But the divine purposes could not be specified in the form of moral or juridical norms; these humanity would have to formulate in response to its needs. The normative force of the "general principles" consists in the necessity to meet human needs as these are known in the history of the species; they specify what is required for human life in society. Our means of knowing these requirements is the empirical investigation of human life as it is and has been lived, and this is what Smith attempted both systematically and historically. The principles that may be found in this way are "general" in the sense that they are generalizations that are derived from empirical mores and historical societies, but while we may be unable to imagine life without some of them, this does not lend them transcendental authority.

What are those "general principles"? In *The Theory of Moral Sentiments* (VII.iv.7–37) Smith discussed what he considered the two main lines of thought concerning moral, including juridical, rules: the casuistry that had become a prominent part of scholastic theology (and been taken over by Protestant moral theology) and the natural law that had flourished in the wake of Hugo Grotius. Smith was critical of both. He rejected the attempt by casuists "to direct by precise rules what it belongs to feeling and sentiment only to judge of" (VII.iv.33); they were so to speak not casuistical enough, in the hackneyed sense of the term. Furthermore, these moral theologians thought that they could formulate such rules into a system that covered all aspects of morals, not only duties to avoid harm, but also injunctions to do good. The latter was futile, as the natural lawyers recognized. The jurists did separate the just from the good, but they did not adhere to the distinction and often seemed to be confused about its implications (VII.iv.15). Smith even referred to three of the leading lawyers, Samuel Pufendorf, Jean Barbeyrac, and Hutcheson, as themselves casuists (VII.iv.11). He continued this criticism in the introduction to the lectures on jurisprudence, where he brushed Pufendorf aside as being no better than "the divines" in answering Hobbes. The Englishman had maintained that only with the contractual creation of civil sovereignty was common human morality possible, whereas Christian natural lawyers, including Pufendorf, had maintained that law and rights were characteristic for humanity also in its natural state. This may not be a very satisfactory reading of Pufendorf, but the point here is that Smith saw this as a meaningless debate, "as there is no such state [as the natural] existing" nor, as mentioned, any basic natural law (LJB 3). All law in the proper sense is positive law, but "[s]ystems of positive law . . . can never be regarded as accurate systems of the rules of natural justice" (TMS VII.iv.36).

The only thinker who escaped relatively unscathed from Smith's brief survey of modern jurisprudence was Grotius. Both in *The Theory of Moral Sentiments* and in the lectures on jurisprudence Grotius was said to have given not only the first, but also "the most compleat work on this subject" (LJB 1; cf. TMS VII.iv.37). Smith's characterization of Grotius's *De iure belli ac pacis* (1625) is remarkable: "It is a sort of casuistical book for sovereigns and states determining in what cases war may justly be made and how far it may be carried on" (LJB 1). This had led Grotius to analyze the internal jurisprudence of states, and although the latter could achieve greater clarity and certainty than was possible in casuistry, it appears that what Smith appreciated in Grotius was his "particularism," namely his focus on rights, conflict, and peace settlement in jurisprudence (cf. Smith's Grotian approach to the law of war, LJB 339–54). It is through these concepts that we can grasp what he meant by the general principles of jurisprudence.

The very earliest preserved statement of Smith's jurisprudence, the Anderson Notes, begins with two principles:

[1] To deprive a man of life or limbs or to give him pain is shocking to the rudest of our species when no enmity or grudge subsists, i.e., where no punishment is due or danger apprehended.

2 Principle[:] We acquire a liking for those creatures or things which we are much conversant with. and thus to deprive us of them must give us pain. (Anderson Notes, p. 467)

The first principle is a simple version of the idea that the integrity of the individual person is something basic in people's mutual recognition of each other, and that it is constituted by third persons' reaction to violations of it. The second principle concerns the "extension" of the individual person because of its pursuit of satisfaction of its desires, which leads to a more complex personality and hence a wider scope for violations of that person. The bulk of the Anderson Notes are concerned with the extension of personality through the acquisition of possessions and property and through contractual relations with others. Smith seems already here to be applying Hume's theory of association to account for the connections between the person and its surroundings. It is remarkable how confident Smith already is in undertaking historical analyses of these matters, and the influence of Montesquieu is evident from his sure-footed criticism of specific points in *The Spirit of Laws*, such as the historical role of bills of exchange, the connection between interest and the quantity of money (where he leans on Hume), polygamy, and other matters that remained in his teaching and writing.

It is the two principles stated at the opening of the Anderson Notes that are developed into Smith's theory of rights as the cardinal point of his jurisprudence. In the case of the first principle, the connecting link is the *Theory of Moral Sentiment*'s analysis of the formation of personal identity.[10] This Smith sees as a sociopsychological process of interchange between each individual and the persons surrounding him or her. As we grow aware that we are the objects of observation simply by living among others, we become observers of ourselves, and this is the root of self-awareness as a person and, eventually, of the formation of our conscience. Since our very being as self-conscious agents is dependent upon our social context, we learn that we are vulnerable to harm not only as physical beings but also as social individuals, namely through multiple forms of misrecognition by others. Our appreciation of this condition can be articulated in the form of claims to our basic natural rights, namely, the rights to life, bodily integrity, freedom to make use of our person in intercourse with the surrounding world, including with other individuals (e.g., right to marriage), and the integrity of one's social identity ("reputation"). The second principle from the Anderson Notes becomes Smith's theory of the "adventitious" (or acquired) rights that arise when the person is associated with things or with other persons in the world; in other words, rights to property and to fulfillment of contracts. The natural and adventitious rights together make up the juridical status of the person considered simply as an individual.

The basis for rights, in Smith's view, is injury. In recognizing something as injury to a person, we ascribe that in which the person has been injured as a right to the injured person—his or her physical integrity, freedom of movement, property in things, voluntary relations with other individuals, and so on. The idea of rights that is the key to his jurisprudence is thus an important part of the spectator theory of justice as developed in *The Theory of Moral Sentiments*.[11] This raises the question of why he singles out some rights as natural; if the ascription of rights is a matter of spectator recognition, are not all rights in a sense social? The simple answer is yes, all rights and, indeed, the whole of morality arise from the interaction of humanity. Smith worked in a conceptual world that had been shaped by repeated discussions about the man-made character of moral, including social, phenomena. First of all there had been the many attempts to formulate this idea in terms of contracts of one kind or another, and these attempts continued right through the seventeenth and eighteenth centuries, not least because of the perceived need to limit, and later to exploit, their radical potential as theories of political authority. Second, and more recently, there had been concerted attempts to replace the idea of contract with theories of spontaneous social interaction. Here the most important effort in Smith's world had been David Hume's theory of the "artificiality" of important sections of morality, notably justice. Smith must be seen as driving Hume's argument more or less to the limit by simply dissolving the distinction between natural and artificial parts of morality, an effort epitomized in his declaration that there is no such thing as a state of nature, his associated neglect of the idea of a fundamental law of nature, and his spectator theory of natural rights. In this perspective the contract theory had cleared a conceptual space in which culture, including economic culture, according to Hobbes and Pufendorf, could arise thanks to the exercise of power, whereas Hume and especially Smith filled the same space with a theory according to which power was an integral part of culture. This is the point where Smith's theory glides over into a historical theory of government, as we shall see.

When Smith counts the rights to personal integrity as natural, despite their social origins, it is because they are obvious and therefore pervasive; they come, as it were, naturally to people "[t]he origin of natural rights is quite evident. That a person has a right to have his body free from injury, and his liberty free from infringement unless there be a proper cause, no body doubts" (LJB 11). He thinks that the injuries that define these rights are among the most generally recognized aspects of the moral life of the species. However, generality is not universality, and Smith accepted that there were societies and periods in which even bodily injury was differently conceived than in contemporary European society. When the "savages in North America" accepted torture or the early Greeks exposure of children as part of their social practice, Smith certainly did not like it, he thought it barbarous, and he had no doubt that modern mores were much preferable, but he did not seem to think that the indigenous Americans or the very early Greeks had set aside a natural right in some cosmopolitan sense. The limit he saw to such customs was, rather, that of the viability of societies that harbored them.[12] Similarly, when he discussed how the idea of incestuous relations has varied greatly, his critical attitude to several of these arrangements was held in terms of social utility and personal revulsion; there is no invocation of natural rights to indict the cases as unjust.

In the big picture of human history, however, natural rights are considered natural because they tend not to change in such a way that one can say that they have a history. This is the crucial difference between them and the adventitious rights. While natural rights are self-referential, in the sense that they refer to the person alone, the adventitious rights are relational, in the sense that they

concern the relationship between the person and the surrounding world, and these relationships vary, giving the rights a history.
The simple human needs for sustenance, shelter, and procreation
could be considered part of the natural history of the animal creation; but the satisfaction of such needs for humans will vary
with opportunities and tastes in different kinds of situations, and
it will therefore have a moral history. Smith sought to order the
situations in which humanity satisfies its needs by describing four
types of subsistence and social organization, namely, those of the
hunter-gatherer society, nomadic society, agricultural society, and
commercial society. Again the concept of injury was a basic tool in
his analysis, for one can say that the four forms of society are characterized by different forms of possible injuries and consequently
have different kinds of rights. The theory may also be regarded as
an extensive replacement of John Locke's labor theory of property,
which Smith clearly had in his sights. It was not the labor as such
that created a property right; labor, or more broadly the productive activity, was instead an important factor in inducing the social
group—the spectators—to recognize the relationship between the
productive person and the thing produced, and it was this recognition that was the basis for property. But what counted as labor
would vary from one type of society to another.

Smith used the theory of the four forms of society to transform
another of the standard issues in natural law, namely, the idea that
government was founded upon a contract, whether explicit, tacit, or
implied. A crucial feature of British political thought in general, the
idea of a social contract was felled by Smith because it had neither
historical nor psychological foundation. Only rarely had government arisen from a contract, and if it had, the grounds for its continuing support over time must be sought elsewhere. Furthermore,
people simply did not think of allegiance as a matter of contractual
duty. Instead political allegiance had to be accounted for in terms
of the social psychology set out in *The Theory of Moral Sentiments*, and this showed that humanity had a general tendency to
sympathize with people of "[s]uperiour age, superior abilities of
body and of mind, ancient family, and superior wealth"; those
"seem to be the four things that give one man authority over an-

other" (LJB 13). In addition, people would always be looking for the benefit of government, especially in providing protection and settling disputes. These two "principles of authority and utility," not contract, provide the basis for government; they are present in all societies, the former being the more prominent in monarchical government, the latter in republican. However, just as with the basis for rights, namely injury, so with authority and utility as the bases for allegiance: they demand a history. What counts as a public benefit (Smith discounts private utility as a historical force in this connection) depends upon the type of society. And among the factors that confer authority, people "give the preference to riches," since "superior abilities of body and mind are not so easily judged of by others" (LJB 13).[13] However, riches, or property, are inherently subject to historical variation, and the four forms of society are models of these variations.

The theory of these four forms is, in other words, about types of social relations, namely, of exclusion, dependence, and power. Hunting and gathering for survival require little social organization, establish only the simplest possession, and cater for only relatively few individuals at a time. Such societies need only powerful warrior figures whose ad hoc utility is obvious but yield nothing that resembles government and law. Nomadic society is dramatically different. Here is real property in moveable goods, as distinct from mere physical possession, and the fourth source of authority, "superiour wealth," accordingly becomes the dominant factor. Property is an objective, external, and potentially alienable feature of the person (in contrast to the subjective characteristics of ability and age). It is in fact an abstract relationship, and as such it can be sustained only by force, and shepherd society therefore produces central features of government and law. Due to the nexus of concentrated wealth, authority, and power in the hands of individual chiefs, this is the most unequal type of society. Agricultural society is again entirely different because it makes social living much more stationary and requires the exclusion of outsiders from the actual ground on which any social group lives. This necessitates much stronger government to provide external security, and when ownership of the land is divided up and transferred from the collectivity to individuals, further strengthening of government as well as elaborate rules of ownership become necessary. Furthermore, the exclusion of some people from the cultivated areas and the need for places of refuge in times of war lead to the concentration of non-agriculturalists in towns and a division of labor between town and country. With the formation of cities, the possibility arises that other forms of "superiour wealth" will support authority, especially in actual city-states. In a purely agricultural society authority arises from the ownership of land, but in cities commercial wealth is decisive. Commerce in the sense of the exchange of goods is, of course, to be found in all types of society, but in commercial society not only the relation between proprietor and property but the property itself is completely abstract, namely, the symbolic property of money and credit for investment. This requires a still more elaborate legal system, and it tends to come about first in small city-states, but eventually it spreads in some degree to larger societies that are also agricultural. This leads to new challenges to existing forms of government, such as the British, as agricultural, commercial, and monetary interests vie for influence.

Smith often talked of the types of society as "ages," which seems to imply a historical sequence, and in some measure he did think in this way. He certainly used the rhetoric of the "natural" order of development, when he needed it to chastise the special interests that exploited government. It is nevertheless misleading to see the theory as simply and straightforwardly historical. First, he offered only relatively little explanation of the factors that will make one age turn into another, and those are mostly the broader circumstances that may make change possible, especially population pressure that requires more productive forms of labor and organization, but also the need for leadership in order to face external threats to the social group. Second, his account of the actual course of history was not a four stages sequence. Ancient Greece and Rome were developing commerce alongside agriculture, and, most crucially for modern Europe, it was the wandering barbarians of Northern Europe who destroyed the agricultural and proto-commercial society of the Roman Empire, thus upsetting the whole of subsequent European history in such a way that commerce developed long before agriculture had reached proper flourishing. Furthermore, Smith was well aware of the existence of both nomadic and hunting societies that interacted with contemporary commercial society; and it was not exactly a historical necessity that all of Europe itself would successfully become commercial.

The difference between the four stages theory and Smith's narrative of the actual course of history is also underlined by the European parochialism of the latter. It has rightly been pointed out that Smith's history was written from an "archipelagic" perspective, hence the pivotal role of the ancient Attic settlements, whereas he did not apply his stages theory to "the river valleys of Asia or Africa. The great cities of Egypt and the Fertile Crescent are excluded from this history."[14] He was simply attempting not a universal history but an analysis of the unique case of Europe. In tune with this, the factors that move things, in Smith's view of history, are particular: physical geography (e.g., Attica's natural inland defenses and access to the sea; elsewhere natural harbors, navigable rivers, etc.), war (invasion of Rome), internal violence (the Dutch and the American rebellions), luck (survival of cities after the fall of the Roman Empire), greed and vanity (feudal landowners), religious fancy (WN V.i.g.iii, passim), technological inventions (oceangoing shipping, armaments), social inventions (paper credit and banking), and other incidental factors. It is this open-endedness that makes it intelligible how government can grasp opportunities and change the course of events, and Smith thought that modern government had a major chance of destroying the remnants of the feudal order, of preventing the perversion of government by the new "moneyed interest" of capitalists, of facilitating social development through education, public works, a stable currency, strong defense, and so on.

The theory of justice that Smith based upon *The Theory of Moral Sentiments* was a theory of rights, and, as indicated, he needed to fuse it with his theory of the four types of society because rights (through injury) were socially determined. However, with the four stages account there is a certain shift of focus from rights to government and law. What is the relationship between rights and law? As we saw, some elementary rights may be recognized even in the first age of society where there is no real government and law. Similarly, in modern Europe there may be recognition of rights between states, but there is no international government to enforce the law of nations, as Smith stresses. Furthermore, people recognize rights that are no part of the law within established government; and in line with this, one of the reasons for Smith's preference for common law was that it was a fund of rights that was independent of the government's law. As might be expected in view of his cavalier attitude to the distinction between natural and conventional—as signaled by his peremptory rejection of the idea of a "natural" state of humankind—the important point for him was not whether rights were "natural" in the technical sense of the natural lawyers. The important thing was that humankind had a distinct tendency to generate rights also independently of government, thus presenting government with its main challenge, namely how to enforce rights.[15] The ability of government to meet this challenge depended on the type of government that was possible, and the latter was itself a historical question that was necessitated by *The Theory of Moral Sentiments*, namely, the necessity of giving contextual content to the two principles of authority and utility.

Smith's overriding ambition was to integrate the theory of rights with the theory of law and government, and it is a mistake to see one or the other as the more fundamental. Both were directly dependent on his moral psychology, and in that sense he provided an alternative naturalism to that of traditional natural law. At the same time, this moral psychology necessitated historical accounts of the key features of civic life, namely, rights, law, and government. This tightly constructed analysis was his solvent for the problems he found in the post-Grotian natural law that provided the framework and much of the idiom with which he worked. If we understand rights to be the core of the theory of justice and allegiance to be equally basic to the theory of government, and if we accept that both rights and allegiance of necessity are historically determined in human life, then we have a reasonable idea of the sort of construction Smith had in mind with his project of a natural jurisprudence that encompassed the general principles of justice and of law and government. This would obviously be distinct, as he maintained, from the specific history of "the different revolutions [the principles] have undergone in the different ages and periods of society," and from the positive jurisprudence of "the particular institutions of any one nation" (TMS VII.iv.37), but it would be a demonstration of why the principles had to have a history and how they functioned in different contexts. Failure to understand this nexus between the permanent ("natural") features of social psychology and the historicity of humanity's mode of living was a failure to understand the "principles that ought to run through and be the foundation of the laws of all nations" (TMS VII.iv.37).

Smith wanted a "system" of such principles, but this does not seem to have meant the systematic derivation of rules of justice from a *Grundnorm*, such as a basic law of nature. There is no such norm in his thought; humanity has to create its own obligations. And the systematicity that he desired seems to have been the comprehensiveness that he found in Grotius. Grotius of course operated with a plurality of sources of norms, which explains why Smith, in approving of it, characterized his work as "casuistical." In other words, for Smith there seemed to be no conflict between a pluralism of norms and a "system" of principles. What Grotius did not have was a social psychology that explained why and how the principles of justice arose in their different forms. If Smith could do this—as he proposed—then he would have added to the authority of the rules of justice; not only were they backed by juridical principles, historical practice, international consensus, and so on, as in Grotius, but also by the psychology of social interaction. In a perspective such as Smith's, the best reason for suggesting that certain rules ought to be heeded was (to echo one of his favorite formulations) that they were heeded, that they could be heeded and under certain circumstances would be heeded, namely, with proper enlightenment—by his "system."

Smith did not leave us this system, and all we have are the brief outlines at the end of *The Theory of Moral Sentiments* and the students' notes from his lectures on jurisprudence. If one ascribes to him our modern notion of normativity, it may seem impossible that he could have completed his project. If one accepts instead the pluralism indicated above, there is no reason why he could not have done so. However, he was both a perfectionist and one of the few major thinkers who actually lived up to the period's ideal of privacy, and so he got his friends to burn what was not ready for the public.

In the records that have survived, it is an open question how he would have preferred to *present* the relationship between the theory of rights and the theory of government. At least since the lectures in circa 1753–55 (the Anderson Notes) and up until his penultimate year of lecturing in Glasgow, he followed the approach that his teacher, Hutcheson, had adapted from Pufendorf:

> The end of justice is to secure from injury. A man may be injured in several respects. 1st, as a man[.] 2dly, as a member of a family[.] 3dly, as a member of a state. As a man, he may be injured in his body, reputation, or estate. As a member of a family, he may be injured as a father, as a son, as a husband or wife, as a master or servant, as a guardian or pupil. . . . As a member of a state, a magistrate may be injured by disobedience or a subject by oppresion, etca. (LJB 6–7)

Even though the arrangement was Pufendorfian, the method of analysis on each topic was by means of Smith's notion of rights defined by injury. Smith's focus on the particular case as the core of the system of justice is further underlined by his emphasis on the role of courts in the history of society, by his high regard for common law, especially the English (e.g., LJA v.31–32; LJB 74; LRBL ii.200–204), and by his idea of the importance of equity, which he virtually identifies with the reasoning of the impartial spectator and with "natural justice" (e.g., LJA ii.28 and 80). This particularism is clearly the background to Smith's liking for Grotius and his "casuistry."

In his final year of lecturing, Smith made a drastic change in this order of presentation, proposing now to deal first with civil society, then familial society, then the individual person: "The civilians begin with considering government and then treat of property and other rights. Others who have written on this subject begin with the latter and then consider family and civil government" (LJB 11). By the unspecific "civilians" Smith must have meant the Roman law as preserved in Justinian's *Institutes* and *Digest*, which remained very much part of contemporary legal culture both in the form of scholarly commentary and in the form of adaptations to domestic law. In this literature there was generally some exposition of governmental authority and lawmaking before turning to rights in the family and then the rights of persons. The specific ideas of government were probably not of importance to Smith, but the reference was a readily understood signal of the general shift he intended away from the "others," by which he meant the natural lawyers whom he had followed hitherto.

The new arrangement might be seen as a means of putting greater emphasis on law and government, but the internal logic of the argument remained the same as it had been in the preceding years. The individual subject areas were not *substantially* changed, only the order of presentation. As Smith said about the two approaches, "There are several advantages peculiar to each of these methods, tho' that of the civil law seems upon the whole preferable" (LJB 11). In other words, it did not matter a great deal, yet he did make a change. We may speculate that Smith was beginning to lay more specific plans for the book on "the general principles of law and government" that he had foreshadowed at the end of *The Theory of Moral Sentiments* (VII.iv.37), and which he knew that he might soon expect to have a freer hand to write. (His departure from Glasgow was more or less certain by the beginning of the session in 1763.)[16] He may have wanted to experiment with an exposition free of the limitations of the natural law system. The latter had been a convenient way of proceeding from the moral philosophy to the jurisprudence section of his course, since the spectator analysis of justice had already been provided in the former. But since the conclusion from this philosophical theory was that justice was a situationally dependent practice and hence the sort of thing that always had a historical aspect, a self-contained treatment of the subject—such as an eventual book—might well seem to benefit from an analysis in terms of that which had an actual empirical history, namely, historical types of society within which the enforcement of rights could be analyzed.

"The first and chief design of every system of government is to maintain justice"; "Justice . . . is the foundation of civil government" (LJA i.1; LJB 5). However, as we have seen, Smith did not consider justice to be the *only* object of law. Also "police," revenue, arms, and the law of nations had to be taken into account, and a great deal of Smith's analysis of society was concerned with the ways in which all of them had challenged justice in the past, did so at present, and were likely to continue to do so in the future. He clearly believed that commercial society with its deep and deepening division of labor offered special opportunities of solving some serious problems, especially those of "cheapness of commodities," the personal independence of working people, the replacement of war by international trade. But at the same time commercial society presented its own problems, such as the "mental mutilation" of the working class due to the ever greater division of labor, the neglect of education arising from the same cause, the loss of public spirit, especially in matters of defense, wealth creation without a firm link to the country, monetary corruption of politics. "To remedy [such] defects would be an object worthy of serious attention" (LJB 333). It all depended on the ability of government to understand these dangers and to take the opportunities, and Smith did not have great faith in this happening. This is shown, not least, by his appreciation of his own voice as part of this contingency: he thought it as absurd to expect his "natural system of liberty" to become reality as More's Utopia or Harrington's Oceana (WN IV.ii.43). Indeed, the system was rather an antisystem, inasmuch as it would be based upon the simple principles of negative justice, or the basic rights, that had to be elaborated into law according to historical circumstance and in competition with other needs, such as defense. Piecemeal steps on this path were the best that one could hope for.

NOTES

1. Though he gave some lectures on the subject already in 1751–52 when he was professor of logic. Cf. I. S. Ross, *The Life of Adam Smith* (Oxford: 1995), chaps. 8–9.

2. R. L. Meek, "New Light on Adam Smith's Glasgow Lectures on Jurisprudence," *History of Political Economy* 8 (1976), pp. 439–77. The transcription of the Anderson Notes is at pp. 467–77.

3. Francis Hutcheson, *Philosophiae moralis institutio compendiaria*, with *A Short Introduction to Moral Philosophy*, ed. L. Turco (Indianapolis: 2007).

4. LJA. For details of the manuscripts and publication history of this and LJB, see the editors' introduction to LJ.

5. Dugald Stewart, "Account of the Life and Writings of Adam Smith, LL.D.," v.8, in Smith, EPS.

6. Ross, *Life*, p. 123.

7. Stewart, "Account," i.16–22, quotation at i.18.

8. Ibid., i.20.

9. See, e.g., A. S. Skinner, *A System of Social Science. Papers Relating to Adam Smith* (Oxford: 1979), chap. 6.

10. Concerning Smith's spectator theory, see also Eric Schliesser's chapter in this volume on *The Theory of Moral Sentiments*.

11. See especially TMS II.2 and VII.4.

12. See TMS V.2.9–16.

13. The most basic starting point for the whole of Smith's moral thought is the skeptical thesis that we have no sure access to the other person's mind, and a similar skepticism is crucial for his politics.

14. See John Pocock, *Barbarism and Religion*, vol. 3, *The First Decline and Fall* (Cambridge: 2003), p. 389.

15. For a conflicting account, see K. Haakonssen, *Natural Law and Moral Philosophy: From Grotius to the Scottish Enlightenment* (Cambridge: 1996), chap. 4.

16. Cf. Ross, *Life*, pp. 151–53.

BIBLIOGRAPHIC ESSAY

J. Cairns, "Adam Smith's Lectures on Jurisprudence: Their Influence on Legal Education," in *Adam Smith: International Perspectives*, ed. H. Mizuta and C. Sugiyama (New York: 1993), pp. 63–83; the professional context of Smith's lectures. K. Haakonssen, *The Science of a Legislator: The Natural Jurisprudence of David Hume and Adam Smith* (Cambridge: 1981); a complete reconstruction of Smith's system of jurisprudence. D. Lieberman, "Adam Smith on Justice, Rights, and Law," in *Cambridge Companion to Adam Smith*, ed. K. Haakonssen (Cambridge: 2006), pp. 214–45; a clear analysis and general overview of the jurisprudence. G. Vivenza, *Adam Smith and the Classics: The Classical Heritage in Adam Smith's Thought* (Oxford: 2001), chap. 3; the relationship between natural jurisprudence and history of law. E. Metzger, "Adam Smith's Historical Jurisprudence and the Method of the

'Civilians,'" *Loyola Law Review* 56 (2010), pp. 1–31; theory of rights versus history of government. P. Wood, "'The Fittest Man in the Kingdom': Thomas Reid and the Glasgow Chair of Moral Philosophy," *Hume Studies* 23 (1997), pp. 277–313; the institutional context.

5

THE *WEALTH OF NATIONS*

Jerry Evensky

The purpose of this chapter is to guide the reader through Adam Smith's *Inquiry into the Nature and Causes of the Wealth of Nations* (hereafter *Inquiry*). Smith's *Inquiry* represents his analysis of the nature and causes of the material progress that he sees in humankind's journey from past to prospect. Smith envisioned that progress as unfolding in four stages: hunting and gathering, pasturage, agriculture, and commerce.[1] Much of Smith's *Inquiry* is focused on the final, commercial stage. He seeks to persuade his readers that his analysis of the principles that drive commerce can explain the observed dynamic of commerce, and therefore the policy implications of his analysis are worthy of the attention of those who guide the nation(s).

As we examine Smith's analysis in his *Inquiry* it will be important to keep in mind that Smith is not an economist; he is a moral philosopher. His *Inquiry* is indeed into a very "economic" topic, but it represents only one dimension of his moral philosophical framework for thinking about the human condition. In Smith's vision of humankind's progress through stages, the social, political, and economic dimensions of human societies form a simultaneous system within which progress in any one dimension is dependent on complementary progress in the other two. An oft-neglected thread that weaves its way through his analysis of the progressive development of the wealth of nations is that such progress is impossible without simultaneous, appropriate development of social and political institutions.

At the level of a nation-state this maturation of the institutional matrix is neither inexorable nor inevitable. Nations progress and decline; they come and they go. It is humankind and not any particular nation that has made progress, slowly in fits and starts . . . but surely, from the rude state to commerce. As noted, the purpose of Smith's *Inquiry* is to represent the principles that promote progress as a guide for policy. His immediate objective is to facilitate the commercial policy in his own Great Britain, but his larger goal is to contribute to the progress of humankind.

Smith's *Inquiry* is divided into five books, each playing a distinct role in his analysis of "the nature and causes of the wealth of nations." Book I lays out the foundation of his analysis: his assumptions, his definitions, his basic framework for optimal wealth creation, and an early introduction to the sources of distortions that impede that optimal process. Book II sets out his analysis of the dynamics of growth, the "cause" of the progress of the *Wealth of Nations*. Book III examines the evolution of European society after the fall of Rome as an empirical case to demonstrate the power of his analysis. Book IV contrasts his analysis with the leading contemporary competing analyses. Book V presents some of the policy principles that follow from his analysis.

The *Wealth of Nations* is a very long work, and present space is very limited. What follows aims to present the analysis Smith offers in each book, trace the threads that weave together his analysis from book to book, and highlight the importance of Smith's moral philosophical vision as the context for his analysis in this *Inquiry into the Nature and Causes of the Wealth of Nations*.

BOOK I: "OF THE CAUSES OF IMPROVEMENT IN THE PRODUCTIVE POWERS OF LABOUR"

Progress begins, and therefore so does Smith's analysis, with the division of labor. If we divide up the tasks of a production process, each of us focusing on a single one, we become more productive at our chosen task because our dexterity improves, we save time not having to move from task to task, and our creativity is engaged. This arrangement "is not originally the effect of any human wisdom" (WN I.ii.1). According to Smith, we essentially stumble into this division of labor in the rude state as we begin to exchange surpluses and in due course recognize the benefits of specialization.

Thus the source of this interdependent, productive arrangement is our "propensity to truck, barter, and exchange" (WN I.ii.1). Smith briefly considers how humans have come to have this propensity, but he quickly leaves the question behind for it "belongs not to our present subject to enquire" (WN I.ii.2).

The division of labor makes each of us more productive. But what am I going to do with the "four thousand eight hundred pins" (WN I.i.3) that I can claim as my share of the daily production of my team of ten? This increased productivity is beneficial to me only if there is a market through which I can vent my surplus. Which brings Smith to his next point: the more extensive the market, the more surplus production it can absorb, and thus the finer and more productive the division of labor it can support.

In the rude state the extent of a market is determined by natural avenues (rivers) or barriers (mountain ranges) that respectively facilitate or impede trade. Humankind's progress beyond this rude state is made possible through our capacity to extend markets artificially by developing a trading/transportation infrastructure. But, and this is crucial to Smith's analysis, there is an important symmetry here: we also have the capacity to diminish the extent of the market by creating artificial barriers to trade.

As trade does expand it quickly runs into an impediment, barter. In even a moderately complex trading environment, barter is extremely inefficient. In Smith's analysis it is again not by rational problem solving but through an evolutionary process that a medium of exchange emerges to facilitate trade: money.

Money is a prickly subject. There's the obvious question as to why some commodities have a value in exchange, a monetary price, which seems to bear no relation to the value of that commodity in use. In Smith's analysis, these peculiar cases are due to naturally imposed scarcity, for example, diamonds and fine wines are naturally scarce relative to the effective demand in the market. But that raises another question. For those items that can be produced in quantities that satisfy the effective market demand, what determines their value in exchange?

For Smith the answer is labor. As he appreciates, it is fairly easy to justify a labor theory of value analysis in the rude state. If, ceteris paribus, someone chooses to toil two hours producing one item and four hours producing another, then he has revealed that the latter has twice as much value to him as the former and he would exchange these items at that ratio. But what is fairly straightforward in the rude state becomes significantly more complex as society progresses because production becomes the fruit of not just labor but of labor and capital combined. So how does one factor the value of this previously embodied labor (the capital) used in production into the measure of a commodity's value? Smith explores this issue, but he doesn't resolve its complexity, a fact he acknowledges noting that "after the fullest explication which I am capable of giving of it . . . [the concept of value may] appear still in some degree obscure" (WN I.iv.18). With that, he moves on to an analysis of price.

For most commodities the natural price reflects the cost of production, and the market price will in an undistorted environment oscillate around this natural price. But distortions do occur. Some are, as noted above, natural, like the natural scarcity of diamonds. Some are the result of artificial distortions. Such artificial distortions are a central theme in the *Inquiry*, for Smith's objective is to represent the natural course of humankind's progress and contrast that with the twists and turns of real human events caused by the opportunities and the incentives individuals have to distort the natural course. Book III is dedicated to laying out an extended historical case as an example of this contrast.

Smith begins to explore the sources of distortions as he examines the elements of price: In the rude state an exchange price is based on labor cost, for there is only labor involved in production. In more complex production systems the cost of production and thus the price includes payments to the workers (wages), the landowner (rent), and the undertaker, a role we might today refer to as that of an entrepreneur, who organizes the production (profit). As we will see, in Smith's analysis wages and rents increase with progress, while profits decrease.

Wages rise with progress, so the immiseration of labor is a prima facie case for the presence of distortions. Given the incentive masters have to keep wages low and the inherent asymmetry of power in the wage relationship ("[t]he masters . . . can combine much more easily"; WN I.viii.12) such distortions are common. Smith notes that in his own Great Britain "the law . . . [exacerbates this distortion by allowing] combinations [of masters], while it prohibits those of the workmen" (WN I.viii.12). And Great Britain is the best case. He goes on to examine how the laws and institutions of China and Bengal have created environments in which labor is grossly exploited, and how these distortions have contributed to China's stagnation and Bengal's decline.

This analysis reflects a central theme of Smith's *Inquiry*: progress is not a one-dimensional, economic process. The trajectory of any given society will be determined by the "nature of its laws and institutions" (WN I.ix.15), including social norms and political structures. If those laws and institutions are distorted to the advantage of any particular faction within society (e.g., masters), the progress of that society will be impeded or reversed.

Profit is included in the price because it is appropriate that the undertaker should be paid for his effort, imagination, and risk taking. It is the undertaker's accumulation and investment that drives the ever-finer division of labor, and thus the increasing productive capacity of society and the growing wealth of the nation. With each cycle of production and sale, a profit rewards the undertaker's effort, imagination, and risk taking, and his stock of capital deepens. This deeper pool of capital leads to ever more intense competition among undertakers, including for labor. This dynamic lowers the return to capital while at the same time raising wages. Thus, as noted above, in a dynamic, undistorted economy we should see higher wages and lower profit rates.

Net profit is a requisite and fair return for entrepreneurial activity. Net profit is the "lowest ordinary rate of profit . . . sufficient to compensate . . . the risk . . . [and to] recompence . . . the trouble of employing the stock" (WN I.ix.18–22). Gross profit includes an unearned return: interest. "[I]nterest of money . . . remains after completely compensating the whole risk and trouble of employing the stock" (WN V.ii.f.3). In the absence of market distortions, capital will flow to the best risk-adjusted rate of return, driving down the profit rate and reducing interest as capital deepens.

But clearly the capital holder prefers high interest, so there is an incentive to distort the market by creating artificial market advantages that protect high interest returns. This incentive is an important theme in Smith's *Inquiry*, for it is the driver in his analysis of the manipulation of the laws and institutions.[2]

Where laws and institutions are mature and undistorted, interest "would be so low as to render it impossible for any but the very wealthiest people to live upon the interest of their money" (WN I.ix.20). Where distortions abound one finds a rentier class. Smith cites for example the high interest rate in China as a function of "laws and institutions . . . [that] establish the monopoly of the rich" (WN I.ix.15). In Smith's *Inquiry*, sustained high interest is a signal of a distortion in economic activity.

Rent, like interest, is an unearned return. But unlike interest, rent is a return to a productive contribution: the natural productivity of a resource, like fertile land. "In agriculture," Smith writes, "nature labours along with man" (WN II.v.12), so the most fruitful and thus the earliest systematic production begins in agriculture. As agricultural productivity grows it generates a surplus that can support tradesmen. These tradesmen form towns. Towns are located based on their proximity to avenues of trade because the more extensive the market the town can reach, the finer the division of labor the town can support. As a town reaches ever more extensive markets its population expands and the town rents rise. The expanding town population expands the demand for foodstuffs, thus raising the rents on agricultural land near the town. Thus the natural effect of expanding economic activity is rising rents.

The unearned character of both rent and interest is important in Smith's presentation in Book V of his *Inquiry*. There, when Smith examines possible sources of tax revenue necessary to support government activity, he identifies rent and interest as two ideal targets. As unearned returns, taxing these shares does not distort productive incentives. But, as we will see, he recognizes the challenges of implementing such taxes on each of these returns.

Also in Book V Smith makes the case that government "police" (regulation) should align incentives to encourage productive and discourage unproductive activity. In this regard, he is keen to see government implement policies that do not facilitate but rather diminish the potential for generating an interest return. Apropos of this Smith closes Book I with a warning. The workers' and the landlords' interests are consistent with that of society, for as society progresses so too do wages and rents. Not so the "merchants and master manufacturers" (WN I.xi.p.10). Gross profits fall with progress. Thus this order of men "has not the same connection with the general interest of the society as that of the other two" (WN I.xi.p.10). "The proposal [therefore] of any new law or regulation of commerce which comes from this order, ought always to be listened to with great precaution" (WN I.xi.p.10). This warning anticipates much of Smith's analysis in Book IV.

BOOK II: "ON THE NATURE, ACCUMULATION, AND EMPLOYMENT OF STOCK"

Book II is the fulcrum of Smith's analysis. It lays out the dynamic *Causes of the Wealth of Nations*.

As individuals in the rude state become more productive they generate a surplus that can be accumulated to smooth their pattern of consumption. When this accumulation grows beyond the level necessary to satisfy personal requirements, the individual "naturally endeavours to derive a revenue from the greater part of it" (WN II.i.2). "His whole stock, therefore, is distinguished into two parts. That part which, he expects, is to afford him this revenue, is called his capital. The other is that which supplies his immediate consumption" (WN II.i.2). Part of this capital is fixed in the form of "instruments of trade which facilitate and abridge labour" (WN II.i.14) and part of it circulates. That portion that circulates takes different forms as it passes through the stages of production and trade from purchased resources to sold product. Money is the instrumental, liquefied form capital takes in order to lubricate exchanges between these stages (WN II.v.2):

- "procuring the rude produce"
- "manufacturing"

- "transporting" or wholesaling
- "dividing" or retailing

Observing that different forms of money are more universally accepted than others, Smith makes the point that domestic fiat money serves well in domestic circuits of production and trade because it is readily accepted there. Using paper currency domestically frees up the more universally accepted forms of money, gold and silver, for use in foreign trade. So, Smith argues, the paper currency should be just sufficient to service the domestic circuits, thus freeing up these metals for those more distant opportunities.

Smith analyzes the potential problems with paper currency at length, citing historical cases, but his point for the purposes of the thread of his *Inquiry* is that a properly managed paper currency can facilitate the progress of the *Wealth of Nations*.

The engine that "causes" the growth of the "wealth of nations" is these circuits of capital flow in production and trade. With every circuit the capital invested is not only replaced; it generates a net product. Labor applied in this circuit is "productive labour" (WN I.iii.1) precisely because it replaces the capital thrown into the circuit and contributes to this net production. "Unproductive labour" does neither.[3] "[T]he whole annual produce, if we except the spontaneous productions of the earth [is] the effect of productive labour" (WN II.iii.3).

Productive labor is dependent on accumulation, for it is accumulation that generates the capital necessary to sustain and equip this productive labor. Accumulation requires that individuals are less prodigal and more parsimonious . . . and parsimony requires security. Thus in Smith's analysis security is the sine qua non of the dynamic of accumulation, investment, and growth.

This focus on the importance of parsimony and security sets Smith's WN analysis into the larger context of his moral philosophy. Progress depends on society being "well governed" (WN I.i.10). The optimal locus of that "government" is individual ethics (à la TMS).[4] An ethical person in Smith's analysis governs his prodigality and is properly prudent and thus parsimonious. An ethical person in Smith's analysis is also just. He plays by the rules that protect rights and property, and thus he makes others feel secure. But in a society of less than angels, society requires an efficient, effective institutional government (à la LJ)[5] to police the behavior of those few who would not otherwise play by the rules.

Having laid out the role of circuits of capital flows in the growth of the wealth of nations, Smith analyzes the *natural* progress of the "wealth of nations." "Natural" here means the path this progress would take through the four stages if there were no distortions impeding that progress.

As noted above, the division of labor begins in the rude state. Pasturage follows once tribes domesticate animals. With this step from stage to stage, as with every such step in this "progress," the increasing complexity of societal arrangements (e.g., the emergence of private property in domesticated animals) requires the development of appropriate laws and institutions to ensure security. Those societies that succeed in this multidimensional evolutionary process are, ceteris paribus, larger, more powerful, and more sustainable.

The real "takeoff" begins in agriculture because, as noted above, "[i]n agriculture . . . nature labours along with man" (WN II.v.12) so the farmer is especially productive. But while the farmer is initially more productive than the merchant, the merchant has two advantages that make his realm, commerce, ultimately the more productive realm. His demand is not limited by the size of the consumers' stomachs, and most of his capital is circulating capital so it is much more mobile and can move with agility to unfolding opportunities in the market.

Capital flows to the best risk-adjusted rate of return. As capital stock deepens in a given circuit its return falls, and when this return falls sufficiently capital will "overflow" (WN II.ii.30) into successively more distant and/or risky circuits. Thus capital will naturally flow, according to Smith, into each of the following circuits in turn (WN II.v.17):

- "improve and cultivate all its lands"—under the immediate eye of the cultivator, this is quickest and least risky circuit (see WN III.i.1–4, 6–7) and it enjoys the advantage of nature's contribution

- "manufacture and prepare their whole rude produce for immediate use and consumption"—these local transaction circuits are quick and secure
- "transport the surplus part either of the rude or manufactured produce to . . . distant markets"

This last circuit, the "wholesale trade" (WN II.v.23), is itself divided by Smith into (WN II.v.24)

- "home trade"—domestic circuits that are not quite so quick and secure as local transactions
- "foreign trade of consumption"—circuits between home and foreign ports, less quick and less secure than home trade
- "the carrying trade"—circuits between two or more foreign ports, the slowest and least secure circuits

The dynamic is clear. Capital starts in the most advantageous circuit, the quickest and most secure circuit, and deepens there. As it deepens the risk-adjusted rate of return in that circuit falls. At some point, given the falling rate of return, the deepening capital will naturally spill into that next circuit with a now relatively attractive risk-adjusted rate of return, and so it goes sequentially from inner to outer circuit.

Apropos of this analysis, Smith writes, "The carrying trade is the natural effect and symptom of great national wealth [i.e., a deep pool of capital]; but it does not seem to be the natural cause of it. Those statesmen who have been disposed to favour it with particular encouragements, seem to have mistaken the effect and symptom for the cause" (WN II.v.35). This line anticipates the heart of his argument in Book IV: mercantilism, by intimidating the legislature (WN IV.ii.43) into favoring the carrying trade, has distorted the economy of Britain and undermined the nation's progress.

At this point in his *Inquiry* Smith has made the natural course clear. In a well-governed society capital flows to its best advantage, and the unintended consequence of this self-interested incentive is the progress of the nation's opulence. But human societies are all too often very perversely governed, or worse yet, ungoverned. Indicative of that is the unnatural development of Europe after the fall of Rome when, contrary to the natural course, progress began in the towns and only later reached the agricultural areas. In Book III Smith traces this dynamic in order to demonstrate the power of his analysis: using his Book II's natural progress analysis as a normative reference, in Book III Smith demonstrates how institutional distortions led to unnatural, inefficient development.

BOOK III: "OF THE DIFFERENT PROGRESS OF OPULENCE IN DIFFERENT NATIONS"

The natural course of human progress is, in Smith's analysis, from hunting and gathering to pasturage to agriculture to commerce, and so it would be "[h]ad human institutions . . . never disturbed the natural course of things" (WN III.i.4). "But though this natural order of things must have taken place in some degree in every . . . society, it has, in all the modern states of Europe, been, in many respects, entirely inverted" (WN III.i.9). This is classic Smith. His method is to tell two stories of humankind's history. One, a "theoretical or conjectural history" (Stewart II.49), describes the natural progress of opulence if laws and institutions evolved in proper alignment for each successive stage. Then, with this as normative reference, he analyzes the actual course of historical development with its unnatural twists and turns. His objective is to demonstrate that while the overall trajectory of humankind's path is progress, localized distortions caused by perverse laws and institutions distort and impede that natural progress. Book III's case in point: "the Discouragement of Agriculture in the antient State of Europe after the Fall of the Roman Empire" (WN III.ii).

In the vacuum left by the fall of Rome there was chaos. Into this chaos stepped individuals, lords, who engrossed the land and established order. The continuity of this order was preserved by entail and primogeniture. While these laws would be an anathema to Smith in a commercial setting, given the exigencies of the times he sees them as functionally valuable for they held chaos at bay.

These lords were the source of security, but they were not "great improvers" (WN III.ii.7). Surpluses were squandered on maintaining many retainers, unproductive laborers who served the whims of the lord.[6] Agriculture stagnated.

Initially the townspeople were just as barren and just as beholden to the local lords as the country folk. But ultimately the inhabitants of the towns escaped from the grip of the lords by allying themselves with the king in his competition with the lords for power (WN III.ii.12). This alliance allowed the occupants of towns to slowly free themselves from the oppression of the lords (WN III.iii.2–3) and to enjoy more security. With security came the incentive to accumulate and invest capital in circuits of production and trade. Thus, contrary to the natural course of things, towns progressed while the countryside remained stagnant.

As towns progressed, the lords began to spend less of their wealth on retainers and more on the material baubles available from the towns. In order to afford ever more of these material goods the lords sought more productivity from their lands. Thus it became worthwhile for the lords to give those living on the land more incentive for production. Rents were fixed and those on the land were given more autonomy and security. This unleashed the potential of agriculture.

By his spending in the market, the lord who once supported thousands of unproductive dependents now supported a fraction of the subsistence of each among a much larger number of productive workers. And, "[t]hough he contributes, therefore, to the maintenance of them all, they are all more or less independent of him, because generally they can all be maintained without him" (WN III.iv.11). Secure independence, energetic participation in the market, productivity . . . these are of a piece in Smith's *Inquiry*.

Book III reflects Smith's belief that in order to understand the course of a nation's progress, or lack thereof, one must examine the evolving structure of its laws and institutions.

Smith believed that the Britain of his day was the most advanced nation in the world precisely because it had, through the serendipitous unfolding of chance, circumstance, and the intended and unintended consequences of individuals' choices, established laws and institutions that protected individuals' independence and security. But he saw this British success as at risk due to the influence of the self-serving principles of the mercantile system. In Book IV Smith turns his attention to two competing views regarding *The Nature and Causes of the Wealth of Nations*, but his primary focus in Book IV is on the one he found most troubling: the principles of the mercantile system.

BOOK IV: "OF SYSTEMS OF POLITICAL OECONOMY"

Smith gives short shrift to the "agricultural systems of political oeconomy" (the physiocrats) because this system "has, so far as I know, never been adopted by any nation . . . [and i]t would not, surely, be worthwhile to examine at great length the errors of a system which never has done, and probably never will do any harm in any part of the world" (WN IV.ix.2).

Not so the mercantile system. Smith's deep and growing concern about the "harm" done by the "errors" of this system is reflected in the energy he pours into debunking this system. It is a policy regime designed not for the benefit of "the great body of the people" (WN IV.iii.c.11) but rather "for the benefit of the rich and the powerful, that is principally encouraged by our mercantile system" (WN IV.viii.4).

Book IV demonstrates that while Smith is writing for the ages, he is also very keen to be a strong voice in the policy debates of his day. He was compulsive about developing Book IV, delaying the initial publication of his *Inquiry* three years, primarily to further develop Book IV; and making his most significant subsequent addition to the *Inquiry* (in the third [1784] edition) an entire new chapter for Book IV: "Conclusion of the Mercantile System."

Smith begins Book IV by examining the evolution of mercantile thought from a simple bullionist argument that wealth comes from hoarding gold to a more textured assertion that trade is a zero-sum game and thus a nation's wealth is augmented by winning at trade. What seems to concern and disturb Smith most about this evolution is that it reflects the transformation of the analysis from an honest, albeit flawed analysis of wealth creation, to a dishonest, distorting, and self-serving policy prescription disguised as honest analysis: "[T]he interested sophistry of merchants and manufac-turers [the mercantile system] confounded the common sense of mankind. Their interest is . . . directly opposite to that of the great body of the people" (WN IV.iii.c.10).

Smith spends most of Book IV demonstrating that mercantilist policies in fact reduce the wealth of the nation. His objective is to unmask the advocates of these distorting policies as powerful play-ers who use their wealth and influence to persuade or, if necessary, "intimidate the legislature" into adopting their self-serving policies (WN IV.ii.43).

Smith begins his analysis of the perversity of mercantile policies by examining restraints on imports. With such restraints "the mo-nopoly of the home-market is more or less secured" (WN IV.ii.1), thus ensuring that the nation will produce for itself rather than spend on the products of others. Seems like a good idea: giving domestic producers advantages to encourage domestic produc-tion. Smith deploys the circuits of capital analysis he developed in Book II to debunk this simplistic thinking. Creating a monopoly for home production generates an unnaturally high rate of profit on this innermost circuit of capital. This in turn artificially dis-torts capital flow, delaying the spillover of capital into successively broader circuits. Thus such a policy "divert[s] a part of it [capital] into a direction into which it might not otherwise have gone" (WN IV.ii.3).

In contrast, in an undistorted market capital naturally flows to its best advantage and, in turn, supports the most productive labor and the ever finer division of that labor. Thus in an unfettered mar-ket, as each capital holder pursues his self-interest he is "led by an invisible hand to promote an end which was no part of his inten-tion": the progress of the *Wealth of Nations* (WN IV.ii.9).

Chapters 4, 5, and 6 of Book IV explore other distortions caused by mercantile policies, but the heart of Smith's attack on mercan-tilism begins in chapter 7, "Of Colonies." Chapter 7 accounts for almost half of Book IV because, for Smith, colonial policies repre-sent the most perverse manifestation of mercantilism.

The essence of the argument is again derived from Smith's Book II circuits of capital analysis. If "Restraints upon . . . Importation"

(WN IV.ii.1) are distorting because they lead to a glut of capital in the home market, then colonial policies are all the more perverse because they artificially drive capital into "a channel much less advantageous [much more slow and insecure] than that in which it would naturally run" (WN IV.v.a.3). "[I]nstead of running in a great number of small channels, [capital] has been taught to run principally into one great channel," the colonial trade (WN IV.vii.c.43), reducing the wealth and the security of the nation.

The only semisuccessful colonial enterprise, according to Smith, has been the British colonies in North America. And that success is not thanks to but rather in spite of mercantilist policies. The blossoming of those colonies reflects the fact that the "security which the laws in Great Britain give to every man that he shall enjoy the fruits of his own labour, is alone sufficient to make any country flourish, notwithstanding these and twenty other absurd regulations of commerce" (WN IV.v.b.43).

Here again Adam Smith the moral philosopher is making that essential connection between dimensions of society. It is the maturity of political institutions that ensures justice and in turn the security of the people, and it is this security that "is alone sufficient to make any country flourish." But even as the colonies themselves have prospered, all that Great Britain has derived from this colonial enterprise is a "loss" (WN IV.vii.c.65): the cost of several wars to protect the mercantile enterprise. While the "pretended purpose . . . [of mercantile colonial policy was] to increase the commerce of Great Britain . . . its real effect has been to raise the rate of merchant profit" (WN IV.vii.c.64) at the expense of British blood and treasure.

Smith closes his assessment of mercantilism with chapter 8 added in 1784. By then Smith had served for several years as a commissioner of customs, a position that gave him an insider's access to the politics and policies of trade. This new chapter is a scathing attack on the mercantile system as an arrangement designed for the "benefit of the rich and the powerful" (WN IV.viii.4) at the expense of "the great body of the people" (WN IV.viii.20). To Smith this is deplorable: "To hurt in any degree the interest of any one order of citizens, for no other purpose but to promote that of some other, is evidently contrary to that justice and equality of treatment which the sovereign owes to all the different orders of his subjects" (WN IV.viii.30). Here again we hear Smith the moral philosopher for whom the analysis is always informed by standards of morality and justice that he has explored elsewhere in detail (TMS and LJ).

So, if mercantilism is a distortion of government policy, what then is the appropriate role of government? In Book V Smith addresses that question.

BOOK V: "OF THE REVENUE OF THE SOVEREIGN OR COMMONWEALTH"

The first order of business for any society is to defend itself. Smith's analysis of the role of government thus begins with defense and is framed by his stages logic. In the hunting and pasturage stages there is little role for government in defense because in the natural course of life people develop mastery of weapons and a culture of courage. What distinguishes these first two stages is the size of the force that can be assembled. Hunting tribes live hand to mouth and are very small. Pasturage supports a larger population because domesticated animals are a steadier source of maintenance. This larger population can assemble a greater fighting force, so as a society evolves from hunting and gathering to pasturage its ability to defend itself is enhanced.

This analysis represents an essential thread in Smith's story of humankind's progress. With each new stage, the productive capacity and thus the sustainable size of the population grow. This larger population and the attendant progress of technology makes the military power of the society more formidable, and thus with its progress into each new stage a given society is, ceteris paribus, naturally more secure relative to a society in the previous stage.

Individual societies may progress through stages and with this progress comes the power to preserve themselves, but invariably internal distortions emerge that cause stagnation and/or decline making them unnaturally vulnerable to external forces (e.g., "the

Fall of the Roman Empire"; WN III.ii). No society is on an inexorable path of progress. Sustained progress occurs only at the level of humankind as the improvements in the capacity for defense that come with material progress advantage that progress.

Having traced the role of government in securing citizens from external threats, Smith turns to the government's role in ensuring justice within the state. As with defense, this "requires too very different degrees of expence in the different periods of society" (WN V.i.b.1). The continuity of Smith's analysis from defense to domestic justice is striking. Both focus on security. In both cases the analysis is framed by the evolution of society through the "different periods." In both cases, the role of government expands as the complexity of society grows. With respect to the administration of justice, as the extent of property holdings and the complexity of the concept of property rights grows from extremely small and simple in a hunting and gathering society to extremely large and complex in a commercial society, the necessity of a government role in defining and securing property grows.

The third fundamental role of government is the provision of "publick Works and publick Institutions" "for facilitating the commerce of the society, and those for promoting the instruction of the people" (WN V.i.c.2).

Always, when it comes to private versus public provision, Smith has his eye on the alignment of incentives. If incentives are naturally, constructively aligned . . . then laissez-faire. If they are perversely aligned in a way that is socially destructive, the first option is to constructively realign the incentives by government regulation. Failing that, more active government intervention (e.g., public provision) is warranted.

As a commercial case in point, Smith distinguishes those avenues of trade that require constant maintenance, canals, from those that continue to be passable with minimal maintenance, high roads. The best way to ensure proper maintenance for the former is to put the toll revenue into the hands of a private person, for his well-being will incentivize him to keep the canal passable. In contrast, a high road does not need such constant care, and so in the hands of a private person it might be neglected as the person simply collects the tools. Better such roads be maintained by the state.

From the state's role in commerce, Smith turns to its role in education. He emphasizes that for its own sake a liberal state must structure institutions that enhance the maturity of its citizens. If working-class citizens' minds are numbed by the monotony of their work, they can become easy prey to the "man of system" (TMS VI.ii.2.17) who offers simplistic solutions to complex problems. Similarly, if citizens are caught up in the enthusiasms of a religion, the power of that religion can become formidable to the state.

State provision of a basic public education for working-class citizens can ameliorate the mind-numbing effect of their work. Screens on access to higher societal pursuits, public or private, that require study of science and philosophy can ensure that those in the higher ranks of society are equipped to resist the simplistic, yet powerful appeals of enthusiasm.

An uneducated citizenry can be led by a demagogue down a path that would destroy the very liberty that gave that demagogue a voice. Smith appreciates that the liberal solution to this potential liberal dilemma is not to still the voices of demagogues, but rather to empower the citizenry to take the measure of all ideas and reject demagoguery.

As noted above, Smith's first choice for government policy is to align private incentives so that the desired public result is efficiently achieved. But as far as Smith is concerned, where the desired result is imperative and incentives cannot be aligned properly, state provision is essential.

State provision implies expenditures. Smith argues that wherever possible these costs should be borne by the beneficiaries. This is not only just, it aligns incentives correctly because the beneficiary will hold the provider accountable. If the benefits are spread more generally, then each citizen should contribute "in proportion to their respective abilities" (WN V.i.i.1).

This brings Smith to the subject of taxation. He lays out four general "maxims" (WN V.ii.b.2) that should guide taxation (WN V.ii.b.3–6):

- Taxes should be based on ability to pay. He suggests that those who "enjoy [more] under the protection of the state" should pay more.
- Taxes "ought to be certain, and not arbitrary."
- Taxes should be levied with the convenience of the payer in mind.
- Taxes should be collected as efficiently as possible.

As noted earlier, rent and interest are theoretically ideal subjects of taxation because, as unearned returns, taxing them does not diminish the incentives for productive activity. But, the practical issues with such taxes are daunting: for example, measuring the level of these revenues, the jointness of some rent and profit returns, the mobility of capital, and the challenge of determining the incidence of taxes imposed in these complex cases. Smith explores these issues in detail and offers his prescription for second best options. He then turns to other potential subjects of taxation: enterprises, transfers (e.g., bequests), wages, or consumption. In each case he points out the complications that make the tax problematic vis-à-vis the principles cited above and explores the effect of the tax on the alignment of incentives.

Absent sufficient tax revenue, the state takes on debt. Smith asserts that a large source of government debt is the financing of wars because government hesitates to raise taxes to cover the cost of a war. He cites two reasons for this: the level of need is often unclear and the public commitment to the war can be eroded by such a tax. Borrowing allows the government to avoid a tax. If the war is remote, then for the people, who feel no real sacrifice, the war can simply be a fascinating "amusement" (WN V.iii.37).

Such borrowing is facilitated by the fact that in the commercial stage there is a ready supply of capital to meet the needs of government borrowing. Those merchants and manufacturers who engage their capital in the circuits of production and trade can divert some of that capital to the government as loans. This withdrawal of accumulation from these circuits reduces the long-term productive capacity of the nation because it is being channeled from support of productive labor into the maintenance of unproductive labor, the military; but it still yields a return for the merchants and manufacturers, the interest on the loan. So while this financing method is problematic for society, it can be a boon to this faction.

Smith argues that in peacetime and even at the outset of a war, government should finance itself on a pay as you go basis . . . by taxes. Doing so protects capital accumulation and under such a system of finance "[w]ars would in general be more speedily concluded, and less wantonly undertaken" (WN V.iii.50). For example, the wisdom of wars to protect the interests of the mercantile faction, wars that account for much of Britain's current debt, may have been more carefully scrutinized if they had been paid for by taxation. This is a keenly salient issue as he closes his *Inquiry* in 1776 with a wary eye on "the present disturbances" in the colonies (WN IV.vii.b.20).

A BRIEF REFLECTION ON SMITH'S *INQUIRY INTO THE NATURE AND CAUSES OF THE WEALTH OF NATIONS*

There are few works in the history of humankind that have had more influence than Adam Smith's *Inquiry into the Nature and Causes of the Wealth of Nations*. In the over two hundred years since his *Inquiry* was published, as market economies have come to dominate the globe commercially and militarily, Adam Smith and his "invisible hand" have been cited as a guiding light by many who believe in the magic of markets. In the past thirty or so years those nations that had emerged as the greatest competitors to the market model of national economic activity, Russia and China, have abandoned their competition and embraced the market system. The world is moving to markets, and Adam Smith "wrote the book" on markets.

Unfortunately Smith's book is sometimes used, as is the Bible or the Koran, to justify a deeply held position by selectively extracting supportive quotations.[7] In Smith's case he is cited by some as the patron saint of laissez-faire. Certainly, Smith believes in liberty. But his view is much more nuanced than "liberty is all." Smith believed that liberty without justice is a road to serfdom under "Lord Faction," or to chaos.

Smith fully appreciated that government can be a most powerful tool for "rent-seeking" when it is captured by faction (see WN IV); but it is also the only collective tool we have to constrain those who would not play by the rules and to provide essential services that private incentives will not provide.

Adam Smith had an abiding faith in humankind's ability to progress. He imagined that progress as moving through stages toward an ideal limiting case: "the liberal plan of equality, liberty and justice" (WN IV.ix.3). His purpose as a moral philosopher was to contribute to that progress. His *Inquiry into the Nature and Causes of the Wealth of Nations* was one piece of that contribution.

NOTES

1. Ronald L. Meek, "Smith, Turgot, and the 'Four Stages' Theory," *History of Political Economy* 3 (1971), p. 24.

2. In modern terminology the term for that dynamic is "rent-seeking." See James Buchanan, R. D. Tollison, and G. Tullock, eds., *Toward a Theory of a Rent-Seeking Society* (College Station, TX: 1980).

3. This is not to say that unproductive labor is not valuable labor. Smith includes "men of letters" (WN II.iii.2) as unproductive labor, but he clearly felt that his work had value.

4. For more detail, see Jerry Evensky, *Adam Smith's Moral Philosophy: A Historical and Contemporary Perspective on Markets, Law, Ethics, and Culture* (Cambridge: 2005), chap. 2. Also see Jerry Evensky, "Adam Smith's Essentials: On Trust, Faith, and Free Markets," *Journal of the History of Economic Thought* 33 (2011), pp. 249–68.

5. For more detail, see Evensky, *Adam Smith's Moral Philosophy*, chap. 3. Also see Evensky, "Adam Smith's Essentials."

6. He offers as an example of the reported extravagances of that age "[t]he great earl of Warwick [who] is said to have entertained every day at his different manors, thirty thousand people; and though the number here may have been exaggerated, it must, however, have been very great to admit of such exaggeration" (WN III.iv.5).

7. See, for example, "God Gave the Law of Segregation (as Well as the 10 Commandments) to Moses on Mount Sinai," in U. M. Gaillot, *God Gave the Law of Segregation (as Well as the 10 Commandments) to Moses on Mount Sinai*, 3rd ed. (New Orleans: 1960), http://digilib.usm.edu/cdm/compoundobject/collection/manu/id/2139/rec/6 (accessed October 5, 2012).

BIBLIOGRAPHIC ESSAY

For a book-length guide to the content of the *Wealth of Nations*, see my *Adam Smith's* Wealth of Nations: *A Reader's Guide* (Cambridge: 2015). Samuel Hollander's *The Economics of Adam Smith* (Toronto: 1973) is a very valuable contribution to Smith scholarship. Hollander's purpose, as he himself notes, is to analyze Smith through a modern lens, applying modern techniques to assess Smith's contributions in the *Wealth of Nations*. Among the best full-length arguments for interpreting Smith as an advocate for laissez-faire is James Otteson's *Adam Smith* (Continuum: 2011), published as vol. 16 in the Major Conservative and Libertarian Thinkers series (John Meadowcroft, series ed.). For a more holistic view of Smith's *Wealth of Nations*, see Jeffrey Young's *Economics as a Moral Science: The Political Economy of Adam Smith* (Cheltenham: 1997).

There are several recent and valuable readers that cover Smith's work including his *Wealth of Nations*. These include *The Cambridge Companion to Adam Smith*, ed. Knud Haakonssen (Cambridge: 2006), *The Elgar Companion to Adam Smith*, ed. Jeffrey Young (Cheltenham: 2009), and *The Oxford Handbook of Adam Smith*, ed. Christopher Berry, Maria Pia Paganelli, and Craig Smith (Oxford: 2013).

If one chooses to tackle the *Wealth of Nations* itself, there is no better edition than the Oxford Edition edited by D. D. Raphael and Andrew Skinner (Oxford: 1976). The exquisite notation by the editors of this edition allows the reader to see how Smith revised the *Wealth* from edition to edition over the course of his lifetime, a valuable tool for understanding the evolution of his views.

THE *ESSAYS ON PHILOSOPHICAL SUBJECTS*

Craig Smith

Adam Smith's *Essays on Philosophical Subjects* (EPS) was published in 1795, five years after Smith's death. The posthumous publication of this collection of essays was provided for in Smith's will. Indeed he mentioned its publication in his original letter appointing David Hume as his executor in 1773. He instructed the executors of his 1790 will, the geologist James Hutton and the medical scientist Joseph Black, that he wished to see his lecture notes and draft material destroyed except for the essays that would eventually become the EPS. His friends duly assisted in burning this material before Smith passed away and then completed the task of publishing the surviving material, together with Dugald Stewart's *Life of Adam Smith*, which had been read to the Royal Society of Edinburgh in January and March 1793.

The essays collected in the volume are of interest for a number of reasons, but perhaps the principal reason is that, of the large amount of draft material that Smith had to hand, they were the only pieces that he felt warranted publication. In his letter to Hume in 1773 he described the essay on *Astronomy* as a "fragment of an intended juvenile work" that he had come to suspect contained "more refinement than solidity" (CAS 137) and that he would leave Hume to judge on its worthiness for publication. Similar instructions were left to Black and Hutton, who state in the advertisement to the 1795 edition that the material "appeared to be parts of a plan he [Smith] had once formed, for giving a connected history of the liberal sciences and elegant arts," a plan that Smith had abandoned as "far too extensive" to be completed in his lifetime.[1] This early, unrealized, project appears to date from Smith's time in Oxford, Edinburgh, and Kirkcaldy prior to taking up his chair at Glasgow in 1751.

The edition of the EPS published in 1795 contains (in order) Stewart's *Life of Adam Smith*; *The Principles Which Lead and Direct Philosophical Enquiries Illustrated by the History of Astronomy*; *The Principles Which Lead and Direct Philosophical Enquiries Illustrated by the History of the Ancient Physics*; *The Principles Which Lead and Direct Philosophical Enquiries Illustrated by the History of the Ancient Logics and Metaphysics*; *Of the Nature of That Imitation Which Takes Place in What Are Called the Imitative Arts*; *Of the Affinity between Music, Dancing, and Poetry*; *Of the Affinity between Certain English and Italian Verses*; and *Of the External Senses*.[2]

In what follows I propose to focus my attention on the more substantive "scientific" essays in this volume.[3] Limitations on space prevent a full exploration of Smith's aesthetics and literary criticism in this chapter (on the latter, see chapter 24 of this volume). The essays in aesthetics in EPS demonstrate the breadth of Smith's intellectual interests and may have formed some part of his projected work on the "elegant arts." *Of the Nature of That Imitation Which Takes Place in What Are Called the Imitative Arts* and its companion piece *Of the Affinity between Music, Dancing, and Poetry* are difficult to date but seem most likely to have been written sometime in the 1760s or 1770s. They represent a careful analysis of the role of imitation in the arts, with a focus on the role of sympathy and the sentimental basis of aesthetic experience. The "hinge" of Smith's analysis in both is that "the disparity between the imitating and the imitated object is the foundation of the beauty of imitation" (IA I.14). His point is that the pleasure of imitation comes not from a direct copy in the same medium, but through the skill involved in producing an imitation of a subject in a different medium. Using the examples of painting, sculpture, music, poetry, and dancing, Smith develops an analysis of different forms of imitation and the aesthetic pleasure that are elicited in each medium. The "art" of imitation is the capacity to invoke an imaginative, emotional experience that pleases us not by the perfection of the reproduction, but by the skill with which the resemblance is brought upon our minds. The psychological approach continues when Smith sketches his views on the capacity of each medium to express complex ideas and argues that dancing is superior to music and inferior to poetry in this regard. *Of the Affinity between Certain English and Italian Verses* probably dates from 1782 and demonstrates Smith's capacity in European languages. It sees him developing a stand-alone essay in comparative literature. He is engaging in an ongoing eighteenth-century debate about poetic style through an examination of the similarity in poetic structure between Italian and English verse. The point is to highlight that in these languages, as opposed to Latin and French, the rhythmic structure of poetry is best understood through variations in stress and accent rather than in the precise syllable count of a verse. The piece may have been intended to be a part of the larger work on the arts, suggesting that Smith may have intended to deploy comparative case studies to illustrate his argument, but this is purely speculative as we have no evidence reliably to link this piece with the preceding essays.

The three histories and the essay *Of the External Senses* reveal an aspect of Smith's wide-ranging academic interests that is often obscured by the moral and economic focus of his more famous works. From his days as an undergraduate at Glasgow studying under the mathematician Robert Simson, Smith maintained an interest in the natural sciences and appears to have read widely on the subject throughout his life. There is some evidence that the material that forms these four essays was something that Smith worked on throughout his career, possibly from his time at Oxford until shortly before his death. In letters dated 1780 (CAS 208) and 1785 (CAS 248) Smith refers to working on his philosophical history of the arts and science. We also have evidence of his regular attendance at and participation in the discussions of the natural sciences at the Royal Society of Edinburgh and the Royal Society in London, together with his own reference to an amateur study of botany at Kirkcaldy (CAS 208) to support the notion of Smith as someone who followed the development of the natural sciences. His executors, Hutton and Black, were both eminent in their own fields of science and were perhaps well chosen to arrange the publication of a volume whose focus was largely "scientific" in the modern sense.

Before discussing the details of the three historical essays it is important to note the title appended to each: they are *The Principles Which Lead and Direct Philosophical Enquiries Illustrated by* . . . . Smith's aim is not really to provide a narrative history of the development of astronomy, ancient physics, and ancient logics and metaphysics. The historical details that he provides here are reasonably accurate for the time and represent a serious scholarly interest in the material, but that is not what is of significance about these essays.[4] The point is that the material is being used to illustrate a wider theory about the practice of science, or even more significantly, about the nature of human intellectual development in a manner akin to Turgot's programmatic *A Philosophical Review of the Successive Advances of the Human Mind* (1750). Smith's aim in these essays is to outline a theory of the growth of human knowledge. The histories serve to illustrate the more general point about the nature of the development of systematic knowledge that forms a common theme throughout Smith's work.

What is particularly interesting about Smith's account of the principles that lead and direct philosophy is that he grounds them firmly in the sentiments. The urge to pursue systematic knowledge, understood as structured, organized, and comprehensive knowledge, is a product of a human need for emotional stability. This in turn prompts the exercise of the imagination to account for phenomena in a way that banishes emotional unease. Smith's analysis begins in the *History of Astronomy* with three emotions: wonder, surprise, and admiration. We wonder at things we have not seen before, we are surprised when familiar objects appear out of their usual setting and we admire an explanatory account that renders these familiar to us. By stressing the emotional origins of philosophical inquiry Smith is not rejecting the view that knowledge can be useful. But what he is doing is stating that usefulness is not the original motive to inquiry (HA III.5). Instead our thirst for knowledge comes from a far more basic part of our shared human psychology. It arises from the fact that humans have emotional responses to the world around them and that they operate with a form of associationist psychology. Smith, largely following Hume, believes that our imagination develops habitual patterns of thought that we use to orientate our lives through the association of ideas drawn from experience. Our thought "glides easily" along the "natural career of the imagination" (HA II.8) when events follow their usual course. Wonder and surprise arise when these habitual expectations are confronted with a completely new phenomenon or with an irregularity in the usual appearance of familiar events.

Surprise, says Smith, is "the violent and sudden change produced upon the mind, when an emotion of any kind is brought suddenly upon it" (HA I.5). Surprises make us uneasy as they interrupt the smooth operation of the imagination, and it is this uneasiness that prompts us to seek explanation. Explanation is achieved when we are able to account for the surprising event in terms that are familiar to our imagination from past experience. Once we have become accustomed to an initially surprising occurrence we are left with a residual uneasiness if we are not able to provide a satisfactory account of the phenomenon. We wonder at the cause of a phenomenon and seek to classify it in terms of our own experience. Once we have successfully placed a phenomenon our minds are able to operate smoothly and are freed from unease. We come to admire the account of the phenomenon that we have developed to the extent that it is familiar to us and "beautiful" in its explanatory reach.[5] At this stage the process that Smith is describing is a general account of human epistemic urges. But he goes on to point out that while many people—the example is "common artizans" (HA II.11)—are satisfied when they can accommodate the phenomena of their everyday lives within a habitual framework uninterrupted by surprising events, there are others for whom wonder becomes a prompt to a deeper curiosity. These individuals are not satisfied with mere habitual acceptance of the world as it appears from experience, but desire to look closer and closer into the relationships between phenomena. Their way of doing this is through the classification of thought by the examination of causes and effects. This, according to Smith, is the pursuit of philosophy understood as "the science of the connecting principles of nature" (HA II.12). The philosopher is engaged in a process of "render[ing] familiar to the imagination" (HA IV.65) chains of events that appear, initially at least, to be chaotic. The philosopher methodizes human experience by illustrating the chains that connect phenomena. The result is the reduction of surprise, the satisfaction of wonder, and the elucidation of admiration. "Who wonders," Smith writes, "at the machinery of the opera-house who has once been admitted behind the scenes?" (HA II.9) The approach is summarized by Smith in the following terms: "Philosophy, by representing the invisible chains which bind together all these disjointed objects, endeavours to introduce order into this chaos of jarring and discordant appearances, to allay this tumult of the imagination, and to restore it, when it surveys the great revolutions of the universe, to that tone of tranquillity and composure, which is both most agreeable in itself, and most suitable to its nature" (HA II.12).

The philosopher, or as we would probably say today, the scientist, becomes an active inquirer into the connections that lie behind phenomena. He undertakes in a self-conscious fashion the general model of human epistemic experience that Smith outlines. Smith would return to this theme in the *Wealth of Nations*, where he would describe the development, through the division of labor, of a distinct profession of philosophers "whose trade it is, not to do anything, but to observe everything; and who, upon that account, are often capable of combining together the powers of the most distant and dissimilar objects" (WN I.i.9).[6]

Smith begins Section III of the *Astronomy* with a significant initial foray. Rather than plunge straight into the astronomical systems that held from ancient times, Smith begins with an account of polytheistic religion. What is startling about this is that he is accounting for primitive religion with the same psychological model that he will later apply to philosophy.[7] Polytheism is the "natural" response of an ignorant people to events that are beyond their everyday experience. Unexpected events are attributed to the intervention of particular deities who disrupt the regular pattern of events. These deities are then understood as operating with anthropomorphic characters and a superhuman intelligence that allows them deliberately to bring about the apparently chaotic events of nature to satisfy their whims. Polytheistic religion, like philosophy, operates from the same general epistemic motivators of surprise and wonder coupled with an associationist psychology.

It is only later in social development, when "order and security" (HA III.3) have been established and "civilized societies" are freed from the most damaging effects of nature upon subsistence, that humans begin to inquire into the regularities of nature and gradually diminish their reliance on invisible beings to account for natural phenomena (and also when the division of labor between artisans and philosophers is able to develop). But the reduced reliance on explanation through the actions of deities is accompanied by a desire to systematize knowledge of the regularities of nature and by the development of systems of thought that seek to satisfy our curiosity.

Smith identifies two principles that he uses to account for the gradual evolution of our thinking about astronomy. The first of these is gap-plugging. A system of explanation, according to Smith's version of Hume's associationist psychology, will successfully convince us to the extent it is able to lead the imagination smoothly through its account of the phenomena at hand. If it fails to account for a part of the observed phenomena the mind will "feel" the gap and fail to be convinced. The second principle is that of explanatory simplicity. If convincingness depends on the ease with which the mind is led through the account of the phenomena at hand, then the system that is able to do this in the simplest fashion will be more satisfactory to our imaginations. Or as Smith would have it, "This system [of Plato and Aristotle] had now become as intricate and complex as those appearances themselves, which it had been invented to render uniform and coherent. The imagination, therefore, found itself but little relieved from that embarrassment, into which those appearances had thrown it, by so perplexed an account of things" (HA IV.8).

Theoretical beauty is a product of coherence (gaplessness) and parsimony, and both of these are assessed in the light of observation of the phenomena concerned. One system of astronomy will come to replace another when it is able to explain everything (and more) that the prior system could explain without resorting to a complexity that will fail to lead the mind smoothly through the explanatory process.

This leads Smith to the history of astronomy. If our admiration of a philosophical account depends upon its ability to banish surprise and satisfy wonder then explanations will compete with each other in terms of their ability to satisfy the desire for calmness of mind in the light of observed phenomena. What Smith proceeds to do in the remainder of the *Astronomy* and in the subsequent two essays is to examine the development and succession of various systems of philosophy. A system is an "imaginary machine invented to connect together in the fancy those different movements and effects which are already in reality performed" (HA IV.19).[8] The acceptance of a system of philosophy depends upon its ability to calm our minds, and to explain the phenomena in question in a fashion that both leads the imagination in a smooth and gap-free fashion, and does so in a more elegant and coherent fashion than alternative accounts.

With this model in place Smith traces the basic ideas of astronomical systems from the ancient Greeks through Ptolemy, Copernicus, Tycho Brahe, Galileo, Kepler, Gassendi, Descartes, and Newton. Smith's account describes the main features of each system and its relationship to its predecessors and successors. His point is that systems of astronomy have a period of dominance when they are widely accepted and when scholars operate within their assumptions "arranging and methodizing" (HA IV.50) the main points of the approach. However dissatisfaction with a system begins to develop when it faces insurmountable gaps that it cannot account for, or when the additions to the main theory lead to overcomplexity. When this happens Smith shows how a new system is introduced that succeeds where the earlier system succeeded and surpasses it in terms of explanatory reach and theoretical elegance. These new systems face initial hostility from those devoted to the existing system and only gradually come to surpass the previous account.[9] The shift to a new system of thinking is prompted, like that between Ptolemy and Copernicus, because the new account explains in "a more simple as well as a more accurate manner"

(HA IV.27) or because, like that of Kepler, the established system becomes "of too intricate a nature to facilitate very much the effort of the imagination in conceiving it" (HA IV.57).

The account ends with a brief discussion of Newton and the success of his system in explaining the movement of the planets through a few simple principles issuing in predictions that can be verified by exploration and measurement (HA IV.72). This success leads to his system supplanting that of Descartes, which though theoretically elegant, failed in scope, coherence, and (crucially) verifiability in comparison to Newton's account when the complex theory of vortices was compared to the simple laws of Newtonian physics and the invocation of gravity. Smith's account of Newton is less complete than the discussion of the earlier thinkers, but as his executors note, they have included it from some imperfect notes as a further "illustration" of the general thesis.[10] Once again this reminds us that the point of the essay is not a discussion of the details of the particular theories, or even the development of a philosophy of science, but rather an account of the evolution of human knowledge illustrated by its advance in a particular discipline. The approach here is clearly one instance of Smith's wider interest in providing evolutionary accounts of the development of phenomena such as language, law, political institutions, and morality.

The subsequent two essays are much shorter and less complete, but continue the general approach of using the shifting positions of the ancient schools to indicate how human understanding of the subject at hand advances through the exposition and refinement of increasingly coherent systems of thought. They also include observations about the difference in approach between the subjects, which suggest that Smith, perhaps as a part of his intended larger account of the arts and sciences, sought to methodize the sciences by the order in which their subject matter provoked wonder and suggested them to our attention. Thus our attention "descended" from the more obviously wondrous phenomena of the heavens to the more mundane, but more complex, details of the earth. The ancient physics, in Smith's view, is intended to "determine wherein consisted the Nature or Essence of every particular Species of things, in order to connect together all the different events that occur in the material world" (HALM 1). It proceeds by the classification of the events of the natural world. Once again the deliberate inquiry follows the more general account of human psychology: "To introduce order and coherence into the mind's conception of this seeming chaos of dissimilar and disjointed appearances, it was necessary to deduce all their qualities, operations, and laws of succession, from those of some particular things, with which it was perfectly acquainted and familiar, and along which its imagination could glide smoothly and easily, and without interruption" (HAP 2). Resemblance and classification systematized our experience of the world, and in the ancient world this took the form of classification as elements—air, earth, fire, and water and various combinations of each. While Smith offers a brief survey of some such approaches he does so while observing that the urge to provide a systematic account in the "infancy of science" often led its practitioners to grasp "at an account of all things before it had got full satisfaction with regard to any one" (HAP 3) and that this led to the creation of fanciful systems of classification where speculation superseded observation.

In the *Ancient Logics and Metaphysics* Smith continues his exploration of the unfolding of human attempts to understand the natural world by tracing how the various ancient schools attempted to account for the nature of the elements as "Universals" (HALM 1), while Logics accounted for the rules by which particular objects were to be distributed into universal classes and for the structure of the relationships between them.

In addition to the details in the latter two essays being less developed, there is also less of an effort made to connect the account of the relationships between the systems of the ancient schools and the more general exposition of surprise, wonder, and admiration. The focus here is on the self-conscious process of classification as a "method" rather than on the longer account of the progress of science through time. It may be that this is a consequence of these essays being in a less finished state than the longer *Astronomy* essay, or it may be that having made his case with relation to astronomy Smith contented himself with illustrating how other branches of philosophy unfold from the way that our attention is led "naturally" through the problems of classification—from the identification of classes to the attribution of their universal quality, the relationships between them, and the rules that assign particular phenomena to general groups. What remains constant throughout the three essays is the attempt to trace how humans attempt to use their imagination to account for the phenomena of the natural world as it presents itself to their attention.

The essay *Of the External Senses* is more difficult to place. Smith scholars are divided on its composition and purpose. We have no evidence to link it in any convincing fashion with the putative wider project on the arts and sciences, and scholars are divided on the timing of its composition.[11] Taken as a text it is, of all Smith's writings, perhaps the closest in format, subject matter, and style to the mainstream philosophy of the early modern period. The essay examines the relationship between our perception of external objects and the sensory organs of the body. Smith's survey is odd in a number of respects, not least of these is his decision to treat the senses in the reverse of their usual order of consideration: moving from touching through tasting, smelling, hearing, and seeing. The unusual structure appears to result from Smith's interest in one particular problem of perception rather than in providing a complete account of sensory perception. He examines each sense in relation to the theory that our senses are confined "in" the organ of perception and then discusses problems that this generates for the explication of the origin of our ideas about the external world. Along the way Smith touches on several points that were of wider interest to eighteenth-century philosophers. He appears at different points to draw on Lockean empiricism and Berkeley's theory of vision without mentioning any wider opposition between their thought. He invokes the widely discussed example of vision and the blind and the problems that it creates for thinking about the relationship between data generated by the various senses. He dwells on the notion of instinctual propensities such as a child seeking breastfeeding, and he illustrates this point by comparing human infants with other animals. All of these points suggest that Smith was familiar with the sorts of mainstream philosophical debates from Descartes onward. However the work is too much of an "essay" for us to form any real view of the details of his thinking on these matters. Intriguingly though Smith ends with what might even be thought to be an anticipation of Darwinian evolutionary thought when he makes the tentative suggestion that "[t]he three senses of Seeing, Hearing, and Smelling, seem to be given to us by Nature, not so much in order to inform us concerning the actual situation of our bodies, as concerning that of those other external bodies, which, though at some distance from us, may sooner or later affect that actual situation, and eventually either benefit or hurt us" (Senses 88).

Although these four essays are clearly insufficient to provide us with a fully worked out philosophy of science, they nonetheless offer us a number of interesting insights into Smith's thought. First, as we noted above, they indicate the breadth of Smith's scholarly interests and his continuing interest in the natural sciences throughout his career. Second, they give us a glimpse into one of the two books that we know Smith began work on but did not finish. These essays may form part of his intended philosophical history of the arts and sciences, which, along with his work on politics and government, was not to see publication. Third, the essays display evidence of those who influenced Smith's early thinking. The account of psychology and the stress on habit and the sentiments that marks the account of the practice of science display the mark of Hume's influence on Smith's thinking, while the interest in systems and systematization displays the influence of French thinkers and in particular perhaps d'Alembert in his *Discours préliminaire* to the *Encyclopédie*. Indeed in his *Letter to the Edinburgh Review* (included in the modern edition of EPS) Smith advocates a combination of what he sees as the English and French approaches to learning: "It seems to be the peculiar talent of the French nation, to arrange every subject in that natural and simple order, which carries the attention, without any effort, along with it. The English seem to have employed themselves entirely in inventing, and to have disdained the more inglorious but not less useful labour of arranging and methodizing their discoveries" (LER 5). This passage and Smith's fascination with evolution of systems of thought have led his most recent biographer, Nicholas Phillipson, to make this the cornerstone of his study of Smith's general method.[12] Fourth, the account of the development of science appears startlingly modern when compared to contemporary philosophy of science. Several commentators have noted the similarities between Smith's account and the more recent account of paradigm shifts offered in the theory of Kuhn, though there appears to have been no direct inspiration.[13]

The understanding of science as a formalization or deliberate application of the underlying principles of the human mind prompted, in the first instance, by our emotional need for explanation is something quite different from the Baconian accounts of science that focus on the desire to control nature that were widespread in the Enlightenment; it is also something that points us toward what might well have been the organizational principle of Smith's unfinished larger work—perhaps what he had in mind was an attempt to trace the unfolding of human art and science from the mode of human sensory perception and the "felt" need to overcome surprise, dispel wonder, and admire the resulting systems of thought that emerge.

Indeed what is perhaps most interesting about the approach outlined in these four essays is that it gives us insight into what Smith thought he was engaged in when he undertook scholarship. His *Theory of Moral Sentiments* and *Wealth of Nations* can be understood as attempts to realize a system of thought in their respective fields. As such we can imagine Smith as holding himself to the principles that he advances here. His accounts must calm the mind and lead the imagination through the invisible chains that bind nature together in a way that avoids gaps and bases itself on simple principles that account for a wide variety of phenomena. Thus TMS gives us natural sociability and sympathy as the basis of morality while WN gives us the division of labor and trade as the basis of a successful economy. In each case alternative systems are superseded as failing adequately to account for the phenomena at hand (e.g., mercantilism's erroneous account of the nature of wealth in WN) or failing to account for the phenomena in as uncomplicated a fashion as possible (e.g., the overcomplexity of Mandeville's selfish system in accounting for apparently benevolent behavior in

TMS).[14] These tentative hypotheses aside, the EPS deserve to be more widely read than they have been in the past.

NOTES

1. "Advertisement by the Editors," in EPS, p. 32.

2. It is worth noting that the standard modern edition of the EPS edited by W.P.D. Wightman as part of the Glasgow Edition of Smith's works does not reproduce this ordering of the essays. Instead Wightman places the Stewart *Life* at the end of the volume and moves the essay on the *External Senses* to a place after the three histories while claiming to follow the text of 1795. This, together with the editor's somewhat caustic attitude to his material, can create a misleading impression of the texts for a reader unacquainted with their original format.

3. The modern Glasgow Edition of EPS also includes Smith's earliest published work from the *Edinburgh Review* (1755–56). These include a review of Johnson's *Dictionary* and a letter to the editor that deals chiefly with the development of European thought with particular reference to Rousseau's views in the *Discourse on the Origin of Inequality*. Also included is Smith's preface to William Hamilton's *Poems on Several Occasions*.

4. Wightman, in his less than charitable introduction to the Glasgow Edition of the *Essays*, notes a number of failures of interpretation and detail on Smith's part when compared with modern scholarship; see Wightman's introduction in EPS, p. 11.

5. The stress on the beauty of explanations has led some to view Smith's account as an aesthetics of science. See H. Thomson, "Adam Smith's Philosophy of Science," *Quarterly Journal of Economics* 79 (1965), pp. 212–33.

6. Smith also appears to refer back to the subject of the *Astronomy* at WN V.i.f.24–25.

7. Though he skillfully avoids charges of irreligion by exempting revealed religion from his account and limiting his discussion of metaphysics and physics to the ancient schools.

8. There is a substantial critical debate about the status of Smith's philosophy of science in relation to modern distinctions between realism and antirealism. Some read his account as realist; see R. Olson, *Scottish Philosophy and British Physics 1750–1880* (Princeton: 1975), and N. Hetherington, "Isaac Newton's Influence on Adam Smith's Natural Law in Economics," *Journal of the History of Ideas* 44 (1983), pp. 497–505, while Kwangsu Kim interprets Smith's general approach as a precursor of critical realism: "Adam Smith's 'History of Astronomy' and View of Science," *Cambridge Journal of Economics* 36 (2012), pp. 799–820. In the antirealist camp are S. Cremaschi, "Adam Smith: Skeptical Newtonianism, Disenchanted Republicanism and the Birth of Social Science," in *Knowledge and Politics*, ed. M. Dascal and O. Greungard (Boulder, CO: 1989), and D. D. Raphael, "Adam Smith, Philosophy, Science and Social Science," in *Philosophers of the Enlightenment*, ed. S. Brown (Brighton: 1979).

9. In an aside Smith takes aim at unoriginal disciples who assume that all human wisdom "was comprehended in the writings of those elder sages" (HA IV.21). This concern about devotion to system appears in a slightly different form in the famous passage in TMS (IV.ii.2.18), where he attacks the "man of system" who is more enamored of the beauty of a system than of its coherence and applicability in a particular setting.

10. See the "Note by the Editors" at EPS, p. 105. For a more detailed discussion of Smith's relationship to Newton see Leonidas Montes, "Newtonianism and Smith," in *The Oxford Handbook of Adam Smith*, ed. C. J. Berry, M. P. Paganelli and C. Smith (Oxford: 2013), pp. 36–53; and E. Schliesser, "Wonder in the Face of Scientific Revolutions: Adam Smith on Newton's 'Proof' of Copernicanism," *British Journal for the History of Philosophy* 13 (2005), pp. 697–732.

11. See Kevin L. Brown, "Dating Adam Smith's Essay 'Of the External Senses,' " *Journal of the History of Ideas* 53 (1992), pp. 333–37; Brian Glenney, "Adam Smith and the Problem of the External World," *Journal of Scottish Philosophy* 9 (2011), pp. 205–23; and Tetsuo Taka, "Instinct as a Foundational Concept in Adam Smith's Social Theory," *History of Economic Thought* 53 (2011), pp. 1–20.

12. Nicholas Phillipson, *Adam Smith: An Enlightened Life* (New Haven: 2010), p. 4.

13. Andrew Skinner, "Adam Smith: Science and the Role of the Imagination," in *Hume and the Enlightenment*, ed. W. B. Todd (Edinburgh: 1974), pp. 164–88, at p. 180.

14. For an account of the relationship between the EPS and Smith's approach to social science, see C. J. Berry, "Smith and Science," in *The Cambridge Companion to Adam Smith*, ed. Knud Haakonssen (Cambridge: 2006), pp. 112–35.

BIBLIOGRAPHIC ESSAY

As mentioned above the EPS has been subject to far less detailed discussion than many other aspects of Smith's work. Biographical and bibliographic details of the texts can be found in I. S. Ross, *The Life of Adam Smith* (Oxford: 1995, 2nd ed. 2010), and Nicholas Phillipson, *Adam Smith: An Enlightened Life* (New Haven: 2010). For an overview of the aesthetic essays in EPS, see C. Labio, "Adam Smith's Aesthetics," in *The Oxford Handbook of Adam Smith*, ed. C. J. Berry, M. P. Paganelli, and C. Smith (Oxford: 2013), pp. 105–24. A good summary of the broader Scottish discussion of science can be found in P. Wood, "Science and the Scottish Enlightenment," in *The Cambridge Companion to the Scottish Enlightenment*, ed. A. Broadie (Cambridge: 2003), pp. 94–116. General discussions of Smith's argument can be found in H. Thomson, "Adam Smith's Philosophy of Science," *Quarterly Journal of Economics* 79 (1965), pp. 212–33; and in C. Smith, *Adam Smith's Political Philosophy* (London: 2006), chap. 2. The relationship between Smith and Newton is discussed by E. Schliesser, "Wonder in the Face of Scientific Revolutions: Adam Smith on Newton's 'Proof' of Copernicanism," *British Journal for the History of Philosophy* 13 (2005), pp. 697–732; and Leonidas Montes, "Newtonianism and Smith," in Berry, Paganelli, and Smith, *Oxford Handbook of Adam Smith*, pp. 36–53. Note 8 lists some of the contributions to the debates concerning Smith's relationship to realism and antirealism in the philosophy of science, and a useful summary of these can be found in C. J. Berry, "Smith and Science," in *The Cambridge Companion to Adam Smith*, ed. Knud Haakonssen (Cambridge: 2006), pp. 112–35.

SMITH AND THE SCOTTISH ENLIGHTENMENT

Nicholas Phillipson

Adam Smith is an interesting philosopher to contextualize. For contemporaries who knew nothing of his university teaching, he was a two-book man, the author of *The Theory of Moral Sentiments* and the *Wealth of Nations*. Since the publication of the Glasgow edition of his published and unpublished texts and the student notes of the lectures on rhetoric and jurisprudence he developed in the 1740s and 1750s, it has become possible to view his life's work as a project devoted to developing that grandest of enlightenment projects, a science of man based on "experimental" foundations, a project of Aristotelian proportions which, with more time and better health, Smith could well have accomplished. Recent revisionist thinking about the Enlightenment and its legacy has made it possible to view this *projet manqué* as one that had roots in the natural jurisprudence of Grotius, Hobbes, and Pufendorf and was to reach its summation in the work of Smith and his fellow Scottish philosophers and historians.[1] It also raises the question that provides this chapter with its starting point; why this particular enterprise should have been pursued with such intellectual energy in this remote and perhaps somewhat unexpected center of enlightenment. It is a question that can best be approached in the first instance by considering the highly distinctive circumstances in which Smith was born, raised, and received his philosophical education.

Adam Smith was born on June 5, 1723, in Kirkcaldy, a small trading port on the east coast of Scotland and in fairly easy reach of Scotland's capital, Edinburgh. His father, who died before his birth, seems to have been an ambitious customs official with the prospect of a decent career in public life before him; his mother was a member of the local gentry. His parents and their families and friends were well-established, ambitious, middle-ranking members of the Whig-Presbyterian establishment that had come to dominate the religious, professional, economic, and cultural life of a country that was being transformed by the Glorious Revolution of 1688 and the Act of Union of 1707. The Revolution had been the occasion of restoring the Presbyterian kirk, and the Union had given Scots merchants the right of free trade with English markets at home and overseas as compensation for the loss of their parliament and political independence. The hope was that these two great measures would bring about "a revival of that spirit and activity," which had been frustrated by the political and religious turmoil of the previous century, foster a spirit of "improvement" among its citizens, and encourage the regeneration of the economy, institutions, and culture of a volatile nation that had been in danger of turning into a failed state.[2] By Smith's day, this belief in the practical and patriotic virtue of "improvement" was penetrating every corner of the public and private life of this Whig-Presbyterian establishment. It was a belief that Smith was to theorize and place at the center of his understanding of sociability, civilization, and progress. It was one of the taproots that established his science of man in the cultural soil of post-Union Scotland.[3]

Smith owed most of his philosophical education to Glasgow University, at which he studied from 1736 to 1740.[4] The university, like that of Edinburgh and Aberdeen, was still feeling the shock waves of a long period of reform made necessary by the restoration of the Presbyterian kirk and by the government's insistence that the universities supplied the restored kirk with a "moderate" clergy rather than the radical and potentially disruptive clergy that had unsettled religious and political life in the previous century. By the 1730s Glasgow University had become a pillar of the Whig-Presbyterian establishment and the cradle of a curriculum designed to satisfy the interests of learning and ideology. Smith was taught natural philosophy well enough for one of his friends to conclude that he was destined for a scientific rather than a philosophical career. He was taught mathematics by Robert Simson, a mathematician of European importance who taught him to value mathematical explanation for its elegance and economy; like Hobbes, Smith would think long and hard about its relevance for the human sciences. But his greatest debts would be to the "never to be forgotten" Francis Hutcheson, the professor of moral philosophy. It was he who provided Smith with a critical introduction to the moral philosophy of the ancient and modern world, and although Smith's philosophical path was to diverge significantly from that of his teacher, he would always acknowledge Hutcheson as one of the founding fathers of the Newtonian, or as contemporaries usually termed it, the "experimental" approach to the study of human nature. Hutcheson taught Smith to think of the classic problems of moral philosophy—the origins of our ideas of morality, justice, political obligation, natural religion, and beauty—as questions about sociability and the means by which it is cultivated in common life. He taught his students to consider the nature of the affections and sentiments that are aroused when we find ourselves ethically challenged by the conduct of others, and about the nature of our responses to their conduct. Orthodox theologians abominated an approach to ethics that appeared to view the principles of virtue as matters of social convenience and a function of selfishness rather than the will of the deity, but Hutcheson was able to reply that experimentation of this sort would show that our conduct was regulated by a moral sense that seemed to be hardwired in the human personality and seemed to work independently of all considerations of reason or interest. It was a conclusion that allowed him to suggest that his work on the moral sense provided new and compelling evidence for the existence of a benevolent deity whose purposes could be realized by cultivating sociability and virtue in civil society and common life. For his admirers, Hutcheson had provided contemporary Scotland with a Christian moral philosophy that regarded religious toleration and freedom of expression as foundation stones on which sociability, virtue, and the future of liberty and godliness depended.[5]

This was a moral philosophy that Smith never forgot but about which he was to have serious reservations. Was it really possible to believe that our social behavior was regulated by a moral sense that no one had noticed before? Was it plausible to think of a sense of morality as the foundation stone on which our capacity for sociability rested? What about the sense of fairness and justice? And, most seriously of all, wasn't Hutcheson introducing theology by the back door by hinting that this curious, hitherto unnoticed faculty had been installed somewhere in the human personality by the deity? All of Smith's understanding of the principles of human nature and all of his views about the human personality worked on the assumption that the moral sensibility we undoubtedly acquire in the course of common life had its roots in social experience and education. These were reservations that were to encourage Smith to develop what was essentially a "non-Christian," sociopsychological approach to a subject that had always been deeply impregnated with theological assumptions. What was to characterize this approach was a determination not to allow his treatment of a theologically sensitive subject to descend into the cynicism and iconoclasm that was characteristic of earlier, non-Christian, and, in contemporary eyes, skeptical or Epicurean systems. What Smith wanted was a science of man to which Christians as well unbelievers could subscribe; the problems this irenic approach aroused were to fertilize debates about the principles of human nature that were to lie at the heart of the Scottish enlightenment.

I am pretty sure that Smith laid the foundations of his own approach to the science of man between 1740 and 1746 when he was in his late teens and early twenties and a student at Balliol College, Oxford. He famously hated Oxford and wrote scathingly about it in the *Wealth of Nations* (V.i.f.5–9), but the college provided him with six years of private study during which he almost certainly came to terms with the philosophy of David Hume, the man who was to become his greatest friend and was to exercise a decisive influence on his philosophy. Hume's devastating assault on claims that reason has the power to regulate the workings of the mind, to determine our understanding of the world, and to inform us of our duties, had reached the inescapable conclusion that the source of our cognitive powers lay in the imagination, the passions, and the customs and habits we acquire in the course of common life. This skeptical philosophy pointed toward a theory of sociability that

Smith was to adopt in its entirety. Hume thought that our capacity for sociability was derived from the sense of fairness and justice we acquire from an early age, competing for scarce resources and learning the meaning of "property." He thought that our willingness to submit to established political authority was rooted in the belief that it was necessary to secure our persons and property. He thought that our ability to function as apparently self-regulating moral agents was an art we acquire when we feel secure enough to regularize our relations with others and reflect on the nature of our duties. Hume's insights pointed to a new approach to the science of man that would involve exploring the anatomy of the moral sensibility we develop in the course of common life. It was an approach that emphasized the importance of understanding the process by which that sensibility was formed in the particular situations in which we are born, are raised, and live our lives. It was an approach to the science of man that was both profoundly skeptical and profoundly aware of the *historicity* of human nature.[6]

But it is important to think of Smith as a critic as well as a disciple of Hume. For example, although Hume had written brilliantly about the processes by which our sentiments and understanding are formed and had fully realized the importance of language and conversation in facilitating these developments, he had conspicuously failed to develop a systematic theory of language. In the same way, although his theory of justice had emphasized the importance of learning the meaning of "property," he had failed to ask the historical question, how that sense of justice would differ in different types of property-owning society. And beyond these specific questions lay the unexplored assumptions on which Hume's entire science of man seemed to rest, that all human behavior is somehow driven by *need* and that needs differ in kind and in quality in different types of society. In other words, while Hume had undoubtedly placed the science of man on what he claimed were "entirely new foundations," he could be criticized for failing to erect the philosophically and historically viable superstructure that would make it possible to formulate general laws about human behavior. Developing such a system, showing how it could be used to educate modern citizens and magistrates about themselves and their duties, and doing so "experimentally" and without skeptical iconoclasm, was to remain Smith's driving ambition for the rest of his life.

Smith set out the fundamentals of his system between 1748 and 1762 in lectures and papers given in Edinburgh in 1748–50, developed in Glasgow as professor of moral philosophy from 1752–63 and published in part in 1759 as *The Theory of Moral Sentiments*. Taken together they added up to an analysis of the different strands of the sensibility the sociable agent needs to acquire if he is to survive and prosper in civil society. The lectures on rhetoric dealt with the sense of propriety we acquire in developing the language skills on which social life and our understanding of the world depend. The lectures on morals he gave in Glasgow, and published in *The Theory of Moral Sentiments*, built on his theory of rhetoric and dealt with the origins of the senses of morality, justice, and political obligation. He also brilliantly addressed the question that Hutcheson and Hume had raised, of explaining the circumstances under which we learn to become self-regulating moral agents.[7] In the lectures on jurisprudence he showed how the sense of fairness and justice will vary in different types of property-owning societies with different types of government; he also paid particular attention to the part governments can unwittingly play in preserving and refining their subjects' sense of justice. His fragmentary papers on the history of philosophy and aesthetics showed that the credibility of any type of art and any system of philosophy will ultimately depend on the taste and the sense of beauty and truthfulness of particular publics. But what underpinned this immensely powerful system was a sophisticated theory of need, first hinted at in the lectures on rhetoric, subsequently developed in the lectures on jurisprudence and latterly used to underpin the system of political economy developed in the *Wealth of Nations*, a theory based on a conjecture about the principles of sociability derived from Mandeville's notoriously cynical *Fable of the Bees* (1723 and 1728).[8]

Like Mandeville, Smith took the potentially skeptical step of arguing that man differed from the brutes simply by virtue of his physical frailty; aboriginal man, living in a world of wild beasts and natural hardship, had learned the hard way that survival depends on cooperation, communication, and a usable language.[9] Society was thus a response to need, and a capacity for sociability depended on effective communication and trust. Accounting for progress would therefore be a matter of accounting for changing patterns of need and above all, for the multiplication of needs characteristic of more advanced types of society. Mandeville had made much of the inherently ridiculous rage of fashion and luxury that caused needs to multiply, economies to flourish, and civilization to progress and had attributed this to the pride and gullibility of our species. For Smith cynicism of this sort missed the essential point; whatever its ultimate cause—and that would always be a matter of dispute—all that mattered to the moral scientist, he conjectured, was that in all societies, men seem to have a natural love of "improvement," which takes the form of a natural disposition to make their lives more "convenient" when they feel secure enough to do so. Thus, in time, primitive man exchanged caves for huts, clothes for nakedness, cooked meat for raw, and so on. But this taste for improvement would have further unintended consequences for men's senses of fairness, justice, and morality, and beyond that, for their expectations of government and their fellow men. It was security, a seemingly natural love of convenience and improvement, not Mandeville's mischievously overstated rage of fashion per se that was the real engine of progress. It was a deeply attractive conjecture to set before the audience of young Edinburgh professionals who first heard Smith's foundational thoughts on the principles of political economy in 1750 and for whom the tumults of the seventeenth century were an all too recent memory.

As Smith was well aware, such conjectures about the principles of human behavior were only conjectures; the task of the philosopher was to enhance their truth-value by means of "illustrations" drawn from common life and history rather than from theologically charged and unproveable assumptions about men's inherent selfishness, rationality, or beneficence. For conjectures were to be treated as axioms to be elaborated and illustrated in the knowledge that their credibility would increase in relation to the quantity and quality of the examples chosen.[10] Smith's erudition was vast and the range and variety of illustration he brought to bear on every division of his thought was one his most admired intellectual characteristics. Nevertheless, while this method allowed Smith to develop the extraordinary stadial—or, as Dugald Stewart famously put it, "conjectural"—histories that invited citizens and magistrates to view their own country's histories in the wider context of the history of civilization, it was a method that embodied a view of science that many of his contemporaries found to be skeptical and deeply troubling.[11] By arguing that all knowledge has its roots in the imagination, passions, and custom and habit, Smith was following Hume's lead in undermining the truth-claims on which the validity of all natural science, mathematics, and theology depended. Neither Smith nor Hume ever claimed that their "science" was prescriptive in the sense of prescribing "laws" on which magistrates, clergy, and citizens could rely in shaping policies and guides to living. All they ever tried to do was to persuade intelligent citizens to test the credibility of the beliefs that regulated their policies and their moral, political, and religious behavior by viewing them in wider historical contexts and by considering their utility in satisfying what they thought of as their own and their country's needs.

By the end of Smith's life the different branches of his science of man, published like *The Theory of Moral Sentiments* and the *Wealth of Nations*, and unpublished, like the lectures on rhetoric and jurisprudence, had entered the mainstream of Scottish philosophy and letters, though it is not always clear exactly how they did so. Paradoxically, the clearest indication of the importance of Smith's philosophy to contemporary discussion comes from the evidence of its least known division, the theory of rhetoric. The rhetoric course, first given in 1748, had been attended by younger members of the clergy, the legal profession, and men about town, and was popular enough to be repeated a year later; after Smith's appointment to a Glasgow chair in 1751, it gave rise to similar successor courses given by Robert Watson, later principal of St. Andrew's and author of a best-selling life of Phillip II, and, more famously, by Hugh Blair, shortly to be appointed first Regius Professor of rhetoric and belles lettres at Edinburgh, and to become the eventual author of one of the biggest-selling textbooks generated by the Scottish enlightenment, the *Lectures on Rhetoric and Belles Lettres* (1783). By that time the study of rhetoric, now coupled with the study of belles lettres, or what we should call literature, had established an important place in the curriculum of every Scottish university as an alternative approach to the study of language and discourse and the formation of the human personality to that traditionally provided by logic and metaphysics. As Smith's pupil, John Millar explained, "the best method of explaining and illustrating the various powers of the human mind, the most useful part of metaphysics, arises from an examination of the several ways of communicating our thoughts by speech, and from an attention to the principles of those literary compositions which contribute to persuasion or entertainment." It was a way of introducing students "to studies of a more interesting and useful nature than the logic and metaphysics of the schools" (Stewart I.16). What Millar was too discreet to mention was that Smith's course had played a crucial part in developing a discipline that was attempting to break the hold of a theology-driven subject on the philosophy curriculum of the Scottish universities.

Smith's moral philosophy began to enter the mainstream of Scottish academic culture with the publication of *Theory of Moral Sentiments* in 1759. It was the book that established his reputation as a moral philosopher of international importance and was admired in Scotland and elsewhere as much for its remarkable illustrations as well as for its analysis of the working of the moral sentiments. In 1759, one of Smith's former students, a young Presbyterian minister, wrote enthusiastically and perceptively about Smith's use of the "experimental" method in moral philosophy, noting the "wonderful profusion of Examples to illustrate the different parts of the theory which seem like so many facts and experiments in Natural Philosophy & seem to confirm & support the author's principles in the most satisfying manner."[12] By the 1760s Smith's moral theory, along with Hutcheson's and Hume's was being discussed in moral philosophy courses throughout Scotland by professors like Thomas Reid, Adam Ferguson, and James Beattie, and a generation later by Dugald Stewart. It was predictable that his theory should have been treated critically as well as with respect; after all, Smith's method had been designed specifically to avoid resting arguments on the unprovable premises about the principles of human nature on which theological discourse then depended. Thus Reid and Kames thought his theory was merely "a refinement of the selfish system," and Ferguson believed that it failed to do justice to man's evident longing for perfection.[13] Smith's moral theory acquired a new lease of life later in his career when it was taken up by two immensely popular polite journals, the *Lounger* (1779–80) and the *Mirror* (1785), which, like Addison's *Spectator*, were designed to bring discussion of taste, morality, and the improvement of manners to a wider public. Most of the authors were lawyers, some of them Smith's former pupils. Their ethics were strongly Smithian, and it was perhaps not surprising that their editor, the novelist Henry Mackenzie, should have invited Smith himself to contribute. It was an invitation he refused. As Mackenzie reported, "My Manner of Writing, said he, will not do for a work of that Sort; it runs too much into Deduction and inference."[14] It would be interesting to know which, if any, of Smith's extensive revisions and clarifications of *The Theory of Moral Sentiments* in subsequent editions were prompted by the need to respond to criticisms in Scottish universities and salons.

The impact of Smith's jurisprudence, and the conjectural history that sustained it, on Scottish philosophy and letters is the hardest to establish. Apart from his students, not many heard his lectures in Edinburgh and Glasgow, and it was not until the publication of the *Wealth of Nations* in 1776 that Smith had anything to say in print about the principles of conjectural history. How far his lectures in Edinburgh and Glasgow shaped Scottish historical thinking before 1776 is not easy to say. The appendices on the feudal system Hume included in the last volume of his *History of England* (1762) and William Robertson's highly influential introduction to the *History of the Reign of Charles V* (1769), which deals with the progress of civilization in Europe from the fall of Rome to the accession of Charles V, are the work of historians who knew Smith well and do indeed provide histories of European feudalism that use the same sort of conjectural history as his; but the precise extent of Smith's particular influence on their thinking is unclear. However it is worth noting that Smith, who was touchy about such matters, often maintained that Robertson had plagiarized him. By that time, two of Smith's best pupils, John Millar and Allan Maconochie, had been appointed to chairs at Glasgow and Edinburgh and were delivering courses on jurisprudence based on a broadly Smithian conjectural history; Millar's was to form the basis of his *Origin of Ranks* of 1771, which offered in print a brilliant exposition and application of Smith's theory to questions about the principles of social organization; Maconochie's was never published.[15] By that time, it was being noticed in Europe that the Scots were developing a historical sensibility that employed various forms of conjectural history to explore the institutions and cultural of different types of civilization. It is tempting to read Hugh Blair's sensational and influential *Critical Introduction to the Poems of Ossian* (1763) as the partial application of Smith's conjectural history to an account of a primitive civilization at a particular stage of transition. And it is hard not to read William Robertson's remarkable *History of America* (1778) as the work of a brilliant historian who had internalized Smith's conjectural history and turned it to his own distinctive purposes.[16]

Smith had laid the foundations of his science of man at an extraordinary moment in his country's history when it had been possible for him to take advantage of a first-rate and distinctive education at Glasgow and early contact with a remarkable philosopher, David Hume. His Edinburgh lectures, given when he was in his mid-twenties, established him as a literatus of major importance who would shortly become vice president of Edinburgh's Philosophical Society in 1752 and a founder member of the Select Society in 1754, the two leading institutions of Edinburgh's burgeoning enlightenment; his lectures also prepared the ground for his appointment to the logic and metaphysics chair at Glasgow in 1751. These were all appointments in which the hands of Henry Home and the Duke of Argyll, the so-called uncrowned king of Scotland, were at work; Smith's first attempts to develop a science of man on non-Christian principles were receiving significant patronage and public recognition. And although Smith was a man who valued his privacy as much as the company of friends, he was one who was fully prepared to play an active role in the world of affairs as well as in the world of letters. As a Glasgow professor he proved to be a notably effective financial and business manager, devoting time and trouble to restocking the library, to encouraging the work of the Foulis Press, which was setting new standards for the publication of literature and philosophy in Scotland, and to abetting the creation of an Academy of the Fine Arts on the grounds that "a seat of the Sciences and Belles Lettres is the perfect nursery for the Fine Arts" and a Riding Academy in the overoptimistic hope that this would attract members of the nobility and gentry to the university. The publication of the *Wealth of Nations* (1776), his appointment as a commissioner of customs, and setting up house in Edinburgh established him in the public eye as the leading light of Scotland's literati, and, in spite of failing health, it was a role Smith was happy to play. He was to live the rest of his life as a celebrity, visited by cultural tourists, a philosopher whose weekly receptions and whose regular appearances at the Oyster Club (more generally known as Adam Smith's Club) were keenly followed by locals and visitors. It was the culmination of the career of a much-liked and respected philosopher who, for all his personal modesty and love of privacy, remained keenly aware that in the modern world of enlightenment it was important for philosophers and men of letters to cut a significant figure in public life.

NOTES

1. See, for example, Istvan Hont, *Jealousy of Trade: International Competition and the Nation State in Historical Perspective* (Cambridge: 2005), esp. chaps. 1, 5, 6.

2. The phrase is that of one of Smith's friends, Sir Gilbert Elliot of Minto. The canonical contemporary statement of the importance of the Union for Scotland's remarkable economic and political development is to be found in the final pages of William Robertson's *History of Scotland* (1759).

3. On the characteristics of the Scottish science of man, as seen from a sociological perspective, see C. J. Berry, *Social Theory of the Scottish Enlightenment* (Edinburgh: 1997); G. Bryson, *Man and Society: The Scottish Inquiry of the Eighteenth Century* (New York: 1968); and R. L. Meek, "The Scottish Contribu-

tion to Marxist Sociology," in *Economics and Ideology and Other Essays: Studies in the Development of Economic Thought* (London: 1967). For pioneering exercises in setting the Scottish enterprise in its historical setting, see D. Forbes's classic " 'Scientific' Whiggism: Adam Smith and John Millar," *Cambridge Journal* 7 (1954), pp. 643–70; and Hont, *Jealousy of Trade*.

4. I have discussed Smith's student career in my *Adam Smith: An Enlightened Life* (London: 2010). See also I. S. Ross, *The Life of Adam Smith* (Oxford: 1995, 2nd ed. 2010) and W. R. Scott, *Adam Smith as Student and Professor* (Glasgow: 1937).

5. The nature of Hutcheson's influence on Smith is a matter for debate among philosophers. I have tried to set his thinking in historical context in my *Adam Smith*, chap. 2. For pioneering work on viewing Hutcheson's thought historically, see J. Moore, "The Two Systems of Francis Hutcheson: On the Origins of the Scottish Enlightenment," in *Studies in the Philosophy of the Scottish Enlightenment*, ed. M. A. Stewart (Oxford: 1990), pp. 37–59.

6. I have developed this line of argument further in my *David Hume: Philosopher and Historian* (London: 2011).

7. Smith's remarkable account of the patterns of experience that make it possible for us to develop as self-regulating moral agents is set out in his discussion of the so-called impartial spectator, the rudiments of which appear in TMS Part III. It is important to note that Smith returned to this discussion when revising his text, in the second and sixth editions. There is much discussion of the significance of these revisions, particularly those of the sixth edition, written in the last months of his life and in the shadow of the French Revolution. See esp. D. D. Raphael's introduction to the Glasgow Edition of the TMS and, for more recent discussions, C. Griswold, *Adam Smith and the Virtues of Enlightenment* (Cambridge: 1999), esp. chaps. 3 and 7; R. P. Hanley, *Adam Smith and the Character of Virtue* (Cambridge: 2009) esp. pp. 136ff.; and F. Forman-Barzilai, *Adam Smith and the Circles of Sympathy* (Cambridge: 2011). My own view is that the fundamentals of Smith's theory do not change. His revisions clarify and illustrate, rather than modify his theory. See my *Adam Smith*, chaps. 7 and 13.

8. E. J. Hundert's *The Enlightenment's Fable: Bernard Mandeville and the Discovery of Society* (Cambridge: 1994) notwithstanding, the influence of Mandeville's memorable text on Smith and his fellow literati is a surprisingly neglected subject. Smith's first serious contact with this text must have been as one of Hutcheson's students; Mandeville's cynicism troubled Hutcheson greatly, to the point that he is said to have dragged him into nearly all of his lectures.

9. Smith's conjectures about the progress of need are set out in the lectures on jurisprudence (see LJB 205–23).

10. Smith's thinking about method was first set out in the lectures on rhetoric (LRBL ii.125–37). He returned to the subject in HA.

11. Stewart's influential discussion of Smith's "conjectural history" is to be found in Stewart II.44–56. For equally influential and more recent discussions, see Forbes, " 'Scientific' Whiggism"; Hont, *Jealousy of Trade*, esp. chaps. 1, 5, 6; and J.G.A. Pocock, *Barbarism and Religion*, vol. 2, pts. 2 and 3 (Cambridge: 1999) and vol. 4, pt. 3 (Cambridge: 2005).

12. Quoted in N. Phillipson, *Adam Smith*, p. 161.

13. J. Reeder, ed., *On Moral Sentiments: Contemporary Responses to Adam Smith* (Bristol: 1997), pp. 65–68. For Ferguson's critique of TMS, see A. Ferguson, *The Principles of Moral and Political Science* (Hildesheim: 1995), vol. 2, esp. pp. 123–34.

14. Phillipson, *Adam Smith*, p. 261. For an extended treatment, see J. Dwyer, *Virtuous Discourse: Sensibility and Community in Late Eighteenth-Century Scotland* (Edinburgh: 1987).

15. Forbes, "'Scientific' Whiggism," pp. 643–70. See also Michael Ignatieff, "John Millar and Individualism," in *Wealth and Virtue: The Shaping of Political Economy in the Scottish Enlightenment*, ed. I. Hont and M. Ignatieff (Cambridge: 1983), pp. 317–43. Maconochie is unexplored.

16. N. Phillipson, "Providence and Progress: An Introduction to the Historical Thought of William Robertson," in *William Robertson and the Expansion of Empire*, ed. S. J. Brown (Cambridge: 1997), pp. 55–73. See also K. O'Brien, *Narratives of Enlightenment: Cosmopolitan History from Voltaire to Gibbon* (Cambridge: 1997).

BIBLIOGRAPHIC ESSAY

All biographies of Smith look back to Dugald Stewart's *Account of the Life and Writings of Adam Smith, LL.D* (1794, reprinted in EPS), the work of a pupil and friend who knew Smith and his world better than most. The most recent biographically sensitive accounts of his life and works are I. S. Ross, *Life of Adam Smith*, 2nd ed. (Oxford: 2010), James Buchan, *Adam Smith and the Pursuit of Perfect Liberty* (London: 2006), and my own *Adam Smith: An Enlightened Life* (London: 2010). Donald Winch's entry in the *New Dictionary of National Biography* is well worth consulting. The history of the Scottish Enlightenment has yet to be written, but by way of general introduction see A. Herman, *The Scottish Enlightenment: The Scots' Invention of the Modern World* (London: 2001), *The Glasgow Enlightenment*, ed. A. Hook and R. B. Sher (East Linton: 1995), and my "The Scottish Enlightenment," in *The Enlightenment in National Context*, ed. R. Porter and M. Teich (Cambridge: 1981).

Much of the most interesting recent work on Smith has been devoted to setting his texts in historical contexts. Donald Winch's *Adam Smith's Politics* (Cambridge: 1978) was a pioneering attempt to read the WN as a contribution to contemporary English political discourse. Emma Rothchild's *Economic Sentiments: Adam Smith, Condorcet and the Enlightenment* (Cambridge, MA: 2002) views Smith's political economy in the context of a Scottish French enterprise. Istvan Hont's *Jealousy of Trade* (Cambridge, MA: 2010) sees Smith's enterprise as the culmination of an enlightenment exercise in developing a science of jurisprudence and politics. The ever-intriguing question of the relationship between the TMS and the WN has recently been fruitfully explored by Ryan P. Hanley in *Adam Smith and the Character of Virtue* (Cambridge: 2009) and Fonna Forman-Barzilai in *Adam Smith and the Circles of Sympathy: Cosmopolitanism and Moral Theory* (Cambridge: 2010).

PART II

Smith's Social Vision

8

ADAM SMITH ON LIVING A LIFE

Ryan Patrick Hanley

Whatever else it may also be, life in our modern world is busy. Our natures and the nature of our world together conspire to pull us in multiple directions, and often all at once. Any given moment thus finds us attempting to navigate multiple identities—from worker and citizen to parent and spouse—multiple associations—from workplace and school to neighborhood and club—and multiple desires—from external goods to internal tranquility. In contemporary philosophical parlance, we today necessarily inhabit a series of overlapping and often competing "lifeworlds." But what effect must all of this have on us?

At the birth of commercial modernity—itself the birth of a great number of these pressures, or at least a more pronounced awareness of them—several efforts were made to diagnose the effects of these competing lifeworlds on the individual. Among the most prominent and most notable was that of Adam Smith's sometime interlocutor, Jean-Jacques Rousseau. Rousseau began his *Emile* by laying out these competing obligations, and then stating their necessary effect on us. "From these contradictions is born the one we constantly experience within ourselves. Swept along in contrary routes by nature and by men, forced to divide ourselves between these different impulses, we follow a composite impulse which leads us to neither one goal nor the other. Thus, in conflict and floating during the whole course of our life, we end it without having been able to put ourselves in harmony with ourselves and without having been good either for ourselves or for others."[1] Thus Rousseau's project in *Emile*—and, arguably, throughout his corpus as a whole: to devise a means by which individuals might recapture that unity imperiled by the pressures of commercial modernity, and thereby establish a means of living that might, as Rousseau says, render us at once good for ourselves and good for others.

Rousseau's answer to these challenges was nothing if not controversial. Yet his voice hardly cried alone in the wilderness. For even if he was alone in defending his particular response to this challenge, his fundamental worry was one shared by several others—including, especially, Adam Smith. Both Smith's life and work are in fact animated to a striking degree by a concern to respond precisely to the challenge outlined by Rousseau: namely to describe a way of life that might enable us today to recover some semblance of unity and also to render ourselves good and useful both to others and to ourselves.

This is, of course, not how Smith's project is often seen. His spirited defense of commercial society—often taken as the whole or at least the core of his thought—hardly seems like fertile ground in which to sow the seeds of a philosophy of living, insofar as it champions precisely the institutions that on Rousseau's diagnosis serve to exacerbate our corruption and division. Even some who have attended both long and carefully to Smith's moral philosophy proper have not found in it evidence of an engagement with concerns of this sort. Thus it has been said that for Smith the aim of moral philosophy is simply to provide "an account of the origin and function" of our moral concepts, and that once we have this "there is nothing more to say," and that "if we want guidance on how to live the good life, we should look elsewhere."[2] Yet this view, however common among scholars today, was not always dominant. In Smith's own day his work was regarded quite differently, and was in fact thought by more than a few to be concerned precisely to provide such guidance. Smith himself claimed that the true aim of ethics is "to establish and confirm the best and most useful habits of which the mind of man is susceptible" (TMS VII.iv.6), and Dugald Stewart, his close associate and first biographer, once said of TMS that "with the theoretical doctrines of the book, there are everywhere interwoven, with singular taste and address, the purest and most elevated maxims concerning the practical conduct of life."[3] A century later, the same judgment was delivered by no less a figure than the future US President Woodrow

Wilson, who, as a Princeton lecturer, insisted Smith "stores his volumes full with the sagest practical maxims, fit to have fallen from the lips of the shrewdest of those Glasgow merchants in whose society he learned so much."[4] And even more recently, the economist Russ Roberts has described TMS as a guide to "what the good life is and how to achieve it," in seeking to recast TMS into a "digestible form" for readers unlikely to "get around to reading all of the original."[5]

Readers of *The Theory of Moral Sentiments* need not look far for the sorts of "practical maxims" these authors have in mind. Whatever else it might contain, TMS is full of pithy sayings delivering direct injunctions, and readers of a practically minded type are sure to find in it answers to at least a few of their questions. Do you wish to be successful? Smith is quick to counsel: be prudent and industrious. Do you wish to be well regarded? Cultivate your talents. You wish to be free? Avoid excess ambition. Are you too sad or too glad? Live with strangers. Hoping to preserve your children's innocence? Homeschool them.[6] All of these injunctions—and many more could be added—clearly attest to Smith's solicitude for the cares and concerns of his most practical and prudent readers. At the same time, we would do Smith an injustice were we to suggest that his concerns with the philosophy of living were limited solely to providing practical maxims of the sort that filled the volumes of his friend Benjamin Franklin. This was part of Smith's project, but it was hardly the whole. In addition to providing practical advice to the upwardly mobile, Smith also provides guidance to another sort of reader, and specifically one concerned to navigate well the challenges of living in a world in which pursuit of upward mobility often leads to psychic fragmentation and comes at the expense of both the well-being of others and ourselves.

Smith's effort to forestall this fragmentation begins with his effort to state clearly the extent to which its seeds have been sown in our very natures. For Smith, the natural condition of a human being is one of division—a point made powerfully in the first line of *The Theory of Moral Sentiments*. "How selfish soever man may be supposed," he notoriously begins, "there are evidently some principles in his nature, which interest him in the fortune of others"

(TMS I.i.1.1). A great deal of work is clearly being done in this opening line and the discussion it introduces. As scholars have long appreciated, Smith in particular here lays the foundation for his alterative to certain familiar conceptions of human nature. On Smith's view human nature is neither simply egocentric (as Hobbes and Mandeville argued), nor simply altruistic (as Shaftesbury and Hutcheson responded). The true condition of human nature is rather more mixed, Smith thinks; our natures contain at once both self-directed and other-directed passions.[7] For our purposes, what is crucial is that Smith regards our natural condition as one of division, and specifically one divided between concerns for others and concerns for ourselves.

Yet this is hardly the only division Smith finds in our natures. For not only are we naturally divided between concerns for self and concerns for others, but our self-concerns themselves exhibit a certain division. In this vein, the self-love that is fundamental to our nature on Smith's account is hardly some sort of static mono-lith that directs us to a single end. On the contrary, for Smith the objects of our natural self-love are multiple; in his idiom, "man naturally desires, not only to be loved, but to be lovely," and so too "he naturally dreads, not only to be hated, but to be hateful." In this sense we desire "not only praise, but praise-worthiness," and dread "not only blame, but blame-worthiness" (TMS III.2.1). Smith states this so simply, and indeed uses this distinction to do so much important philosophical work, that it is easy to miss a fundamental implication of his observation. In short, our natural desires for both praise and praiseworthiness pose a foundational challenge to the individual's efforts to live well insofar as in the world the least praiseworthy are often praised the most and the most praiseworthy praised the least (see, e.g., TMS I.iii.3.2). And this being the case, the fact that "nature" has endowed us "not only with a desire of being approved of, but with a desire of being what ought to be approved of" would seem to guarantee that our nature in its entirety is unlikely to be fully satisfied in the world as it is (TMS III.2.7). And even if we assume that it might be possible to discover a path whereby both of these natural desires might be gratified, it is by no means clear what this path would look like. As

Smith explains, "two different roads are presented to us" as means of gratifying our dual desires "both to be respectable and to be respected." Smith's locutions here are suggestive; four times in this brief passage he divides our options into "two different roads," "two different characters," "two different models," or "two different pictures" (TMS I.iii.3.2). The lesson seems clear: we may want it all, but we who have only one life to lead must make a choice, and quite simply it may be that no single option that we choose will gratify both of our natural desires. So far from relieving the division of our natures then, our entrance into the world seems only to inflame it.

And it hardly ends here. Our experience of living in the world only serves to exacerbate the division already inflamed by our entrance into it. Nowhere is this so clear as in Smith's thoughts on anxiety. Anxiety and remorse are strikingly common and recurrent concepts in his work, yet rare have been the commentators who have called attention to "his awareness of the possible social dislocation of the individual, of psychic terror, and loneliness," and the degree to which such an awareness places him "among those who saw the shadows lurking in the dark corners of the bright world of the enlightenment."[8] But even a casual reader cannot help but be struck by the force and ubiquity of his accounts of the "avenging furies of shame and remorse" that torture those of bad conscience.[9] And while Smith reserves his most poignant accounts of these avenging furies for the grossly criminal and egregiously negligent, to the degree that all human beings are necessarily less than perfect—a claim made more than once in *The Theory of Moral Sentiments* (e.g., TMS I.i.5.9–10; VI.iii.23–25)—it would seem that none of us, however virtuous, are likely to be free from some degree of anxiety in our lives.

All of this poses a profound challenge. We are divided by nature, our lives in the world exacerbate this division, and yet we seem to require some degree of unity for our happiness. How then can we achieve it? Smith's answer is surprising. In the first place, he seems to suggest that the alleviation of our division must begin with an embrace of division itself. This, at any rate, seems a fundamental element of the concept of the impartial spectator, presented by

Smith as a key to the alleviation of our anxiety and our pursuit of praiseworthiness. What then are we in fact doing when we attempt to enter into the perspective of the impartial spectator? Smith's answer is that we are engaged in an effort at further self-division: "When I endeavour to examine my own conduct, when I endeavour to pass sentence upon it, and either to approve or condemn it, it is evident that, in all such cases, I divide myself, as it were, into two persons; and that I, the examiner and judge, represent a different character from that other I, the person whose conduct is examined into and judged of" (TMS III.1.6). This is a striking and clever response to a fundamental problem Smith has laid out for himself. The whole reason we are compelled to strive to become "spectators of our own behaviour" is that we have "become anxious to know" not only how others judge us but also "how far we deserve their censure or applause" (TMS III.1.5). Put differently, our competing desires for both praise and praiseworthiness give rise to an anxiety that is best assuaged only by the further division of the self. And this is not only a clever argument but also one that deserves recognition as a precursor to contemporary psychotherapeutic anxiety management techniques which similarly encourage suffers of anxiety to become disinterested and disengaged spectators of their own mental activity.

In any case, the impartial spectator emerges in the first instance as an effort to recover some degree of psychic unity in the face of division. But how successful is it likely to be at solving the fundamental problem that Smith has set out for himself? Here a certain challenge arises. Smith clearly thinks that impartial spectatorship of the self can help restore the tranquility so often disturbed by anxieties prompted by the world's judgments of our characters and our merits. And this, to be sure, is not to be sniffed at. Insofar as it can make good on this, the impartial spectator is able to do what Smith elsewhere pointedly says "reason and philosophy" cannot do (TMS I.i.1.12). Furthermore, if indeed "happiness consists in tranquillity and enjoyment" and indeed "without tranquillity there can be no enjoyment" (TMS III.3.30), the efforts of the impartial spectator to promote such tranquility are to be greatly welcomed. At the same time, even if tranquility is a necessary condition for happiness, it seems not to be a sufficient condition for such. Smith himself on occasion will suggest it is: "What can be added to the happiness of the man who is in health, who is out of debt, and has a clear conscience?" (TMS I.iii.1.7) But one need only read a bit further into TMS to see that genuine happiness, and indeed genuine virtue, require a great deal else besides, even on Smith's own account. At the very least, true happiness seems to require not merely the clean conscience of the man who knows that he has done no harm to others, but also the self-approbation of the man who knows that he has done positive good for others. Put slightly differently, even if the impartial spectator succeeds in helping to establish the tranquility that renders us good for ourselves, it yet remains to be supplemented by a type or form of commitment that renders us good for others.

Smith is clearly aware of this problem. His notorious portrait of the just man whose virtue consists merely in "sitting still and doing nothing" attests to the degree to which he is conscious of the difference between mere tranquility and being good for others (TMS II.ii.1.9). In particular, where the former can be done passively, the latter requires activity. Fortunately Smith thinks we are inclined precisely to such activity by our natures: a point he makes especially clear in what is to my mind the most striking passage to be found in the entirety of his corpus:

> Man was made for action, and to promote by the exertion of his faculties such changes in the external circumstances both of himself and others, as may seem most favourable to the happiness of all. He must not be satisfied with indolent benevolence, nor fancy himself the friend of mankind, because in his heart he wishes well to the prosperity of the world. That he may call forth the whole vigour of his soul, and strain every nerve, in order to produce those ends which it is the purpose of his being to advance, Nature has taught him, that neither himself nor mankind can be fully satisfied with his conduct, nor bestow upon it the full measure of applause, unless he has actually produced them. (TMS II.iii.3.3)

This is an arresting statement for more reasons than one. But most important for present purposes, Smith here suggests that our natures not only incline us toward both praise and praiseworthiness, but also incline us to seek praiseworthiness in a particular way: namely through an activity that we have been fashioned to pursue in a wholehearted and unified sense, and indeed with the entirety of our body and the entirety of our soul.

But how might a naturally divided individual pursue a single end in a single-minded manner? And how can an individual naturally divided between concerns for himself and concerns for others come to dedicate himself to others in the way Smith recommends, and thereby reach those "ends" that he claims "Nature" has intended for us? Simple exhortation will not be enough; what is needed is a means by which we might overcome not only the internal division of ourselves, but also our external division of ourselves from others. And how is this to be done? Here too Smith offers an answer that may at first seem counterintuitive. If we hope to be in harmony with others, our first obligation is to pursue the perfection of ourselves. But what saves this pursuit of perfection from devolving into selfishness and alienation from others is the unique nature of this vision of perfection itself: "And hence it is, that to feel much for others and little for ourselves, that to restrain our selfish, and to indulge our benevolent affections, constitutes the perfection of human nature; and can alone produce among mankind that harmony of sentiments and passions in which consists their whole grace and propriety" (TMS I.i.5.5). Several things are immediately striking here. The first concerns the way in which Smith conceives of the pursuit of self-perfection. On his view, the pursuit of such efforts to better the self is hardly an egocentric enterprise. So far from leading us further back into the self, self-perfection, when properly pursued, leads us out of ourselves, toward others; so far from being at odds, the perfection of the self and the harmony of society are commensurate with each other. And if we take Smith at his word, it would even seem that he thinks not only that these are commensurate, but also that our pursuit of self-perfection is indispensable to social harmony, insofar as it "can alone" produce such harmony.

This in turn suggests a second striking element of this account. For Smith, self-perfection substantively consists not in a greater love of the self but rather in a transcendence of self-love that brings us closer to others. Hence, in his most explicit account of "perfect virtue," Smith claims, "The man of the most perfect virtue, the man whom we naturally love and revere the most, is he who joins, to the most perfect command of his own original and selfish feelings, the most exquisite sensibility both to the original and sympathetic feelings of others" (TMS III.3.35). With this we begin to see what else will be needed to close the gap between and to transcend the natural divide between our self-concern and our concern for others. It is virtue, and indeed "perfect virtue"—and indeed perfect virtue of a very specific sort—that alone can affect this transcendence. In particular, it is the perfect virtue of the individual who has cultivated at once "two different sets of virtues"—on the one hand, "the virtues of candid condescension and indulgent humanity" that lead us out of ourselves to others, and on the other hand, "the virtues of self-denial, of self-government, of that command of the passions" that come from appreciation of the judgments of others on ourselves (TMS I.i.5.1). Thus even self-perfection, we might say, consists in overcoming self-division, insofar as it so consciously requires us to cultivate two very different sorts of virtues that are very rarely found together in a single person—what Smith, following Hume, calls the "amiable" virtues that lead us out of ourselves to others, and the "awful" virtues that limit our self-centeredness and make it possible for us to move beyond self-concern in the first place.

As Smith's comments on virtue and perfection attest, a principal aim of his conception of self-perfection, or perfect virtue, is the transcendence of our division, and indeed on two levels. Insofar as the "man of the most perfect virtue" exhibits both amiable and awful virtues, his perfection aims to synthesize those two sides of our nature, selfish and altruistic, to which TMS calls our attention in its opening line. Insofar as the "perfection of human nature" serves to "produce among mankind that harmony of sentiments and passions" that enables us to live with others, such perfection overcomes our separation from others. Smith's theory of virtue itself thus deserves to be seen as his answer to both the division within the self and the division of the self from others. But yet we might wonder, even if virtue can cure these divisions, how can we achieve it in practice? Is it enough merely to will it, or is some other action or capacity necessary as well?

In Smith's response to this challenge lies, I think, what is perhaps the most interesting and important element of his moral theory. If we wish to pursue virtue—and indeed to cultivate not only the excellence that leads us to seek the well-being of others but also to develop a capacity to restrain our ever-present self-concern—a good will is again necessary but not sufficient. What we also need is the capacity to reimagine our place in the world, and indeed to reimagine our very relationship to others. This is an extraordinarily challenging and demanding enterprise. Smith in fact himself calls it the "hardest of all the lessons of morality" (TMS III.3.8). Yet it is indispensable to his entire moral project. At the core of this enterprise lies an effort to transcend the self-love that leads us always to prefer ourselves to others. The key task on this front is for us to move ourselves beyond nature. By nature, Smith often tells us, we are animated by a self-concern that inclines us to value our own well-being over that of others—what Smith himself calls "the natural preference which every man has for his own happiness above that of other people" (TMS II.ii.2.1). Smith celebrates this disposition when well channeled and well regulated; the illustration of its practical benefits is of course largely taken to be his primary aim as an economist. But as a moral philosopher, Smith is concerned to illustrate the ways in which this same natural capacity, when left unregulated, impedes and imperils our efforts to be good for both ourselves and for others.

The effect of excessive self-preference on the self is a prominent theme in Smith; one thinks immediately of his cautionary parable of the poor man's son and the misery his ambition brings upon him (TMS IV.1.8). But rather than revisit this familiar ground here, I want to focus instead on Smith's vision of the danger such excessive self-preference poses to our relationships to others. In this vein Smith is prone to insist that an individual who enters the world believing that others ought to regard him in that same light in which he is naturally inclined to view himself is necessarily bound for disappointment and misery; what seems natural to him "must always appear excessive and extravagant to them" (TMS II.ii.2.1). Thus our dilemma as naturally self-loving individuals who must yet live together with other self-loving individuals: nature inclines us to one view, but social harmony demands that we adopt another. And it is for the sake of overcoming nature in this sense that we need not merely virtue, or even a good will, but the capacity to reimagine ourselves. Thus Smith's striking call—repeated three times over the course of TMS—for us to correct the "natural inequality of our sentiments" and indeed compensate for "the natural misrepresentations of self-love" by coming to appreciate "that we are but one of the multitude, in no respect better than any other in it" (TMS III.3.3–4; cf. II.ii.2.1, VI.ii.2.2). Short of this fundamental reimagining of the self—and specifically such a reimagining that leads us to appreciate the equality of our interests with those of others—not only will we remain susceptible to that "absurd self-love" or "unjust preference" that has had such devastating effects on our hopes for peace and justice (e.g., TMS II.iii.1.5, III.3.6), but we will be unable to cultivate that "sense of what is due to [our] fellow-creatures which is the basis of justice and of society" (TMS II.iii.2.8; cf. II.iii.3.4).

Genuine excellence thus consists in transcending our self-love and coming to dedicate ourselves to the promotion of the well-being of others. But what will this in fact look like in the world? Smith gives us a portrait of such an individual in action, in the form of "the wise and virtuous man." This is the peak figure in Smith's ethics, and the excellence of his character lies in his cultivation of two specific dispositions. First, the wise and virtuous man achieves unity within himself. In contrast to others whose lives are animated by their solicitude for the external goods of wealth and recognition, and hence divided by their need for tranquility and their desires for goods that take them out of themselves, the wise and virtuous man exhibits a certain indifference to fortune—what Smith himself calls a "magnanimous resignation" or "reverential submission" that leads him to welcome the sacrifice of his own "inferior interests" to those of "the greater interest of the universe" (TMS VI.ii.3.3–4, VII.ii.1.45). But it is important to be clear about what this submission will and will not demand. At first glance it seems akin to the apathy that leads the Stoic sage to regard "all the events of human life" as "in a great measure indifferent" (TMS VII.ii.1.21). With the Stoic sage, Smith's wise man shares a detachment from the self that preserves the tranquility of the self. But he differs from the Stoic sage in rejecting any suggestion that we ought to regard as indifferent all the events of human life—and especially the events that cause misery and suffering to others. For Smith, the pursuit of unity and tranquility within the self must never lead to disengagement from others, for it is at this moment that one's concern to be good for one's self becomes inimical to one's calling to be good for others.

And herein lies the second element of the wise and virtuous man's excellence. The wise and virtuous man, Smith believes, not only embodies the perfection of the awful virtues that afford us the proper perspective on ourselves, but he also exhibits the perfection of the amiable virtues that testify to the degree of our commitment to others. A wise and virtuous man thus not only exhibits a magnanimous resignation to the world and embraces his humble status in it, but also comes to appreciate and indeed delight in his essential equality with others—an equality that not only leads him to overcome the "excessive self-admiration and presumption" that often plagues even the most virtuous (TMS VI.iii.30; see also TMS VI.iii.27 and 33), but also leads him to be good for others in the most practical of senses: "far from insulting over their inferiority, he views it with the most indulgent commiseration, and, by his advice as well as example, is at all times willing to promote their further advancement" (TMS VI.iii.25).

But how does a wise and virtuous man do this? Smith offers some hint in his life. Yet to see this we must see that life in a new light. To many today Adam Smith remains the "awkward Scotch professor" memorialized by Walter Bagehot, "choked with books and absorbed in abstractions" if endearing for a sort of "lumbering *bonhomie*."[10] However fair such a sketch may or may not be to Smith the man, it has overshadowed another arguably more crucial side of both his life and character—a side that fortunately did not escape Stewart, who, alongside his reports of Smith's notorious eccentricities, also called attention to his "ruling passion, of contributing to the happiness and the improvement of society."[11] It is a passion evident in several episodes in Smith's life and per- haps especially in his activities as a teacher, indeed one profoundly dedicated to the well-being of his students, and his actions as a philanthropist, indeed one who donated extensively in "offices of secret charity."[12]

But ultimately it is in his activities as an author that we see the clearest evidence of Smith's consciousness of the responsibilities of the wise and virtuous man. In the *Lectures on Jurisprudence* it is argued that the provision of life's basic necessaries—"meat, drink, rayment, and lodging"—is the proper end of wisdom and virtue (LJA vi.20–21). And while Smith certainly never became himself a butcher or brewer or spinner or joiner, his literary life aimed to further this end. Indeed his *Wealth of Nations*—of all the accom- plishments of his life, certainly the most famous—was itself dedi- cated precisely to promoting such wise and virtuous ends insofar as it sought to render the necessities and conveniences of human life more accessible to all. In so doing, Smith gave us reason to include him among that class of wise and virtuous men who have furthered those arts "which contribute to the subsistence, to the conveniency, or to the ornament of human life" (TMS III.2.35). And insofar as the execution of this work proved such a joy to Smith himself, we are given a model of how indeed one might live a life both good for one's self and good for others.

NOTES

Earlier versions of this chapter were delivered to student audiences at Zhejiang University, Mercer University, and St. Anselm's College. I am very grateful to the audiences on these occasions for their enthusiastic engagement, and to Luo Wei- Dong, Charlotte Thomas, Will Jordan, and Peter Josephson for their very kind invitations to these events. I am also grateful to the Earhart Foundation for a fellowship that supported my work on this project.

1. Jean-Jacques Rousseau, *Emile; or, On Education*, trans. Allan Bloom (New York: 1976), p. 41.

2. Knud Haakonssen and Donald Winch, "The Legacy of Adam Smith," in *The Cambridge Companion to Adam Smith*, ed. Haakonssen (Cambridge: 2006), p. 385.

3. Dugald Stewart, "Account of the Life and Writings of Adam Smith, LL.D.," in *Essays on Philosophical Subjects*, p. 2:42, ed. W.P.D. Wightman and J.C. Bryce (Indianapolis: 1982), p. 291.

4. Woodrow Wilson, *An Old Master, and Other Political Essays* (New York: 1893), pp. 17–18.

5. Russ Roberts, *How Adam Smith Can Change Your Life* (New York: 2014), pp. 3, 10.

6. See, respectively, TMS I.iii.2.5 and I.iii.3.5, VII.ii.2.13, I.iii.2.7, III.3.39–40, VI.ii.1.10.

7. For important early discussions of this opening line, see Joseph Cropsey, *Polity and Economy*, 2nd ed. (South Bend: 2001), pp. 124, 162; for a nuanced recent discussion, see Samuel Fleischacker, "David Hume and Adam Smith on Sympathy: A Contrast, Critique, and Reconstruction," in *Intersubjectivity and Objectivity in Adam Smith and Edmund Husserl*, ed. Dagfinn Føllesdal and Christel Fricke (Frankfurt: 2012).

8. R. F. Brissenden, "Authority, Guilt and Anxiety in *The Theory of Moral Sentiments*," *Texas Studies in Literature and Language* 11 (1969), p. 961. The most acute recent study is likely Charles Griswold, *Adam Smith and the Virtues of Enlightenment* (Cambridge: 1999), pp. 221–25.

9. TMS I.iii.3.8; cf. II.ii.2.3, III.2.9, III.2.11.

10. Walter Bagehot, "Adam Smith as a Person," in *The Works and Life of Walter Bagehot*, vol. 7 (London: 1915), pp. 247, 262; see also pp. 254–55, 261, 275, 280.

11. Stewart, "Account of the Life," 1.8; see also 3.20, 4.12.

12. Stewart, "Account of the Life," 1.21, 5.4 and n.

BIBLIOGRAPHIC ESSAY

The traditional association of philosophy with the art of living has not been a main focus of most contemporary academic philosophy. One important attempt to revive this approach to philosophy can be found in Alexander Nehamas, *The Art of Living* (Berkeley: 1998). Students of Adam Smith seeking to understand the relationship between the life he lived and the principles he articulated in his books would do well to begin with the portraits of Smith's life as presented especially in the three key modern biographies: Ian S. Ross, *The Life of Adam Smith*, 2nd ed. (Oxford: 2010), Nicholas Phillipson, *Adam Smith: An Enlightened Life* (London: 2010), and James Buchan, *The Authentic Adam Smith* (New York: 2006). In addition, older but still of interest for the light they shed on Smith's life and character are W. R. Scott, *Adam Smith as Student and Professor*

(Glasgow: 1937), John Rae's *Life of Adam Smith* with Jacob Viner's *Guide* (New York: 1965), and Walter Bagehot's essay "Adam Smith as a Person," in *The Works and Life of Walter Bagehot* (London: 1915). An engaging popular account of Smith's practical wisdom in the style of a modern self-help book has been recently provided in Russ Roberts, *How Adam Smith Can Change Your Life: An Unexpected Guide to Human Nature and Happiness* (New York: 2014). I examine Smith's activity as a philosopher in light of his study of the wise and virtuous man at greater length in chap. 6 of *Adam Smith and the Character of Virtue* (Cambridge: 2009). And Charles Griswold's *Adam Smith and the Virtues of Enlightenment* (Cambridge: 1999) offers a preeminent example of how revealing a dialectical engagement with *The Theory of Moral Sentiments* can be, and stands as an essential point of departure for serious study of Smith.

9

ADAM SMITH: SELF-INTEREST AND THE VIRTUES

Leonidas Montes

1. INTRODUCTION

During Smith's lifetime, TMS went through six editions (1759, 1761, 1767, 1774, 1781, and 1790) and WN went through five (1776, 1778, 1784, 1786, and 1789). Although the two last lifetime editions of WN did not suffer any major alterations, the sixth edition of TMS contained substantial revisions and extensive additions. Indeed, almost one-third of the definitive TMS corresponds to his final years' work. But it is important to point out that in this last and definite edition there is, as the editors of TMS have argued, "development but no fundamental alteration" (TMS intr., p. 20). And this development is rather important.[1]

It is noteworthy that Smith, who became the father of economics, dedicated the last years of his life to TMS, almost ignoring further revision to his treatise on political economy. Historically TMS has been overshadowed by WN.[2] However, the publication of the scholarly edition of TMS in 1976, as part of the definitive Glasgow Edition of Smith's Works and Correspondence (1976–87) and its republication in paperback by the Liberty Fund, brought about a renaissance in scholarship on TMS.[3] In fact, TMS has influenced the thought of well-known contemporary moral philosophers such as Martha Nussbaum, Stephen Darwall, Ernst Tugendhat, and Charles Larmore, among others. Moreover, recently economists, following the example of Nobel laureates Amartya Sen and Vernon Smith, have been paying more attention to TMS.

Despite the early acclamation of TMS upon its publication, during the nineteenth century and greater part of the twentieth century this philosophical work was, with a very few exceptions, either misinterpreted or simply ignored.[4] The almost overwhelming influence of Bentham's utilitarianism and Kant's deontological approach eclipsed TMS. Adam Smith became mainly known as the author of WN, and Smith's book on ethics was largely dismissed as a minor proto-utilitarian piece.[5] Alec Macfie was an early exception when he bluntly stated that Smith "was not a utilitarian."[6] And more recently Samuel Fleischacker has suggestively labeled Smith as "a clear ancestor of Kant's purposiveness without purpose."[7] If nowadays there is a general consensus that Adam Smith is not a proto-utilitarian, and there are good grounds to defend a deontological position as Fleischacker has proposed,[8] the emerging virtue ethics interpretation of Smith's TMS is perhaps the most interesting contribution to recent Smith scholarship.[9]

Of course WN also provides a ground for virtues. Indeed "the liberal plan of equality, liberty, and justice" rests upon "allowing every man to pursue his own interest his own way" (WN IV.ix.3) and thereby "bring both his industry and capital into competition with those of any other man, or order of men" (WN IV.9.51). As Rousseau, in his *Discourse on the Origins of Inequality*, distinguishes between *amour propre* and *amour de soi*, for Smith self-love is not necessarily the same as self-interest. *Amour propre* can have the pejorative sense of vanity, just as self-love can suggest selfishness. However, self-interest has a moral foundation that principally relies on the Stoics and is underpinned and enhanced by Smith's moral virtues. Indeed, the virtues of commercial society, supported by self-interest, are crucial to both WN and TMS: "Regard to our own private happiness and interest, too, appear upon many occasions very laudable principles of action. The habits of oeconomy, industry, discretion, attention, and application of thought, are generally supposed to be cultivated from self-interested motives, and at the same time are apprehended to be very praise-worthy qualities, which deserve the esteem and approbation of every body" (TMS VII.ii.3.16). As human beings we naturally seek our own improvement: "the principle which prompts to save is the desire of bettering our condition, a desire which, though generally calm and dispassionate, comes with us from the womb, and never leaves us till we go into the grave" (WN II.iii.28). And behind this pursuit lies the idea of the "industrious and frugal peasant" (WN I.i.11), which suggests that fostering social and economic development requires moral virtues.

Smith recurrently insists on the virtues of industriousness, hard work, austerity, frugality and parsimony. The protestant ethic, suggestively developed by Max Weber, is in the background of his moral and economic thought. But commercial virtues are not limited strictly to self-interest. Sympathy, the impartial spectator—the "man within the breast"—and the Smithian virtues interact with self-interest. Thus the famous Adam Smith Problem, a confusion that emerged within the German Historical School, is spurious: there is no difference between the Smith of TMS and the Smith of WN, since his moral defense of self-interest is present in both books.[10] In an effort to demonstrate this, what follows examines the moral principle of sympathy as well as what we might call Smith's cardinal virtues of prudence, justice, beneficence, and self-command, with an eye toward how they complement and interact with this moral defense of self-interest.

2. SMITH'S SYMPATHY

Sympathy and the idea of the impartial spectator are the foundations of Smith's original approach to moral philosophy. Its influence and importance today crosses several disciplines. The first sentence of TMS—"[h]ow selfish soever man may be supposed, there are evidently some principles in his nature, which interest him in the fortune of others, and render their happiness necessary to him, though he derives nothing from it except the pleasure of seeing it" (TMS I.i.1.1)—already defines sympathy as a complex principle in human nature. But Smith is aware that common language might mislead us on what he really means by sympathy: "Pity and compassion are words appropriated to signify our fellow-feeling with the sorrows of others. Sympathy, though its meaning was, perhaps, originally the same, may now, however, without much impropriety, be made use of to denote our fellow-feeling with any passion whatever" (TMS I.i.I.5). Sympathy is not merely a kind of fellow-feeling related to pity, as it pertains to "any passion whatever." Differentiating from Hume's sympathy and its relationship with pleasure, Smith reiterates that sympathy has to do with "joy and grief," and that it is necessary for moral judgment.[11] The Greek word for sympathy is *sumpátheia*. The prefix *sun* means "together" or "with," which is joined to *pathos*. The analogous word in Latin is *com-passion* (the Latin prefix *cum* is the equivalent of the Greek *sun*). Therefore the etymological origin of the word *sumpátheia* would simply imply "feeling with" or "together with." Literally it would merely mean sharing a fellow-feeling.

But Smith is aware that there is another side to sympathy as well, so he carefully explains its broader meaning. In this sense, the causes that motivate the passions are fundamental. Sympathy not only is related to feelings, but also requires a process of deliberation. Smith concludes that "[s]ympathy, therefore, does not arise so much from the view of the passion, as from that of the situation which excites it" (TMS I.i.1.10). Sympathy thus goes beyond its literal etymological meaning, as it not only implies being in the person's shoes, but also requires knowing or assessing where those shoes are standing. Of course I will have fellow-feeling with any passion, but I cannot sympathize "till informed of its cause" (TMS I.i.1.8). I can feel and share your passion, but that does not necessarily mean that I can sympathize with it. Smith's sympathy requires a rational assessment of the circumstances, which implies a deliberative process. Actually sympathy would more precisely correspond to empathy (feeling "in" the other). Therefore, Smith's sympathetic process has both moral and intellectual components.[12] Simply stated, the attainment of mutual sympathy requires both heart and head.

Within Smith's framework of sympathy, virtues play an important role. There is a continuous interaction between sympathy and virtues. Sympathy requires social interaction. And the reason is simple: Smith follows the Aristotelian tradition of regarding human beings as naturally social (*zoon politikón*). There is no place for Robinson Crusoe. For Smith ethics is a social phenomenon simply because a man without society cannot have a sense of good or bad: "Were it possible that a human creature could grow up to manhood in some solitary place, without any communication with his own species, he could no more think of his own character. . . . Bring him into society, and he is immediately provided with the mirror which he wanted before. It is placed in the countenance and behaviour of those he lives with . . . and it is here that he first views the propriety and impropriety of his own passions" (TMS III.1.3). For Adam Smith human nature is predominantly social, and sympathy, underpinned by the relevance of the impartial spectator, is the core of moral judgment. As human conduct is fundamentally moral—we live and learn our *mores* in society—social interaction shapes moral approbation.[13]

To the sixth and last edition of *The Theory of Moral Sentiments* Adam Smith added a complete new section titled "Of the Character of Virtue." The title of this part signals his late concern with virtues. Although virtues are pervasive throughout TMS and WN, we will concentrate on Part VI of TMS as here Smith puts forward his four chief virtues: prudence, beneficence, justice, and self-command. In what follows I will briefly analyze Smith's four main virtues, perfunctorily comparing them with the cardinal virtues (justice, prudence, temperance, and fortitude), stressing the distinctive and original role of self-command.

3. SMITH'S VIRTUES

3.1. Prudence

Adam Smith shares with many of the philosophes of the Scottish Enlightenment, and particularly David Hume, a realistic and pragmatic view of human nature. Even if we aim at moral perfection, as human beings we must necessarily fall short of absolute perfection. For example, Smith distinguishes between inferior and superior prudence:

> Wise and judicious conduct, when directed to greater and nobler purposes than the care of the health, the rank and reputation of the in-

dividual, is frequently and very properly called prudence . . . superior prudence . . . necessarily supposes the utmost perfection of all intellectual and of all the moral virtues. It is the best head joined to the best heart. It is the most perfect wisdom combined with the most perfect virtue. It constitutes very nearly the character of the Academical or Peripatetic sage, as inferior prudence does that of the Epicurean. (TMS VI.i.14)

As Norbert Waszek has persuasively argued, Smith conceives two levels of morality: one for the wise few, and one for the common man.[14] Regarding prudence, or the cardinal virtue of *prudentia*, this intuition is clearly explicit when Smith distinguishes between superior prudence, which requires the "most exact propriety," and inferior prudence. Smith concentrates on inferior prudence, following the more practical and simple concept of prudence developed by the Epicureans.[15] With an emphasis on "a steady perseverance in the practice of frugality, industry and application" (TMS IV.2.6), prudence represents the pragmatic and worldly face of this virtue that is present in TMS and WN. In this sense, prudence is the cardinal virtue of Smith's moral system that most clearly serves to promote self-interest and commercial society.

Smith restricts prudence to "our own happiness . . . originally recommended to us by our selfish . . . affections" (TMS VI.concl.1). His liberal—in the classical tradition—understanding of prudence is worth reproducing: "The care of the health, of the fortune, of the rank and reputation of the individual, the objects upon which his comfort and happiness in this life are supposed principally to depend, is considered as the proper business of that virtue which is commonly called Prudence. . . . Security, therefore, is the first and the principal object of prudence" (TMS VI.i.5 and 6). Prudence, as here described, is clearly related to self-interest, insofar as "the habits of oeconomy, industry, discretion, attention, and application of thought . . . deserve the esteem and approbation of everybody" (TMS VII.ii.3.16). It is a self-regarding virtue that fosters Smith's recurrent defense of the right of all people to pursue the "bettering of our condition." The latter does not entail the cold individualism of the *homo œconomicus* as a socially detached acquisitive individual.[16] Prudence demands not only the "propriety of self-command," a theme that will be developed below, but also the approval of the impartial spectator and the supposed impartial spectator within each of us (see TMS VI.i.11).

In short, self-interest is a motivation behind prudence, but prudence is not the blind pursuit of one's own wishes, wants, or desires regardless of others. Compare the story of the poor man's son who admires the rich and "labours night and day to acquire talents superior to all his competitors" but does not realize that "wealth and greatness are mere trinkets of frivolous utility" that "gratify that love of distinction so natural to man" but bring "no real satisfaction." The moral, with an underlying Aristotelian sense of *eudaimonia* and human flourishing, is obvious: "power and riches" can lead "to anxiety, to fear, and to sorrow" (TMS IV.1.7, pp. 181–83).

Summing up, inferior prudence is related to well-being as "the habits of oeconomy, industry, discretion, attention, and application of thought, are generally supposed to be cultivated from self-interested motives, and at the same time are apprehended to be very praiseworthy qualities, which deserve the esteem and approbation of everybody" (TMS VII.ii.3.16). But it is a self-regarding virtue, rather than a manifestation of selfishness.

3.2. Justice and Beneficence

For Smith, as for Hume who considers justice as an artificial virtue, justice does not have the preeminent role it had for Plato and all those ancients who regarded it as the primary and connecting cardinal virtue. Of course Smith repeatedly refers to the "the most sacred law of justice" (TMS II.ii.2.2), but it is a human virtue. From a social point of view justice "is the main pillar that upholds the whole edifice" (TMS II.ii.2.2). But Smith simply defines justice in its commutative sense as "when we abstain from doing him [our neighbor] any positive harm, and do not directly hurt him, either in his person, or in his estate, or in his reputation" (TMS

VII.ii.1.10, p. 269). It is "a negative virtue, and only hinders us from hurting our neighbour" (TMS II.ii.I.9, p. 82). Moreover, the simple laws of justice "guard the life and person of our neighbour; the next are those which guard his property and possessions; and last of all come those which guard what are called his personal rights, or what is due to him from the promises of others" (TMS II.ii.2.2, p. 84). Following Locke, life, property, and contracts are basic principles implied in the "sacred and religious regard not to hurt or disturb in any respect the happiness of our neighbour" (TMS VI.intro.2). In his definition of commutative justice Smith is following Grotius, whom he praises at the end of TMS.[17]

Beneficence, as the virtue of doing good to others (as opposed to benevolence, which is the "will" or simple "desire" to do good), appears to entail a sense of duty. But Smith is clearly aware of the "limited powers of beneficence" (TMS VI.ii.intro.2), as it "is the ornament which embellishes, not the foundation which supports the building. . . . Justice, on the contrary, is the main pillar that upholds the whole edifice" (TMS II.ii.3.4). At the individual level, beneficence plays a role. And this virtue also relates to our relationship with society, which might have political implications (see TMS VI.ii.2). However, if Smith praises and develops the public spirit and love of our country in this passage on beneficence, in his final edition of TMS he ends up underlining the risk of the "man of system" who "seems to imagine that he can arrange the different members of a great society with as much ease as the hand arranges the different pieces upon a chess-board," but he forgets that "in the great chess-board of human society, every single piece has a principle of motion of its own" (TMS VI.ii.2.18).

Smith is conscious that "we may often fulfill all the rules of justice by sitting still and doing nothing" (TMS II.ii.1.9). This is what Grotius calls "*justitia expletrix*, which consists in abstaining from what is another's" (TMS VII.ii.I.10). But Smith also calls attention to "what some have called distributive justice, and with the *justitia attributrix* of Grotius, *which consists in proper beneficence*" (TMS VII.ii.I.10, last emphasis added). Smith's account of justice has been often criticized for considering only its negative definition. Some have even stated that his "notion of justice" is "not well developed in the TMS or in any of Smith's writings."[18] Others have argued that Smith could not develop a proper theory of justice, and this would explain his final request to burn his writings on this subject.[19] However, distributive justice, in its *grand* but elusive sense, is also implicit in Smith's account of virtues. At the individual level, distributive justice, an imperfect right in the Grotian tradition, is included under the virtue of beneficence.[20]

Smith probably focuses on inferior prudence and negative justice in order to bring the "excellences of character" closer to men. He assumes a pragmatic stance very much influenced by the jurisprudential tradition, or perhaps an "eclectic" position that suggests he knows what to select among the classics.[21] But we may say that sympathy and the impartial spectator "command" the restricted sense of negative justice:

> [W]e are said not to do justice to our neighbour unless we conceive for him all that love, respect, and esteem, which his character, his situation, and his connexion with ourselves, render suitable and proper for us to feel, and unless we act accordingly. It is in this sense that we are said to do injustice to a man of merit who is connected with us, though we abstain from hurting him in every respect, if we do not exert ourselves to serve him and to place him in that situation in which the impartial spectator would be pleased to see him. (TMS VII.ii.I.10)

Prudence and justice are related to the language of rights, the former as my right to better my own condition, and the latter as my right to life, property, and contracts; in this sense, justice, like prudence, is also a virtue that concerns my self-interest. Beneficence in certain cases might involve a language of duties,[22] so there is a combination of what pertains to the self and to the community. But even if "[t]he man who acts according to the rules of perfect prudence, of strict justice, and of proper benevolence, may be said to be perfectly virtuous" (TMS VI.iii.1) passions might mislead him. Therefore, "[t]he most perfect knowledge, if it is not supported by the most perfect self-command, will not always enable him to do his duty" (TMS VI.iii.1).

3.3. Self-Command

In the conclusion of the sixth part of TMS, Smith sums up his four main virtues: prudence, justice, beneficence, and self-command, the cardinal "Smithian virtues." Smith's prudence and justice differ from the classical and Christian cardinal virtues tradition, which also include temperance and fortitude. In fact, inferior prudence and negative justice deviate from the grand classical sense of *phrónesis* and *dikaiosúne*. But his most original claims concern self-command, which plays a unique and important role insofar as it is "principally and almost entirely recommended to us by . . . the sense of propriety, by regard to the sentiments of the supposed impartial spectator" (TMS VI.concl.2). Smith's crucial virtue of self-command, which appears more often and acquires greater relevance in the final edition of TMS, is related to propriety and the impartial spectator. Moreover, Smith states that self-command "is not only a great virtue, but from it all the other virtues seem to derive their principal lustre" (TMS VI.iii.11). As justice does within Plato's cardinal virtues, this passage suggests that for Smith self-command has a foundational and connecting character within his four main virtues.

The actual sense of self-command is complex. Prior to the sixth edition, Smith's self-command seems to have many meanings. First, it appears related to control of passions as "the great, the awful, and respectable, the virtues of self-denial, of self-government, of that command of the passions which subjects all the movements of our nature to what our own dignity and honour, and the propriety of our own conduct require" (TMS I.i.5.1). Elsewhere it resembles the Epicurean *ataraxia*, or tranquillity of mind, governing the natural passions of our nature (e.g., TMS I.i.5.3). Smith even refers to the "absolute" self-command of the American savages (TMS V.2.9), which rests on a complete physical and psychological self-denial. For the final and sixth edition of TMS, it is even related to the martial virtues: "hardships, dangers, injuries, misfortunes, are the only masters under whom we can learn the exercise of this virtue [self-command]" (TMS III.3.37), and therefore to the cardinal virtue of fortitude. And Smith also considers that in "the great school of self-command" we study how "to be more and more" masters of ourselves (TMS III.3.22; see also III.3.25).

A first reading gives the impression that self-command is related to control of the passions, to the cardinal virtue of temperance that would imply a kind of self-denial. But self-command is an original and distinctively Smithian virtue that appears as the foundation of all other virtues, not only supporting them, but giving them a sense of direction—a key point, since it serves to reiterate how the cultivation of self-command is itself in the self-interest of individuals seeking to flourish.

Following the editors of TMS, it has been commonly argued that self-command "is distinctively Stoic" (TMS intr., p. 6). Although the influence of the Stoics on the Scottish context is significant, the importance of the Stoics for Adam Smith has been overestimated.[23] A deeper analysis of the virtue of self-command is a good example to understand that Smith's account of virtues is much more complex than a simple Stoical inheritance.

The general argument that has been given for considering self-command as essentially Stoic is, explicitly or implicitly, related to the widely discussed Stoical concept of *apátheia*. But this connection vanishes if we consider what Smith actually said, and what the Stoics really meant. Smith wrote "The Theory of Moral *Sentiments*." Not surprisingly he argues that "the stoical apathy is, in such cases, never agreeable, and all the metaphysical sophisms by which it is supported can seldom serve any other purpose than to blow up the hard insensibility of a coxcomb to ten times its native impertinence" (TMS III.3.14). Smith rejects the common and particular interpretation of *apátheia* that literally translates it as "without passions or emotions." This reading would explain the Stoics' indifference toward worldly events.[24] But this is debatable. Against the vernacular use of the word "stoical," some scholars maintain that "*apátheia* does not imply a wise man without emotions, but that all his emotions are rationally controlled."[25] In fact, morally indifferent things for the Stoics, such as wealth, rank, or reputation, are neither good nor bad, but simply indifferent.[26] Their moral content is neutral. However, we can pursue these indifferent things provided they spring from a literally "good" impulse or sentiment, what the Stoics called *eupátheia*. This idea proves that the Stoics had no intention of "eradicating" emotions, sentiments, or passions. A narrow reading of *apátheia*, as devoid of morality and sentiments, is simply one questionable interpretation of Stoic philosophy, an interpretation that distorts their philosophical legacy. And Smith was fully aware of this.

Evidently, nowadays our knowledge of the Stoics through new sources is deeper and more sophisticated. Nevertheless, Smith rejects the literal translation of *apátheia* and develops a complex meaning for self-command that is not related to *apátheia*. Smith's self-command is most probably inspired by the Socratic virtue of *enkráteia*, with some important nuances in its meaning. It has its roots in the Greek virtue of *enkráteia*. For example Xenophon's *Memorabilia*, which was widely read during the eighteenth century, portrays Socrates as referring to *enkráteia* as the "foundation of all virtues."[27] This statement resembles Smith's account of its importance (cf. TMS VI.iii.11). Besides, the notion of "self-command" was not widely employed in eighteenth-century moral discourse. It was much more common to hear about self-control or even self-restraint in the neo-Stoic tradition of control of passions. What distinguishes Smith's self-command from simple self-control is that "command" gives this virtue a sense of direction.[28] The actual meaning of *enkráteia* confirms this very simple intuition. The Greek word *eg-kráteia* literally means "inner power" or "power within oneself"—as for example *démos-kráteia* is power of the people—making "self-command" a fairly good literal translation of the term *enkráteia*.

Self-command also implies a person "possessed of himself," somebody who knows what to do and not to do. Therefore it is not simply a Stoical virtue that denies passions and focuses on plain indifference. In fact, self-command has an important classical philosophical tradition with which Smith was probably familiar.[29] Self-command as *enkráteia* is not exclusively related to the restraint of passions. Indeed, for Aristotle, *enkráteia* means not only endurance of pain, but also victory over desire.[30] This implies a sense of direction and possession of oneself as we learn to become masters of ourselves (cf. TMS III.3.22). Indeed, self-command is connected to the cardinal virtue of temperance (*sophrosúne*), and to all other Smithian virtues as well.[31]

As it has a sense of direction, self-command must also be seen as related to individual free choice.[32] Therefore, it could be argued that the complexity and distinctiveness of Smith's self-command combines a negative and a positive aspect. That is, it evolves from a negative virtue (self-assessment) to a positive one (self-direction), one capable of prompting our self-interest by guiding our self-direction. Therefore, the meaning of self-command combines negative and positive liberty.

Moreover, self-command is the only Smithian virtue assessed by its *propriety*, regardless of its effects or consequences (cf. TMS I.i.3.5 and II.i.I.1). In this sense, the propriety of self-command implies that rhetoric, deliberation, persuasion, and moral conduct are interrelated.[33] In Part VI Smith claims that "in our approbation of the virtues of self-command, complacency with their effects sometimes constitutes no part, and frequently but a small part, of that approbation" (TMS VI.concl.6). In relation to the virtues of prudence, justice, and beneficence, Smith simply speaks "of their agreeable effects, of their utility." But the broader sense of self-command is linked to our conscience, to the supposed impartial spectator who is capable of assessing the *propriety* of our behavior, regardless of its consequences. In this setting, self-command is a virtue that enables proper moral behavior, providing a kind of moral structure for virtuous behavior. As has been already underlined, from self-command "all the other virtues seem to derive their principal lustre" (TMS VI.iii.11). The role of self-command, as an enabling virtue, reflects Smith's interplay between *propriety* and merit, that is, moral motivations and consequences. This feature has been summarized by Knud Haakonssen as "a most extraordinary combination of an ideal of intentions with an actual ethics of consequences."[34] The virtue of self-command, as *enkráteia* for the classics, sustains the morality of the Smithian virtues.

In summary, self-command is a distinctively Smithian virtue that contrasts and complements the specific nature of Smith's more consequentialist or more utilitarian virtues (prudence, justice, and beneficence). If these three virtues have a utilitarian nuance, self-command has a Kantian overtone or a deontological insinuation over an Aristotelian background.

4. CONCLUSION

In TMS Smith presents four virtues that differ in their nature and spirit from the four virtues central to the classical cardinal virtue tradition. The cardinal virtue of fortitude does not appear explicitly in Smith's catalogue, but is implicit in self-command. Smith continuously refers to prudence (*phrónesis*) and justice (*dĭkaiosúne*), but he mainly concentrates on inferior prudence and negative justice. Smith also adds beneficence, the virtue of doing good to others. And if his central virtue of self-command is related to the cardinal virtue of temperance (*sophrosúne*), it has its origins in the Socratic virtue of *enkráteia*. All four Smithian virtues are interrelated insofar as they all play a crucial role in the moral life of a human being who is naturally though not exclusively self-interested. And self-command has a special position in this scheme. The other three virtues—beneficence, prudence, and justice—are judged by their consequences. Only self-command is related to *propriety*. In this interpretation, the motives underlying Smith's virtue of self-command support the consequentialist nature of his other virtues. Or better said, in relation to other Smithian virtues, self-command infuses a moral character that is behind and beyond utilitarianism and consequentialism. With its emphasis on self-direction, it enhances all other virtues, including self-interest.

Of course we cannot fully understand Smith's position on virtues without the sympathy-impartial spectator framework. But beyond the interpretation in this chapter, Smith's final attempt to give an account of the significance of his four main virtues in the sixth part of TMS, duly titled *Of the Character of Virtue*, is more than a mere foreshadowing of virtue ethics.[35] In fact, the Aristotelian catalogue of virtues, and his notion of *in medio virtus*, is present throughout TMS. And self-command is not an exception.

If Adam Smith came to be known mainly as the father of the "science" of economics, as the prophet of cold self-interest indifferent to virtue, this narrow and erroneous perception has changed. The renaissance of scholarship on his moral philosophy is the best proof. Recent academic interest on Smith's TMS acknowledges the originality and importance of his ethical thought. A proper understanding of the meaning of Smith's virtues, the moral character of self-interest and the neglected importance of self-command, is necessary to recover the classic connection between political economy and moral philosophy. Definitely this would be the best tribute to the legacy of the father of economics.

NOTES

This chapter owes much to Ryan Hanley's rigorous and challenging editorial suggestions. I am also indebted to Stephen McKenna for his comments.

1. Eckstein, in his excellent introduction to the 1926 German translation of the TMS, compares Smith's six lifetime editions. W. Eckstein, "Introduction to *The Theory of Moral Sentiments*" (1926), reprinted in *Adam Smith: Critical Responses*, vol. 1, ed. H. Mizuta (London: 2000), pp. 12–49. Also Dickey underlines some differences between the first and the sixth edition. L. Dickey, "Historicizing the 'Adam Smith Problem': Conceptual, Historiographical, and Textual Issues," *Journal of Modern History* 58, no. 3 (1986), pp. 579–609.

2. During the nineteenth century and the first half of the twentieth, TMS only "had four reprint editions without new introductions or notes" (H. Mizuta, *Adam Smith: Critical Responses*, 6 vols. [London: 2000], vol. 1, p. xxvi), and WN had more than ten.

3. For recent scholarship, see S. Fleischacker and V. Brown, "The Philosophy of Adam Smith. Essays Commemorating the 250th Anniversary of *The Theory of Moral Sentiments*," *Adam Smith Review* 5 (2010), pp. 1–11, and on this renaissance, see also review essays by Horst Claus Rechtenwald, "An Adam Smith Renaissance Anno 1976? The Bicentenary Output—A Reappraisal of His Scholarship," *Journal of Economic Literature* 16, no. 1 (1978), pp. 56–83, Vivienne Brown, "Mere Inventions of the Imagination," *Economics and Philosophy* 13 (1997), pp. 281–312, and Keith Tribe, "Adam Smith: Critical Theorist?," *Journal of Economic Literature* 37, no. 2 (1999), pp. 609–32.

4. In the twentieth century, up to the publication of the Glasgow Edition of the TMS in 1976, not a single edition of TMS had been published in Great Britain. See K. Tribe and H. Mizuta, *A Critical Bibliography of Adam Smith* (London: 2002), pp. 276–308.

5. For example, Thorstein Veblen affirms that "Smith might well be classed as a moderate utilitarian" (T. Veblen, "The Preconceptions of Economics," in *The Place of Science in Civilization and Other Essays* [New York: 1933 (1899–1900)], p. 131) and even John Rawls labels TMS as a preutilitarian work (J. Rawls, *A Theory of Justice* [Oxford: 1992 (1971)], p. 20, n. 9). Galbraith sums up this trend, arguing that TMS was "a work now largely forgotten and largely antecedent to his interest in Political Economy." J. K. Galbraith, *A History of Economics: The Past as the Present* (London: 1989 [1987]), p. 60.

6. A. L. Macfie, "Adam Smith's Moral Sentiments as Foundation for His Wealth of Nations," reprinted in *The Individual in Society: Papers on Adam Smith*, ed. Macfie (London: 1967), pp. 59–81, at p. 48.

7. S. Fleischacker, *A Third Concept of Liberty: Judgment and Freedom in Kant and Adam Smith* (Princeton: 1999), p. 147.

8. See also S. Fleischacker, "Philosophy in Moral Practice: Kant and Adam Smith," *Kant-Studien* 82, no. 3 (1991), pp. 249–69; L. Montes, *Adam Smith in Context. A Critical Reassessment of Some Central Components of His Thought* (London: 2004), pp. 118–22.

9. See esp. D. McCloskey, *The Bourgeois Virtues* (Chicago: 2006); McCloskey, "Adam Smith, the Last of the Former Virtue Ethicists," *History of Political Economy* 40 (2008), pp. 43–71; R. P. Hanley, *Adam Smith and the Character of Virtue* (Cambridge: 2009); Hanley, "Adam Smith and Virtue," in *The Oxford Handbook of Adam Smith*, ed. C. Berry, M. P. Paganelli, and C. Smith (Oxford: 2013); M. Carrasco, "Adam Smith: Virtues and Universal Principles," *Revue internationale de philosophie* 68 (2014), pp. 223–50.

10. For the historical context, origins, and intellectual evolution of the Adam Problem, see L. Montes, "Das Adam Smith Problem: Its Origins, the Stages of the Current Debate, and One Implication for Our Understanding of Sympathy," *Journal of the History of Economic Thought* 25, no. 1 (2003), pp. 64–90.

11. Smith's sympathy is broader than Hume's, and it deviates from Hume's proto-utilitarian approach. Emma Rothschild has correctly argued that Smith rejects Hume's position as in the Smithian sympathetic process "the convergence of sentiments depends on judgements about motives, as well as about consequences." E. Rothschild, *Economic Sentiments: Adam Smith, Condorcet, and the Enlightenment* (Cambridge, MA: 2001), p. 231.

12. The relationship of sympathy and Smith's intellectual virtues is worth exploring (on Smith's intellectual virtues, see R. P. Hanley, "Adam Smith and Virtue," in *The Oxford Handbook of Adam Smith*, ed. C. Berry, M. P. Paganelli, and C. Smith [Oxford: 2013], pp. 230–36).

13. In a way, the etymology of ethics, distinguishing *ethos* with *epsilon* or *etha*, that is, character or habit, respectively, acquires a virtuous Aristotelian interaction in Smith's legacy. For Smith, the experience of conduct, that is, the exercise of sympathy, also shapes our moral character.

14. N. Waszek, "Two Concepts of Morality: A Distinction of Adam Smith's Ethics and its Stoic Origin," *Journal of the History of Ideas* 45, no. 4 (1984), pp. 591–606. On Smith's practical reason, the moral minimum, and perfect virtue, see M. Carrasco, "Adam Smith's Reconstruction of Practical Reason," *Review of Metaphysics* 58, no. 1 (2004), pp. 81–116.

15. Gloria Vivenza appropriately refers to Smith's "domestic" prudence. G. Vivenza, *Adam Smith and the Classics: The Classical Heritage in Adam Smith's Thought* (Oxford: 2001), p. 197.

16. George Stigler, for example, narrowly defines self-interest as "the crown jewel" of the WN that "became, and remains to this day, the foundation of the theory of the allocation of resources." G. J. Stigler, *The Economist as a Preacher* (Oxford: 1982), p. 147.

17. See TMS VII.iv.37, and VII.ii.I.10. The development of the natural law tradition initiated by Grotius, reformulated by Pufendorf, and adapted by Locke, is fundamental to the Scottish Enlightenment and also to the shaping of Smith's virtues.

18. Patricia H. Werhane, *Adam Smith and His Legacy for Modern Capitalism* (Oxford: 1991), p. 43.

19. See Samuel Fleischacker, *On Adam Smith's* Wealth of Nations (Princeton: 2004).

20. Griswold also develops this connection. C. L. Griswold, *Adam Smith and the Virtues of Enlightenment* (Cambridge: 1999), p. 252.

21. On Smith and the classics' influence, see Vivenza, *Adam Smith and the Classics*.

22. On the language of duties, Smith's position of the standing army versus militia debate is a good example to show that he represents the twilight of the classical republican tradition. See L. Montes, "Adam Smith on the Standing Army versus Militia Issue: Wealth over Virtue?," in *The Elgar Companion to Adam Smith*, ed. Jeffrey Young (Cheltenham: 2009), pp. 315–35.

23. On Smith and the Stoics, see L. Montes, "Adam Smith as an *Eclectic* Stoic," *Adam Smith Review* 4 (2008), pp. 30–56.

24. For example, Martha Nussbaum refers to the concept of *apátheia* as "what the Stoics said it was. It is extirpation" or "the Stoic does not hesitate to describe the wise person as totally free from passion." Nussbaum, *The Therapy of Desire: Theory and Practice in Hellenistic Ethics* (Princeton: 1994), pp. 401, 390.

25. J. M. Rist, "The Stoic Concept of Detachment," in *The Stoics*, ed. J. M. Rist (Berkeley: 1978), pp. 259–72, at p. 259; see also A. A. Long, *Stoic Studies* (Cambridge: 1996), p. 177; F. H. Sandbach, *The Stoics* (London: 1975), p. 59.

26. A. A. Long and D. N. Sedley, *The Hellenistic Philosophers*, 2 vols. (Cambridge: 1987), vol. 1, pp. 419–23.

27. Xenophon, *Memorabilia*, ed. G. P. Goold (Cambridge, MA: 1997), I.v.4, p. 67.

28. See, for example, J. R. Otteson, *Adam Smith's Marketplace of Life* (Cambridge: 2002), pp. 55, 238–39, 291.

29. Evidence is found in the collection of works by classical writers in Smith's library (H. Mizuta, *Adam Smith's Library: A Supplement to Bonar's Catalogue with a Checklist of the whole Library* [Cambridge: 2008 (1967)]). We also know

that Smith managed Latin and Greek quite well. Therefore, it is very likely that Smith was well aware of the Greek word *enkráteia*, its nature and meaning, and its relationship with the cardinal virtue of temperance or *sophrosúne*.

30. Aristotle, *Nicomachean Ethics*, ed. and trans. H. Rackham (Cambridge, MA: 1994), VII 1150.a.32, p. 415.

31. In the classical tradition, the cardinal virtue of temperance or *sophrosúne* is related to *enkráteia*. For the history of this cardinal virtue and its relationship with *enkráteia*, see H. North, *Sophrosyne: Self-Knowledge and Self-Restraint in Greek Literature* (Ithaca, NY: 1966).

32. Edward Harpham suggests that "[o]ne could argue that the ideal of self-command itself demands a certain amount of negative liberty." Harpham, "The Problem of Liberty in the Thought of Adam Smith," *Journal of the History of Economic Thought* 22, no. 2 (2000), pp. 215–37, at p. 236.

33. Smith's rhetoric of propriety, as McKenna has argued, combines an interaction between propriety of moral action and propriety of speech. S. J. McKenna, *Adam Smith: The Rhetoric of Propriety* (Albany, NY: 2006).

34. K. Haakonssen, *The Science of a Legislator: The Natural Jurisprudence of David Hume and Adam Smith* (Cambridge: 1981), p. 65.

35. As Ryan Hanley has argued, "his virtue theory is both important and understudied." Hanley, *Adam Smith and the Character of Virtue* (Cambridge: 2009), p. 11.

BIBLIOGRAPHIC ESSAY

The best advice for understanding Smith's virtues is certainly reading TMS and WN. There is a vast literature on Smith and virtues in different books and especially in specialized journals. Of most recent contributions, Charles Griswold's classic *Adam Smith and the Virtues of Enlightenment* (Cambridge: 1999) is a good start. Samuel Fleischacker's *A Third Concept of Liberty: Judgment and Freedom in Kant and Adam Smith* (Princeton: 1999) might follow. Then, James Otteson's *Adam Smith's Marketplace of Life* (Cambridge: 2002) is a suggestive and deep reading of Smith's morality and the importance of markets, a theme also taken up in Deirdre McCloskey's book *The Bourgeois Virtues* (Chicago: 2006). Also it is worth looking at the collection of essays in *Wealth and Virtue* (Cambridge: 1983) edited by Istvan Hont and Michael Ignatieff, Leonidas Montes's *Adam Smith in Context* (New York: 2004), and Athol Fitzgibbons's *Adam Smith's System of Liberty, Wealth, and Virtue* (Oxford: 1995). Of more recent developments, Ryan Hanley's

Adam Smith and the Character of Virtue (Cambridge: 2009) is the best account for a virtue ethics interpretation of Smith. Fonna Forman-Barzilai's *Adam Smith and the Circles of Sympathy* (Cambridge: 2010) is worth reading on how virtues relate to sympathy, and Gloria Vivenza's *Adam Smith and the Classics* (Oxford: 2001) provides an important source for understanding the classics influence on Smith. From these recent works, cross-references might lead the interested reader to previous and fascinating earlier contributions.

10

ADAM SMITH ON EQUALITY

Elizabeth Anderson

1. TYPES OF EGALITARIANISM

Moral egalitarianism is the view that, from a moral point of view, everyone counts equally: all have equal moral standing to claim rights and have their interests count in moral assessment. This idea can be taken in radical or moderate directions. Radical egalitarians call for the abolition of social hierarchy in one or more domains, replacing it with individual autonomy (as in anarchism) or, where joint action is needed, democratic governance (as in participatory democracy). Moderate egalitarians accept various forms of social hierarchy, but insist that authority relations be tempered by egalitarian norms.[1] A moderate principle of *political egalitarianism* claims that the state is obligated to impartially enforce a set of equal basic rights, and to give equal consideration to every member's interests in public policy. A moderate form of *esteem egalitarianism* holds that one's social rank should not affect how much anyone esteems one's merit or sympathizes with one's suffering. A moderate form of *social egalitarianism* prefers that individuals relate to one another in civil society on terms of equality and personal independence, rather than on terms of domination and dependent subordination.

Smith is a moderate egalitarian in all these senses.[2] The next section demonstrates how his assessments of public policy reflect a moderate political egalitarianism, founded on a principle of moral equality. Section 3 considers Rousseau's objection that commercial society, with its extreme economic inequality, violates esteem egalitarianism. It argues that Smith shares Rousseau's concern, but his different psychology of esteem offers openings to resolve the problem. Section 4 shows how Smith thinks commercial society can meet

Rousseau's objection. Smith's argument turns on the idea that commercial society replaces relations of domination and dependence with relations of cooperation among independent persons, mediated by mutual recognition of people's rights and interests in market transactions. This chapter concludes with reflections on the distance not closed by Smith's answers to radical egalitarians.

2. SMITH'S MODERATE MORAL AND POLITICAL EGALITARIANISM

Smith argues that when we undertake a moral assessment of someone, we consider how others view that person—or how they would view that person if they were informed and impartial. When we take up this moral point of view on ourselves, we discover that we are "but one of the multitude in no respect better than any other in it" (TMS III.3.4). Thus, we are fundamentally moral equals. The person of moral conscience acts on principles of which an impartial observer could approve. Given our moral equality, such principles can only be those that others are willing to "go along with" (TMS II.ii.2.1).

What principles are those? We care not simply about our physical and material well-being, but about how others regard us. What angers us most when another injures us is not the "mischief which we have suffered," but "the little account which he seems to make of us, the unreasonable preference which he gives to himself above us" (TMS II.iii.1.5). We care about our *respectability* in the eyes of others, a recognition of ourselves as entitled to have our interests taken into account in others' decision making.

When the state is the decision maker, Smith insists that everyone's rights and interests be regarded *equally*. The state's duty to administer justice requires equal treatment under the law for all, thereby ensuring that the rights of "the meanest British subject" are "respectable to the greatest" (WN IV.7.c.54). It is unjust for the state to harm the interests of some for no other purpose than to benefit another class of citizens, and thereby create inequality (WN IV.8.30).

This principle of political egalitarianism lies at the heart of Smith's public policy assessments. Smith focuses his criticisms on policies that create privileges for some at the expense of others. Virtually all the policies he condemns exacerbate inequality by unjustly favoring the rich at the expense of workers and consumers, especially the poor. These unjust policies include state grants of monopoly and corporation (WN I.10.2); tariffs that enrich protected producers by raising prices for everyone else (WN IV.3.2.9–10); bounties on grain exports, which raise the price of bread at the expense of the poor (WN IV.5); primogeniture and entail, aimed at maintaining a monopoly of property on the part of a few great families (WN III.2.6); laws permitting employers to combine (WN I.8.12–13); and all forms of forced labor, including slavery, serfdom, sharecropping (WN III.2.8–13, IV.7.2.54), and apprenticeship (a form of indentured servitude in which the master kept the proceeds of the apprentice's work) (WN I.10.2.12). Worst of all, imperialism—a system designed to serve monopoly interests—is a system of cruel oppression, "ruinous and destructive," a "savage injustice" that Europeans inflicted on others (WN IV.1.32), leading to famine in Bengal (WN I.8.26), the enslavement of Africans, and plunder and murder of indigenous peoples (WN IV.7.2.7; IV.7.3.80, 101).

Against the view that Smith is a political egalitarian, one might object that the free market system he endorses generates unjust distributive inequality. Contemporary egalitarians argue that for the state to treat everyone with equal consideration requires that it regulate the distribution of income and wealth so as to satisfy egalitarian principles of distributive justice. This objection is anachronistic. The idea of distributive justice—principles for assessing the justice of distributive patterns produced by a whole economic system—was not fully conceived until shortly after Smith died.[3] Nevertheless, while not using the language of distributive justice, Smith often takes up distributive considerations in assessing institutions. Four features of Smith's assessments stand out.

First, unlike many who claim to follow him, Smith is not dogmatically opposed to state regulation or redistributive measures that reduce inequality.[4] He praises institutions for promoting distributive equality, or for improving the prospects of the poor. He supports modestly progressive taxes (WN V.1.d.5), state funding of schools for the working class (WN V.1.f.54–55), and laws protecting farmers from eviction by their landlords (WN III.2.14). He endorses public roads and canals because they equalize the condition of country people to townspeople (WN I.11.b.5). He argues that state regulations on behalf of the workers, such as laws requiring that their wages be paid in cash rather than in kind, are "always just and equitable" (WN I.10.c.61).

Second and most famously, the *Wealth of Nations* defends high and growing wages for the working classes. Against those who claim that low wages are needed to force the poor to work just to survive, Smith argues that the motive to better one's condition is common to all. Higher wages increase production by providing an incentive to work more (WN I.8.42–44). Even apart from their utility, equity demands that the workers, who provide everyone else with food, clothing, and shelter, should have decent levels of these goods themselves (WN I.8.36).

Third, where Smith endorses distributive inequality, it is on behalf of the least advantaged. "[A] people who are all on an equality will necessarily be very poor" (LJA iii.139). It takes a commercial society to raise productivity enough to generate "universal opulence" (WN I.1.10). Although this creates inequality, it is likely that the least advantaged would rather enjoy a decent standard of living and "go along with" inequality, than stay poor.

Fourth, for an advocate of commercial society, Smith is surprisingly skeptical of the benefits of great wealth. People grossly overrate the supposed advantages of great wealth, which are mostly illusory (TMS III.3.31). These suppositions are based on vanity, and on the false belief that wealth brings peace of mind. Riches are not worth the trouble it takes to acquire them: they cause their owners anxiety about maintaining them and distract wealth seekers from what is really valuable in life, which is the love and respect of people in one's social circle (TMS I.iii.2.1; IV.1.6–8). People who climb quickly from poverty to riches are unhappy, because they lose their older and poorer friends but never gain acceptance in the richer circles they try to enter (TMS I.ii.5.1). Hence, while the distribution of wealth is very unequal in commercial societies, the distribution of well-being, at least where the lowest ranks enjoy a decent standard of living, is nearly equal. Nevertheless, the *illusion* that great riches are beneficial is useful, because it motivates people in commercial societies to be economically active in ways that raise the prospects of the least well-off (TMS IV.1.10).[5]

The growth of a consumer society providing diverse opportunities for consumption may cast doubt on Smith's suggestion that wealth, beyond serving modest needs, serves only to slake people's vanity. Indeed, Smith makes more room for the value of moderate accumulation in the *Wealth of Nations*.[6] To the extent that wealth delivers genuine goods, concerns about fairly dividing the gains from cooperation become more important. Smith's thought, while it lacks a theory of distributive justice, provides two resources for developing a metric of justice. Consider his famous defense of a living wage: "No society can surely be flourishing and happy, of which the far greater part of the members are poor and miserable. It is but equity, besides, that they who feed, cloath and lodge the whole body of the people, should have such a share of the produce of their own labour as to be themselves tolerably well fed, cloathed and lodged" (WN I.8.36). Smith's metric of welfare is not expressed in monetary terms, but in terms of what Amartya Sen has called *functionings*—valuable states of being or doing—in this case, of adequate levels of nutrition, clothing, and housing.[7] What levels count as adequate depends on various factors, including climate, the energy requirements of one's occupation, one's physical condition (for example, pregnancy), and social norms. Smith observes that the clothing one must wear to be able to appear in public without shame varies across societies, according to their general level of prosperity. In the England of his day, a respectable worker required leather shoes, but not in somewhat poorer France. "Under necessaries therefore, I comprehend, not only those things which nature, but those things which the established rules of decency have rendered necessary to the lowest rank of people" (WN V.2.k.3). Advanced societies today include access to decent medical care among the necessities. Smith's view thus includes a concept of relative poverty that, like any egalitarian measure, is concerned with interpersonal comparisons. The concept of relative poverty accommodates the possibility that economic growth will deliver genuine goods beyond subsistence, over the fair division of which it makes sense to be concerned.

Smith consistently views public policies in terms of how well they serve the interests of the less advantaged in society—workers, and the poor—because they are society's most numerous members (WN I.8.36). Their interests include not only higher income but freedom, especially freedom of occupation and personal independence from their masters. These are fundamental for any egalitarian whose concerns extend beyond resource distribution to relations of domination and subjection. And, as Smith argues, securing freedom for workers usually raises their incomes as well. This is just what a moderate political and social egalitarian would recommend.

3. ROUSSEAU'S CHALLENGE: ESTEEM INEQUALITY IN COMMERCIAL SOCIETY

If Smith's free market commercial society fares well from the perspective of moderate political egalitarianism, it faces a deep challenge from the perspective of moderate esteem egalitarianism. Societies marked by great wealth inequality inflict undeserved contempt and obscurity on the poor, and admire the wealthy simply for being rich. Esteem competition in unequal societies may generate spite and envy throughout all social classes.

Rousseau articulates this challenge most forcefully. His 1755 *Discourse on the Origin of Inequality* argues that people would be content to satisfy simple needs if they did not compete with one another for the admiration of their fellows.[8] At first they compete for esteem by displaying personal merits—beauty, eloquence, strength, agility—(2D 144)—that is, features that deserve admiration. However, once human beings value what others think about them, they "know how to live only in the opinions of others" (2D 161). The desperate need for recognition leads people to seek counterfeits. "Being something and appearing to be something became two completely different things; and from this distinction arose grand ostentation" (2D 147). The acquisition and conspicuous display of wealth substitute for merit. Esteem competition thus leads to private property, industry, and commerce.

Esteem competition leads to inequality (2D 144) because the economy of esteem is positional, and structured as a zero-sum game: one person can rise in the opinion of others only if others descend. The perverse and destructive incentives built into esteem competition are the origin of inequalities in wealth and power. For people do not merely seek wealth and power, they seek to have *more* than others, and to keep others deprived: "if one sees a handful of powerful and rich men at the height of greatness and fortune while the mob grovels in obscurity and misery, it is because the former prize the things they enjoy only to the extent that others are deprived of them; and because, without changing their position, they would cease to be happy, if the people ceased to be miserable" (2D 158). To the charge that envy drives egalitarianism, Rousseau retorts that the envy is the natural response to the spitefulness of the rich and powerful. The rich, out of "zeal for raising the relative level of . . . [their] fortune" seek to "profit at the expense of someone else." The powerful, seeking "the pleasure of domination," enlist their subordinates to put ever more people into subjection (2D 148).

Rousseau argues for radical political and economic equality to overcome the competitive economy of esteem that produces spite and envy, rich and poor, masters and slaves. Recognizing that there is no going back to the psychic self-sufficiency of savages, Rousseau argues for institutions that restructure the economy of esteem so that access to recognition is universalizable.[9] Life in a republic under the social contract aims to achieve this. When all citizens are united as equals under laws willed by and for all, then everyone enjoys the mutual respect enshrined in the laws. To prevent the degeneration of a free republic of equals into a plutocracy, public policy must ensure that all have enough property to secure their personal independence, and none so much as to buy others' subordination. There should be "neither rich men nor beggars" because both threaten republican liberty (SC 2.11, 46).

Smith accepts central elements of Rousseau's analysis. He agrees that vanity—the desire for the unmerited esteem of others—is the basic motive for seeking luxury (TMS I.iii.2.1). This is one of the driving forces behind commercial society, generating both great wealth and great inequality. Commerce and manufactures arise to gratify "the most childish, the meanest, and the most sordid of all vanities" (WN III.4.10), and thus lead to a prosperous society, while corrupting our standards of esteem and generating unjust esteem inequality.

While agreeing with Rousseau on these points, Smith softens Rousseau's moral psychology by rejecting the idea that, outside of a republic of equals, people win esteem only by putting others down. The economy of esteem in commercial societies is not *essentially* a zero-sum game, and hence is not essentially driven by spite and envy. These feelings do not dominate psychic relations between rich and poor, for everyone, even the poor, naturally, spontaneously, and *disinterestedly* sympathizes with the rich! "Our obsequiousness to our superiors more frequently arises from our admiration for the advantages of their situation, than from any private expectations of benefit from their good-will. . . . We are eager to assist them in completing a system of happiness that approaches so near to perfection; and we desire to serve them for their own sake, without any other recompense but the vanity or the honour of obliging them" (TMS I.iii.2.3). This tendency radically reduces the extent of envy in commercial society. Smith traces it to an asymmetry in our sentiments: we sympathize more with others' joy than with their sorrow (TMS I.iii.1.5). This asymmetry follows from the fact that sympathy involves sharing the same feelings as the target of our sympathy. Sympathizing with joy is pleasurable, while sympathizing with sorrow is painful. So we are eager to share others' joy and reluctant to share their sadness (TMS I.iii.1.9). This explains why spite does not dominate the economy of esteem. We generally want to avoid viewing anyone's suffering, because the sight of it is painful. The chief vice underlying the injustice in the economy of esteem is therefore not spite but "hard-heartedness" (TMS I.iii.1.9).

Hard-heartedness makes the fortunate indifferent to the suffering of the poor. They think the wretched should hide so as not to disturb their tranquility. Because people desire to have others feel in concord with them, and understand the asymmetry of sympathy between rich and poor, the poor strive to hide their misfortunes, while the rich parade their fortunes. This inflicts further injustices on the poor: in addition to shame, they suffer obscurity (TMS I.iii.2.1). Observers feel "ten times more compassion and resentment" on behalf of the rich, when they suffer injury, than when the poor suffer the same injury, because injury to the former ruins the vicarious pleasure they feel in the illusory fantasy they have constructed of the bliss of the rich (TMS I.iii.2.2). People also respect the rich and powerful more than the poor and humble for the same degree of merit (TMS I.iii.3.4).

Smith condemns this inequality of sympathy. It is "the great and most universal cause of the corruption of our moral sentiments" and causes "contempt . . . [to be] most unjustly bestowed upon poverty and weakness" (TMS I.iii.3.1). Yet the facts that this injustice is not essentially founded on a zero-sum game and does not cause pervasive envy and spite offer Smith room to address this injustice within commercial society.

An asymmetry in the injustice of the economy of esteem provides additional room. While the poor may justly complain of the obscurity and contempt from which they suffer, they have no just complaint in the fact that the rich receive undeserved esteem. Offering *more* esteem to some than others, even when it is undeserved, does no injury to anyone else. Others may envy it, but envy has no moral standing.

This conclusion is reinforced by the fact that unmerited esteem is worthless. Wealth, power, and rank do not deserve respect, although people do respect it (TMS I.iii.3.4). When people offer excessive regard to the rich and powerful, they are therefore paying in false coin. The rich are contemptible fools to seek it. They are contemptible, because seeking such regard is vanity. They are fools, because the anxious quest for wealth and power, and the troubles that need to be taken to maintain it, displace the real joys of friendship and comity in one's social circle that are equally available to the humble, and the main source of true happiness (TMS III.3.31).

Smith's diagnosis of the ills of esteem inequality in commercial societies, due to their fostering of extreme wealth inequality, provides *openings* for remedies to be found *within* commercial society. The next section explains Smith's moderate egalitarian remedies.

4. SMITH'S MODERATE EGALITARIAN REPLY TO ROUSSEAU

Smith's defense of commercial society rests on two great benefits it bestows on the less advantaged: prosperity, and personal independence from their superiors. Although it exacerbates property inequality in comparison with primitive societies (WN I.i.11), it lifts the masses out of poverty. By extending the market and enabling a finer, more productive division of labor, commercial society creates a "universal opulence which extends itself to the lowest ranks of the people" (WN I.1.10). A society that enforces material equality could never achieve this, because "a people who are all on an equality will necessarily be very poor" (LJA iii.139). Thus, in line with the tradition of moderate egalitarianism from Condorcet to Rawls, Smith justifies these inequalities as necessary to improve the prospects of the least well-off.

While "universal opulence" is beneficial, "by far the most important" of the effects of commercial society are the introduction of good government, and the liberation of people from "servile dependency upon their superiors" (WN III.4.4). Before the rise of commercial society, the rich could spend their wealth only by directly maintaining servants, retainers, slaves, serfs, and tenants. The latter received subsistence but owed obedience in return. Their superiors exercised despotic and arbitrary dominion over them. Commercial society enabled the rich to spend all their wealth on themselves, by purchasing manufactured luxuries. "Thus, for the gratification of the most childish, the meanest, and the most sordid of all vanities they gradually bartered their whole power and authority" (WN III.4.10). Workers, instead of being dependent on one master, left their lords' estates for employment in manufacturing, retail trades, and shipping, and became wage earners. They thereby gained personal independence from their superiors—a moderate form of social equality.

These two great goods—prosperity and personal independence—are not merely compensation for the unjust esteem inequalities inflicted on the poor. They provide partial remedies for these psychic injustices. Eventually, economic growth should spread wealth far enough to end poverty. With the abolition of poverty, no one will suffer its humiliation and obscurity. Being "tolerably well fed [and] cloathed" (WN I.8.36), all can appear in public without shame (WN V.2.k.3).

The personal independence of workers also shifts the terms on which they receive resources from the wealthy. As dependents, they had to bow and scrape before their superiors, virtually begging for subsistence. Their humiliating condition as real or virtual slaves to their superiors satisfied the latter's love of dominion. Upon becoming free and independent workers, their superiors, to get what they wanted from them, were "obliged to condescend to persuade" them that it was to their advantage to exchange goods with them (WN III.2.8–10). The market nexus thus makes individuals respectable in the eyes of those with whom they transact, as people who must be persuaded rather than ordered to serve others (WN I.2.2). Commercial society distracts the vanity of the rich from exercising oppressive dominion over others to displaying frivolous ornaments on their persons and estates. Wages also enable workers to get what they want from others by appealing to their self-interest rather than their vanity. Instead of offering their "servile and fawning attention" to others, they offer cash (WN I.2.1). This more dignified mode of obtaining what they want from others enhances their respectability.

Good government does even more to raise the respectability of inferiors. Just governments observe scrupulous impartiality in enforcing laws protecting property and persons, upholding as vigorously the rights of the less as the more advantaged. The rich thereby understand that their inferiors are entitled to respect (WN IV.7.c.54). In addition, public funding of education for the working class enhances their intelligence and makes them more respectable, in their own eyes and in the eyes of their superiors (WN V.1.f.61). Commercial society thus generates prosperity and good institutions that reduce the injustices of esteem inequality.

Does Smith offer a complete answer to radical egalitarians? At least four objections remain. First, Rousseau's republican objections to wealth inequality in commercial society are not confined to its corruptions of the economy of esteem. He also worries that great wealth inequality undermines democracy, because it leads to plutocracy. Recent experience with the corrupting effects of increasing inequality on politics in contemporary democracies supports Rousseau's concern. Smith confesses that he has no answer to this (WN IV.3.c.9). He takes it for granted that the rich will rule, because wealth is the fundamental natural basis for authority, even though it does not correspond with merit or talent (WN V.1.b.5, 7–8, 11). There are no innate differences in talent among different classes; observed differences are due to environmental causes, particularly in the different work people do (WN I.2.4). Yet the rich will rule even though landowners are stupid, and even though merchants and manufacturers make the worst governors, having interests opposed to those of the general public (WN I.11.p.8, 10; V.1.e.26).

Second, and related to this point, Smith admits that the "disposition to admire, and almost to worship, the rich and the powerful" (TMS I.iii.3.1) leads people to underrate the virtues of the less advantaged. This poses a serious obstacle to equality of opportunity, even in ostensibly meritocratic selection processes.

Third, Smith's celebration of the liberation of workers from their superiors in the transition from feudal to market society, while vitally important, failed to anticipate the rise of large-scale productive enterprises in the Industrial Revolution, and hence the extent to which workers in manufacturing and commerce have become subject to the dominion of their employers. Smith offers penetrating criticisms of industrial production, stressing in particular the stultifying effects of a fine-grained division of labor (WN V.1.f.50). However, he expected that the rise of commerce and manufacturing, conjoined with the abolition of monopolizing regulations, would lead to an economy dominated by independent craftsmen running small workshops, shopkeepers, and yeoman farmers.[10] By the mid-nineteenth century, the scale and intensity of factory work involved a minute, disciplined, oppressive form of employer governance of employee's conduct. Notwithstanding the changing content of work in the postindustrial era, today's egalitarians remain concerned about the despotical character of employer governance of employees' lives on and even off the job, including issues such as sexual harassment, employers' invasions of employee privacy, and employers' control of workers' speech and political activity.

Finally, Smith wrote at a time when virtually all state interference with the "system of natural liberty" was on behalf of the rich. In that context the interests of market freedom and equality coincide. By the nineteenth century, workers were mobilizing for minimum wages, maximum hours, factory safety regulations, the right to demand that employers negotiate with labor unions, and comprehensive social insurance. Opponents of such regulations have long invoked Smith against these demands. While a closer reading of Smith demonstrates that he was a friend of equality and no dogmatist about laissez-faire, it is harder to glean from his texts general principles that could guide us in the sorts of cases that concern us today, where interests in equality and market freedom appear to conflict.[11]

Nevertheless, Smith's work is a milestone in the history of egalitarianism. His moderate egalitarianism offers a great deal to the less advantaged. His defense of commercial society helpfully reminds us of the deep connections between equality and freedom—especially free labor, and personal independence from superiors. His defense also helpfully sets an example of how to avoid the two great vices of political economy—dogmatic condemnation, and uncritical worship, of market institutions.

NOTES

I thank Ryan Hanley and Sam Fleischacker for helpful comments on this essay.

1. For example, most liberals accept the hierarchical governance of the firm, but insist on antidiscrimination laws to protect workers.

2. Norbert Waszek, in "Two Concepts of Morality: A Distinction of Adam Smith's Ethics and Its Stoic Origin," *Journal of the History of Ideas* 45, no. 4

(1984), pp. 591–606, suggests that Smith is a moral elitist, distinguishing the vulgar masses, capable of merely proper action, from the few, who are capable of true virtue. Whatever the merits of this interpretation of Smith's theory of virtue, it is irrelevant to his social and political views. Smith argues that authority must be based on objectively discernible features, while people's virtues are invisible and subject to endless dispute (WN V.1.b.5). This and his frequent criticisms of the vanity, selfishness, and stupidity of the upper classes, show that he rejects any suggestion that distinctions of virtue do or ever could ground social institutions of hierarchy or inequality. David Levy and Sandra Peart, in *The Street Porter and the Philosopher: Conversations on Analytical Egalitarianism* (Ann Arbor: 2008), agree, stressing Smith's frequent references to the broad natural equality of human beings in their needs, motives, and capacities.

3. Samuel Fleischacker, *A Short History of Distributive Justice* (Cambridge, MA: 2004).

4. Amartya Sen, "Uses and Abuses of Adam Smith," *History of Political Economy* 43, no. 2 (2011), pp. 257–71.

5. Sam Fleischacker argues that in WN, Smith retreats from the suggestion of TMS IV.1 that vanity and illusion are needed to drive economic improvements. Ordinary desires for a decent standard of living and moderate advancement are enough. See *On Adam Smith's* Wealth of Nations: *A Philosophical Companion* (Princeton: 2004), chap. 6.

6. Ibid.

7. Amartya Sen, *Development as Freedom* (New York: 1999), pp. 75–76. Sen cites Smith's use of functionings on p. 74.

8. Jean-Jacques Rousseau, *On the Social Contract and Discourses*, trans. Donald Cress (Indianapolis: 1983). Subsequent citations to the *Discourse on the Origins of Inequality* included in this text are noted as 2D. Citations to *The Social Contract* are noted as SC.

9. See Joshua Cohen, *Rousseau: A Free Community of Equals* (Oxford: 2010) for a leading account of this argument.

10. The abolition of primogeniture and entail would lead to the breakup of vast estates, which were too large to be managed productively (WN III.4.19, III.2.7). Land sold in a free market would end up in the hands of the most productive. These were the yeoman farmers, who, as self-employed and owning their own capital, were the chief improvers of the land, and more productive than large estates farmed by wage workers, sharecroppers, or slaves (WN III.2.8–13, 20, III.4.19). Smith expected that the most productive nonfarm enterprises would also be small. His famous pin factory employed only ten workers (WN I.1.3). Large-scale joint-stock corporations were justified only for the four types of enterprise that required large concentrations of capital: banking, insurance, canals, and water utilities (WN V.5.i.e). The abolition of guilds and mercantilist barriers to trade would end monopolies, leading to the entry of smaller-scale enterprises and greater competition. This would reduce the rate of profit. Low profit rates reduce the scale of fortunes, forcing nearly all capital owners to work for a living (WN I.ix.20). Thus, while a free market economy would be more unequal than a primitive economy, it would be more equal than a mercantilist one. For further discussion, see Deborah Boucoyannis, "The Equalizing Hand: Why Adam Smith

Thought the Market Should Produce Wealth without Steep Inequality," *Perspectives on Politics* 11, no. 4 (2013), pp. 1051–70.

11. Smith was no ideologue; he did not theorize from first principles of political philosophy. Hence his thought remains today, as it did for his immediate successors, a resource for thinkers on both the left and the right. This point is widely recognized by Smith scholars. See, for example, Charles Griswold, *Adam Smith and the Virtues of Enlightenment* (Cambridge: 1999), pp. 295–96; Emma Rothschild, *Economic Sentiments: Adam Smith, Condorcet, and the Enlightenment* (Cambridge, MA: 2001), p. 62; and Samuel Fleischacker, *On Adam Smith's* Wealth of Nations: *A Philosophical Companion* (Princeton: 2004), pp. 263–69.

BIBLIOGRAPHIC ESSAY

Until recently, Smith was regarded as a laissez-faire theorist who repudiated any interest in substantive equality. Gertrude Himmelfarb's *The Idea of Poverty* (New York: 1984) played a pivotal role in reinterpreting Smith as an advocate of high wages and friend of the poor. Gareth Stedman Jones, in *An End to Poverty?* (New York: 2004), continues the project of situating Smith as an optimist in debates about abolishing poverty. Emma Rothschild's *Economic Sentiments* (Cambridge, MA: 2001) offers an extensive reinterpretation of Smith as a liberal egalitarian, and details how Smith's reputation as a dogmatic libertarian and admirer of the rich was forged in the nineteenth-century British reaction to the French Revolution. Samuel Fleischacker's *On Adam Smith's* Wealth of Nations (Princeton: 2004) and *A Short History of Distributive Justice* (Cambridge, MA: 2004) place Smith at the threshold of an egalitarian theory of distributive justice. Amartya Sen, in *Commodities and Capabilities* (Amsterdam: 1985) and later works, pioneers the capabilities approach to measuring justice, partly on a reading of Smith. Another pivotal development regarding Smith on equality connects his *Theory of Moral Sentiments* to a foundational moral egalitarianism, and reads his account of mutual recognition in market transactions in egalitarian terms. See Fleischacker, *On Adam Smith's* Wealth of Nations, and Charles Griswold, *Adam Smith and the Virtues of Enlightenment* (Cambridge: 1999). For critical commentary on this development, see Stephen Darwall, "Sympathetic Liberalism: Recent Work on Adam

Smith," *Philosophy and Public Affairs* 28 (1999), pp. 139–64 and Remy Debes, "Adam Smith on Dignity and Equality," *British Journal for the History of Philosophy* 20 (2012), pp. 109–40. The most important work considering Smith's response to Rousseau's critique of commercial society is Ryan Hanley's *Adam Smith and the Character of Virtue* (Cambridge: 2009).

ADAM SMITH ON JUSTICE AND INJUSTICE

Nicholas Wolterstorff

The theory of justice that Adam Smith develops in his *Theory of Moral Sentiments* grounds justice in human nature, in particular, in our emotional nature. One of the goals Smith had in mind in developing his theory was that it would enable us to determine to what extent the laws and practices of our actual societies are just and to what extent they are unjust.

His theory is highly original. Most theories of justice that have been developed in the West are either of the Aristotelian or the Ulpian type. The theory Smith develops belongs to neither of these types.[1]

Justice, as Aristotle explained it, consists of fairness or equity in the distribution of benefits and burdens and in our exchanges with each other. Justice is equality of treatment—with the understanding that the equality of treatment that constitutes justice will often be not a flat equality but an equality proportioned to relevant differences in the recipients.[2] This way of thinking about justice has been dominant in the West. John Rawls's theory of justice, for example, is of the Aristotelian type; justice for Rawls is fairness in distribution.

The ancient Roman jurist Ulpian defined justice as *suum ius cuique tribuere*—rendering to each what is his or her right or due. Persons are assumed to have a right to certain things; certain things are due them. Justice, then, consists of rendering to them whatever be their right or due. The idea of equality nowhere appears in Ulpian's formula.

Smith's account is distinctly different from both of these. Smith never explicitly tells us what justice is; his theory proves to be, strictly speaking, a theory of injustice rather than a theory of justice. Let me describe, in my own words, the feature of injustice that Smith places at the center of his theory; later we will see how Smith himself describes that feature.

When one is wronged, or treated unjustly, one thereby acquires the permission-right to treat the wrongdoer negatively in certain ways—to be angry at him, to feel resentment for what he did, perhaps to shun him, perhaps to punish him or support his being punished by some social institution, and so forth. In other words, being treated unjustly generates in one the permission-right to impose "evils" of certain sorts on the person who wronged one. At the center of Smith's theory of injustice is that phenomenon, though, as I have suggested, described somewhat differently from how I have described it just now. I know of no other theory of justice or injustice that is anything like this. Smith's theory is idiosyncratic.

Smith set his account of justice in *Theory of Moral Sentiments* within the context of a general theory of the virtues; I will have to neglect what he says about the other virtues and focus exclusively on justice. Until late in his life Smith worked on a manuscript on jurisprudence in which he once again took up the topic of justice; he asked that the manuscript be destroyed at his death. However, student notes of his lectures survived and have now been published under the title *Lectures on Jurisprudence*. I will have to neglect what Smith says there about justice and focus my attention here on what he says in his published work, *Theory*. Last, both in *Theory* and in *Lectures*, Smith spends some time engaging other theories of justice current at his day; I will have to focus exclusively on Smith's development of his own theory. In the bibliographic essay at the end of this article I refer the reader to some of the books and essays that take a more comprehensive approach to Smith on justice.

In the opening chapters of *Theory of Moral Sentiments* Smith develops an original and intricate moral psychology. He employs that psychology when articulating his theory of justice. So it is with his moral psychology that we must begin.

The title of Smith's treatise, *Theory of Moral Sentiments*, announces that at the center of his moral psychology will be what he calls *sentiments* or *emotions*. He assumes that sentiments arise in a person because they are evoked by something that happens to him or her. Fundamental to his entire discussion is the further assumption that a sentiment may be either a proper or an improper response to whatever it is that evoked it. Anger, for example, would be a patently improper response to someone's doing one a favor.

The treatise opens with a discussion of the sentiment of sympathy; of all sentiments, sympathy is beyond a doubt the most important for Smith's moral psychology as a whole. Nonetheless, I will begin my exposition of Smith's theory not with what he has to say about the particular sentiment of sympathy but with his idea of *proper* sentiments, since this pertains to sentiments in general.

Though the opening section of TMS is titled "Of the Propriety of Action," neither here nor elsewhere does Smith define "proper" or explain what he means by the term; he takes for granted that his readers already have an adequate grasp of the concept he has in mind and devotes the section to discussing various issues pertaining to propriety.

One wonders initially whether the concept of *proper* that he has in mind is the proper-functioning concept; we speak of something as functioning properly or improperly. No doubt there was in the back of Smith's mind the idea of a person's moral psychology functioning properly or improperly. But the synonyms that he uses for "proper" indicate that he has something different in mind.

A proper sentiment, as Smith understands it, is one that, in his words, *fits* its cause, one that is *suitable* to its cause, *appropriate* to it. When a person's moral psychology is functioning properly, the sentiments evoked by what happens to her will *fit* what happened; they will be *proper* to it. That point cannot be made if we equate *proper sentiment* with *sentiment that is evoked when one's moral psychology is functioning properly*. A proper sentiment is one that, again in Smith's words, *befits* its cause, *harmonizes with* its cause. Smith notes that what determines whether a sentiment is proper to its cause is not just the nature of the sentiment but also its intensity. For example, though the sentiment of resentment is a proper response to many harms, intense resentment does not befit a minor harm.

Smith builds a large part of his moral psychology on this concept of a sentiment as befitting its cause. He notes that we typically disapprove of an improper sentiment; and that we sometimes blame a person for an action motivated by an improper sentiment. So *proper* is a moral, or quasi-moral, concept in Smith's scheme.

Smith thinks of actions as motivated by sentiments. He does not explicitly declare that sentiments are the only springs of action. But nowhere in *Theory of Moral Sentiments*, so far as I know, does he indicate that there are other springs of action.

What about acting out of duty, one might ask. Isn't acting out of duty an alternative spring of action? In the course of discussing what he calls "the sense of duty," Smith makes the following remark: "That the sense of duty should be the sole principle of our conduct, is no where the precept of Christianity; but that it should be the ruling and the governing one, as philosophy, and as, indeed, common sense directs. It may be a question, however, in what cases our actions ought to arise chiefly or entirely from a sense of duty, or from a regard to general rules; and in what cases some other sentiment or affection ought to concur, and have a principal influence" (TMS III.6.1). In that last sentence, Smith is clearly assuming that acting from a sense of duty, or from regard for some general rule, is a special case of being motivated by some sentiment or affection.

A given sentiment does not motivate actions of any sort whatsoever; sentiments of a certain sort motivate actions of a certain sort. This fact enables Smith to speak not only of propriety in sentiments but, derivatively, of propriety in actions: "In the suitableness or unsuitableness, in the proportion or disproportion which the affection seems to bear to the cause or object which excites it, consists the propriety or impropriety, the decency or ungracefulness of the consequent action" (TMS I.i.3.6).

I take it that Smith is here distinguishing *suitableness* in sentiments from *proportion*, and distinguishing *unsuitableness* from *disproportion*. The *suitableness* or *unsuitableness* of a sentiment to its cause is determined by whether or not a sentiment of this *nature* befits what caused it. By contrast, the *proportion* or *disproportion* of a sentiment is determined by whether or not a sentiment of this *intensity* befits its cause. That, then, gives us a corresponding pair of distinctions in actions: whether an action is *proper* or *improper* is determined by whether or not the nature of the sentiment that caused it is suitable to its cause; whether an action is *decent* or *ungraceful* is determined by whether or not the intensity of the sentiment that caused it is proportionate to its cause.

Let us now move on to the sentiment that Smith discusses in the opening pages of *Theory of Moral Sentiments*, and that is more important for his moral psychology than any other, namely, sympathy. He explains sympathy as follows:

> As we have no immediate experience of what other men feel, we can form no idea of the manner in which they are affected, but by conceiving what we ourselves should feel in the like situation. Though our brother is upon the rack, as long as we ourselves are at our ease, our senses will never inform us of what he suffers. . . . It is by the imagination only that we can form any conception of what are his sensations. . . . By the imagination we place ourselves in his situation, we conceive ourselves enduring all the same torments, we enter as it were into his body, and become in some measure the same person with him, and thence form some idea of his sensations, and even feel something which, though weaker in degree, is not altogether unlike them. (TMS I.i.1.2)

This fellow-feeling Smith calls sympathy.

He goes on to explain that sympathy is sometimes evoked not by knowing what befell the other person but by gaining cognizance of the emotion he feels. "The passions, upon some occasions, may seem to be transfused from one man to another, instantaneously and antecedent to any knowledge of what excited them in the person principally concerned. Grief and joy, for example, strongly expressed in the look and gestures of any one, at once affect the spectator with some degree of a like painful or agreeable emotion" (TMS I.i.1.6). For the most part, though, sympathy "does not arise so much from the view of the passion, as from that of the situation which excites it" (TMS I.i.1.10).

Suppose, now, that I am not only aware of what caused the emotions of the other person but, by interpreting her gestures, her facial expressions, her cries, and the like, have gained some cognizance of her emotions themselves. Then, if "the original passions of the person principally concerned are in perfect concord with the sympathetic emotions of the spectator, they necessarily appear to this last just and proper, and suitable to their objects; and, on the contrary, when, upon bringing the case home to himself, he finds that they do not coincide with what he feels, they necessarily appear to him unjust and improper, and unsuitable to the causes which excite them" (TMS I.i.3.1). Indeed, "when we judge . . . of any affection, as proportioned or disproportioned to the cause which excites it, it is scarce possible that we should make use of any other rule or canon but the correspondent affection in ourselves. If, upon bringing the case home to our own breast, we find that the sentiments which it gives occasion to, coincide and tally with our own, we necessarily approve of them as proportioned and suitable to their objects; if otherwise, we necessarily disapprove of them, as extravagant and out of proportion" (TMS I.i.3.9).[3]

For his theory of injustice Smith needs, in addition to these concepts of proper and improper sentiments and actions, the concepts of meritorious and nonmeritorious actions. Here is how he explains them.

Any sentiment, he says, can "be considered under two different aspects, or in two different relations: first, in relation to the cause or object which excites it; and, secondly, in relation to the end which it proposes, or to the effect which it tends to produce" (TMS II.i.intro.2). In our discussion thus far we have considered sentiments under the former aspect. The relation of a sentiment to its cause determines the propriety or impropriety of the sentiment; and that determines, in turn, the propriety or impropriety of the action that the sentiment motivates. By contrast, the merit and demerit of actions is determined by the relation of the sentiment that motivates it "to the end which it proposes, or to the effect which it tends to produce" (TMS I.i.3.5).

We now have in hand the main concepts from his moral psychology that Smith uses in his account of justice. In his account, Smith also appeals to some general theses from his moral psychology concerning the relation among harm, resentment, and punishment, and among beneficence, gratitude, and reward. So let us turn next to that.

Begin with the action of rewarding, which Smith understands as returning "good for good received," and with the action of punishing, which he understands as returning "evil for evil that has been done" (TMS II.i.1.4). Rewarding and punishing are like all actions in that they are motivated by sentiments. "The sentiment which most immediately and directly prompts us to reward, is gratitude; that which most immediately and directly prompts us to punish, is resentment" (TMS II.i.1.2).

And to what way of being treated is the sentiment of gratitude the proper response? Whatever it is, it will be the sort of action to which reward is the proper response in action. Smith reasons as follows: if the sentiment of gratitude is the proper emotional response to some way of being treated, then, given that gratitude is the sentiment that most immediately and directly prompts us to reward, it follows that reward is the proper action in response to that way of being treated. In general, an action is proper if the sentiment that motivates it is proper.

And to what way of being treated is the sentiment of resentment the proper response? Whatever it is, it will be the sort of action to which punishment is the proper response in action. Smith's reasoning is parallel to that for gratitude. If the sentiment of resentment is the proper emotional response to some way of being treated, then, given that resentment is the sentiment that most immediately and directly prompts us to punish, it follows that punishment is the proper action in response to that way of being treated. To say it again: actions in general are proper if the sentiments that motivate them are proper.

Smith speaks of actions as *deserving* reward and of actions as *deserving* punishment: that action deserves reward, which is the proper object of gratitude, and that action deserves punishment, which is the proper object of resentment (TMS II.i.1.3). And he then declares that the qualities of merit and demerit in actions are "the qualities of deserving reward, and of deserving punishment" (TMS II.i.intro.1). I judge that when Smith says that some way of being treated *deserves* reward or *deserves* punishment, he simply means that reward or punishment is the proper response of action to that way of being treated.

Let me postpone, for just a bit, my answer to the two questions I posed, to what way of being treated is gratitude the proper response and to what way of being treated is resentment the proper response, in order to bring sympathy into the picture.

Thus far I have presented Smith's thoughts about gratitude and resentment, reward and punishment, merit and demerit, from the first-person standpoint. To certain ways of being treated by another person, the sentiment of gratitude is the proper response on my part. This sentiment immediately and directly prompts me to seek to reward that person. The way he treated me deserves reward; reward is the proper action on my part in response to what he did. Counterpart things are to be said concerning resentment.

But of course Smith does not want his thought on these matters to be limited to the first-person case; he wants it to apply to the second-person and third-person cases as well. Given his moral psychology, this requires that he now complicate things by introducing sympathy into his account of merit and demerit in actions. Here is what he says: "He, therefore appears to deserve reward, who, to some person or persons, is the natural object of a gratitude which every human heart is disposed to beat time to, and thereby applaud; and he, on the other hand, appears to deserve punishment, who, in the same manner is to some person or persons the natural object of a resentment which the breast of every reasonable man is ready to adopt and sympathize with" (TMS II.i.2.3).[4] The passage is dense and compact. Here's the basic idea. Suppose that I take note of what was done to you, that I am also cognizant of your emotional response of gratitude, and that I resonate sympathetically with this emotional response. When this happens, I judge that the person who treated you in this way deserves to be rewarded for how he treated you; in other words, I judge that his action is meritorious. The counterpart thing is to be said concerning my resonating sympathetically with your resentment.

Back now to the questions, to what way of being treated is gratitude the proper response and to what way of being treated is resentment the proper response? For Smith, those questions are closely related to these other two questions: to what way of being treated is reward the proper response in action, and to what way of being treated is punishment the proper response in action?

Smith answers these questions in the following passage: "Actions of a beneficent tendency, which proceed from proper motives, seem alone to require reward; because such alone are the approved objects of gratitude, or excite the sympathetic gratitude of the spectator" (TMS II.ii.1.1). "Actions of a hurtful tendency, which proceed from improper motives, seem alone to deserve punishment; because such alone are the approved objects of resentment, or excite the sympathetic resentment of the spectator" (TMS II.ii.1.2).

One can easily surmise what Smith means here by *approved* objects of gratitude or resentment. But he makes his meaning explicit: "To be the proper and approved object either of gratitude or resentment, can mean nothing but to be the object of that gratitude, and of that resentment, which naturally seems proper, and is approved of" (TMS II.i.2.1). This explains the idea of approved *objects* of gratitude or resentment in terms of approval of the sentiments of which those are the objects. Earlier we saw how he thinks of approval of sentiments themselves. Let me quote another passage on the matter, in which he explains approval of sentiments by analogy to approval of opinions: "To approve of another man's opinions is to adopt those opinions, and to adopt them is to approve of them. To approve or disapprove, therefore, of the opinions of others is acknowledged, by every body, to mean no more than to observe their agreement or disagreement with our own. But this is equally the case with regard to our approbation or disapprobation of the sentiments or passions of others" (TMS I.i.3.2).

We now have enough of Smith's intricate moral psychology in hand to understand his account of injustice. Smith introduces his account by pointing to a certain feature of beneficence; he then contrasts beneficence on this point with justice. Crucial for the point he wants to make is the triple distinction among the following: actions of doing good to someone, actions of doing "real and positive hurt" to someone, and instances of refraining from doing either of these to someone.

Beneficence, says Smith, "is always free, it cannot be extorted by force, the mere want of it exposes to no punishment." That is "because the mere want of beneficence tends to do no real positive evil" (TMS II.ii.1.3). It is the doing of real positive evil to someone that deserves punishment and to which the proper emotional response is resentment.

A person's failure to treat someone beneficently may be a failure to do that "which in propriety he ought to have done" (TMS II.ii.1.3). He may be "blamable, . . . the proper object of disapprobation" (II.ii.1.6). He may be the proper object of hatred, "a passion which is naturally excited by impropriety of sentiment and behavior" (TMS II.ii.1.3). But he is not the proper object of "resentment, a passion which is never properly called forth but by actions which tend to do real and positive hurt to some particular persons" (TMS II.ii.1.3). And because resentment would not be proper, it would not be proper to punish him.

The virtue of justice stands in contrast to the virtue of beneficence on these points. Justice is that virtue whose "violation exposes to resentment, and consequently to punishment" (TMS II.ii.1.5). Injustice, the violation of the virtue of justice, "does real and positive hurt to some particular persons, from motives which are naturally disapproved of. It is, therefore, the proper object of resentment and of punishment" (TMS II.ii.1.5).[5]

This is an explanation of injustice; as I remarked earlier, Smith never explicitly says what he thinks constitutes justice. Any Smith-type explanation of justice has to take account of the fact that one may impose "real and positive hurt" on someone without thereby treating the person unjustly. Surgery is a familiar example of the point; so too, obviously, is the action that plays a central role in Smith's account of injustice, namely, punishment.[6] There are various, slightly different, ways of explaining justice that take account of this fact and are compatible with, and in the spirit of, Smith's account of injustice. Here is one: to treat someone justly is either to refrain from imposing real and positive hurt on that person or to do so only from a proper motive.[7]

Smith takes note of a peculiarity of the virtue of justice when understood along these lines.

> Though the breach of justice . . . exposes to punishment, the observance of the rules of that virtue seems scarce to deserve any reward. There is, no doubt, a propriety in the practice of justice, and it merits, upon that account, all the approbation which is due to propriety. But as it does no real positive good, it is entitled to very little gratitude. Mere justice is, upon most occasions, but a negative virtue, and only hinders us from hurting our neighbour. The man who barely abstains from violating either the person, or the estate, or the reputation of his neighbours, has surely very little positive merit. . . . We may often fulfil all the rules of justice by sitting still and doing nothing. (TMS II.ii.1.9)

Having erected his account of injustice on his emphatic claim that only real and positive hurt deserves punishment, Smith proceeds to introduce a wide range of exceptions. The abuse of a child by a parent sometimes takes the form not of doing "real and positive hurt" to the child but of standing by and doing nothing—letting the child starve, for example, or letting the child die of some disease or injury. About such cases, Smith says this:

> The laws of all civilized nations oblige parents to maintain their children, and children to maintain their parents, and impose upon men many other duties of beneficence. The civil magistrate is entrusted with the power not only of preserving the public peace by restraining injustice, but of promoting the prosperity of the commonwealth, by establishing good discipline, and by discouraging every sort of vice and impropriety; he may prescribe rules, therefore, which not only prohibit mutual injury among fellow-citizens, but command mutual good offices to a certain degree. When the sovereign commands what is merely indifferent, and what, antecedent to his orders, might have been omitted without any blame, it becomes not only blamable but punishable to disobey him. (TMS II.ii.1.8)[8]

Smith adds the wise comment that nothing else so requires good "judgment" on the part of a lawgiver as discerning which blamable acts that do not cause hurt should be forbidden in law. "To neglect [the passage of such laws] altogether exposes the commonwealth to many gross disorders and shocking enormities, [but] to push it too far is destructive of all liberty, security, and justice" (TMS II.ii.1.8).

The obvious question that the passage poses is how we are to fit together Smith's concession here, that the lack of beneficence is sometimes punishable, with his earlier emphatic insistence that only real and positive harm deserves punishment. Smith himself does not make a point of explaining how he is thinking. But he does offer a hint. He says that "even the most ordinary degree of kindness or beneficence . . . cannot, among equals, be extorted by force" (TMS II.ii.1.7); and then, a bit later, he says that "a superior may . . . sometimes . . . oblige those under his jurisdiction to behave . . . with a certain degree of propriety to one another" (TMS II.ii.1.8). In short, the principle, that only real and positive harm deserves punishment, holds if neither of the two parties has authority over the other; if one of the two parties does have authority over the other, then the principle does not hold.

This leaves open the question: if the failure to exercise beneficence deserves punishment in some case because some authority has commanded it, is that a case of injustice? Does injustice track with the imposition of harm out of an improper motive, or does it track with what deserves punishment? Smith does not address the question; but my guess is that, if asked, he would say that injustice tracks with what deserves punishment. If I deserve to be punished for what I did to you, whether because I inflicted real and positive harm on you or because I violated the command of some authority to treat you beneficently, then I have treated you unjustly.

And how does resentment fit in? If I violated the command of some authority to treat you beneficently but did not harm you, is resentment on your part proper? Does proper resentment track with the infliction of harm or does it track with deserving punishment? Again, Smith does not address the question. In this case, I have no guess as to how he would answer if asked.

Before we move on, let me note that the passage just quoted makes unmistakably clear that, on Smith's view, government is not properly confined to stopping people from hurting each other. Sam

Fleischacker, in *On Adam Smith's* Wealth of Nations,[9] notes that Smith has been enlisted by both sides in the debate between libertarians and welfare state proponents. If one considers only what Smith has to say about justice when neither of the two parties has authority over the other, then Smith's insistence, that I treat you justly when I refrain from causing you real and positive hurt, would lead one to guess that he was a libertarian. But the debate between libertarians and welfare state proponents pertains to legitimate actions by the state; and the passage quoted above makes unmistakably clear that Smith was not a libertarian. How far a given state should go in the direction of the welfare state was, for him, a matter of judgment: lawgivers have to balance preventing "gross disorders and shocking enormities" against damaging the interests of "liberty, security, and justice."

Lest Smith's thought be misunderstood on this point, it should be added that he did not regard justice as merely one among other virtues but as the socially and politically indispensable virtue. Justice, he said, "is the main pillar that upholds the whole edifice [of society]. If it is removed, the great, the immense fabric of human society . . . must in a moment crumble into atoms" (TMS II.ii.3.4). "Society cannot subsist unless the laws of justice are tolerably observed, as no social intercourse can take place among men who do not generally abstain from injuring one another" (TMS II.ii.3.6).

As we saw earlier, Smith presents his account of justice in the context of contrasting justice with beneficence. But he also draws an interesting and provocative contrast between justice, on the one hand, and all the other virtues—in addition to the point, just made, that justice is the socially and politically indispensable virtue.

For most of the virtues we can formulate "general rules which determine what are the offices of prudence, of charity, of generosity, of gratitude, of friendship," and so on (TMS III.6.9). Typically, however, these rules are at best rules of thumb. They "are in many respects loose and inaccurate and admit of many exceptions, and require so many modifications, that it is scarce possible to regulate our conduct entirely by a regard to them" (TMS III.6.9). A "pretty plain rule" for gratitude would seem to be that "as soon as we can we should make a return of equal, and if possible of superior value to the services we have received. . . . Upon the most superficial examination, however, this rule will appear to be in the highest degree loose and inaccurate, and to admit of ten thousand exceptions" (TMS III.6.9). Smith then points to a variety of exceptions.

Justice is different. "The rules of justice are accurate in the highest degree, and admit of no exceptions or modifications, but such as may be ascertained as accurately as the rules themselves. . . . If I owe a man ten pounds, justice requires that I should precisely pay him ten pounds, either at the time agreed upon, or when he demands it" (TMS III.6.10).

Smith then draws a fascinating comparison between rules of justice and rules of grammar. The passage deserves to be quoted in its entirety:

> The rules of justice may be compared to the rules of grammar; the rules of the other virtues, to the rules which critics lay down for the attainment of what is sublime and elegant in composition. The one, are precise, accurate, and indispensable. The other, are loose, vague, and indeterminate, and present us rather with a general idea of the perfection we ought to aim at, than afford us any certain and infallible directions for acquiring it. A man may learn to write grammatically by rule, with the most absolute infallibility; and so, perhaps, he may be taught to act justly. But there are no rules whose observance will infallibly lead us to the attainment of elegance or sublimity in writing; though there are some which may help us in some measure, to correct and ascertain the vague ideas which we might otherwise have entertained of those perfections. And there are no rules by the knowledge of which we can infallibly be taught to act upon all occasions with prudence, with just magnanimity, or proper beneficence: though there are some which may enable us to correct and ascertain, in several respects, the imperfect ideas which we might otherwise have entertained of those virtues. (TMS III.6.11)[10]

There is more that could be said by way of presenting Smith's account of injustice. But we now have enough in hand to be able to stand back and reflect critically on his account. Since Smith does not really offer an account of justice, only of injustice, and since a number of slightly different accounts of justice are compatible with his account of injustice, I will confine myself to comments on what he says about injustice and not consider what is to be said for and against one and another compatible account of justice.

I will also refrain from critical comments on the moral psychology within which Smith embedded his account of injustice. In particular, I will refrain from reflecting on when resentment is an appropriate response to what was done to one; Smith seems to have had a much more refined sense of when resentment is proper than I do. And rather than discussing the concept of *harm* that lies at the center of Smith's theory, let me refer the reader to Fleischacker's discussion in which he shows how hazy the concept is.[11] I will confine myself to offering some counterexamples to Smith's theory.

First, it's easy to find examples of treating someone unjustly that are not cases of hurting them. Wronging goes beyond hurting. Suppose, for example, that someone violates my privacy for purely prurient reasons. He does nothing whatsoever with what he discovers other than to enjoy it by himself at home; neither I nor anyone else ever discovers what he has done. Nonetheless, he has wronged me, treated me unjustly. I would say that if his deed comes to the light of day, it would be appropriate to punish him whether or not there is a law forbidding such conduct. But he has not imposed on me any real and positive hurt. Though Fleischacker is correct in arguing that the concept of harm or hurt, on which Smith places so much weight, is far from being clear, what is clear from Smith's discussion is that a necessary condition of something's being a harm to one is that it enter one's consciousness.

Or consider slavery. I dare say that most slave masters imposed on their slaves real and positive hurt. But imagine a case of benevolent slavery in which this was not the case, a case in which the slave master treats his slave as if he were one of his own children. His enslavement of the other person would nonetheless be a violation of justice. Buying a person, owning a person, putting a person up on the block for sale, these are violations of justice whether or not the person is in any way hurt and whether or not the person minds being treated in this way. Smith was in fact an active opponent of slavery. But on his account of injustice, benevolent slavery is not a case of injustice.

Injustice, says Smith, consists of imposing real and positive hurt on someone out of an improper motive. Just as it is easy to find cases of injustice in which no hurt was imposed on the victim, so too it is easy to find cases of injustice in which the hurt imposed was not out of an improper motive. Unjust paternalism comes to mind; often it is noble motives that lead parents to impose hurt on their children of such a sort as thereby to treat them unjustly. The parent does not deny that he is hurting the child; but he sincerely believes that it is for the child's good. And the twentieth century provided us with examples in abundance of political regimes and revolutionary movements that imposed real and positive hurt on masses of people, thereby wronging them, for the sake of some great social good to be achieved.

Let me conclude. Suppose we distinguish between the life-goods and life-evils of a person, on the one hand, and the worth or dignity of the person whose life it is, on the other hand. And correspondingly, suppose we distinguish between promoting the life-goods and diminishing the life-evils of a person, and paying due respect to the worth of the person.

Eudaimonism and utilitarianism are ethical systems that work only with the former in each of these pairs. They work with the ideas of life-goods and life-evils, and with the ideas of promoting the former and diminishing the latter; their systems make no use of the idea of the worth or dignity of a person, and hence none of paying due respect to that dignity or worth. In my *Justice: Rights and Wrongs*,[12] I argued that it is impossible to construct an adequate theory of justice if one works only with the ideas of life-goods and life-evils, and of promoting the former and diminishing the latter. One needs, in addition, the idea of the worth or dignity of those whose lives these are, and the idea of paying due respect to their worth or dignity.

Smith's account of injustice in TMS is one more example of a theory that speaks only of life-goods and life-evils; the idea of the worth and dignity of human beings plays no role in the account he gives there of injustice.[13] This is not to say that the idea of human dignity plays no role in Smith's thought generally; most definitely it did. My claim is that in his theory of justice in TMS it plays no role. It is fundamentally for that reason that the account he there gives of justice fails. It is the dignity of the child that is violated when the parent stands by and lets her starve or die from some disease; that's why it is a case of injustice. It is the dignity of the slave that is violated when he is bought, owned, and sold; that's why it is a case of injustice no matter how well he is treated. It is the dignity that is violated of those who are shuffled around or killed for the sake of some great social good to be achieved; that's why it is a case of injustice.

NOTES

1. At the end of this essay I will point out that one can also classify theories of justice into those that appeal only to life-goods in their account and those that appeal to something in addition to life-goods, typically dignity. Smith's theory is an example of the former type.

2. Aristotle's account of justice is to be found in Book V of the *Nicomachean Ethics*.

3. A bit earlier Smith said that "to approve of the passions of another . . . as suitable to their objects, is the same thing as to observe that we entirely sympathize with them; and not to approve of them as such, is the same thing as to observe that we do not entirely sympathize with them" (TMS I.i.3.1). I think that this reductionist way of thinking of approval is mistaken. The fact that I approve of the passion as suitable to its object is not identical with the fact that I sympathize with the passion of the other person. I think that what Smith should have said is that the former of these facts is the *ground* or *basis* for my approval of the passion as suitable to its object. D. D. Raphael makes this same point in *The Impartial Spectator: Adam Smith's Moral Philosophy* (Oxford: 2007), pp. 17–20.

4. In the immediately preceding sections, Smith spoke of sympathy in the heart of every *impartial spectator*. In the passages we are considering, Smith very seldom employs the concept of an impartial spectator. It did play a significant role in his thought overall, however. For a full discussion, see Raphael, *Impartial Spectator*.

5. The extraordinary role given to resentment in Smith's theory of justice makes one think of the role that resentment plays in Nietzsche's account of the origins of morality.

6. Smith says the following at one point: "There can be no proper motive for hurting our neighbour, there can be no incitement to do evil to another, which mankind will go along with, except just indignation for evil which that other has done to us" (TMS II.ii.2.1). Was Smith overlooking such an obvious counterexample as surgery? Perhaps. But maybe he understood "hurt" in such a way that the surgeon does not hurt the patient, the idea being that the good of continued or restored health that the surgeon expects to result from the surgery outweighs the evil of the pain. I know of no passage, however, in which Smith explains that this is how he understands "hurt."

7. In Sam Fleischacker's otherwise excellent account of Smith's theory of justice/injustice in *On Adam Smith's* Wealth of Nations: *A Philosophical Companion* (Princeton: 2004), he takes no note of the fact that justice, for Smith, is not just the imposition of harm but the imposition of harm *from an improper motive*. He says that injustice for Smith is "primarily a matter of harm to individuals" (159), and he cites surgery as a counterexample to Smith's theory (156). But though surgery does indeed impose harm, it does not do so from an improper motive.

8. The passage strongly suggests, though it does not quite say, that a parent is appropriately punished for standing by and letting his child die of starvation only if there are laws in force that forbid such abuse. That seems to me mistaken.

9. Fleischacker, *On Adam Smith's* Wealth of Nations, p. 145.

10. Ryan Hanley discusses Smith's contrast between rules for justice and rules for the other virtues in his *Adam Smith and the Character of Virtue* (Cambridge: 2009), pp. 72–78. David Lieberman discusses the contrast in "Justice, Rights, and Law," in *The Cambridge Companion to Adam Smith*, ed. Knud Haakonssen (Cambridge: 2006), pp. 216–18.

11. In Fleischacker, *On Adam Smith's* Wealth of Nations.

12. Nicholas Wolterstorff, *Justice: Rights and Wrongs* (Princeton: 2008). The theory of justice that I develop there is of the Ulpian type. In the course of developing my theory, I defend what I call the Principle of Correlatives: if X is the sort of thing that can have rights, then X has a right to Y's doing so-and-so if and only if Y has an obligation to X to do so-and-so. Smith's way of thinking about injustice leads him to an emphatic rejection of this principle.

13. There is one passage in TMS in which Smith is on the verge of appealing to dignity in explaining why it is that some action is unjust. "What chiefly enrages us against the man who injures or insults us, is the little account which he seems to make of us, the unreasonable preference which he gives to himself above us, and that absurd self-love, by which he seems to imagine, that other people may be sacrificed at any time, to his conveniency or his humour. The glaring impropriety of his conduct, the gross insolence and injustice which is seems to involve in it, often shock and exasperate us more than all the mischief which we have suffered. To bring him back to a more just sense of what is due to other people, to make him sensible of what he owes us, and of the wrong that he has done to us, is frequently the principal end proposed in our revenge" (TMS II.iii.1.5).

BIBLIOGRAPHIC ESSAY

Two very good accounts of the general theory of morality that Smith develops in *Theory of Moral Sentiments* are D. D. Raphael's *The Impartial Spectator: Adam Smith's Moral Philosophy* (Oxford: 2007) and Ryan Patrick Hanley's *Adam Smith and the Character of Virtue* (Cambridge: 2009). Smith says a fair amount about justice in the *Lectures on Jurisprudence*, taking a somewhat different approach from that in TMS. Knud Haakonssen, in his *The Science of a Legislator* (Cambridge:1981), discusses Smith's *Lectures*, including then a discussion of what Smith says there about justice. David Lieberman, in his essay "Adam Smith on Justice, Rights, and Law," in *The Cambridge Companion to Adam Smith*, ed. Knud Haakonssen (Cambridge: 2006), pp. 214–45, makes a few comments about justice in TMS, but devotes most of his attention to the *Lectures*. Spencer J. Pack and Eric Schliesser, in their essay "Smith's Humean Criticism of Hume's Account of the Origin of Justice," *Journal of the History of Philosophy* 44, no. 1 (2006), pp. 47–63, compare and contrast Smith's account of justice with Hume's.

ADAM SMITH AND THE SYMPATHETIC IMAGINATION

Remy Debes

My aim in this chapter is to explain Smith's account of sympathy as it figures into his moral theory, but also how that account bears on Smith's closely connected conception of human social nature.[1] This secondary aim will draw out some of the subtler aspects of sympathy, as Smith conceives it, especially the importance of his novel articulation of sympathy as a primarily imaginative phenomenon. I begin, however, with a bit of historical contextualization.

HUMAN NATURE AND HUMAN SOCIABILITY

We miss something crucial about eighteenth-century Scottish sentimentalism (represented by Hutcheson, Hume, and Smith) if we fail to recognize that it was partly motivated by its opposition to early modern forms of egoism, and, in particular, Bernard Mandeville's then notorious *Fable of the Bees*. But it was not Mandeville's apparent egoism or cynical critique of virtue alone that agitated Hutcheson, Hume, and Smith. Mandeville also attacked the English moralist and forebear of Scottish sentimentalism, Shaftesbury, specifically on the question of human sociability. "This Noble Writer," Mandeville wrote of Shaftesbury, "Fancies, that as Man is made for Society, so he ought to be born with a kind Affection to the whole, of which he is a part, and a Propensity to seek the Welfare of it. . . . His Notions I confess are generous and refin'd: They are a high Compliment to Human-kind, and capable by the help of a little Enthusiasm of Inspiring us with the most Noble Sentiments concerning the Dignity of our exalted Nature: What Pity it is that they are not true." Instead, Mandeville argued, human sociability is the product of various manifestations of self-love. This was a claim the Scots could not let stand.

However, the Scots did not offer a uniform reply to Mandeville. To explain sociability, Hutcheson defended a conception of humans as originally benevolent, thus attempting to rebut Mandeville head-on. And Hume, despite distancing himself in various ways from Hutcheson on the point of benevolence (especially to explain justice), nevertheless did retain an element of original benevolence in his explanation of human sociability, albeit Hume combined benevolence with a contagion theory of sympathy (the latter of which was based on Hume's more fundamental associationist theory of mind—more on this below). By contrast, Smith broke almost entirely from the idea of original benevolence. Thus Smith writes in the middle of TMS, "It is not the soft power of humanity, it is not that feeble spark of benevolence which Nature has lighted up in the human heart, that is thus capable of counteracting the strongest impulses of self-love . . . It is a stronger love, a more powerful affection, which generally takes place upon such occasions; the love of what is honorable and noble, of the grandeur, and dignity, and superiority of our own characters" (TMS III.3.4). In short, for Smith, it is not an agent's love for others that is fundamental to human sociability, but a love of virtue, and, in particular, an agent's desire that she *herself* be virtuous.

Of course, without an anchor in innate benevolence, Smith needed some other ground for his view if he was to provide a genuine alternative to self-love explanations of sociability. Thus enters his peculiar imaginative conception of sympathy, or what scholars today would call his "simulation" theory of sympathy. My goal here is to outline the basic elements of this "simulation" theory with the further aims (1) to illustrate how even the basic elements of sympathy play into Smith's view of human sociability and (2) to sketch, very roughly, Smith's attending attempt to *ground* our "stronger love" of virtue, and, in turn, human sociability, on sympathy.

SMITH'S BASIC ACCOUNT OF SYMPATHY

Smith's basic account of sympathy can be broken into (1) a reconceptualization of the nature of sympathy and (2) a metaethical account of moral judgment (i.e., an account of the nature or meaning of moral judgment). Regarding the first, according to Smith, "sympathy" denotes "our fellow-feeling with any passion whatever" (TMS I.i.1.5). It thus has more in common with present connotations of "empathy," although much more would need to be said to situate Smith's concept of sympathy into contemporary empathy theory. More important, Smith radically reconceived how sympathy works, and, in particular, how Hume thought sympathy works. Hume explained sympathy as a kind of "contagion" process, wherein passions "communicate themselves" more or less passively through a mechanistic association of ideas. "The passions are so contagious," Hume writes at one point in the *Treatise*, "that they pass with the greatest facility from one person to another, and produce correspondent movements in all human breasts" (T 3.3.3.5; SBN 605).[2] Or, even more eloquently, "As in strings equally wound up, the motion of one [man's mind] communicates itself to the rest; so all the affections readily pass from one person to another, and beget correspondent movements in every human creature" (T 3.3.1.7; SBN 576). Less metaphorically, though still very roughly, Hume argues that whenever we observe the "external signs" of emotion (i.e., facial or other behavioral emotional displays; see, e.g., T 2.1.11.3), we form an idea of the emotion itself through an association with general ideas we already have of that same emotion. This idea of what another person is feeling is then typically "enlivened" into an "impression"—"impressions" being, for Hume, the vivacious counterparts to ideas, and which include, crucially, the passions.[3] Thus do we come actually to feel what others feel, according to Hume.

How striking, then, that Smith's first task in TMS is to recast the nature of sympathy. On his view, "it is by changing places in fancy with the sufferer, that we come either to conceive or to be affected by what he feels" (TMS I.i.1.3). That is, "spectators" *imagine* being in the place of "actors" to generate original emotional responses to the object or objects in question—namely, to whatever is causing actors to feel as they do. Sympathy thus operates primarily through a kind of simulation of the *situation* that provoked the emotion in question. It does not arise, as Hume would have it, by a contagion-like response to emotional displays. Or as Smith puts the same point, signaling his difference with Hume, sympathy does not arise "merely from the view of a certain emotion in another person" (TMS I.i.1.6). For example, suppose you see someone smiling over a letter. You do not, Smith thinks, feel happy as an upshot of merely having *seen* the smiling. Not in an ordinary case anyway.[4] You must have an idea of the cause of that smiling. Only once you have some idea of *why* the letter has caused the actor to smile—say, because you learn it is a prestigious invitation letter—can you begin to sympathize. And even then, it isn't merely your idea of "why" the actor is smiling that does the work. Spectators don't *infer* their way to emotions. Instead, Smith argues, the idea of the cause (the "why") becomes the attentional focus of an imaginative simulation. You imagine *being* the recipient of a prestigious invitation letter (i.e., like the actor actually is), and only then do you "conceive" or are "affected by" the actor's presumably joyful affective response. Indeed, Smith pushes this point so far as to say that even in cases where it seems the mere appearance of an emotion moves us sympathetically, that is, by a kind of Humean contagion, in fact it is only because those appearances suggest to us the "general idea of some good or bad fortune that has befallen the person in whom we observe them" (TMS I.i.1.8). In other words, what explains seeming cases of contagion is that spectators *supply* the "why" necessary to spark simulation. This is why, Smith argues, contagion-like cases yield only weak affective responses in spectators. We always simulate very imperfectly "before we are informed of the cause" (TMS I.i.1.9)—that is, before we, the spectators, know the *real* cause that moved the actor, as opposed to the *general* cause we supplied. Smith writes, "The first question which we ask is, What has befallen you? Till this be answered, though we are uneasy both from the vague idea of his misfortune, and still more from torturing ourselves with conjectures about what it may be, yet our fellow-feeling is not very considerable" (TMS I.i.1.9).[5]

Now for the metaethical part of Smith's view: If the spectator feels anything at all like the actor—that is, if she feels a sentiment that matches the actor's in kind but not necessarily in degree—then, strictly speaking, this "fellow-feeling" counts as a case of "sympathy" for Smith. However, not all cases of sympathy are alike. Thus, the *degree* of match matters greatly on Smith's view. This is because the spectator's sentiment is simultaneously the basis for a moral judgment, namely, of the *propriety* of the actor's passion (which passion, it bears noting, is also the motive or potential motive of action on Smith's view). Smith writes, "To approve of the passions of another, therefore, as suitable to their objects, is the same thing as to observe that we entirely sympathize with them; and not to approve of them as such, is the same thing as to observe that we do not entirely sympathize with them" (TMS I.i.3.1). Moral judgment thus turns out to be what is known in contemporary ethics as a "fittingness" assessment. In Smith's theory it breaks down as follows: (1) If, upon imaginatively adopting the actor's situation, the spectator feels the same *kind* of sentiment as the actor, and feels it approximately to the same *degree*, then the spectator, assuming she is aware of this match, will feel a pleasure of "mutual sympathy," which pleasure constitutes the spectator's *approbation*, yet a third passion;[6] (2) this approbation "expresses" the spectator's judgment that the actor's feeling *fits* its object, namely, the situation that provoked it (usually some particular object embedded in a context, e.g., a *given* person in a *given* set of circumstances).[7]

* * *

Thus goes the basic account. Smith complicates it in myriad ways, but four are especially important. Three of these I pass over quickly, simply to ensure the reader is aware of them. The last I linger on for a moment. First, Smith actually says there are two "aspects" or "relations" according to which an actor's sentiment can be evaluated: (1) propriety, which I explained above; and (2) merit, which is based on "the beneficial or hurtful effects which the affection proposes or tends to produce" (TMS II.i.intro.2). But, according to Smith, merit (and demerit) hang largely on a further judgment about propriety, namely, of whether it would be fitting to feel gratitude (or resentment) toward the actor for what-ever her original sentiment motivated her to do. Thus, Smith's ac-count of propriety and his basic account of mutual sympathy are plainly more fundamental. Second, Smith is careful to observe that a perfect match of sentiments between spectator and actor rarely, if ever, occurs (TMS I.i.4.7). Smith is equally clear, however, that a perfect match or "accord" isn't psychologically necessary for one to feel the pleasure of mutual sympathy. In turn, perfect accord between the sentiments of spectator and actor isn't sociologically necessary. As Smith puts it, these "two sentiments" may have "such a correspondence with one another, as is sufficient for the har-mony of society. Though they will never be unisons, they may be concords, and this is all that is wanted or required" (TMS I.i.4.7). Third, as much as I want to stress the "socializing" potential of imaginative sympathy, it must be noted that Smith is keen to point out that imagination has a variety of corrupting effects—indeed, also through the operation of sympathy—on the moral and social character of persons. There is simply not enough room to cover these details here.[8]

The fourth elaboration of sympathy demands a few more words. Smith eventually moves from explaining what moral judgment *is* (his metaethics) to offering a *normative* theory for moral judg-ment. Thus, while every case of a spectator's awareness of mutual sympathy generates the pleasure that constitutes an instance of approbation, Smith makes clear that every instance of approbation isn't necessarily an instance of *moral* judgment, strictly speaking. Moral judgment proper does not arise from mutual sympathy with any old spectator, but from the mutual sympathy of the "impar-tial" spectator (see, e.g., TMS II.i.2.2 or VI.intro.2). The impartial spectator is sometimes an actual spectator: our impartial neighbor, as it were. But in Smith's theory the most crucial manifestation of the impartial spectator is in self-reflection, when we try to imag-ine how our impartial neighbors *would* view our sentiments and motives, *if* they could know those sentiments as well as we do. Smith writes, "We endeavour to examine our own conduct as we imagine any other fair and impartial spectator would examine it. If, upon placing ourselves in his situation, we thoroughly enter into all the passions and motives which influenced it, we approve of it, by sympathy with the approbation of this supposed equitable judge. If otherwise, we enter into his disapprobation, and condemn it" (TMS III.1.2). Thus, Smith argues, we set up an ideal "man within," "the great judge and arbiter of our conduct" (TMS III.3.4) as the normative standard for approbation: "If we place ourselves completely in his situation, if we really view ourselves with his eyes, and as he views us, and listen with diligent and reverential attention to what he suggests to us, his voice will never deceive us. We shall stand in need of no casuistic rules to direct our conduct" (TMS VI.ii.1.22). I will return to the idea of the impartial spectator at the end of this chapter.

THE BASIC SOCIALIZING EFFECTS OF SYMPATHY

Sympathy has both simple (in the sense of textually straightforward) and sophisticated socializing effects. By "socializing," I mean that sympathy motivates us not simply to be *in* society with others, but rather, in a normatively richer sense, to *be social*, that is, to cooperate with, forward the interests of, or care about other persons. In this section I detail a few of the simple effects. In the next section I turn to some more sophisticated ones, albeit only with the hope to gesture at the potential depth of Smith's theory, as it would take more space than is available here to give a full account of these more sophisticated effects.

Smith says in the first sentence of TMS that the sheer existence of man's sympathetic capacity "interests him" in the "fortune of others" (TMS I.i.1.1). It is no accident that the object of the verb in this sentence is the generalized person "him"—really, us. The point of Smith's overture is that *we* are originally, and to some extent passively, social, if only weakly (after all, having an "interest in" someone is a far cry from "caring for" her).[9]

However, what is crucial is that it is not the mere capacity for sympathy that explains its most interesting socializing effects. It is the fact that this capacity works through the imagination. In the first place, Smith's overture is fully defensible only because sympathy involves taking the viewpoints of others. Consider: it is not the mere display of another person's joys or sorrows, or the violence or apathy with which she seems to feel that joy or sorrow, that Smith claims we cannot help taking an interest in. It is her "fortune." It is what befalls *her*. At the same time, as already noted, Smith rejects any appeal to a strong innate disposition of humanity or benevolence. We do not love or care about other persons merely as such (or if we do, we do so only weakly). Thus, *if* sympathy operated only by mechanistic contagion, then Smith's overture would be suspect. For without recourse to something like innate benevolence, how could the mere "transfer" of emotion from an actor to a spectator cause the spectator to *care about* or *for* the actor in any sense? Hence it is crucial for Smith that it is the whole passionate experience we are sympathetically forced into. Our sympathetic nature means that we cannot help engaging in the actual lived experience of other lives *as* those others persons themselves experience their lives. This is what entitles Smith to speak in terms of "interest" at all. Sympathy *interests* us in the welfare of other persons, as opposed to simply *notice* persons, precisely because sympathy imaginatively pulls us into their viewpoints, their situations, their lives.[10] This aspect of Smith's theory is monumentally important.

Second, because sympathy works through imagination, it is drawn with special force to passions that arise from the imagination (which Smith contrasts with those arising from the body). This fact itself has socializing upshots. On the one hand, it allows Smith to argue that we are disposed against sympathizing with self-centered happiness and suffering. That is, we are disposed against sympathizing with passions that depend on objects having peculiar interest only to the agents affected by them, precisely because such objects or causes derive most of their power to enliven the imagination from the idiosyncratic tendencies and experiences of the actors who feel them. Such idiosyncraticity stymies the indifferent imagination—that is, the imagination of "anyone" on "anyone else": the spectator with no familiar relationship to, or peculiar favorable bias for, or special knowledge of, the actor in question. On the other hand, and inversely to the last point, it is precisely those passions that are not self-centered, those raised by objects of *general* concern—that is, objects that concern most persons on average—that indifferent spectators more readily sympathize with because the imagination, aided by familiarity, quickly latches onto and is enlivened by such objects. Taken together, if we want to cultivate the pleasure of mutual sympathy and approbation for our sentiments, we are naturally encouraged to focus our attention on objects of general concern and away from objects of peculiar, self-centered interest.

Third, the simulative nature of sympathy leaves us disposed against sympathizing with what Smith classifies as the "unsocial" passions of hatred and resentment ("unsocial" because, while necessary for Smith's theory of justice, they nevertheless tend to breed violence, dissent, and strife). We have this negative disposition partly because such sentiments are prima facie unpleasant: both the primary sentiment felt by the actor (e.g., resentment) and the usual reactive feelings *to* such sentiments (e.g., anger or fear by the one resented) are in themselves negative and painful. But more important, even when we sympathize and approve passions like resentment, such passions "divide" our sympathy between the actor who feels them and whoever is the target of them (TMS I.i.3.1). For, according to Smith, the fear or reactive anger, which hatred and resentment naturally provoke in the targeted person, almost always draw us, the spectators, in.[11] The upshot is that our *imagination* is distracted. In turn we struggle to reach full mutual sympathy with the actor's unsocial passion—a result, it should be underlined, a contagion model of sympathy does not predict. Moreover, and for similar reasons, Smith claims we are peculiarly disposed *to* sympathize with the "social" passions of generosity, humanity, kindness, compassion, mutual friendship, and esteem (TMS I.ii.4.1). Not only are such sentiments pleasurable in themselves, but also these sentiments lead to a "redoubled sympathy": we sympathize *both* with the original passion of the actor and the satisfaction of whoever is the object of these passions. Thus, exactly opposite to the unsocial passions, we get a redoubled pleasure—first with the passions themselves, and second from the mutual sympathy we feel both with the actor and whoever is the object of the actor's passions.

SOMETHING SUBTLER: SOCIABILITY, SYMPATHY, AND THE "STRONGER LOVE"

I have stressed that it is because sympathy is primarily simulative that it has its most important socializing effects in Smith's theory. In this section, I want to leverage the same point, but now focusing specifically on the phenomenon of "mutual sympathy." Thus consider: the fact that mutual sympathy between two people is pleasurable, if it really is a fact, is already a socializing force, insofar as all things pleasant are potentially motivating.[12] But it would be facile to say that, for Smith, we strive for mutual sympathy *only* because it is pleasurable. Thus, Smith is keen to point out a number of related psychological and moral functions this pleasure plays, some of which are peculiarly enlivened by the simulative form of sympathy, others which depend on simulation. In what follows I describe three such functions. The third, however, is by far the most important. For it is the bridge back to my overarching interest, namely, Smith's strategy to ground our "stronger love" for virtue in sympathy. Or so I will tentatively suggest.

I. The pleasure of mutual sympathy has secondary hedonic effects: it *ameliorates* grief and suffering and *enlivens* joy. Thus does Smith explain why, for example, when others sympathize with our suffering, such commiseration soothes our pain, even if it doesn't eliminate it; or why sharing good news with those who genuinely care for us can make our triumphs even sweeter than we privately felt them; and so on. Obviously, then, these secondary hedonic effects are socializing (though perhaps not in a normatively rich sense). What may not be obvious is why these effects are distinctly enhanced by imaginative sympathy. So consider: both effects *could* occur without imaginative simulation. That is, conceivably we could be similarly affected by a pleasurable mutual sympathy that arises merely by contagion.[13] Nothing in principle makes this impossible. But it requires very little argument to conclude that both effects will be enhanced immensely by simulative sympathy. Take only the case of suffering. How much more likely will you be to sympathize with a friend's grief, and to what a greater degree of sensitivity and depth, and, in a word, accuracy, if your own sorrowful response to her grief involves your *imagining* her life and her loss as *she* sees it—that is, as opposed to reacting to the mere countenance of sadness she wears on her face? Indeed, if we flip perspectives to that of the grieving actor, it seems clear that we would feel little if any amelioration from the sympathy of others (our own spectators) if it were to occur to us consciously that they were moved to tears *merely* because they had seen us weep, and not because we believed they had in some sense considered what had *caused* our grief; that is, if we did not think they had *imagined* our loss as if it were their own.[14]

II. Recall that the pleasure of mutual sympathy is what is "expressed" by judgments of propriety. Thus, it is not merely the pleasure of mutual sympathy, but the idea of being approved of, that motivates us toward affective harmony with others. Indeed, from the fact that mutual sympathy expresses approbation arises a complex and dynamic form of social interaction—a kind of moral "commerce" of the affections, as Smith describes it. In this commerce actors and spectators are always trying to adjust their feelings to reach the point of mutual concord.[15] This commerce of the affections is socializing in a variety of ways, but one demands special mention. From the perspective of the actor, the pleasure in question *depends* on the judgments of others. There is thus a psychologically primitive sense in which the agential consequence of simulative interaction involves, intrinsically, the transferring of *authority* outside oneself, namely, by recognizing others as judges of one's feelings and motives.[16] However primitive, this is a case where sympathy leads us to care about, in a normative sense, the sentiments of others. For, again, according to Smith's metaethics, it is the sentiments of others that serve as the basis of their judgments of us.

III. Near the middle of TMS Smith introduces what he clearly takes to be an important further insight into human nature. He writes, "Man naturally desires, not only to be loved, but to be lovely; or to be that thing which is the natural and proper object of love . . . not only praise, but praise-worthiness" (TMS III.2.1). Equally important is the explicit connection Smith draws between this quality of our nature and sociability. Man's desire for praise, Smith argues, "would not alone have rendered him fit for that society for which he was made" (TMS III.2.7). Only the "second" desire to be praiseworthy could do this. Smith thus elaborates, "The first desire could only have made him wish to appear to be fit for society. The second was necessary in order to render him *anxious* to be really fit" (TMS III.2.7, emphasis added). This is not the place to explore Smith's defense of these claims or their implications. But the following two points are crucial to my own final remarks.

First, Smith's argument for why the desire to be praiseworthy is "anxious," is, at least in part, conceptual. The *nature* of this desire conditions its satisfaction on a peculiar self-scrutiny. Mere praise (from others) can't satisfy it. We must "know" that we deserve such praise: we must have a sense of what Smith often calls "self-approbation." Thus, Smith argues, once we are sensible to it, the desire for praiseworthiness essentially instills, or cultures in us, a relentless need to verify *internally* that we have the characters others think we do. This is just what he means by calling it an "anxious" desire. Second, and part and parcel of the first point, this anxiety depends on simulative sympathy. Satisfying the desire to be praiseworthy depends on our imaginatively taking up the viewpoints of spectators *on* ourselves. Thus in the background of this conception of humans as naturally desirous of praiseworthiness is again that crucial product of sympathetic imagination mentioned at the start, the "impartial spectator." As Smith himself says in the same stretch of text where he introduces the praiseworthiness claim, "But, in order to attain this satisfaction [the full satisfaction of emulation], we must become the impartial spectators of our own character and conduct. We must endeavour to view them with the eyes of other people, or as other people are likely to view them. When seen in this light, if they appear to us as we wish, we are happy and contented" (TMS III.2.3).

This brings us to my final claim. The foregoing might seem to suggest an irony in Smith's moral theory, and, in particular, his account of human sociability. For, this drive to self-approbation and the attending reliance on the impartial spectator arguably cuts against a positive theory of human sociability, by ultimately releasing each of us (individually) from the need for approval by *actual* other persons. That is, it may seem that we become, in a certain sense, independent of the actual "commerce" of mutual sympathy.

In one sense, this is right. Indeed, it is precisely this aspect of Smith's normative theory, made possible by the imaginative nature of sympathy, that allows Smith to answer a variety of possible objections to his view, not the least of which is that his metaethical account of moral judgment lends itself to moral relativism. For, Smith's appeal to the impartial spectator allows him to explain the objectivity typically ascribed to morality, if not the means to justify such objectivity—though readers may well disagree whether Smith really aspired to the latter.

And yet, I suggest it would be a mistake to think Smith's appeal to the impartial spectator presents a conceptual problem for attributing to him an optimistic, antiegoist account of human sociability. As I said at the outset, Smith's goal is not to explain our motive to be simply *in* society. The goal is normative. I first explained it as an attempt to explain why we are social in the sense of having a *reason to care* about others. But, arguably, our reflections in this final section have shown us that Smith took the task one step further. He wanted to explain not just why we have a reason to care about others, but why we have a reason to make ourselves *worthy to be cared about*—or as Smith put it, to be "really fit" for society. This is the account of human sociability I'm now suggesting Smith offers us. This is the sense in which human sociability, for Smith, is "grounded" in simulative sympathy. Indeed, it should now be said that, according to Smith, being anxious about "self-approbation," which is what the desire for praiseworthiness raises in us, though not identical with, is very close to the love of virtue itself. Thus Smith writes, in the same stretch of text discussing the desire for praiseworthiness, "This self-approbation, if not the only, is at least the principal object, about which [a wise man] can or ought to be anxious. The love of it, is the love of virtue" (TMS III.2.8). At a minimum, we've come close enough to glean why Smith feels entitled to say that it is a "stronger love" of virtue that makes most of us truly sociable creatures. For, as a consequence of our natural and lively sympathetic imagination, together with our desire for praiseworthiness, we become sensitive to the judgment of the impartial spectator, and, in turn, unable to rest content with the mere appearance of being praiseworthy, virtuous, or moral. We become anxious to be *actually* praiseworthy, virtuous, and moral. And on Smith's view, to make this last claim just is to say that we desire to be "really fit" for society.

NOTES

1. The faculty of imagination is central to Smith's larger philosophical system, not just the account of sympathy. The best concise but still comprehensive treatment can be found in Charles Griswold's "Imagination: Morals, Science, and Arts," in *Cambridge Companion to Adam Smith*, ed. Knud Haakonssen (New York: 2006).

2. All citations to Hume's *Treatise* are to *A Treatise of Human Nature*, ed. David and Mary Norton (Oxford: 2000), hereafter abbreviated with "T," followed by book, part, section, and paragraph numbers; and to the Selby-Bigge/Nidditch edition (Oxford: 1978), abbreviated with "SBN," followed by page numbers. Hume gives his first account of sympathy at *Treatise* 2.1.11. He uses the language of "contagion" in connection with "sympathy" in both *Treatise* and *Enquiry* (see, e.g., *Enquiry* sec. 7 [all citations to Hume's *Enquiry* are to the Clarendon Critical Edition of *An Enquiry Concerning the Principles of Morals*, ed. Tom Beauchamp (Oxford: 1998)]). He also applies the concept in his *History of England* (see, e.g., vol. 5.LIV: "By stronger contagion, the popular affections were communicated from breast to breast, in this place of general rendezvous and society"). For more on Hume's account of sympathy, see my paired articles: "Humanity, Sympathy, and the Puzzle of Hume's Second Enquiry," *British Journal for the History of Philosophy* 15, no. 1 (2007), pp. 27–57, and "Has Anything Changed? Hume's Theory of Association and Sympathy after the Treatise," *British Journal for the History of Philosophy* 15, no. 2 (2007), pp. 313–38. For an excellent dissection of the differences between Hume and Smith's account of sympathy, see Samuel Fleischacker, "Sympathy in Hume and Smith: A Contrast, Critique, and Reconstruction," in *Intersubjectivity and Objectivity in Adam Smith and Edmund Husserl*, ed. Christel Fricke and Dagfinn Føllesdal (Frankfurt: 2012). For more on the "passivity" of Hume's notion, see Ryan Hanley, "Hume and Smith on Moral Philosophy," in *Oxford Handbook of David Hume*, ed. Paul Russell (Oxford: forthcoming).

3. This "enlivening" step is the most contentious part of Hume's theory, in large part because of Hume's own dubious suggestion that it is explained by a kind

of transfer of "energy" *from* the awareness one has of one's "self" *to* the idea of the passion in question (i.e., the idea of the other person's passion). For more on this, see my "Has Anything Changed?"

4. My description of both Smith and Hume is of their "primary" models. Thus Smith's opening analysis of sympathy in TMS is marked by qualifying clauses and expressions that leave room for a Humean analysis of sympathy, albeit only in atypical cases. As to the reverse question—whether Hume has the resources to incorporate aspects of Smith's simulative view—this is a live question. For more on this issue, see again Fleischacker, "Sympathy in Hume and Smith."

5. Obviously how one is "informed" of the cause varies. More to the point, as much as Smith wants to argue, contra Hume, that mere observation of how others feel yields (at best) imperfect ideas of the causes of those feelings, it must be underlined that Smith means only that observation of emotional displays per se is impotent. He doesn't mean that observation of an emotional display *in context* is never potent. Thus, if you are watching me run fearfully from a bear through the woods, you don't need me to *tell* you why I'm scared in order to form an accurate idea of what's scaring me. Also important, sometimes we try to simulate an actor's situation *first*—that is, before we have any clear idea of the cause—precisely as a means of trying to "conjecture" as to the cause. Even so, it is only the conjunction of simulation *and* an idea of the cause (some aspect of the situation we are imagining), which raises some emotion in us.

6. This detail—that approbation is itself a distinct feeling, identical to what Smith calls "mutual sympathy"—seems to trip up readers of Smith. But that this is the correct rendering of his account is made clear in Smith's famous footnote at TMS I.iii.I.9, which replies to a demand Hume made to clarify this very point.

7. To put it this way is to borrow liberally from the language of contemporary metaethics. Nevertheless, this is basically what Smith means.

8. But see Griswold, "Imagination."

9. Smith argues that sympathy often occurs instantaneously (TMS I.i.4.10), but also sometimes irresistibly (e.g., TMS I.ii.3.5).

10. Smith is clear that, strictly speaking, we are ultimately epistemologically locked in our own viewpoints, and it is thus really *our* interpretation, our guess, or imagined idea of another person's experience that drives sympathy (TMS I.i.I.2; TMS I.i.4.7). But this doesn't change the driving point. However much we fail to perfectly simulate the lives of others, it remains the most basic feature of Smith's account of sympathy that we *try and do* simulate.

11. Paradoxically, given my stress on simulation over contagion, this is partly because Smith admits that cries of misery and fright typically provoke sympathy even when we do *not* know the cause—i.e., even before we properly simulate; see TMS I.ii.3.5.

12. It must be admitted that, just as sympathy itself isn't necessarily simulative, so too the pleasure of mutual sympathy doesn't necessarily depend on the imagination, and thus neither is its motivational role necessarily dependent on imagination. That is, this pleasure *could* arise through cognitive-poor channels. For example, it is conceivable that the mere observational recognition that another person feels as we feel do might raise this peculiar pleasure in us, assuming we and he are obviously faced with the same object—i.e., are literally *in* the same

situation. But as I say above, all the interesting socializing effects of the fact that mutual sympathy is pleasurable stem from its simulative form.

13. See note 9.

14. Or, at a minimum, if he had insufficient time to actually simulate our terrible situation, we must think he arrived at his expression of grief for our grief by consulting his own past experiences of loss and sorrow. Smith introduces this "general rules" caveat at TMS I.i.3.3–4.

15. Though Smith talks ubiquitously of the sort of back-and-forth exchange of sentiments I'm referring to, he calls it a "commerce" of affections only once, at TMS I.ii.4.1. The metaphor, however, is poignant. For more, see James Otteson, *Adam Smith's Marketplace of Life* (New York: 2002).

16. Granted, in Smith's system we are not necessarily beholden to the approval of spectators, insofar as we can court the appeal of a higher authority, namely, Smith's famous "impartial spectator." I return to the impartial spectator below.

BIBLIOGRAPHIC ESSAY

Sympathy is the central concept of Smith's moral theory, and there is a correspondingly extensive secondary literature devoted to it. The indispensable and already classic commentary, however, is contained in Charles Griswold's 1999 comprehensive analysis of Smith's moral theory, *Adam Smith and the Virtues of Enlightenment* (Cambridge: 1999). Other influential analyses of Smith's theory of sympathy can be found in Vivienne Brown's *Adam Smith's Discourse: Canonicity, Commerce and Conscience* (London: 1994), and, with respect to Smith's economic theory, Samuel Fleischacker's *On Adam Smith's Wealth of Nations* (Princeton: 2004). For a moderately revisionist account of the nature and import of sympathy in Smith's thought, see Ryan Hanley's recent *Adam Smith and the Character of Virtue* (Cambridge: 2009). For a general analysis of the faculty of imagination in Smith's larger philosophical system (not just sympathy), see Charles Griswold's "Imagination: Morals, Science, and Arts," in *The Cambridge Companion to Adam Smith*, ed. Knud Haakonssen (Cambridge: 2006). For a general treatment of the concept of sympathy, its historical origins in antiquity, its development up to and during the modern era, and its contemporary significance, turn to Eric Schliesser's commanding anthology, *Sympathy: A History* (Oxford: 2015).

13

ADAM SMITH ON FREEDOM

David Schmidtz

Adam Smith did not present readers with a theory of freedom per se. He did, however, reflect on prospects for autonomy and self-esteem in market society, inspiring capitalism's critics almost as much as he did capitalism's defenders. In the process he gave us elements of a theory about what sort of freedom market society makes possible, what sort of challenge this freedom represents, and how and why such freedom is (or is not) achieved in particular cases. This essay discusses four such elements: first, market society frees us from starvation; second, market society frees us from servility; third, however, the liberating impact of markets is not guaranteed because markets can be corrupted by crony capitalism (that is, by monarchs and merchants buying and selling political privilege); fourth, markets can fail to be all they should be because of how much people want. Strikingly, the latter worry on Smith's part is not the obvious problem of people wanting too much so much as more subtle problems that go with wanting too little.

1. FREEDOMS MADE POSSIBLE

1.1. Freedom from Starvation

Ryan Hanley says, "the fundamental departure point for Smith's defense of commercial society is its capacity to provide for the poor."[1] To Smith, "no society can be flourishing and happy, of which the far greater part of its members are poor and miserable" (WN I.viii.36). Smith observed commercial society liberating the poor from desperate need.

In a village, a poor man's son *might* grow up to become a doctor, but it is *certain* that no one will be pushing the frontier of oral surgery, for in a village there are not enough customers to sustain specialized trades. To see specialized trades, we go to a commercial hub such as London. In London, someone who otherwise would have been the village carpenter can specialize in making violins. To Smith, economies of scale enable fine-grained specialization, thereby making possible new dimensions of pride in being able to perform superlatively at a particular kind of work. In port cities, arts proliferate and people innovate, because port cities are hubs of commerce; they are where cultures meet, and where entrepreneurs come looking for ideas.[2] When trade goes global, enabling trade with customers by the millions, someone can get rich by inventing the window envelope. Wal-Mart can become stunningly profitable not by making millions from each customer, but by netting a few pennies each from untold millions of transactions per day. The volume of trade is so massive that Wal-Mart can net billions even if nearly all of the surplus value created by transactions involving Wal-Mart is captured by Wal-Mart's customers.

How would we ensure that when London needs more carpenters, more people go into carpentry? Smith's answer is one of his signature insights. Given price signals, we check whether there is a problem (and in the process acquire a reason to help solve the problem) by checking the price of a carpenter's wage. This simple, elegant mechanism, intuitively grasped by everyone who buys and sells, coordinates the productive efforts of people who may share neither a religion nor even a language, and who are indeed only dimly aware of each other's existence. A spike in the wages of carpenters, more reliably than anything else, alerts consumers to a need to be more economical in their use of carpentry services, simultaneously alerting prospective suppliers to a community's rising need for carpentry services. Falling prices, more reliably than anything else, signal would-be suppliers that a community already has more than it needs. From such economic coordination, made possible by free-floating price signals, the wealth of nations is made. What comes to be classified as poverty will be what previous generations would have called opulence, such that even the poorest members of market societies will have, for example, life expectancies exceeding fifty years.

Where Plato supposed the wealth of nations must ultimately depend on a guardian class assigning to each worker tasks appropriate to that worker's nature, Smith realized that no guardian class could ever know enough (or reliably care enough) to handle such a task. Only a price mechanism can track the incomprehensibly vast torrent of daily feedback from buyers and sellers regarding whether X is worth producing and if so where X needs to be shipped so as to reach consumers to whom X is worth what it costs to get it to them.

And yet, the manifest clarity of Smith's vision of the liberating power of markets notwithstanding, Smith is no giddy cheerleader but is instead one of history's most probing critics of commercial society even as he so insightfully defends it. He says, for example, that the pleasures of success and wealth "strike the imagination as something grand and beautiful and noble" (TMS IV.1.9) but immediately adds that this useful *illusion* induces us to be so overly productive that we produce vastly more than we need, leading at some point to our having nothing better to do than sell our surplus to neighbors who have more use for it. He concludes (in one of the only explicit uses of the metaphor for which Smith is most famous) that high achievers "are led by an invisible hand to make nearly the same distribution of the necessaries of life, which would have been made, had the earth been divided into equal portions among all its inhabitants" (TMS IV.1.10). The result, as Smith put it: in terms of material comfort and peace of mind, the different ranks of life are nearly level, and even a beggar sunning himself by the side of a highway ends up with much of that security for which kings must fight.

1.2. Freedom from Servility

A second freedom transforming Europe's economy by Smith's time was the freedom of ordinary people to contract with persons other than their lord. In a feudal system, if you are born a serf, you are entitled to your lord's protection, but you lack many rights that today we take for granted. In a feudal system, you live where your lord tells you to live. You grow what the lord tells you to grow. You sell your harvest to the lord *at a price of the lord's choosing*. If you want to leave, you need your lord's permission. When you meet your lord, you bow. Your lord does not see you as his equal. For that matter, neither do you.

As market society supplanted this system, the effect was liberating for all, especially the poor. As Hanley puts it, "commerce substitutes interdependence for direct dependence and makes possible the freedom of the previously oppressed."[3] Your dependence on a particular lord's mercy is replaced by your autonomous interdependence in a loose-knit but functional community of customers and suppliers (WN 3, esp. 3.3).

If you choose to work for an employer instead of launching a business of your own, then you delegate to your employer many key decisions and relegate to your employer much of the risk that comes with those decisions. You remain a free agent in the pivotal sense that when you decide to leave, you will not need permission. Even as an employee, you are in crucial ways a partner, not a mere possession. You won't necessarily *prefer* being a partner to being a serf. You may feel insecure. But you will be free.

Throughout history, the strong have subjugated the weak. In Smith's mind, commercial society changed the frontier of possibility in such a way that the strong often have a better option: namely, learning to do business in such a way that the community is better off with them than without them. As Hanley sees it, "this fascination with and gratitude for the harnessing of the powers of the strong for the relief of the weak is the fundamental fact uniting Smith's seemingly separate defenses of both commercial society and his specific vision of virtue." Commercial societies "promote not only universal opulence but also a universal freedom of which the weak are the principal beneficiaries."[4]

The crucial bottom line is that when people achieve freedom in commercial society, such freedom will involve *depending* on many, yet being at the *mercy* of none.

2. FREEDOMS THREATENED

However, as Hanley notes, "Smith is not only a founding father of commercial society, but also a father of a critique of it that would come to dominate European political thought in the next two centuries."[5] A society of free and responsible persons must solve a twofold problem. First, people tend to be too intent on running other people's lives. Second, people are insufficiently intent on properly running their own. One problem corrupts the polis; the other corrupts the soul. This pair of problems arguably is a driving focus of Smith's two major works.

2.1. Corrupting the Polis

First, we labor under a ubiquitous threat of being shackled by crony capitalists. Smith wondered how internally stable a free market could be in the face of a tendency for its political infrastructure to decay into crony capitalism. (The phrase "crony capitalism" is not Smith's. I use it to refer to various of Smith's targets: mercantilists who lobby for subsidies for exporters, protectionists who lobby for tariffs and other trade barriers, monopolists who pay kings for a license to be free from competition altogether, and so on.) Partnerships between big business and big government lead to big subsidies, monopolistic licensing practices, and tariffs. These ways of compromising freedom have been and always will be touted as protecting the middle class, but their true purpose is (and almost always will be) to transfer wealth and power from ordinary citizens to well-connected elites. As a result, an ordinary citizen's pivotal relationships are not with free and equal trading partners but with bureaucratic rulers: people whose grip on our community is so pervasive that we cannot walk away from such terms of engagement as they unilaterally propose. Thus, we reinvent feudalism. We are at the mercy of lords.

Adam Smith fought mercantilism, protectionism, and other forms of crony capitalism because such policies stifle innovation.[6] Smith remarks on the good, the bad, and the ugly of industrial motivation:

> To widen the market and to narrow the competition is always the
> interest of the dealers. To widen the market may frequently be agree-

able enough to the interest of the public; but to narrow the competition must always be against it, and can serve only to enable the dealers, by raising their profits above what they naturally would be, to levy, for their own benefit, an absurd tax upon the rest of their fellow-citizens. The proposal of any new law or regulation of commerce which comes from this order, ought always to be listened to with great precaution, and ought never to be adopted till after having been long and carefully examined, not only with the most scrupulous, but with the most suspicious attention. It comes from an order of men, whose interest is never exactly the same with that of the public, who have generally an interest to deceive and even to oppress the public, and who accordingly have, upon many occasions, both deceived and oppressed it. (WN I.xi.p.10)

Resistance to such oppression requires eternal vigilance, with no hope of final victory.

People of the same trade seldom meet together, even for merriment and diversion, but the conversation ends in a conspiracy against the public, or in some contrivance to raise prices. It is impossible indeed to prevent such meetings, by any law which either could be executed, or would be consistent with liberty and justice. But though the law cannot hinder people of the same trade from sometimes assembling together, it ought to do nothing to facilitate such assemblies; much less to render them necessary. (WN I.x.c.27)

Unfortunately, kings wanting to fights wars employing expensive mercenaries are driven to sell monopoly licenses to generate revenue. This market for political power has a singularly unhappy logic. Namely, kings adopt policies systematically favoring merchants who have lost their economic edge, because inferior competitors are the ones most willing to pay for the imposition of tariffs and other legal barriers to competition. As David Hume saw, the easy transfer of external goods was both an enormous opportunity and an enormous problem, a foundation of both the promise and the downfall of capitalism. It makes piracy possible, and enables crony capitalists to enlist the help of kings to bureaucratize piracy and make it routine.

Second, we labor under a related and equally ubiquitous threat of being shackled by "men of system." As Samuel Fleischacker says, "the limitations Smith describes on what anyone can know about their society should give pause to those who are confident that governments can carry out even the task of protecting freedom successfully. Taken together with his scepticism about the judiciousness, decency, and impartiality of those who go into politics, this is what gives punch to the libertarian reading of Smith."[7] As Smith saw it, the "man of system"

> is apt to be very wise in his own conceit. . . . He seems to imagine that he can arrange the different members of a great society with as much ease as the hand arranges the different pieces upon a chessboard. He does not consider that the pieces upon the chess-board have no other principle of motion besides that which the hand impresses upon them; but that, in the great chess-board of human society, every single piece has a principle of motion of its own, altogether different from that which the legislature might cause to impress upon it. (TMS VI.ii.2.17)

A "man of system" moves pawns in pursuit of his goals, but pawns tend to respond in an irritatingly contrarian way. First, they have interests of their own. Second, their interests are not always narrow but may be bound up in a constellation of loyalties, habits, and mutual expectations that make communities what they are; moreover, part of what communities are is resistant to change. So, Smith says, public spirit leads people both to respect their traditions but also to want to see their institutions perfected. In peaceful times the potential conflict between these two impulses is not a problem, but in times of strife the two impulses of public spirit can come apart, and a "man of system" gripped by a vision of perfection can do great damage. A man of system moves the pieces, but the pieces respond as if they have minds of their own, which, after all, they do. Pieces respond with a view to their own hopes and dreams, but also with their own sense of what their society is about and where it needs to go from here (TMS VI.ii.2.17).[8] Incensed by the pawn's contrarian response, men of system make adjustments, now seeking more to dominate "pawns" than to help them, and any virtue these would-be public servants initially brought to public office is corroded. Compounding the problem, reins of power come at a price. Anyone acquiring the reins will be a person to whom such power is worth the price. Moreover, the more power there is to acquire, the more it will be worth, the more people must invest to acquire it, and thus the more that such power gets concentrated in the hands of people intent on using it for all that it is worth. So, the process by which people gain political appointment will systematically tend, and *increasingly* tend, to select the wrong person for the job.

Consequently, there is a predictable even if not inevitable disconnect between what truly benevolent people seek and what men of system deliver. Such tension is driven by the logic of offices that align bureaucratic interests with that of "dealers" in particular rather than of the public in general. As Smith sees it, the law cannot circumvent this logic, but at least it can avoid requiring dealers and bureaucratic men of system alike to be driven by it. Thus there is a presumption of liberty, allowing ordinary merchants a measure of freedom from regulation by dealers and such men of system as the dealers co-opt.

It bears mentioning that Smith was by no means extreme in his pessimism about the possibility of good governance. He was merely a realist. He outlines a role for civil magistrates in upholding the basic infrastructure of a commercial society's limited government (at, for example, TMS II.ii.1.8), expressing hope, if not exuberant overconfidence, that magistrates will take his message to heart regarding their proper role. And they might; after all, they too have an expansive as well as a narrow self-interest, and among other things aim to earn self-esteem. Smith likewise reflects (see, for example, TMS IV.1.11) on what it would take to instruct people in the art of true public spirit, and when he says this he himself is self-consciously providing such instruction and exhortation to the would-be public servants to whom his work was addressed.

2.2. Corrupting the Person

I mentioned two factors that corrupt the polis, dividing a community against itself: first, some capitalists end up being pirates rather than producers; second, many public servants become men of system—treating people like pawns to be patronized at best and squashed at worst and who themselves eventually become pawns of crony capitalists.

A person's soul likewise can be divided against itself.

1. First, after acquiring enough to meet genuine needs, workers tend to keep working. Why? Part of the reason is that they seek to amass enough wealth to make themselves more visible to others. Smith speaks of the "poor man's son" whose drive for visibility translates into a simplistic drive to *win* (TMS IV.1.8). The poor man's son is among other things an embryonic form of the crony capitalist and the man of system, the seed from which they grow. Tormented by envy and untutored ambition, the son's quest for opulence comes to revolve around keeping up with the Joneses (or keeping the Joneses in line) rather than around a meaningful life. He loses sight of the difference between creating wealth and merely capturing it, thereby helping to turn what should have been an effervescent positive sum society into a dreary zero-sum game where players spend much of their time waiting in line to beg bureaucrats for permission to make a move. And Smith sees the poor man's son everywhere he looks. Smith is glad people work as hard as they do for their customers, but laments that people come to care so little for themselves. It takes maturity and true self-centeredness to transcend this drive and to develop the habitual serenity that goes with *deeply* minding one's own business. Not everyone has what it takes.

What makes market society unique, however, is not that it makes alienation inevitable but that it raises the frontier of human possibility. The fact that we achieve so much less than we could is partly a function of how much we have been liberated to achieve.[9] Market society also gives us *free time* to indulge such laments, but that is not a bad thing. Thus, Smith's discussion of this failure to hit the rising ceiling of our potential was merely a lament, not a damnation: not a critique of capitalism so much as a reflection on how much capitalism makes possible but also how little it guarantees. A precondition of free society is people accepting (1) that they inhabit a world thick both with possibilities and responsibilities and (2) that not all possibilities will be realized. We trust people to do their best. We accept that many of them won't.

Using leisure time well is a skill. Developing that skill is an achievement. Both individuals and cultures need practice to fully capitalize on the potentials of new opportunities.[10] The surpassing compliment to commercial society that Smith wants to pay is to say that members of commercial society, even in failing to be all that they could be, make life better for their trading partners. Laborers working overtime for trinkets make our world a better place even while squandering opportunities to enjoy their earnings in more thoughtful, creative, self-fulfilling ways. (Part of the problem with the feverish quest for happiness via the acquiring of toys and trinkets is that it embodies a mistake. It confuses the faux-visibility that comes from conspicuous consumption with the estimable visibility that comes from conspicuous production.) To Smith, our concern to be validated by others can drive our maturation through a certain stage, but then we will need to outgrow that drive. Otherwise, it becomes a psychological shackle. Why? Because to care greatly about external validation is to be controlled by the hoped-for source of validation. It is good for growing children to feel a need to insinuate themselves into socializing networks and to learn the rudiments of being a good neighbor and good citizen, but for an adult, the liberating ideal is Stoic indifference.[11]

2. Specialization is the source of the greatest benefits of human civilization, but Marx would come to share Smith's worry that repetitive factory floor work would make the mind drowsy.[12] Here is Smith's classic statement: "The man whose whole life is spent in performing a few simple operations, of which the effects are perhaps always the same, or very nearly the same, has no occasion to exert his understanding or to exercise his invention in finding out expedients for removing difficulties which never occur. He naturally loses, therefore, the habit of such exertion, and generally becomes as stupid and ignorant as it is possible for a human creature to become" (WN V.i.f.50). According to E. G. West, Smith feared that without a rigorous education, factory workers would have no idea what to fight for and what against, and would become dupes of (often equally uncomprehending) revolutionaries.[13] West says, "the root of alienation in Rousseau as in Marx—is economic

interdependence and exchange based on private property."[14] To Smith, by contrast, "property, wealth, and commodity production are preconditions for the non-alienated state. And in this state individuals pursue refinement and art."[15] West goes on to remark that what may appear to a Marxist as a pointless, interminable quest for marginal advances in productivity becomes an art form, a healthy expression of the creative impulse.[16] Innovators experience commercial and technological breakthroughs as liberating affirmations of their exquisitely refined commitment to excellence rather than as never-ending turns in a cosmic rat race.

3. Marx anticipated, as did Smith, that alienation would not be confined to the factory floor but instead would some day be found even among well-paid white-collar workers. Alienation does not presuppose dismal working conditions. It can happen in posh offices (1) to executives who no longer see a connection between their labors and the possibility of satisfaction from a job well done; (2) to creators who work only through intermediaries, losing contact with products and customers on the ground, thus losing some of the sense of the estimable place in the communities that their excellence creates; (3) to investors, when investments begin to present themselves as nothing more than gambles rather than as estimable opportunities to help worthy producers achieve excellence. Indeed, large organizations spawn legions of "Dilberts" whose main challenge every day is to cover their tracks in large bureaucracies where the drive to deliver an excellent product has been replaced by a drive to secure a less vulnerable position in the office hierarchy. Smith's and Marx's concerns are related, albeit not identical. It is easy to see why Smith would have inspired Marx as he did.[17]

4. Less obviously, a different kind of risk to a person's soul goes with the fact that one of life's great pleasures is the finding of *kindred* souls—people with whom we can reach a concurrence of sentiment. We actively seek out companionship.[18] Because this desire for concord runs so deep, it can corrupt us in the following way. We tend not to notice our tendency to adjust our attitudes to fit those of people around us. Adjusting subconsciously makes us more vulnerable to social pressure.[19] If we *noticed* ourselves "going along to get along" then we could resist, or at least go along self-

consciously. But if we do not even notice ourselves adjusting as needed so as to become agreeable company for potential allies, our ability to master this ever-present threat to our autonomy is compromised.[20] The abdication is motivated by self-preservation, but also in a way by a deficiency of self-love. One is letting oneself become a self that one cannot afford to examine too closely—a self unworthy of esteem.

Yet, as James Otteson observes, Smith sees our sociality as a key to accurate self-perception. It is upon being introduced into society that a solitary man takes stock of his appearance and character for the first time.[21]

> Were it possible that a human creature could grow up to manhood in some solitary place, without any communication with his own species, he could no more think of his own character, of the propriety or demerit of his own sentiments and conduct, of the beauty or deformity of his own mind, than of the beauty or deformity of his own face. . . . Bring him into society, and he is immediately provided with the mirror which he wanted before. It is . . . here that he first views the propriety and impropriety of his own passions, the beauty and deformity of his own mind. (TMS III.1.3)

The image is lovely, although it hardly seems that Smith needed so bold a premise to make the simple point that solitary life is not among our serious options. A *human* life is a *social* life. Therefore, the life of a trader, someone who needs suppliers and customers but who needs no particular trading partner, is as independent a life form as a humanly rational agent wants. We may not have what it takes to be indifferent to whether we are visible to others.[22] If we cannot be indifferent, however, we still have what it takes to distinguish between *being* esteemed and *deserving* esteem, and to preserve our psychological independence by reminding ourselves that we aren't seeking sympathy for our false facades. It is our real core selves for which we want to achieve a sense of belonging.

That need for recognition—deep visibility—leaves us open to various disappointments.

First, when a partner starts appealing directly to my benevolence rather than to my self-interest, that makes the relationship a one-way street, and its failure to sustain me materially eventually translates into a failure to sustain me emotionally as well. I am being treated as a mere means.

Second, if I start to feel like a feudal serf, having no choice about whom I do business with, or at what price—if I am not merely depending on others but at their *mercy*—then that is another way in which commerce becomes alienating rather than affirming.

Third, if my way of making partners better off involves no particular *alertness* on my part to their needs—if I feel like a cog in a wheel, endlessly repeating a mindless task of someone else's design—then that too is a relationship that fails to make me feel visible as an esteemed member of a community of estimable traders. So, that too leads me to stop caring about the excellence of my craft. I cannot see myself as visible, and from there it is a short step to being unable to see myself as estimable. Thus, I fail to be all that a member of market society can be, and instead I become the kind of creature lamented by Marx and Dickens.

3. LIBERATING SELF-LOVE

Smith's second great work seems to treat self-interest as the fundamental human motivation, while the first privileges sympathy and a drive to earn esteem. This has been treated as a remarkable inconsistency, an "Adam Smith problem."[23] My diagnosis is this.

3.1. Is the Propensity to Truck and Barter More Fundamental Than Self-Interest?

First, there is some evidence that, to Smith, self-interest was not as fundamental a psychological foundation as some readings of *Wealth of Nations* have suggested. Strikingly, when Smith opens WN, Book I, chapter 2 by asking what accounts for the evolution of specialization, his opening remark refers not to the profit motive but to the propensity to truck and barter. This propensity, Smith says, is a necessary attribute of social beings whose ability to cooperate is mediated by faculties of reason and speech. Taking what Smith says at face value, it would seem that trucking and bartering is not grounded in the profit motive but is itself a primordial human motive.[24] A drive to truck and barter is not only a drive to make money but more fundamentally a drive to make deals. It is a drive to reciprocate favors, cultivate allies, and be part of a community of people who each bring something good to the table—free and responsible reciprocators who warrant esteem and whose esteem is thus worth something in return. This esteem for Smith is the ultimate coin of the realm (TMS VI.i.3).[25] The desire for esteem cannot be eliminated, but it can be educated.[26] A merchant learns how to bring something to the community that makes it a better place to live and work for everyone with whom that merchant deals. The overall result may be no part of a trader's intention, as Smith says in places, but neither is a successful trader's intention simply a matter of self-absorbed acquisitiveness.

A person of true benevolence puts himself in a customer's shoes not simply for the sake of predicting what customers will find irresistible but also for the sake of making it true that his partners are better off with him than without him. That is what enables a merchant to go home after work, look in the mirror, and like what he sees, having affirmed that he is good at what he does; moreover, his community needs him to be that good. When he dies, he will pass from this earth knowing that it mattered that he was here. As Otteson says, being affirmed in that mundane way becomes a person's reason for living.

By contrast, being tormented by raw ambition—a naked desire to be an object of envy unrefined by a desire to be praise*worthy* —is a feverish, heteronomous, lamentable condition. Something is wrong with the poor man's son, and it may have no remedy.[27] Worries about lack of authenticity remain to haunt any reflective person, and there is no such thing as addressing it "once and for all." And yet, we do have what it takes to worry about the possibility, and at least to want to avoid being that kind of person. We spend a lot of time grooming, and some of that quiet time is for reflecting on what lies beneath the surface.

3.2. Is Benevolence More Fundamental Than Self-Interest?

Second, it makes perfect sense for the author who treated benevolence as primary in his first book to subsequently analyze market virtue as a matter of treating the self-love of trading partners as primary. As a benevolent person hoping to truck and barter with the brewer and baker, you think first of their self-love because you want them to be better off. Smith does not say bakers are motivated solely by self-love. What he says is that we do not *address ourselves* to their benevolence but to their self-love. This is not to deny that bakers are benevolent. Rather, it is to reflect on what it takes to be benevolent oneself in one's dealings with bakers.[28] In sum, the author of *Moral Sentiments* gives center stage to virtue and benevolence, but in elaborating the substantive content of these ideas, the author of *Wealth of Nations* notes what should be obvious: namely, a man of true benevolence wants his partners to be better off with him than without him.

This trader, consistently the subject of all Smith's writings, cannot address his own benevolent concern except by addressing the brewer's and baker's self-love. The point of addressing each other's self-love is to give each other's self its due. That is what it is like to succeed in one's attempt to be sympathetic. From such sympathetic, indeed impartial, consideration of the ubiquity of self-interest and of manifestly real albeit contingent ways in which self-interest can be consonant with the common good, there emerges the complementary understanding of how the liberty of butchers, bakers, and their customers likewise serves the common good. The harmony of interests among free persons is not remotely to be taken for granted, yet is manifestly a real possibility. So long as people can see a way of building a community of partners who are better off with them than without them, and so long as they see themselves as having reason to cherish such an achievement, their self-interest will bring them together to form a free and thriving community.

3.3. Sympathy for Self-Love in a Free Society

When it is time to reflect on an evolving culture and legal infrastructure, and perchance to modify it, true benevolence is not about counting on people to be unselfish. True benevolence does not embrace an ideal of suppressing self-love; it instead embraces an ideal of guiding self-love to constructive rather than destructive ends.

Moreover, we do not count on the poor man's son being magnanimous. We encourage people to be magnanimous, but what honestly encourages people to be magnanimous is putting them in a position where they can afford to believe in each other—where they are not at the mercy of people who may be, or who may one day become, something other than magnanimous. When they are free to make their own decisions about whom to trust, and when they have some liberty to exit from relationships that have gone sour, they will in that sense be more free to enter those relationships (that is, more able to afford the risk) in the first place.

4. CONCLUSION

Smith has a story about the wealth of nations: how wealth grows, liberating us in the process, but how we systematically fail to take full advantage of opportunities for liberation that wealth creates. Smith sees commercial society emerging, in the process liberating people economically from the shackles of destitution. He sees commercial society liberating people culturally from shackles of feudalism. He sees commercial society potentially liberating people psychologically, too, opening a door to a gusher of human possibility. Yet, Smith also wonders who will have what it takes to stride into that limitless future. (Will people, enough people, be sufficiently educated? Will the working class be a reservoir of talent, from whose ranks children will have an opportunity to lift the ceiling of human progress? Market society teaches us how to create wealth, but will we teach ourselves what wealth is for? Will we teach ourselves that money can buy precious time?) So long as people are trading freely—trading only when their partners consent—they will be led as if by an invisible hand to do right by their trading partners. Yet, they are *not* led as if by an invisible hand to do right by themselves. We face an abiding risk of waking some day to find that we have been shackled by crony capitalists, or by "men of system." We also face risks from within—risks that we will *not* wake up, and will not realize we have been shackled by social pressure. Practicing true self-love, in ways newly made possible by technological and commercial progress, is life's greatest challenge. The market throws down the gauntlet; there is no guarantee that we will be up to the challenge it offers us.

NOTES

Work on this essay was supported by a grant from the John Templeton Foundation. The opinions expressed here are those of the author and do not necessarily reflect the views of the John Templeton Foundation. I thank Chad Van Schoelandt for organizing a session at the University of Arizona, Mike Munger and Geoff Brennan for sponsoring a guest lecture in their Philosophy, Politics, and Economics seminar at Duke University, Jim Otteson for invitations to Yeshiva University, Colin Bird for including me in a workshop on "Work and Worth" at the University of Virginia, Justin Weinberg for inviting me to the University of South Carolina, Virgil Storr and Pete Boettke for hosting me at George Mason University, Gary Chartier for inviting me to La Sierra University, and Jon Mahoney and Amy Lara for bringing me to Boğaziçi University to team-teach a graduate seminar on liberalism. I thank all who attended these events, and especially Paul Aligica, Dan Brudney, Richard Dagger, Sam Freeman, Erin Kelly, David Lefkowicz, Loren Lomasky, and Allan Megill for helpful conversation. I also thank the Property and Environment Research Center in Bozeman, Montana, for supporting me in the summer of 2012 when I was finishing this article. And finally, I thank Ryan Hanley for editing my essay with such consummate tact that he managed not to impose his own standards so much as to induce me to raise mine.

1. Ryan Patrick Hanley, *Adam Smith and the Character of Virtue* (New York: 2009), p. 18.

2. Tyler Cowen, *In Praise of Commercial Culture* (Cambridge: 1998).

3. Hanley, *Adam Smith*, p. 20. Smith's claim is that commercial society is the society wherein "the person who either acquires, or succeeds to a great fortune does not *necessarily* acquire or succeed to any political power" (WN I.v.3, emphasis added). That Smith would feel a need to add the italicized qualifier reflects a realism found throughout Smith's writings (but see Jacob Viner, "Adam Smith and Laissez Faire," *Journal of Political Economy* 35 [1927], pp. 198–232, for an argument that WN is more realistic than TMS).

4. Hanley, *Adam Smith*, p. 19.

5. Ibid., p. 24.

6. The story in WN I.1.8 of how an innovative boy invents a labor-saving improvement on extant fire engines would be greeted by many labor unions as the sort of "jobs-killer" against which they have a right to be cushioned.

7. Samuel Fleischacker, *On Adam Smith's* Wealth of Nations: *A Philosophical Companion* (Princeton: 2004), p. 235. See also ibid., p. 233, on the delusions of the sovereign and the folly of the statesman who fancies himself fit to exercise the power to impose a central plan. See also WN IV.ii.10 and WN IV.ix.51.

8. My remarks here about the matrix of habit and tradition that thwarts the best-laid plans is indebted to Jacob Levy. See chaps. 3 and 7 of Levy's "Rationalism, Pluralism, and Freedom" (manuscript, 2012). See also Vincent Ostrom's discussion of "habits of the heart" and historically embedded structures of shared meaning. Although Ostrom was thinking mainly about Tocqueville, it seems likely that Smith too had such things in mind as part of the constellation of factors, distinct from self-love narrowly conceived, that men of the system are all too prone to ignore, at the expense of untold suffering. Vincent Ostrom, *The Meaning of Democracy and the Vulnerability of Democracies: A Response to Tocqueville's Challenge* (Ann Arbor: 1997).

9. One of Smith's abiding laments was that for a typical laborer, it was becoming increasingly true that "their work through half the week is sufficient to maintain them, and through want of education they have no amusement for the other but riot and debauchery" (LJW 330).

10. For comparison, see F. A. Hayek, *Constitution of Liberty* (Chicago: 1960), p. 129.

11. I do not pretend to any expertise regarding Stoic philosophy, but my colleague Dan Russell discusses the Stoic view of disordered emotions, and why the way to deal with disorder is to get rid of emotions altogether, in sections 2 and 3 of "Why the Stoics Think There Is No Right Way to Grieve," http://www.danielcrussell.com/faculty/videos/169. Stretching the point even further, we might suppose that Rousseau's "noble savage" characteristically "lives in himself; a man of society always out of himself cannot live but in the opinion of others." (This is Smith's translation, from his 1755 *Edinburgh Review* of Rousseau's *Discourse on the Origin of Inequality*.) Rousseau's noble savage, however, is not a paragon of Stoic indifference; neither is it Smith's ideal. Smith, siding with the Stoics, treats the prior stage of socialization as a necessary stage through which maturing humans must pass in order to emerge as genuine grown-up members of society. (It is tempting to read this as hinting at Nietzsche: the will to power drives a person to transcend the ideal types of unselfconscious "beast" on one hand and "ascetic priest" on the other, emerging from the process as a turned-inward exemplar of self-control.)

12. Had Smith seen automation coming, he might have worried less about drowsiness, because he would have foreseen that the "drowsy" jobs are the ones that automation would eliminate.

13. E. G. West, "Adam Smith and Alienation: A Rejoinder," *Oxford Economic Papers* 27 (1975), pp. 295–301, at p. 296.

14. Ibid., p. 297.

15. Ibid., p. 298.

16. Ibid., p. 298.

17. I thank Dan Brudney (but don't hold him responsible) for the thought that "[f]rom each according to ability to each according to need" is not a principle of distribution but a description of how an economy ideally would work. People produce X and bring it to market because X is the best they have within them. They consume as necessary to sustain their best work. But communism is Marx's *ideal* theory; socialism is his nonideal theory. The *ideal* Marx is uninterested in

the size of shares because, ideally, goods are no longer scarce, so shares are immaterial.

Contrast this with *nonideal* Marx, and with Rawls. Rawlsian ideal justice is very much about the size of shares; moreover, it aggressively denies that share size should be proportional to contribution. Nonideal Marx, circa 1844, was incensed about workers getting less than they deserve, which sounds like a concern about distributive justice. And yet, Rawls's question of whether workers can accept their *share* is not Marx's question. The nonidealist Marx's question is whether workers can accept how their *productivity* is treated.

18. James R. Otteson, *Adam Smith's Marketplace of Life* (New York: 2002), p. 207.

19. Thus, Smith acknowledges various circumstances in the "earliest period of society" conspired to make infanticide pardonable, but it was condoned in the latter ages of ancient Greece as well, even by philosophers such as Plato and Aristotle, for no better reason than because it was "commonly done." A brooding Smith worries that "[w]hen custom can give sanction to so dreadful a violation of humanity, we may well imagine there is scarce any particular practice so gross which it cannot authorize" (TMS V.2.15).

20. Smith does not lament that commercial society is disordered and chaotic (unproblematic in and of itself) so much as "that the soul of the commercial man replicates this chaotic disorder" (Hanley, *Adam Smith*, p. 39).

21. Otteson, *Adam Smith's Marketplace*, p. 298. See also Hanley, *Adam Smith*, p. 137.

22. In particular, we are prone to a slide from wanting people to be *able* to depend on us to wanting people to *need* us. People of true benevolence, though, transcend needing to be needed and instead aim to help people to be independent. We succeed as parents, teachers, or investors by making ourselves dispensable, and ultimately less visible. Our ultimate consolation, when we look in the mirror, is that we will know we were there when it counted.

23. Otteson (*Adam Smith's Marketplace*, chap. 4) addresses that problem squarely; Smith's impartial spectator would see a prudent partiality toward oneself as having a prominent place in a constellation of virtues. See also Leonidas Montes, *Adam Smith in Context* (New York: 2004), chap. 2.

24. I owe the point to a discussion with Geoff Brennan.

25. The desire to be proper objects of esteem may be "the strongest of all our desires" and for good reason. Nowadays, our bodily needs are easily met, whereas the esteem of our peers is a hard-fought daily battle that on any given day may hold the key to our fate.

26. Hanley, *Adam Smith*, p. 118.

27. For a sober yet reasonably optimistic discussion of corrupting elements in market society, see chap. 7 of Charles Griswold, *Adam Smith and the Virtues of Enlightenment* (New York: 1999).

28. Although this does not posit self-love as primary, it does invite reflection on the fragility of all motivations, self-love and benevolence included. Benevolence needs nurturing. One way to nurture it is to avoid leaning too hard on it, and celebrate when it culminates in flourishing rather than self-sacrifice. To Smith, self-love likewise needs nurturing, and our failure to keep our true interest

in focus is lamentably common. See David Schmidtz, "Reasons for Altruism," in *Person, Polis, Planet* (New York: 2008), pp. 62–77.

BIBLIOGRAPHIC ESSAY

The books cited by Fleischacker, Griswold, Hanley, Montes, and Otteson are important contributions to a notable recent surge of interest in Adam Smith in particular and Scottish Enlightenment philosophy in general. On the more general topic, important works include Michael Gill, *The British Moralists on Human Nature and the Birth of Secular Ethics* (Cambridge: 2006), and Knud Haakonssen, *Natural Law and Moral Philosophy: From Grotius to the Scottish Enlightenment* (Cambridge: 1996).

PART III

Smith and Economics

14

ADAM SMITH AND MODERN ECONOMICS

Agnar Sandmo

In his 1776 book *An Inquiry into the Nature and Causes of the Wealth of Nations* (WN), Adam Smith created an agenda for economic theory whose outline can still be seen in the structure of modern economics. Some central areas in which this is particularly true are his theory of price formation, his ideas about the relationship between the market economy and the public interest, his reflections on the role of the state, and his analysis of the sources of economic growth. The present essay describes the core of his contributions to these areas and relates them to the state of economics as it has developed in particular over the past fifty years.

PRICE THEORY

Smith begins his analysis of the determination of the relative prices of goods and services with a story of price formation in a primitive society of hunters. The point of the example was obviously not to present a theory that could immediately be applied to contemporary economic conditions, but to construct a pedagogical case that would lead the reader to understand more complicated issues. In this society hunters aim to kill beavers and deer, both of which are desired by consumers. If it takes twice as many hours to kill a beaver than to kill a deer, it follows, Smith argues, that the price of a beaver will be twice that of a deer. Since the prices are determined exclusively by the labor time of the hunters, this is a clear and simple illustration of what became known as the labor theory of value.

The modern reader, accustomed to think of price formation in terms of the joint effects of supply and demand, may be puzzled by the neglect of the demand side in this example. Is demand irrelevant for the understanding of prices? In fact, demand does play a role in the determination of the market outcome, but given the simple assumptions made about costs, the role of demand is solely that of determining quantities, that is, the number of beavers and deer that are actually caught and brought to the market. Costs determine prices, demand determines quantities.

Smith generalized the example to the case where costs have more components than simply labor time. If costs also include necessary expenditure on weapons and the possible costs related to the use of the land, the total costs of production have three components that reflect the payment to the three factors of production, labor, capital, and land. When all three factors earn their normal reward, this defines the "natural price" of the commodity in question. With this extension, Smith's original labor theory of value became a more general cost of production theory of value. However, in the real world the actual market price may deviate from the natural price, as in his celebrated example of a public mourning. The death of a king increases the demand for black cloth, but since the supply of cloth in the short run is a given quantity, the effect of the rise in demand is to push up the price. In the longer run, the fact that the market price is above the natural price may lead to the entry of additional suppliers who are attracted to the market by the prospect of earning more than the normal reward to their resources. Moreover, once the period of public mourning has come to an end, demand diminishes and the price falls back to its normal level. This is the normal operation of a free market. However, there are other reasons why the market price may stay above its normal level, the most important of which is a public monopoly that has been established because the government has combined the privilege of exclusive rights of production with the prohibition of entry by other firms. While the competitive price—the price under "the system of perfect liberty" (WN I.vii.30)—is "the lowest which the sellers can commonly afford to take, and at the same time continue their business," the monopoly price is "the highest that can be squeezed out of the buyers, or which, it is supposed, they will consent to give" (WN I.vii.27). To a large extent, Smith's reasoning is well in line with modern analysis of competition and monopoly. The distinction between the natural and market price corresponds to the modern distinction between the long-run and short-run equilibrium price under perfect competition, where the cost-based constancy of the long-run equilibrium price is the result of the twin assumptions of constant returns to scale for the industry as a whole and free entry.[1] Thus, the modern notion of the long-run equilibrium price is essentially equivalent to Smith's natural price, and deviations of the market price from its long-run equilibrium are explained by the modern economist in terms that are essentially similar to Smith's discussion of the example of public mourning.

But there are also aspects of Smith's analysis that are unsatisfactory. His characterization of the equilibrium price under monopoly is loose and suffers from the lack of an explicit analysis of profit maximization. There is also a notable lack of a general equilibrium perspective when he seems to consider the natural price as caused by the normal rewards to the factors of production instead of—as in modern theory—regarding both commodity and factor prices as being jointly determined by preferences, technology, and market structure.

The system of perfect liberty and monopoly are the limiting cases of competition. What about the cases in between, referred to by later economists as imperfect competition? On this point, there is some ambivalence in Smith's writing. On the one hand, he sometimes expresses himself as if effective competition simply means the absence of monopoly, and the crucial condition for the existence of effective competition is free entry. If an existing monopoly position can be challenged by new entrants it is simply not viable, and competition will reign in the long run. But he also admits that even a fairly large number of producers may not be a guarantee of effective competition. A famous passage in the *Wealth of Nations* argues that "people of the same trade seldom meet together, even for merriment and diversion, but the conversation ends in a conspiracy against the publick, or in some contrivance to raise prices"

(WN I.x.c.27). The fundamental insight that producers have individual incentives to deviate from the competitive conditions for their own benefit underlies modern ideas of competition policy, designed to uphold effective competition in the interests of society as a whole.

What is it that makes such conspiracies against the public likely to occur? Smith points to the role played by the number of producers, and his argument, remarkably, is not the simple and mechanistic one that as the number of producers grows large, each of them will take the market price as given. If trade in a town is divided between two grocers instead of being in the hands of just one, this will make both of them sell cheaper. Suppose now that it is divided between twenty. Then "their competition would be just so much the greater, and their *chance of combining together*, in order to raise the price, so much the less" (WN II.v.7, emphasis added). This line of analysis bears a striking resemblance to the modern game-theoretic analysis of the core that points out that as the number of competitors increases, the difficulty of forming coalitions that cannot be challenged by other coalitions increases until the only equilibrium outcome that remains is that of the competitive equilibrium. Thus, Smith's theoretical insight was confirmed by the analysis of mathematical economists and game theorists during the 1960s and 1970s.[2]

THE INVISIBLE HAND

Modern economics can be thought of as divided into two main branches, positive and normative economics, the former being concerned with descriptive analysis of how the economy works, the latter with evaluation of its performance. Smith's theory of competition as outlined above clearly belongs to the branch of positive economics. Equally clearly, the most famous of all his ideas, his theory of the invisible hand, belongs to normative economics. His central statement of the idea is the following:

> [E]very individual necessarily labours to render the annual revenue of society as great as he can. He generally, indeed, neither intends to

promote the publick interest, nor knows how much he is promoting it. . . . [H]e intends only his own gain, and he is in this, as in many other cases, led by an invisible hand to promote an end which was no part of his intention. Nor is it always the worse for society that it was no part of it. By pursuing his own interest he frequently promotes that of the society more effectually than when he really intends to promote it. (WN IV.ii.9)

The context in which this quotation appears has caused some difficulties to interpreters of Smith who are sympathetic to the thought that the private pursuit of self-interest is beneficial to society.[3] In fact, the passage appears not as part of a general discourse on the benefits of markets but in a much more specific discussion of the benefits of home versus foreign investment. However, there are in fact a number of similar statements in the *Wealth of Nations* that justify the common interpretation that Smith thought that markets and competition were beneficial to the public interest. But this proposition also raises a number of questions. One concerns the nature of the competition that is supposed to have these beneficial effects. Another is the more precise meaning to be attached to the concept of the public interest in order for the statement to be meaningful. These questions are so central for one's understanding of the market economy that they have engaged the efforts of theoretical economists ever since.

Regarding the nature of competition it seems clear that Smith's minimum requirement for markets to work in the public interest was the absence of monopoly. This again was based on the assumption of free entry, meaning that anyone could establish a business if a particular industry were to offer a more than normal return on the resources invested. But as the example of the number of grocers in a town shows, competition works better if there are many producers. This provides a check to private efforts to limit competition, and the benefits of the system of perfect liberty may accordingly be realized.

A more intriguing question is raised by Smith's notion of the public interest. His claim is that private entrepreneurs who move their capital from declining to expanding industries act in the interests of society. But this process inevitably means that some individuals, for example, the workers in the declining industries, lose while others gain. How can we decide whether there is a net gain to society? In his invisible hand statement, Smith refers to the annual revenue of society or the national income, as we would say today. This indicates that society gains if the winners in the process of structural change gain more that the losers lose. But this is not an entirely convincing argument. Suppose that those who gain are already well off while the losers live in poverty. Would we not in this case hesitate to say that the invisible hand of the market works in the interests of society? And if so, what principles should guide our aggregation of individual interests into a measure of the interest of society as a whole?[4]

There are several indications in the text of the *Wealth of Nations* that Smith would indeed attach greater weight to the losses of the poor than to the gains of the rich. A reasonable interpretation of his postulate that competition works in the interests of society is that in the long run, everyone would benefit from living in a wealthy society. This interpretation receives support from another use that Smith makes of the metaphor of the invisible hand. This occurs in the other of his two major works, *The Theory of Moral Sentiments* (TMS), which was first published in 1759. There he makes the claim that the rich, without intending to do so, promote the interests of the poor. Although the sole end of the rich in employing the poor "[is] the gratification of their own vain and insatiable desires, they divide with the poor the produce of all their improvements. They are led by an invisible hand to make nearly the same distribution of the necessaries of life, which would have been made, had the earth been divided into equal portions among all its inhabitants, and thus without intending it, without knowing it, advance the interest of the society" (TMS IV.1.10). Here the term "the interest of society" obviously refers to all of its members, rich and poor included. The reference to the equal proportions of the earth is not easy to interpret, but in any case the claim is clearly that the rich provide for the necessaries of life that the poor need, although the result is not that there is any complete equalization of the standard of living.

The reasonable conclusion to draw from Smith's references to the invisible hand as well as from other related passages in his books is that the market economy tends to generate a maximum of "the general revenue of society" or the national income. However, there is no guarantee that the distribution of this income will turn out to be fair or equitable, even if one admits that fair and equitable are concepts of which there are no generally accepted definitions.

With his notion of the invisible hand Adam Smith may be regarded as having founded modern normative economics. The claim that the market mechanism tended to promote the public interest led later generations of economists to explore both the concept of competitive markets and measures of the public interest in order to discover the conditions under which Smith's claim could be justified in more precise analytical terms. The part of economic theory that embodies the results of these explorations is known as welfare economics, and the core of the theory is the establishment of an equivalence between a competitive equilibrium and what is known as a Pareto optimum. A competitive equilibrium is a situation where all firms and consumers take prices as given in the market and where these prices have adjusted so as to bring about equality between demand and supply in all markets. A Pareto optimum—named after the Italian economist Vilfredo Pareto—is essentially a situation where there is no waste in the economy: it is impossible to improve the outcome for one individual without making somebody else worse off. Consequently, the conclusion is that the market economy under ideal conditions generates a situation where there is no waste; society's resources are used in an efficient manner.

How are we to judge this conclusion seen in the light of Smith's original statement? On the one hand it marks the results of careful theoretical research that resolves the ambiguities contained in the *Wealth of Nations* regarding the concepts of competition and the public interest. On the other hand, it may come as a disappointment to those who have found inspiration in Smith's vision of the market economy as a system working for the common good. For Smith's "system of perfect liberty" modern theorists have substituted a notion of perfect competition that is so abstract and stylized that it is hardly recognizable as a representation of actual markets.[5] And instead of the public interest they have introduced the concept of Pareto optimality that avoids the troublesome aggregation of individual interests but at the cost that hardly any institutional or political reform can unequivocally be said to be in the interest of society as a whole.

However, when it comes to the practical applications of economic theory to issues of economic policy, many modern economists would probably adopt a position that is in fact not very far from that of Smith. While acknowledging the result of economic theory that efficiency will result only when competition is "perfect," they would be inclined to believe that actual markets, if reasonably free from unwarranted public regulations and private restraints on competition, might in fact offer good approximations to the theoretical ideal. And regarding the public interest, many would subscribe to the opinion that such a system of free markets would be the best guarantee for an economic and social development that in the long run would benefit all classes in society. They would probably also emphasize that this conclusion hinges not on the analysis of the market system alone but also on the nature of the coexistence between markets and government. This is another topic to which Smith contributed important insights.

THE ROLE OF THE STATE

For a long time a common interpretation of Adam Smith's economics was that he was a propagandist for laissez-faire, that is, for the view that the best policy was to leave the economy to the free play of market forces. It also seemed to follow from this interpretation that the state—at least with respect to its role in the economy—should be as small as possible. To some extent, this reading of the *Wealth of Nations* was inspired by Smith's polemics against the contemporary view of economic policy, which he called mercantilism and which was based on detailed economic regulation of the market mechanism. However, when one takes a broader view of his work and distinguishes between his polemics and his theoretical perspectives on the relationship between markets and government, between the roles of the private and public sectors, a more balanced view emerges.

One important role of the government, according to Smith, was to provide the institutional framework required for competitive markets to function. A legal system that provided a secure framework for private contracts was essential for the market system to work efficiently. More broadly, the role of the state was to protect the members of society, both as participants in market transactions and in their private lives, from violence and invasion from other societies and oppression by other members of society. As we have seen, Smith also acknowledged that, although well-functioning markets were good for society, individual producers might well find it in their individual interests to limit competition by entering into "conspiracies against the publick." Therefore, an important role for government was to design an economic system that as far as possible discouraged the creation of private cartels and monopolies.

A further role of the state is to provide goods and services for which the market system does not provide the right incentives for private producers to supply them. Such goods are known in modern economics as public goods, and in regard to these Adam Smith argues that the role of the state consists in "erecting and maintaining certain publick works and certain publick institutions, which it can never be for the interest of any individual, or small number of individuals, to erect and maintain; because the profit would never repay the expence to any individual or small number of individuals, though it may frequently do much more than repay it to a great society" (WN IV.ix.51). Just as in the modern theory of public goods, Smith's emphasis is on the failure of private incentives when it comes to providing public goods at the efficient level.[6] The individual producer of a public good will compare his private cost with his private benefit, but he does not take into account the benefits that accrue to other individuals; hence he underestimates the total benefit to society, and too little of these goods will be provided in a pure market economy. In the language of modern economics these are cases of market failure. The economic agent that can overcome these failures is the government; thus we are presented with another positive argument for the role of the state in the economic system. It is together with a well-functioning state that the case for a competitive market system is strongest. Smith also provides a number of examples from different areas of the economy that illustrate the application of this general principle.

Another contribution that Smith makes to the economics of the public sector comes in his analysis of taxation. Taxes are required to finance the provision of public goods and services. But the form of taxation is a matter for public concern since taxes can be more or less harmful for the efficient performance of the private sector. In the design of the overall system of taxation, Smith argues, account should be taken of some general principles that relate to both the equity and efficiency of taxation. Regarding equity he argues that "[t]he subjects of every state ought to contribute towards the support of the government, as nearly as possible, in proportion to their respective abilities; that is, in proportion to the revenue which they respectively enjoy under the protection of the state" (WN V.ii.b.3). While later economists drew a distinction between taxation according to ability to pay and to benefits received, in Adam Smith's thought there appears to be no conflict between the two principles. The individual's income is a measure both of his ability to pay taxes and of the benefits that he receives from the government. The larger his income, the greater the benefits that he receives from a safe environment for his economic activities.

Regarding the efficiency of the tax system, Smith's main proposition is that "every tax ought to be so contrived as both to take out and to keep out of the pockets of the people as little as possible, over and above what it brings into the publick treasury of the state" (WN V.ii.b.6). What is the difference between the amount of taxes paid by the people and that received by the state? Smith's statement can be given both a narrow and a broad interpretation. In the narrow interpretation, the difference is simply the costs of tax collection, such as the salaries of the tax inspectors. But in a broader perspective, the costs of taxation should also be taken to include the inefficiencies that arise in the private sector because taxes have adverse effects on individual incentives to work, save and invest. It is clear from the context that Smith had the broader interpretation in mind, and that his thoughts regarding these issues therefore point forward to modern discussions of the social costs of taxation where the cost of these inefficiencies are taken into account in cost-benefit analysis of public projects.

THE ECONOMIC SYSTEM AS AN ENGINE OF GROWTH

The very title of the *Wealth of Nations* suggests that the main topic of the book is economic growth. But for the modern economist who has been taught economic growth in terms of a series of specialized models of an expanding economy, reading the book may actually be a puzzling experience, since he may easily conclude that there are hardly any chapters that are explicitly concerned with economic growth, at least not according to modern notions of what growth is about.

However, the modern reader has to adopt a different perspective on growth than the one he has been taught in current textbooks, in which economic growth is typically studied in terms of a few macroeconomic aggregates such as saving, investment, and technical progress, and with few references to markets and institutions.[7] Smith does acknowledge the importance of capital accumulation for economic progress. But it must also be kept in mind that he saw his theory of the market mechanism and the invisible hand as an integral part of a theory of social and economic progress. Institutional and political reforms that made markets function more efficiently meant that the return on capital investment for society as a whole would become higher; consequently, national income would expand. Well-functioning markets, free international trade, and a wisely designed public sector were all elements that would contribute to economic growth. However, in the long run there must clearly be a limit to how much growth can be achieved through institutional and political reform without increasing the amount of productive resources in the economy.

In a prominent place in the introductory chapter of the *Wealth of Nations* Smith discusses the division of labor, and the example that he uses for this purpose is that of a pin factory. The production of a pin is a complicated task, and a single worker with little experience would find it a demanding task to produce a single pin in the course of a day's work. But in the pin factory where the production of pins has been broken down into a number of separate operations, specialized workers are able to produce several thousand times as many pins as an individual worker could do if operating on his own. So division of labor is an important source of productivity growth and economic development.

The question then becomes, what determines the extent of division of labor? Smith's famous answer was that the division of labor is determined by the extent of the market. In the thinly populated regions of the Scottish highlands, every farmer has to be his own slaughterer, baker, and blacksmith. With increasing density of population the conditions for division of labor improve, and society is able to reap the benefits from the use of more efficient technologies. This theory of economic progress also throws an interesting light on Smith's price theory. As noted above, this was essentially a cost theory; natural prices were determined by the cost of production, independent of demand. But the theory has to be modified to take account of the gains from the division of labor. An expanding market will improve the scope for specialization in industrial production, so that there is a feedback on costs from the demand side. Production will expand, and goods—especially industrial products—can be provided at lower prices.

This is of course not the whole story of economic growth, according to Smith. Workers, both in pin factories and in other sectors of the economy, cannot exploit more specialized technologies without having more real capital available to assist them. The source of real capital accumulation is individual saving. Savers will both invest in real capital on their own and lend to others who in turn will make capital investments. Together with population growth, the accumulation of capital leads to more division of labor and thereby to improved productivity and increasing prosperity.

PERSPECTIVES

In 1971 Kenneth Boulding posed the interesting question, "After Samuelson, who needs Adam Smith?"[8] No doubt, some will find the question provocative because it seems obvious to them that we need to be acquainted with the work of one of the greatest economists in history, just like philosophers need to study the work of Smith's great contemporary and friend David Hume. Others may react differently, arguing that all that is of lasting value in Smith's work has been incorporated into modern economics, which—unlike philosophy—is a cumulative science, built up by gradually substituting better theories and more substantive empirical knowledge for the less solid insights of the economists of earlier centuries. Who is right?

It is impossible to argue that there is not much truth in the view of economics as a cumulative science. Moreover, it is a fact of life that there are many contemporary economists who do excellent work in research, teaching, public administration, and private business with only a very superficial knowledge of the contributions of Adam Smith and the other great figures in the history of economics. Indeed, the time may come when modern economists no longer have much firsthand acquaintance with the work of Paul Samuelson, a giant of economics in the twentieth century, whom Boulding used as the embodiment of modern economics as seen from the perspective of 1971. For someone who aspires to be a leading economist in the twenty-first century or to acquire a good understanding of the frontiers of economic knowledge, reading Adam Smith is no substitute for studying contemporary textbooks and journal articles. But in the economic theory of consumption, goods are classified as substitutes and complements; two goods are complements if the consumption of one increases the benefits from consuming the other. Perhaps this is a fruitful way to regard the study of the history of economic thought in general and Adam Smith in particular: it increases the benefits from learning modern economics.

These increased benefits are of several kinds. On the one hand, it is instructive to see how Smith develops concepts and ideas that still form central elements of contemporary economics. In witnessing this early struggle to formulate a consistent theoretical framework for the study of economic life, we learn how ideas and abstractions that we now take for granted were once problems at the research frontier of economics.

During the almost two and a half centuries that have passed since the publication of the *Wealth of Nations*, economics has become a very different discipline. Theories of markets and competition, of the invisible hand and economic growth have been reformulated in terms of mathematical models, and the study of empirical data utilizes advanced statistical methods. A modern economist who wishes to be at the top of his subject needs to master the new analytical tools. But the mastery of techniques is not sufficient to make a good economist. He or she must also be able to develop a more intuitive grasp of the connection between the abstract models and the real economy. In this respect Adam Smith is still a good role model. Of course, the society that was his frame of reference is very different from today's world. But his combination of theoretical analysis and broad perspectives on history, institutions, and politics is still capable of inspiring his colleagues in the twenty-first century.

NOTES

1. The distinction between the short-run and long-run equilibrium price under perfect competition received its first analytical formulation by Knut Wicksell in a book published in Swedish in 1901; this has been translated as *Lectures on Political Economy, Vol. 1: General Theory* (London: 1934). The essence of his theory can be found in any modern textbook on microeconomic theory.

2. A pioneering contribution was that by Gerard Debreu and Herbert Scarf, "A Limit Theorem on the Core of an Economy," *International Economic Review* 4 (1963), pp. 235–46. The essential idea can also be found, however, in F. Y. Edgeworth, *Mathematical Psychics* (London: 1881).

3. See Sandmo, *Economics Evolving* (Princeton: 2011), chap. 3, for a discussion of alternative interpretations and further references.

4. In modern welfare economics, this aggregation takes place through the theoretical notion of a social welfare function that weighs the utility functions of individuals together to arrive at a measure of aggregate welfare. A special case

of this is utilitarianism, where social welfare is taken to be the sum of individual utilities. But this analytical approach was foreign to Smith's way of thinking.

5. This model of the competitive economy is usually referred to as the Arrow-Debreu model after its two originators. For a compact statement of it, see Gerard Debreu, *Theory of Value* (New York: 1959).

6. The modern theory of public goods was founded by Paul Samuelson in his article "The Pure Theory of Public Expenditure," *Review of Economics and Statistics* 36 (1954), pp. 387–89, which has been a major influence on all later discussions. In this and later contributions, Samuelson emphasizes, just like Smith, the failure of individual incentives to provide public goods at an efficient level.

7. The seminal contribution to modern growth theory is Robert Solow's article, "A Contribution to the Theory of Economic Growth," *Quarterly Journal of Economics* 70 (1956), pp. 65–94. The present discussion should not be interpreted as a criticism of the literature that stems from Solow's work, which has taught us a lot about the process of growth. But formal model building inevitably involves some narrowing of vision, and it is useful to keep in mind the broader view of Adam Smith.

8. Kenneth E. Boulding, "After Samuelson: Who Needs Adam Smith?," *History of Political Economy* 3 (1971), pp. 225–37.

BIBLIOGRAPHIC ESSAY

A broader presentation of Adam Smith's economic theories as well as his views on public policy is contained in Agnar Sandmo, *Economics Evolving. A History of Economic Thought* (Princeton: 2011). While Smith for a long time was regarded as an unqualified spokesman for market liberalism, this view of him has in more recent times been much modified. The modern reevaluation of Smith's and the other classical economists' opinions regarding economic policy and the role of government in a market economy began with the book by Lionel Robbins, *The Theory of Economic Policy in English Classical Political Economy* (London: 1952). A more recent study is Emma Rothschild, *Economic Sentiments: Adam Smith, Condorcet, and the Enlightenment* (Cambridge: 2001). This book discusses Smith's theories as part of the general body of thought in the period of the Enlightenment. Amartya Sen's "Uses and Abuses of Adam Smith," *History of Political Economy* 43 (2011), pp. 257–71, considers both Smith's economics and his wider views on social institutions and justice.

The Glasgow Bicentenary Edition of the *Wealth of Nations* includes a very informative introduction by the editors Richard H. Campbell and Andrew S. Skinner. A companion volume of articles on Smith's economics is Thomas Wilson and Skinner, eds., *The Market and the State: Essays in Honour of Adam Smith* (Oxford: 1976). This contains essays on various aspects of Smith's economic thought, including some that have not been touched upon in the present essay. Another volume, Skinner and Wilson, eds., *Essays on Adam Smith* (Oxford: 1975), also includes some articles on economics in addition to contributions on more philosophical topics.

ADAM SMITH AND THE HISTORY OF ECONOMIC THOUGHT: THE CASE OF BANKING

Maria Pia Paganelli

Adam Smith's analysis of banking is often studied as part of the history of banking in Scotland, of free banking, or of the Real Bill doctrine debate[1]—topics that are not part of traditional mainstream economic doctrines. It is seldom center stage in the Smith scholarship. Banking in Smith's thought is also mentioned, but not generally analyzed in depth, in Smith's analysis of the relation between free market and state intervention.[2] Smith believes in the free market, but he also supports banking regulations that would seem to violate that same "natural liberty" associated with free markets.

I suggest that there is more in Smith's analysis of banking than a historical account of free banking in Scotland and than a contribution to a technical issue of economic theory. When historians of economics look at Smith on banking and focus only on the historical or technical aspects of Smith, they often narrow the focus, often narrowing (or losing) the picture of the bigger project Smith seems to envision, generating what seem like contradictions in Smith's thought. I suggest instead that Smith's analysis of banking is a reflection of Smith's bigger picture of society[3]—the banking systems that Smith describes, like markets, through a complex web of relationships, create efficiency and are able to develop and support moral social life—resolving, at least in part, some of the tensions presented by the literature regarding otherwise puzzling calls for regulations and state interventions in an economy that should be self-regulating instead.[4]

According to Smith banks should be allowed to issue their own money and compete in a minimally regulated environment. On the one hand, competition, including the possibility of bank failures, generates discipline, and discipline generates prudent behavior. On the other hand, competition in the banking sector is generated and maintained by prudent behavior. The prudent behavior of morally responsible banks is rewarded with economic success and supports the economic and moral development of society; and the economic success of banks allows for morals to flourish.

In recent years there have been an increasing number of calls for a more integrated view of economics in general,[5] and of Adam Smith in particular.[6] Markets are powerful promoters of social well-being, but they cannot be conceived outside their legal and moral framework. Laws and regulations, if enlightened and designed with communal well-being in mind (a heroic assumption, granted, as Smith was well aware), enhance the powers of the market. If not, they can destroy the benefits originating from the market. Banking is, like any other part of Smith's analysis, an integral part of a complex web of entangled relationships among the economy, the polity, laws, and morals—an example of the complexity of the natural system of liberty that promotes prosperity and the development of moral, free, and responsible individuals. And if banking is an example of how symbiotic individuals, society, morals, the market, and its legal framework are for Smith, state regulation and self-regulation may no longer be in contradiction.

If we see that for Smith wealth develops in conjunction with morals and justice, we can appreciate his commitment to both free banking and banking regulations. Given the multiplicity of individuals in society, it is possible that some have conflicting goals. As a result there will be times when some individuals may benefit at the expense of the majority of members of their communities, and other times when the majority of members of a community may benefit at the expense of some minority of individuals.[7] In cases where there are conflicting interests, Smith tends to side with the one that makes the majority of the individuals better off. David Levy describes Smith as a median utilitarian, that is to say that one of Smith's major concerns is the well-being of the median, of the majority of the population.[8]

Smith favors the formal and informal institutional arrangements that align the interest of individuals with the interest of society and that allow society to prosper peacefully and ethically. Competition, morals, the rule of law, and, occasionally, regulation are part of these formal and informal institutional arrangements. In this light, we may understand Smith's position on banking. The competition of free banking enhances the majority of the people both materially and morally, and if some regulations are needed to support the smooth functioning of the banking system, those regulations are welcomed. On the other hand, if some banking regulations favor some at the expense of the majority, therefore inhibiting material growth and incentivizing immoral behaviors, those regulations are, in Smith's view, to be criticized and hopefully avoided. Using the vision that historians of economics recognize in Smith also for understanding Smith's views of banks may help us not only to use a more coherent method of analysis of Smith, but also to decrease some of the alleged contradictions attributed to Smith.

SMITH AND BANKING

The banking system that Smith describes is a commodity money system, different from the fiat money system we have today. Commodity money is a form of money that has an alternative use. Gold and silver can be used as money, as well as, say, jewelry. Fiat money is instead a form of money without an alternative use. A banknote that one has in the wallet today can be used only as money: it does not have any alternative use. In a commodity money system, like the one that Smith describes, paper money can circulate in place of gold and silver money. But paper money can be redeemed for gold and silver on demand, meaning that a holder of a paper note can go to a bank and ask to exchange that note for gold and silver. With fiat money, this is not possible. If one goes to a bank and asks to exchange a banknote for something else, one would get more banknotes only. While today only one bank, usually the central bank of a country, can issue money, in Smith's Scotland, the banking system consisted of several competing banks, each issuing its own notes: "It is chiefly by discounting bills of exchange, that is, by advancing money upon them before they are due, that the greater part of banks and bankers issue their promissory notes" (WN II.ii.43) and "[by] invent[ing] . . . another method of issuing their promissory notes; by granting, what they call, cash accounts, that is by giving credit to the extent of a certain sum . . . to any individual who could procure two persons of undoubted credit and good landed estate to become surety for him, that whatever money should be advanced to him, within the sum for which the credit had been given, should be repaid upon demand, together with the legal interest" (WN II.ii.44). In stark contrast to David Hume, who fears inflation and wishes the abolition of banks and paper money,[9] Smith sees banks and banking as facilitators of economic development, and therefore of the material well-being of the majority of people, while at the same time improving the moral behavior of individuals by encouraging individual responsibility. We could speculate that Smith may actually care more about presenting this vision than a meticulous description of reality:[10] Smith's analysis of the Scottish banking system seems to have some elements that are historically quite accurate,[11] but others that are not, despite Smith's familiarity with the banking system that he describes.[12]

Smith tells us that he favors banking because of its role in the development of Scotland: "That the trade and industry of Scotland . . . have increased considerably during this period, and that the banks have contributed a good deal to this increase, cannot be doubted" (WN II.ii.41). But Smith's praises are qualified. It is judicious banking that is beneficial. He repeats the word several times in a few pages. It is the "judicious operations of banking" that contribute to popular well-being and align the self-interest of the bankers and of the merchants with society's benefits. "The *judicious* operations of banking enable [a dealer] to convert his dead stock into active and productive stock; into materials to work upon, into tools to work with, and into provisions and subsistence to work for; into stock which produces something both to himself and to his country"

(WN II.ii.86, emphasis added). It is the *"judicious* operations of banking" that increase productivity by, figuratively, freeing some fertile fields, previously used as highways to transport goods, by moving the highways from the ground to the air:

> It is not by augmenting the capital of the country, but by rendering a greater part of that capital active and productive than would otherwise be so, that the most *judicious* operations of banking can increase the industry of the country. . . . That part of his capital which a dealer is obliged to keep by him unemployed, and in ready money for answering occasional demands, is so much dead stock, which . . . produces nothing either to him or his country. . . . The *judicious* operations of banking, by substituting paper in the room of a great part of this gold and silver, enables the country to convert a great part of this dead stock into active and productive stock. . . . The gold and silver money which circulated in any country may very properly be compared to a highway, which, while it circulates and carries to market all the grass and corn of the country, produces itself not a single pile of either. The *judicious* operations of banking, by proving, if I may be allowed so violent a metaphor, a sort of wagon-way through the air; enables the country to convert, as it were, a great part of its highways into good pastures and corn fields, and thereby to increase very considerably the annual produce of its land and labour. (WN II.ii.86, emphasis added)

Banks, *judicious* banks that is, provide a useful service to the community by creating credit and using fractional reserves. Gold and silver do not have to be hoarded or used as coins to transact. Paper credit and paper notes can be used as money at home, allowing gold and silver to be invested abroad, where paper money cannot go as easily. For Smith, therefore, judicious banks should be supported.

That said, we cannot assume that bankers are moved by public spirit rather than self-interest. And indeed Smith does not make that move. For Smith bankers are moved by their self-interest. But their self-interest aligns with the interest of the community and with morality—at least in the long run. If banking is left as a competitive industry, markets will do their work of channeling self-interest in the direction of virtuous responsibility and the community's interest through competition.

For Smith, borrowers have the tendency to overborrow as they overestimate their probability of success because of the natural overconfidence in one's good fortune that any man in reasonable good health has. They also tend to like promissory notes (credit) more than loans in precious metals because the notes free idle capital, and because they can pay back a little at a time, while regular loans require full payment at the end of the loan's term. For Smith, bankers, inexperienced bankers at least (see below), have incentives to overissue paper money (promissory notes and other circulating lending instruments) because they gain from the interest on the notes. The interest on the notes is revenue to the bank. The more notes issued, the more interest collected, the more revenue generated, and allegedly the higher the profits for the bank. If banks discount bills of exchange with promissory notes rather than with gold and silver, they can make even more profit (WN II.ii.43). Creditors, therefore, are tempted to ask for overissuing of credit, and banks are tempted to overissue credit.

There is therefore a tendency to overissue paper and cause crises. But if a bank overissues, for whatever reason, that bank not only will fail to make profits, but may actually fail. If a bank overissues, the extra notes will be considered as extra notes in the hands of the note holder. Rather than holding paper money, the merchant has incentives to go to the bank and redeem the paper money for specie and send that specie abroad for a more fruitful investment. The bank is under obligation to pay on demand, and it will have to, unless it is willing to face a bank run, which would mean the potential for bankruptcy (WN II.ii.48). To pay for the incoming notes the bank needs specie. If it overissues, that specie will not be readily available. The bank must get specie by borrowing from another bank, or more commonly from London. This is expensive because of the transaction and transportation costs and because often the rate at which it can draw from other local banks and/or London is higher than the interest it receives from its borrowers. Indeed, "[t]he Scotch banks, no doubt, paid all of them very dearly for their own imprudence and inattention" (WN II.ii.56). This can be done on occasion, but not regularly. If it is done regularly, the bank will eventually fold. Indeed that was the case of the Ayr Bank. To avoid losing profits and a bank run, banks learn to decrease the amount issued (WN II.ii.49–56) and learn how to be judicious.

Competition among issuers allows banks, via trial and error, to understand what allows for individual profits and what instead leads to bankruptcy and social distress. It is this learning that characterizes "judicious" banking, and it is the competition among issuers that allows for the development and strengthening of this judiciousness. Smith is also convinced that competition and the risk of failure will (and did) teach bankers individual and social responsibility.[13] Moreover, if something goes wrong, the damage is more limited because each bank is small and its failure has a limited effect (WN II.ii.106).

Once banks understand what they have "not always understood," they will not (and did not) overissue. And because every man is driven by his desire to better his condition, there is no reason to believe that banks will continue to "not attend[] to [their] own particular interest." In fact, Smith also observes, the learning process of banking companies leads them to innovation and to the development of innovative institutions that promote banking stability: the establishment of the Note Exchange is a successful example of private institutions that promote the stability and therefore the long-term development of individual banks, the banking system in general, and the well-being of the community.

The competition generated by a self-regulated banking system, according to Smith, generates incentives to have a successful system of development of individual banks, the community, and individual responsibility. Irresponsible and "greedy" bankers would paint themselves into a corner and face the losses, up to bankruptcy, that the discipline of competition imposes. What Smith favorably describes seems therefore to be a system of incentives generated by competitive forces that promote the development of an ethical system and of a system of justice, based on prudence and judiciousness. The system of credit that the competitive banking system uses, especially regarding cash accounts, utilizes virtue as a signal of creditworthiness. Smith echoes Wallace's claim that "none will give credit but to men of integrity, prudence, and activity, or to men of substance. Here then are natural checks and limits, beyond which credit will not be extended."[14] Chiara Baroni elaborates how Smith sees a "man of credit" as a virtuous man to whom it is worth lending.[15]

Smith had a favorable view of a system of self-regulated banks because its competitive pressures incentivize individuals to act prudently and judiciously so that the banking system can be stable and generate prosperity for the entire community.

SMITH ON BANKING REGULATION

But what about regulation? After all Smith not only lauds free banking but also calls for regulation of it, as we are often reminded by historians of economics.[16] I believe this is consistent with Smith's focus on the well-being of the majority of the individuals, that is, of the community. I show why this may be the case by looking at Smith's reaction to regulation of notes and coins.

Smith favors two regulations of notes: a ban on issuing of small notes, and a ban on the "option clause," a clause that allows temporary suspension of convertibility of notes into specie. In Scotland at the time of the banking boom, there was a chronic lack of specie. The emergence of bank notes may be seen as either an answer to the scarcity of coins, or the cause of the scarcity of coins. Regardless, the lack of small-denomination coins was a problem, especially since wages could not be paid in the absence of coins. Small-denomination notes could substitute for coins, and laborers' wages could be paid in notes.

But, Smith points out,

> [w]here the issuing of bank notes for very small sums is allowed and commonly practiced, many mean people are both enabled and encouraged to become bankers. A person whose promissory note for five pounds, or even for twenty shillings, would be rejected by every body, will get it to be received without scruple when it is issued for so small a sum as a sixpence. But the frequent bankruptcies

to which such beggarly bankers must be liable, may occasion a very considerable inconveniency, and sometimes even a great calamity to many poor people who had received their notes in payment. (WN II.ii.90)

Smith therefore advocates banning notes of less than five pounds. This ban would confine notes to transactions between dealers and dealers, and not extend them to transactions between dealers and consumers. On top of stability, this policy would, according to Smith, allow the reintroduction of coins (WN II.ii.92).

What is interesting about this call for regulation is the distinction Smith makes between the effects of a failure of a bank that issues large-denomination notes, and those of a failure of a bank that issues small-denomination notes. In the case of large-denomination notes, the negative effects are limited and the positive effects are large. In the case of small-denomination notes, the opposite seems true: if a "beggarly banker" goes bankrupt, the poor may face something like a "great calamity." The protection of the poor, and, given their large numbers in the total population, the consequent protection of the well-being and stability of society, seems therefore to take priority over a minor convenience. Smith himself says that such regulations might seem to be a "violation of natural liberty. But those exertions of natural liberty of a few individuals, which might endanger the security of the whole society, are and ought to be, restrained by the laws of all governments; of the most free as well as of the most despotical. The obligation to build party walls, in order to prevent the communication of fire, is a violation of natural liberty, exactly of the same kind with the regulation of the banking trade which are here proposed" (WN II.ii.94). In addition, small-denomination notes are afflicted with another problem. Especially, but not only, with these small-denomination notes there is a tendency to overissue. Some banks accept small-denomination notes from rival banks. They may collect enough notes and then go to the issuer and ask for their redemption all at once. The issuing bank must have sufficient reserves to honor the notes. If not, the bank risks a run and a failure. This has the beneficial effect of putting a check on the amount issued by each bank and to maintain the appropriate level of reserves. But it is also true that the risk of bankruptcy increases and the consequences may become catastrophic for the poor. To prevent the depletion of their specie reserves, banks start temporarily suspending convertibility.

Banks start issuing notes with an "option clause," meaning that the bank will convert the notes back to precious metals upon demand, but with a delay of up to six months, while paying interest for those months. The clause, when exercised, buys the bank time to acquire the precious metals it does not have in reserve. While prima facie the option clause seems an instrument of stability, in reality it is not: the option clause, temporarily suspending convertibility, generates instability as it dilutes the incentive to restrain overissuing. There is now an increased threat of bank runs. Bankers eventually realize it and wish to eliminate this clause. But "as voluntary agreement to ban the clause was not possible because of the bad feelings amongst the banks, it was decided, independently by the bankers in Edinburgh and Glasgow, that legislation should be sought to put an end to it and to the issue of bank notes of small denomination."[17] In 1765, Parliament passed an act abolishing the option clause and limiting the issuing of notes above the value of one pound. The implication of this was that banks had to pay their notes on demand. But while banning notes below one pound contracted the banking system, banning of the option clause increased the popularity of notes and allowed the system to expand. Smith supports this idea and favors the legal banning of the option clause.

Notice that at the same time as restrictions on the denomination of notes were proposed, the two Scottish public banks petitioned for monopoly privileges and the extinction of the provincial banking companies in exchange for an annual fixed payment to the Trustees for Improving Fisheries and Manufactures. The petition failed, finding a strong opposition among Scottish MPs. And Adam Smith, while supporting the ban on small notes and the option clause, does not support bank privileges in particular and monopoly privileges in general:[18] these regulations favor a few at the expense of the majority of the people in the community.

Smith is indeed ready to criticize most of the other banking regulations because those rules help some at the expense of many. The community not only does not benefit from them, but is actually hurt by them. For example, Smith claims that in North America paper money comes not from banks, but from the government. Government paper is made into legal tender.

> But allowing the colony security to be perfectly good, a hundred pounds payable fifteen years hence, for example, in a country where interest is at six per cent. is worth little more than forty pounds of ready money. To oblige a creditor, therefore, to accept of this as full payment for a debt of a hundred pounds actually paid down in ready money, was an act of such *violent injustice*, as has scarce, perhaps, been attempted by the government of any other country which pretended to be free. It bears the evident marks of having originally been, what the honest and downright Doctor Douglas assures us it was, a scheme of *fraudulent* debtors to cheat their creditors. (WN II.ii.100, emphasis added)

Regulations and institutional settings that favor some at the expense of many—as was also the case, for example, in cases of sovereign coin debasement (see, e.g., WN I.iv.10)—receive strong criticism because they are thought of as immoral and incentivizing immoral behaviors such as, but not limited to, fraud.

So, it is wrong to say that Smith favors regulation of the banking system, just as it is wrong to say that Smith favors an unregulated banking system. He favors regulation in very specific cases: Smith favors self-imposed regulation, emerging from practice and experience, and generating positive effects both in terms of the morality of the incentives generated and in terms of the diffused benefits generated. He also favors government-enforced regulations for cases in which self-regulation is desired but fails to take shape, but with the consciousness that "I have never known much good done by those who affected to trade for the publick good" (WN IV.ii.9).

The two cases of regulation presented above both describe situations in which the government intervenes to regulate something that individuals would want to have regulated because it is to their benefit, but they somehow fail to do it themselves. Banks eventually realized the option clause was not to their benefit and wanted to eliminate it. They were unable to do so on their own because of their history of rivalry. Small notes, similarly, are something individuals would not want, and the benefits of their elimination would spread to everybody in the long run, even if a few individuals would have to bear the cost. Other regulations, which benefit a few at the expense of most, are judged as detrimental for material and moral growth and are not supported.

CONCLUSION

Economists and historians of economic thought generally think of Adam Smith as a well-rounded thinker who cares not just about efficiency but also about justice. Yet, for some topics, they seem to forget their own analysis and concentrate only on technical aspects of Smith. This narrowing of focus without reference to the broader picture has led some to see Smith as inconsistent. I use the case of Smith's analysis of banking to illustrate the point. My hope is that in the future, before accusing Smith of inconsistency, we might take a closer look at his vision of the economy and of society as integrated systems of natural liberty that promote both efficiency and justice.

When his bird's-eye view is set aside, Smith tends to be described as inconsistent: he is a vigorous promoter of the free market but also favors a heavy regulatory hand in some parts of the economy. But Smith seems to promote neither an unregulated market nor a government-regulated one. Smith's major concern seems instead to be the material and moral well-being of the majority of the people. He favors the institutional structure that would benefit the community the most, and often this is a mix of self-regulated and minimally government-regulated markets.

The free banking system of Scotland at his time is for Smith the most effective institutional banking setting to promote both moral and material prosperity for the majority of the people. The competitive discipline of many small banks that must convert notes into specie on demand generates the incentives for a stable banking system that allows for economic development as well as the virtues of prudence and judiciousness. Given the multiplicity of interests in society, it is possible that those interests will conflict with each other and not attain a mutually beneficial solution. In these cases Smith believes regulation would make society both morally better and materially better off, as long as the regulation benefits the majority of the people, and not some at the expense of many. Indeed, the banking and monetary regulations that create concentrated benefits and disperse costs receive strong condemnation. The banking regulations that Smith calls for seem to be just a definition of the rules of the game that will allow competition to function at this best. And competitive forces allow for a fruitful moral and material development of the majority of the individuals.

Economists have taken major steps toward integrating technical issues into the big picture that Smith offers us. I think and hope that this will be an increasing trend in the future.

NOTES

1. Sydney George Checkland, "Adam Smith and the Bankers," in *Essays on Adam Smith*, ed. Andrew Skinner and Thomas Wilson (Oxford: 1975), pp. 504–23; Charles W. Munn, *The Scottish Provincial Banking Companies, 1747–1864* (Edinburgh: 1981), p. 1; David Glasner, "A Reinterpretation of Classical Monetary Theory," *Southern Economic Journal* 52, no. 1 (1985), p. 46; George A. Selgin, "The Analytical Framework of the Real-Bills Doctrine," *Journal of Institutional and Theoretical Economics* 145, no. 3 (1989), pp. 489–507; David Glasner, "The Real-Bills Doctrine in the Light of the Law of Reflux," *History of Political Economy* 24, no. 2 (1992), pp. 867–94; James A. Gherity, "The Evolution of Adam Smith's Theory of Banking," *History of Political Economy* 26, no. 3 (1994), pp. 423–41; Lawrence White, *Free Banking in Britain: Theory, Experience, and Debate, 1800–1845* (London: 1995 [1994]); Arie Arnon, *Monetary Theory and Policy from Hume and Smith to Wicksell: Money, Credit, and the Economy* (Cambridge: 2011); Hugh Rockoff, "Upon Daedalian Wings of Paper Money: Adam Smith and the Crisis of 1772," *Adam Smith Review* 6 (2011), pp. 255–84; Hugh Rockoff, "Adam Smith on Money, Banking, and the Price Level," in *The Oxford Handbook of Adam Smith*, ed. Christopher Berry, Maria Pia Paganelli, and Craig Smith (Oxford: 2013), pp. 307–32.

2. Jacob Viner, "Adam Smith and Laissez Faire," *Journal of Political Economy* 2 (1927), p. 198; George J. Stigler, "Smith's Travels on the Ship of State," *History of Political Economy* 3, no. 2 (1971), pp. 265–77.

3. James M. Buchanan, "The Justice of Natural Liberty," in *Adam Smith and the Wealth of Nations: Bicentennial Essays 1776–1976*, ed. Fred R. Glahe (Boulder, CO: 1978), pp. 61–81; Jerry Evensky, *Adam Smith's Moral Philosophy* (New York: 2005).

4. E.g., Viner, "Adam Smith and Laissez Faire," p. 198; Stigler, "Smith's Travels on the Ship of State," pp. 265–77; Leonard Billet, "Justice, Liberty, and Economy," in Glahe, *Adam Smith and the Wealth of Nations*, pp. 83–109.

5. Vernon L. Smith, *Rationality in Economics: Constructivist and Ecological Forms* (Cambridge: 2008); Richard E. Wagner, *Deficits, Debt, and Democracy: Wrestling with Tragedy on the Fiscal Commons* (Cheltenham: 2012).

6. Maria Pia Paganelli, "Adam Smith and Entangled Political Economy," *Advances in Austrian Economics* 18 (2014), pp. 37–54.

7. Maria Pia Paganelli, "Approbation and the Desire to Better One's Condition in Adam Smith: When the Desire to Better One's Condition Does Not Better One's Condition and Society's Condition," *History of Economics Society Bulletin* 31, no. 1 (2009), pp. 79–92.

8. David M. Levy, "A Partial Spectator in the Wealth of Nations: A Robust Utilitarianism," *European Journal of the History of Economic Thought* 2 (1995), pp. 299–326.

9. Maria Pia Paganelli, "David Hume on Banking and Hoarding," *Southern Economic Journal* 80, no. 4 (April 2014), pp. 968–80.

10. Glenn Hueckel, "'In the Heat of Writing': Polemics and the 'Error of Adam Smith' in the Matter of the Corn Bounty," in *The Elgar Companion to Adam Smith*, ed. Jeffrey Young (Cheltenham: 2009).

11. James A. Gherity, "The Option Clause in Scottish Banking, 1730–65: A Reappraisal," *Journal of Money, Credit and Banking* 27, no. 3 (1995), pp. 713–26; Neil T. Skaggs, "Adam Smith on Growth and Credit—Too Weak a Connection?," *Journal of Economic Studies* 26, no. 6 (1999), pp. 481–96; Rockoff, "Adam Smith on Money," pp. 307–32.

12. Checkland, "Adam Smith and the Bankers," pp. 504–23.

13. Tyler Cowen and Randall Kroszner, *Explorations in the New Monetary Economics* (Oxford: 1994); White, *Free Banking in Britain*.

14. Robert Wallace, *Characteristics of the Present Political State of Great Britain* (London: 1969 [1758]).

15. Chiara Baroni, "The Man of Credit: An Aristocratic Ethics for the Middle Class?" (manuscript, 2002).

16. Viner, "Adam Smith and Laissez Faire," p. 198; Stigler, "Smith's Travels on the Ship of State," pp. 265–77.

17. Munn, *Scottish Provincial Banking Companies*, p. 19.

18. Checkland, "Adam Smith and the Bankers," pp. 504–23.

BIBLIOGRAPHIC ESSAY

On the historical account of banks in Scotland, see Sydney George Checkland, *Scottish Banking: A History, 1695–1973* (Glasgow: 1975).

On the alleged tensions between intervention and laissez-faire in Smith, see Jacob Viner, "Adam Smith and Laissez Faire," *Journal of Political Economy* 2 (1927), p. 198. On the moral components in Smith's opus, see Jerry Evensky, *Adam Smith's Moral Philosophy* (New York: 2005). On the complex web of relations in Smith, see Maria Pia Paganelli, "Adam Smith and Entangled Political Economy," *Advances in Austrian Economics* 18 (2014), pp. 37–54.

ADAM SMITH AND EXPERIMENTAL ECONOMICS: *SENTIMENTS* TO *WEALTH*

Vernon L. Smith

Adam Smith has had little impact on experimental economics, and that impact is very recent.[1] But he has had a transforming impact on my thinking about experimental economics especially within the past two decades. This essay tells that story, illustrating by example how the substance of experimental economics can be enhanced through engagement with Smith.

SMITH'S PROGRAM

The program begins in the conception of a pre-civil world that (1) develops a systematic treatment of human sentiments, (2) leads to the rules we live by in our intimate cultural groupings, and (3) evolves into property in the civil order.[2] With third-party enforcement of property in support of civil justice, the necessary conditions were laid for the extended order of exchange and specialization, essential for wealth creation and human material betterment.[3]

In *Sentiments*, particularly Part I (TMS I.i.1.3–I.i.5.10 and TMS I.ii.2.1–I.iii.1.15), individual actions are driven by the propriety of our conduct, not outcome utility; Smith models relational processes, not a welfare end-maximizing equilibrium of outcomes. "Pleasure" flows from fellow-feeling and mutual sympathy via the metaphor of the impartial spectator through which we see and judge others, and see ourselves as others see and judge us. Within this experiential social process of consent there emerge the general rules of propriety that ultimately govern us primarily through self-command (TMS II.i.1.1–II.ii.1.10). Out of this proving ground of sociability originate the rules of property that govern the civil order; that is, in effect, the *propriety* rights that emerge in close-knit communities shape the subsequent civil form of *property* rights (TMS II.ii.2.1–II.ii.2.4).

In *Wealth* property is necessary but not sufficient, and Adam Smith supplies the essential *Discovery Axiom* that fuels wealth creation: "the propensity to truck, barter and exchange" (WN I.ii.1). Just as in *Sentiments*, it is process all the way up; it's not about the whiteboard mechanics of market clearing prices and outcomes, based on specialization, that creates wealth; it's about the discovery of prices, whose very existence calls for comparisons that otherwise would not be made between one's own circumstances and that of all others as revealed in prices as they form; prices provide the connection between the individual and all others in economic commerce, just as the "impartial spectator" is the connecting link between the individual and all others in social commerce. This price discovery perspective in *Wealth* was lost in the neoclassical marginal revolution and its aftermath. Instead of supplementing the price discovery process in *Wealth*, it was displaced by equilibrium market statics until revived by Hayek's critique of price theory and the unexpected results of laboratory market experiments.

The relevance of the *Sentiments* model persists in our daily lives, and has followed markets in going global in the multibillion-dollar social media corporations like Facebook. Moreover, in markets *Sentiments* continues to be significant wherever the maintenance of relationships in the performance of contracts is important to human achievement.

Each of Smith's two books models human betterment: *Sentiments* is devoted to social psychological betterment achieved through mutual sympathy and consensual rules of conduct, rules that define the boundaries within which our actions are not subject to resentment by others and may invoke gratitude from others; *Wealth* is about how exchange and specialization enable economic betterment, based on rules of property that define the boundaries within which we are free to take action.

EARLY ENCOUNTER WITH SMITH

My early encounter with Smith would eventually become significant, but the beginning carried no hint of this future. At the University of Kansas, as a candidate for a master's in economics in 1950–51, I enrolled in Dick Howey's course, "The Development of Economic Thought." After going through some of the precursors of Smith (Petty, the physiocrats), we read *Wealth*, including, as Howey put it, "even the 80-page digression on silver." My course notes (Duke University Archives) record no mention of *Sentiments*. Most likely I learned of it through Jacob Viner,[4] as cited in my essay "The Two Faces of Adam Smith."[5]

The second semester of Dick Howey's course had a far larger impact on me until the 1990s. We discussed the big three after Smith—Malthus, Ricardo, and Mill—but the main task was to read Jevons, Menger, and Walras, fomenters of the 1870s marginal revolution. It is no exaggeration to say that Dick is one of the leading scholars of the history of the marginal utility school; so it is to be expected that he would influence me.[6] This exposure to equilibrium theory was reinforced by subsequent graduate work at Harvard, and it would follow me into experimental economics.[7] But experiments would teach me that equilibrium could be discovered by naïve market traders far better than equilibrium economics could articulate a theoretical process for discovering the equilibrium, and that discovery would eventually return me to a new appreciation of *Wealth*.

EXPERIMENTAL SUPPLY AND DEMAND MARKETS, INSTITUTIONS, AND THE HAYEK CONNECTION

Beginning in January 1956, and continuing for the next three decades, I and my coauthors and many others would learn a great deal about how the rules of trading (bid-ask double auctions, sealed bid procedures, posted offer pricing, the standard auctions) that defined an institution enabling decentralized agents to find efficient market outcomes, and respond to external changes. Although this research was the topic of my first published report,[8] others such as Sidney Siegel and Reinhard Selten were almost simultaneously recording congruent findings.[9]

Upon reflection I came to the view that the only satisfying treatment of the issues we were uncovering in these experiments had been provided by Friedrich Hayek, whose many works emphasized how economic order derives from rules.[10] This connection was important because it was a pathway back to the eighteenth century, directly to David Hume and indirectly to Smith's *Sentiments*. Hayek's debt to Hume was transparent to me, and called for the study of Hume; Hayek's debt to *Sentiments* was not transparent, and it was only later that it became clear to me that Hayek's "two worlds" dichotomy (see below) was precisely what Smith's two books were all about.[11]

In retrospect the beginning of the end of that early learning was summarized in my essay "Microeconomic Systems as an Experimental Science."[12] That was a break point in the sense that my attention turned to asset market trading in which the results would contradict the rapid convergence performance of the supply and demand environments studied earlier.[13] The key to understanding the behavior underlying asset markets was to recognize that their durability (and retradability) made them vulnerable to false price signals mediated by the money supply, a topic whose pursuit must not distract us here.[14]

TRUST GAMES: SELF-LOVE FAILS TO PREDICT

A second break point, leading me ultimately back to *Sentiments*, was Hayek's important contributions to the idea that economic order, in small groups as well as markets, arises from rules.[15] This juncture came with experiments in an investment trust setting that originated with Berg et al.,[16] and motivated my collaboration on two-person extensive form trust, ultimatum, and dictator games.[17] Subject behavior in these experiments was baffling within the traditional modern economic or game-theoretic framework.

To provide an example, individuals in groups of twelve or sixteen people, all sitting at a private computer monitor screen in a lab, are randomly pairwise matched. All have complete payment information, and anonymity with respect to each other in their decisions. One in each pair is selected to be Person 1, the other Person 2, and they make choices in the following sequence:

- Person 1 chooses either (1) payments of ($10 to Person 1, $10 to Person 2), or (2) pass choice to Person 2.
- If Person 1 chooses the first option, the experiment is over, and the indicated payments are made privately.
- If the choice is "pass choice to Person 2," then the latter chooses either ($15 to Person 1, $25 to Person 2) or ($0 to Person 1, $40 to Person 2). The experiment ends and each is paid privately the amount indicated by the choice of Person 2.

The typical outcome from thirty pairs of people in this experiment is for about half of the Persons 1 to choose ($10 to Person 1, $10 to Person 2) and about half to "pass choice to Person 2." Between two-thirds and three-fourths of Persons 2 choose ($15 to Person 1, $25 to Person 2) while between one-third and one-fourths choose ($0 to Person 1, $40 to Person 2). These results have been replicated and extended in many experiments, under differing payoffs (and conditions); changing the payoffs causes only minor variations and the qualitative outcomes persist. Thus, consider a second variation of this game in which Person 1 still chooses between ($10 to Person 1, $10 to Person 2) and "pass choice to Person 2." But in the second game Person 2 chooses either ($12.50 to Person 1, $17.50 to Person 2) or ($5 to Person 1, $25 to Person 2). In this second game 56 percent of Persons 1 choose the first option, 46 percent pass to Person 2. And two-thirds of Persons 2 choose to cooperate ($12.50, $17.50) while one-third defect for ($5, $25).

The traditional analysis, based on own-payoff maximizing choice, predicts that Person 1 will not pass to Person 2 in either of these games, because Person 2 will select the option yielding $40 in the first game, $25 in the second game.[18] The experimental results are not only contrary to this prediction, but differ sharply from the hundreds of market experiments over the years in which people behave in a quite consistently own-maximizing manner. On average in the first game, Persons 1 make more money by passing to the other player than by choosing the sure thing of $10. (In the second they about break even.) These actions are hardly irrational, although they are inexplicable by the traditional concept of individual rationality.

UTILITY FUNCTIONS TO THE RESCUE?

The experimental and behavioral economic communities both tend to resolve the confrontation between the trust (and other two-person) game observations and traditional theory by modifying people's utility functions. The "fix" is to assume that people might derive utility from both own and other payoffs.[19] These exercises leave untouched the underlying assumptions of game theory, such as the concept of the single play game between strangers with no history or future. Only the utility function is modified to account for the results, and consequently the theory-repair mechanics becomes a technical twist that fails to deepen our understanding of why self-love accounts for market decisions but not small group relational decisions, or fails to articulate what might be the specific process that generates the largesse in small groups, but not in impersonal markets.[20]

RECIPROCITY AND EXCHANGE:
THE TWO FACES OF ADAM SMITH?

The first attempt of my coauthors and me to come to terms with this discrepancy between theory and observations was to appeal to the evolutionary (biology and psychology) concept of reciprocity (or "reciprocal altruism").[21] Also by this time I was reading *Sentiments* and trying to relate it to what I was learning from experiments. In my lecture at the Southern Economic Association meetings of 1997, I cited both of Smith's books as well as Viner and developed the idea that Adam Smith's two books are both about "the propensity to truck, barter and exchange";[22] in *Sentiments* people are exchanging favors and gifts; and in *Wealth* they are exchanging goods.[23] This was an important stage in my thinking—recognizing a unity in Smith's program—but it fell short of a full appreciation of the intellectual depth of *Sentiments*. Smith did not postulate reciprocity; rather he derived it from more fundamental axioms qua principles!

In retrospect, my SEA lecture contained a significant omission—like Sherlock Holmes's dog that didn't bark, Hayek's work was not cited.

HAYEK'S TWO WORLDS

Within a few years Hayek gave me greater insight into why these disparate results prevailed, and ultimately I was able to appreciate not what was wrong, but what was simply inadequate, concerning the reciprocity-exchange interpretation of *Sentiments*. Thus, in Hayek's last work we get this gem:

> Part of our present difficulty is that we must constantly adjust our lives, our thoughts and our emotions, in order to live simultaneously within different kinds of orders according to different rules. If we were to apply the unmodified, uncurbed rules of the microcosmos (i.e., of the small band or troop, or of, say, our families) to the macro-cosmos (our wider civilisation), as our instincts and sentimental yearnings often make us wish to do, *we would destroy it*. Yet if we were always to apply the rules of the extended order to our more intimate groupings, *we would crush them*.[24]

In Hayek, all socioeconomic order derives from rules that were not given innately but arose out of human experience, an idea developed well in Hume, and acknowledged by Hayek. These ideas, however, were more extensively articulated in *Sentiments* and in a manner that frees it from utilitarian justification.

HUMAN MOTIVATION: ACTIONS ARE ABOUT CONDUCT AND SELF-COMMAND, NOT ONLY SELF-LOVE

Axioms of motivation and principles of self-command in *Sentiments* include these:

- Man "desires, not only praise, but praiseworthiness" (TMS III.2.1).
- And "dreads, not only blame, but blameworthiness" (TMS III.2.1).
- "But in order to attain this satisfaction, we must become the impartial spectators of our own conduct" (TMS III.2.3). Or, "endeavor to examine our own conduct as we imagine any other fair and impartial spectator would examine it" (TMS III.1.3).
- From birth every person is disciplined by "those he lives with, which always mark when they enter into, and when they disapprove of his sentiments; and it is here that he first views the propriety or impropriety of his own passions, the beauty and deformity of his own mind" (TMS III.1.3).
- "When he views himself in the light in which he is conscious that others will view him, he sees that to them he is but one of the multitude in no respect better than any other in it. If he would act so as that the impartial spectator may enter into the principles of his conduct . . . he must . . . humble the arrogance of his self-love, and bring it down to something which other men can go along with" (TMS II.ii.2.1).

Smith's impartial spectator is a metaphor for the social commerce through which we observe and judge the conduct expressed in the actions of others, in turn see how others view and judge us by our actions, and thus to develop self-command. We learn to humble our self-love in congruence with what others will "go along with," but "kindness . . . cannot . . . be extracted by force" (TMS II.ii.1.5–7); rather, the humbling of self-love derives from our experience of the "fellow-feeling," "pleasures of mutual sympathy," "praise and praise-worthiness" ("avoid blame and blame-worthiness") that grow out of our interaction with others. The outcome may yield "profit" in our own interest (as in a trust game), but for Smith that is *not why we do it.* Smith brilliantly describes a social (moral) betterment process entirely distinct from utilitarian outcomes.

One proposition governing conduct is Smith's

- *Beneficence Proposition:* "Actions of a beneficent tendency, which proceed from proper motives, seem alone to require reward; because such alone are the approved objects of gratitude, or excite the sympathetic gratitude of the spectator" (TMS II.ii.1.1).[25]

Applying Smith's Beneficence Proposition to the above trust game, we see that it predicts that some or perhaps many people in the position of Person 2 will feel gratitude and be moved to reward Person 1 for her action. Moreover, to the extent that pairing any anonymous humans invokes some "fellow-feeling," Person 1 may expect that Person 2 will cooperate, although to a lesser extent (50 percent) than Persons 2 (two-thirds to three-fourths); this follows because sequential play means that Person 2 chooses in directly linked knowledge of the choice by Person 1, whereas Person 1 faces uncertainty about Person 2 and whether that person will be sensitive to an action that seeks to define a relationship.[26]

A variation on these game results is reported by Cox and Deck,[27] using a procedure that ensures that subject decisions are anonymous with respect to the experimenter or anyone who might see the data, and compare behavior under this condition with behavior where subjects are anonymous with respect to each other only (double anonymity vs. single anonymity).[28] They find that many more Persons 2 choose to defect on offers to cooperate under double anonymity (71 percent) than under single anonymity (32 percent). Hence the defection rate more than doubles when no one can know your decision. This comparison relates to Smith's axioms on motivation and his careful distinction between praise and praiseworthiness: "Those two principles, though they resemble one another, are yet, . . . distinct and independent" (TMS III.2.2) and "it often gives real comfort to reflect, that though no praise should actually be bestowed upon us, our conduct, however, has been such as to deserve it" (TMS III.2.5). The results suggest that in a treatment where no one can know and judge the praiseability of a person's action, then praiseworthiness alone sustains a much lower cooperative response frequency.[29]

Coricelli et al. report a comparison of faculty to undergraduate students in a trust game: only 28 percent (five of eighteen pairs) of faculty offer cooperation, compared with 72 percent (thirteen of eighteen pairs) of the student subjects.[30] The time taken to decide also differs dramatically in the two groups: Faculty Persons 1 average 43.5 seconds deciding to choose the equilibrium outcome, 36.9 seconds to offer cooperation; corresponding undergraduate times are only 14.8 and 16.6 seconds, respectively. Faculty Persons 2 average 17.6 seconds deciding to defect, 24.1 to cooperate; corresponding undergraduate times are 17.3 and 12.4.[31] Coricelli et al. conclude, "We find that assistant professors take longer, trust less and do worse in terms of final payoffs than undergraduates. However, within each group, levels of trust are well matched with the resulting levels of reciprocity. This suggests that individuals are quite successful in reading the intentions of their randomly paired in-group partner."[32]

A second proposition governing conduct is Smith's

- *Injustice Proposition:* "Actions of a hurtful tendency, which pro-ceed from improper motives, seem alone to deserve punishment; because such alone are the approved objects of resentment, or ex-cite the sympathetic resentment of the spectator. . . . Resentment seems to have been given us by nature for defence, and for de-fence only. It is the safeguard of justice and the security of inno-cence" (TMS II.ii.1.2–4).

Consider an application of Smith's Injustice Proposition to a vari-ation on the second trust game discussed above. Suppose in this variant that if Person 2 decides not to cooperate and opt for the outcome ($5, $25), he cannot choose that option directly; he must first pass play back to Person 1, and then Person 1 chooses between the outcome ($5, $25) and the outcome ($0, $0). Hence, if Person 2 defects on the offer to cooperate, Person 1 can, at a cost to herself, punish Person 2. The Injustice Proposition predicts that resentment on the part of Person 2 may lead to punishment, but in order to give the resentment teeth we require that its expression be costly.

In this new version of the second game, 50 percent of Persons 1 choose ($10, $10) and 50 percent pass to Person 2; only 42 percent of Persons 2 choose to cooperate ($12.50, $17.50), and 58 percent defect, returning play to Person 1, whereupon 71 percent accept the defection and 29 percent choose the punishment outcome ($0, $0). Hence, the existence of the punishment option reduces cooperation from two-thirds to 42 percent. Kindness declines where it can be perceived as extracted by force!

In *Sentiments* these propositions work to explain the origins of property in the civil order.

FROM PROPRIETY TO PROPERTY

Property in the civil order emerges gradually from our long experience of the rules of propriety in the social order:

> As the greater and more irreparable the evil that is done, the resentment of the sufferer runs naturally the higher; so does likewise the sympathetic indignation of the spectator. . . . Death is the greatest evil which one man can inflict upon another, and excites the highest degree of resentment. . . . Murder, therefore, is the most atrocious of all crimes which affect individuals only, in the sight both of mankind, and of the person who has committed it. To be deprived of that which we are possessed of, is a greater evil than to be disappointed of what we have only the expectation. Breach of property, therefore, theft and robbery, which take from us what we are possessed of, are greater crimes than breach of contract, which only disappoints us of what we expected. The most sacred laws of justice, therefore, . . . are the laws that guard the life and person of our neighbor; the next are those which guard his property and possessions; and last of all come those which guard what are called his personal rights, or what is due to him from the promises of others. (TMS II.ii.2.2)

The distinction drawn here between a loss of "what we are possessed of" and loss due to the violation of promises that "only disappoints us of what we expected" shows that Smith is much aware of the psychological asymmetry between gains and losses,[33] a proposition prominently associated with the experiments of Kahneman and Tversky.[34]

But what is justice? On this Smith is specific and clear, and we here state it as a proposition:

- *Justice Proposition:* "Though the breach of justice . . . exposes to punishment, the observance of the rules of that virtue seems scarce to deserve any reward. There is . . . a propriety in the practice of justice. . . . But as it does no real positive good, it is entitled to very little gratitude. Mere justice is, upon most occasions, but a negative virtue, and only hinders us from hurting our neighbour. . . . The man who . . . merely abstains from hurting his neighbours, can merit only that his neighbours in their turn should respect his innocence, and that the same laws should be religiously observed with regard to him." (TMS II.ii.1.9–10)

Consequently, justice is secured by suitably punishing acts of injustice, not by rewarding justice, which is your duty. *Justice is the residual (a negative virtue) that consists in what remains, or is left over, after the civil order has instituted proportioned punishments for unjust actions.* No reward should be expected or given for driving through a green light; but if you drive through a red light you are subject to a citation and a penalty.

FROM PROPERTY TO *WEALTH*

Once we have third-party enforcement of promises, trusting actions that require trustworthy responses to capture mutual gains from exchange and specialization, or prevent confiscation, can be secured by the rules of property. Reciprocity in exchange is no longer entirely dependent on gratitude for the voluntary reward of beneficent action, and on resentment for the private provision of punishment of malfeasance. In the trust games above, cooperation is now supported by publicly financed sanctions that penalize self-loving unsocial acts of defection. This interpretation is largely implicit, not explicit, in *Wealth*, although toward the end of his second book his reflections on property hark back to a significant theme in *Sentiments* (he does not cite himself). Thus:

> The affluence of the rich excites the indignation of the poor, who are often both driven by want, and prompted by envy, to invade his possessions. It is only under the shelter of the civil magistrate that the owner of that valuable property, which is acquired by the labour of many years, or perhaps of many successive generations, can sleep a single night in security. He is at all times surrounded by unknown enemies, whom, though he never provoked, he can never appease, and from whose injustice he can be protected only by the powerful arm of the civil magistrate continually held up to chastise it. The acquisition of valuable and extensive property, therefore, necessarily requires the establishment of civil government. Where there is no property, or at least none that exceeds the value of two or three days labour, civil government is not so necessary. (WN V.i.b.2)

From *Sentiments* we learn of the "invisible hand" significance of the rich as the source of improvements that benefit rich and poor alike, because they serve the roles of savers, investors, and custodians of capital wealth: "though they mean only their own conveniency . . . they divide with the poor the produce of all their improvements" (TMS IV.1.10).

More commonly, only the shadow of key concepts in *Sentiments* is cast into passages in *Wealth*, and without the first work in mind the reader may not appreciate the significance of important passages in the second. For example:

- Just prior to Smith's oft-quoted and misunderstood, "It is not from the benevolence of the butcher . . ." (WN I.ii.2) we read the following, which message is easily misconstrued by anyone not primed by *Sentiments*: "In civilized society he (man) stands at all times in need of the cooperation and assistance of great multitudes, while his whole life is scarce sufficient to gain the friendship of a few persons. . . . But man has almost constant occasion for the help of his brethren, and it is in vain for him to expect it from their benevolence only. He will be more likely to prevail if he can interest their self-love in his favour, and shew them that it is for their own advantage to do for him what he requires of them. Whoever offers to another a bargain of any kind, proposes to do this. Give me that which I want, and you shall have this which you want, is the meaning of every such offer; and it is in this manner that we obtain from one another the far greater part of those good offices which we stand in need of" (WN I.ii.2).

The words "civilized society," "friendship," "brethren," "benevolence" (or "beneficence"), "self-love," and "good offices" are all central to the vocabulary of *Sentiments*. Before speaking of the appeal to their self-love, he first makes it plain that "benevolence only" is insufficient, a qualification hardly surprising from the author of *Sentiments*.

- ". . . allowing every man to pursue his own interest his own way, upon the liberal plan of equality, liberty and justice . . ." (WN IV.ix.3).
- "All systems either of preference or of restraint, therefore, being thus completely taken away, the obvious and simple system of natural liberty establishes itself of its own accord. Every man, as long as he does not violate the laws of justice, is left perfectly free to pursue his own interest his own way, and to bring both his industry and capital into competition with those of any other man, or order of men" (WN IV.ix.51).

From *Sentiments* we learn that the liberal plan of justice consisted in not violating the laws of justice, justice being a negative virtue in which every person's rights to action are entirely free within the ruling bounds of what constitutes foul play. The impartial spectator was the metaphor used to model the emergence of social rules that incentivized self-command through the discipline of resentment and punishment—rules that in civil society became the means of defining the field of fair play outlined by defining the edges beyond which civil society will not "go along with."

CONCLUSION

Sentiments, already eclipsed by *Wealth* in 1790 when the sixth and final edition was published, represents not so much a legacy lost, as one that failed to achieve traction, an entire means of thinking that established no foothold on economics as the nineteenth and particularly the twentieth centuries turned to utilitarianism. The acclaim of *Wealth* was spectacularly justified but obscured Smith's equally penetrating examination of the pre-civil rules of order that emerge in culture.

In my view, *Sentiments* provides a nonutilitarian framework for modeling small group interactions in which actions signal conduct, or responses to such signals, in social contexts governed by the rules of propriety. Under such rules people acquire culture-specific expectations of what actions find approval and what actions encounter disapproval. I have used the familiar class of trust games to illustrate the power of this way of thinking and modeling that leads naturally to predictions that contrast sharply with those of neoclassical Max U. I believe that *Sentiments* provides the potential for a much larger program of pursuit by experimental economists than is indicated in these examples. Thus, over and over we find that context matters in small group experiments, and context is a principal theme in *Sentiments*. I have introduced a sharp demarcation between *Sentiments* and *Wealth* based on the idea that the consensual rules of propriety became externally enforced property. Of course this is a simplification since contracts cannot cover every margin of mutual benefit and protect from destabilizing invasions motivated by self-love. Actions on these margins may acquire discipline by the kind of self-command principles that are modeled in *Sentiments*. These examples open a much larger potential for further laboratory explorations.

NOTES

1. Maria Pia Paganelli, "Smithian Answers to Some Experimental Puzzles," in *The Elgar Companion to Adam Smith*, ed. Jeffrey Young (Cheltenham: 2009), pp. 181–92.

2. This is the project of Smith's *Theory of Moral Sentiments*. See Jeffrey T. Young, "Adam Smith and New Institutional Theories of Property Rights," in *The Adam Smith Review*, vol. 2, ed. Vivienne Brown (London: 2006).

3. This is the project of Smith's *Wealth of Nations*.

4. Jacob Viner, "Adam Smith," in *Essays on the Intellectual History of Economics*, ed. Douglas A. Irwin (Princeton: 1991), pp. 248–61.

5. Vernon L. Smith, "The Two Faces of Adam Smith," *Southern Economic Journal* 65 (1998), pp. 2–19.

6. Richard S. Howey, *The Rise of the Marginal Utility School* (New York: 1989).

7. Howey also taught the graduate course in mathematical economics that I devoured with relish. As a thought scholar, he was well versed in its required language tools: mathematics, German, French, and Italian.

8. Vernon L. Smith, "An Experimental Study of Competitive Market Behavior," *Journal of Political Economy* 70 (1962), pp. 111–37.

9. Samuel Messick and Arthur Brayfield, *Decision and Choice: Contributions of Sidney Siegel* (New York: 1964); Heinz Sauermann and Reinhard Selten, "Ein Oligopolexperiment," *Zeitschrift für die gesamte Staatswissenschaft/Journal of Institutional and Theoretical Economics* 115 (1959), pp. 427–71, would be the first of a great many contributions to experimental economics over Selten's distinguished career.

10. Friedrich Hayek, "The Use of Knowledge in Society," *American Economic Review* 35 (1945), pp. 519–30.

11. Friedrich Hayek, *The Fatal Conceit*, ed. W. W. Bartley III (Chicago: 1988), p. 18.

12. Vernon L. Smith, "Microeconomic Systems as an Experimental Science," *American Economic Review* 72 (1982), pp. 923–55.

13. Vernon L. Smith, Gerry L. Suchanek, and Arlington W. Williams, "Bubbles, Crashes and Endogenous Expectations in Experimental Spot Asset Markets," *Econometrica* 56 (1988), pp. 1119–51.

14. See the experiments reported in John Dickhaut, Shengle Lin, David Porter, and Vernon L. Smith, "Commodity Durability, Trader Specialization, and Market Performance," *Proceedings of the National Academy of Sciences* 109 (2012), pp. 1425–30, comparing perishable goods, which yield a surplus to buyer and seller immediately, with durable retradable goods; each of the components in this comparison is examined with low versus high cash endowments. High cash interacts with retradability to exacerbate the problem of discovering the static equilibrium prices that maximize surplus.

15. Friedrich Hayek, *Law, Legislation and Liberty, Rules and Order*, vol. 1 (Chicago: 1983); Hayek, *Fatal Conceit*.

16. Joyce Berg, John Dickhaut, and Kevin McCabe, "Trust, Reciprocity, and Social History," *Games and Economic Behavior* 10 (1995), pp 122–42.

17. A summary with connections to *Sentiments* is in Vernon L. Smith and Bart J. Wilson, "Fair and Impartial Spectators in Experimental Economic Behavior," in *Sympathy: A History*, ed. Eric Schliesser (Oxford: 2015).

18. In the first game we say that ($10, $10) is the equilibrium outcome ($15, $25) the cooperative outcome, and ($0, $40) the defection outcome.

19. For an excellent summary and an extension of these utilitarian models to include "emotions," see James Cox, Daniel Friedman, and Steven Gjerstad, "A Tractable Model of Reciprocity and Fairness," *Games and Economic Behavior* 59 (2007), pp. 17–45.

20. I use Smith's term "self-love" here, rather than the traditional "self-interest," because as Smith would say, "[w]e address ourselves, not to their humanity but to

their self-love, and never talk to them of our own necessities but of their advantages" (WN I.ii.2).

21. Kevin A. McCabe, Stephen J. Rassenti, and Vernon L. Smith, "Game Theory and Reciprocity in Some Extensive Form Experimental Games," *Proceedings of the National Academy of Sciences* 93 (1996), pp. 13421–28.

22. Viner, "Adam Smith."

23. Smith, "Two Faces of Adam Smith."

24. Hayek, *Fatal Conceit*, p. 18.

25. Smith and Wilson's "Fair and Impartial Spectators" applies a second proposition on beneficence to the ultimatum game, arguing that because the game as usually presented projects the features of extortion, choices cannot be interpreted in terms of the calculus of being either beneficent or hurtful: "Beneficence is always free, it cannot be extorted by force, the mere want of it exposes to no punishment; because the mere want of beneficence tends to do no real positive evil. It may disappoint of the good which might reasonably have been expected, and upon that account it may justly excite dislike and disapprobation: it cannot, however, provoke any resentment which mankind can go along with" (TMS II.ii.1.3). Consistent with this proposition, experiments that define or frame a voluntary choice path to a final ultimatum interaction yield outcomes that are much nearer to the equilibrium prediction.

26. These results are modified, yielding less trusting and trustworthy behavior, if the game is played in "strategic form," wherein each person indicates his choice independently, and the outcome is then determined accordingly by the computer. Kevin A. McCabe and Vernon L. Smith, "A Comparison of Naïve and Sophisticated Subject Behavior with Game Theoretic Predictions," *Proceedings of the National Academy of Sciences* 97 (2000), pp. 3777–81, table 3, report data for a trust game in which offers to cooperate fall from 46 percent to 29 percent (acceptances fall from 50 percent to 14 percent) when comparing the extensive to the strategic form. Hence, offering (or responding to offers of) cooperation under simultaneous contingent-play conditions is not equivalent to directly experiencing the interaction in sequence. The latter, I would suggest, is critical in invoking a sense of "fellow-feeling," that of being linked in a personal relationship, as distinct from a separation that mechanically executes the consequence of the two separate decisions. Game theory assumes the equivalence of the two forms.

27. James C. Cox and Cary A. Deck, "On the Nature of Reciprocal Motives," *Economic Inquiry* 43 (2005), pp. 623–35.

28. Elizabeth Hoffman, Kevin McCabe, Keith Shachat, and Vernon L. Smith, "Preferences, Property Rights and Anonymity in Bargaining Games," *Games and Economic Behavior* 7 (1994), pp. 346–80, had found that dictator games were sensitive to this double anonymity treatment.

29. In interpreting motivation in *Sentiments*, Smith and Wilson, "Fair and Impartial Spectators," write that an action taken by i depends on its propriety given the circumstances:

$$a_i \,(\text{Propriety}|C) = \alpha_i(C)(PR) + \beta_i(C)(PR){\bullet}(PW) + \gamma_i(C)(PW) + \delta_i(C).$$

PR and PW are (0, 1) indicator variables that an action would be socially praised (1), or not (0), or is praiseworthy (1), or not (0); and α_i, β_i, γ_i, and δ_i are nonnegative functions of C (circumstances, including game structure and pay-offs). In the second term, PW adds leverage to PR, while the third term expresses the sentiment that PW may contribute to self-command, where it can never re-ceive praise. In the text we are supposing that double anonymity suppresses the effect of the first two terms on the choice of action, or $\alpha_i = \beta_i = 0$.

30. Georgio Coricelli, Kevin McCabe, and Vernon L. Smith, "Theory-of-Mind Mechanism in Personal Exchange," in *Proceedings 13th Annual Toyota Confer-ence on Affective Minds*, ed. G. Hatano, N. Okada, and H. Tanabe (Amsterdam: 2000), p. 258.

31. A recent report of ten studies across several experimental designs shows that subjects cooperated more when they reached decisions more quickly whether under time constraints or under reflective or intuitive prompts: David G. Rand, J. D. Greene, and Martin Nowak, "Spontaneous Giving and Calculated Greed," *Nature* 489 (2012), pp. 427–30.

32. Coricelli, McCabe, and Smith, "Theory-of-Mind Mechanism," p. 259.

33. For example, "We suffer more, it has already been observed, when we fall from a better to a worse situation, than we ever enjoy when we rise from a worse to a better" (TMS VI.i.6; also see I.iii.1.5–8).

34. Daniel Kahneman and Amos Tversky, "Prospect Theory: An Analysis of Decision under Risk," *Econometrica* 47 (1979), pp. 263–91.

BIBLIOGRAPHIC ESSAY

For those who are venturing into the world of Adam Smith for the first time or reentering it after a long hiatus, I recommend Nicho-las Phillipson, *Adam Smith: An Enlightened Life* (London: 2010). Phillipson provides the reader with a sense of Smith's eighteenth-century associates, social, political, and intellectual. Smith was much more than an unusually learned scholar of science and the classics; he was a remarkably careful and thoughtful observer who under-stood that the evolutionary processes of cultural change were in-visible to the participants. Like his friend, David Hume, he sought reasonable conjectural (theoretical) explanations of these observa-tions, but recognized that these were idle speculations of the mind if left unchallenged by confrontation with cases as "experiments" that serve to test the validity of the constructions. Be warned that Adam Smith's *Theory of Moral Sentiments* (1759) is a difficult read. His words are chosen carefully to convey depths of meaning that will be missed again and again. It is a work in psychology, in particular social psychology, written 125 years before it would become a field separate and distinct from natural philosophy. I believe it is Smith's most important work, and a good case can be made that he thought so also. His second and much more celebrated book cannot be properly understood without a thorough familiarity with his first book, hence, the widespread and incorrect view that he championed the unfettered expression of self-interest. I have explored the relationships of these books in several articles, including my first attempt in "The Two Faces of Adam Smith," *Southern Economic Journal* 65 (1998), pp. 1–19; and "Adam Smith: From Propriety and Sentiments to Property and Wealth," *Forum for Social Economics* 42 (2013), pp. 283–97.

17

ADAM SMITH AND ECONOMIC DEVELOPMENT

Amartya Sen

Adam Smith's claim to be the father of modern economics is strong—arguably stronger than that of any other economist. But is his work, including the departures that he initiated in economics, of significant interest specifically to problems of *economic development*? This question has not been much examined, and the reasons for this abstinence are not difficult to see. Smith's economic writings concentrated particularly on problems faced by Britain, France, and more generally Europe (rather than those of the non-Western world), and his ideas had a major impact on the understanding of the political economy—and policy making—in these countries. The context of Smith's economic writings, with their focus on the countries at the center of the Industrial Revolution (and at the metropolis of the growing imperial world), is so prominent, that it might seem a bit odd to think of Smith as a theorist of economic development.

And yet it can be argued that Smith was, in fact, a major development economist, and even that he pioneered the subject of development economics, as a part of his work in initiating modern economic analysis. Indeed, many of the insights and innovative economic thinking for which Smith is famous are quite central to development economics.

How is this dual role possible? How can the major contributions of the same person be central both (1) to mainstream economics, which has been geared particularly toward the understanding of economic and social relations in the rich economies of the world, *and* (2) to development economics, the concentration of which has to be, in one way or another, on the so-called developing economies—the world of the poor rather than of the rich?

This apparent puzzle cannot, however, be a deep mystery for at least three distinct reasons. First, when Smith was writing in the eighteenth century (his definitive book on economics, the *Wealth of Nations*, was published in 1776), Britain and France—and Europe in general—were not particularly rich economies. The problem these economies faced then were not vastly different from the challenges that the developing economies of today have to wrestle with. This applies to the choice of institutions (for example, how to make good use of the market economy as well as the transformative agency of the state) and to ways and means of increasing productivity (in particular, how to generate new skills and advance efficiency) and reducing the incidence of poverty (how to aid the indigents, including those covered by the Poor Laws of Britain).

The big divergence in prosperity between the rich and the poor countries of the world gathered momentum in the nineteenth century. This largely happened *after* Smith—and the development strategies that were pursued followed principles and policies on which Smith had thrown pioneering light. There is nothing really surprising in the fact that the principles on which Smith concentrated have much pertinence for the developing economies of today, no matter how relevant they may have remained even for the rich countries in the contemporary world.

Second, Smith's economics was much influenced by his moral and political philosophy. Smith saw his second book, the *Wealth of Nations* (WN), to be largely an extension of the philosophical work that presented in his first book, *The Theory of Moral Sentiments* (TMS), published in 1759, seventeen years before the *Wealth of Nations*. Aside from the importance of TMS for moral philosophy itself (which is very substantial), the intellectual connections between TMS and WN are quite central for enlightened economic analysis and policy making, in *any* country—rich or poor. Problems of normative evaluation as well as of having an adequate understanding of human motivations and social interrelations among people, analyzed by Smith, remain as fundamental for the problems faced by contemporary Brazil or India or Ghana, as they are to the challenges faced by today's Britain or Japan or the United States.

Third, development economics is a much broader subject than the economics of developing countries. When, for example, the economic crisis hit the richest economies of the world in 2008, beginning with the United States, the issues that came into focus, with telling rapidity, were, in many ways, developmental concerns, such as the need for an efficiently functioning market economy, the role of public regulation in restraining restless searches for expected profit (ignoring prudential as well as social concerns), and the predicament of the impoverished and the deprived even in an otherwise successful economy. Similarly, if the birth of the so-called welfare state in Europe at the end of the Second World War was a "developmental" move (as it certainly was), the forces demanding, right now, the removal—or sharp curtailment—of welfare provisions in parts of postcrisis Europe are also setting up developmental challenges.

The economics of structural change, and of long-run implications of short-run moves, can be very much a part of what can be called development economics. It would be arbitrarily restrictive to try to identify development economics exclusively with the economics of poor or developing countries. In the light of all this, the rationale of seeing Adam Smith as an outstanding development economist is not hard to find.

THE MARKET ECONOMY

The pioneering work of Smith included his far-reaching discussion of the usefulness and creativity of the market economy, and *why*—and particularly *how*—that dynamism worked. Smith never used the term "capitalism" (as far I have been able to determine), but his explication of the rationale of the market economy is central to the understanding of what is now seen as the basic success of capitalism in the modern world. Smith's causal investigation provided an illuminating diagnosis of the principles of the market economy just when that dynamism was powerfully emerging, and the contribution that the *Wealth of Nations* made to the understanding of this part of economics, among others, was absolutely monumental. Smith showed how the freeing of trade can very often be extremely helpful in generating economic prosperity through specialization in production and division of labor and through making good use of economies of large scale.

Those lessons remain crucially relevant even today. Indeed, the economic analyses that followed those early expositions of markets and capitals in the eighteenth century have succeeded in solidly establishing the understanding of the rationale of the market system in the corpus of mainstream economics. Central to Smith's approach to the achievements of the market economy is the critical importance of trade and exchange (departing from the mirage of tradeless prosperity). It is also crucial to Smithian analysis of economic progress—and of development—to understand the importance he attached to the economy of large scale and the formation of human skill and productivity through specialization.

One of the economists—also a great contributor to the world of economic ideas—namely David Ricardo, followed Smith in focusing on the importance of trade, but to a great extent departed from him in explaining the rationale of trade in terms of comparative costs of different countries—or regions—in the world.[1] In fact, the main thrust of "Ricardian" advocacy of trade lies in the variations in the resource bases of different countries (for example, country A may be richer in iron and country B in agricultural land), and they can all benefit through exchanging commodities, the production of which draws on the resources respectively plentiful in the different regions, giving them differential comparative advantages in the production of diverse commodities that can be exchanged with mutual profit.

While Ricardian reasoning and its variations have been central to a great deal of trade theory, the Smithian reasoning, focusing on benefits of specialization, and economies of scale and cultivated skill formation, have been a huge source of trade opportunities in the world. Even if all countries had the same mixture of resources, they could still greatly benefit from trade through specialization in different types of production. The benefits of trade do not depend only on the contingent circumstances of the different countries (in particular, having divergent availability of natural resources), and the people of the world can greatly benefit from more trade even if there were exactly the same natural resources everywhere. The benefits of specialization, economies of scale, and skill formation create and expand opportunities for trade and exchange. To get the benefits of specialization in some field, a country does not have to be, Smith's reasoning indicated, blessed with a preexisting resource base giving it a natural advantage: specialization creates its own resource base, through skill formation and learning, as well as economies of large scale. These Smithian lessons are very central to development economics, and remain as relevant today as they have been over the centuries.[2]

SMITH'S ANALYSIS OF EARLY DEVELOPMENT AND TRADE

Based on his analysis of the importance of trade for economic development, Smith even attempted a sketchy history of ancient civilizations in terms of the navigational opportunities they respectively enjoyed. He talked particularly about "of those great inlets, such as the Baltic and Adriatic seas in Europe, the Mediterranean and Euxine seas in both Europe and Asia, and the gulphs of Arabia, Persia, India, Bengal, and Siam, in Asia, to carry maritime commerce into the interior parts of that great continent." While the role of the Nile in the civilization of Northern Africa fell into the general pattern of Smith's analysis of ancient splendors, he attributed the backwardness of much of the rest—for example, "inland parts of Africa"—to the absence of navigational opportunities: "the great *rivers* of Africa are at too great a distance from one another to give occasion to any considerable inland navigation." Smith saw in the same light the historical backwardness of economies in that part of "Asia which lies any considerable way north of the Euxine and Caspian seas, the ancient Scythia, the modern Tartary and Siberia": "The sea of Tartary is the frozen ocean which admits of no navigation, and though some of the greatest *rivers* in the world run through that country, they are at too great a distance from one another to carry commerce and communication through the greater part of it" (WN I.iii.8).

If this line of analysis, related to the importance of physical conditions for trade and commerce, led Smith to emphasize the role of geography in early economic prosperity, he went on to comment also on the relevance of political boundaries for allowing easy development of exchange across regions. Smith observed:

> The commerce besides which any nation can carry on by means of a river which does not break itself into any great number of branches or canals, and which runs into another territory before it reaches the sea, can never be very considerable; because it is always in the power of the nations who possess that other territory to obstruct the communication between the upper country and the sea. The navigation of the Danube is of very little use to the different states of Bavaria, Austria and Hungary, in comparison of what it would be if any of them possessed the whole of its course till it falls into the Black Sea. (WN I.iii.8)

Smith's speculations on history were not, of course, as fully informed as those a modern historian, with a much greater informational base, can provide today. But it is striking how Smith used his basic analysis of the importance of trade and exchange to attempt some understanding of the history of economic successes, and related to it, the development of old civilizations. There is a link between Smith's pure economic theory and his ideas on the history of human civilization, and that link has some foundational connections with development economics. One of the interesting features of Smith's intellectual journey was his constant attempt to relate ideas from different disciplines to each other. This is itself an important precursor to the recognition of the need for multidisciplinary analysis of the process of development—a need that would be gradually recognized and celebrated as the field of development studies would be born and mature over the centuries.

LIMITS OF THE MARKET MECHANISM: OMISSIONS

Even as the positive contributions of market processes and profit motives were being clarified and explicated in a pioneering way by Adam Smith, their negative sides were also becoming clear—to Smith himself. The balancing of the power and achievements of the market mechanism, on one side, against the limitations of that mechanism (particularly the dangers of relying exclusively on it), on the other, was quite central to Smith's analysis of political economy. A balanced investigation remains critically important for development economics even in the contemporary world.

A number of socialist critics (including Karl Marx and also, to a great extent, John Stuart Mill), in the century following Smith's own writings, would present the case for censuring and ultimately supplanting capitalism. What is, however, particularly interesting is that even to Smith—the trailblazing exponent of the rationale of the market economy—the huge limitations of relying entirely on the market economy and only on the profit motive were clear enough (he sought substantial *supplementation* of the market mechanism, though he would not endorse any proposal to *supplant* it). Indeed, while Smith took the market economy to be an essential requirement for successful development, he did not take the pure market mechanism to be a free-standing performer of excellence, nor did he take the profit motive to be all that is needed for good economic performance.

Even though the so-called welfare state that would emerge later on in Europe was far away from ideas current in Smith's own time, he expressed with much clarity, in his various writings, his overwhelming concern about the fate of the poor and the disadvantaged, whose needs, he feared, would often not be met even by a very efficient market economy.

The most immediate failure of the market mechanism lies in *omissions* rather than commissions—the necessary pursuits that the market leaves *undone*. Smith was not only a defender of the role of the state in providing public services, such as education and poverty relief (but with greater freedom for the indigent than the Poor Laws of his day provided), but also deeply concerned about the inequality and poverty that might survive in an otherwise successful market economy. As it happens, Smith would also identify some errors of *commission* that the market mechanism would generate, but the basic limitations of the markets on which Smith particularly focused were matters of omission, rather than of commission.

Lack of clarity about that distinction between omission and commission has been responsible for some misdiagnosis of Smith's assessment of the market mechanism, and the insights on development economics that can be obtained from Smith's work. Consider, for example, Smith's analysis of the need for state action to prevent hunger and famines. Adam Smith's defense of private trade in food grains and criticism of prohibitory restrictions imposed by the state on free trade have often been interpreted as a proposition that state interference can only make hunger and starvation worse.

For example, when the governor of Bombay rejected in 1812 a proposal of government help to aid the victims of a growing famine in Gujarat by going beyond the market mechanism, he justified his decision to do nothing by referring to "the celebrated author of the *Wealth of Nations* concerning Corn-trade." Colonel Baird-Smith rapped the interventionist Warren Hastings on the knuckles in 1783 for moving food into a famine-affected Bengal, and traced this "mistake" to Hastings's failure to understand Adam Smith's economic analysis and policy advice. Baird-Smith was, however, generous enough to forgive Hastings because in 1783 many would not have yet understood "the first dawn of the revolution of thought on such questions produced ultimately by the publication of Adam Smith's *Wealth of Nations* in 1776."[3]

All this is, in fact, based on a complete misinterpretation of Smith's contentions. His defense of private trade, in this context, took the form only of disputing the belief, common among policy makers at his time, that allowing trade, particularly in food, would tend to produce serious distortions, and through that, an intensification of hunger. Smith strongly criticized that general belief, and argued that trade can greatly help to relieve shortage in a particular area by bringing in food (for example, food grains) from other areas that were not comparably stricken. Similarly, if income of those who have been pauperized could somehow be enhanced, then the market can help to feed these people. The problem, however, lies in the fact that the market need not generate any new income for those who have been pauperized, for example by crop failure, or a collapse of employment through floods or droughts, or by wars or social disorders.

The importance of the basic economic understanding that trade can help in moving food across regions, or between consumer groups, does not undermine in any way the need for state action to supplement the operations of the market by creating incomes for the indigent (for example, through work programs) because the market will typically not do this, on its own. If employment were to go down sharply thanks to bad economic circumstances or bad public policy, the market would not, on its own, re-create the lost incomes of those who are destituted. The new unemployed "would either starve, or be driven to seek a subsistence either by begging, or by the perpetration perhaps of the greatest enormities," and "want, famine, and mortality would immediately prevail" (WN I.viii.26). Smith rejected *market-excluding* intervention, but was in favor of *market-including* interventions aimed at doing the necessary things that the market may leave undone (in particular generating income, for example through public employment programs, and then allowing the market to respond by bringing food to meet the newly created demand coming from erstwhile indigents).[4]

POVERTY AND THE ROLE OF THE STATE

Despite all Smith did to explicate the contributions of the market mechanism, he was deeply concerned about the incidence of poverty, illiteracy, and relative deprivation that might remain despite an otherwise well-functioning market economy. This broader analysis profoundly complemented Smith's specialized championing of the market mechanism and the profit motive for specific purposes. As was mentioned earlier, Adam Smith is not known to have used the word, or the idea, of "capitalism," but, in addition, it would also be hard to carve out from his works any theory of the *sufficiency* of the market economy (as opposed to the *necessity* of markets).

Smith wanted institutional diversity and motivational variety—not monolithic markets and singular dominance of the profit motive.[5] Markets were seen as doing good work within their context, but they required support from other institutions for viability and success in securing human well-being and freedom.

Most importantly, Smith saw the task of political economy as the pursuit of "two distinct objects": "first, to provide a plentiful revenue or subsistence for the people, or more properly to enable them to provide such a revenue or subsistence for themselves; and secondly, to supply the state or commonwealth with a revenue sufficient for the publick services" (WN IV.intro.1). Smith's priorities for good economic performance and rapid economic development included, in addition to a well-functioning market economy, the role of the state in providing adequate public services: he talked particularly about universal—and free—education as well as intelligent and humane poverty relief.

Indeed, even in dealing with regulations that restrain the markets, Smith saw the case for intervention in the interest of the poor and the underdogs of society. At one stage he gave a formula of disarming simplicity: "When the regulation, therefore, is in favour of the workmen, it is always just and equitable, but it is sometimes otherwise when in favour of the masters" (WN I.x.c.61). It is doubtful that Smith would have meant this rather extremist remark, made in a particular context, to be taken literally, with universal application, but underlying the plural institutional structure that Smith proposed was not only Smith's skepticism of the reach of the market (important as the market economy is), but his attempt to marry the pursuit of the interests of the poor and the deprived with combined use of the market economy and well-chosen state intervention.

THE STATE AND UNIVERSAL EDUCATION

The Smithian development strategy, thus, is not one of relying just on the market mechanism, but to have a *market-inclusive* broad institutional structure with specific roles of the state to cater to the well-being and freedom of the less fortunate, and also to help build up human capability to participate in fast and sustained economic growth. One area of state intervention on which Smith attached special importance is that of education in general, and school education in particular. He wanted much greater use of state resources for public education and argued, "For a very small expence the publick can facilitate, can encourage, and can even impose upon almost the whole body of the people, the necessity of acquiring those most essential parts of education" (WN V.i.f.54). To be sure, the immediate context of Smith's remark was the removal of the continuing curse of unschooled "stupidity," with its penalties and destabilizing effects, but the transformative role of universal schooling fits in well with Smith's general focus on skill formation as an engine of development.

In focusing on the central role of universal education as a revolutionary strategy, Smith was both visionary and prophetic, in the eighteenth-century world of widespread illiteracy in Europe. The experiences of Europe—and of America—bring out most forcefully the pervasive role of education, led typically by governmental initiatives, in facilitating and sustaining economic and social development. That understanding also inspired the rising economic powers in Asia. Already in the mid-nineteenth century, following the Meiji Restoration in 1868, the transforming role of school education was seen with remarkable clarity in Japan—the pioneering country to undertake modern economic development in Asia. After Japan, other East Asian economies, such as South Korea, Taiwan, Singapore, Hong Kong, and of course China, followed similar routes and firmly focused on basic education, largely delivered by the state. In explaining the rapid economic progress of East Asia, its willingness to make good use of the global market economy has been rightly emphasized. But that process was greatly helped by the achievements of these countries in public education. Widespread participation in a global economy would have been hard to accomplish if people could not read or write. The so-called East Asian strategy of economic development, combining rapid progress in universal education and widespread use of the global market economy, can perhaps be best understood in terms of the strategy for economic progress and development that Adam Smith was powerfully advocating.

ERRORS OF COMMISSION OF THE MARKET ECONOMY

If Adam Smith's reservations on the market economy about errors of omission of the market have tended to be drowned in the stylized representation of Smith as a "free marketeer," the challenge is even greater in understanding that Smith also had much to say—of great interest—about errors of commission of the market. It was not only that the market leaves many important tasks undone, but also that the operation of an unregulated market can lead to serious mistakes in the performance of the economy. That part of Smith's analysis also has significant relevance to development economics, both for poor countries that are trying to initiate rapid development and for rich countries that can get into instability and downturns through an overreliance on the market economy (despite the market being such a general engine of economic expansion and performance).

This applies particularly to Smith's analysis of the promoters of excessive risk in search of profits, whom he called "prodigals and projectors." Smith's use of these terms was quite pejorative. For example, by "projector" Smith did not mean those who "form a project," but specifically used it in the derogatory sense, apparently common from 1616 (so it appears from *The Shorter Oxford English Dictionary*), meaning, among other things, "a promoter of bubble companies; a speculator; a cheat." Indeed, Jonathan Swift's unflattering portrayal of "projectors" in *Gulliver's Travels*, published in 1726 (fifty years before the *Wealth of Nations*), corresponds closely enough to Smith's deployment of that word.[6] Unwavering faith in the wisdom of the stand-alone market economy, which has had considerable responsibility in the removal of the established regulations in a number of countries, including the United States, tends to assume away the activities of prodigals and projectors in a way that would have shocked the pioneering exponent of the rationale of the market economy.[7] In addition to possibly generating a financial crisis, the ability of the "prodigals and projectors" to take capital away from really productive investment to bubbles and exuberances of one kind or another can, Smith argued, lead to misallocation of investment resources of a country. Indeed, Smith warned that relying entirely on an unregulated market economy can easily pave the way for "a great part of the capital of the country" being "kept out of the hands which were most likely to make a profitable and advantageous use of it, and thrown into those which were most likely to waste and destroy it" (WN II.iv.14–15).

Smith's reservations about the market economy—not just about its omissions but also about commissions—may seem quite strange to those who see Smith as being an unqualified admirer of the pure market mechanism. Interestingly enough, Smith's reservations about the market mechanism were subjects of discussion in his own days, and even for a decade or so after his death. There was a major reinterpretation of Smith around the beginning of the nineteenth century, when the radical Smith, critical of blind allegiance to any one institution (including the market), was remolded into the image, which flourishes to this day, of a deeply conservative Smith, who constantly sings unqualified praise of the stand-alone market. In his own time, Smith's ideas were often invoked by revolutionary authors across the Channel, and there can be little doubt that he was a very established figure in the French radical—and indeed revolutionary—circles (led particularly by the influential Marquis de Condorcet), who were inspired by Smith's writings. The view of a conservative and single-mindedly promarket Smith would emerge and become the standard view of Smith, particularly in England, well after Smith's death.[8]

In one of the really interesting, if largely forgotten, intellectual debates of the eighteenth century, Jeremy Bentham grumbled about Smith's inability to understand enough about the virtues of the market economy, and took Smith to task in a long letter he wrote to Smith suggesting that he—Smith—was unreasonably antimarket. Smith should, Bentham argued, leave the market alone, rather than criticize—and propose to interfere with—the market for its inability to control those whom Smith called "prodigals and projectors" and that he should give up supporting state regulation of financial transactions.[9] Bentham may have missed the force of Smith's reasoning on this subject (indeed I believe he certainly did that), but his diagnosis of Smith's skepticism of the market was not really mistaken.

RATIONALITY, SELF-INTEREST, AND BROADER MOTIVATIONS

One of the central issues for successful development is the role of human motivation in generating rapid economic expansion and the sharing of the fruits of that expansion. Even though Smith gave much room for emotions in guiding people's thoughts as well as actions, he did think that even our instinctive attitudes to particular behavior cannot but rely—if only implicitly—on our reasoned understanding of causal connections between conduct and consequences in "a vast variety of instances." Furthermore, first perceptions may also change in response to critical examination, for example on the basis of causal empirical investigation that may show, Smith noted in *The Theory of Moral Sentiments*, that a certain "object is the means of obtaining some other." And in the pursuit of reasoning (and this is the central issue here), a great deal more than self-interest and selfishness can—and does—come into Smith's investigation. In this broad understanding of the role of reasoning in human behavior, we can see one of the basic ingredients of development economics.

Mischaracterization of Smith's analysis of reasons for action has been a rampant feature of twentieth-century economics. For example, in two well-known and forcefully argued papers, the famous Chicago economist George Stigler has presented his "self-interest theory" (including the belief that "self-interest dominates the majority of men") as being "on Smithian lines."[10] Stigler was not really alone or idiosyncratic in that diagnosis—this is indeed the standard view of Smith that has been powerfully promoted by many writers who constantly invoke Smith to support their belief in the unique importance—and rationality—of the profit motive.

There is no room in the beliefs of this "as if Smith" for moral values of various kinds, from altruism to social commitment—values the reasonableness of which Smith discussed in considerable detail in *The Theory of Moral Sentiments*. Indeed, that book—Smith's first—opens with the following sentence: "How selfish soever man may be supposed, there are evidently some principles in his nature, which interests him in the fortunes of others, and render their happiness necessary to him, though he derives nothing from it except the pleasure of seeing it" (TMS I.i.1.1). The analysis of plural objectives and a broader understanding of human motivation are further developed by Smith as the book proceeds, and he makes particular use of his thought experiment of "the impartial spectator" as a device for reasoned self-scrutiny, of which, he thought, reasoning human beings are perfectly capable (TMS III.1.2).

Instead of the naïve simplicity of the "as if" Smith's behavioral beliefs, the real Smith distinguishes between the different kinds of reasons people have in taking an interest in the lives of others, separating out "sympathy," "generosity," "public spirit," and other motivations, each of which differs from the others, and yet all of which have the implication of taking people away from purely selfish pursuit of their own interests.

MOTIVATIONAL DEMANDS OF ECONOMIC DEVELOPMENT

The fact that profit seeking is an important part of human motivation is not, of course, in doubt, but the question is whether that is the *only* motivation that can move people—a question that has major implications for development studies. In providing incentives for economic activities—from investment to work—economic gain can be a major factor, and a development plan that ignores that elementary connection can do it only at its own peril. And yet there is so much more to people's motivation than can be captured within the limited box of profits. The development of good work habits, spontaneous punctuality, regular diligence, attention to work performance, ability to work cooperatively with others— all this is much aided by broader motivations.

Smith did note that sophisticated reasoning about self-interest can cover a larger ground by taking note of incentives developed in situations that are repeated or paralleled over time. In making use of what in today's terminology of game theory would be called "repeated games," Smith developed his own theory of the rewards of good reputation, including the benefits arising from people having reason to develop "trust" in decent behavior and reliability of each other. Smith noted that the credit of the trader depends on the way in which he is judged by other people, about their "probity, and prudence" (WN I.x.b.20).[11] While Smith emphasized the need for long-run prudential considerations in developing good reputation based on trustworthy behavior, he also pointed out that the success of an economy, no less than that of a society, depends, among other things, on people's spontaneous sense of responsibility and on people having a basic sense of owing each other.

A great deal of the confusion surrounding Smith's presumptions about human motivation and his assessment of the usefulness of different kinds of motives has tended to arise from not distinguishing between (1) people's reasons for seeking trade and (2) the motivations that make different kinds of economic activities, including trading, successful and stable. It is in answer to the first question that Smith noted the adequacy of the motive of self-seeking. He noted that to explain why people seek trade and pursue exchange, we do not have to go beyond the simple pursuit of self-interest. In his most famous and widely quoted passage from the *Wealth of Nations* (very popular in mainstream economics as well as in the specialized discipline that has come to be called "law and economics," and also in so-called rational choice politics), Smith wrote, "It is not from the benevolence of the butcher, the brewer, or the baker that we expect our dinner, but from their regard to their own interest. We address ourselves, not to their humanity but to their self-love" (WN I.ii.2). The butcher, the brewer, and the baker want to get our money in exchange for the meat, the beer, and the bread they make, and we—the consumers—want their meat, beer, and bread and are ready to pay for them with our money. The exchange benefits us all, and we do not have to be raving altruists to find reason to seek such exchange. This is a fine point about motivation for trade—interesting in itself—but it is not a claim about the adequacy of self-seeking for the success of a society or even of the market economy, or even the success and sustainability of trade and exchange.

Indeed, a market economy demands a variety of values for its success, including mutual trust and confidence, whether derived from the discipline of "repeated games" (when that works) or from reasoning of other kinds that do not draw only on self-interest. Smith made this basic point with several illustrations. He argued, for example, "When the people of any particular country has such confidence in the fortune, probity, and prudence of a particular banker, as to believe he is always ready to pay upon demand such of his promissory notes as are likely to be at any time presented to him; those notes come to have the same currency as gold and silver money, from the confidence that such money can at any time be had for them" (WN II.ii.28). Smith discussed why such confidence need not always exist. Even though the champions of the baker-brewer-butcher reading of Smith, enshrined in many economic books, may be at a loss about how to understand the recent economic crisis of 2008 (since people—even bakers, brewers, and butchers—still had excellent reason to *seek* more trade even during the crisis, but had far less *opportunity* to sell their wares), the devastating consequences of mistrust and the shattering of mutual confidence that was an important feature of the crises would not have appeared puzzling to Adam Smith.

Furthermore, going beyond just the smooth working of the market economy, Smith also discussed the need for various institutions that can do what the markets may not be able to achieve. He was deeply concerned about the incidences of poverty, illiteracy, and relative deprivation that might remain despite a well-functioning market economy, and our determination to do something about these failures demands more than the pursuit of self-interest and even of self-centered prudence. Smith wanted institutional diversity and motivational variety—neither monolithic markets nor the singular dominance of the profit motive.

REASONING AND HABIT FORMATION

Development economics demands a realistic understanding of the variety of motivations that enter into human behavior, and the institutional demands of economic development have to take note of these variations. On one side, many well-meaning but overtrusting development initiatives have foundered in the world because of unanticipated self-seeking behavior—for example by public servants making use of their power to seek bribes and other personal advantages—and there is need for more realism in setting up these arrangements. And yet, on the other side, a failure to develop work ethics and disciplined conduct restricts the feasibility of many institutional arrangements on which many successful development experiences across the world have standardly depended.

Smith's contribution here did not take the form of asserting the existence of an insatiable thirst for self-seeking by all people, nor affirming the preexistence of a tradition of morally upright behavior by all. He recognized the fallibility of human conduct in moral terms, but emphasized the possibility both of the influence of reasoning on human behavior, and of the formation of good conduct based on reasoning that might become habitual, even when the original reasoning does not remain uppermost in people's thinking. As Smith put it, "Many men behave very decently, and through the whole of their lives avoid any considerable degree of blame, and who yet, perhaps, never felt the sentiment upon the propriety of which we found our approbation of their conduct, but acted merely from a regard to what they saw were the established rules of behaviour" (TMS III.5.1). In the development of "established rules of behaviour" lies one of the most important challenges of economic development. Smith was as skeptical of naïve faith in people's morality and honesty as he was of universal and unchangeable corrupt behavior. A combination of accountability and enhancement of new rules of behavior remains as important for development efforts today—from India to Brazil—as it was for the development experiences in Smith's own time.

IMPERIALISM, INEQUALITY, AND HUMANITY

I end this essay with some remarks on Adam Smith's attitude to different people across the world, divided by race, culture, class, and economic and social fortunes. The subject of development economics suffered for a long time from a tendency of theorists from the rich and developed countries to assume, if only implicitly, that what their nations have actually accomplished might not be at all achievable by other nations—no matter what policies they followed. A sense of racial or civilizational superiority has served, for a long period, as a barrier to open-minded assessment of developmental thinking in a world of imperial dominance.

Smith was fundamentally opposed to trying to understand observed inequalities in achievements in different parts of the world by any presumption of differences in intrinsic qualities of human beings. In fact, he found that general presumption to be not only false, but also so revolting that he often opted for considerable exaggeration in the opposite direction in repudiating such beliefs, which he took to be empirically shoddy and psychologically nasty.

In Smith's own time, the issue of slavery had raised questions of human inequality in quite a prominent way. Smith not only was totally hostile to the institution of slavery, but also expressed forcefully his indignation at the presumption of the superior racial endowments of the white man over black Africans. Breaking into something of hyperbole, the indignant Smith remarked in *The Theory of Moral Sentiments*, "There is not a negro from the coast of Africa who does not, in this respect, possess a degree of magnanimity which the soul of his sordid master is too often scarce capable of conceiving" (TMS V.2.9).[12]

Nearer his home, Smith was similarly angered by the tendency of the English to blame the culture of the Irish for their own woes—a tendency that went back a long time, at least to Edmund Spenser's *Faerie Queene* in the sixteenth century. Indeed, during the notorious Irish famines of the 1840s—almost a century after the *Moral Sentiments*—the often-repeated English diagnosis that the Irish culture had a big responsibility in causing Ireland's terrible problems would be dusted up again. The Irish were, of course, accused of indolence and other traditional vices, but even the Irish dependence on the potato, it was argued in London, generated a culturally inflicted vulnerability that, it was argued in London, directly contributed to the great Irish famines.

Smith found this kind of cultural racism, already common in the eighteenth century, quite contemptible. And this perhaps explains why he launched into an oddly emphatic defense of the potato, closely linked with a defense of the Irish people, despite Smith's lack of expertise (it would be fair to presume) on the subject. He remarked, "The chairmen, porters, and coalheavers in London, and those unfortunate women who live by prostitution, the strongest men and the most beautiful women perhaps in the British dominions, are said to be the greater part of them from the lowest rank of people in Ireland, who are generally fed with this root [potato]. No food can afford a more decisive proof of its nourishing quality, or of its being peculiarly suitable to the health of the human constitution" (WN I.xi.b.42). Even if one is not converted by Smith's arguments about relying on the potato for one's nutrition, it is easy to see what incensed Smith so much to take up the subject matter at all.

Going beyond Smith's resistance to racial and ethnic prejudices, Smith is also firmly resistant to the idea that people's fortunes relate to their inborn merits. On the contrary, Smith argued, the fortunes of the rich—often acquired without any special talents—create the impression that they are benefitting from the special nature of their inborn qualities. Smith argued, "The difference of natural talents in different men is, in reality, much less than we are aware of; and the very different genius which appears to distinguish men of different professions, when grown up to maturity, is not upon many occasions so much the cause as the effect of the division of labour. The difference between the most dissimilar characters, between a philosopher and a common street porter, for example, seems to arise not so much from nature as from habit, custom, and education" (WN I.ii.4). Poverty, Smith argues, is "extremely unfavourable to the rearing of children."

The educational disadvantage applies, Smith argued, not only in the rearing of children, but also throughout the lives of the working classes precisely because of their economic disadvantage and poverty:

> People of some rank and fortune are generally eighteen or nineteen years of age before they enter upon that particular business, profession, or trade, by which they propose to distinguish themselves in the world. They have before that full time to acquire, or at least to fit themselves for afterwards acquiring, every accomplishment which can recommend them to the public esteem, or render them worthy of it. . . . It is otherwise with the common people. They have

little time to spare for education. Their parents can scarce afford to maintain them even in infancy. As soon as they are able to work they must apply to some trade by which they can earn their subsistence. That trade, too, is generally so simple and uniform as to give little exercise to the understanding, while, at the same time, their labour is both so constant and so severe, that it leaves them little leisure and less inclination to apply to, or even to think of, anything else. (WN V.i.f.53)

Smith's strong desire to see all human beings in symmetrical terms is at least as important for the moral attitude surrounding his political economy as it is in understanding the epistemic presumptions about human potentials that appealed to Smith. It is certainly possible to fault the details of Smith's general empirical claims about human equality, and yet those presumptions reflect an attitude about humanity that serves well as a moral backdrop to Smith's analysis of developmental possibilities for all people. As it happens, all the policy wisdom that emerges from Smith's analyses, discussed earlier, remain unaffected even if there are interindividual variations (as there may well be, unrelated to race-based or class-based stereotyping that Smith challenged).

Adam Smith's stubborn opposition to the racism, imperial prejudice, ethnic snobbery, and intellectual arrogance common among influential people in the world around him, indicates how far ahead of his time Smith was as a morally sensitive thinker. As it happens, Smith's insightful contributions to development economics, which I discussed earlier, are not in any way compromised by the fact that he wanted to see all human beings in the best possible light. The rough world of empirical details need not, even for practical purposes, tarnish the intellectual power and humane reach of perhaps the finest political economist of all time.

NOTES

1. David Ricardo, *On the Principles of Political Economy and Taxation* (1817), reprinted *The Works and Correspondence of David Ricardo*, ed. Piero Sraffa, with the assistance of Maurice Dobb, vol. 1 (Cambridge: 2005).

2. For modern economic reasoning involving these dynamic aspects of trade, see particularly Paul Krugman, *Rethinking International Trade* (Cambridge, MA: 1990). Also see Paul Krugman and Elhanan Helpman, *Market Structure and Foreign Trade* (Cambridge, MA: 1985); and Paul Roemer, "Increasing Returns and Long Run Growth," *Journal of Political Economy* 94 (1986), pp. 1002–37.

3. For these and many similar references citing Smith to justify the policy of nonintervention in developing famines, see S. Ambirajan, *Classical Political Economy and British Policy in India* (Cambridge: 1978).

4. That combination of market-inclusive but state-dependent policies has been widely used in recent years in successful attempts of famine prevention both in India and in Africa. On this, see Jean Dreze and Amartya Sen, *Hunger and Public Action* (Oxford: 1987).

5. See Emma Rothschild, *Economic Sentiments: Adam Smith, Condorcet and the Enlightenment* (Cambridge, MA: 2001).

6. I am grateful to Giorgio Basevi for drawing my attention to the importance of the similarity of terminology between Smith and Swift.

7. There is a similarity here with the causation of the recent economic crisis of 2008, in which overspeculative financial investment in search of a "quick kill" paid a big part.

8. See Rothschild, *Economic Sentiments*.

9. Bentham included this letter in the second of the two prefaces he wrote for the second edition of his combative defense of the market economy against regulations that restrain usury: *Defence of Usury* (London: 1790).

10. See George Stigler, "Smith's Travels on the Ship of State," in *Essays on Adam Smith*, ed. A. S. Skinner and T. Wilson (Oxford: 1975), esp. p. 237, and "Economics or Ethics?," in *Tanner Lectures on Human Values*, vol. 2, ed. S. McMurrin (Cambridge: 1981), esp. p. 176.

11. See also WN II.ii.68–69, III.i.4, III.iv.1–4, IV.ix.13.

12. For this reference and many similar ones, see Emma Rothschild and Amartya Sen, "Adam Smith's Economics," in *The Cambridge Companion to Adam Smith*, ed. Knud Haakonssen (Cambridge: 2006).

PART IV

Smith beyond Economics

ADAM SMITH AND RELIGION

Gordon Graham

The title "Adam Smith and Religion" potentially covers three quite different aspects of its subject. There is first the matter of Smith's personal religious beliefs, and the extent to which they were reflected in the events of his life. Second, there is the matter of the theological components and implications, if any, of his philosophical work. Third, there is his "philosophy of religion" properly so called, which is to say, his account of the place and nature of religion in human life. On this topic he shows himself to be engaged in philosophical anthropology rather than philosophical theology, and thus importantly demonstrates the possibility of a "philosophy of religion" quite different in style to the kinds of arguments that have dominated the subject in recent decades. This chapter considers these three topics in turn.

SMITH'S PERSONAL FAITH

The degree to which religious beliefs and interests colored Adam Smith's life is evidently a matter of biography. This already presents us with a difficulty. Those who have undertaken to write biographies of Adam Smith almost invariably begin by noting the paucity of evidence with which they have to work. Smith left a great deal of written material, but very little of it relates to his personal life. He did not keep a diary, and though reasonably gregarious, he does not appear to have been a regular correspondent. He made some strong and enduring friendships, but they were not much maintained by the exchange of letters. Even his mother received fewer letters than his evident devotion to her would have warranted, a neglect he himself acknowledged. If we had more biographical material of this kind, however, it would probably tell us relatively little about his personal faith. Smith seems to have been a strikingly private individual, unlikely to commit such intimate thoughts to writing, and in any case cautious about giving hostages to fortune.

Accordingly, any account of Smith's own religious sentiments must be largely conjectural, based partly on the circumstances of his life and upbringing in the society and family to which he belonged, and partly on inferences drawn from his published works. On the strength of these two sources, it seems safe to conclude that he was both highly conversant with the religious and theological questions of the day, and at home in a society in which religion figured prominently. His father's library was well stocked with theology, his mother was a devout Presbyterian, and he had many clerical friends, acquaintances, and former students. We have little evidence on personal attendance at church services, but he certainly supported the church as an institution, and paid for a pew at the Canongate church where he is buried. His letters show he knew the Bible well, and TMS and WN reveal his reflective acquaintance with both theological and ecclesiastical issues. Though it is impossible to say anything about his personal religious practices, or his attitude to the sacraments, it is clear from his writings that he was more than broadly sympathetic to the "Moderate" variety of Presbyterianism that was culturally ascendant in Scotland for most of his life. Smith admired his teacher Francis Hutcheson and his friend David Hume in equal proportions, but he tended rather more to the religious moderation of Hutcheson than to the religious skepticism of Hume, especially when it might prove the occasion of trouble or conflict. This explains, in all likelihood, his reluctance to expedite the publication of the *Dialogues* after Hume's death. Given Smith's great admiration for Hume, this is a significant fact. Commentators have generally supposed that on the subject of religion Smith and Hume were of one mind. But there is reason, both textual and circumstantial, to think that Smith's admiration did not mean that he found himself in perfect agreement with Hume on the matter of religion. In particular, it seems plausible to think that for Smith, but not for Hume, religious sentiments are to be included among the "natural beliefs" without which we cannot function properly.[1]

Yet the difference between their two positions is not as great as might be supposed. Smith may be said to have had a firmer belief in "true religion" than Hume did, describing it in WN as "pure and rational" (WN V.i.g.8). On the other hand, he was no less wary of the "superstition" and "enthusiasm" with which Hume contrasts it. On his appointment as a professor at Glasgow, Smith, like Hutcheson before him, was obliged to sign the Westminster Confession. He freely did so, but petitioned to be exempted from the standard practice of beginning each lecture with prayer. When Smith's request was denied, however, he did as he was required—though it is said that his prayers were perfunctory in comparison to the more fulsome prayers that were the norm. It is hard to say just what such a petition and subsequent compliance meant. Hume, after all, knew of these requirements when he hoped to be appointed to the chair of logic at Glasgow. Had he been successful he would, presumably, have done the same as Smith. Perhaps Smith's request arose more from a belief that religious observance should be kept separate from academic instruction, than from personal doubts. However this may be, it is a petition one cannot imagine Francis Hutcheson making, but then, Hutcheson was an ordained minister. There is no solid evidence that Smith ever meant to emulate him in this. The requirement that a Snell Exhibition be awarded to students who had Anglican ordination in mind was scrapped two years before Smith was awarded his. If, in reality, Smith's personal attitude to religion lay a little closer to Hume's than to Hutcheson's, he nevertheless successfully avoided the imputation of skepticism. One contemporary reviewer of the TMS (a Presbyterian minister and former student) captures his successful balancing act: "The Author seems to have . . . a regard for Religion at least it does not appear to me that the book has any licentious tendency like the most part of David Hume's writing . . . tho' perhaps the Principles are at bottom the same."[2]

Religion (in contrast to theology) is an essentially practical matter. It is about how one is to conduct oneself, and how life is best led. On this score something can indeed be said about Smith's "personal faith." His conformity to the conventional religion of his times was not insincere; he believed that religion had an important social function, even if this function was best served by a religion that is (so to speak) theology-lite, and that this, broadly ethical, function worked by grounding action in reason. At the same time, his famous commendation of Hume "as approaching as nearly to the idea of a perfectly wise and virtuous man,"[3] combined with his denunciation of "the futile mortifications of the monastery" (TMS III.2.35) makes it reasonable to infer that Smith's own ideal of how human life should be lived did not include much, if anything, of what is usually meant by "Christian spirituality."

SMITH AND THEOLOGY

In 2001 Lisa Hill published an essay titled "The Hidden Theology of Adam Smith."[4] Her purpose was to reverse an interpretative trend that had stripped Smith's social theory of its more explicitly theological elements. This trend argues that the theological references in TMS and WN constitute little more than an invocation of the traditional language of piety that the culture of contemporary readership then required. Conventional expressions like "the Author of Nature," which Hume uses as easily as Smith, can be replaced by concepts of biological and/or social evolution without significant loss to his system of ideas. Smith's "invisible hand," on this account, is not a hidden device, and certainly not the hand of God.

Contrary to this line of thought, Hill's contention is that a thoroughly secularized version of the "science of human nature" that underlies both TMS and WN simply will not work. Divine teleology and providential guidance are *essential* elements. Intentional design and deliberate regulation on the part of human beings, individually or collectively, cannot ensure that all things work together for social and economic good. That much Smith and his secular interpreters agree upon, of course. But a "blind" process, like spontaneous "order" or market "forces," cannot secure this either.

Nor did Smith think it could. There must be a natural ordering principle built in, which, if it is not hampered or distorted, will have the general good as its outcome. And there must be both an originating source, and final regulator, of this ordering principle if it is to have the result it is supposed to have. This originating source and final regulator can only be a divine Being with the benevolence, omniscience, and omnipotence required to make the otherwise competing and divergent actions and desires of human beings combine in ways that are conducive to the general good. As Smith himself puts it, "The administration of the great system of the universe . . . the care of the universal happiness of all rational and sensible beings, is the business of God and not of man" (TMS VI.ii.3.6). It can be argued, of course, that in the explanations of social forms that Smith offers, efficient causes do all the work, and final causes little or none.[5] The issue, though, is not simply an interpretative one, since there are philosophical reasons for holding that within a providentialist framework efficient causes work only because of the teleological ends they serve.

It is not quite clear what the force of "hidden" is in Hill's title. At one point she alludes to Smith's having been "deliberately evasive about his precise personal convictions."[6] The thesis of the essay, however, suggests something different—that a "hidden or 'secret' theology is revealed by examining and disclosing the working of his . . . 'invisible hand.' "[7] Yet, this interpretation is not entirely satisfactory either, because Hill is at pains to show just how *evident* Smith's reference to divine agency and providential oversight are to anyone who reads the text dispassionately. All attempts to dismiss them as merely pious platitudes that do no real work are hugely implausible, precisely because, if she is to be believed, the theological dimension of his thought is there for all to see. Part III of TMS, for example, is devoted to uncovering "the foundations of our judgments concerning our own sentiments and . . . sense of duty." It then lists religion among these foundations, and includes a chapter (chapter 5) with a title expressly declaring that "the general rules of morality . . . are justly regarded as the laws of the Deity." This, Smith goes on to claim, is an "opinion which is first impressed by nature, and afterwards confirmed by reasoning and philosophy" (TMS III.5.3). If this is what is meant by Smith's "theology," it cannot on any reasonable interpretation be said to be "hidden."

One further possible interpretation is this. While there are indeed *evident* theological components in Smith's system, perhaps its *full* theological implications are "hidden." That is to say, if we take Smith's system as our starting point, contrary to what many have supposed, we will find suggestive material for *further* theological work. This third interpretation is implied by the title of a collection of essays published in 2011—*Adam Smith as Theologian*.[8] Inspired in part by Hill's paper, the book's title, together with its inclusion in a series called "Studies in Religion," suggests that Smith was a significant theologian as well as a moral philosopher and social theorist. But if this *is* the suggestion, then it is a very implausible one. Hill argues persuasively that "[f]ar from being incidental to his scheme, it is the theological constructs—the design principle and a teleology which embodies first, final and efficient causes—which make the system work."[9] Let us suppose this to be true. Even so, very little of theological substance follows. The theology presupposed by Smith's system is minimal and entirely "natural." In fact, it differs very little from the "thin" deism to which, it can be argued, even David Hume subscribed. In the opening of Book XII of the *Dialogues* Hume famously declares, in the voice of the skeptical Philo, that "a purpose, an intention, or design strikes everywhere the most careless, the most stupid thinker; and no man can be so hardened in absurd systems, as at all times to reject it."[10] Yet the conversation that occupies the remainder of this book concludes that the most we can infer from this incontrovertible "evidence" of design is that "the cause or causes of order in the universe probably bear some remote analogy to human intelligence."[11]

Smith's natural theology, it is true, goes rather further than this. He attributes omniscience and omnipotence to the "Author of Nature," and more importantly, where Hume argues that the natural order of the world is morally neutral, Smith supposes that the final end of the system is the promotion of happiness. Moreover, he accords to God the role of a judge in matters of moral conduct.

These further attributes, though, are not explicitly Christian; the revealed theology of God's incarnation in Christ plays no part in them.[12] The key question, however, is what the logical relation of Smith's slightly richer natural theology is to the theory of moral sentiments and the generation of wealth that he is principally concerned to advance. Hill seems correct in arguing that the secularists seriously misinterpret Smith's texts when they try to excise or discount his use of theological concepts. There is still the possibility that an alternative explanation of moral life and social progress, formulated within something like Smith's system, might successfully *discard* the theological components. This, after all, is the impact that the advent of Darwin has been widely thought to have on other eighteenth-century versions of the "design" argument. The theory of evolution appears to offer an alternative, nontheological explanation of precisely those elements of "design" that even "the most stupid thinker" cannot deny. If it is successful in this, then appearances of "design" lend no support to the "remote analogy" that Hume was prepared to concede.[13]

Is there such an alternative explanation for the order we find in the social world as well as the natural world? Evolutionary explanations of moral and political life are less obviously successful than evolutionary explanations of plants and animals. This fact raises a further possibility. Might Smith's providentialist explanation of social phenomena provide support for theology on the basis of an "inference to the best explanation"? The argument would go like this:

(1) Smith's system is the best explanation we have of moral life/economic development.

(2) Smith's system presupposes a Divine Author.

Therefore, and in the absence of better explanations,

(3) the existence of social order/economic development, gives us reason to infer the existence of a Divine Author.

Abductive arguments of this form (IBE) that take the natural world as their starting point are widely employed in contemporary philosophy of religion and elsewhere, to explain, for instance the "fine tuning" of the universe that makes biological life possible.[14] Perhaps the social world provides an interestingly different starting point. The logical cogency of IBE is a matter of some debate, however, not least because it relies crucially on an estimate of the "prior probability" of the *explanans*. How probable is the postulation of a Divine Author in advance of any evidence? To those who regard it as highly improbable, or just imponderable, any IBE argument will be wholly unpersuasive. For present purposes, though, it is enough to observe that Smith does not use his observations on morality, economy, and society to offer any argument of this kind. Had he done so—implicitly or explicitly—there would perhaps be reason to consider him a natural theologian with a new slant on an old argument. But there is no "hidden" theology of this kind. If any argument of this sort is to be made plausible, someone else must do all the work. Adam Smith "as a theologian," it seems reasonably clear, has so little to offer us, that it scarcely seems plausible to call him a "theologian" at all—a conclusion, I am inclined to think, with which Smith himself would readily concur.

SMITH AND RELIGION

In both TMS and WN, Smith writes about "religion" more often than he writes about "God." This reflects his chief interest in the subject, namely, the source of religion in human nature and its place in the development of a social life. In this regard, Smith engages in a kind of philosophy of religion more characteristic of his period than the philosophical theology that the posthumous publication of Hume's *Dialogues* eventually made dominant. For Smith and his contemporaries, the identification of "true religion" was both a descriptive and a normative task. It required careful empirical inquiry about the natural impulses and inclinations that human beings exhibit, the religious practices of modern and ancient societies, and a critical discrimination separating religion, superstition, and dogma based on emotion ("enthusiasm"). Superstition and enthusiasm are the dangerous forms in which the religious inclinations of human beings show themselves. "True" religion, by contrast, can play a beneficial role in the lives of individuals and the well-being of societies. That is why "pure and rational religion, free from every mixture of absurdity, imposture or fanaticism [is] such as wise men in all ages of the world [have] wished to see established" (WN V.i.g.8).

By Smith's account, the benefits of true religion lie first and foremost in the psychological and moral lives of individuals. Human beings have moral sentiments "implanted" in their nature as deeply as the appetite for food or sex. Contra the Stoics, they cannot help caring more about their own happiness than that of others, and contra the "whining and melancholy moralists" (TMS III.3.9), they do not need to feel guilty about this. At the same time, human beings are not the rampant egoists of Hobbes and Mandeville. The good opinion of others matters to them, and they have a rational faculty that enables them to make an impartial assessment of their own conduct. Still, in the ordinary course of life, the average human being cannot be expected to deliberate with "exact justness" about the best way of "acting upon all occasions with the most delicate and accurate propriety." "The coarse clay of which the bulk of mankind are formed, cannot be wrought up to such perfection. There is scarce any man, however, who by discipline, education and example, may not be so impressed with a regard to general rules, as to act upon almost every occasion with tolerable decency, and through the whole of his life to avoid any considerable degree of blame" (TMS III.5.1).

Moral rules work to the general good because they are the commands and laws of a Deity "who will finally reward the obedient and punish the transgressors of their duty" (TMS III.5.3). Here Smith's providentialism comes into play. At the same time he observes that this final outcome may sometimes be hard to see and to believe in. Life does not always go well for us, a fact about the human condition that easily weakens our moral resolve to keep these rules. And it may sometimes appear decidedly advantageous to ignore them. What is needed is a "sacred regard to general rules," and this is where religion comes into play. The rules of justice, truth, and so on are insufficient in themselves to secure universal adherence, when there are "so many strong motives to violate" them. Neither impartiality nor self-interest is sufficient to motivate enough of the people enough of the time, and so "nature" steps in by giving us a deep seated "reverence for those important rules of conduct," without which "the very existence of human society . . . would crumble into nothing" (TMS III.5.2). These rules are "sacred" insofar as we revere them, and we revere them because of the religious sentiments that are built in to our nature. "Religion, even in its rudest form, gave a sanction to the rules of morality long before the age of artificial reasoning and philosophy. That the terrors of religion should thus enforce the natural sense of duty, was of too much importance to the happiness of mankind, for nature to leave it dependent upon the slowness and uncertainty of philosophical researches" (TMS III.5.4).

Natural religion is to be distinguished from natural theology. It consists not in a set of metaphysical beliefs, but in human emotions and dispositions, including the "natural pangs of an affrighted conscience . . . from which no principles of irreligion can entirely deliver [us]" (TMS III.2.9). The religious impulse, however, is not merely negative. It includes "reverence" as well as "terror," and it does not only result in injunction and prohibition. It also generates moral confidence and sustains hope in times of adversity. Religion locates the ultimate vindication of the just over the unjust beyond human welfare and belief. It thus enables moral motivation to survive the potentially baneful effects of personal temptation, popular opinion and susceptibility to "the empire of Fortune" (TMS II.iii.1.7). In all these ways, and especially the last, religion is superior to philosophy.

> To persons in such unfortunate circumstances, that humble philosophy which confines its views to this life, can afford, perhaps, but little consolation. . . . Religion alone . . . can tell them, that it is of little importance what man may think of their conduct, while the all-seeing Judge of the world approves it. She alone can present to them . . . a world of more candour, humanity, and justice, than the present; where their innocence is in due time to be declared, and their virtue to be finally rewarded. . . . The same great principle which can alone strike terror into triumphant vice, affords the only

effectual consolation to disgraced and insulted innocence. (TMS III.2.12)

The rules of morality constitute the basis of both personal happiness and social well-being, and by giving these rules a "sacred" character, the natural religious impulses of human beings give them a firmer foundation than anything else can. On the other hand "false notions of religion are almost the only causes which can occasion any very gross perversion of our natural sentiments." This is what happens when "superstition" and "enthusiasm" prevail over "true religion." That is why Smith devotes a lengthy section of WN to discussing the proper attitude that political rulers should take to religion.

The evils of superstition and enthusiasm are best averted by education in "science and philosophy," and by public entertainments. Public religion serves both these purposes in the form of communal ceremonies and edifying sermons. Its special solemnity means that religion does this better than any combination of schools and playhouses would. When religion falls prey to sectarianism, however, the result is a "gross perversion of our natural sentiments" that turns them in divisive and destructive directions. Accordingly, a wise ruler will create an "established" religion and support a professional clergy to lead it, while preventing the church to which those clergy belong from being structured in ways that promote clericalism, the sort of personal and professional aggrandizement that leads to the vices of what in the Protestant world is called "priestcraft." For Smith, the church establishment that prevailed in the Scotland of his day offers one of the best illustrations of how religion, properly instituted, can serve the best interests of society.

> The equality which the presbyterian form of church government establishes among the clergy [generates] a more learned, decent independent, and respectable set of men . . . who are obliged to follow that system of morals which the common people respect the most. . . . The presbyterian clergy, accordingly, . . . have more influence over the minds of the common people than perhaps the clergy of any other established church. . . . It is . . . in presbyterian countries

only that we ever find the common people converted, without per-
secution. (WN V.i.g.37–38)

The most opulent church in Christendom does not maintain better
the uniformity of faith, the fervor of devotion, the spirit of order,
regularity, and austere morals in the great body of the people, than
this very poorly endowed church of Scotland. All the good effects,
both civil and religious, which an established church can be supposed to produce, are produced by it as completely as by any other.
(WN V.i.g.41)

These remarks may suggest a somewhat unwarranted complacency
about the church in his native land, along with a Protestant prejudice against Roman Catholicism. In the course of defending them,
though, Smith has some very insightful observations on the workings of different forms of ecclesiastical organization. The principal
point here, however, is that by Smith's account, religion is chiefly
significant for the twofold *function* that it has. First, religious sentiments are part of human nature and therefore have a key role to
play in the life of human beings as moral agents. Second, social
organization can channel these sentiments in directions that are
either beneficial or destructive to society at large. "True" religion,
therefore, both helps the individual to live well, and fosters a social
order that is beneficial to all. It is, we might say, the proper fulfillment of one aspect of our nature, both as individual human beings
and as social creatures.

Two questions arise. Does there have to be anything supernat-
urally true about "true" religion for it to fulfill its function successfully, or would traditional "myths" serve just as well? Second,
are the ecclesiastical forms and practices of which Smith approves
adequate to the sentiments to which he directs attention? While
Smith writes in ways that strongly suggest that he himself sub-
scribes to the *truth* of a providential natural theology, the answer
to the first of these questions seems to be "No." The function of
religion is to give powerful backing to moral rules. It does so by
threatening evildoers with hell and promising heaven to the righ-
teous, regardless of earthly appearances to the contrary. The motivating force of this sanction, though, rests entirely on the strength

of an individual's conviction. It is enough to *believe* in heaven or hell; the belief does not need to be true, while the reality of heaven and hell cannot motivate the person who believes them to be pious fictions. Furthermore, *any* religious belief, however ill founded, is as good as any other, provided that it adequately serves the purpose of powerfully inclining those who believe it to act in accordance with the moral rules that social life requires.

In the *Critique of Practical Reason*, Kant famously argues that God, freedom, and immortality are *necessary* presuppositions of moral agency, an a priori argument that rests upon the logical structure of practical reason. By contrast, Smith's account of the relation between morality and religion simply rests upon empirical observation—the fact that in many times and places fear of hell and hope of heaven have proved to be powerful incentives to morally decent conduct. Perhaps so, but such a contention fails to address the problem Kant was addressing. Does a sense of duty give us *reason* to believe in God and the afterlife? Smith may well have thought that it did, but his system of ideas cannot ground this thought.

There is a different argument to be made however, and one that suggests an interesting lacuna in Smith's treatment of religion. Among the sentiments that Smith identifies as components of a truly virtuous life, there are three that he characterizes in notably religious language, and whose connection with right and wrong action is not intelligible simply in terms of conformity with moral rules.

The first of these occurs in his discussion of the two standards by which we might judge the adequacy of our own moral conduct. The second of these standards is based on human norms. We can judge ourselves to have acted in accordance with what it is reasonable to expect of anyone if we equal the "degree of excellence" that decent people "commonly arrive at." But the standard Smith ranks first goes beyond empirically observable human norms. When we apply this standard, we hold ourselves accountable to an "archetype of perfection" by which we seek to imitate "the work of a divine artist, which can never be equalled." This "first" standard, Smith tells us, is the one to which the "wise and virtuous man directs his principal attention" (TMS VI.iii.25). The pursuit of perfection, then, though it exceeds what we can expect of human behavior in general, is nonetheless an admirable human trait.

A second human sentiment that Smith identifies and commends is this: "A man of humanity, who accidentally, and without the smallest degree of blameable negligence, has been the cause of the death of another man, feels himself piacular, though not guilty," and though he is not guilty, he will seek means by which "to atone for what has happened, and to propitiate" (TMS II.iii.3.4). Once more, this "piacular" sentiment, though it does not flow from the requirements of justice, is not the less commendable.

Third, there are those "natural pangs of an affrighted conscience" referred to earlier. Smith actually describes them as "dæmons" that "haunt the guilty" and may "drive them to despair and distraction." The language of "dæmons" may be figurative, but it serves to underline his important contention that "no principles of irreligion can entirely deliver" us from these (TMS III.2.9).

By implication, religion can perform this psychological function. But what kind of religion can adequately assuage this haunting guilt, accommodate the piacular feelings of those who are innocent of acting unjustly, and underwrite the pursuit of a moral perfection that only God can realize? The first duty that true religion requires of us, he says, is "to fulfil all the obligations of morality" (TMS III.5.13). That is why he commended the model of Scotland's "Moderate" Presbyterianism, which favored services of worship centered on sermons by means of which the clergy edified, encouraged, warned, and chastised their congregations, and thus would reinforce in the minds of listeners the moral rules to which their consciences naturally subscribed. But sacrificial atonement and the striving after divine perfection exceed what "rational" endorsement of moral rules requires, because they look to ideals beyond the fulfillment of duty. And haunting guilt arises, and lingers, precisely to the extent that the sacred authority of those rules is acknowledged. All three, we might say, are *exceptional* sentiments, and cannot accordingly be accommodated by what is plainly "reasonable."

Smith is not merely skeptical, but dismissive of "the public and private worship of the deity" (TMS III.2.34) in many forms. He discounts "frivolous observances," "sacrifices," "ceremonies," and "vain supplications" (TMS III.5.13) as having any value in themselves, and roundly condemns "the futile mortifications of a monastery" (TMS III.2.35). Unlike virtually all the other moralists of his time, he does not include "piety" among the list of virtues, and does not specify any "duties to God." Yet it is by means of just this kind of practice that human beings in almost all cultures have sought to accommodate the religious sentiments that Smith himself identifies. How is unattainable perfection to be venerated except in worship? How is atonement to be made without sacrifice? How is guilt to be relieved except by confession? Even if Smith is right to make morality the centerpiece of virtue, the traditional practices of prayer, worship, and sacrifice of which he is deeply suspicious may have a more significant role than he is willing to allow.

NOTES

1. See Ryan Hanley, "Scepticism and Naturalism in Adam Smith," in *Adam Smith Review*, vol. 5, ed. Vivienne Brown and Samuel Fleischacker (London: 2010).

2. Rev. James Wodrow, quoted in Nicholas Phillipson, *Adam Smith: An Enlightened Life* (London: 2010), p. 161.

3. "Letter from Adam Smith to William Strahan," in *Hume's Dialogues Concerning Natural Religion*, 2nd ed. with supplement, ed. Norman Kemp Smith (London: 1947), p. 248.

4. Lisa Hill, "The Hidden Theology of Adam Smith," *European Journal for the History of Economic Thought* 8 (2001), pp. 1–29.

5. See Knud Haakonssen, *The Science of the Legislator: The Natural Jurisprudence of David Hume and Adam Smith* (Cambridge: 1989), chap. 3.

6. Hill, "Hidden Theology," p. 4.

7. Ibid., p. 1.

8. Paul Oslington, ed., *Adam Smith as Theologian* (London: 2011).

9. Hill, "Hidden Theology," p. 22.

10. Hume, *Dialogues*, p. 214.

11. Ibid., p. 227.

12. Famously, for the sixth edition of TMS Smith eliminated a brief reference to the doctrine of the Atonement. Just why he did this has been a matter of some debate (see Hanley's "Scepticism and Naturalism in Adam Smith"). Still, the fact that he did so shows that he regarded it as inessential to the central ideas he was expounding.

13. Some prominent philosophers of religion deny that the theory of evolution, properly understood, does obviate the need for a theistic explanation of "design." See, for instance, Alvin Plantinga, *Where the Conflict Really Lies* (Oxford: 2012).

14. See, for instance, pt. 2 of Neil Manson, ed., *God and Design: The Teleological Argument and Modern Science* (New York: 2003).

BIBLIOGRAPHIC ESSAY

Adam Smith's treatment of religion is largely concentrated in Part III of *The Theory of Moral Sentiments*, and Book V, chapter 1 of the *Wealth of Nations*. It has not received extensive critical discussion. There is, for example, no section on religion in *The Cambridge Companion to Adam Smith*. Jacob Viner's book *The Role of Providence in the Social Order* (Princeton: 1972) set out the case for thinking that natural theology plays a central role in Smith's philosophy, and Lisa Hill's 2001 essay "The Hidden Theology of Adam Smith" in the *European Journal for the History of Economic Thought* 8, no. 1 renewed the debate on this topic. Knud Haakonssen argues for the theoretical irrelevance of religion in *The Science of the Legislator: The Natural Jurisprudence of David Hume and Adam Smith* (Cambridge: 1989). D. D. Raphael included a short chapter on "Ethics and Theology" in *The Impartial Spectator* (Oxford: 2007), his study of Smith's moral philosophy. Ryan Patrick Hanley's "Scepticism and Naturalism in Adam Smith," in *Adam Smith Review*, vol. 5, ed. Brown and Fleischacker (London: 2010), argues that Smith treats religion is a species of Humean "natural belief," and Hanley's *Adam Smith and the Character of Virtue* (Cambridge: 2009) offers a sustained exploration of the place of Christian virtue in Smith's social theory. *Adam Smith as Theologian* (Routledge: 2011), edited by Paul Oslington, is a collection of specially commissioned essays that explicitly connect themes in Smith with both major Christian theologians such as Augustine, Aquinas, and Calvin, and central theological topics including natural law, theodicy, and providence. In "The Problem of Natural Religion in Smith's Moral Thought," *Journal of the History of Ideas* (forthcoming), Colin Heydt notes the major points on which Smith's treatment of religion in the context of practical ethics differs from that of his contemporaries.

ADAM SMITH AND POLITICAL THEORY

Lisa Hill

Adam Smith (1723–90) is undoubtedly the most important ideological source of laissez-faire liberalism, and the effect of his thought on economics is undisputed. But because he is commonly conceived as either an economist or a moral philosopher, his place as a political thinker has been somewhat neglected. Furthermore, in the literature that does address his politics there is a perception that his political project lacks coherence. Some even deny that he was interested in political ideas at all.

Smith's interest in political thought is partly obscured by his determination to develop a new politics; he rejected the hitherto dominant virtue- and power-focused approaches to statecraft, because, in his opinion, they were "unscientific"; took no account of the changes wrought by commerce, global trade, and material progress; and failed to consider the welfare of ordinary subjects. He therefore sought to reinvent the art of governing as the science of welfare maximization under commercial conditions.

Aside from exploring this reinvention by reference to his theory of spontaneous order, a related aim of this chapter is to challenge the perception that there is no coherent political project in the material available on Smith by showing how confusion about the coherence and even existence of a Smithian politics has been obscured by his attempts to make the art of governing more social-scientific. Despite his importance as a liberal thinker who urged reform of existing practices of governance, Smith was also a conservative who valued order and social tranquility and disliked rapid change. This has led to the perception that his politics is conflicted and even muddled, a perception this discussion seeks to correct.

ADAM SMITH'S POLITICS?

Determining Smith's political project is hampered by the fact that he provided no aggregated account of the topic. He had long promised to write a treatise on the "science" of "law and government" (TMS VII.iv.37), and he was still referring to it in 1785 as "upon the anvil" (CAS 286–87). The manuscript was eagerly anticipated by scholars and the public alike, but it never saw the light of day because Smith died before it could be published. Even so, there is a wealth of political material in the work that he did publish.

But, this is not the same as saying that Smith's political views are easily accessible. Many Smith scholars have expressed frustration at Smith's elusiveness here.[1] Some have even denied that he had any interest in politics.[2]

It is true that Smith's politics often seems inconsistent and even contradictory. One example is his apparently conflicted attitude to "capitalism" and the free market, which has baffled some scholars and even given rise to suggestions that he is proto-Marxist.[3] Another is his simultaneous embrace of liberal and conservative ideas, while his views on war, imperialism, and free trade have often struck commentators as inconsistent.[4] Because Smith's politics seeks to break free of classical political science and eschews the traditional left-right dichotomy (such as it existed in the eighteenth century),[5] he has perplexed many of those who seek to classify his political thought. For instance, there has been debate over whether he was a Whig or a Tory;[6] whether he is a "real" liberal,[7] or else a "civic humanist";[8] whether or not he was egalitarian,[9] or stood for "social justice";[10] and whether he was genuinely a free marketeer.[11]

The problem with these kinds of debates is that they focus on the wrong questions: so far as I can tell, despite his apparently "Whiggish" tendencies, Smith was not on any particular ideological side, except the side aligned with the laws of nature as he understood them. When appreciated in the context of his underlying social science—the unifying framework of his thought—many of the apparent contradictions identified in the secondary literature are dispelled. Specifically, this framework is the spontaneous order elaboration; the belief that the human universe is a self-ordering, self-equilibrating unit that has been designed to work by secondary laws of nature. This is the system of "natural liberty" in which the "invisible hand" is constantly at work. In the absence of a proper comprehension of Smith's social science, the integrated character of his politics has been missed, even denied.[12] Smith's political thought isn't merely an artifact of his economic theory as is sometimes suggested;[13] rather *both* his politics and economics are artifacts of his social science and, being artifacts of the same "scientific" system, are intimately bound together.

PROGRESSIVE WHIG OR CONSERVATIVE TORY?

Did Smith have a political loyalty that might have underpinned or unified his general program? This question is difficult to determine and has generated some debate on whether Smith's sympathies lay with the Tories or Whigs. Although most commentators have labeled him as a Whig of one form or another, he has also struck some as more Tory in inclination. For example, his intense aversion to radical reform and innovation has led one commentator to conclude that in his later years he developed into a kind of Tory.[14] Yet, Smith saw value in both Tory and Whig ideas and believed the world needed a political theory that was able to reconcile the Whig principle of "public utility with the allegedly opposed Tory principle of authority."[15] I will say more about Smith's attitude to order and change presently, but my point for the moment is that, at first sight, Smith defies easy political categorization. This is partly because he actively resisted existing categories; indeed he sought to forge new ones driven by—and consistent with—his social science.

A NEW POLITICS

Smith was a highly original and independent thinker, therefore it does not make much sense to try to pigeonhole him as a political theorist. He seems to have taken each issue case by case, assessing it within what he believed to be a social-scientific framework. He tended to remain aloof from political ideology because he saw it as a product of rancorous faction and unreflective, un-social-scientific commitments. For Smith, one should begin by working out how the social and economic system actually works and thereafter *respond* with the politics.

Smith's reinvention of political science sought to focus on previously neglected aspects of public management. Classical approaches were eschewed because they were normative, utopian, and overly concerned with means for "perpetuating" and "extending the glory of the state."[16] The more recent and more realist Machiavellian and Hobbesian approaches were also rejected, first because they inevitably led to endless, destructive war and ultimately national debilitation;[17] and second, because they took no account of the effects of commerce, modern trade, manufacture, consumerism, and material refinement that had become "*the* distinctive attributes of modern states."[18] Commerce now took center stage as a natural development to be embraced and understood: Locke had been wrong to conceive commerce as a threat to liberty. Rather, commerce meant progress and had therefore effectively "created modern liberty."[19]

Smith was interested in the proper management of people and mass societies as they really were, and he did not care much about classical virtues or even national greatness. He sought to develop a statecraft that maximized welfare, that enabled governors to "regulate the social order" and "make as equitable a distribution as possible" throughout the polity of the "advantages" of living in "political union."[20] As Donald Winch has noted, Smith's "work marks an important watershed in the history of liberal political thought" in which "a 'scientific' conception of a self-regulating social and economic realm assumed dominance over what, for better or worse, had previously been an exclusively moral and political domain."[21] The legislator should no longer seek to unduly control or enlist the people in programs of national virtue or aggrandizement, or to direct their morality (except where it interfered with public order and commutative justice) but to provide the right conditions for their self-management, including any infrastructure necessary to support and encourage commercial effort, hence Smith's violent attack upon mercantilism with its condemnation of arbitrary restrictions, profligacy, corruption, and class privilege. "Political œconomy" or "the science of a statesman or legislator," as Smith called it, was an important and hitherto underdeveloped "branch" with two key and urgent "objects": first to enrich and provide for the people ("or more properly to enable them to provide such a revenue or subsistence for *themselves*"), and second to supply the "commonwealth with a revenue sufficient for the publick services" (WN IV.intro.I.138). Political economy thus proposes not only to benefit the people, but to ensure that the state has sufficient wealth to provide for those public works that the market cannot deliver spontaneously (WN IV.intro.I.138).

It is significant that the indicators Smith used to test how well states were governed did not include traditional markers like extent of conquered territory or the amount of stockpiled gold but referred to factors that directly affected the lives of the average person: available food supply, population levels, productivity and employment levels, general living conditions, education standards, and mortality rates. He was concerned with welfare and positive outcomes for the population in general rather than with the conventional concerns of government elites.

POLITICAL THEORY AND THE SCIENCE OF THE LEGISLATOR

It is not that Smith's goals weren't highly political ones; it was just that he was attempting to redefine what the political consisted in. It was not about virtue, constitutional taxonomy, statecraft (understood as written exclusively from the perspective of elites and primarily concerned with the maintenance of power), and national aggrandizement at any cost. Rather, it was about economic growth, prosperity, and social and political stability, all of which could be achieved via sound principles of politico-economic management and a better understanding of human behavior and the natural laws governing it.

It is sometimes assumed that Smith sees politics as transcended by the market and that he reserved no significant role for legislators in political action. However, Smith saw certain types of leaders—namely wise ones—as key to a properly functioning, flourishing state. Unfortunately wise leaders were in short supply, a fact of which Smith was painfully aware when he wrote of "that insidious and crafty animal, vulgarly called a statesman or politician" (WN IV.ii.39). But the good leader will operate according to "the science of a legislator," by which Smith means, a mode of "deliberatio[n]" that is informed by "general" and invariable "principles" rather than "momentary fluctuations of affairs" as per the style of the calculating, opportunistic types that tended to dominate politics (WN IV.ii.39). As Ryan Hanley has suggested, Smith wanted to "provide a mechanism capable of elevating statesmanship above the politics of interest."[22] Above all, it was a practical science for the achievement of welfare, order, economic prosperity, peace, and security.

The "science" to which Smith alludes is not scientific in the purely descriptive, "hard science" sense but in the sense particular to eighteenth-century usage, namely, as a "body of systematic knowledge" with normative implications for what, practically, ought to be done, in this case, by legislators.[23] The "science of the legislator" was "a system of what might properly be called natural jurisprudence" to serve as the "foundation of the laws of all nations." Such principles, being "general" and natural, were universalizable and "independent of all positive institution" (TMS VII.iv.37). Although Smith's promised synthetic account of these "general principles of law and government" never eventuated there is ample material in his published works to indicate that it was to be built around the idea of a basically self-equilibrating universe, or what Smith referred to as the system of "natural liberty" (TMS VII.iv.36–37). Smith's attempt to forge a new welfare-focused science of politics thus began with his spontaneous order theory. This was an enterprise founded on what he saw as a systematic understanding of universal social and economic laws and an appreciation of the full extent of civil society.

SPONTANEOUS ORDER AND THE
SYSTEM OF "NATURAL LIBERTY"

As far as Smith was concerned, the solution to many of the urgent political problems of his day was already in place, but, due to ignorance, it was being stifled and suppressed by legislators. This solution was, of course, the market, which was, as Lisa Herzog puts it, "a natural 'problem solver'" for Smith.[24] The realm of uncoerced collective action was naturally very large: beneath the cumbersome layers of artificially imposed institutional constraints on human action, there was a system of spontaneous social and economic relations that, when left undisturbed, would function more or less harmoniously. Order is the product, not of conscious planning and design, but of mainly subrational, internal processes played out at the micro level of individual human action. Our institutions, when allowed to develop naturally, insensibly, and by degrees, embody the collective genius of generations over time (e.g., WN III.iv.20).

According to Smith, the entire universe is a vast equilibrium generated and upheld by divinely endued natural laws while the human universe is upheld by laws that inhere in the human constitution. Our self-interested and/or psychologically individualized actions on the individual level inadvertently give rise to social-systems benefits. "Hunger, thirst, the passion which unites the two sexes, the love of pleasure and the dread of pain" all generate "beneficent ends which the great Director of nature"—but not the human actors involved—"intended to produce by them" (TMS II.i.5.10). In the system of natural liberty, each person is by nature the best judge of her own interest and should therefore be left unhindered to pursue it in her own way. In pursuing her own advantage, Smith wrote famously, each individual was "led by an invisible hand to promote an end which was no part of [her] intention," namely the general welfare and prosperity of the nation (WN IV.ii.9).

Smith's is a two-tiered explanatory model, with the first tier represented by the individual goal level and the second by the social systems level. There is a distinct demarcation between the individual and social systems realms. Because the social systems benefits are generated from the bottom up by the self-regarding actions of individuals, neither private individuals nor the state should seek to interfere in the latter sphere of activity, which is the realm of final causes and therefore reserved for the Author of Nature, who has "from all eternity, contrived and conducted the immense machine of the universe" (TMS II.ii.3.5). Humans are merely efficient causes of Nature's plan; only the divine "Architect" is cognizant of the full meaning of the events in progress, hence the emphasis on the synoptic blindness of its efficient causes: individual human beings (TMS VI.ii.3.6). This reliance upon Nature and the invisible hand is a recognition on Smith's part that the social order embodies a rationality that is more than the rationality of human capabilities.

In this irrationalist scheme legislators ought to eschew social engineering and large-scale planning. Smith derided "systems" and the utopian schemes of the legislator who "fancies himself the only wise and worthy man in the commonwealth" (TMS VI.ii.2.18). Why should "his fellow citizens . . . accommodate themselves to him and not he to them" (TMS VI.ii.2.18)? Just as legislators should steer clear of constructivist hubris, so the average actor should mind "his" own business, responding only to immediate drives and personal interests. Meddling in other people's welfare and worrying about the "general good" will produce more harm than good. As Smith says, "To man is allotted a much humbler department, but one much more suited to the weakness of his powers and narrowness of his comprehension; the care of his own happiness" (TMS VI.ii.3.6). After all, Nature would never leave her "darling care" (the welfare of human beings) to so flimsy and fallible a faculty as "the slow and uncertain determinations of our reason" (TMS II.i.5.10; see also TMS VII.ii.1.44–46). Every person "so long as he does not violate the laws of justice" should be "left perfectly free to pursue his own interest in his own way." The "sovereign is completely discharged from a duty," of which only the dangerously deluded would consider himself under obligation to perform, namely "of superintending the industry of private people and of directing it towards the employments most suitable to the interest of society" (WN IV.ix.51). Accordingly, Smith condemned monolithic, paternalistic, and intrusive forms of governance, including any institutional and legal impediments to the free play of the market and the development of independent moral character. Such impediments included monopolies, poor laws, corporation laws, patronage and nepotism, apprenticeship laws, and laws regulating the institutions of entail and primogeniture. These restrictions obstructed individual effort and threatened the prosperity and security of entire nations; they should, therefore, be eliminated wherever possible.

Smith's discourse on the proper sphere of state action seems to constitute the classic liberal statement of the night-watchman state. Due to market failures and the existence of a number of collective action problems (the causes of which Smith never bothers to explore) he outlines "three proper duties of government," which, though of "great importance . . . are plain and intelligible to common understanding" (WN IV.ix.51). These are, first, to protect society from the invasion of other societies (defense); second, to establish and administer a system of justice; and finally, to provide essential public works and infrastructure (WN IV.ix.51).

Paradoxically, without some degree of state interference in the realm of "natural liberty," liberty itself could not be enjoyed and economic activity would be pointless, even impossible. Only when "[t]he natural effort of every individual to better his own condition" is protected and secure will the society be prosperous and flourishing (WN IV.v.b.43, WN V.i.a.39–40, WN I.xi.i).

As if to underline the futility of attempting to typecast him ideologically, Smith adds a further state function that, from a contemporary perspective, looks like something a social democrat might propose: a publicly funded, compulsory education system. Public schools are necessary, Smith says, to offset the problems generated by economic development. Among the "lower" metropolitan orders, the education of children is "greatly neglected"; this leaves young people with no ideas of "amusement" and so, when at leisure, they fall into bad habits of "drunkenness and riot" (LJB 330; see also WN V.i.i.5–6, WN V.i.f.57). Therefore, for the sake of public order and general civility Smith advocates the establishment of a compulsory and publicly funded school system (WN V.i.f.54).

Smith never explains why markets sometimes fail, nor does he deem it necessary to defend the degree of state intervention he advocates beyond its obvious utility. By the same token, at no point does he suggest that markets are infallible mechanisms, so it is probable he saw no tension here. Unfettered by the kind of ideological constraints retrospectively imposed on him by those keen to locate him on the left-right spectrum, he saw himself as simply working out from observation when the system of natural liberty needed a little help.

At this point it might be objected that the self-evident deficiencies and inconveniences of human existence disqualify Smith's spontaneous order model as genuinely providentialist. In fact, Smith was never one to gloss over the often harsh realities of market life. He drew attention to the adverse side effects of commercial progress such as the problems of isolation and alienation that came with urbanization; the alienating effects of the division of labor; the undermining effects of commerce on education levels; and the inequality and even exploitation that commercial labor often entailed.[25] Yet, he did not see these things as fatal to his theory of self-equilibration. Rather, they were regrettable but tolerable (and in most cases ameliorable) by-products—even symptoms—of material prosperity that could be addressed through the application of sound policy. Smith nowhere claimed that the world is literally perfect or that complete equilibrium is attainable. As a realist he could not suggest otherwise; yet, as a sincere Deist, neither could he concede that the world's deficiencies were evidence of a lack of design. His solution was to balance his realist tendencies with a Deistic faith in the laws of spontaneous order by resort to theodicy, that is, by an insistence that life's apparent evils are ultimately either adaptive or, at the very least, necessary evils.[26]

NATURAL LIBERTY AND SMITH'S CONSERVATISM

Smith saw that there was much work to be done in order to realize his ideal of a system of natural liberty, and he had moments of deep pessimism about the possibility of it ever being allowed to establish itself. Even in his more optimistic moments he doubted whether such a system could "ever be *entirely* restored" due to "the prejudices of the publick" and the "unconquerable . . . private interests of many individuals" (WN IV.ii.43, emphasis added). Yet, Smith made it his personal mission to correct these prejudices and to guide legislators toward policies that were compatible with the natural laws already regulating—or attempting to regulate— human affairs. Importantly, he saw this advice not as utopian or interventionist but as conservative, even revisionist, hence his reference to "*restor[ing]*" rather than instituting the system of natural liberty. The system of natural liberty already existed; it just needed to be revealed and allowed to operate properly. As Smith put it, when "[a]ll systems either of preference or of restraint" are "completely taken away, the obvious and simple system of natural liberty establishes itself of its own accord" (WN IV.ix.50).

Despite his fervent desire for change, as a spontaneous order theorist, Smith could only ever urge cautious reform.[27] Gradualism is key here: the wise legislator respects the delicate concatenation of social and historical forces that have brought existing arrangements into being insensibly and by degrees. "He" will "accommodate, as well as he can, his public arrangements to the confirmed habits and prejudices of the people; and will remedy as well as he can, the inconveniencies which may flow from the want of those regulations which the people are averse to submit to" (TMS VI.ii.2.16). And "when he cannot establish the best system of laws, he will endeavour to establish the best that the people can bear" (TMS VI.ii.2.16) and what the "interests, prejudices, and temper of the times would admit of" (WN IV.v.b.53). Legislators, if they are sensible, will "respect the established powers and privileges" of individuals as well as "the great orders and societies, into which the state is divided" (TMS VI.ii.2.16). Even if they are "in some measure abusive," he will have the wisdom to "content himself with moderating, what he often cannot annihilate without great violence" (TMS VI.ii.2.16). And even the dangerous and deep-seated "prejudices of the people" will be treated, not with force, but with "reason and persuasion" (TMS VI.ii.2.16).

Smith sought to advise leaders on when action was needed and when history and the mechanisms of spontaneous order should be allowed to do their steady work. The wisdom of the legislator consists in understanding where the limits of state action begin and end, in understanding where the system of natural liberty was working well and where it needed some help. The legislator schooled in a thorough knowledge of the laws of nature knows the importance of proceeding "by trial and error and . . . retain[ing] what experience shows to be valuable."[28] It is not only wisdom but real patriotism that is called forth when such a leader is compelled to determine whether the "authority of the old system" ought to be "support[ed]" and "re-establish[ed]" or to "give way to the more daring, but often dangerous spirit of innovation" (TMS IV.ii.2.12). Smith's advice to legislators, as Dugald Stewart saw it, had "no tendency to unhinge established institutions, or to inflame the passions of the multitude."[29]

Yet, Smith's expressed desire to restore the system of natural liberty seems at odds with his conservatism and has sometimes led to the perception that his politics is either conflicted or incoherent (see above). But in reality, he was attempting to balance two key tenets of the spontaneous order theory, namely, liberty and gradualism. Smith's struggle to balance his liberal progressivism with his cautious, order-seeking streak is reflected in the following two examples: his approach to British imperialism and his attitude to the working poor. In both cases this tension is shown to be a function of Smith's determination to solve practical political problems within the limits of his social-scientific commitments.

IMPERIALISM, MERCANTILISM, AND REFORM

Smith was a fierce critic of British imperialism and its economic counterpart, mercantilism. He thought the world was—and should be—opening up and becoming more integrated, therefore he can be thought of as an early theorist of globalization. Although Smith did not use the term specifically (it was yet to be coined), he took a keen interest in the process of increasing global connectivity, integration, and interdependence and was especially optimistic about economic globalization, the process whereby prices, products, wages, rates of interest, and profits converge toward the norms of developed countries.

The colonial system was "invidious and malignant" for many reasons, but primarily because it allowed empires to monopolize the markets of their colonies (WN IV.vii.c.18). The monopoly of trade of the "mother country" that unavoidably accompanied British imperialism had not enriched "the mother country"; rather, it was an egregious "clog" that "cramp[ed]" and depressed "the enjoyments and industry of all . . . nations," imposing a "dead weight" upon trade and commercial effort in general. Monopolistic impediments on the right to choose how best to employ one's resources and labor were "a manifest violation of the most sacred rights of mankind" (WN I.x.c.12; WN IV.v.b.43), and they imposed a kind of "slavery" upon the colonies (WN IV.vii.b.44). Smith referred to "[t]he real futility of all distant dominions" and thought that decolonization and the opening of the international market was not only highly desirable but historically inevitable, "necessary" and "natural" (CAS 383). He therefore advocated not only the dismantling of mercantilism, but the complete emancipation of the colonies (CAS 382). Henceforth "Britain should by all means be made a free port . . . and *liberty of exchange should be allowed with all nations and for all things*" (LJB 262–69, emphasis added; WN IV.vii.c.44). This is Smith in the rhetorical mood for which he is best known: a champion of liberty, progress, economic freedom, personal enterprise, economic cosmopolitanism, and free trade, all of which are key values in his theory of spontaneous order.

And yet, while Smith was extremely desirous of what were clearly far-reaching reforms in the international system, as a spontaneous order theorist he also cautioned against abrupt and radical change. Establishing the system of "perfect liberty" throughout the globe was a potentially damaging enterprise; therefore it had to be executed with considerable "reserve and circumspection" (WN IV.ii.40). "Humanity" required that the market be opened "only by slow gradations" and a "moderate and gradual relaxation" of the relevant laws (WN IV.vii.c.44). Were "duties and prohibitions taken away all at once," home markets would be immediately saturated with "cheaper foreign goods" that would suddenly deprive "many thousands of our people of their ordinary employment and means of subsistence" (WN IV.ii.40). To open up "the colony trade . . . all at once to all nations" would also occasion "great permanent loss" to investors. Restoring "the natural system of perfect liberty and justice" was a process that should occur over time and under the supervision of successive generations (WN IV.vii.c.44). This advice was fully consistent with Smith's emphasis on gradualism in his theory of self-equilibration. The system of "natural liberty" must be restored from the bottom up; therefore any introduced changes should allow time for adaptation and adjustment. What is significant about Smith's advice here is that he does not permit the liberal concerns to dominate the gradualist, conservative ones; his first commitment is to social science and welfare rather than to any political ideology.

THE WORKING POOR AND REFORM

We see the same kind of thinking at work in Smith's treatment of the working poor, where, again, he seems at first sight to be conflicted about reform, evincing at once social-democratic, conservative, and libertarian values. Smith called for reform of the wage system to relieve the misery of workers; indeed he was the most influential high wages advocate of his time.[30] Part of his argument rested on considerations about economic efficiency and productivity and the importance of incentivizing workers: "when wages are high . . . we shall always find the working-men more active, diligent and expeditious, than when they are low" (WN I.viii.44). But part of it also rested on equity grounds: "no society can surely be flourishing and happy, of which the far greater part of the members are poor and miserable." "[E]quity" demands that "they who feed, cloath and lodge the whole body of the people, should have such a share of the produce of their own labour as to be themselves tolerably well-fed, cloathed and lodged" (WN I.viii.36).

And yet, despite Smith's concern for the poor and his demands for a fairer wage system, he was not a progressive egalitarian in the standard, late-modern liberal mold. Like many eighteenth- and nineteenth-century progressives he did not necessarily equate progress with substantive equality (bear in mind that even J. S. Mill argued for weighted votes).[31] Class inequalities were not only acceptable; they were natural, inevitable, and socially adaptive, an indispensable part of the architecture of a self-equilibrating society. Smith saw social order in functionalist terms as a direct consequence of a well-structured system of rank distinctions: "the peace and order of society," he opined, "are, in a great measure, founded upon the respect which we naturally conceive" for the "rich and powerful" (TMS VI.ii.1.21). According to Smith, "Nature has wisely judged that the distinction of ranks, the peace and order of society" rests "more securely upon the plain and palpable difference of birth and fortune, than upon the invisible and often uncertain difference of wisdom and virtue." He concedes that this seems like a rather unfair arrangement, but since "the peace and order of society is of more importance than even the relief of the miserable" it is all for the best. In fact, it is a clear sign of nature's "benevolent wisdom" (TMS VI.ii.1.21). Furthermore, rank distinctions are structurally indispensable because they provide a vital spur to industry via the mechanism of invidious comparison (TMS I.iii.2.2; TMS IV.i.10). We must tolerate the conspicuous consumption of the rich and the exaggerated esteem in which they are held so that the poor can be incentivized to productive activity. For Smith, the system of rank distinctions was a natural aspect of civil society, a spontaneous product of natural human dispositions, and therefore something to be valued and preserved. It was one thing to demand higher wages so that workers did not starve, quite another to undermine the very basis of an orderly society.

Smith's concern for the poor was balanced and constrained by his desire for order and prosperity and by his prior spontaneous order commitments. Respecting such commitments would, he believed, deliver lasting benefits to everyone in the long run. Again, Smith does not privilege liberal concerns with equity, freedom, and merit over the conservative need for order. Rather, he attempts to balance them within his social science, which is, after all, a much better guide to securing welfare.

CONCLUSION

Those attempting to understand Smith's politics should be wary of the political categories that dominated his time, not only because he sought to sidestep them, but because he was consciously attempting to forge new ones. For Smith, politics was not a constructivist, virtue-focused enterprise, and it could not be abstracted from the conditions of commercial modernity: it involved attending to conditions as they really were, detecting the laws already driving history, and regulating human interaction and drawing out the political and legal implications of all of this. Neither politics nor economics should be allowed to dominate the other; rather, both should be subservient to a social-scientific understanding of how best to manage commercial polities. In this regard, Smith offers an important insight to contemporary debates about government spending: what counts in the end is not ideology, but whether or not a policy is effective in securing human flourishing in a manner that does not have destructive long-term consequences.

Welfare, not ideology—libertarian, conservative, or otherwise—should be the decisive criterion for public policy, but welfare had to be understood as something that could only be delivered once legislators learned to work within the system of natural liberty that was already on hand to organize human interaction. This attitude often gave Smith the appearance of being conflicted, particularly where change and order were at stake.

NOTES

1. See, for example, D. Forbes, "Skeptical Whiggism, Commerce, and Liberty," in *Essays on Adam Smith*, ed. Andrew S. Skinner and Thomas Wilson (Oxford: 1976), p. 182.

2. See, for example, E. Halévy, *The Growth of Philosophical Radicalism* (London: 1934), p. 142; S. Justman, *The Autonomous Male of Adam Smith* (Norman: 1993); J. Robertson, "Introduction," in Andrew Fletcher, *Political Works* (Cambridge: 1997), p. xxx.

3. E.g., D. Drosos, "Adam Smith and Karl Marx," *History of Economic Ideas* 4, nos. 1–2 (1996), pp. 325–51; S. Pack, *Capitalism as a Moral System:*

Adam Smith's Critique of the Free Market (Aldershot: 1991); R. Heilbroner, "The Paradox of Progress: Decline and Decay in *The Wealth of Nations*," *Journal of the History of Ideas* 34, no. 2 (1973), pp. 243–62.

4. See K. E. Knorr, *British Colonial Theories, 1570–1850* (Toronto: 1944), p. 185; D. O. Wagner, "British Economists and the Empire I," *Political Science Quarterly* 46, no. 2 (1932), pp. 248–76, p. 74; and L. Hill, "Adam Smith's Cosmopolitanism: The Expanding Circles of Commercial Strangership," *History of Political Thought* 31, no. 3 (2010), pp. 449–73.

5. Craig Smith has addressed the issue of where Smith sits on the left-right spectrum by exploring whether he can be associated "with the modern egalitarian idea of social justice" (C. Smith, "Adam Smith: Left or Right?," *Political Studies* 61, no. 4 [2013], pp. 784–98). Ryan Patrick Hanley's recent study of Smith's treatment of China and Tartary shows that it "cuts a useful new path between 'right' and 'left' on the issue of the legitimate extent of state action" (R. P. Hanley, "The 'Wisdom of the State': Adam Smith on China and Tartary," *American Political Science Review* 108, no. 2 [2014]).

6. E.g., E. C. Mossner and I. S. Ross, "Introduction," in CAS, pp. 18–19.

7. E.g., K. Haakonssen, *Traditions of Liberalism* (St. Leonards: 1988).

8. E.g., V. Brown, *Adam Smith's Discourse* (London: 1994); D. Winch, *Adam Smith's Politics: An Essay in Historiographic Revision* (Cambridge: 1978).

9. I. McLean, *Adam Smith: Radical and Egalitarian* (Edinburgh: 2006).

10. A. Sen, *The Idea of Justice* (London: 2009); S. Fleischacker, *On Adam Smith's* Wealth of Nations: *A Philosophical Companion* (Princeton: 2004).

11. E.g., W.A.S. Hewins, "The Fiscal Policy of the Empire," *Times*, June 5, 1903.

12. E.g., Halévy, *Philosophical Radicalism*, p. 142; Robertson, "Introduction," p. xxx; E. G. West, "Adam Smith's Economics of Politics," *History of Political Economy* 8, no. 4 (1976), pp. 515–39, at p. 515.

13. E.g., S. Wolin, *Politics and Vision* (Boston: 1960); P. Minowitz, *Profits, Priests, and Princes: Adam Smith's Emancipation of Economics from Politics and Religion* (Stanford: 1993).

14. Eckstein, cited in Mossner and Ross, "Introduction," pp. 18–19.

15. I. Hont, "Adam Smith's History of Law and Government as Political Theory," in *Political Judgement: Essays for John Dunn*, ed. R. Bourke and R. Geuss (Cambridge: 2009), pp. 139–40.

16. Smith in D. Stewart, "Account of the Life and Writings of Adam Smith, LL.D.," in *Essays on Philosophical Subjects*, ed. W. P. D. Wightman, J. C. Bryce, and I. S. Ross (Oxford: 1980 [1793]), pp. 309–10.

17. See Hill, "Adam Smith's Cosmopolitanism."

18. F. Oz-Salzburger, "The Political Theory of the Scottish Enlightenment," in *The Scottish Enlightenment*, ed. A. Broadie (Cambridge: 2003), p. 165.

19. Hont, "Adam Smith's History," p. 149.

20. Smith in Stewart, "Account of the Life and Writings," pp. 309–10.

21. Winch, *Adam Smith's Politics*, p. 7.

22. R. P. Hanley, "Enlightened Nation Building: The Science of the Legislator in Adam Smith and Rousseau," *American Journal of Political Science* 52, no. 2 (2008), p. 221.

23. W. Letwin, "Was Adam Smith a Liberal?," in *Traditions of Liberalism*, ed. K. Haakonssen (St. Leonards: 1988), p. 68; K. Haakonssen, *The Science of the Legislator* (Cambridge: 1981), p. 2.

24. L. Herzog, *Inventing the Market: Smith, Hegel and Political Theory* (Oxford: 2013), p. 11 and chap. 2, passim.

25. For a fuller discussion, see L. Hill, "Adam Smith, Adam Ferguson and Karl Marx on the Division of Labour," *Journal of Classical Sociology* 7 (2007), pp. 339–66.

26. The term "theodicy" refers to any attempt to reconcile a belief in a benign and omnipotent God with the apparent evils of existence. All theodicies attempt to answer the age-old question, "If God is good, why is there evil?" In order to avoid heterodoxy, such an answer should not diminish or compromise any of "God's" attributes. For Smith, every feature of the created universe, even its seemingly harsh and maladaptive aspects, are accommodated within his theodicy. Nothing in the universe is truly evil since all of creation performs some positive role in the benign master plan. On this account, the world, from the long view, is basically benign, progressive, and driven by natural laws. There is a "natural progress of things towards improvement" despite human errors and perverse policy and institutions (WN V.i.g.24, pp. 802–3). The human universe need not be perfect or unremittingly congenial for it to be self-regulating and ultimately benign. It might experience adversity, but, ultimately, it operates as an organic, self-righting unit able to restore to itself its own "health and vigour" (e.g., WN II.iii.31, p. 343). For a fuller discussion, see L. Hill, "Further Reflections on the Hidden Theology of Adam Smith," *European Journal of the History of Economic Thought* 11 (2004), pp. 629–35.

27. For a fuller discussion of the gradualism and conservatism of spontaneous order models in the Scottish Enlightenment, see L. Hill, "The Invisible Hand of Adam Ferguson," *European Legacy* 3, no. 6 (1998), pp. 42–65.

28. West, "Adam Smith's Economics," p. 523.

29. Stewart in Smith, *Essays*, pp. 309, 311.

30. M. G. Marshall, "Luxury, Economic Development, and Work Motivation: David Hume, Adam Smith, and J. R. McCulloch," *History of Political Economy* 32 (2000), pp. 631–48.

31. Thanks to an anonymous referee for the suggestion of this important qualification.

BIBLIOGRAPHIC ESSAY

The classic treatments of Smith's political thought are Donald Winch's *Adam Smith's Politics: An Essay in Historiographic Revision* (Cambridge: 1978) and Duncan Forbes, "Skeptical Whiggism, Commerce, and Liberty," in *Essays on Adam Smith*, ed. Andrew S. Skinner and Thomas Wilson (Oxford: 1976). A pioneering and influential account of the natural jurisprudence underpinning Smith's political economy is found in Knud Haakonssen's *The Science of the Legislator* (Cambridge: 1981).

For further reading on Smith's political theory, see Lisa Herzog, *Inventing the Market: Smith, Hegel and Political Theory* (Oxford: 2013) and Istvan Hont, "Adam Smith's History of Law and Government as Political Theory," in *Political Judgement: Essays for John Dunn*, ed. R. Bourke and R. Geuss (Cambridge: 2009).

A detailed study of Smith's international political thought, including his attitude to war, global integration, and British imperialism, is found in Lisa Hill's "Adam Smith's Cosmopolitanism: The Expanding Circles of Commercial Strangership," *History of Political Thought* 31 (2010), pp. 449–73. Smith's importance as a theorist of political corruption is explored in chaps. 5 and 6 of Bruce Buchan and Lisa Hill, *The Intellectual History of Political Corruption* (London: 2014).

For a reading of Smith that challenges the received wisdom, see Samuel Fleischacker, *On Adam Smith's* Wealth of Nations: *A Philosophical Companion* (Princeton: 2004). Fleischacker offers an interpretation of Smith as an egalitarian who anticipates a modern conception of distributive justice.

ADAM SMITH AND MODERN ETHICS

Lisa Herzog

The modern self is under attack. The autonomous, sovereign individual that Enlightenment thinkers imagined is challenged from various angles, not only from "postmodern" theories,[1] but also within Anglophone philosophy. Virtue ethicists and so-called communitarian thinkers have long criticized the mainstream of liberal theory for working with an overly idealized and overly atomized conception of the self.[2] They have called attention to the importance of the psychological mechanisms through which moral principles are internalized, and to the role of communities for the development of our moral identities. More recently, the debate has taken yet another turn. Critics of virtue ethics have claimed that there is no such thing as a moral character; drawing on various pieces of social-scientific evidence, they argue that situational pressures, rather than character, are the main determinants of moral and immoral behavior.[3] For example, the infamous Milgram experiments have shown that "normal" human beings can be brought to torture another human being (an actor, in the experiment) with electric shocks, simply by putting them in a situation in which a person in a lab coat tells them to do so.[4] Friends and foes of "character" have engaged in a heated debate about what such experiments show, and whether it is true that the notion of an autonomous subject with a stable character is a chimera. Arguably, if the latter is the case, this is a threat not only to virtue ethics, but also to Kantian ethics and consequentialism, which equally assume that there is more to human behavior than the pressures of social situations.

But even if there is such a thing as "character," questions arise about where it comes from. As communitarian thinkers remind us,

as human beings we are formed by social contexts, we are socialized into a particular culture, and many of our moral convictions
are not autonomously chosen, but taken over from others. They
are formulated in a language that we have not created ourselves,
but which we have inherited from our ancestors. Our behavior, and
arguably also our moral intuitions, are to a large extent shaped by
participating in social practices that have existed before us, and we
take up, or stumble into, social roles that carry normative expectations with them.

Thus, there has been an ongoing debate in which critics have
charged the mainstream of modern ethics with presupposing an idealized picture of the autonomous individual, and with focusing on
individual decisions, judgments, and character without paying sufficient attention to social contexts. This argument has been raised by
thinkers from various backgrounds, for example, postmodernism,
feminism, postcolonialism, or social psychology. What these approaches have in common is a strong emphasis on the basic fact that
human beings are social animals, and that "the social" needs to be
taken seriously when we think about the nature of morality. "The
social" is reducible neither to individual agency nor to the "basic
structure" of a society. It is the realm of human interactions and
shared practices in historically grown cultures, which often have
a massive impact on individual thought and individual behavior.[5]

This essay turns to Adam Smith's moral philosophy in order to
reflect on ways in which moral theorizing can take human sociality
seriously, but without giving up the idea of a moral self that can, to
some degree at least, emancipate itself from situational pressures
and social and cultural contexts.[6] Smith was a keen observer of social and psychological processes, and much of what he wrote about
human interaction stands up to the scrutiny of modern empirical
research.[7] His *Theory of Moral Sentiments* offers ample resources
for reintroducing "the social" into ethical theorizing. At the same
time, he puts his ethical theory on a firm egalitarian basis,[8] and
retains a strong sense of individual moral responsibility. This can
deflect worries that a reintroduction of "the social" would lead
one into conservative or culturally relativistic waters. What can be

gained from Smith's theory is an account of how the moral self is the result of a (successful) process of socialization, and how it can gain distance from its immediate surroundings and develop a perspective that can claim objectivity, at least as much objectivity as is possible in human affairs.[9]

The next section describes Smith's account of human sociality. It is followed by a discussion of how, for Smith, individuals can develop a moral perspective that emancipates itself to considerable degree from the immediate social context, and in which the "impartial spectator," the central figure of his moral theory, plays a central role. The remainder of this essay sketches some of the inspirations that modern ethics can take from Smith in theorizing "the social."

SMITH ON HUMAN SOCIALITY

Although today Smith is mainly known for his emphasis on the role of self-interest in markets, *The Theory of Moral Sentiments* opens with a denial that self-interest is the only principle of human action: "How selfish soever man may be supposed, there are evidently some principles in his nature, which interest him in the fortune of others, and render their happiness necessary to him, though he derives nothing from it except the pleasure of seeing it" (TMS I.i.1.1). For Smith, a basic feature of human nature is the ability to feel sympathy, our "fellow-feeling with any passion whatever" (TMS I.i.1.5). Sympathy is based on the ability of imagining one's self in another person's position (TMS I.i.1.3), which is pleasurable for both the sympathizer and the one sympathized with (TMS I.i.2.1). Hence, many aspects of human behavior—including the striving for economic success!—can be explained by the human desire to gain other people's sympathy. Men want to have "the respect of their equals" and "credit and rank in the society [they] live in" (TMS IV.1.3). "Emulation," an important motive for action, arises from the desire "[t]o be observed, to be attended to, to be taken notice of with sympathy, complacency, and approbation" (TMS I.iii.2.1). Human beings also have a "desire of being believed, . . . of persuading, of leading and directing other people," which no other animal has (TMS VII.iv.25). A central element of human happiness is "the consciousness of being beloved" (TMS I.ii.5.1).

Living a good human life, for Smith, thus crucially depends on our relations with others. In fact, human beings could not even develop self-consciousness if they lived in isolation. They need the "looking-glass" (TMS III.1.5) of others in order to direct their attention back to themselves. Also, the need to tone down one's passions to a degree that others can sympathize with is a strong motivation to acquire self-command (TMS I.i.4.4). Central elements of what it means to be a human being, rather than an unconscious, instinct-driven creature more akin to an animal, are, for Smith, acquired only in society. The dependence on, and embeddedness in, human communities is for him the starting point of all moral theorizing.[10]

What this also implies, however, is that human beings automatically pick up moral norms and evaluations from those around them: "Bring [man] into society, and all his own passions will immediately become the causes of new passions. He will observe that mankind *approve of* some of them, and are *disgusted* by others. He will be elevated in the one case, and cast down in the other" (TMS III.1.3, emphasis added). In addition, human beings quickly develop habits of thinking, for example, when they are used to seeing "two objects . . . frequently . . . together" (TMS V.1.2). "Custom and fashion" influence not only our aesthetic perception, but also "the Sentiments of *Moral* Approbation and Disapprobation" (title of Part V of TMS, emphasis added). Smith critically describes these influences as "the chief causes of the many irregular and discordant opinions which prevail in different ages and nations concerning what is blameable or praise-worthy" (TMS V.1.1). For Smith it is obvious that different countries, with their different "customs and fashions," have different standards of politeness: what would be "thought effeminate adulation" in Russia would be "regarded as rudeness and barbarism at the court of France" (TMS V.2.7). But "custom and fashion" also have an impact on virtues that are closer to the core of morality than norms of politeness. For example,

Smith observes a distinction between "civilized nations" and "savages and barbarians" with regard to the question of what counts as virtue: the former value virtues that are "founded upon humanity," for the latter virtues based on "self-denial" are more important; the former are "frank, open, and sincere," whereas the latter are forced by their socioeconomic situation to "acquire the habits of falsehood and dissimulation" (TMS V.2.8ff.). Within a given society, the moral standards an individual develops depend to a large degree on whether he or she has been "educated in what is really good company" or "amidst violence, licentiousness, falsehood, and injustice" (TMS V.2.2). Age, profession, and "state of life" also influence people's moral sentiments, and "naturally form in them very different characters and manners" (TMS V.2.4). And although Smith holds that "the sentiments of moral approbation and disapprobation . . . cannot be entirely perverted" (TMS V.2.1), he himself seems to deliver a counterexample when discussing the custom of infanticide, which was a common practice in ancient Greece, and which even Aristotle and "the humane Plato" considered normal (TMS V.2.15).[11] Smith does not offer an explanation or excuse, except for stating that this practice might have lingered on from the "rudest and lowest state of society," in which it was "undoubtedly more pardonable" (TMS V.2.15), and holding that such "pervert[ed]" sentiments can only ever concern individual practices, otherwise a society could not subsist (TMS V.2.16).

The Smithian subject may thus seem quite weak and vulnerable, and at a far distance from the picture of the sovereign, autonomous individual that much ethical theorizing, implicitly or explicitly, presupposes: Smithian individuals are embedded in cultural communities, and take over their standards of right and wrong. Smith's account may have the advantage of being psychologically realistic, and close to everyday life in its concreteness[12]—but does it not come at the cost of giving up the idea of a subject that is sufficiently autonomous to be the addressee of normative claims? But the socially embedded self described so far is only the starting point of Smith's reflections. He offers a rich and subtle account of how individuals can, to some degree at least, emancipate themselves from these influences, and develop a strong and independent moral character.[13] In this way, he offers inspiration for the contemporary debates about how to think about the self and its social context.

SMITH ON THE DEVELOPMENT OF THE MORAL INDIVIDUAL

One basic insight is crucial for understanding how, for Smith, a moral self can develop despite the fact that human beings are socially embedded and depending on a community: holding one another responsible, and treating one another as subjects with moral responsibility, is *itself* part of these social practices. During their socialization into a community, children learn to recognize one another as moral agents, who are more than a bundle of instinctive reactions to a social context. Smith analyzes this process by describing a child who enters school: "When it is old enough to go to school, or to mix with its equals, it . . . naturally wishes to gain their favour, and to avoid their hatred or contempt . . . and it soon finds that it can do so in no other way than by moderating, not only its anger, but all its other passions, to the degree which its play-fellows and companions are likely to be pleased with. It thus enters into the great school of self-command, it studies to be more and more master of itself" (TMS III.3.22). The community teaches human beings to control their instincts and emotions (see also TMS I.i.4.7), and to become agents who can be held responsible for what they do; this is simply part of what it means to be a human being. In a different but related context, namely in the debate about free will and determinism, Peter Strawson has drawn attention to the sheer impossibility of *not* addressing one another as responsible agents, toward whom we hold "reactive attitudes" such as resentment, anger, or forgiveness, and to whom we apply moral categories.[14] Similarly, we cannot see one another as exclusively shaped by our social context; rather, our social practices themselves include an understanding of human agents as being more than the result of external forces.

But *what* is it that agents are held morally responsible for, and that other agents feel gratitude or resentment about? What has been said so far implies that individuals can hold one another responsible, but nothing has been said about whether the standards according to which they do so can ever be more than an internalization of the expectations of those around them. Is it ever possible to emancipate oneself, to some degree at least, from the conventional morality that one is embedded in, and to develop more objective standards? Smith's answer is positive, but it involves a long process, which starts with the social context in which the individual finds herself.

For Smith, human beings have a natural desire to attain objective standards: "Man naturally desires, not only to be loved, but to be lovely; or to be that thing which is the natural and proper object of love. He naturally dreads, not only to be hated, but to be hateful; or to be that thing which is the natural and proper object of hatred" (TMS III.2.1). In order to understand what the "natural and proper object[s] of love" are, Smith introduces the notion of the "impartial spectator," the "great judge and arbiter of conduct": "[I]n order to attain this satisfaction [to have done the right thing], we must become the impartial spectators of our own character and conduct. We must endeavour to view them with the eyes of other people, or as other people are likely to view them" (TMS III.2.3). The impartial spectator corrects the distortions of one's own perspective caused by one's selfish desires, by taking into account the perspectives of others. An agent learns to see himself "in the light in which the impartial spectator naturally and necessarily views him, as but one of the multitude . . . of no more consequence than any other in it" (TMS VI.ii.2.2).

The desire to achieve certain moral standards thus leads individuals to cultivate their sentiments in ways that accord with the perspective of the impartial spectator. They start a lifelong journey of developing their character, in order to stabilize it against the influences of the immediate social context. In this process, moral rules play an important role, because they can help to control short-term impulses, and without "a sacred regard to general rules, there is no man whose conduct can be much depended upon" (TMS III.5.2; see also TMS III.4.7ff.). These rules are derived from the moral sentiments by reason (cf. TMS VII.iii.2.6–7).[15] Reason can then, in turn, correct our moral sentiments, as Smith discusses in a hypothetical example in which the loss of a finger is compared to an earthquake in China: the former excites our sentiments, whereas the latter does not trouble our sleep. But nonetheless, we can come to a different evaluation of the relative importance of these two events: "It is not the soft power of humanity, it is not that feeble spark of benevolence . . . that is thus capable of counteracting the strongest impulses of self-love. It is a stronger power, a more forcible motive, which exerts itself upon such occasions. It is reason, principle, conscience, the inhabitant of the breast, the man within, the great judge and arbiter of our conduct" (TMS III.3.4). Inner dialogue is a crucial element in the process in which individuals learn to behave according to the dictates of this impartial spectator. Smith describes the "impartial spectator" as an "inmate who, in the evening, calls us to account for all those omissions and violations" and whose "reproaches often make us blush inwardly both for our folly and inattention to our own happiness, and for our still greater indifference and inattention, perhaps, to that of other people" (TMS VI.concl.1). By reflecting on the perspective that an impartial spectator would take on, one can strengthen one's character, and develop habits of thought and behavior that live up to his scrutiny. One thus becomes, to some degree at least, an autonomous self, not unlike the one presupposed in many strands of modern ethics—but this is an achievement, not something one can simply presuppose.

But moral agents remain nonetheless embedded in social contexts in which they hold one another responsible for their actions. As Smith puts it, the "man within the breast, the abstract and ideal spectator of our sentiments and conduct" often has to be "awakened and put in mind of his duty, by the presence of the real spectator" (TMS III.3.38). Smith's morality does not transfer agents into a realm of abstract principles; they remain tied to the lived experiences of their social context.[16] Nonetheless, there are criteria that can be used to evaluate these contexts, and moral agents can develop their character in ways that offer answers to the challenges for the self that have been discussed at the beginning of this essay.

A morally mature person has developed the "man within the breast" in a way that makes his judgment more important to her than the judgment of other people (TMS III.2.32); she acts not out of "love of praise," but out of "love of praiseworthiness" and "love of virtue" (see, e.g., TMS III.1.8 and III.1.14). Smith emphasizes the importance of self-command—which is valuable in itself, and from which "all other virtues seem to derive their principal lustre" (TMS VI.iii.11)—in particular for the fight against selfish desires.[17] He holds that "[t]he most perfect knowledge, if it is not supported by the most perfect self-command, will not always enable him [the virtuous man] to do his duty" (TMS VI.iii.1), and takes inspiration from ancient philosophy in his reflections on how self-command can be acquired and strengthened (TMS VI.iii.2). Such self-command, and the constant attention to the internalized voice of the impartial spectator, however, are weapons not only in the fight against the selfish corruption of one's sentiments, but also against the kind of thoughtlessness, or instinctive reaction to triggers from the social environment that threaten the moral autonomy of the self. A moral person can also develop some independence from the moral standards of her time. Not everyone may be able to develop his or her character up to the status of the "wise and virtuous" (TMS I.iii.3.2). But, Smith holds, "there exists in the mind of *every* man, an idea of [exact propriety and perfection]" (TMS VI.iii.25, emphasis added), and everyone can internalize basic moral rules, which offer a certain protection against social influences.

TAKING "THE SOCIAL" SERIOUSLY

In his subtle account of human beings as both socially embedded, and capable of transcending their immediate social context, Smith offers rich food for thought for a rediscovery of "the social" and its relevance for moral theorizing and moral agency. Taking social contexts seriously means acknowledging their importance for moral agency, but also our collective responsibility for them. As Sally Haslanger recently wrote, "As individuals, we aren't responsible for social meanings (though we must constantly navigate them) or social practices (though we can act to resist or sustain them)." But this fact does not condemn us to inactivity, she argues;

rather, in order to change social meanings and social practices we need "social change, collective change."[18]

Concepts, images, and practices from earlier periods can have a grip on us, simply by appearing "normal," that is equally strong as the grip of tradition on those ancient Greeks who did not consider infanticide as morally problematic. Haslanger points to the ways in which prejudices about gender and race pervade the very ways in which we talk about social phenomena. Ethical theory needs to explore how such social meanings and social practices influence individual behavior, and how they could be changed. How can we make sure that we prevent practices in which individuals might be led to immoral actions, such as the scenario in the Milgram experiments? How can we change our language and our practices in order to stop injustices toward minorities, or anyone who seems "not normal"? Thinking about the ways in which social practices shape our moral behavior and our character, and building and maintaining institutions and practices in which this happens in a positive way, is a joint task. This, by the way, is also an answer that has been given to the "situationist challenge" in the debate about "lack of character." As Merritt argues, rather than thinking about the development of character about a matter of "inner" resources, we should acknowledge that these resources come, to a large degree, from the "outer," even if they may come from other social settings than the ones in which we are immediately involved.[19] Therefore, she holds, a central demand of virtue ethics must be "the exercise of care in your choice of [social situations],"[20] because our character is "dependent, in an ongoing way and in maturity (not just during early development) upon involvements in social life."[21]

The imperative to maintain morally viable social practices raises complicated questions about responsibility: How to translate the collective responsibility for maintaining morally viable practices into individual responsibility? Who is responsible, in which ways, for the use of words and images, and for the standards that are considered "normal"? It is likely that in answering such questions we cannot stop short of also looking at the more formal institutions that often underlie social practices, or interact with them in other ways. For example, how do the hierarchies in the organizations in which we work shape individuals' thought and behavior? One of the gems of *The Theory of Moral Sentiments* is a scene in which Smith describes "the courts of princes," "the drawing-rooms of the great," where "success and preferment depend, not upon the esteem of intelligent and well-informed equals, but upon the fanciful and foolish favour of ignorant, presumptuous, and proud superiors." The result is, he writes, that "flattery and falsehood too often prevail over merit and abilities" (TMS I.iii.3.6), with predictable effects on the character of those who participate in those social practices. While we may not have eighteenth-century-style courts any more, private companies and civil bureaucracies remain to a considerable degree shaped by hierarchies. How can individuals retain an independent sense of judgment in such institutions, which enables them, for example, to speak up if they encounter violations of basic standards of morality?

But just as individuals are shaped by their social contexts, these contexts, whether formal or informal, are shaped by the larger societal framework within which they operate, including its most basic socioeconomic structures. Therefore, it is worth thinking about these structures as well, not only from a perspective of justice, but also with another set of questions in mind: what kind of meso- and micro-level organizations do the macro-structures create, and how do all three levels influence individuals and their ability to develop their moral character and to act morally? This takes us back to Smith the economist, who was very attentive to the fact that different economic regimes lead to different social practices. Toward the end of his life, in the sixth edition of *The Theory of Moral Sentiments*, he offered some reflections that sound extremely relevant for today. The tendency to admire rich and powerful individuals, and to look down on poorer members of society, is for Smith "the great and most universal cause of the corruption of our moral sentiments" (TMS I.iii.3.1).[22] This disposition leads individuals to regard positions of wealth or power with "the respect and admiration which are due only to wisdom and virtue" (TMS I.iii.3.1). Not only does it entice individuals to desperately try to climb the rungs of society, sacrificing their happiness and tranquility of mind, like the "poor man's son" whose fate Smith colorfully depicts (TMS

IV.1.8). It also distorts moral judgment, because individuals give undue weight to the perspectives of the rich and powerful, and discount the perspectives of the poor (TMS I.iii.3.1). Hanley argues that Smith developed his theory of the virtues in the sixth edition of the *Theory* in part as a response to the problems of "commercial corruption."[23] But the *Wealth of Nations* also contributes to this endeavor, because many of the policy suggestions that Smith makes work against the inequalities of the previous feudal era, and improve the situation of the working poor.[24] Smith's moral egalitarianism—his view that all individuals have an equal moral worth—certainly pushes him in this direction.[25] But attention to the ways in which moral selves are shaped by their social contexts also pushes him there. For different social contexts can make it easier or harder to emancipate oneself from them, and to attain a certain standard of impartiality. For moral life to be possible, we need a society in which impartiality is possible. This relates ethical theorizing to questions about the political and economic structures of society. Modern ethics can take inspiration from Smith in this regard as well: to take both human sociality and the possibility of emancipation from the immediate context seriously, we may have to go beyond the traditional focus on the moral individual, and address new questions about social practices and social structures.

NOTES

1. For a summary of the debate on "the death of the subject," see the insightful (and critical) discussion by James Heartfield in *The "Death of the Subject" Explained* (Sheffield: 2000).

2. For overviews of these debates, see, e.g., Rosalind Hursthouse, "Virtue Ethics," in *The Stanford Encyclopedia of Philosophy*, Fall 2013 ed., ed. Edward N. Zalta, http://plato.stanford.edu/archives/fall2013/entries/ethics-virtue/; and Daniel Bell, "Communitarianism," in Zalta, *Stanford Encyclopedia*, http://plato.stanford.edu/archives/fall2013/entries/communitarianism/.

3. See esp. John Doris, *Lack of Character. Personality and Moral Behavior* (Cambridge: 2005).

4. Stanley Milgram, *Obedience to Authority* (New York: 1974).

5. Cf. similarly Sally Haslanger, "What Is the Domain of Social (Not Political?) Justice?" (2014), http://politicalphilosopher.net/2014/01/31/featured-philosop-her-sally-haslanger/.

6. On the role of sociality in the thought of the Scottish Enlightenment, see also Christopher Berry, *The Social Theory of the Scottish Enlightenment* (Edinburgh: 1997).

7. Cf., for example, recent discoveries of behavioral economics, many of which Smith anticipated. See, e.g., N. Ashraf, C. Camerer, and G. Loewenstein, "Adam Smith, Behavioural Economist," *Journal of Economic Perspectives* 19 (2005), pp. 131–45.

8. Cf. esp. Stephen Darwall, "Sympathetic Liberalism: Recent Work on Adam Smith," *Philosophy and Public Affairs* 28 (1999), pp. 139–65.

9. On Smith's views of how much distance from her historical context a moral person can ever achieve, see Lisa Herzog, "Adam Smith's Account of Justice between Naturalness and Historicity," *Journal of the History of Philosophy* 52, no. 4 (2014), pp. 703–26.

10. Cf. also Charles Griswold, *Adam Smith and the Virtues of Enlightenment* (Cambridge: 1999), p. 205, who holds that for Smith we could not have a moral self outside of a community. See also Jack Russell Weinstein, "Sympathy, Difference, and Education: Social Unity in the Work of Adam Smith," *Economics and Philosophy*, 22, no. 1 (2006), pp. 79–111; he describes Smith's view of the self as "relational," thus transcending the dichotomy between liberalism and communitarianism (p. 83).

11. Another example in which cultural influences lead to the acceptance of what is, from Smith's perspective, a moral perversion is slavery, which he treats in the LJ (181ff., 452–53). For a discussion, see, e.g., Griswold, *Adam Smith*, pp. 198ff.

12. This has been emphasized in particular by Griswold, *Adam Smith*.

13. In fact, Smith added some of the relevant passages in later editions of the *Theory*, having received criticisms that he was reducing morality to convention after the publication of the first edition (see Ian Simpson Ross, *The Life of Adam Smith* [Oxford: 1995], 190ff.). I cannot discuss the differences between the various editions in the scope of this essay.

14. Peter F. Strawson, "Freedom and Resentment," *Proceedings of the British Academy* 48 (1962), pp. 1–25, at p. 7.

15. As Maria Alejandra Carrasco has argued, Smith's "impartial spectator" can be read as a metaphor for the "faculty of judgment" ("Adam Smith's Reconstruction of Practical Reason," *Review of Metaphysics* 58, no. 1 [2004], pp. 82–116, at p. 94).

16. Cf. also Weinstein, "Sympathy, Difference, and Education," p. 86; Griswold, *Adam Smith*, p. 68.

17. See also Griswold, *Adam Smith*, p. 138.

18. Haslanger, "What Is the Domain?"

19. Maria W. Merritt, "Virtue Ethics and Situationist Personality Psychology," *Ethical Theory and Moral Practice* 3 (2000), pp. 365–83.

20. Ibid., p. 378.

21. Ibid., p. 374.

22. Smith also holds that this admiration is "necessary both to establish and to maintain the distinction of ranks and the order of society." This creates a tension in Smith's treatment of inequality for which he offers no solution (see also

TMS VI.iii.30). One does not have to share this position, however, in order to share his worries about the influence of inequality on the moral sentiments. For a discussion of this "corruption" of the moral sentiments, see also Griswold, *Adam Smith*, pp. 127–28.

23. Ryan Patrick Hanley, *Adam Smith and the Character of Virtue* (Cambridge: 2009).

24. Lisa Herzog, *Inventing the Market: Smith, Hegel and Political Theory* (Oxford: 2013), pp. 101ff.

25. On the connections between the *Wealth* and egalitarianism, see esp. Samuel Fleischacker, *On Adam Smith's* Wealth of Nations: *A Philosophical Companion* (Princeton: 2004).

BIBLIOGRAPHIC ESSAY

Important treatments of Smith's ethics include Charles Griswold, *Adam Smith and the Virtues of Enlightenment* (Cambridge: 1999) and Ryan Patrick Hanley, *Adam Smith and the Character of Virtue* (Cambridge: 2009). On the views of human nature held by Smith and other thinkers of the Scottish Enlightenment, see Christopher Berry, *The Social Theory of the Scottish Enlightenment* (Edinburgh: 1997). For a discussion of Smith's view on human sociality, see also Lisa Herzog, *Inventing the Market: Smith, Hegel and Political Theory* (Oxford: 2013), chap. 4, and, with a somewhat different emphasis, Fonna Forman-Barzilai, *Adam Smith and the Circles of Sympathy* (Cambridge: 2010), chaps. 3 and 4.

ADAM SMITH AND FEMINIST ETHICS: SYMPATHY, RESENTMENT, AND SOLIDARITY

Jacqueline Taylor

Adam Smith, David Hume, and other Scottish Enlightenment thinkers sought to balance justice and benevolence as the central virtues of a modern society that aims at fostering economic flourishing, education and knowledge, sociability, and a sense of our shared humanity. These values and the virtues required for promoting them still stand at the forefront of much of contemporary ethics. In particular, Smith's moral philosophy, with its normative conceptions of sympathy, propriety, compassion, and resentment, and its emphasis on human dignity and justice, provides powerful resources for *feminist ethics*. Some of the key concerns in contemporary feminist ethics include the role of care and the particularity of persons; inequality, oppression, and the need for an account of justice that focuses on how to achieve greater equality between persons and societies; the cultivation of human capabilities; and the importance of solidarity and working across boundaries, such as those of class, race, or sexual orientation, that otherwise divide women in terms of their interests and aims. The feminist *ethics of care* initially aimed to reclaim ethical aspects of caring for particular individuals with attention to the concreteness of individuals and their situations, and often opposed making justice, rights, and obligations the most central moral concepts. Subsequently, work in feminist ethics has combined a focus on empathy and identification with, for example, recognition of the emotional cost of caring labor and so advocating for its greater material worth.[1] Other feminist approaches, including feminist liberalism and feminist phenomenology, focus on the role of sympathy and recognition of others for achieving solidarity with disadvantaged others in order to promote understanding, empathic identification, and a collective motivation to better their social and political conditions.[2] Thus it makes sense to explore the affinities, and some differences, between certain feminist approaches to ethics and moral psychology and the moral sentimentalist approach of Smith. My aim is to show that Smith's moral psychology and ethics can be an important resource for the concerns of contemporary feminist thinkers.

Smith has important relevance not only for those interested in the ethics of care and compassion, but also for another feminist concern, namely, how to achieve solidarity among women who are very differently situated in terms of socioeconomic and political standing. Sandra Bartky, for example, appeals to the work of Max Scheler, to argue for the importance of sympathy in achieving solidarity. I will argue that Scheler's negative critique of what he calls *ressentiment* and its association with women and other marginalized groups makes him badly inadequate as a resource for feminist ethics. In contrast, Smith's virtues of propriety make his emphasis on sympathy more germane than that of Scheler for feminist solidarity. Importantly, Smith's account of resentment, human dignity, and justice can inform and supplement accounts such as Bartky's that want to explain how to promote collective social and political reform.

1

We begin with a brief survey of Smith's discussions of women. It is important to note that Smith's moral philosophy regards women as inherently capable of sympathy and other moral attitudes as well as moral agency. Yet we should acknowledge that Smith does not much discuss women's moral education or capacities. In discussing parental affection, Smith mentions only the father's affection (e.g., TMS III.3.13, VI.ii.1.1–14). The wife appears not to be an object of her husband's affection: "After himself, the members of his own family, those who usually live in the same house with

him, his parents, his children, his brothers and sisters, are naturally the objects of his warmest affections" (TMS VI.ii.1.2). He
mentions the unfaithful wife, the difficulty of the husband having
affection for children who are not his own, and the dishonor to
himself and disgrace to his family that her infidelity has wrought
(TMS VI.ii.1.14). Smith ridicules romantic love, a position that
Sophie de Grouchy rightly criticizes; de Grouchy offers her own
account of the importance of the emotional and physical aspects of
intimate loving relationships (but see TMS III.5.1).[3] According to
Smith, the "breach of chastity dishonours irretrievably," and "even
a rape dishonours, and the innocence of the mind [of the victim]
cannot, in our imagination, wash out the pollution of the body"
(TMS VII.iv.13). As Edith Kuiper reminds us, Smith wrote TMS
as a work to educate boys in the cultivation of morality and the
moral sentiments, yet that does not excuse his view of women as
weak minded.[4]

Smith also distinguishes between female and male virtues: "Humanity is the virtue of a woman," and is merely an "exquisite fellow-
feeling" with others. "The most humane actions require no self-denial,
no self-command, no great exertion of the sense of propriety"; they
are simply those prompted by a natural sympathy. Men in contrast have the virtue of generosity, which requires sacrifice and the
preference of another's interest to our own (TMS IV.2.10). Nevertheless, humanity, along with "justice, generosity, and public spirit,
are the qualities most useful to others" (TMS IV.2.9). Moreover,
an "indulgent humanity" is part of the amiable virtues of propriety
(TMS VII.ii.4.2). And Smith explicitly argues that civilized nations
tend to cultivate those virtues founded on humanity in contrast
to the prevalence of self-denial in more barbarous societies (TMS
V.2.8). Both humanity and benevolence contribute to public spirit
(TMS VI.ii.2.16).[5] Smith does not explicitly exclude women from
cultivating the virtue of self-command, although he regards it as a
difficult virtue that few manage to acquire.[6]

In his *Lectures on Jurisprudence*, Smith takes up the history of
women's legal situation, especially regarding marriage and property, and surveying laws from ancient Greece and Rome up to
the present time. He is critical of easy divorce, as it corrupted the

morals of women, giving "but very loose notions of chastity and good behaviour" (LJA iii.11). On the other hand, he is much more critical of polygamy as a particularly inhumane form of marriage. While polygamy may be legal in those countries where it is practiced, it has unfortunate consequences, especially for women. It turns them into jealous competitors for their husband's affection, and makes them interested only in their own children. The women are miserable, with no real friends, often severely treated by the eunuchs, and reduced to the status of slaves of their husband. Husbands suffer too, since they cannot let other men near their wives; they are also not properly affectionate toward their children since they have so many of them (LJA iii.49–53). Smith also criticizes the marriage of female children, suggesting that it essentially involves rape (LJA iii.38). As Kuiper notes, Smith thus shows in his *Lectures* more sensitivity about women's legal situation.[7] It is also well worth recalling here that Smith's student John Millar gives a central place to the condition of women in his empirically informed account of the stages of social development in *The Origin of the Distinction of Ranks*.

While Smith is no feminist, in the sense of explicitly advocating for political rights and protections for women, and for promoting gender equality, he does not deny women's intelligence or capacity for sympathy, sociability, and morality. We will see that Smith's moral psychology provides powerful resources, especially his emphasis on sympathy and resentment, that can inform the feminist end of achieving solidarity across the socially constituted barriers that often divide them.

2

Sandra Lee Bartky is prominent feminist philosopher who has championed sympathy as an aspect of human nature that can help us to achieve solidarity with women across such barriers as race, religion or sexual orientation. In looking at Bartky's account of the importance of sympathy, which draws on while also modifying the work of Max Scheler, I shall suggest that we should not overlook the relevance of the justified resentment of those who have been disadvantaged in significant social and political ways such as economic inequality. The feminist appeal to Scheler faces limits, especially when we turn to Scheler's concept of *ressentiment*. In contrast, Smith argues for a warranted resentment that feminists can more readily embrace as pertinent to forming solidarity and achieving social and political reform. In her essay, "Sympathy and Solidarity," Bartky begins by asking how we can appropriately sympathize with persons whose experiences of oppression or disadvantage are different, especially when they are worse than one's own experience.[8] Bartky uses the term *sympathy* much as Smith does; it does not mean pity but is closer to our contemporary term *empathy*. As Smith observes, sympathy denotes "our fellow-feeling with any passion whatsoever" (TMS I.i.1.5). For Bartky, an appropriate sympathy with those who are (more) oppressed seeks above all to forge ties of solidarity, to gain understanding, and to share in the task of ameliorating political suffering. Appropriate sympathy is thus not first and foremost about the interests of the sympathizing non-other, although she may well have a deep interest in gaining an understanding of others as well as contributing to a betterment of their affective life and welfare. Bartky appeals to sympathy precisely because it goes beyond mere cognitive understanding of the experiences and situations of others. Sympathy makes us susceptible to and affectively aware of the emotional lives of others. Throughout her work, Bartky has emphasized the significance of the phenomenology and "affective taste" of the experiences of those with particular social identities, and whose oppression results from such social markers as gender, sexual orientation, race or ethnicity, socioeconomic class, and religious commitment. To achieve solidarity with disadvantaged others, she suggests, is a political action that leads to self-transformation on the part of the sympathizer, since she will both gain an appreciation of and be positively responsive to those with whom she appropriately sympathizes. I take this to mean, among other things, that the sympathizer will acquire a new affectively infused awareness of others' relationship to and awareness of her in a way that helps her to respond meaningfully and positively.

Bartky thinks we best sympathize with others when we move beyond our own self-concern. She argues that mere cognitive understanding of others is inadequate for achieving solidarity. To be appropriately responsive, the sympathizer needs to access the affective taste of otherness, especially what it is like to experience oneself as different from a dominant majority, which may give a negative valence to self-awareness and to feelings about oneself in relation to others. Sympathy with that phenomenology and affective taste is thus revelatory insofar as the sympathizer herself is made more affectively aware of and attuned to the experience of those who have been made to feel subordinate in relation to others.

Bartky appeals to Scheler's work on fellow-feeling or *Mitgefühl* because of her interest in the relevance of the phenomenology and affective awareness of the experience of oppression and Scheler's emphasis on transcending oneself to engage in loving participation in the world.[9] Scheler, who is aware of the accounts of sympathy of Hume and Smith, recognizes the phenomenon of emotional contagion. For Scheler, we should resist this catching of others' emotions or moods, since it is an unreflective and "herd like" way of sympathizing. Bartky finds the need to revise Scheler's rejection of emotional contagion. As she notes, those who are passionate about a cause, especially one that promotes greater justice and inclusion, can be inspirational to one another in the process of contagious collective protest. For Smith, emotional contagion may be positive as in the sharing of laughter, as well as negative, so it is not necessarily something that should be resisted. I will discuss later how Smith's account of sympathetic resentment has relevance for the kind of collective movements toward greater justice that Bartky seeks to promote.[10]

For Smith the majority of situations in which we appropriately sympathize with others take us well beyond contagion, and require that we reconstruct imaginatively the details of those situations. This process, which I call *imaginative reconstruction*, is similar to what Bartky describes as *vicarious visualization* and which forms the key component of Scheler's conception of *genuine* sympathy. On Bartky's reading of Scheler, genuine sympathy renders as intentional objects the signs of another's emotions, thus allowing the sympathizer to vicariously visualize her situation and emotional state. In turn vicarious visualization allows the sympathizer to be appropriately responsive to and aware of how the other feels, and of the value of those feelings for her. For Smith too we have no immediate experience of what others feel, so we must conceive what we would feel in the situation that another is in. As Smith writes, "By the imagination we place ourselves in his situation, . . . we enter as it were into his body, and become in some measure the same person with him, and then form some idea of his sensations, and even feel something which, though weaker in degree, is not altogether unlike them" (TMS I.i.1.2). By imaginatively reconstructing the situation and feelings of the other person, we position ourselves to be appropriately responsive, for example, to take pleasure in his pleasure, or console him in his sorrow. Here we should consider too the important influence that Smith's concept of sympathy has had on feminist philosophy with aims similar to those of Bartky; Martha Nussbaum's capabilities approach to human development emphasizes the necessity of sympathetically taking up the perspective of marginalized others precisely in order to be appropriately responsive to ways of improving social conditions that best fit the needs of others.[11]

3

A primary aspect of Scheler's thought at odds with the feminist aim of solidarity is his denunciation of the phenomenon he calls, following Friedrich Nietzsche, *ressentiment*. In his introduction to the English translation of Scheler's work, *Ressentiment*, Manfred S. Frings writes that the French word *ressentiment* "possesses a peculiar strong nuance of a lingering hate that our English word 'resentment' does not always carry."[12] *Ressentiment* is "an incurable, persistent feeling of hating and despising which occurs in certain individuals and groups," and has its roots "in equally incurable *impotencies* or weaknesses that those subjects constantly suffer from," and that generate "negative emotive attitudes" and "false moral judgments."[13] Scheler describes *ressentiment* as "a self-poisoning of the mind which has quite definite causes and consequences. It is *reactive*, a lasting mental attitude, caused by the systematic repression of certain emotions and affects which, as such, are normal components of human nature. Their repression leads to the constant tendency to indulge in certain kinds of value delusions and corresponding value judgments." The emotions and affects that constitute *ressentiment* are "revenge, hatred, malice, envy, the impulse to detract, and spite."[14] The desire for revenge exists, but the subject cannot act on it, typically because she is subordinated or marginalized in her society; it thus produces in her feelings of impotence and the negative emotions Scheler lists. In repressing the desire for revenge, it becomes detached from the original object and subsequently attaches to any individual possessing certain qualities, becoming, for example, a general class hatred of the wealthy or powerful.

As Scheler notes, *ressentiment* is strongest "where approximately equal rights (political and otherwise) or formal social equality, publicly recognized, go hand in hand with wide factual differences in power, property, and education."[15] Scheler follows Nietzsche in valorizing the noble man, the one who realizes the highest objective values, and he contrasts the noble's values with "the value judgments of those who are vitally inferior, the pariahs of the human race!"[16] Comparison of oneself with others is key to *ressentiment*. And "the noble man experiences value *prior* to any comparison, the common man *in* and *through* comparison."[17] Unfortunately, Scheler follows also Nietzsche in the latter's elitism and misogyny. Scheler finds that those most susceptible to *ressentiment* include the disabled, Jews, and women; soldiers suffer least from it. Of women, he writes that "she is the weaker and therefore the more vindictive sex," forced to compete with other women for man's favor."[18] Feminine *ressentiment* is "extraordinarily" compounded "because both nature and custom impose upon woman a reactive and passive role in love, the domain of her most vital interest." In addition, particular kinds of women suffer from variations of *ressentiment*, including "old maids," prostitutes, and mothers-in-law.[19]

Scheler recognizes as positive an active, impulsive, and aggressive taking of vengeance as well as the venting of one's spleen to others.[20] But between Scheler's characterization of the impotent rage of those suffering from *ressentiment* on the one hand, and impulsive rage and revenge on the other, we find in Smith's work a form of resentment that can, when appropriately expressed, solicit a sympathetic resentment on the part of others and lead to *collective* action (including penal punishment, seeking recompense, remuneration, and other forms of redress).[21] Smith provides an important voice on the *necessity* and even the *nobility* of resentment. Smith writes,

> When we bring home to ourselves the situation of the persons whom those scourges of mankind insulted, murdered, or betrayed, what indignation do we not feel against such insolent and inhuman oppressors of the earth? Our sympathy with the unavoidable distress of the innocent sufferers is not more real or more lively, than our fellow-feeling with their just and natural resentment. The former sentiment only heightens the latter, and the idea of their distress serves only to inflame and blow up our animosity against those who occasioned it. (TMS II.i.5.6)

I first examine the importance of resentment for the moral sentimentalist approach before turning to show how it has relevance for the prospect of feminist solidarity with marginalized or oppressed others. Before Smith, David Hume had drawn attention to the importance of resentment in relation to justice. Hume asks us to imagine a species of rational creature (and he accords rationality or powers of causal reasoning to a wide range of species), vastly inferior to us in mental and bodily capacity. Their inferiority to us suggests, according to Hume, that our interaction with them cannot be called *society*, since that supposes a degree of equality. Because we can have an absolute command over them, and they must obey us, justice is *useless* "in so unequal a confederacy."[22] When Hume claims these creatures cannot make their resentment felt, he means they cannot *conceive* of having been wronged or injured, as in some sense having a legitimate claim on us, for example, a rights claim, and so cannot communicate intelligibly any such claim. Annette Baier regards the Humean passion of resentment, not as a form of hopelessness, but as a *power* of rational creatures of equal strength insofar as they can make others feel the force of their resentment for injury and wrongs. Baier sees resentment as potentially a good, a proto-moral sentiment that motivates avenging oneself against wrongdoers. She reminds us that in the *Treatise*, resentment is one of the calm, instinctive passions, a basic desire to retaliate against injury. The proper objects of resentment, according to Baier, include dispossession, expropriation, oppression, and humiliation.[23] As Hume notes, modern legal systems revise their laws to reflect social progress and greater inclusion, in terms of extending rights and privileges, often in response to the collective resentment and solidarity of those who claim rights they previously have lacked.[24] Smith too sees resentment, including the sympathetic resentment of impartial spectators, as natural and instinctive. He goes into more depth than Hume in examining resentment, both in terms of the moral psychology of individuals and with respect to punishment and justice. With Smith, resentment becomes a fully moral attitude.

4

Let us briefly review Smith's account of the significance of sympathy to understand its role with regard to resentment. As he observes, sympathy is a principle that interests us in others, and is the source of our fellow-feeling with them (TMS I.i.1.1). Our capacity to imagine the grief or joy another feels produces in us a similar sympathetic emotion. When others sympathize with us, it is satisfying to have them mirror and share in our joy and pleasure. More important, Smith thinks, is that others can alleviate our painful emotions such as grief, sorrow, or sadness. We actually seem to distribute the intensity of the feeling, to lessen its weight. The "sweetness" of the other's sympathy "more than compensates the bitterness of that sorrow" that their sympathizing enlivened in us, their healing compassion helps us to be less isolated in our painful emotional state (TMS I.i.2). It is more important to us that others sympathize with our pains than with our pleasures, and Smith contrasts the *impoliteness* of failing to sympathize with someone's joy with the *inhumanity* of ignoring his sorrow. Exercising our capacity to sympathize with others is also important to us. By doing so we share in their experiences, taking pleasure in their joys and successes, or consoling them when they grieve. Because the sympathizer lacks direct access to another's emotions, and must imaginatively reconstruct the other's situation to discover what feelings the situation would produce in her, she aims not for an emotional unison with the same pitch of feeling but rather to achieve a concord of emotion (TMS I.i.4.7).

This concord is properly achieved when both the sympathizer and the person sympathized with cultivate the virtues of propriety, that is, of sympathizing appropriately. The person experiencing the emotion must moderate his passion so that the sympathizer, who does not feel the intensity of the other's emotional agitation, can more easily take up the moderated emotion (TMS I.i.4.7). To cultivate the ability to moderate or tamp down one's passions is to have the virtue of self-command, what Smith refers to as an awful or respectable virtue. With self-command one can, in particular, rise above or strongly moderate negative emotions such as grief or anger. The sympathizer's corresponding amiable virtues, reflecting her humanity, compassion, or benevolence, allow her to go along with others' emotions (TMS I.i.5). To have the amiable virtues also helps one to cultivate a more delicate sensibility, making one more attuned to the salient features of the circumstances faced by the person with whom one sympathizes. Smith acknowledges the difficulty of cultivating fully the virtues of propriety. They are rare, but also represent the perfection of human nature because "we feel much for others and little for ourselves" (TMS I.i.5.5).

Smith observes that it is particularly in the case of negative emotions such as anger, hatred, or resentment that those who sympathize must work to imaginatively re-create the situations of others, while those who want others to sympathize with them must lower the pitch of their emotion. By nature, "the discordant voice of anger," or expressions of hatred or resentment, make the negative emotions "the objects of our aversion" (TMS I.ii.3.5). This set of negative emotions is likewise disagreeable to the person who feels them. They poison her happiness, produce physically distressing symptoms such as "harsh tears," and destroy the mental tranquility that comes with greater sympathetic sociability (TMS I.ii.3.7). And at first, the sympathy of others "is divided between the person who feels them, and the person who is the object of them"; sympathy is here divided between conflicting interests (TMS I.ii.3.1). Resentment thus requires not only the imaginative reconstruction by the sympathizer of the resentful person's situation but also her compassion, that amiable virtue of propriety. Because of the inherent uneasiness that resentment produces both in the person who feels it and in those who observe it, the resentful person must modulate her resentment and distress.

Resentment can, however, become "graceful and agreeable," and even noble (TMS I.ii.3.1). We naturally resent many of the injuries done to others. The person who actually suffers the injury naturally feels resentment more than others, and he must be careful not to make uneasy those whom he would have sympathize with him. The resentful person must thus balance his emotions, retaining his "patience, his mildness, his humanity," yet not appearing to be without spirit, or a sense of dignity and what is his due (TMS I.ii.3.2). Smith thinks it is part of human character not to always turn the other cheek (TMS III.6.13). We should resent those who injure or disrespect us. The person who accepts or is indifferent to the disrespectful behavior of others toward her strikes us as too submissive, slavish, or subordinate; if she is without self-respect she is unlikely to earn respect from us. If she is properly indignant or resentful, that enlivens the sympathetic resentment of others, who are glad to see her stand up for herself. Making one's resentment felt also has utility insofar as it puts others on notice that insults and injuries will be avenged or redressed.

For others to sympathize with resentment, it must be the proper response to injury. We can be improperly resentful. Smith invokes his notion of the impartial spectator to help someone ascertain whether her feeling of resentment is well grounded. He also appeals to a person's sense of magnanimity, having a sense of self-respect and dignity, because these "ennoble the expression" of resentment. Magnanimity will characterize the conduct and attitudes of the resentful person; she is "plain, open, and direct; determined without positiveness, elevated without insolence; not only free from petulance and low scurrility, but generous, candid, and full of all proper regards, even for the person who has offended" her. This shows that she has retained her sense of humanity, a sense of the sameness of our shared human nature with respect to our desire to be well thought of and treated well by others. And, Smith writes, "when resentment is guarded and qualified in this manner, it may be admitted to be even generous and noble" (TMS I.ii.3.8). The nobility of a just resentment in the magnanimous person suggests that others' sympathy with someone can provide the sense of solidarity that makes possible social and political progress and reform.[25]

In a section on the merit or demerit of actions, Smith examines the relation between resentment and ill desert and punishment.[26] My concern here will be with how collective resentment can serve as a force for social and political change. Actions that have harm as their proposed end or a tendency to harmful effects lack merit, and may deserve punishment or require some recompense or remuneration. Resentment is the passion that most directly seeks the punishment of the injuring party, just as gratitude moves us to reward those whose actions are beneficial. Smith contrasts resentment with dislike or hatred, arguing that the latter do not lead us to punishment. Resentment actively participates in the punishment, making the other repent for his misdeed. The passion is thus gratified by the repentance or grief of the person punished (TMS II.i.5). Here resentment has the status of a moral attitude, and Smith writes that its gratification produces "all the political ends of punishment; the correction of the criminal, and the example to the public" (TMS II.i.1.6). As Stephen Darwall has emphasized, resentment is a *reactive* attitude (in P. F. Strawson's sense), one that seeks recognition of one's dignity and meeting the demands of justice, rather than mere retaliation.[27]

The sympathy of impartial spectators confirms the moral status of proper resentment. When she disapproves of the motives of the person who injures someone, renouncing her sympathy for him, the impartial spectator goes along with the attitude of the resentful person, agreeing with the need for punishment and even rejoicing at the punishment of the wrongdoer. The spectator enters sympathetically into the other's abhorrence of his injury or loss. Her heart "beats time to his grief," and her fellow-feeling with his resentment produces in her a "vigorous and active sentiment" that goes along with his effort to repel or avoid injury or loss. The resentment of the injured person and our fellow-feeling with him are both natural: "Nature, antecedent to all reflections upon the utility of punishment, has in this manner stamped upon the human heart, in the strongest and most indelible characters, an immediate and instinctive approbation of the sacred and necessary law of retaliation" (TMS II.i.2.5).

5

Bartky acknowledges that our sympathetic outrage or indignation on behalf of disadvantaged others can motivate us to learn more about their situation. But she is unlikely to draw upon Scheler, given his views on *ressentiment*. Smith, on the other hand, offers accounts of sympathy and of proper resentment that nicely serve feminist interests.[28] Consider one of Bartky's examples, that of Egyptian feminist doctor and author Nawal El Saadawi's description in *The Hidden Face of Eve* of her mother and other women performing genital cutting on her during the night. No anesthesia was used. Bartky describes the effort to vicariously visualize the terror, pain, and confusion of the very young girl, and to imaginatively re-create what it was like for the child to have her trust betrayed in this way. To be made vividly aware of what some women experienced as children, something very few Western women will experience, is to begin to achieve some solidarity with them; as Bartky puts it, one's "intentional objects have proliferated," and one is positioned to learn more about their experiences and lives.[29]

Given El Saadawi's political activism—she founded the Arab Women's Solidarity Association—Smith's account of resentment has real relevance here. She argues that genital cutting brutalizes young girls and forms a key component of the legal inequality that many Muslim women face.[30] Smith's moralized resentment that motivates legal action can be expressed collectively by those advocating solidarity and real legal and political reform. This is not avenging oneself so much as turning to legal authorities such as legal theorists who can argue for revisions in the law, or magistrates who should be enforcing the laws that offer protection for women, for example, laws for the prosecution of domestic violence or rape. Smith's individual resentment can be a powerful way of asserting one's dignity and sense of self-respect. It also expresses the expectation that those who are the object of resentment acknowledge the respect and dignity owed to the resentful. Smith emphasizes the resentful person's magnanimity, making one's case calmly and plainly. At the same time, he invokes the shared humanity between the disadvantaged or subordinated, on the one hand, and those who oppress or have been indifferent, on the other. Sympathy both with collective resentment and advocacy and with individuals helps us to become aware of the lived experience of others who are very differently situated in society. Our shared humanity connects us, their distress, resentment, and sense of dignity move us to learn more about how progressive reform can be effected. Smith's moral psychology thus contributes to the arenas of feminist thought and activism.

NOTES

1. For an excellent volume on early work in the ethics of care, see Eva Kittay and Diana T. Meyers, eds., *Women and Moral Theory* (Lanham, MD: 1987). Annette C. Baier presents a range of views in *Moral Prejudices: Essays on Ethics* (Cambridge MA: 1995). Joan C. Tronto provides a particularly astute politically informed account of the significance of care in *Moral Boundaries: A Political Argument for an Ethic of Care* (New York: 1994).

2. For a fine example of the feminist liberal approach, see Martha Nussbaum, *Sex and Social Justice* (Oxford: 2000); for feminist phenomenology, see Sandra Bartky, *"Sympathy and Solidarity" and Other Essays* (Lanham, MD: 2002).

3. Sophie de Grouchy, *Letters on Sympathy* (1798), trans. James E. McClellan III (Philadelphia: 2008). In advocating intimate relations between parent and child and between partners, De Grouchy, far more than Smith, anticipates one strand of the ethics of care, namely, maternal ethics. For a fine example of recent work, see Sara Ruddick, *Maternal Thinking* (Boston: 1999). On the other hand, Nel Noddings draws particularly on Hume and Smith for the ethics of care in *The*

Maternal Factor: Two Paths to Morality (Berkeley: 2010), while acknowledging that some different virtues will arise from women's experience and the maternal instinct.

4. Edith Kuiper, "Adam Smith and His Feminist Contemporaries," in *New Voices on Adam Smith*, ed. Leonidas Montes and Eric Schliesser (London: 2006), pp. 40–60. For other feminist investigations of Smith's work, see Maureen Harkin, "Adam Smith on Women," in *The Oxford Handbook of Adam Smith*, ed. Christopher J. Berry, Maria Pia Paganelli, and Craig Smith (Oxford: 2013), pp. 501–20; Jane Rendall, "Virtue and Commerce: Women in the Making of Adam Smith's Political Economy," in *Women in Western Political Philosophy: Kant to Nietzsche*, ed. Ellen Kennedy and Susan Mendus (Basingstoke: 1987), pp. 44–77.

5. See Henry C. Clark, "Women and Humanity in Scottish Enlightenment Social Thought: The Case of Adam Smith," *Historical Reflections/Reflexions Historiques* 19 (1993), pp. 335–61; republished in Knud Haakonssen, ed., *Adam Smith* (Aldershot: 1998), pp. 383–409.

6. Karen Valihora regards Fanny in Jane Austen's *Mansfield Park* as embodying the wise judgment of an impartial spectator. See Karen Valihora, *Austen's Oughts: Judgment after Locke and Shaftesbury* (Newark, DE: 2010), chap. 8.

7. Kuiper, "Adam Smith and His Feminist Contemporaries." On the other hand, Maureen Harkin is critical of Smith's stance on women in LJ, since he allows women no domestic influence in the private sphere to which they have been assigned; see "Adam Smith on Women."

8. Sandra Lee Bartky, "Sympathy and Solidarity," in *"Sympathy and Solidarity" and Other Essays* (Lanham, MD: 2002), pp. 69–89.

9. Max Scheler, *The Nature of Sympathy*, trans. Peter Heath (London: 1954).

10. Within the tradition of liberalism and cosmopolitanism, feminist-informed adaptations of Smith's approach include Sharon Krause, *Civil Passions: Moral Sentiment and Democratic Deliberation* (Princeton: 2008), and Rebecca Kingston, *Bringing the Passions Back In: The Emotions in Political Philosophy* (Vancouver: 2008).

11. Martha C. Nussbaum, *Creating Capabilities: The Human Development Approach* (Cambridge, MA: 2011).

12. Max Scheler, *Ressentiment*, trans. Lewis B. Coser and William W. Holdheim (Milwaukee: 1994), p. 5.

13. Ibid., p. 6.

14. Ibid., p. 29.

15. Ibid., p. 33.

16. Ibid., p. 142.

17. Ibid., p. 37.

18. Ibid., p. 42.

19. Ibid., pp. 43–46.

20. Max Scheler, *On Feeling, Knowing, and Valuing* (Chicago: 1992), pp. 118–19.

21. In a paper comparing Nietzschean *ressentiment* with Smith's resentment, Michael Ure asks whether the two attitudes are different "evaluations of the same basic 'unsocial passion' or are they concepts deriving from incommensurable

conceptual orders?" He concludes that we should recognize three forms of resentment: the moral resentment, as discussed by Smith, a sociopolitical resentment that allows for collective alleviation of injustice, and an ontological *ressentiment*, as discussed by Nietzsche. The sociopolitical resentment has its roots in Smith's account, but Ure notes that it could turn into *ressentiment* if unchecked. See "Resentment/Ressentiment," *Constellations: An International Journal of Critical and Democratic Theory* 21, no. 4 (2014).

22. David Hume, *An Enquiry Concerning the Principles of Morals* (Oxford: 2006), 3.18, p. 88.

23. Annette C. Baier, "Hume on Resentment," in *The Cautious Jealous Virtue* (Cambridge, MA: 2010), pp. 149–62.

24. In "Adam Smith and the Limits of Sympathy," Duncan Kelly discusses both Hume and Baier on resentment; in Berry, Paganelli, and Smith, *Oxford Handbook of Adam Smith*, pp. 211–13.

25. See Kingston, *Bringing the Passions Back In.*

26. For more on the connections Smith draws among resentment, justice, and punishment, see Fabrizio Simon, "Adam Smith and the Law," in Berry, Paganelli, and Smith, *Oxford Handbook of Adam Smith*, esp. pp. 400–407; Stephen Darwall, *The Second-Person Standpoint: Morality, Respect, and Accountability* (Cambridge, MA: 2006), pp. 84–85, 178–79; and Knud Haakonssen, *The Science of a Legislator: The Natural Jurisprudence of David Hume and Adam Smith* (Cambridge: 1981), pp. 114–15, 119.

27. Darwall, *Second-Person Standpoint*, pp. 85, 179.

28. See Krause, *Civil Passions*, and Kingston, *Bringing the Passions Back In.*

29. Bartky, "Sympathy and Solidarity," p. 85.

30. Nawal El Saadawi, *The Hidden Face of Eve: Women in the Arab World*, 2nd ed. (London: 2007).

BIBLIOGRAPHIC ESSAY

For more on Adam Smith's views and women and gender relations, see "Symposium: Smith and Women," *Adam Smith Review* 7 (2013). For more on the importance of resentment in Smith's work, see Alice MacLachlan, "Resentment and Moral Judgment in Smith and Butler," *Adam Smith Review* 5 (2010), pp. 161–77; and Ryan Hanley, "Hume and Smith on Moral Philosophy," in *Oxford Handbook of David Hume*, ed. Paul Russell (Oxford: forthcoming).

ADAM SMITH'S JURISPRUDENCE: RESENTMENT, PUNISHMENT, JUSTICE

Chad Flanders

The topic, and even the name, of "jurisprudence" today seems to suggest something bloodless, abstracted from the day-to-day realities of trials and courts and even of the particular laws of any country. The legal philosopher Ronald Dworkin, in one of his late essays, cautioned that the debate over legal positivism that had dominated contemporary jurisprudence was becoming (and mostly had already become) unduly "scholastic," where this was intended as a term of abuse.[1]

That Adam Smith's name is not common in contemporary debates about jurisprudence is the product of many causes. One is surely the fact that Smith never finished his tome on jurisprudence. Indeed, in a move that has been the occasion of much speculation, Smith ordered the manuscript of his work on jurisprudence to be consigned to the flames after his death.[2]

What we have of Smith's that directly addresses jurisprudence is two series of lecture notes, which survive only accidentally. From these we may not be able to reliably infer what Smith thought about jurisprudence. The goals one has in teaching a subject can be very different from the goals one might have in writing about a subject. The former may be largely informational and expository, as would befit a set of instructional lectures; the latter may be more persuasive and assertive, even speculative.

But there is a deeper reason why Smith has been largely ignored in modern debates about jurisprudence, which reflects the state of jurisprudence that Dworkin bemoaned. Smith's approach was to begin with history, either the history of a particular country, or a history grounded in particular facts about human nature. If a critique of much modern analytical jurisprudence is that what it finds to be "necessary" features of a legal system are in fact features of presently existing Anglo-American legal systems, Smith *begins* with the history of those Anglo-American legal systems, and tries to show how those rules change and progress over time. Smith held out hope that we might in the end find principles of a "natural jurisprudence," but those principles could be found only by doing historical research into existing societies and not by abstracting from them. This, at least, was the plan of Smith's never-to-be-completed book on jurisprudence.

Although we do not have a finished book by Smith on jurisprudence to guide us, we do have something equally valuable, and equally important to contemporary debates on law and philosophy: his considered account of the origins of justice, and especially just punishment, in *The Theory of Moral Sentiments* (TMS). Where his lectures on jurisprudence present law as a product of history, TMS gives us the prehistory, or the anthropology, of justice. While several recent scholars have recognized the importance of Smith's writing on punishment, they have done less to place it in the context of Smith's overall thought, as well as his proposal for a "natural jurisprudence."[3] This essay does so.

There may also be an immediate payoff to a focus on Smith's writing on resentment and punishment. Recent years have seen a renewed interest in the relationship of the moral emotions to law, and especially to the criminal law.[4] Emotions such as resentment and hatred seem to fuel the desire to punish, and possibly to justify the institution of punishment. But are those emotions themselves justified, and if so, what justifies them? How do we prevent those emotions from spilling over into revenge? Smith's writings on resentment and punishment provide an extended meditation on the problem of the sentiments when it comes to punishment, both their necessity and their dangers, and the way to structure legal institutions so as to both exploit as well as restrain those sentiments.[5]

1. THE STRUCTURE OF RESENTMENT

If the primal scene of contemporary political philosophy is a contract (real or imaginary),[6] the primal scene for Smith is one of conflict: someone has been injured, and he and those close to him naturally want to retaliate (TMS II.i.1.6). This emotional response is so basic that it sometimes happens in relation to *things* that have done us harm (as someone who has stubbed his toe against a rock or slammed a door on his finger will recognize) or animals who have injured us (TMS II.iii.1.3; LJA ii.119). In the moment, the injury demands a response, and that response is first resentment, and then (closely related) a desire to retaliate and punish. The problem of law and politics for Smith is in large part how to deal with injury and with the resentment that it begets.[7]

Resentment has a complex structure that Smith contrasts with what we can call simply "wishing ill" on another person. If someone we know has a disagreeable character, we might wish that bad things happen to him. But we would not necessarily want to be the instruments of harming him; indeed, if we have any "spark of justice" in us, we do not go around causing harm to anybody who has not caused us harm, even though we might take a "malicious pleasure" when he suffers misfortune (TMS II.i.1.6). But things are quite different when we become aware that someone has caused another person an undeserved injury. Then resentment kicks in: not only do we want bad things to happen to the person who has caused the suffering, *we want to do those bad things to him*. Resentment is not gratified, Smith says, just when a bad thing happens to someone who has hurt us; resentment is gratified only when *we make that person* "grieve for that particular wrong which we have suffered from him" (TMS II.i.1.6). Not only this, we want to teach him and others like him a lesson: to make them feel sorry for what they have done, and to make others fearful of injuring us.

As usual, Smith's moral psychology proves sound when we test our own feelings against his descriptions. He accurately distinguishes between what we now call schadenfreude ("the malicious pleasure in the misfortune of the man" who is disagreeable to us;

TMS II.i.1.6) and genuine resentment, where we have the desire to be the instruments of a person's misfortune. But Smith goes further, and sees incipient in our immediate reactions the structure not only of resentment, but the beginnings of the political nature of our moral emotions. We not only want to gratify our desire for justice—to see wrong done to the person who has done us wrong—we also want to induce remorse in the offender, and to deter others from doing similar things to us. Thus in the "natural gratification" of our resentment, we see implicitly "all the political ends of punishment; the correction of the criminal, and the example to the public," not as by-products of resentment but as parts of it (TMS II.i.1.6). Placing Smith's theory of punishment as solely backward-looking, as for the satisfaction of our resentment alone, is too quick: it ignores what resentment does, and what we want it to do, even going forward.

But it is important for the structure of Smith's moral and political philosophy that it explains our feelings of resentment not just in our own case (where we are the objects of the injury) but in cases where another has been injured. Resentment is not just about us and our injuries or even only about the injuries to those who are close to us (family and friends). We do not even need the person to be alive for us to feel sympathy with the injured person's resentment. We can sympathize even with the injury of a dead person, "who is no longer capable of feeling" resentment "or any other human sentiment." But "we put ourselves in his situation, as we enter, as it were, into his body, and in our imaginations, in some measure" and "animate anew the deformed and mangled carcass of the slain" (TMS II.i.2.5). Our sympathies pull us out of our concern with our own injuries and into the larger moral community, a community that includes even the dead. We hear their call for vengeance, even when they can no longer speak out loud.

In a sense (albeit an attenuated one), this is because when we sympathize with the person's injury *we ourselves* are also injured, or at least feel the injury. Thus, we *also* want ourselves to be the instruments of retaliation. The analytical structure of resentment does not change when we move from our own injury to that of another: we still want to be the instruments of misfortunate against the person who has caused the injury. But sympathy means that what counts as an injury to us has been expanded. The other person's resentment *becomes our resentment*; his anger, our anger; his desire to punish, our desire to punish. Our sense of resentment defines us not just as individuals defending ourselves, but as members of a moral community who sympathize with one another. When someone is injured, we not only learn about our emotional response, we also learn about what community or communities we are members of.

2. THE UTILITY OF RESENTMENT AND THE FOUNDATIONS OF PUNISHMENT

So far we have been looking at Smith on resentment descriptively, how people behave and how they tend to react. Our sympathy means that not only can we respond with resentment toward an injury of another person, but that we usually do. Smith early on in his discussion of punishment and resentment is careful to speak in terms of not what people really deserve for what they have done, but what they appear to deserve, or what they seem to deserve (see, e.g., TMS II.i.2.3). He is describing our moral phenomenology: how things appear to us to be. And we might think that this is where Smith begins and ends his inquiry, on matters of fact and not of right (TMS II.i.iii.6n.a), of describing how people behave, not how they should behave. We might see him simply as engaged in a kind of "descriptive sociology" of our emotions and the institutions (criminal law and punishment) those emotions give rise to.[8]

But the text cannot support this reading. First, Smith speaks not only of resentment when it happens, but also of resentment going wrong and becoming "excessive" (TMS II.i.iii.6n.a). Some people show too much resentment, and then we come to resent them in turn. Here again Smith may only be describing matters, but it does not seem so: those who resent too much, who slip into revenge, aren't just apt to be the objects of resentment; rather they are *mistaken* in their resentment. They feel in a way that is disproportionate to the wrong that has been committed. Thus Smith is not dealing merely with "matters of fact," but with matters of how we *ought* to feel, which leads to the second point.

Smith does not simply rest content to describe the reactions of ordinary spectators and their feelings of injury; he also speaks of those injuries with which the impartial spectator sympathizes (TMS II.i.2.2). The impartial spectator judges not simply how most people react, but how people ought to react. The spectator is correctly attuned to the world: he responds to it as he ought to respond (he never lacks an "objective correlative"). We test our own judgments against the impartial spectator, to see how they match up, and we should correct them if they do not correspond.

The introduction of the impartial spectator may only raise a further question, namely, why the judgments of the *spectator* are the correct ones. Why should the judgments of the impartial spectator, one who is removed from the immediate situation, be more authoritative than those of the person involved? We might even think that the person *injured* may have a better understanding than the impartial spectator, who has not been injured, and who is at most an "indifferent by-stander" (TMS II.i.2.2). The impartial spectator, for all the prestige that attends the title "impartial," is just another point of view. What justifies the (limited) resentment of the impartial spectator, which, ideally, is *our* resentment? This worry may seem especially pressing, especially because in the heat of the moment, the passions seem to justify themselves as long as we continue to feel them (TMS III.4.2). How could an impartial spectator know better than we do, in our immediate response to the situation?

Smith has little tolerance for the above type of skeptical inquiry.[9] He thinks that most people, if they are human beings and have been raised tolerably well, will not usually question the judgments of the impartial spectator. They know better than to trust their immediate emotional reactions as the "right" ones, and will frequently criticize themselves as impetuous or rash. Even if they do not use the language of the impartial spectator, this is what they mean. At best, we will see things instinctively or intuitively as the impartial spectator sees them. At our worst, we will recognize how much we diverge from the impartial spectator's viewpoint (as we might wonder why a friend's distress leaves us cold, or we cannot share in the joy of the success of a colleague). Most of the time, we will try to behave as if we saw things as the impartial spectator sees them, to try to have our sentiments track his.

But in one passage in TMS on merit and demerit, Smith does directly if somewhat impatiently address the skeptic, and his answer to him gives us a valuable insight into the nature of resentment, punishment, and ultimately justice.[10] Smith says that we may respond to the person who questions why we must resent, why we have these attitudes in the first place, by reminding him that if we did not have them society would be in a state of "disorder and confusion" (TMS II.ii.3.8). Unless we resented and also punished those who harmed us, society would simply disintegrate, "crumble into atoms" (TMS II.ii.3.4).

So it is good, in the sense of useful, that we have these sentiments, chief among them resentment for injury. Although we do not calculate that society needs resentment before we actually *feel* resentment, on reflection we can see that our resentment at injustice is necessary. "Nature has implanted in the human breast that consciousness of ill-desert," Smith says, "those terrors of merited punishment which attend upon its violation, as the great safeguards of the association of mankind, to protect the weak, to curb the violent, and to chastise the guilty" (TMS II.ii.3.4). Resentment, not love, is what holds society together.

It might be tempting to see Smith's response here as not really his own: he speaks of what is "commonly" believed about the utility of our sentiments (TMS II.ii.3.7). Or it might be only a second line of defense for Smith against the skeptic, the first line being the commonsense reply that our sentiments simply are (usually) appropriate.[11] But Smith's answer to the skeptic is no brush off, but the culmination of an *entire section* on the utility of our moral sentiments, in which Smith in no uncertain terms explains that the survival of society requires that we have punishment and resentment, and even calls utility the "final cause" of these sentiments (TMS II.ii.3.5). The fact that this justification does not often come up (most of us will not question that we hate and detest things because they are hateful and detestable) does not mean that it is not true and important, even foundational. We need the sentiments to preserve society.

3. JUSTICE: PUNISHMENT AND RESTRAINT

But not all rules and not even all laws need to be enforced if society is going to survive. Those rules that are the most important to the preservation of society are those that protect people from injury. "As society cannot subsist unless the laws of justice are tolerably observed," Smith says, "as no social intercourse can take place among men who do not generally abstain from injuring one another" (TMS II.ii.3.6). The threat presented by hurt and injury in fact runs two ways. First, and most obviously, if people rob and murder and rape without being punished, then society will not long endure. "Injustice," Smith writes, "necessarily tends to destroy" society (TMS II.ii.3.6), and if injustice is prevalent, society will be destroyed "utterly" (TMS II.ii.3.3).

There is a second side to enforcing the rules of justice that is important. That side is what people will do to the robbers and murderers and rapists if there is no formal mechanism of punishment in place. The people will take the law into their own hands, and attack those who have injured them, and society will be swallowed up in "mutual resentment and animosity" and its members will be "dissipated and scattered abroad by the violence and the opposition of their discordant affections" (TMS II.ii.3.3). Punishment thus serves what John Gardner has recently called a "displacement function" in political life.[12] If we focus too much on the purpose of punishment, Gardner writes, we forget about the *origin* of punishment, which was "as a response to the activism of *victims*, together with their families, associates and supporters."[13] Punishment takes the resentment of those who are angry and funnels it into an appropriate (even "gentle and fair") response (TMS II.ii.3.6). The problem with those who resent too much, whose resentment tips into revenge, is that *they too* threaten the order of society.[14] Without the enforcement by magistrates of the criminal law, Smith revealingly writes, "civil society would become a scene of bloodshed and disorder" because of "every man revenging himself at his own hand whenever he fancied he was injured" (TMS VII.iv.36).

If these two forces—on the one hand crime, and on the other hand the violent response to crime—are what make the enforcement of justice necessary, then we should find them helpful in discerning the specific content of justice as well. Thus the importance of negative duties over positive ones may have to do less with any intrinsic property of the negative than with the importance negative duties have in protecting society (TMS II.ii.3.3). Negative duties may be more likely to be duties of justice (hence enforceable by legal sanctions; see TMS II.ii.3.5) because when they are violated, they threaten the order of society, either directly by the harm they cause or indirectly by occasioning strong resentment against the people who do them. The priority given to "negative duties" is contingent on these social facts,[15] not on any conceptual priority.

But we can still comprehend the contingent relationship between negative duties and justice. Negative duties usually are easier to comply with than positive ones; as Smith says, most of the time we can fulfill all of our duties of justice by sitting still "doing nothing" (TMS II.i.1.9). There are usually no complicated calculations we need to make in order to be just people as opposed to being good people (TMS III.6.11). It is not that hard, for instance, to go through the day without intentionally murdering someone. Because these duties are easy to follow, it is also easier to resent someone when he does not fulfill them, even when the duty he breaches is minor.

We also tend to resent it more when someone does us a positive injury (hurts us or steals from us) rather than when he omits to do something nice to us;[16] so too with even those small violations of fair play which may cause us immense outrage (TMS II.ii.2.1).[17] In these cases, punishing the wrong may be more necessary to displace our resentment, rather than essential to preventing any real injury to society. These are rules of justice because our resentment is a powerful force, which the laws have to take account of.[18] Law both legitimately expresses our resentment but also restrains that resentment from going overboard. Most of the time those things that really cause the most harm will be the most resented. "As the greater and more irreparable the evil that is done," Smith says, "the resentment of the sufferer runs naturally the higher, so does likewise the sympathetic indignation of the spectator" (TMS II.ii.2.2). But sometimes we will resent a minor slight against us and punishment will be designed to help *us* get over the hurt, to prevent *us* from going overboard. Law restrains both those who would unjustly injure and those who would unjustly punish, and law's story is the story of this ongoing restraint.[19]

4. THE PROPRIETY OF RESENTMENT AND THE LAWS OF JUSTICE

But justifying the laws in terms of their utility does not capture all of what justifies our sentiments, because it does not explain their internal logic: we think we punish because people deserve it *because they have injured us*. Nature has not made resentment originally a matter of utilitarian calculation, where we punish only because the costs outweigh the benefits even if utility is the deep reason we have those sentiments (TMS II.ii.2.5). It is the rare circumstance where we approve of a punishment "merely from a view to the general interest of society" (TMS II.ii.3.11).

The general interest of society may be what justifies the sentiments as a whole, but in each case we have to test our sentiments: is the resentment and/or punishment appropriate to the injury? We do not live day to day from an external point of view that looks at only the utility of punishment, nor can such an external point of view fully explain all of our sentiments. If the need for punishment was solely about securing the general interest of society, then we should have no interest in giving people what they deserved if they no longer posed a threat to society. When a murderer dies of a fever in jail before he is executed, our resentment may feel cheated (TMS II.i.1.6; TMS II.ii.3.11). We did not merely wish harm to befall him, we ourselves (or so our sentiments reveal) wanted to be the mechanism of his harm; we did not merely want him to die, we wanted to *cause* his death. What is the *use* of such resentment, which persists after the death of its object? Is it irrational?

Smith thought not: it is not irrational to hope that the evil are punished, even after their death. Thus we hope that the murderer we could not punish ourselves will receive his proper punishment in the afterlife. Just as we have sympathy for the dead, we can also have resentment for the dead; in both cases, our sense of desert pursues its end "even beyond the grave" (TMS II.ii.3.12). We earnestly hope that he be punished, for "the justice of God," we think, "still requires . . . that he should hereafter avenge the injuries of the widow and the fatherless" (TMS II.ii.3.12). God hates vice and loves virtue, *as do we*, for their own sakes. There are things that we resent and punish because they deserve resentment and punishment, and not merely because it is useful to do so.

5. TOWARD A NATURAL JURISPRUDENCE

It should not be too surprising that our sentiments about what is hateful and what is destructive of society should converge, nor do we need to attribute this convergence to the Author of Nature. After all, those who cause damage to society and threaten its existence *are* hateful. We do not need to posit an Author of Nature who creates this convergence to see that it is so. But the idea that there is a someone who hates what is bad because it is bad and not simply because it serves societal purposes shows that when we resent we are trying to get something right. We are trying to be appropriately resentful of the right things in the way that God, or the impartial spectator, is.[20]

To say this is to raise the prospect of a "natural jurisprudence," that is to say, a system of justice that positive laws should attempt to approximate. Even if we do not posit a God who is the author of the natural laws, we can still make sense of laws that are more or less just taken against a standard of natural justice, which is all Smith needs. Although "[e]very system of positive law may be regarded as a more or less imperfect attempt towards a system of natural jurisprudence" (TMS VII.iv.36), Smith certainly seemed to think that some societies are further along in getting their sentiments and laws right than others. Some nations are rude and barbarous and others are civilized, sometimes due to the laws and sometimes due to the characters of the people (which may themselves be the product of prior institutional arrangements) (TMS VII.iv.36). A nation can even see itself as more civilized than it once was. It may have expanded the scope of those whom it can sympathize with, and so widen the circle of humanity; it may see certain things as injuries that it did not before. Thus our sentiments progress and our laws become closer to what natural jurisprudence requires.

As for the subject matter of a "natural jurisprudence," Smith finds it above all in protecting against violations of the rules of justice, for without a magistrate enforcing those rules, there would be "bloodshed" and "disorder" and people would "revenge" themselves at their own hands whenever they were injured (TMS VII.iv.34). In other words, the need for justice is a need in *all* nations. As a result, the best place to look for the process of a truly international natural jurisprudence is in the international criminal law, where nations try to agree on and codify norms about what sorts of things *all* nations should resent, and which threaten the foundations of all societies. We call certain things, such as genocide or mass rape and other atrocities, "crimes against humanity." It is not that these things are wrong because most nations agree that they are wrong. Rather, they are all trying to get something right in their international treaties and covenants. They are trying to outlaw those things that a "well-governed state" would not—and could not—tolerate (TMS VII.iv.36), and which deserve the world community's collective resentment. A law of crimes against humanity would be, unabashedly, part of a natural jurisprudence, reflecting universal norms that are binding on all societies, and the "foundation of the laws of all nations" (TMS VII.iv.37).

Smith at the end of TMS saw international law as a possible place for the emergence of a natural jurisprudence. In the closing paragraphs of TMS he points to the law of nations as the place to look for a natural jurisprudence, and holds up Grotius as the one person who has begun along this path, someone who had begun articulating the universal norms that are binding on all societies (TMS VII.iv.37). Smith did not see a natural jurisprudence as impossible; indeed, he saw Grotius as *already doing* natural jurisprudence. If there is a reason Smith did not finish his project (besides being busy), it might have been because the progress toward universal norms is one that is ongoing, and in this sense "open-ended."[21] To write a history of a natural jurisprudence is to only write a chapter in the progress toward a fully natural jurisprudence, of which the positive laws of every nation are "records of the sentiments of mankind in different ages and nations, yet can never be regarded as accurate systems of the rules of natural justice" (TMS VII.iv.36). It is through history that we approach more fully a realization of the system of the rules of natural justice.[22]

Smith may have also believed that a natural jurisprudence could go beyond the broad and basic norms of international law to specific regimes and be complete; he may have believed that there are rules of justice that are both reasonably specific and universal. But for Smith, rules of justice are some of the more basic norms of society, the ones that society needs for its preservation. It does not seem implausible to say that there are some domestic, mostly criminal laws that every "well-governed" society *should* have.

But how do we know that we are getting closer to what natural justice requires? Here is perhaps where Smith's jurisprudential theory needed the most development. He needed a theory that could explain how we, through history, are able to make progress on developing a natural jurisprudence. He would have to not only explain "general principles of law and government, and of the different revolutions they have undergone in the different ages and periods of society" (TMS VII.iv.37), but how those revolutions had also been *evolutions*, not merely the different laws of different societies.[23] For Smith clearly believed that there was a process of evolution in society, and that later societies were getting better at approximating what ideal justice requires. In short, Smith needed a theory to explain how a process of *immanent, historical criticism* might get us closer to finding what *transcendental, universal norms of justice* require.[24] Such a theory is not indefensible, still less incoherent or impossible, but it does need to be defended.[25]

CONCLUSION

Smith in TMS gives us a prelude to a theory of a natural jurisprudence. It lays the foundation, and from that foundation we can see what that theory would look like. The basis for the laws of each society would be necessity: for the survival of society, so that society does not become a "scene of bloodshed and disorder" (TMS VII.iv.36). This basis, however, would not rule out that the laws have their own internal logic, and be related to the resentment we naturally and appropriately feel. A theory of jurisprudence would explain this internal logic, but also how it relates to the utilitarian foundations of justice. This combination of things explains most of what is going on in Smith's *Lectures on Jurisprudence* (LJ). The focus is on the content of the laws of England, in minute and somewhat excruciating detail.

But never far from view is how these laws relate to our natural sentiments, and at bottom relate to the preservation of society. Also at play in brief moments of LJ is a description of how, by means of internal criticism, those sentiments change over time. It is only through history that we come to approximate a system of natural jurisprudence, only through time that we can escape time. A description of positive laws, no matter how exhaustive or comprehensive, can be only the story of a journey to *approximating* a natural jurisprudence.

Although we can tell ourselves stories that we are more enlightened and civilized now than we were centuries ago, how we see some injuries more clearly than before, we can never be entirely certain of our progress. We can only hope that as we change our laws, we are getting closer to getting those laws right, or as right and just as we can make them given our imperfections. Whether this hope for Smith was based in a belief in an Author of Nature, or grounded in an Enlightenment belief in historical progress, he clearly felt it was not in vain.

NOTES

Thanks to Ryan Hanley, Michael Frazer, Eric Schliesser, Daniel Green, Zak Calo, and Danny Priel for comments on previous drafts.

1. Ronald Dworkin, "Thirty Years On," *Harvard Law Review* 115 (2012), p. 1676.

2. Nicholas Phillipson, *Adam Smith: An Enlightened Life* (London: 2010), p. 279.

3. R. F. Salley, "Adam Smith and the Theory of Punishment," *Journal of Scottish Philosophy* 10 (2012), p. 69; Eric Miller, "Sympathetic Exchange: Adam Smith on Punishment," *Ratio Juris* 9 (1996), p. 182; Alan Norrie, "Punishment and Justice in Adam Smith," *Ratio Juris* 2 (1989), p. 227; Chad Flanders, "Retribution and Reform," *Maryland Law Review* 70 (2010), p. 87.

4. See, e.g., Susan Bandes, ed., *The Passions of Law* (New York: 2001); Jeffrie Murphy, *Punishment and the Moral Emotions* (Oxford: 2012).

5. A topic I consider in Flanders, "Retribution and Reform," with reference to Smith.

6. Christine Korsgaard, *Creating the Kingdom of Ends* (Cambridge: 1996), p. 275.

7. See Spencer J. Pack and Eric Schliesser, "Smith's Humean Criticism of Hume's Account of the Origin of Justice," *Journal of the History of Philosophy* 44, no. 1 (2006), p. 47.

8. H.L.A. Hart described his project as of this nature in *The Concept of Law*, 3rd ed. (Oxford: 2012).

9. Charles Griswold, *Adam Smith and the Virtues of Enlightenment* (Cambridge: 1999), at p. 246.

10. We might imagine the skeptic's viewpoint being motivated not by churlishness but by a Stoic or Buddhist desire to be free of emotion and especially of all resentment.

11. See also Knud Haakonssen, "Natural Jurisprudence and the Theory of Justice," in *The Cambridge Companion to the Scottish Enlightenment*, ed. Alexander Broadie (Cambridge: 2003), p. 117.

12. John Gardner, "Crime: In Proportion and in Perspective," in *Fundamentals of Sentencing Theory*, ed. Andrew Ashworth and Martin Wask (Oxford: 1998).

13. Ibid., p. 31.

14. Note that the spectator's feelings will often "fall short of the violence of what is felt by the sufferer" (TMS I.i.4.7).

15. Haakonssen, "Natural Jurisprudence," p. 213.

16. "It is a common saying, that he who does not pay me what he owes me, does me as great an injury as he who takes as much from me by theft or robbery. It is very true the loss is as great, but we do not naturally [look] upon the injury as at all so heinous" (LJA ii.44).

17. Smith here finds support in behavioral economics. See Christine Jolls, Cass Sunstein, and Richard Thaler, "Behavioral Approach to Law and Economics," *Stanford Law Review* 50 (1998).

18. See Paul Robinson, "Empirical Desert," in *Criminal Law Conversations*, ed. Paul Robinson, Stephen Garvey, and Kim Ferzan (Oxford: 2009).

19. Haakonssen, "Natural Jurisprudence," p. 115.

20. See Chad Flanders, "The Mind as a Whole," *Adam Smith Review* 7 (2012).

21. Griswold, *Adam Smith*, p. 257.

22. See Eric Schliesser, "Articulating Practices as Reasons," *Adam Smith Review* 2 (2006), p. 69.

23. Salley, "Adam Smith," p. 84.

24. For doubts about this project, see Griswold, *Adam Smith*, p. 37, n. 61; Samuel Fleischacker, *On Adam Smith's* Wealth of Nations: *A Philosophical Companion* (Princeton: 2004), p. 147; Haakonssen, "Natural Jurisprudence," p. 217.

25. For a contemporary attempt at a defense, see Charles Larmore, *The Autonomy of Morality* (Cambridge: 2008). See also John W. Cairnes, "Legal Theory," in *The Cambridge Companion to the Scottish Enlightenment*, ed. Alexander Broadie (Cambridge: 2003), pp. 233–34 for a discussion of Lord Kames's and John Millar's attempts at such a theory.

BIBLIOGRAPHIC ESSAY

As noted above, there is little extended writing on Adam Smith and punishment. Notable exceptions include R. F. Salley, "Adam Smith and the Theory of Punishment," *Journal of Scottish Philosophy* 10 (2012), p. 69; Eric Miller, "Sympathetic Exchange: Adam Smith on Punishment," *Ratio Juris* 9 (1996), p. 182; Alan Norrie, "Punishment and Justice in Adam Smith," *Ratio Juris* 2 (1989), p. 227; and Chad Flanders, "Retribution and Reform," *Maryland Law Review* 70 (2010), p. 87. Important recent works on punishment and the moral emotions are Susan Bandes, ed., *The Passions of Law* (New York: 2001) and Jeffrie Murphy, *Punishment and the Moral Emotions* (Oxford: 2012). The classic modern essay on moral responsibility, punishment, and the reactive attitudes (and which bears obvious, if unacknowledged, debts to Smith) is Peter Strawson, "Freedom and Resentment," now in *Freedom and Resentment and Other Essays* (London: 2008). Smith's position on punishment as developed in this essay resembles in some respects the contemporary theories of John Gardner, "Crime: In Proportion and in Perspective," in *Fundamentals of Sentencing Theory*, ed. Andrew Ashworth and Martin Wask (Oxford: 1998) and Paul Robinson, "Empirical Desert," in *Criminal Law Conversations*, ed. Paul Robinson, Stephen Garvey, and Kim Ferzan (Oxford: 2009).

ADAM SMITH AND RHETORIC

Stephen McKenna

The place of Adam Smith's rhetorical thought in the academy is tricky to gauge for several interconnected reasons. One is that while it was widely known that Smith had begun his career with a public lecture series on rhetoric sponsored by Henry Home, Lord Kames, until the publication of a set of student notes on them in 1963 (thought to have been recorded in 1762–63, after Smith had conjoined his rhetoric lecturing to his professorial duties at the University of Glasgow), his teaching was known at best in a very general way. Telling remarks in his major published works about the pervasiveness of persuasion in human society suggested that rhetoric was important, but anything like the rich and innovative belletristic theory indicated by the notes published as *Lectures on Rhetoric and Belles Lettres* would have been far too much to infer. Even after the discovery of the notes, scholarly caution has been well warranted, as they are literally unauthorized. While they have come to be regarded as a reasonably accurate representation of Smith's lectures, Smith clearly intended his major published works to stand on their own. Another difficulty in assessing Smith's place in rhetorical studies has to do with the status of the field itself. Arguably the oldest humanistic discipline in Western civilization, and what we would now label as the most "interdisciplinary," comprising concerns overlapping with grammar, logic, dialectic, ethics, psychology, politics, and poetics, the study of rhetoric in the academy today is a product of its own long, often conflicted, and always protean history; it thus takes vastly different forms in different places and hands. There are scholars who study the history and theory of "the rhetorical tradition" as it was formulated by ancient Greek and Roman theorists, adapted to a range of medieval purposes, rediscovered by Renaissance humanists, and revised by enlightened thinkers such as Smith, just as there are scholars engaged in poststructuralist modes of cultural and media studies who see themselves equally part of the field after what might be termed its epistemic turn in the twentieth century.[1] Still, rhetoric's durability as an art studied as a method for the production and interpretation of persuasive discourse has much to do with this very capacious interdisciplinarity, which has seen it seep into other fields of study, only to have its articulations there percolate back into its home domain. As Walter Ong remarks, "The persistent presence of rhetoric as a recognized force in Western culture can be seen in the number of major intellectual figures known today chiefly for their work in a variety of other subjects who at one time taught rhetoric or wrote about it." Ong cites as English-speaking examples Joseph Priestley, Thomas De Quincey, John Quincy Adams, Herbert Spencer, and, of course, Adam Smith.[2]

Indeed, Smith's lectures have been seen as a key juncture in rhetoric's history, if a purportedly inauspicious one for having led, intentionally or not, a trend largely dismissive of the traditional rhetorical corpus and subsequently contributing to a marked demotion of the status of rhetoric as an academic field in the nineteenth and early twentieth centuries.[3] It remains a curious fact that the discovery and publication of the student notes on Smith's lectures coincided almost exactly with a vigorous reanimation of rhetoric as an academic discipline in the latter half of the twentieth century under the varied influence of such major theorists as Richard Weaver, Kenneth Burke, Richard McKeon, Wayne Booth, and others. As we now know from these notes, Smith's interest in rhetoric was itself capacious, extending to a range of subjects such as historiography, visual aesthetics, and moral epistemology in ways that adumbrate the expansive twentieth- and twenty-first-century undertakings by many rhetoric scholars and theorists. It should be no surprise that Booth contended that, with the discovery of the notes, "our understanding of [Smith] and his writing should be radically revised."[4] But Smith's rhetoric should also prompt rhetoric scholars to see that much of what passes for contemporary innovation in the field has a vital history rooted in the eighteenth century.

Discussion of some of this revised understanding will follow, but first it is worthwhile to examine the role of Smith's early lecturing on rhetoric within the academy of his own day and just after. In terms of the direct influence of his rhetoric lectures upon the shape of advanced rhetorical and literary education, that role was surely less than it might have been had Smith opted to publish them. Discounting several versions of a speculative history of the origins of language derived in part from Lecture 3 ("Considerations Concerning the First Formation of Languages," most notably appended to the third and later editions of *The Theory of Moral Sentiments*), he did not; he had his manuscript copies burned shortly before his death. *Lectures on Rhetoric and Belles Lettres* as scholars know it today has increasingly been understood as reflecting core ideas about communication that are integral to the full system of Smith's thought and as being of value for understanding related academic and cultural developments associated with what is now known as the Scottish Enlightenment. In his time, Smith's lectures on rhetoric earned considerable public notice and surely had some effect within the wider post-Union project of Scottish improvement led by enlightened literati such as Kames, if only in championing a model of polite sociability based on the study and practice of rhetorical propriety.[5] But his lectures' influence upon the academy is best understood as indirect.

For being indirect, however, that influence was not inconsiderable. It is widely accepted among historians of rhetoric that Smith's belletristic approach was groundbreaking in Great Britain in several significant ways. His method was largely nonpreceptive: rather than enumerate a body of rules and devices, Smith centered his lectures on the idea that discourse is made effective when writers and speakers appropriately adapt their language to the elements of the situation—the character of the speaker, the nature of the subject matter, the limitations of the audience, and so on—so as to sympathetically communicate sentiments, and he sought to demonstrate this mainly through critical examples. This approach marked a decisive turn away from then more typical neoclassical approaches, even while reconstituting some classical concerns; it imported ideas from French belletrists such as Bernard Lamy,

Dominique Bouhours, François Fénelon, Charles Rollin, and Jean-Baptiste Dubos;[6] it took a significant step in the direction of expanding rhetoric from an art of persuasion to a methodology of effective communication in general; it shifted rhetoric's critical focus from spoken to written discourse by putting forward the study of vernacular prose as a means of understanding character and the mind as well as improving communication between minds; it gave a prominent place to the analysis of historiography. Moreover, Smith advanced ideas that were wholly original, such as his theory of indirect description, according to which some objects, most particularly passions and sentiments, are best disclosed by describing their effects on a spectator (see Lecture 15). In the words of Wilbur Samuel Howell, the most important twentieth-century historian of eighteenth-century British rhetoric, "Smith may confidently be called the earliest and most independent of the new British rhetoricians of the eighteenth century."[7] The lectures gained renown over the fifteen years they were delivered, first in Edinburgh (1748–50) as a public series sponsored by Kames, then at the University of Glasgow, where Smith continued delivering them in conjunction with his teaching there, first as professor of logic and rhetoric (1751) and then as professor of moral philosophy (1752–63). When Smith left for Glasgow, the lectureship in Edinburgh was continued for another five years by Robert Watson, who almost certainly had been in one of Smith's earlier audiences, and who later spread the teaching of belletristic rhetoric to St. Andrews, where he assumed the position of professor of logic, rhetoric, and metaphysics.[8] Following Watson came Hugh Blair, whose success in the public lectures led to his appointment in 1760 as Regius Professor of rhetoric and belles lettres at the University of Edinburgh, considered to be the first chair of English literature in history. Blair certainly had been in Smith's audience, one among an illustrious group that included Alexander Wedderburn and John Millar. Blair's extraordinarily popular *Lectures on Belles Lettres* (1783, and numerous later editions) was less philosophical and more prescriptive than Smith's, and it more directly addressed the needs of the ministry, but Blair's continuation of Smith's belletristic approach became one of the most important forces shaping the institutionalization of vernacular literary studies in Great Britain, America, and beyond, a historical trajectory sometimes labeled "the Scottish invention of English literature."[9] Contributing further to this development were several of Smith's Glasgow students, Archibald Arthur, later Glasgow chair of moral philosophy, and George Jardine, later professor of logic and rhetoric at Glasgow, both of whom brought belletristic concerns to their teaching.[10] Undoubtedly the rise of English as an academic discipline is a complex affair, but any account of its history must assign significant moment to the innovation of Scottish belletrism, a signal development in the history of modern rhetoric that had Smith at its vanguard.

Prior to the discovery of the student notes of Smith's rhetoric lectures, scholars had long noted, though perhaps necessarily undervalued, that persuasion occupied a significant place in Smith's thought, and not only because his years of lecturing on rhetoric were well known. It is likely that Smith had included a treatment of rhetoric drawn in part from his lectures in one of the "great works" he had ambitions to complete, as mentioned in a letter of 1785: one "a sort of Philosophical History of all the different branches of Literature, of Philosophy, Poetry, and Eloquence; the other . . . a sort of theory and History of law and Government." Alas, although Smith wrote that the works were "a great measure collected, and [that] some Part of both is put into tolerable good order," he did not live to complete the project (CAS 248). It is tantalizing to wonder not only what those works contained, but also whether there might have been an explicit rhetorical connection between them, for Smith famously held at the outset of the *Wealth of Nations* that the human "propensity to truck, barter, and exchange one thing for another" is probably "the necessary consequence of the faculties of reason and speech" (WN 1.2.1–2). Smith wagered this speculation more pointedly in his *Lectures on Jurisprudence* (also known from student notes), where he argued that this commercial propensity rests on "the naturall inclination every one has to perswade" (LJA vi.57; see also LJB 221). Rhetoric's importance to Smith was evident too in the centrality of propriety in *The Theory of Moral Sentiments*. The concept of propriety (in forms such as Greek *tò prépon* and Latin *decorum*) had always lived a double life in the disciplines of rhetoric and ethics. No reader with even a modest background in the history and theory of rhetoric, especially knowing Smith's own background steeped in the classics, could mistake the rhetorical timbre in his deployment of propriety as a pivotal concept in TMS.

Not surprisingly, persuasive communication as elemental in the formation of moral conscience and as occupying important roles in social discourse is a running motif in TMS; reception of LRBL has only increased scholars' attention to this. If rhetoric is the art of making reputable opinions (*endoxa* in Aristotle) acceptable to others as the basis for linguistically motivated action, then the opening section of TMS, "Of Propriety," puts the operation of sympathy in explicitly rhetorical terms:

> To approve of another man's opinions is to adopt those opinions, and to adopt them is to approve them. If the same arguments which convince you convince me likewise, I necessarily approve of your conviction; and if they do not, I necessarily disapprove of it: neither can I possibly conceive that I should do the one without the other. To approve or disapprove, therefore, of the opinions of others is acknowledged, by every body, to mean no more than to observe their agreement or disagreement with our own. But this is equally the case with regard to our approbation or disapprobation of the sentiments or passions of others. (TMS I.i.3.2)

Propriety in TMS is a mode of action, often taking the form of speech, by which agents communicate passions to others so that they may earn approbation. The credible agreement symptomatic of sympathy, wrote Smith, gives rise to "the great pleasure of conversation and society" and is also essential for successful leadership. "But this delightful harmony cannot be obtained unless there is a free communication of sentiments and opinions" (TMS VII. iv.28). The publication of LRBL has afforded scholars opportunities to cautiously gauge the qualities and operation of such communication, weighing its importance broadly for the interpretation of Smith's system as a whole.

The earliest focused studies of LRBL, such as Howell's mentioned above, were largely descriptive and concerned with determining the accuracy of the notes as a record of Smith's lectures, as well as with contextualizing them in and against the Western rhetorical tradition. These preliminary studies paved the way for wider and more analytical assessments, engagements that have been somewhat scattered and varied, but that can be seen traversing one or more of the following categories. (1) They have examined more extensively the classical, early modern, and contemporaneous influences Smith's rhetorical thought. (2) They have examined Smith's own rhetorical practices more closely. (3) They have enlisted Smith's theory of rhetoric as yet more evidence against the old "Adam Smith Problem," showing that the same kind of communication can abet both the flourishing of commerce and a decent social milieu conducive to the formation of moral conscience. (4) They have examined propriety as a central concept in both LRBL and TMS. (5) They have weighed the lectures' role in the early formation of vernacular literary study, as already mentioned, and (somewhat curiously) in the rise of the novel in particular as an object of study in that field. (6) They have made recourse to LRBL in describing Smith's contribution to both contemporary discourse about and the philosophy of moral character. (7) They have examined the implications of Smith's rhetorical thought for understanding his views on jurisprudence.

It would be impossible here to examine this range of scholarship, so focus will be given to the latter two interconnected topics.[11] The matter of character has perhaps been the most focused and fruitful area of academic attention to Smith's rhetoric in recent years. Nicholas Phillipson, Smith's most recent biographer, succinctly states the reason for such focus: in LRBL, "Smith was proposing to show that the art of using language with propriety is a skill which would refine our manners and morals as well as our powers of communication, and would help us to develop that 'character' which played such a large part in influencing the way in which others responded to our sentiments."[12] In this respect, Smith's rhetorical theory can be seen as a specifically modern chapter in rhetoric's long historical debate over whether rhetorical study and practice can promote the formation of moral character, or ethos. Richard Lanham has called this "the 'Q' question" after Quintilian, the Roman rhetorician who most prominently entertained it, albeit tautologically, in his definition of eloquence as "the good man skilled in speaking."[13]

We should not be surprised that classical rhetoric raised this question (far earlier than Quintilian in fact), and not only because serious political and philosophical concerns about the morality of rhetoric—understood as the theory and practice of persuasive speechmaking—had dogged it since the first controversies over whether the sophistic paideia—the sophists' body of teaching that comingled grammar, rhetoric, and ethics—was morally salutary or depraved. The most elaborate and philosophically grounded classical system of dialectical invention, Aristotle's *topoi*, was imported into his rhetorical theory in part to answer Plato's critique of rhetoric as a morally corrupting pseudo-art. For Aristotle, rhetoric is not the art of persuasion, but the art of *discovering* the available means of persuasion in any given case. Other methods of argument discovery, such as the Hermogenaic *stasis* questions and the Ciceronian *loci communes*, likewise functioned not only as devices for the creation of discourse, but disclosed rhetoric as an art of practical reason as much as an art of persuasion. It is largely on these bases that rhetoric has been thought at various moments in its history to serve moral education at least as much as it has been a practical guide for constructing persuasive speech.[14] As such, formal study of the theory of rhetoric can be an ethical hedge against the abuse of persuasion for corrupt political ends; Smith was all too aware of the dangers of demagoguery and sophistry.[15] But one of the defining characteristics of the belletristic turn in rhetoric is the dismissal of formal heuristics (i.e., a methodology for generating arguments). For his part, Smith agreed with what he took to be a dominant classical attitude toward invention as "very slight matter, and of no great difficulty" (LRBL ii.139). The other defining characteristic of belletrism is a concomitant emphasis on style, aesthetic taste, and the performance of literary criticism. It has been argued that invention may yet be carried on anyway via the figures of speech, but belletrism's stylistic theory likewise jettisons the formulaic study of schemes and tropes.[16] Smith regarded both ancient and modern treatises on figuration as "generally a very silly set of Books and not at all instructive" (LRBL i.v.59).

And yet TMS has been interpreted quite persuasively as offering a system of practical reasoning conducive to persuasion.[17] And LRBL has been interpreted as offering an art of character at least as much if not more than as a work offering prescriptions for effective communication across a range of discursive genres.[18] This goes to the heart of what Charles Griswold has called "a second 'Adam Smith problem'" (not to say the first ever had real substance): namely, the relation between LRBL and TMS.[19] Can we read LRBL as an ethics? Can we read TMS as a rhetoric? Is there value in doing so? If LRBL can be read as underwriting TMS with the kind of linguistic and epistemological detail about communication otherwise largely only implied in Smith's ethics, then his rhetoric is ample warrant for the idea that belletristic education can indeed shape an ethical character that is morally sound, given the natural psychology of the human person, as well as conducive to social harmony and commercial progress under capitalism. In exemplifying this so well—far better than the belletrism of Blair, which lacks much philosophical rigor—Smith's rhetoric can help us see that in well-constructed belletristic rhetoric, invention has not been banished but sublated, shifted from the task of forming persuasive and stylistically effective arguments to forming the kind of character from which reasonably persuasive and stylistically effective (that is, as a whole, sympathy-inducing) arguments would naturally flow. Seen this way, Smith's contribution to the "new rhetoric" that arose in eighteenth-century Britain gives powerful credence to Richard McKeon's dictum that rhetoric must be understood as an "architectonic productive art": when new approaches to humanistic disciplines are needed, or indeed where entirely new disciplines surface, humans inevitably mine rhetoric for the conceptual vocabulary and practical tools needed to structure those disciplines.[20] Perhaps we can see this mining in action in LRBL, which gives so much attention to character: the central element of rhetorical propriety for Smith consists in deploying a style well suited to the author's character—a reanimation of the classical concept of ethos. Smith devotes five full lectures (7–11) to this topic, and another (15) to the proper method of character description.

One useful way to delve into some implications of this, and one that simultaneously demonstrates the value of rhetoric outside its more traditional disciplinary boundaries, porous as they are, while bridging us to questions regarding rhetoric and jurisprudence, is via an important recent reading of propriety in Smith's political philosophy. Duncan Kelly features Smith as one among a number of prominent modern political thinkers who theorize liberty as a form of propriety, where propriety is understood as agency made responsible through the inward regulation of passions while being performed outwardly through judgments that articulate a common sense of justice. Kelly thus reads propriety in Smith as exploiting its dual quality as both a moral and a rhetorical concept. Indeed this is evident in the very title of TMS, as "sentiment" for Smith is not just a feeling or passion, but a feeling that issues as and is most often verbally expressed as a judgment that must succeed in persuading others of its aptness to a particular set of circumstances. The dynamics of such persuasion are critical in modern society. Politics emerges in commercial society from the interplay between the human inclinations to superiority, domination, and vanity with the tempering need for social approval. Thus for Smith, writes Kelly, "We must therefore learn . . . to see social life as an exercise in persuasion of a very particular sort, where others approve of the claims we make on them and judge the actions we undertake on the basis of how persuasive our claim to their approval or sympathy might be. To be persuasive requires a standard of judgement, and that standard of judgement in Smith is propriety."[21] Kelly adverts to Smith's comments in LJ and WN on the rhetorical underpinnings of humans' commercial propensities, but he also argues that "the true propriety of language" as adduced in LRBL—communication made perspicuous through apt adjustment to the psychosocial circumstances of context—is at the core of successful persuasion. Drawing on Smith's view of the tempering "mediocrity" required of passions if they are to be sympathized with by a spectator (TMS I.ii.intro.1), Kelly labels the form this propriety takes in commercial society as "persuasive mediocrity."[22] Failure in this propriety of liberty is ultimately a threat to political justice, which depends on the spectatorial disapproval of injustice. The rules of justice themselves derive from such disapproval, and so propriety also accounts for the core tenet of Smith's politics and jurisprudence as a system of natural liberty: the "rigorous, severe, and exemplary" enforcement of law (LJA vi.2). Kelly's adversion to LRBL thus bolsters his analysis of the role of propriety in the historiography of liberalism as involving processes best understood as rhetorical.

The notion of "persuasive mediocrity" may also be read as an indicator of the type of character requisite for individual happiness (for Smith this might be better understood as personal "tranquility") and for simultaneous social harmony and commercial progress within an unnatural economic system prone to causing kinds of human unhappiness, whether drudgery of specialization under the division of labor or the vain attraction to ephemeral goods. As Catherine Labio has pointed out, Smith's approach to character in LRBL has much to do with a fundamental eighteenth-century shift in the sense of what character itself was.[23] Unlike the ancient tendency to suffice with relatively broad character typologies, modern character—and thus modern character description—must partake of extensive nuance and color. In Smith's words, "It is not so much the degree of Virtue or Vice, probity or dishonesty, Courage or Timidity that form the distinguishing part of a character, as the tinctures which these severall parts have received in forming his character" (LRBL i.190). Can specifically eighteenth-century British conceptions of law likewise have something to do with Smith's belletristic recasting of rhetoric?

The answer would seem to be yes. Mark Longaker has shown that far from the view according to which belletristic rhetoric abetted, as one ideological critic put it, "a civil society that defined its members as tasteful consumers and not political participants," Smith's pedagogy in generic and stylistic criticism directly prepared students for the kind of practical reason that they would have to exercise in the determination of just punishments in criminal cases, as well as in the presentation of honest character in commercial transactions.[24] The practice of indirect description is of particular value, since it teaches one to discern the linkage between actions and the complex, often invisible motivating circumstances, psychological and social, that underlie them. While the rules of justice themselves may be analogous to the strict rules of grammar, "precise, accurate and indispensible," the actual carrying out of justice, such as in criminal sentencing, requires recourse to ethical judgment, whose "rules" are analogous to those "which critics lay down for the attainment of what is sublime and elegant in composition"—and which are "vague" and "indeterminate" (TMS III.6.11). "Judgment of punishment," observes Longaker, "depends on an awareness of emotional propriety, a sense that circumstances warrant the victims' pathos."[25] Moral aptitude thus conceived is nowhere better learned than through belletristic theory and practice.

If we attend to eighteenth-century changes in contract jurisprudence, we may likewise see an inherent practical value in the kind of rhetorical education Smith pioneered in Great Britain. As laid out in P. S. Atiyah's *The Rise and Fall of Freedom of Contract*, by the late eighteenth century, English law had evolved away from a concept of contract reliant on "consideration"—what may be thought of as a socially mediated consensus about just terms of relation between contracting parties. Obviously this restricted who could enter into contracts, and who could prosecute claims for breach of contract. Contracts untethered to preexisting conditions of obligation and unsupported by communal standards of equity were seen as nonbinding, but after roughly 1770, a new conception of "promissory" contract emerged. Here, the basis of contract is no more than the spoken or written utterance of the promise, and liability becomes a rather strange metaphysical entity, something that must be inherent in the contract itself.[26] This important chapter in the transition from feudal to free market economics was a boon to commerce, but it also brought new forms of risk: contracts thus easily entered into were literally "inequitable" in the sense of not relying on the moral sanction of communal notions of obligation for their guarantee. But what has this to do with belle-tristic rhetoric?

We should recall first that the patron of Smith's rhetoric lectures, Kames, was a prominent legal practitioner and theorist who was as strong an advocate for Scottish legal reform as he was for the cause of Scottish linguistic improvement; he most particularly sought a rapprochement between Scots and English law that would eclipse elements of the Roman *jus communus* that were, in their adherence to consideration-based contract, an obstacle to commerce.[27] Smith's student John Millar was likewise such an advocate, due directly to Smith himself, who held that such "remains of the old jurisprudence should be removed" (LJA, ii.40–41) and who bore witness to the very shift Atiyah describes, noting that in earlier society, contracts were of a much more communal nature because the trials required to enforce them or punish breach of contract were highly demanding on the community, drawing members away from their occupations. "Besides this," he wrote, "there are several reasons which retard the validity of contracts, as the uncertainty of language. Language at all times must be somewhat ambiguous, and it would be more so in the [primitive] state of society. . . . This must render it very difficult to conclude with exactness the intention of the contracting parties, and determine whether it was their inclination to produce a reasonable expectation or only to signify a design which they had at the time of acting in such a manner" (LJA ii.46). Even though under promissory contract, "a bare promise produces an obligation under law" (LJA ii.49), it would seem that the expansion of promissory contract would yet put different demands on language. There must be a sense in which the simple clarity of contractual language yet ensures the possibility of interpreting intention accurately and reasonably points to the legitimate authority of law. Discursive clarity, it might be said, must be understood to have a socially recognizable "character" of its own. In LRBL, Smith's advocacy for a "plain, distinct, and perspicuous Stile" (ii.245) indicates just this: his is not a recourse to some naïve correspondence theory of *res* and *verba*, but an instance wherein clarity is undergirded by propriety, in all its reliance on the recognition of socially persuasive character and therefore mutual trust. Linguistic propriety in a modern legal context can thus be seen to reconstitute contractual consideration, albeit on a far less parochial or local scale.

As these prolusions are meant to suggest, there is a good deal more work to be done to fully appreciate the place of rhetoric in Smith's corpus and in relation to the social and economic transformations of his day. Likewise, more remains to be done to interpret and value Smith's full intellectual accomplishment for the field of rhetorical studies today, most particularly at a moment when the humanities are thought to be in crisis, due at least in part, it is often said, to utilitarian pressures of capitalism driven by neoliberalist politics. Scholars and teachers of rhetoric should continue to read Smith so they can see both the legitimacy and the value of expanding their field to comprise human communication as a whole, though not as a means to promote some Spencerian efficiency in communication (whatever that would be). Smith can help disclose how rhetoricians working in such a broad field in a pluralistic society yet need succumb neither to the position that rhetoric is thoroughly epistemic (i.e., the skeptical stance that rhetoric is constitutive of our knowledge of reality), nor to any of the range of poststructuralist convictions that the rhetorically informed study of literary excellence is reducible to cultural politics, nor to the view that clear and effective expression is a stealthy handmaiden to hegemonic capitalism. Indeed, as much as to save the humanities from their current etiolation in the academy, it is to save the system of ascendant capitalism from its own darker rapacities, and thereby the just flourishing of humanity under it, that a Smithian art of rhetoric could be envisioned once again at the center of a liberal arts education, as an essential part of the conscious design of a decent society.[28]

NOTES

1. A brief overview of the complex and varied landscape of twentieth-century rhetoric may be had in "Modern and Postmodern Rhetoric: Introduction," in

The Rhetorical Tradition: Readings from Classical Times to the Present, 2nd ed., ed. Patricia Bizzell and Bruce Herzberg (New York: 2001), pp. 1183–1205. A valuable bibliographic essay on this is Krista Ratcliffe, "The Twentieth and Twenty-First Centuries," in *The Present State of Scholarship in the History of Rhetoric*, ed. Lynée Lewis Gaillet and Winifred Bryan Horner (Columbia, MO: 2010), pp. 185–236.

2. Walter Ong, "Foreword," in Gaillet and Horner, *Present State of Scholarship*, p. 5.

3. On the role of belletristic rhetoric in the marked eclipse of classical rhetoric in the nineteenth-century American academy, with specific reference to Smith, see S. Michael Halloran, "Rhetoric in the American College Curriculum: The Decline of Public Discourse," in *PRE/TEXT: The First Decade*, ed. Victor Vitanza (Pittsburgh: 1993), pp. 93–113.

4. Wayne C. Booth, *The Rhetoric of Rhetoric: The Quest for Effective Communication* (Blackwell: 2004), p. 28.

5. On Kames and Smith as agents of Scottish "improvement," see Nicholas T. Phillipson, *Adam Smith: An Enlightened Life* (London: 2010), pp. 72–88.

6. On French sources of British belletrism, see Barbara Warnick, *The Sixth Canon: Belletristic Rhetorical Theory and Its French Antecedents* (Columbia, SC: 1993).

7. Wilbur Samuel Howell, *Eighteenth-Century British Logic and Rhetoric* (Princeton: 1971), p. 576.

8. On Watson's lectures, see Paul Bator, "The Unpublished Rhetoric Lectures of Robert Watson, Professor of Logic, Rhetoric and Metaphysics at St. Andrews, 1756–1778," *Rhetorica* 12, no. 1 (1994), pp. 67–113.

9. On the complex publishing history of Blair's lectures, see "Editors' Introduction," in Hugh Blair, *Lectures on Rhetoric and Belles Lettres*, ed. Linda Ferreira-Buckley and S. Michael Halloran (Carbondale, IL: 2005), pp. xv–liv. On the history of English as a discipline emerging from Scottish belletrism, with reference to the contested role of Smith, see Franklin E. Court, *Institutionalizing English Literature: The Culture and Politics of Literary Study, 1750–1900* (Stanford: 1992); Ian Duncan, "Adam Smith, Samuel Johnson and the Institutions of English Literature," in *The Scottish Invention of English Literature*, ed. Robert Crawford (Cambridge: 1998), pp. 27–54; and Thomas P. Miller, *The Formation of College English, Rhetoric and Belles Lettres in the British Cultural Provinces* (Pittsburgh: 1997), pp. 178–204.

10. On the rhetoric teaching of the too little-known Jardine, see Lynée Lewis Gaillet, "George Jardine: Champion of the Scottish Philosophy of Democratic Intellect," *Rhetoric Society Quarterly* 28, no. 2 (1998), pp. 37–53.

11. A bibliographic essay on the bulk of scholarship on Smith and rhetoric up to 2005 is in Stephen McKenna, *Adam Smith: The Rhetoric of Propriety* (Albany, NY: 2006), p. 150–56.

12. Phillipson, *Adam Smith*, p. 93.

13. Richard A. Lanham, *The Electronic Word: Democracy, Technology, and the Arts* (Chicago: 1993), pp. 154ff.

14. The exemplary study in this regard is Eugene Garver, *Aristotle's Rhetoric: An Art of Character* (Chicago: 1994).

15. See David Gore, "Sophists and Sophistry in the Wealth of Nations," *Philosophy and Rhetoric* 44, no. 1 (2011), pp. 1–26.

16. For example, in the pseudo-Ciceronian *Rhetorica ad Herrenium*, some devices that appear first as topics of invention—i.e., tools for developing lines of argument, such as definition and reasoning by contraries—resurface among the figures of speech. See also Jeanne Fahnestock, *Rhetorical Figures in Science* (Oxford: 1999), which persuasively demonstrates how verbal style can function as an aid to discovery.

17. Maria Alejandra Carrasco, "Adam Smith's Reconstruction of Practical Reason," *Review of Metaphysics* 58, no. 1 (2004), pp. 81–116.

18. Stephen J. McKenna, "Adam Smith's Rhetorical Art of Character," in *Character, Self and Sociability in the Scottish Enlightenment*, ed. Susan Manning and Thomas Ahnert (New York: 2011), pp. 49–65.

19. Charles Griswold, "Smith and Rousseau in Dialogue: *Pitié*, Spectatorship, and Narrative," in *The Philosophy of Adam Smith: The Adam Smith Review Vol. 5, Essays Commemorating the 250th Anniversary of the Theory of Moral Sentiments*, ed. Vivienne Brown and Samuel Fleischacker (Routledge: 2010), p. 73

20. Richard P. McKeon, "The Uses of Rhetoric in a Technological Age: Architectonic Productive Arts," in *Selected Writings of Richard McKeon, Vol. 2: Culture Education and the Arts*, ed. Zahava K. McKeon and William G. Swenson (Chicago: 2005), pp. 197–214.

21. Duncan Kelly, *The Propriety of Liberty: Persons, Passions and Judgment in Modern Political Thought* (Princeton: 2011), p. 119.

22. Ibid., p. 121.

23. Catherine Labio, "Adam Smith's Aesthetics," in *The Oxford Handbook of Adam Smith*, ed. Christopher J. Berry, Maria Pia Paganelli, and Craig Smith (Oxford: 2013), pp. 113–14.

24. Mark Garrett Longaker, "Adam Smith on Rhetoric and Phronesis, Law and Economics," *Philosophy and Rhetoric* 47, no. 1 (2014), p. 27, quoting Miller, *Formation of College English*, p. 190.

25. Longaker, "Adam Smith on Rhetoric and Phronesis," p. 30.

26. P. S. Atiyah, *The Rise and Fall of Freedom of Contract* (Oxford: 1979), p. 154.

27. On the relation between the teaching of rhetoric and law and Scottish legal reform, see John W. Cairns, "Rhetoric, Language and Roman Law: Legal Education and Improvement in Eighteenth-Century Scotland," *Law and History Review* 9, no. 1 (1991), pp. 31–58.

28. The final phrase here borrows from the title of Jerry Z. Muller's *Adam Smith in His Time and Ours: Designing the Decent Society* (Princeton: 1995).

BIBLIOGRAPHIC ESSAY

In 1958, John Lothian discovered a manuscript of "Notes of Dr. Smith's Rhetoric Lectures" and published them with an introductory essay as *Lectures on Rhetoric and Belles Lettres* (London:

1963), but readers should begin with the critical edition published as volume 4 in *The Glasgow Edition of the Works of Adam Smith* (Oxford: 1983), with J. C. Bryce's rich and detailed introduction. Alongside the excellent early assessment of W. S. Howell cited in this chapter, it is still worthwhile to consult Vincent M. Bevilacqua, "Adam Smith's *Lectures on Rhetoric and Belles Lettres*," *Studies in Scottish Literature* 3 (1965), pp. 41–60, the same author's "Adam Smith and Some Philosophical Origins of Eighteenth Century Rhetorical Theory," *Modern Language Review* 63 (1968), pp. 559–68, and James L. Golden, "The Rhetorical Theory of Adam Smith," *Southern Speech Journal* 33, no. 3 (1968), pp. 200–215, whose differing views map interesting intellectual fault lines during the midcentury resuscitation of rhetoric in the academy. For histories of the discipline of English that attend to the early role of Scottish belletrism in general and Smith in particular, see note 6 to this chapter. Both Paul Bator ("Rhetoric and the Novel in the Eighteenth-Century British University Curriculum," *Eighteenth Century Studies* 30, no. 2 [1997], pp. 173–95) and Rae Greiner ("Sympathy Time: Adam Smith, George Eliot, and the Realist Novel," *Narrative* 17, no. 3 [2009], pp. 291–311) have analyzed the rise of the novel as an object of study within English with recourse to Smith. The one monograph dedicated to LRBL, Stephen J. McKenna, *Adam Smith: The Rhetoric of Propriety* (Albany, NY: 2006) examines the classical and modern heritage of rhetorical propriety as Smith knew it, provides a close reading of the lectures as a coherent theory of communication, argues that his treatment of rhetorical propriety should be understood as propaedeutic and infrastructural to his account of sympathy and conscience formation in TMS, and weighs what this means for understanding that account in the context of contemporary ethical and critical theory. It also provides a bibliographic essay on the more important work pertaining to Smith and rhetoric up to 2005. Political philosophers have increasingly taken LRBL into account in their readings of Smith's corpus, often looking closely at Smith's own rhetorical practices: see Duncan Kelly, *The Propriety of Liberty: Persons, Passions and Judgment in Modern Political Thought* (Princeton: 2011), but also Charles L. Griswold, *Adam Smith and the Virtues of Enlightenment* (Cambridge: 1999) and Ryan Patrick Hanley, *Adam Smith and the Character of Virtue* (Cambridge: 2009). See also Paddy Bullard, *Edmund Burke and the Art of Rhetoric* (Cambridge: 2011), for an insightful reading of Smith's synthesis of classical and early modern accounts of rhetorical ethos and his subsequent influence on Burke. The first major work to interpret Smith through the lens of his rhetorical practice is Vivienne Brown, *Adam Smith's Discourse: Canonicity, Commerce and Conscience* (London: 1994). Readers interested in other more recent rhetorical interpretations of Smith should see Colin Heydt, "'A Delicate and an Accurate Pencil': Adam Smith, Description, and Philosophy as Moral Education," *History of Philosophy Quarterly* 25, no. 1 (2008), pp. 57–73; David Gore, "Sophists and Sophistry in the *Wealth of Nations*," *Philosophy and Rhetoric* 44, no. 1 (2011), pp. 1–26; and Lisa Herzog, "The Community of Commerce: Smith's Rhetoric of Sympathy in the Opening of the Wealth of Nations," *Philosophy and Rhetoric* 46, no. 1 (2013), pp. 65–87.

ADAM SMITH'S NARRATIVE LINE

Karen Valihora

Of the range of Smith's work, literary scholars and critics are primarily interested in Smith's *Theory of Moral Sentiments*, and, to a lesser extent, the *Lectures on Rhetoric and Belles Lettres*. Perhaps the most influential reading of the TMS is David Marshall's analysis of the text as a theater, one that turns relations between people into performances for spectators. "I ask what it means that the impartial spectator is a spectator. What is at stake in the inherently theatrical situation that Smith describes when he pictures us appearing before each other as spectators and spectacles."[1] Since his 1984 essay, literary critics have understood the spectatorial dynamics that mark the TMS almost exclusively through models of theatricality and performance—with a consequent shortchanging of attention to Smith's demand that the spectator be impartial—even, or especially, in the matter of feeling. This essay highlights recent scholarship that challenges the theatrical model, to suggest that despite the apparent emphasis on spectators and spectacles, the real force of the TMS is in its narration.[2]

Smith's attention to the specific kinds of point of view narratives can offer, in particular the way they can shift almost imperceptibly from first-person to third-person considerations—and back again—turns the emphasis on images, spectacles, performances, and spectatorship in Book I into the primarily inward drama, the drama of conscience, or internal spectatorship, in Book III. Over the course of the TMS, in other words, Smith moves from the appraisal of others to the crucial matter of judging ourselves. The development of our critical and reflective powers, both exemplified and enabled in Smith's own complex uses of narrative, enables new levels of autonomy, independence, and authority. To that end,

I argue that the real hero of the TMS, the emerging "man of abilities" who challenges the social rank and authority of the aristocrat, is constructed not primarily as a spectator, nor even necessarily as an actor, but as a reader—the reader of the TMS.

Shared standards—of judgment, of propriety, of what composes merit and demerit, virtue, and perfection—are at the heart of the TMS. They compose its narrative line. While Smith opens with a careful notation of how our sympathy for others begins and ends with ourselves, of how we experience someone else's suffering or pain only in imagination—"I neither have, nor can have, any other way of judging about them"—he also shows just how keenly we can imagine others seeing, and judging, us (I.i.3.10). Our ability to take on an external, impartial, or distanced perspective, to imagine how other people might see, is, I argue here, a capacity specifically addressed and sharpened in Smith's mastery of narrative structures, the structures of point of view.

Our ability to respond to the feelings of others not only expresses, but forges, common standards. Finding agreement with others, forging mutual understanding: such activity is at the heart of our moral sentiments. "Though they will never be unisons, they may be concords, and this is all that is wanted or required" (I.i.4.7). Meeting others on their own terms requires exertion; Smith cites Grotius to suggest that falling short of an active regard and respect for others does not do them justice. "We are said not to do justice to our neighbour unless we conceive for him all that love, respect, and esteem, which his character, his situation, and his connexion with ourselves, render suitable and proper for us to feel, and unless we act accordingly" (VII.ii.1.10). Morality unifies; it forges connections between people, drawn together through the shared feelings that become mutual respect and esteem.

And yet, Smith's emphasis on concords, even unities, is in tension with a model of spectatorship that many have seen as antithetical to the sympathy it supposedly seeks. It is no secret that Smith is on the side of the spectator, that his morality is "spectatorial." "We constantly pay more regard to the sentiments of the spectator, than to those of the person principally concerned, and consider rather how his situation will appear to other people, than how it will appear to himself" (IV.1.8). Even when we ourselves suffer, "[w]e are immediately put in mind of the light in which [a spectator] will view our situation, and we begin to view it ourselves in the same light; for the effect of sympathy is instantaneous" (I.i.4.9). The "sympathy" here, again, is for the spectator, or, more precisely, for the distanced, detached point of view he or she represents.[3]

And yet, all of Smith's spectacles are narrated, stories told to us; they are therefore framed not only by narrative commentary but a particular kind of perspective, the kind only a narrative can generate, directs our apprehension of them. Furthermore, if it is, as Smith writes, "the thought of his situation" that creates sympathetic feeling in the breast of "every attentive spectator," "the situation" is what matters. "Sympathy . . . does not arise so much from the view of the passion, as from that of the situation which excites it" (I.i.1.10). "We" are carried along with passion only through the arc, the trajectory, of a plot. The narrative, the backstory, the invisible: that is what we want to know. "The first question which we ask is, What has befallen you? Till this be answered, though we are uneasy . . . our fellow feeling is not very considerable" (I.i.1.9). When it comes, however, to, not just feeling, or the immediate reproduction of feeling, but moral feeling, that knowledge is everything.[4]

In the sympathetic appraisals at the heart of the *Moral Sentiments*, we move immediately from the present occasion to its context. "In every passion of which the mind of man is susceptible, the emotions of the by-stander always correspond to what, by bringing the case home to himself, he imagines should be the sentiments of the sufferer" (I.i.1.4). The modal verb suggests congruence between what "should be" the sufferer's sentiments and what one imagines them to be.[5] The fear and pain of the man who has had his leg shot off by a cannon, for example, ought to be quelled by self-command. Smith counters immediate reality with the idea of what it could or should or ought to be—a strategy he shares with the realist novels of the eighteenth and nineteenth centuries, where the standard of sentiment is not reality, but propriety, linked not to how things are but to how they ought to be.[6]

In the justly famous opening pages of the TMS, Smith elaborates on the power of a perspective that is shared. "When the sentiments of our companion. . . . not only coincide with our own, but lead and direct our own; when in forming them he appears to have attended to many things which we had overlooked, and to have adjusted them to all the various circumstances of their objects; we not only approve of them, but wonder and are surprised at their uncommon and unexpected acuteness and comprehensiveness, and he appears to deserve a very high degree of admiration and applause" (I.i.4.3). This passage moves from describing easily shared perspectives—the kind we enjoy when appraising paintings, or landscapes, or "the conduct of a third person," or "the composition of a discourse"—things that have "no peculiar relation to either ourselves or to the person whose sentiments we judge of" (I.i.4.2)—to a subset of these, the special case of sharing a perspective that at the same time leads one's own in appraising something else. Smith argues that in judgments of works of art, "[w]e both look at them from the same point of view, and we have no occasion for sympathy, or for that imaginary change of situations from which it arises, in order to produce, with regard to these, the most perfect harmony of sentiments and affections." Yet in the special case where the judgments of our more acute companion "lead and direct our own," we do experience a shift in point of view: we see not just with our own eyes, but with his. We see things we wouldn't otherwise have seen, and we note the differences between what we see ourselves and what we see through his eyes. Insofar as our companion leads us to see as he sees, we experience precisely that sympathetic approval—heightened to admiration—that is such a profound source of, not just pleasure, but concord throughout the TMS.

This paragraph, not so coincidentally, both describes and exemplifies the narrative situation of the *Moral Sentiments*. As we read, we follow a superior observer, the narrator, who conscripts us to his perspective every time he says "we" or "our." At the heart of the TMS, there is a complex and powerful identification between ourselves, as readers, and our "companion," the narrator. This identification necessarily precedes and informs—frames—every judgment the text describes and every other sympathetic identification it promotes.

This narrative line is flexible; it may give way at any time to a different form of address and exemplification. When the narrator moves from first-person plural—"we"—into first-person singular, for example, he offers an invitation to identify with him, to see oneself as in a mirror. Consider Smith's description of self-division:

> When I endeavour to examine my own conduct, when I endeavour to pass sentence upon it, and either to approve or condemn it, it is evident that, in all such cases, I divide myself, as it were, into two persons; and that I, the examiner and judge, represent a different character from the other I, the person whose conduct is examined into and judged of. The first is the spectator, whose sentiments with regard to my own conduct I endeavour to enter into, by placing myself in his situation, and by considering how it would appear to me, when seen from that particular point of view. The second is the agent, the person whom I properly call myself, and of whose conduct, under the character of a spectator, I was endeavouring to form some opinion. (III.1.6)

The self-reflecting person, who conceives of himself as at once the "spectator" (also "examiner," and "judge") and the "agent," has not just internalized the division between narrator and reader described in the first paragraph cited above, but is aware of this self-relation. In the first paragraph, from Book I, the constellation of leading narrator and admiring, agreeing reader prefigures and directs our own internal self-division into impartial spectator and agent in the second passage, from Book III. Taken together, the passages suggest both the structure of the identification between reader and narrator, and our awareness of that identification: I experience myself as a reflecting, spectating observer and an "agent, the person whom I properly call myself," with immediate feelings and desires—and I shift back and forth between these perspectives. Smith's sheer narrative control turns the emphasis on images, spectacles, performances, and spectatorship in Book I into the primarily inward drama, the drama of conscience, or internal spectatorship, in Book III.

Smith's narration, in other words, offers an extended demonstration of what it means to be able to shift from first-person to third-person perspectives. This interplay may become so natural and automatic, Smith argues, we do not even realize we are doing it. In what can be read as a commentary on his own narration, so subtle it takes a special kind of parsing to apprehend it, Smith notes, "habit and experience have taught us to do this so easily and readily, that we are scarce sensible that we do it; and it requires . . . some degree of reflection, and even of philosophy, to convince us, how little interest we should take in the greatest concerns of our neighbour, how little we should be affected by whatever relates to him, if the sense of propriety and justice did not correct the otherwise natural inequality of our sentiments" (III.3.3). Propriety and justice require that we move from first- to third-person considerations.

In this way, Smith's own narrative line offers another version of the self-division that generates moral sentiment. As Charles Griswold and Vivienne Brown have shown, there are two key narrators at work in the text.[7] The first, or at least, the one who attracts our notice, is the one I have been describing: he builds an alliance with the reader through the enjoining "we." Brown calls this an "all-inclusive first person plural . . . 'we' refers not only to the author and his readers but to all of humanity. It is the voice of reasonable and humane opinion and it carries along with it a considerable part of the story of TMS" (28). There is also a second, even more authoritative narrator, perhaps Adam Smith himself, the "Professor of Moral Philosophy at the University of Glasgow"—as he is identified on the title page of the first edition.[8] This narrator adopts, in a rhetorical sleight of hand, an impersonal position, beyond that of the "we" and its habitual, commonsense impressions. This impersonal narrator comments on and in this way contains, and sometimes corrects, the sentiments and judgments of the narrator of common experience. It narrates almost exclusively in third person.[9] It often identifies its pronouncements with those of "nature," or "mankind" in general.

For example, Smith writes, "*It is because mankind are disposed to sympathize more entirely with our joy than with our sorrow*, that we make parade of our riches, and conceal our poverty" (I.iii.2.1). The impersonal narrator—in my italics—observes the general rule, the preference for joy over sorrow, and makes "mankind" into the spectator of "our joy." Meanwhile the second narrator—our companion—offers an example from our own experience—"we" are invited to see ourselves here, the way we "make parade of" our riches, if we have them, or, if not, try to "conceal" our poverty as much as possible from public view. We are participant in the general folly, and observed by the impartial spectator, whose mere observation, both of "mankind" and ourselves, suggests a better way of being.

Here is another example: "*Upon this disposition of mankind, to go along with all the passions of the rich and powerful, is founded the distinction of ranks, and the order of society.* Our obsequiousness to our superiors more frequently arises from our admiration for the advantages of their situation, than from any private expectations of benefit from their good will" (I.iii.2.3). Again, the general, impersonal rule, claiming universal authority—although in this case a bit strained, putting the cart before the horse—and then "our" narrator appears again to show us, as in a mirror, our own "obsequiousness" to our superiors, and our—perhaps misplaced—admiration.

This impersonal, observational, impartial, and authoritative voice is a familiar presence in the realist novels of the nineteenth century, and is developed with particular brilliance in the novels of Jane Austen. In the quiet interplay between these two narrators, I wish to suggest, we have an early version, a forerunner, of what will become known as free-indirect discourse. This is impersonal, third-person narration that contains, or filters, the voices, viewpoints, wishes, thoughts, and feelings of characters. A rhetorical tour de force, free-indirect discourse (FID) is associated with novelistic narrative—Frances Ferguson calls it "the novel's one and only formal contribution to literature"—and Jane Austen is considered the "inventor" of FID in the English novel.[10]

The famous first sentence of *Pride and Prejudice* (1813), for example, directly compares with these from Smith—if one allows for an extra layer of irony: "It is a truth universally acknowledged, that a single man in possession of a good fortune, must be in want of a wife."[11] If this pronouncement, at once sententious and trivial, seems to target the invisible authority of the impersonal narrative voice—it also reinforces it, as a voice capable of irony, of self-aware reflexivity. Furthermore, the supposed universality of its claim, "a single man in possession of a good fortune, must be in want of a wife," is also ironic; it masks wishful thinking—identified in the next few pages not with the narrator, who is above such things, but with the hopes of Mrs. Bennet, the mother of five marriageable daughters, who has just learned that a single man in possession of a very good fortune has moved in next door.

The authority of Austen's impersonal narrative voice is accrued and sustained in the contrast, which also marks the TMS, between this pronouncing authority, and the limited and subjective viewpoints it at once echoes and contains. Consider Austen's rendition of Emma's thoughts upon realizing Mr. Elton has presumed to think she might want to become his wife—or to put it another way, proposed: "Perhaps it was not fair to expect him to feel how very much he was her inferior in talent, and all the elegancies of mind. The very want of such equality might prevent his perception of it; but he must know that in fortune and consequence she was greatly his superior. He must know that the Woodhouses had been settled for several generations at Hartfield, the younger branch of a very ancient family—and that the Eltons were nobody."[12] The passage casts Emma's first-person, private, thoughts into third-person narration. This is free-indirect discourse. There is no narrator overtly mediating the thoughts, there are just the thoughts. Furthermore, although we have direct access to Emma's thoughts, we are not directly implicated as hearers or spectators, which means Emma performs for nobody; she does not imagine an audience here at all; she just thinks.

One important effect of Austen's FID is the blurring of narrative authority. The unsuspecting reader, for example, at first takes this passage for the impartial appraisal of the narrator—she may well find herself identifying with Emma's point of view, and agreeing with Emma's assessments of Mr. Elton. Yet, the passage has markers that give it away: the repeated, impatient, "He must know . . . he must know"; the abrupt, "the Eltons were nobody." The arrogance is Emma's: consumed with her own importance and failing to appreciate anybody else's; so impressed with her own rung on the ladder of rank and property she cannot see an equal. When the reader discovers the trick, that this is not impartial narration but a narration of Emma's thoughts amounting to an exposure of them, then not only Emma's thoughts, but our own wishful identification with her superiority are exposed: subject to third-person scrutiny, that of the impersonal, impartial narrator implied in the very repetition of the passage. Through the combination of first-person thought and third-person overhearing Austen achieves the desired effect: self-reflection. We see ourselves, and our private, unspoken snobberies and judgments, as in a mirror.

I wish to suggest that our ability to occupy two subject positions at once is precisely an effect of narrative, one formalized in this special narrative invention of the eighteenth century. FID has several crucial features that locate it as the special product of the spectatorial dynamics Smith explores in the TMS: it mediates sensation and reflection, allowing moments for both immediate, absorbed first-person experience and more distanced, third-person reflection on that experience. It subjects the first person to third-personal forms of scrutiny. If it forces first persons into line with propriety—the general complaint about the spectatorial emphasis in the TMS echoes the general complaint about Austen's use of FID—it is also true that it allows for the expansion of private life: our sense of propriety shifts to take account of inner experience as much as inner experience is inflected by considerations of propriety in the TMS. As a narrative line, it goes both ways.[13]

Before I turn back to the TMS, consider one more set of passages from Austen. These juxtapose Emma's thoughts with those of the impersonal narrator. The subject is visiting Miss Bates. Emma hates visiting Miss Bates; she sees her as poor and therefore pathetic. "She had had many a hint from Mr. Knightley and some from her own heart, as to her deficiency—but none were equal to counteract the persuasion of its being very disagreeable,—a waste of time—tiresome women—and all the horror of being in danger of falling in with the second-rate and third-rate of Highbury, who were calling on them forever." One day, however, in order to put an end to Harriet's tedious whining about Mr. Elton while they are out walking, Emma decides to visit Miss Bates and her mother. "There, in the very moderate sized apartment, which was everything to them, the visitors were most cordially and even gratefully welcomed; the quiet neat old lady, who with her knitting was seated in the warmest corner, wanting even to give up her place to Miss Woodhouse, and her more active, talking daughter, almost ready to overpower them with care and kindness, thanks for their visit, solicitude for their shoes, anxious enquiries after Mr. Woodhouse's health, cheerful communications about her mother's, and sweet-cake from the beaufet" (II.i).

The first paragraph—self-centered, bad-tempered, fearful of contagion by the "second- and third-rate"—in other words, all Emma —is illuminated by the valuing and appreciative notations of the second, which show the Bates in a different light. The contrast between the impartial spectator's narration and Emma's private thoughts creates the effect of mimicry, even parody.[14] Her internal, private thought is overheard, repeated, exposed. Anyone who has ever thought of others in terms of "all the horror of being in danger of falling in" with them must see themselves here, as in a mirror.[15]

Smith writes a passage on bringing the point of view of the impartial spectator to bear on the self that echoes the amplifications of impersonal narration.

> We either approve or disapprove of our own conduct, according as we feel that, when we place ourselves in the situation of another man, and view it, as it were, with his eyes and from his station, we either can or cannot entirely enter into and sympathize with the sentiments and motives which influenced it. We can never survey our own sentiments and motives, we can never form any judgment concerning them, unless we remove ourselves, as it were, from our own natural station, and endeavour to view them as at a certain distance from us. But we can do this is no other way, than by endeavouring to view them with the eyes of other people, or as other people are likely to view them. Whatever judgment we can form concerning them, accordingly, must always bear some secret reference, either to what are, or to what, upon a certain condition, would be, or to what, we imagine, ought to be the judgment of others. (III.1.2)

The subject of the TMS is the same as that of Austen's *Emma*: both texts are interested in the relation between truly superior character and social rank—in Smith's terms, the relation between those who receive praise and those who are truly praiseworthy. Both texts mount a sustained interrogation of the ways and means of attaining impartiality. In particular, the movement between first- and third-person considerations that must characterize our appraisals of both others and the self forms the substance of the narrative in both texts.

Smith's crucial distinction between the praised and the praiseworthy announces in itself a shift from theatrical dynamics— dynamics of public performance that court public approbation—to narrative negotiations, the careful inward scrutiny, for example, that narrative both enables and exemplifies.[16] Any self-respecting person, from the point of view of the TMS, will be interested in being praiseworthy, not merely praised. And yet, as Smith notes, praise, for external trappings such as riches and rank, will substitute, for many kinds of people, for being truly praiseworthy (see, for example, the extended discussions of the vain versus the proud man; of how riches command admiration; and how many of our goals, for large houses for example, will prove of illusory value once we've attained them). As Austen's narrator notes of Emma, whose vanity forms the hidden subject of her story, "She was not . . . sorry to know her reputation for accomplishment often higher than it deserved" (I.vi).

Early in the TMS, two crucial obstacles to the activities of the impartial spectator come into view. The first concerns the forms of public propriety and convention, the second our own capacities for self-delusion—mistaking praise, for example, or rank, for an indication of praiseworthiness. A chapter added in 1790, for the sixth edition, addresses precisely "the corruption of our moral sentiments" caused by our admiration for wealth—and on which rests "the distinction of ranks, and the order of society" (I.iii.1). The very order of society, in other words, threatens moral sentiment. The remedy is to subject public, theatrical performances— the display required to maintain rank and order—to the forms of reflection made possible in the narrative line.

By what important accomplishments is the young nobleman instructed to support the dignity of his rank, and to render himself
worthy of that superiority over his fellow-citizens, to which the
virtue of his ancestors had raised them? Is it by knowledge, by industry, by patience, by self-denial, or by virtue of any kind? As all
his words, as all his motions are attended to, he learns an habitual
regard to every circumstance of ordinary behaviour, and studies to
perform all those small duties with the most exact propriety. As he
is conscious how much he is observed, and how much mankind
are disposed to favour all his inclinations, he acts, upon the most
indifferent occasions, with that freedom and elevation which the
thought of this naturally inspires. His air, his manner, his deportment, all mark that elegant and graceful sense of his own superiority, which those who are born to inferior stations can hardly
ever arrive at. These are the arts by which he proposes to make
mankind more easily submit to his authority, and to govern their
inclinations according to his own pleasure: and in this he is seldom
disappointed. (I.iii.2.4)

The scene Smith describes includes not only the nobleman, but
the admiring onlookers who at once constitute and consolidate
his power. The interplay, made the object of our reflections, is that
between actor and audience: "*As all his words, as all his motions
are attended to*, he learns an habitual regard to every circumstance
of ordinary behavior, and studies to perform all those small duties with the most exact propriety. As he is conscious *how much
he is observed*, and *how much mankind are disposed to favour
all his inclinations*, he acts, upon the most indifferent occasions,
with that freedom and elevation which the thought of this naturally inspires." This is a parody of the operations of the impartial
spectator: the spectators the nobleman imagines and addresses are
not exactly what Smith has in mind when he admonishes us to
consider how we look to others. The nobleman's performance is
theater—but nowhere more so than in Smith's text.

Smith's impersonal narrator models an impartial perspective for
the reader, while the onlookers who attend to the nobleman's "every
word, every motion" mirror that reader—who has not been, even

momentarily, captivated by the spectacle of royalty, nobility, or celebrity? The bifurcation is familiar by now. We identify with the nobleman (wishfully), we identify with his audience (shamefully); we attend to the narrator, and reflect on his reflections on the scene. We are engaged as first persons, second persons, and impartial third persons and move between these positions, appraising the whole.

As Smith elsewhere points out, in any narrative, the nobleman is the star of the show; he is the traditional hero of romance and tragedy because his apparent superiority over his fellow citizens invites the spectator's idealizing identification and sympathy. Yet his series of direct questions interrupts that circuit of identification; they address the reader in second person, asking him to appraise the foundations of the nobleman's superiority. "Is it by knowledge, by industry, by patience, by self-denial, by virtue of any kind?" The list offers a new, and superior, set of identifications: those that define a reader as much as the emerging hero of the TMS, the "man of abilities."

Most of these merits, are, naturally, invisible—they are quite different from the arts of deportment in which the nobleman excels. "Why should the man, whom nobody thinks it worthwhile to look at, be very anxious about the manner in which he holds up his head, or disposes of his arms while he walks through a room?" His very invisibility leads him, allows him, to cultivate the inner virtues, while he searches out an opportunity to display them.

> If ever he hopes to distinguish himself, it must be by more important virtues. . . . [H]e must acquire superior knowledge in his profession, and superior industry in the exercise of it. He must be patient in labour, resolute in danger, and firm in distress. . . . With what impatience does the man of spirit and ambition, who is depressed by his situation, look round for some great opportunity to distinguish himself? No circumstances, which can afford this, appear to him undesirable. He even looks forward with satisfaction to the prospect of foreign war, or civil dissension. (I.iii.2.5)

While Smith's invisible man longs for a revolution, to bring a new actor onto the historical stage, into visibility, or, more importantly, legibility, "the man of rank and distinction," for whom "to figure at a ball is his great triumph," hates the prospect of war or bloodshed—"not from the love of mankind, for the great never look upon their inferiors as their fellow-creatures"—but "from a consciousness that he possesses none of the virtues which are required in such situations, and that the public attention will certainly be drawn away from him by others." The voice is still third person, but by the end of the sentence, with that "conscious-ness," and that "certainly"—"the public attention will certainly be drawn away from him by others"—the point of view is that of the nobleman. We feel his "consciousness" of his own incapacity, we see from his perspective—his quiet, inward, invisible thought: the real specter raised by the prospect of war is his own disappear-ance. Smith continues in a more distant, moralizing vein, but the damage—our felt sense of the real inferiority and cowardice of the nobleman, his limited prospects and his limited perspective—has been done. The moment of private thought makes palpable how the nobleman really feels, what his performances conceal.

These are all narrative effects. Not just the silent switch in point of view, but the making visible the invisible, interior, inward thought of persons become characters. The emphasis within the TMS on first- and third-person perspectives leads it ineluctably forward along a road charted by the historical development of a public culture that could support and further the ends of integrated, inward, and au-tonomous selves—in developing invisible capacities for judgment and sympathy, we find reflective distance on the immediate force of external, and conventional, perspectives. At the same time, then, as Smith emphasizes the crucial ability to bring external and conven-tional perspectives to bear on the self, he develops our first-person capacities to think on our own terms. "Propriety" in the TMS names, not a near-inert set of rules, although for some it may serve this purpose, but exertion—the active justice of Grotius. Insofar as Smith insists we move outside of ourselves, he insists we move beyond the conventional. This movement is built into the narrative structures Smith employs: when first-person thoughts and feelings are cast into third-person terms, inner thoughts are spoken aloud, as it were, in another man's voice. Convention and propriety, as well as vanity and self-absorption, become the subjects of the nar-rative line—they become objects of reflection.

NOTES

1. See David Marshall, "Adam Smith and the Theatricality of Moral Sentiments," *Critical Inquiry* 10, no. 4 (June 1984), p. 593, as well as Marshall, *The Figure of Theatre: Shaftesbury, Defoe, Adam Smith and George Eliot* (New York: 1986).

2. Charles Griswold notes in *Adam Smith and the Virtues of Enlightenment* (Cambridge: 1999), "There is a narrative dimension to sympathy as analysed in TMS; and TMS tends to occlude that fact by advancing a non-narrativistic, ocular conception of sympathetic spectatorship with which the narrative dimension is in tension" (73). Hereafter cited parenthetically. Rae Greiner argues in "Sympathy Time: Adam Smith, George Eliot, and the Realist Novel," *Narrative* 17, no. 3 (October 2009), that the emphasis on spectacles and images both within the TMS and in criticism of the TMS has led to a real underestimation of its importance, "a result of the mistaken assumption that it offers a primarily theatrical account of sympathy production." She suggests instead that Smith's sympathy is the effect of a specifically narrative form: "the book [is] a work of narrative theory" (294). Likewise, Ian Duncan, in "Adam Smith, Samuel Johnson and the Institutions of English," in *The Scottish Invention of English Literature*, ed. Robert Crawford (Cambridge: 1998), notes that Smith's *Lectures on Rhetoric and Belles Lettres* suggest "the constitution of a new kind of modern subject through the techniques of literacy—specifically, they constitute the modern subject as a *reader*" (42).

3. A spectator is then the more useful, paradoxically, the more unsympathetic he is. A "common acquaintance," is more consoling than an intimate friend, because his presence requires that we temper our suffering. "An assembly of strangers" encourages our fortitude even more effectively (I.i.4.9). In every case, it is our ability to imagine an impartial view, to bring it to bear on our own selves, that helps us to acquire it, to internalize it.

4. Smith counters David Hume's model of sympathetic feeling as a kind of "contagion." For Smith, moral feeling is not about sensation, or immediate feeling, but reflection on what is proper to be felt. This has meant, however, that Smith's treatise on sympathy has been interpreted as coldly unfeeling. John Mullan, in *Sentiment and Sociability: The Language of Feeling in the Eighteenth Century* (Cambridge: 1988), describes propriety in Smith as a system of "willed uninvolvement" (46), the spectator as aloof. The opposite is, however, equally true: Smith refers to many occasions when feeling is visceral, too easily shared, and notes how strong feelings push others away from us as much as draw them closer. Which feelings we ought to cultivate and promote is his concern.

5. I look in more detail at Smith's persuasive employment of propriety in "The Judgement of Judgement: Smith's *Theory of Moral Sentiments*," *British Journal of Aesthetics* 41, no. 2 (2001), pp. 138–61.

6. For the ways in which realism refers to an ideal moral order, rather than a real one, see my *Austen's Oughts: Judgment after Locke and Shaftesbury* (Newark, DE: 2010).

7. I am particularly indebted in this essay to Vivienne Brown's line-by-line analysis, in *Adam Smith's Discourse: Canonicity, Commerce and Conscience* (Rout-

ledge: 1994), of the interplay between the impersonal narrator and the commonsense one we tend to see and identify with. Hereafter cited parenthetically. Charles Griswold gives a detailed and insightful discussion of the complexity of Smith's rhetorical techniques, with particular emphasis on the many rhetorical effects of the protreptic "we" (pp. 49–50).

8. David Marshall, "Adam Smith," makes this observation, p. 606.

9. Dorrit Cohn notes, astutely, that narration in third person always implies a narrator, a background presence informing and directing all interpretation. See *Transparent Minds: Narrative Modes for Presenting Consciousness in Fiction* (Princeton: 1978).

10. Frances Ferguson, "Jane Austen, *Emma*, and the Impact of Form," *Modern Language Quarterly* 61, no. 1 (March 2000), p. 159. Blakey Vermeule, in *Why We Care about Literary Characters* (Baltimore: 2009), tracks the development of FID as one of the ways in which eighteenth-century novelists learn to evoke mental life in narrative. Like most critics, she finds FID originates with Austen, but also finds early versions in Frances Burney and William Godwin.

11. Jane Austen, *Pride and Prejudice* (1813), ed. Donald Gray (New York: 2001), I.i.

12. Jane Austen, *Emma* (1816), ed. Stephen Parrish (New York: 2000), I.xvi. Hereafter cited parenthetically in the text.

13. Karen Diane Leibowitz, in "The Reticence Effect: Narrative Interiority in the Nineteenth Century British Novel" (doctoral diss., University of California, Berkeley, 2008), connects Smith's impartial spectator and impersonal narration in the novel; both stances are imagined, and both "can articulate community norms without reference to an individuated perspective" (p. 6).

14. Louise Flavin, "Free Indirect Discourse and the Clever Heroine of *Emma*," *Persuasions* 13 (1991), emphasizes the effect of Austen's free indirect renderings of Emma's thoughts in particular as mimicry verging on parody.

15. About the efficacy of this mirror image, Smith writes, in a sentence reminiscent of Shaftesbury on the same subject, "If we saw ourselves in the light in which others see us, or in which they would see us if they knew all, a reformation would generally be unavoidable. We could not otherwise endure the sight" (III.4.6).

16. In "Smith's Ambivalence about Honor," in *The Philosophy of Adam Smith: Essays Commemorating the 250th Anniversary of* The Theory of Moral Sentiments, ed. Vivienne Brown and Samuel Fleischacker (Routledge: 2010), Stephen Darwall notes Smith moves between the standards of an "honor culture" and the developing standards of a merit culture, with its cultivation of and reliance on the inward sense of the dignity of persons—capable of honoring even private contracts, and personal promises. In an honor culture, appearances are everything: an injury is an insult to rank or status; there is little sense of a self separate from these. Smith refers as often to the moral standards of an honor culture—for example, "the sacred and necessary law of retaliation" (II.i.2.5)—as he does to those of an inward, merit-based culture, where "honor" designates the sense of one's own integrity, responsibility, and, finally, autonomy.

BIBLIOGRAPHIC ESSAY

A very few landmark readings of Adam Smith's TMS connect this work to the eighteenth-century literary scene. John Mullan's *Sentiment and Sociability: The Language of Feeling in the Eighteenth Century* (Cambridge: 1988), reads key works of eighteenth-century literature—by Richardson, Sterne, and Mackenzie—through the emphasis on feeling in works by David Hume and Adam Smith, showing how sympathy was understood to undergird a felt sense of community, and how literary texts are particularly able to produce such sympathy. David Marshall's *The Figure of Theatre: Shaftesbury, Defoe, Adam Smith and George Eliot* (New York: 1986), situates the theatrical performances between people that inflect his reading of the spectatorial dynamics of the TMS within the larger, equally theatrical culture of the second half of the eighteenth century. Charles Griswold's *Adam Smith and the Virtues of Enlightenment* (Cambridge: 1999) advances a reading of the TMS that is at once philosophically grounded and highlights Smith's literary art, particularly his emphasis on narration, in drawing readers into his work. Vivienne Brown's relatively overlooked *Adam Smith's Discourse: Canonicity, Commerce and Conscience* (London: 1994) asks not so much what the TMS and WN say, but how they are to be read. She identifies Smith's apparent emphasis on clear, straightforward prose in the LRBL as misleading, showing how his own writing is intricately metaphorical and, crucially, speaks in different voices—placing the reader in different subject positions and points of view, and so formally enacting the emphasis on switching positions throughout the TMS. Very recent scholarship, such as Rae Greiner's *Sympathetic Realism in Nineteenth-Century British Fiction* (Baltimore: 2012) extends Smith's influence into the nineteenth century: the structure of sympathetic feeling as articulated in the TMS is linked to the narrative strategies of realism in the novel from Jane Austen to Joseph Conrad and Henry James.

ADAM SMITH AND THE HISTORY OF PHILOSOPHY

Michaël Biziou

The history of philosophy can be understood both as an academic discipline (the study of past philosophies) and as the object of it (the development of philosophies through ages). Therefore, examining the relationship between Adam Smith and the history of philosophy requires answering two interconnected questions. First, why should history of philosophy (taken as a discipline) consider Smith as a proper object of study, and along which lines should it study him? Second, what place can be attributed to Smith in the history of philosophy (taken as the historical succession of philosophies), and how does his thought map on to various philosophical traditions? The two sections of this essay address respectively these two questions. In the first section, methodological considerations concerning the task of historians of philosophy are examined, specifically applied to Smith's case. In the second section, a research program for historians of philosophy interested in Smith is sketched out, in order to highlight some of the various philosophical contexts in which his writings need to be understood.

1. METHODOLOGICAL CONSIDERATIONS: SMITH, A PROPER OBJECT FOR THE HISTORY OF PHILOSOPHY

1.1. From the Philosopher to the Economist, and Backward

Readers in Smith's time, and up until the first half of the nineteenth century, unquestionably considered him as a philosopher. In so doing they simply conformed to his own self-conception. Smith presents himself on the title page of both his published books, *The Theory of Moral Sentiments* and the *Inquiry into the Nature and Causes of the Wealth of Nations*, as a "professor of moral philosophy." His third great piece of writing, the *Lectures on Jurisprudence*, belongs to that same field of moral philosophy, which Smith explicitly takes to include not only "ethics" but also "jurisprudence" (TMS VII.iv.7 and VII.iv.34). Moreover Smith investigates "the principles which lead and direct philosophical enquiries," as his essays on the history of science are subtitled. The rest of his scattered writings and lectures he describes as "a sort of philosophical history of all the different branches of literature, of philosophy, poetry and eloquence" (CAS 248). Therefore "philosophy," "philosophical enquiry," and "philosophical history" appear as general headings under which all of Smith's works can be classified.

Indeed, like many writers of his time, Smith has a broad definition of philosophy: "Philosophy is the science of the connecting principles of nature" (HA II.12). The "nature" referred to here is both physical and human. So this definition applies to what was then generally called "natural philosophy" (HALM 1)—that is to say, physics—as well as to what Smith calls, following Hume, the "science of human nature" (TMS VII.iii.2.5). It can also apply to logic and metaphysics, since these consist in nothing but redoubled abstractions upon the objects of the other sciences (HALM 1). Accordingly, Smith's philosophy covers a wide scope of subjects: moral philosophy (TMS), political theory and law (LJ), economics (WN), epistemology (HA, HAP, HALM), linguistics (CL), rhetoric and literary theory (LRBL), and aesthetics (IA).

Smith however came to be viewed almost exclusively as an economist during the second half of the nineteenth century and into the twentieth century. Several reasons can account for this shift. First, the powerful and impressive epistemological development of economics as an autonomous science during these two centuries drew much attention to the economic aspects of Smith's thought, leading to an eclipse of other aspects. Second, the political and ideological debates pitting free trade against socialism and communism, raging from the Industrial Revolution to the Cold War, furthered the view of Smith as exclusively a capitalist economist. Finally, contingent variations in intellectual fashions and philosophical trends further contributed to the neglect of Smith's philosophy, favoring other doctrines more in vogue at the time.[1]

Yet at the end of the twentieth century and into the beginning of the twenty-first, the pendulum has tended to swing back toward the initial understanding of Smith as a philosopher. A substantial and ever-growing bibliography of history of philosophy studies dedicated to Smith testifies to this. Indeed the several reasons that accounted for the general economist bias in the previous period have largely given way to a different set of commitments and debates. First, economic science has evolved into a standard theory mainly inspired by the neoclassical school, whose orthodox grip heterodox economists try to loosen, sometimes in light of investigations of the philosophical aspects of Smith's economics.[2] Second, political and ideological debates have been deeply impacted by the disappearance of communism as an alternative regime. Most discussions now take place instead inside the free market paradigm, to which Smith is generally recognized as a principal contributor. Yet even in recognizing Smith's contributions as a free market thinker, most scholars have come to reject the oversimplified image of Smith as a fierce advocate of absolute laissez-faire, focusing instead on presenting the complexity of his philosophy.[3] Finally, and with regard to the contingent variations in intellectual fashions and philosophical trends, Smith studies have benefitted from a growing appreciation of the way in which Smith's thought can contribute to current philosophical debates—a phenomenon especially evident in the way in which moral philosophers have recently engaged Smith's concepts of sympathy and virtue.[4]

1.2. Systematization, Contextualization, and Retrospection

If Smith can be considered as a philosopher, then he is no doubt a proper object for the history of philosophy. Now, the history of philosophy is itself one way, among others, of doing philosophy, specifically through reading texts of the past and taking seriously their historicity. One can perhaps be a philosopher without opening old books—or, even if one opens them, without caring about how old they are. However, for historians of philosophy old books matter, because they contain still fruitful ideas; in this sense, historians of philosophy believe, like interlocutors in a conversation, that it is not always the case that the last to speak is necessarily the most interesting. Moreover, the historicity of these old books matters, because neglecting it can lead to many misunderstandings. Understanding the words and terms in which philosophical concepts are expressed demands a historical perspective because their meaning can change from one period to another. Understanding arguments similarly demands a historical perspective, because these often emerge out of controversies that have been long forgotten.

As there are different ways of doing philosophy—the history of philosophy being one of them—so there are different ways of doing the history of philosophy. Two are especially important. These two methods are not necessarily exclusive of one another, and are often used together. The first is an internal method of reading, or systematization. It tries to estimate to what extent the different writings of an author can, or cannot, be seen as a coherent whole. Systematization must include a historical dimension because the entire corpus of an author often takes decades to emerge, a new book confirming or contradicting the others, or a new edition of the same book completing or amending previous ones. In Smith's case, the successive editions of his two published books, or the existence of two versions of his lectures on jurisprudence, clearly invite an internal reading. The sixth edition of TMS (1790) is a particularly rich field of inquiry. Its numerous changes and additions raise important questions concerning Smith's judgment upon commercial society (TMS I.iii.3), the significance of his theory of virtues (TMS VI), his position toward religion (TMS II.ii.3), the importance he gives to Stoicism (TMS VI.iii, VII.ii.1), and a possible alteration in his concept of impartial spectator (TMS III.2).[5] The famous "Adam Smith Problem," that is, the problem of the intriguing relationship TMS and WN have with each other, also calls for an internal reading or systematization.[6] Finally, a last reason to attempt this method in studying Smith is the vast plan he seems to have in mind for all his other unpublished writings (CAS 248).

A second method in the history of philosophy is an external method of reading, or contextualization. It tries to interpret the text of an author in light of other texts written by other authors. Contextualization can also possibly refer to social, political, or economic contexts, but the history of philosophy mainly deals with textual context. The other texts can be anterior, contemporary, or even posterior to the main text under study, but in any case it is crucial to know their chronology. The point is to study how a philosopher exploited and possibly altered his sources, and how his legacy was collected and possibly distorted. This is a matter not of erudition but, again, of good philosophical understanding. Contextualization is somewhat analogous to etymology. Just as retracing a word's linguistic history from its ancient forms to its present uses helps to grasp its meaning better, so replacing an author among his predecessors, his contemporaries, and his successors allows us to understand his philosophy better. In Smith's case, his wide philosophical culture, his extensive engagement with his contemporaries, his early-begun and long-lasting influence on many following thinkers—all of these demand an external reading or contextualization.[7] The second section of this essay outlines such an approach.

Whether it resorts to systematization or to contextualization, ultimately the major theoretical problem that the history of philosophy has to face is retrospection. Retrospection is the act of asking contemporary questions of old texts. It is unavoidable, because historians of philosophy are children of their time. Try as he might, a commentator cannot completely rid himself of the terminology, interests, and ways of thinking of his own historical period. Nor would such an enterprise make sense to those concerned to investigate the past precisely because we find it interesting from our present point of view. So, as much as retrospection is not avoidable, it is not detestable either. But it definitely poses a problem, and indeed a thorny one, insofar as retrospection badly handled can lead to anachronism. Anachronism occurs when retrospection is naïve, or even unconscious of itself. To avoid it, therefore, one should always strive to distinguish as clearly as possible the questions that past philosophers asked themselves from the questions that commentators might wish to ask them in retrospect. The problem of retrospection in Smith's case is particularly vivid since many present-day commentators make use of categories totally unknown to him, but to which he is supposed to have given a noteworthy contribution or even a first foundation: classical liberalism,[8] classical economics,[9] spontaneous order theory,[10] school of moral sense,[11] Scottish enlightenment,[12] the Scottish historical school[13]—not to mention capitalism,[14] individualism,[15] egalitarianism,[16] sentimentalism,[17] and so on.

1.3. Smith as a Historian of Philosophy

Smith is all the more interesting for the history of philosophy insofar as he is not only a philosopher, but also a historian of philosophy in his own right. He proposes histories of almost all the fields he studies; some of these are quite elaborate—as in the case of his history of moral philosophy in TMS VII, and in his essays on the history of sciences—while others are less comprehensively developed—as when he retraces the history of early modern natural jurisprudence (LJB 1–4), or the "two different systems of political economy" that preceded his own (WN IV.intro.2). Smith is in fact so historically minded that he even offers two lectures on "the history of historians" (LRBL ii.44). And in these various histories we find Smith making use of the two methods discussed above: systematization, as when he summarizes Plato's or Aristotle's theory of virtue (TMS VII.ii.1.1–14), and contextualization, as when he presents Cudworth's system as a reaction to Hobbes (TMS VII.iii.2.4). And he too has to find his own way through the problem of retrospection. The questions Smith poses to previous philosophical texts are often expressed from an eighteenth-century perspective, as when he declares that the moral rationalism of the preceding century is the product of "a time when the abstract science of human nature was but in its infancy" (TMS VII.iii.2.5).[18]

Because Smith is himself a historian of philosophy, present-day historians of philosophy studying him are confronted with a double historical task. First, they have to recur to the same authors and problems that Smith explicitly does, given that he intends to draw his readers' attention to these as necessary to understand his philosophy. Second, they have to compare his systematization, his contextualization, and his retrospection to theirs. This redoubled work takes the form of double questions: What do we understand of Smith's concept of sympathy, and what do we understand of what Smith says about Hume's concept of sympathy (TMS VII. iii.3.17)? What is the benefit of reading Smith through the present-day category of classical liberalism, and what is the benefit of using this category for commenting Smith's own category of mercantilism (WN IV.i)? To what extent can we properly consider Smith as a philosopher according to our present-day conception of philosophy, and how does this present-day conception fit with Smith's own historical perspective on what he calls "philosophical enquiry"? Historians of philosophy thus might be led to ask questions in retrospect to a Smith who is himself asking questions in retrospect.

In other words, Smith's own history of philosophy explicitly provides us with a primary list of authors and problems who require our attention and study in order to understand Smith himself. To this we have to add a supplementary list that contains authors and problems either that Smith left implicit in his texts (because it would have been too obvious, too tedious, or too audacious for him to make them plain), or that he might never himself have thought of (because they arise from retrospective questions that historians of philosophy are allowed to ask, as we have seen, provided they are cognizant of what they are doing). Of course, in practice the two lists are necessarily mingled, because the search for the implicit cannot be separated from the statement of the explicit, and because retrospection cannot be disconnected from comprehension.

2. A RESEARCH PROGRAM: SMITH'S PLACE IN THE HISTORY OF PHILOSOPHY

Before sketching out a research program regarding the various philosophical contexts in which Smith's writings need to be understood, two caveats are necessary. First, in order to keep our contextualization inside the length granted to the present study, we focus only on Smith's predecessors and contemporaries, leaving aside the way his thought was taken up by later philosophers (e.g., Hegel,

Mill, Marx, Hayek, Rawls, etc.). Second, and with regard to the problem of retrospection, what follows restricts itself to authors generally considered to be philosophers by present-day historians of philosophy, leaving aside other thinkers who might have been considered philosophers in a comparatively looser eighteenth century sense (e.g., rhetoricians such as Hugh Blair or George Campbell, polymaths such as Samuel Johnson or Joseph Addison, scientists such as Isaac Newton, etc.).[19]

2.1. Contextualizing Smith: Predecessors

A. *Greco-Roman classics.* Smith's concept of the "impartial spectator" (TMS I.i.5.4) is often regarded as one of his primary contributions in the history of philosophy, and as an innovating step in the progressive invention of the autonomous moral subject of modernity.[20] But Smith is nonetheless an admirer of the ancients, and his role in the history of philosophy can also be described as an attempt to recover and update important elements of classic thought.[21] Thus, though he cannot but reject Plato's intellectualist definition of virtue, he is however interested in the tripartite division of the soul that grounds it. The irascible part of the soul in the Platonic tripartition helps Smith to formulate his own conception of "magnanimity" (TMS VII.ii.1.17) as a concern for one's reputation and dignity, which is directly linked to his category of the "respectable virtues" (TMS I.i.5.1, VII.ii.4.2).[22] From Aristotle, Smith takes the fundamental idea of virtue as a middle quality. This corresponds to his "point of propriety" (TMS I.ii.intro.2) as the exact degree of a passion coming to be equilibrated and shared, through the process of sympathy, by the agent and the spectator. Smith is also quite Aristotelian in his use of the concept of "character" (TMS VI.concl.6, VII.ii.1.13) and, more generally speaking, in his articulation of a conception of morality that we today would call virtue ethics.[23] Stoicism is of even greater importance to Smith. Key elements of his moral theory, including his concepts of "self-command" (TMS III.3.20, VI.iii), "universal benevolence," and "good offices" (TMS VI.ii.3), as well as his distinction between "perfect virtue" and mere "propriety" (TMS I.i.5.7, VII.ii.1.42), can be easily traced back to Stoicism. So too is it possible to trace back to Stoicism certain of Smith's metaphysical and teleological tenets, including the way individuals or societies are "recommended by Nature" (TMS VI.i.1, VI.ii.1, VII.ii.1.18) to our attention, or the way the universe is offered to philosophical "contemplation" as a well-ordered "system" under the care of "Providence" (TMS VI.ii.3.5, VII.ii.1.20).[24] Epicureanism is another object of reflection for Smith. Much is to be gained from interpreting his concepts of "self-love," "prudence," "tranquility of mind" (TMS VII.ii.2.7), or the complex interdependence he establishes between "pain" and "pleasure" (TMS I.iii.1.3, VII.ii.2.6), "virtue" and "utility" (TMS VII.ii.2.9), through the lens established by Epicurus and Lucretius. Smith's other important philosophical engagement with antiquity concerns his comments on the school he calls the "Eclectics" or the "later Platonists" (TMS VII.ii.3.1), meaning what is known today as Middle Platonism. The typically Eclectic manner in which Antiochus of Ascalon or Plutarch try to show how the moral philosophy of Plato, Aristotle, and Zeno can be conciliated, while disproving Epicureanism, is quite similar to Smith's own view (TMS VII.ii.2.15). It would be interesting to study whether the Middle Platonists' theme of a "resemblance or participation" (TMS VII.ii.3.2) to God's excellence as the only path to human perfection might have any remote echo in Smith's conception of the ascent from the "man without" to the "demigod within the breast," up to the "all-seeing Judge of the world" (TMS III.2.32–33).

B. *Christian theology.* Smith is often said to have contributed to the liberation of the study of human nature from older normative discourses such as theology.[25] However, as a philosopher living and writing in eighteenth-century Presbyterian Scotland, he naturally and inevitably brought to his work a Christian intellectual background. It is well known that Smith's Glasgow teaching began with lectures on natural theology, now lost. Therefore Smith's place in the history of philosophy needs to be studied, if not in the light of plain Christian theology, at least in the light of the process of the secularization of Christian concepts. In particular, he can be seen as undertaking a synthesis or combination of Classics and Christians. For example, his insistence on Providence wisely ruling the universe is indebted no less to Christianity than to Stoicism. So too his conciliation of the "amiable" with the "respectable" virtues (TMS I.i.5, VII.ii.4.2) might be seen as an attempt to reach a balance between Christian love of one's neighbor and Stoic self-command.[26] True, Smith mentions only cursorily the "ancient fathers of the Christian church" and the "divines [of] the Reformation," as upholders of the "system which makes virtue consist in benevolence" (TMS VII.ii.3.1–3). But it is tempting to explore the parallels between Augustine's theory of the two cities—the city of man and that of God—which emphasizes the limits of human virtue and politics as compared to a heavenly realm, and Smith's own reservations toward human agency and politics as compared to the larger order governed by the "invisible hand" (TMS IV.1.10; WN IV.ii.9). Selfishness, that great sin of human nature, could then be considered as the occasion of some secular and economic salvation, achieving the scheme of Augustinian theodicy and meeting the hopes of Augustinian eschatology.[27] As to those Reformation divines, most important for Smith would have been Calvin insofar as Calvinism formed the foundation of Scottish Presbyterianism. According to Calvinist theology, the chief end of the Christian when he acts righteously is to glorify God. To this might be compared Smith's assertion that "by acting according to the dictates of our moral faculties" we may be said "to co-operate with the Deity, and to advance as far as is in our power the plan of Providence" (TMS III.5.7).[28] Other religious sources important to Smith are "the casuists of the middle and latter ages of the Christian church" (TMS VII.iv.7; WN V.i.f.28). Casuistry is rejected by Smith as a "tiresome" and "useless" (TMS VII.iv.31) branch of morals, but the reasons why he thinks so deserve exploration insofar as they relate directly to his conception of rules, both moral or legal.

C. *Natural law theory.* Natural law was an important philosophical tradition in which Smith himself played a considerable part. These contributions are especially evident in the *Lectures on Jurisprudence* and its treatments of rights, the "impartial spectator," and the four stages of society. Appreciating the full significance of Smith's contributions on these fronts requires returning to such early modern theorists as Thomas Hobbes, Hugo Grotius, Samuel Pufendorf,

Richard Cumberland, John Locke, Henry and Samuel Cocceius, Jean-Jacques Burlamaqui, and Jean Barbeyrac. Particular attention needs to be given to two authors who preceded Smith as professors of moral philosophy at the University of Glasgow and taught natural jurisprudence: Gershom Carmichael and Francis Hutcheson. Their natural law theory is especially important insofar as it structured the curriculum Smith taught at Glasgow, and therefore is the mould in which Smithian political economy progressively matured. Smith's contribution to the history of the natural law tradition can itself be described as a decisive evolution of what is called today classical liberalism: from the political version of liberalism, as exemplified by Locke's doctrine of social contract and natural right of resistance, to the economical version of liberalism, as exemplified by Smith's "natural system of perfect liberty and justice" (WN IV.vii.c.44).[29]

D. *Other seventeenth-century philosophical traditions.* Apart from the early modern theory of natural law, four other seventeenth-century philosophical traditions constitute suggestive if less central contexts in which to assess Smith's place in the history of philosophy. The first of these is the Cambridge Platonists, including such thinkers to whom Smith explicitly refers as Ralph Cudworth, Henry More, and John Smith (TMS VII.ii.3.3, VII.iii.2.4). Their moral philosophy is rationalist, and therefore offers a sharp and important contrast to a sentimentalist moral theory, even as it might reasonably be seen as having positively influenced Smith via Shaftesbury's conception of the moral sense. The second tradition worthy of notice is that of the French Moralists, including especially Blaise Pascal, Pierre Nicole, Jean de La Bruyère, and La Rochefoucauld. Turning Augustinian theology into social anthropology, they consider that human virtue is mostly a fallacious pretence, and that a low-flying politics dedicated to equilibrating conflicting self-loves between sinners is the only way to organize society in our postlapsarian world. This, of course, looks much like the "invisible hand" managing competing interests on the market. In addition, Smith's deep interest in court culture, which he often distinguishes from the way of life of "men of inferior rank" in order to draw various moral, political, and sociological conclusions

(TMS I.iii.2.3–5, V.2.3, VI.iii.39; WN V.i.g.10), seems partly inspired by his reading of certain of these court Augustinians. Smith also explicitly refers to La Rochefoucauld on self-love (TMS VII. ii.4.6),[30] his description of the "vain and empty distinction of greatness" (TMS IV.1.8) might allude to Pascal's concept of entertainment, and his use of character as a rhetorical device in TMS is likely indebted to La Bruyère's book on characters, on which he comments in LRBL (i.194).[31] A third tradition is that of the seventeenth-century English empiricists. Smith's epistemology, detailed in his essays on the history of sciences, seems to perpetuate a line of thought emerging from Francis Bacon and John Locke, even though Hume's theory of the imagination is its direct source.[32] Last, a fourth tradition, somewhat opposed to the preceding one, is the Cartesian philosophers. Smith praises the coherence of Descartes' natural philosophy (HA IV.66), the originality of his metaphysics (Letter 10), and the efficiency of his method (LRBL ii.134). He also appreciates Malebranche's theory of passions (TMS III.4.3), which contains several observations on the imitation of affects that seem to point toward a theory of sympathy. But he does not seem much interested in the system of a minor Cartesian as Pierre-Sylvain Régis, though he calls it to the attention of the readers of the *Edinburgh Review* (LER 10).[33]

2.2. Contextualizing Smith: Contemporaries

A. *Tradition of moral sentiments.* One of the principal reasons for Smith's significance in the history of philosophy is suggested by the very title of his treatise on morals. Smith is the philosopher who claims to have succeeded at grounding morals on sentiments, as opposed to other foundations such as reason. From this point of view, the proper context for the study of Smith's moral theory is the eighteenth-century tradition of moral sentiments, consisting mainly of Lord Shaftesbury, Francis Hutcheson, and David Hume. Smith can be seen as developing this tradition of moral sentiments to its fullest by giving it a systematic form grounded in the central concept of sympathy. Thus Shaftesbury's and Hutcheson's moral sense, as the principle of moral judgment on oneself and others, is to be meticulously compared to the "impartial spectator." For example, when Smith describes moral conscience as the process in which I "divide myself, as it were, in two persons" (TMS III.1.6), this echoes Shaftesbury's conception of soliloquy as a technique for cultivating one's moral sense. Hume's theory of sympathy, which sought to provide an original explanation for the concept of moral sense, obviously prefigures Smith's. Identifying the exact difference between them is still a very difficult problem. From a metaphysical point of view, Shaftesbury and Hutcheson adopt the Stoic and Christian vision of the universe as a well-ordered system governed by Providence, and Smith's teleological perspective is partly indebted to them. However, Hume's metaphysical skepticism may have warned Smith against a dogmatic understanding of finalism, and it is a fascinating and open question whether for him the "invisible hand" and "Nature's recommendations" are unconditional teleology or subtle pieces of rhetoric.[34]

B. *Commercial society's contents and discontents.* A large part of Smith's economic arguments might be better understood through the lens of the history of economics rather than that of the history of philosophy. However, Smith plays an important part in the history of philosophy as a particularly knowledgeable theorist of the relationship between commerce and society, and especially by his renewal of the concept of civil society. Here the theme of the unintended consequences of human actions giving rise to a spontaneous social order is joined to a lucid analysis of the political, moral, and intellectual benefits or dangers of commercial society. To put it retrospectively, Smith can be seen as an advocate of economic liberalism who is, however, far from insensitive to the concerns of civic humanism or classical republicanism.[35] On this subject, Bernard Mandeville's paradox that private vices promote public benefits is an important source of reflections for Smith, even if he condemns it as "wholly pernicious" (TMS VII.ii.4.6).[36] Hume's historical considerations on how civil liberty and economic prosperity often reinforce each other, as well as Montesquieu's defense of the spirit of commerce,[37] are also explicit references. On the other hand, Smith has probably been warned about the dark side of commercial society by Jean-Jacques Rousseau's discourse on inequality, lengthily quoted in LER (13–15).[38] Adam Ferguson also helped Smith not to lose sight of the delicate balance to be maintained between commercial society's contents and discontents. Though Smith never explicitly names him, it seems likely that he is one of those "men of republican principles" (WN V.i.a.41) mentioned by Smith who are worried by the loss of public spirit. Ferguson's history of civil society also provides a striking parallel with Smith's concern about the "torpor of mind" inflicted on the laboring poor by the repetitive tasks of the division of labor (WN V.i.f.50).

C. *The Scottish Enlightenment.* Another context for appraising Smith's position in the history of philosophy is to regard him as one of the great representatives of that period of Western culture known as the Enlightenment, and the Scottish Enlightenment in particular. Smith was anything but a recluse, and he benefited from the rich philosophical spirit that breathed through eighteenth-century Scotland. He was in touch with his fellow academics, participated in the highly sociable literati clubs, kept himself informed of the Scottish publishing market, and was aware of political and religious debates of his nation. We have already mentioned Carmichael, Hutcheson, Hume, and Ferguson for their influence on various aspects of Smith's philosophy. We can add, as a further example, that his distinction between justice as a "strict obligation" and "all the other social virtues" (TMS II.ii.1.5) seems to be directly drawn from Lord Kames. However, Smith is remarkably silent about the philosophical influence of other Scots. The extent of this influence is therefore an object of inquiry as interesting as it is complex, partly owing to matters of chronology. Indeed, apart from the names just quoted above, to which can be added George Turnbull, few Scottish philosophers could have inspired the first edition of TMS (1759) or LJ (1762–64). But several of them could have influenced WN (1776) or the last edition of TMS (1790). Thus both James Steuart in his treatise on political economy and William Robertson in his history of Charles V offer arguments concerning the beneficial relationship between "commerce" and "good government" (WN III.iv.4) similar to Smith's.[39]

D. *English Age of Reason.* Even if Scotland is Smith's immediate context as an Enlightenment philosopher, to ignore his engagement with other quarters of the United Kingdom would risk suggesting the erroneous image of a provincial thinker. As an advocate of moral sentiments, Smith also studied the opposite theory, that is, moral rationalism, as found especially in Samuel Clarke and William Wollaston. He presents them under the heading of "those systems which make virtue consist in propriety" (TMS VII.ii.1), but the debate between sentimentalism and rationalism certainly deserves a closer treatment by Smith scholars. Much can also be gained by further investigating philosophical discussions of the period about the nature of moral conscience. Joseph Butler's conceptions on this front have parallels in many pages of TMS, especially concerning the "badges of [the] authority" (TMS III.5.5) of moral conscience. Other interveners in this debate, such as John Balguy, John Gay, David Hartley, or Richard Price, are also of potential interest. In addition, many of these moral philosophers elaborated a natural theology, often linked to Newtonian natural philosophy, and Smith's teleology certainly partakes of this context.[40] Also deserving mention is the Irish philosopher George Berkeley, whose theory of vision is one of the main inspirations for Smith's early essay "Of the External Senses" (Senses 43).

E. *French Lumières.* Smith is no more an insular thinker than he is a provincial one, and his Enlightenment is almost as French as it is Scottish or English. Smith traveled in France, mastered its language, and was personally acquainted with some of its cultural circles. Without even mentioning the political economy of Turgot and of the physiocrats, whose influence on Smith has long been recognized, we might reiterate the importance of Montesquieu and Rousseau for Smith's views on commercial society. Smith's publications and correspondence are padded with references to other French philosophers of the eighteenth century, from the most famous (including Voltaire, Bernard Le Bouyer de Fontenelle, Jean-Baptiste Dubos, Claude-Adrien Helvétius, d'Holbach, Jean Le Rond d'Alembert, and the Encyclopedists) to the more obscure (such as Claude Buffier or Jean-Louis Levesque de Pouilly). To determine if these authors have really had some detailed and specific influence on Smith's ideas supposes precise inquiries, but it is clear anyway that they all together compose for him a general philosophical background not to be overlooked.

NOTES

1. Most of the commentaries on Smith during this period focus on his economics, and deal with his other writings—including his moral theory—rather superficially. There are of course interesting exceptions, for example, J. A. Farrer, *Adam Smith* (London: 1881); A. Delatour, *Adam Smith, sa vie, ses travaux, ses doctrines* (Paris: 1886); G. R. Morrow, *The Ethical and Economic Theories of Adam Smith* (New York: 1923).

2. See the use of Smith's concepts in the work of such economists as J. C. Harsanyi, *Essays on Ethics, Social Behaviour and Scientific Explanation* (Dordrecht: 1976); A. K. Sen, *On Ethics and Economics* (Oxford: 1991). See also R. Manstetten, *Das Menschenbild der Ökonomie. Der homo oeconomicus und die Anthropologie von Adam Smith* (Freiburg: 2002).

3. See, for example, the following, which eloquently declare a critical distance toward the traditional interpretation of Smith as a dogmatic laissez-faire economist: S. J. Pack, *Capitalism as a Moral System: Adam Smith's Critique of the Free Market Economy* (Aldershot: 1991); J. T. Young, *Economics as a Moral Science: The Political Economy of Adam Smith* (Cheltenham: 1997). See also, following a similar line of reinterpretation, G. Kennedy, *Adam Smith's Lost Legacy* (Basingstoke: 2005).

4. See, for example, C. L. Griswold Jr., *Adam Smith and the Virtues of Enlightenment* (Cambridge: 1999); S. Fleischacker, *A Third Concept of Liberty: Judgment and Freedom in Kant and Adam Smith* (Princeton: 1999); G. J. Andree, *Sympathie und Unparteilichkeit. Adam Smiths System der natürlichen Moralität* (Paderborn: 2003); C. Fricke and H.-P. Schütt, eds., *Adam Smith als Moralphilosoph* (Berlin: 2005).

5. The problem of the coherence of Smith's ethics through the various editions of his *Theory* is investigated by L. Dickey, "Historicizing the 'Adam Smith Problem': Conceptual, Historiographical, and Textual Issues," *Journal of Modern History* 58 (1986), pp. 579–609; J. Dwyer, *Virtuous Discourse: Sensibility and Community in Late XVIIIth-Century Scotland* (Edinburgh: 1987); D. D. Raphael, *The Impartial Spectator: Adam Smith's Moral Philosophy* (Oxford: 2007); R. P. Hanley, *Adam Smith and the Character of Virtue* (Cambridge: 2009).

6. Concerning the question of the coherence of Smith's ethics with his economics, the following books are of particular interest: A. S. Skinner, *A System of Social Science: Papers related to Adam Smith* (Oxford: 1979); Pack, *Capitalism as a Moral System*; V. Brown, *Adam Smith's Discourse: Canonicity, Commerce and Conscience* (London: 1994); A. Fitzgibbons, *Adam Smith's System of Liberty, Wealth and Virtue: The Moral and Political Foundations of the Wealth of Nations* (Oxford: 1995); Young, *Economics as a Moral Science*; J. R. Otteson, *Adam Smith's Marketplace of Life* (Cambridge: 2002); M. Biziou, *Adam Smith et l'origine du libéralisme* (Paris: 2003); J. Evensky, *Adam Smith's Moral Philosophy: A Historical and Contemporary Perspective on Markets, Law, Ethics, and Culture* (Cambridge: 2007).

7. The contextualist approach can be found in A. O. Hirschman, *The Passions and the Interests: Political Arguments for Capitalism before Its Triumph* (Princeton: 1977); M. L. Myers, *The Soul of Modern Economic Man: Ideas of Self-Interest from Thomas Hobbes to Adam Smith* (Chicago: 1983); R. F. Teich-

graeber III, *Free Trade and Moral Philosophy: Rethinking the Sources of Adam Smith's* Wealth of Nations (Durham, NC: 1986); P. Force, *Self-Interest before Adam Smith: A Genealogy of Economic Science* (Cambridge: 2003); L. Montes, *Adam Smith in Context: A Critical Reassessment of Some Central Components of His Thought* (Basingstoke: 2004); D. J. Den Uyl, ed., "Symposium: Adam Smith and His Sources," *Adam Smith Review* 4 (2008), pp. 1–206. See also all the references of the second part of the present study.

8. For a "liberal" Smith, see R. D. Cumming, *Human Nature and History: A Study of the Development of Liberal Political Thought* (Chicago: 1969); D. Winch, "Adam Smith and the Liberal Tradition," in *Traditions of Liberalism: Essays on John Locke, Adam Smith and John Stuart Mill*, ed. K. Haakonssen (St. Leonards: 1988); F. Vergara, *Introduction aux fondements philosophiques du libéralisme* (Paris: 1992); Biziou, *Adam Smith et l'origine du libéralisme*.

9. On Smith and classical economics, see S. Hollander, *The Economics of Adam Smith* (London: 1973); E. G. West, *Adam Smith and Modern Economics: From Market Behaviour to Public Choice* (Aldershot: 1990); A. Oakley, *Classical Economic Man: Human Agency and Methodology in the Political Economy of Adam Smith and John Stuart Mill* (Cheltenham: 1994); P. Demeulenaere, *Homo œconomicus. Enquête sur la constitution d'un paradigme* (Paris: 1996); J. Peil, *Adam Smith and Economic Science: A Methodological Reinterpretation* (Cheltenham: 1999).

10. For a "spontaneous" Smith, see R. Hamowy, *The Scottish Enlightenment and the Theory of Spontaneous Order* (Carbondale: 1987); C. Petsoulas, *Hayek's Liberalism and Its Origins: His Idea of Spontaneous Order and the Scottish Enlightenment* (London: 2001).

11. On Smith and the moral sense tradition, see J. Bonar, *The Moral Sense* (New York: 1930); L. Jaffro, ed., *Le sens moral. Une histoire de la philosophie morale de Locke à Kant* (Paris: 2000).

12. For a "Scottish" Smith, see N. Waszek, *Man's Social Nature: Topic of the Scottish Enlightenment in Its Historical Setting* (Frankfurt: 1986); C. J. Berry, *Social Theory of the Scottish Enlightenment* (Edinburgh: 1997); J. A. Dwyer, *The Age of the Passions: An Interpretation of Adam Smith and Scottish Enlightenment Culture* (East Linton: 1998).

13. For a "historian" Smith, see M. S. Phillips, *Society and Sentiment. Genres of Historical Writing in Britain, 1740–1820* (Princeton: 2000).

14. For a "capitalist" Smith, see A. O. Hirschman, *Passions and the Interests*; Pack, *Capitalism as a Moral System*; P. H. Werhane, *Adam Smith and His Legacy for Modern Capitalism* (Oxford: 1991); P. Rosanvallon, *Le capitalisme utopique. Histoire de l'idée de marché* (Paris: 1979).

15. For an "individualistic" Smith, see L. Infantino, *Individualism in Modern Thought: From Adam Smith to Hayek* (London: 1998).

16. For an "egalitarian" Smith, see I. McLean, *Adam Smith, Radical and Egalitarian: An Interpretation for the 21st Century* (Edinburgh: 2006); J. E. Hill, *Democracy, Equality, and Justice: John Adams, Adam Smith, and Political Economy* (Lanham: 2007),

17. For a "sentimental" Smith, see J. G. Barker-Benfield, *The Culture of Sensibility. Sex and Society in Eighteenth-Century Britain* (Chicago: 1992).

18. On Smith's history of science and philosophy, see Biziou, *Adam Smith et l'origine du libéralisme.*

19. These two limits of our study (leaving aside posterior philosophers and nonphilosophical references) will be partly made up for by other chapters in the present volume.

20. On Smith's place in the history of modern moral philosophy, see H. D. Kittsteiner, *Die Entstehung des modernen Gewissens* (Frankfurt: 1991); J. B. Schneewind, *The Invention of Autonomy: A History of Modern Moral Philosophy* (Cambridge: 1998).

21. On Smith and the Classics, see G. Vivenza, *Adam Smith and the Classics* (Oxford: 2001); S. J. McKenna, *Adam Smith: The Rhetoric of Propriety* (Albany, NY: 2005).

22. On Smith and Plato, see L. Hill, "The Role of *Thumos* in Adam Smith's System," in *New Perspectives on Adam Smith's* The Theory of Moral Sentiments, ed. G. Cockfield, A. Firth, J. Laurent (Cheltenham: 2008).

23. On Smith and Aristotle, see M. J. Calkins and P. Werhane, "Adam Smith, Aristotle, and the Virtues of Commerce," *Journal of Value Inquiry* 32 (1998), pp. 43–60; R. Temple-Smith, "Adam Smith's Treatment of the Greeks in *The Theory of Moral Sentiments*: The Case of Aristotle," in Cockfield, Firth, and Laurent, *New Perspectives*; R. P. Hanley, "Adam Smith, Aristotle and Virtue Ethics," in *New Voices on Adam Smith*, ed. L. Montes and E. Schliesser (London: 2008).

24. On Smith and the Stoics, see N. Waszek, "Two Concepts of Morality: A Distinction of Adam Smith's Ethics and Its Stoic Origin," *Journal of the History of Ideas* 45, no. 4 (1984), pp. 591–606; F. Forman-Barzilai, *Adam Smith and the Circles of Sympathy* (Cambridge: 2010).

25. Smith's vindication of economic liberty might be seen as emancipation from arbitrary norms enacted both by the state and the church; see P. Minowitz, *Politics, Priests, and Princes: Adam Smith's Emancipation of Economics from Politics and Religion* (Stanford: 1993).

26. On the combination of Greco-Roman and Christian philosophies, see Hanley, *Adam Smith and the Character of Virtue.*

27. On Smith and Augustine, see E. Gregory, "Sympathy and Domination: Adam Smith, Happiness and the Virtues of Augustinianism," in *Adam Smith as a Theologian*, ed. P. Oslington (Abingdon: 2011).

28. On Smith and Calvin, see J. Blosser, "Christian Freedom in Political Economy: The Legacy of John Calvin in the Thought of Adam Smith," in Oslington, *Adam Smith as a Theologian.*

29. On Smith and the theory of natural law, see H. Medick, *Naturzustand und Naturgeschichte der bürgerlichen Gesellschaft. Die Ursprünge der bürgerlichen Sozialtheorie als Geschichtsphilosophie und Sozialwissenschaft bei Pufendorf, Locke und Smith* (Göttingen: 1973); P. Stein, "From Pufendorf to Adam Smith: The Natural Law Tradition in Scotland," in *Europäisches Rechtsdenken in Geschichte und Gegenwart*, ed. N. Horn (Munich: 1982); K. Haakonssen, *Natural Law and Moral Philosophy: From Grotius to the Scottish Enlightenment* (Cambridge: 1996); G. Nonnenmacher, *Die Ordnung der Gesellschaft. Mangel und Herrschaft in der politischen Philosophie der Neuzeit: Hobbes, Locke, Smith, Rousseau* (Weinheim: 1989); M. Biziou, "A l'articulation du libéralisme politique et

du libéralisme économique: le jugement individuel face à l'Etat chez Locke et Smith," in *La pensée libérale. Histoire et controverses*, ed. G. Kévorkian (Paris: 2010).

30. On Smith and La Rochefoucauld, see J. Lafond, "De la morale à l'économie politique, ou de La Rochefoucauld et des moralistes jansénistes à Adam Smith par Malebranche et Mandeville," in *De la morale à l'économie politique*, ed. P. Force and D. Morgan (Pau: 1996); M. Biziou, "Lien social, norme morale et institutions civiles chez La Rochefoucauld, Mandeville et Adam Smith," in *La production des institutions*, ed. C. Lazzeri (Besançon: 2002).

31. On Smith and La Bruyère, see M. Biziou, "Commerce et caractère chez La Bruyère et Adam Smith: la préhistoire de l'*homo œconomicus*," *Revue d'histoire des sciences humaines* 5 (2001), pp. 11–36.

32. On Smith and Hume's empiricism, see D. D. Raphael, "The True Old Humean Philosophy and Its Influence on Adam Smith," in *David Hume: Bicentenary Papers*, ed. G. P. Morice (Edinburgh: 1977).

33. On Smith and Cartesianism, see V. Foley, *The Social Physics of Adam Smith* (West Lafayette: 1976).

34. On Smith and the tradition of moral sentiments, see Bonar, *Moral Sense*; V. M. Hope, *Virtue by Consensus: The Moral Philosophy of Hutcheson, Hume and Adam Smith* (Oxford: 1989); M. Biziou, *Le concept de système dans la tradition anglo-écossaise des sentiments moraux, 1699–1795. De la métaphysique à l'économie politique (Shaftesbury, Hutcheson, Hume, Smith)* (Lille: 2000).

35. On Smith and civic humanism or classical republicanism, see D. Winch, *Adam Smith's Politics. An Essay in Historiographic Revision* (Cambridge: 1978); I. Hont and M. Ignatieff, eds., *Wealth and Virtue: The Shaping of Political Economy in the Scottish Enlightenment* (Cambridge: 1982); J. Robertson, "Scottish Political Economy beyond the Civic Tradition: Government and Economic Development in the *Wealth of Nations*," *History of Political Thought* 4, no. 3 (1983), pp. 452–82; E. J. Harpham, "Liberalism, Civic Humanism, and the Case of Adam Smith," *American Political Science Review* 78 (1984), pp. 764–74.

36. On Smith and Mandeville, see T. A. Horne, "Envy and Commercial Society: Mandeville and Smith on 'Private Vices, Public Benefits,' " *Political Theory* 9, no. 4 (1981), pp. 551–69; C. Gautier, *L'invention de la société civile. Mandeville, Smith, Ferguson* (Paris: 1993); J. Hurtado-Prieto, "The Mercantilist Foundations of 'Dr Mandeville's Licentious System': Adam Smith on Bernard Mandeville," in Montes and Schliesser, *New Voices on Adam Smith*.

37. On Smith and Montesquieu, see B.C.J. Singer, "Montesquieu, Adam Smith, and the Discovery of the Social," *Journal of Classical Sociology* 4 (2004), pp. 31–57; H. C. Clark, "Montesquieu in Smith's Method of 'Theory and History,' " *Adam Smith Review* 4 (2008), pp. 132–57.

38. On Smith and Rousseau, see D. C. Rasmussen, *The Problems and Promise of Commercial Society: Adam Smith's Response to Rousseau* (University Park, PA: 2008); R. P. Hanley, "Commerce and corruption. Rousseau's diagnosis and Adam Smith's cure," *European Journal of Political Theory* 7, no. 2 (2008), pp. 137–58.

39. On Smith and the Scottish Enlightenment, see Waszek, *Man's Social Nature*; Hamowy, *Scottish Enlightenment*; Berry, *Social Theory*; Dwyer, *Age of the Passions*.

40. On Smith and eighteenth-century natural theology, see P. Harrison, "Adam Smith, Natural Theology, and the Natural Sciences," in Oslington, *Adam Smith as a Theologian.*

BIBLIOGRAPHIC ESSAY

Any investigation of Smith's sources can benefit from Hiroshi Mizuta, *Adam Smith's Library: A Catalogue* (Oxford: 2000). Smith's own history of philosophy is examined at length in Michaël Biziou, *Adam Smith et l'origine du libéralisme* (Paris: 2003).

Smith's relationship with ancient philosophy is documented in Gloria Vivenza, *Adam Smith and the Classics* (Oxford: 2001); Ryan Patrick Hanley, *Adam Smith and the Character of Virtue* (Cambridge: 2009); and Fonna Forman-Barzilai, *Adam Smith and the Circles of Sympathy* (Cambridge: 2010). The influence of Christian theology on Smith is studied by Claudius Luterbacher-Maineri, *Adam Smith. Theologische Grundannahmen* (Freiburg: 2008); and Paul Oslington, ed., *Adam Smith as Theologian* (Abingdon: 2011).

The study of Smith in the context of the two rival traditions of liberalism and republicanism can be seen in Donald Winch, *Adam Smith's Politics* (Cambridge: 1978); and Knud Haakonssen, *Natural Law and Moral Philosophy: From Grotius to the Scottish Enlightenment* (Cambridge: 1996). The tradition of moral sentiments is examined by Vincent M. Hope, *Virtue by Consensus: The Moral Philosophy of Hutcheson, Hume and Adam Smith* (Oxford: 1989); and Michaël Biziou, *Le concept de système dans la tradition anglo-écossaise des sentiments moraux, 1699–1795. De la métaphysique à l'économie politique (Shaftesbury, Hutcheson, Hume, Smith)* (Lille: 2000).

Smith's connection with the Enlightenment can be seen in Claude Gautier, *L'invention de la société civile. Mandeville, Smith, Ferguson* (Paris: 1993); John A. Dwyer, *The Age of the Passions: An Interpretation of Adam Smith and Scottish Enlightenment Culture* (East Linton: 1998); Charles L. Griswold Jr., *Adam Smith and the Virtues of Enlightenment* (Cambridge: 1999); Samuel Fleischacker, *A Third Concept of Liberty: Judgment and Freedom in Kant and*

Adam Smith (Princeton: 1999); Emma Rothschild, *Economic Sentiments: Adam Smith, Condorcet and Enlightenment* (Cambridge: 2001); and Dennis C. Rasmussen, *The Problems and Promise of Commercial Society: Adam Smith's Response to Rousseau* (University Park, PA: 2008).

ADAM SMITH AND ENLIGHTENMENT STUDIES

Fredrik Albritton Jonsson

Few scholars would deny Adam Smith a central place in the Enlightenment. Yet most of us would also find it exceedingly difficult to agree on the precise origin, timing, character, and legacy of the movement. Recent interpretations include Jonathan Israel's Spinozan Enlightenment, Dan Edelstein's moderate *lumières*, John Robertson's Scottish-Neapolitan Enlightenment, Joel Mokyr's "industrial Enlightenment," and John Gascoigne's naturalist networks. Besides these "cosmopolitan" studies of the Enlightenment, scholars have also taken a strong interest in the national context of Smith's thought, focusing on the peculiarities of Scottish society and culture. There is little hope of cutting this tangled knot and arriving at a single unified theory of the Enlightenment, at least in the confines of a single short essay, but a survey of these different historical approaches can greatly enrich our understanding of Smith's thought and life, shedding much needed light on several long-standing concerns. The first part of my essay introduces the basic quarrel between Edelstein, Israel, and Robertson. We then move to the economic literature on the "industrial Enlightenment" to consider the meaning of Smith's manufacturing vision. The third part of the essay examines the place of empire in Smith's thought. The final section places Smith's works in the realm of eighteenth-century natural history in order to show how a liberal vision of the environment was crucial to Smith's political economy. My essay ends with a plea for scholars to rethink the meaning and orientation of Enlightenment studies in the age of anthropogenic climate change.

1

The basic rift in Enlightenment scholarship concerns the origin, chronology, and character of the movement. For Jonathan Israel, the authentic impetus for the Enlightenment came from Baruch Spinoza in the *Tractatus theologico-politicus* (1670) and the *Ethics* (1677). His materialist philosophy provided philosophical unity to a European-wide movement. But this radical challenge to the old regime was betrayed and eclipsed by a moderate version of the Enlightenment spearheaded by Voltaire and Hume. To Israel, the force and complexity of Smith's thought present little more than an eloquent justification for political and philosophical compromise. The true legacy of the radical Enlightenment was the French Revolution, not the triumph of free trade. It was Rousseau, not Smith, who transmitted the message of Spinoza to the French revolutionaries.[1]

Israel's provocative views have not gone unchallenged. Dan Edelstein rejects the Spinozentric model as reductive and insufficient. He too looks to the late seventeenth century for the origin of the Enlightenment, but is more interested in how the movement named and imagined itself; when did savants first think of themselves as enlightened? Edelstein's finds his answer in the Quarrel of Ancients and Moderns in the French Academies. On this score, the Enlightenment was first and foremost a historical and literary debate over the relation of society to the state, characterized by intellectual diversity and acts of appropriation rather than philosophical coherence and linear diffusion. The social dominance of patronage structures strongly molded the form and substance of the movement. Scotland figures in Edelstein's account as the first stop for the spread of the *esprit philosophique* beyond France. Edelstein recounts the familiar story of Hume's sejour in Paris as well as Smith's encounter with Voltaire and his debt to Rousseau and the physiocrats. Much like the philosophes, Hume favored a "synthesis of ancient and modern achievements." But Hume, Smith, and other Scottish savants also modified the "basic model" by introducing into it a much greater stress on "commerce, political freedom, [and] the rule of law."[2]

For John Robertson, this Scottish interest in material improvement supplies a crucial reason to disagree with both Israel and Edelstein. While Robertson insists on the intellectual unity of the Enlightenment, he locates that common ground in the realm of political economy rather than a philosophical defense of materialism. Scotland and Naples rather than France furnish Robertson with his geographic setting. The Enlightenment was the peculiar preoccupation of smaller nations and provinces concerned with their own "backwardness relative to the richer and more powerful nations of Europe." The debates of political economy were attempts to establish how poor nations could catch up with the modernity of the English economy and polity. In stressing the perspective from the periphery, Robertson skirts close to an older approach. To what degree was the Scottish Enlightenment a product of peculiarly Scottish social, political, and economic forces? This emphasis on the periphery might also help solve a mystery of English intellectual history. Why did England, despite its unprecedented degree of prosperity, urban civilization, and imperial power, fail to sustain an Enlightenment of its own? Why did London or Liverpool not yield a savant comparable to David Hume or Adam Smith?[3]

2

For Joel Mokyr, eighteenth-century England was at the heart of the European-wide Enlightenment. But he defines the movement in terms of knowledge-sharing and technological innovation as much as a commitment to liberal political economy. In Mokyr's view, a culture of "scientific literacy" created common ground for natural philosophers, inventors, political economists, entrepreneurs, and artisans. They rejected guild monopolies and alchemical secrets in favor of the public diffusion of useful information, through new kinds of technical education, popular science, and encyclopedias. Mokyr here builds on earlier research by Margaret Jacob, Larry Stewart, and others. He pinpoints the origins of the "industrial enlightenment" in the ideal of information gathering set forth by Francis Bacon. Science supplied "a rich storehouse, for the Glory of the Creator and relief of Man's estate." This model of knowledge-driven technological innovation inspired the great encyclopedic impulse of Diderot and D'Alembert. Mokyr thus sees the Enlightenment as the fulfillment of Bacon's project: the beginning of an unprecedented phase in the history of technology characterized by continuous innovation. The key to success for Mokyr was the decreasing access cost for information in the eighteenth century, which in turn made possible sustained invention. Like the economists of the "new growth theory," Mokyr believes that shared knowledge defies the principle of scarcity: "Ever faster and cheaper access to huge stores of knowledge has shown little evidence so far of diminishing returns." He explicitly compares the Enlightenment to the "open source" system of the Internet age. In short, Mokyr reorients our understanding of the Industrial Revolution, away from environmental and economic factors like coal and high real wages, toward the idea of an eighteenth-century information economy.[4]

In Mokyr's model, Adam Smith was a leading advocate of the "industrial Enlightenment." Mokyr sees the information economy of the mid-eighteenth century as part and parcel of a broader shift in policy toward liberal conditions of trade, market integration, and an "open economy." Smith's famous defense of the division of labor at the outset of the *Wealth of Nations* could indeed be read as a plea for rational information, insofar as it assumes that the manufacturer had the power and knowledge to reorganize production into its most basic elements. Smith seems to have recognized this link between knowledge and the division of labor already in the *Essay on Astronomy*: "when we enter the work-houses of the most common artisans" we are moved first to wonder at the skilled labor of "dyers, brewers [and] distillers." But soon the philosopher uncovers the "connecting principles of nature" that bind "together all these disjointed objects" (HA II.11). William Sewell and Celina Fox have explored the visual dimension of eighteenth-century labor management. For Sewell, the plates of the *Encyclopédie* reflected a concerted effort to make the mysteries of skilled labor accessible to the public. Fox in turn argues that the eighteenth century saw the maturation of a new artistic genre she calls the "arts of industry," which offered a "visual exposition" of "rational explanation." In a painstaking study of Smith's sources, Jean-Louis Peaucelle has concluded that Smith indeed was deeply indebted to the *Encyclopédie* for his analysis of the division of labor in pin manufactures.[5]

Yet there are well-known objections to Mokyr's image of Smith. Hiram Caton and E. A. Wrigley have made a forceful case for the "pre-industrial" character of Smith's thought. Bob Allen notes that the account of pin production in the *Encyclopédie* was drawn from the manufacture at L'Aigle in Normandy. Yet the most advanced techniques of the era were in fact deployed at the Dockwra Copper Company and the Warmley works near Bristol. Both were powered by waterwheels, and at Warmley there was also an auxiliary Newcomen steam engine to pump water into the mill pond. Arthur Young gave a vivid account of the latter in his 1771 tour of the southern counties of England. Why did Smith not take notice of best practice? Wrigley in turn suggests that the philosopher greatly overestimated the efficiency of manual dexterity in the division of labor. Smith claimed that ten men could make forty-eight thousand pins per day. Yet a simple calculation using Smith's own data casts serious doubt on this assertion. Since it took eighteen distinct operations to manufacture an individual pin, this means that every laborer had to perform "2.4 distinct operations each second." Was Smith consciously exaggerating the power of the division of labor, or was this an elementary mistake of arithmetic? Either way, Smith here looks oddly out of touch with the phenomenon of the "industrial Enlightenment."[6]

For Wrigley, Smith's misguided optimism about manufacturing specialization was coupled with a fundamental misunderstanding about the true character of the industrial economy. Wrigley defines the Industrial Revolution primarily as a shift in fuel consumption, from an "organic" economy to a "mineral energy" system. The second half of the eighteenth century was a period of multiplying environmental strains. Demographic pressure and economic development put increasing stress on the natural resources of the island. A finite supply of land had to produce raw materials for "food, clothing, lodging and firing." In the end, mineral energy and colonial expansion saved Britain from a Malthusian trap. But Wrigley stresses that Smith and his successors in classical political economy failed to foresee the revolutionary consequences of coal and steam technology. On this count, Smith was merely an ingenious analyst of the "advanced organic economy." His economic model envisioned expansive opportunities for growth within pre-industrial society, but remained blind to the economic promise of steam technology pioneered by his contemporaries Boulton and Watt. Instead, Smith's future was Dutch. All advanced commercial economies were headed inexorably toward the stationary state. This was the condition in which each nation "acquired its full complement of riches" such that "every particular branch of business" was saturated with the "greatest quantity of stock that could be employed in it." This stage of development was marked by very low interest rates, as capital could no longer find profitable outlets for investment. According to Smith, "the province of Holland"— the most advanced economy in Europe—was "approaching near to this state" (WN I.ix.20). The political economist reserved his greatest hopes of demographic growth and economic expansion for the American colonies. Whereas populations in Great Britain and "most other European countries" took five hundred years to double, in the British colonies they doubled "in twenty or five-and twenty years" (WN I.viii.23). With so much cheap land available and so small a population, wages were high, people married young, and famine was unknown. Smith impishly concluded that the political center of the British Empire would shift to the New World in "little more than a century" (WN IV.vii.c.79).[7]

3

In recent years, the scholarship on Enlightenment and empire has expanded prodigiously. Historians of political thought Jennifer Pitts and Sankar Muthu have drawn attention to the entanglements of political philosophy with the problems of imperial rule. Seymour Drescher and Christopher Brown have investigated the Enlightenment roots of British abolitionism. Intellectual and political historians of the Atlantic world such as Paul Cheney, Sophus Reinert, and Gabrielle Paquette have explored how the success of long-distance trade reshaped the language of political economy and encouraged new patterns of state building and economic reform. Historians of science and technology have charted the uses of the enlightened sciences to European empires. Eighteenth-century savants provided vital expertise to the colonial state in mapping resources and populations from the West Indies to Bengal. In this thriving historiography, Smith occupies an ambiguous place. His political economy is often taken as the sine qua non of anti-imperial political economy, though Smith's critique is shot through with contradictions and ambiguities. Moreover, serious gaps remain in the historiography, despite the heroic labors of Smith scholars. We still do not have a clear picture of Smith's sources of knowledge about different parts of the empire and the wider world. We also lack a systematic account of Smith's work as a government advisor and bureaucrat.[8]

The Paris peace treaties of 1763 and 1783 make useful bookends for this sort of investigation. Victory in the Seven Years' War shattered once and for all any illusions about the character of the British Empire. Massive new territorial acquisitions made the myth of a Protestant trading empire implausible. In P. J. Marshall's words, "The alternatives facing British policy-makers were . . . either to try to assimilate the King's new subjects to British norms or to accept the existence of a new diversity within the empire by incorporating into it hitherto alien religions, laws, and modes of government." British politicians and savants were now forced to reckon with a multiethnic territorial empire that resembled the Pax Romana more than many would have preferred. Would the new empire beget moral corruption, crippling debt, and military disaster, as some predicted? It is hardly a coincidence that the discussion of colonies in Smith's *Wealth of Nations* begins with a meditation on the contrast between Greek and Roman styles of empire (see WN IV.vii.a.1–3 and WN IV.vii.b.6).[9] The peace of 1763 opened the door for a host of competing types of expertise in the administration and reform of the new empire. Richard Drayton dates the beginnings of state patronage for the British sciences of empire to the Seven Years' War. Linnaean natural history gained in popularity as a powerful tool of resource inventory and ecological exchange. The conquest of Bengal encouraged new ventures in colonial knowledge gathering, including the Orientalism of William Jones and the physiocratic reforms of Philip Francis. By situating Smith's political economy in this wider history of expertise, we see more clearly how politics, society, and knowledge were connected in the high Enlightenment. Boundaries between emerging fields were permeable, encouraging wide circulation of information and cross-fertilization of ideas. But different types of expertise also competed for patronage and influence. The authority of a particular kind of technical knowledge depended in great part on its social appeal and fit with a given institutional context.[10]

What did Smith really know about the empire? Emma Rothschild suggests a social and cultural approach to this problem in her microhistory of the Johnstone family. The Johnstones were friends and allies of Smith over several decades. Like many Scottish families, their lives were closely intertwined with the fate of the empire, through their trading ties and political careers. Hence Smith's experience of colonial affairs, despite his relatively sedentary life, was much more intimate and personal than we have suspected. Yet such cozy relation with the elite of the empire did not blunt Smith's sympathy for the plight of colonial subjects. Jennifer Pitts stresses the commitment to cultural diversity which underpinned Smith's stadial history. People in different stages of history varied in their material circumstances and customs but not their mental sophistication or moral probity. The history of medicine provides an additional social context to understand Smith's cosmopolitanism. Physicians at the Edinburgh Medical School like Smith's friend William Cullen led the way in mapping the physiology of nervous sensibility. But sensibility was not just a problem in anatomy and pathology. It also offered a fashionable way of explaining the character of moral judgment and human sociability. "A humane and polished people," Smith observed in *The Theory of Moral Sentiments*, had "more sensibility to the passions of others" (TMS V.2.10). Sensibility was at the same time universal and culturally specific: a faculty common to all mankind but also a force that could be cultivated, constrained, and commanded, according to the customs of any given society. Pitts sees Smith's account of cultural difference in the *Lectures on Jurisprudence* (presented at the end of the Seven

Years' War) as the groundwork for the discussion of empire and colonies in the *Wealth of Nations*. Smith's scathing attack on the "golden dream" of empire was informed by a deep sense of the fundamental equality of the conquered and the conquerors. However, Smith's pragmatic and cautious approach to political change seems to have prevented him from embracing the more radical implications inherent in cosmopolitan sensibility (an end to the slave trade, independence for Bengal). He recognized the legitimate right of resistance only in the case of the thirteen North American settler colonies.[11]

The case of New World slavery gives us a useful measure of the strengths as well as the blind spots in Smith's account of empire. Christopher Brown has shown how the American War of Independence laid the political groundwork for abolitionist mobilization. Once again, imperial crisis triggered an appeal to expert knowledge. Political economy, demographic data, and parliamentary testimony were common weapons in the growing storm over the slave trade. According to Seymour Drescher, Smith played a decisive role by delivering a comprehensive economic argument against the efficiency of slavery. Smith categorically defended the "sacred and inviolable" right of every worker to the fruits of one's labor (e.g., WN I.x.c.12). Coerced labor was wasteful, costly, and ineffective because it undermined any incentive to improvement in the slave: "A person who can acquire no property, can have no other interest but to eat as much and to labor as little as possible" (WN III.ii.9). Smith's economic analysis was combined with a sharp sense of moral outrage. He insisted on the "heroic . . . firmness" of slaves in the face of adversity: "There is not a negro from the coast of Africa who does not . . . possess a degree of magnanimity which the soul of his sordid master is too often scarce capable of conceiving." Slaves had to familiarize their imagination with the "most dreadful misfortunes" (TMS V.2.9). The moral force of this argument relied in part on the culture of sensibility among Smith's readers. To fathom the horrors of empire required an act of expansive sympathy. But for all the technical and rhetorical power of Smith's account, his portrait of plantation society was not without a number of omissions. There was no "cost analysis of colonial slavery," no discussion of indenture, and no treatment of the transatlantic slave trade. Instead Smith included an odd aside on the superior productivity of French sugar plantations, which according to him stemmed from the paternal and benevolent management of the slaves there. Like Drescher, J.G.A. Pocock finds Smith's historical approach uneven. In the New World, Smith's vision was firmly fixed on the northern British colonies rather than the West Indies. And even here, the account of the settler colonies figured principally as an extension of "the progress of society in Europe."[12]

At first glance, the final decade of Smith's life seem to mark a retreat from the problems of empire. Much of Smith's time was now occupied with his work as a commissioner of customs (beginning in 1778). What little attention he could spare for academic writing was spent on a significant revision of *The Theory of Moral Sentiments*. Yet we might plausibly argue that these seemingly disparate activities in fact represented a coherent approach of Smith to the question of empire. In their study of the minutes of the Scottish Customs Board, Gary Anderson, William Shugart, and Robert Tollison have recovered a revealing picture of Smith the diligent official, firmly devoted to making tax collection as effective as possible. This version of Smith looks a lot like the model bureaucrat John Brewer has unearthed in the parallel organization of the eighteenth-century excise. Excise and customs revenue were crucial in serving the interest on the national debt. Fiscal efficiency made the financial burden of prolonged warfare possible to bear; without administrative probity, no empire. We might well understand Smith's activities at the customs office as a form of practical yet principled support for the empire in a period of severe crisis. This ethos of probity in turn seems congruent with Smith's other great concern during the 1780s, the final changes to *The Theory of Moral Sentiments*. A major portion of these revisions were preoccupied with a defense of the pagan virtue of magnanimity, what Ryan Hanley calls the yearning for "true glory characteristic of the hero, the statesman, or the legislator." Defeat in the American War of Independence triggered dramatic reforms. The leading statesmen of the period—Lord Shelburne and William Pitt the Younger—appeared to embody a new kind of enlightened politician. Linda Colley argues that the British aristocracy as a whole reinvented itself in the aftermath of the American war. In such unsettled times, Smith's urgent wrestling with the question of how to synthesize pagan and Christian virtues must have seemed timely and prudent. Might we not read Smith's last revisions as an urgent commentary on the prospect and dangers of a new kind of politics: the liberal reform of empire?[13]

4

Natural knowledge and the environment provide the final lens for our survey of Smith's Enlightenment. A rich harvest of works on natural history, conservationism, and ecological exchange now covers the full range of the Enlightenment from Scotland and Sweden to Mauritius and the South Seas. Yet the scholarship on Smith and nature still tends to follow a well-beaten path that leads to the Newtonian inspiration for self-regulating markets on the one hand and the physiocratic conception of soil fertility on the other. It is high time to move beyond this narrow remit.

In the eighteenth century, ecological exchange became the object of statecraft. Belatedly, ministers and monarchs recognized that the transfer of plants and animals shaped the course of empire. New methods of classification facilitated surveys and exchange, especially the binomial and sexual schema pioneered by the Swedish naturalist Carolus Linnaeus. This brand of natural history offered a way to move useful plants from one region or colony to another. Nation-states, empires, and chartered trading companies sponsored inventories of colonial resources, founded botanical gardens, and established forest preserves. Natural historians, physicians, and surveyors found in the spoils of empire a bounty of new data to mine. In the decades after the American War of Independence, Sir Joseph Banks organized a global network dedicated to diversifying colonial economies with cash crops and securing self-sufficiency in important raw materials. But, natural history also promised to subvert the traditional division of labor between metropole and colony. Linnaeus and his disciples believed that they could acclimatize tropical crops to northern regions, making the nation of Sweden into a miniature empire. British landlords and voluntary associations also experimented with acclimatization trial to undercut the trading monopolies of charted companies. During the American

War of Independence, Scottish physicians and farmers introduced tobacco plantations on a large scale in the Borders.[14]

There is ample evidence that Adam Smith was cognizant of this movement. Numerous traces of early modern agriculture and ecology shape the argument of the *Wealth of Nations*, from the ungulate irruption of cattle herds on the American frontier to the effects of potato diet on Irish porters and prostitutes. Smith's basic argument about exchange and labor was predicated on the bounty of the natural world. "The land constitutes by far the greatest, the most important, and the most durable part of the wealth of every extensive country" (WN I.xi.n.9; see also I.xi.b.33, I.xi.b.41, I.xi.l.1–3, III.i.1, IV.v.b.5–7). At critical points, Smith turned to the eighteenth-century environment in search of ecological warrants to justify his economic concepts. The force of soil fertility was the green fuse of Smith's "natural Progress of Opulence." Natural knowledge about the diffusion of tobacco plants in Europe informed his attack on the logic of imperial protectionism. Assumptions about the average yield of corn and rice harvests sustained his argument against famine relief and public granaries. While it is not yet clear from what sources Smith culled this information, the inventory of his library makes some educated guesses possible. Brian Bonnyman also uncovers fascinating new evidence regarding Smith's tasks as a tutor to the future Duke of Buccleuch, including the improvement of the magnate's estates. Moreover, Smith's network in Scotland—including savants such as William Cullen and Joseph Black—very likely contributed to his understanding of natural history. Finally, Smith's profession as a commissioner of customs involved the active pursuit of natural knowledge.[15]

Smith shared with the natural historians a preoccupation with self-regulating properties. Linnaeus suggested that divine providence had organized the natural world in a system of equilibrium between food supply and consumption, predator and prey, scavenger and carrion. Smith rooted his hopes of economic growth and political liberty in the positive feedback loop between pasture and arable land, manure production and soil fertility, manufacturing and agriculture. But he diverged from the naturalists on one crucial point. Where naturalists frequently stressed the fragility of the natural world, Smith and other liberal political economists emphasized the resilience and robustness of these systems. Natural historians used the argument from instability to insist on the importance of long-term management of natural resources by the state and aristocratic landowners. Liberal political economists instead treated timber, grain, and other important resources as common commodities rather than objects of national security. Smith was pleased to announce that the New Town of Edinburgh, the glory of the Scottish Enlightenment, scarcely contained "a single stick of Scotch timber" (WN I.xi.c.16).[16]

This great divergence left a momentous legacy for the modern world. By recovering the environmental assumptions of Smith and his opponents among the natural historians, we can chart the emergence of two rival ecologies of commerce: on the one hand, a form of expertise that used a nascent notion of ecological fragility to assert its own authority along with that of the state; on the other hand, a celebration of markets that marginalized environmental knowledge in the name of a benevolent natural order.[17] These rival ecologies have arguably persisted down to the present day. Neoliberal economists still assume that free markets respond promptly and effectively to all environmental problems. In contrast, environmental scientists emphasize the high ecological cost of economic development and a growing planetary emergency marked by accelerating climate change, mass extinction, and the rapid deterioration of basic ecological services. The outcome of this debate may well be the most important legacy of the Enlightenment for us and future generations.

NOTES

1. Jonathan Israel, *Radical Enlightenment: Philosophy and the Making of Modernity, 1650–1750* (Oxford: 2001), p. 715.

2. Dan Edelstein, *The Enlightenment: A Genealogy* (Chicago: 2010), pp. 107–8.

3. John Robertson, *The Case for the Enlightenment: Scotland and Naples, 1680–1760* (Cambridge: 2005), p. 391. For the national approach, see Roy Porter and Mikuláš Teich, *The Enlightenment in National Context* (Cambridge: 1982);

Roger L. Emerson, *An Enlightened Duke: The Life of Archibald Campbell (1682–1761) Earl of Ilay, 3rd Duke of Argyll* (Kilkerran: 2013).

4. Joel Mokyr, *The Enlightened Economy: An Economic History of Britain 1700–1850* (New Haven: 2009), pp. 41, 91; cf. Larry Stewart, *The Rise of Public Science: Rhetoric, Technology, and Natural Philosophy in Newtonian Britain, 1660–1750* (Cambridge: 1992); Margaret C. Jacob and Larry Stewart, *Practical Matter: Newton's Science in the Service of Industry and Empire, 1687–1851* (Cambridge, MA: 2004); Peter M. Jones, *Industrial Enlightenment: Science, Technology and Culture in Birmingham and the West Midlands 1760–1820* (Manchester: 2008); Celina Fox, *The Arts of Industry in the Age of Enlightenment* (New Haven: 2009); Joel Mokyr, *The Gifts of Athena: Historical Origins of the Knowledge Economy* (Princeton: 2002), p. 154.

5. Mokyr, *Enlightened Economy*, p. 58; William H. Sewell, Jr., "Visions of Labor: Illustrations of the Mechanical Arts Before, In, and After Diderot's *Encyclopédie*," in *Work in France: Place, Practice, Organization, and Meaning*, ed. Steven Kaplan and Cynthia Koepp (Ithaca, NY: 1986), pp. 258–86; Celina Fox, *The Arts of Industry in the Age of Enlightenment* (New Haven: 2009), pp. 1, 9; Jean-Louis Peaucelle, *Adam Smith et la division du travail* (Paris: 2007).

6. E. A. Wrigley, *Continuity, Chance and Change: The Character of the Industrial Revolution* (Cambridge: 1993), p. 126; Hiram Caton, "The Preindustrial Economics of Adam Smith," *Journal of Economic History* 45 (1985), pp. 833–53; Robert C. Allen, *The British Industrial Revolution in Global Perspective* (Cambridge: 2009), pp. 146–47.

7. Wrigley, *Continuity, Chance and Change*, pp. 48, 52. The notion of a late eighteenth-century ecological bottleneck also features in Kenneth Pomeranz, *The Great Divergence: China, Europe and the Making of the Modern World Economy* (Princeton: 2000); James Belich, *Replenishing the Earth: The Settler Revolution and the Rise of the Anglo World 1783–1939* (Oxford: 2009).

8. Uday Mehta, *Liberalism and Empire* (Chicago: 1999); Sankar Muthu, *Enlightenment Against Empire* (Princeton: 2003); Jennifer Pitts, *A Turn to Empire: The Rise of Imperial Liberalism in Britain and France* (Princeton: 2005); Gabriel Paquette, *Enlightenment, Governance, Reform in Spain and Its Empire 1759–1808* (London: 2011); Paul Cheney, *Revolutionary Commerce: Globalization and the French Monarchy* (Cambridge, MA: 2010); Sophus Reinert, *Translating Empire: Emulation and the Origins of Political Economy* (Cambridge, MA: 2011); Simon Schaffer et al., *The Sciences in Enlightened Europe* (Chicago: 1999); James McLellan III, *Colonialism and Science: Saint Domingue in the Old Regime* (Chicago: 2010 [1992]); John Gascoigne, *Joseph Banks and the English Enlightenment: Useful Knowledge and Polite Culture* (Cambridge: 1994).

9. P. J. Marshall, *The Making and Unmaking of Empires: Britain, India, and America, c.1750–1783* (Oxford: 2007), p. 183.

10. Richard Drayton, "Knowledge and Empire," in *Oxford History of the British Empire: The Eighteenth Century*, ed. P. J. Marshall (Oxford: 1998), p. 244; Ranajit Guha, *A Rule of Property for Bengal*, 2nd ed. (Durham, NC: 1996); C. A. Bayly, *Empire and Information* (Cambridge: 2000).

11. Emma Rothschild, *The Inner Life of Empires: An Eighteenth-Century History* (Princeton: 2011), pp. 215–16; Pitts, *Turn to Empire*, pp. 28–29, 54–

55; Christopher Lawrence, "The Nervous System and Society in the Scottish Enlightenment," in *Natural Order: Historical Studies of Scientific Culture*, ed. Barry Barnes and Steven Shapin (London: 1979); John Dwyer, *The Age of the Passions: An Interpretation of Adam Smith and Scottish Enlightenment Culture* (East Linton: 1996); Anne C. Vila, *Enlightenment and Pathology: Sensibility in the Literature and Medicine of Eighteenth Century France* (Baltimore: 1997).

12. Christopher Brown, *Moral Capital: Foundations of British Abolitionism* (Chapel Hill: 2006), pp. 48, 113, 174, 233–34; Seymour Drescher, *The Mighty Experiment: Free Labor versus Slavery in British Emancipation* (Oxford: 2002), pp. 5–6, 20, 27, 31; J.G.A. Pocock, "Adam Smith and History," in *The Cambridge Companion to Adam Smith*, ed. Knud Haakonssen (Cambridge: 2006), p. 286.

13. Gary M. Anderson, William F. Shugart, and Robert Tollison, "Adam Smith in the Customhouse," *Journal of Political Economy* 93 (1985), pp. 740–59; John Brewer, *The Sinews of Power: War, Money and the English State 1688–1783* (Cambridge, MA: 1988); Ryan Patrick Hanley, *Adam Smith and the Character of Virtue* (Cambridge: 2009), p. 160; Nigel Aston and Clarissa Campbell Orr, *An Enlightenment Statesman in Whig Britain: Lord Shelburne in Context, 1737–1805* (Suffolk: 2011), pp. 268–61; Linda Colley, *Britons: Forging the Nation 1707–1837* (New Haven: 1992), chap. 4.

14. See, for example, Joyce E. Chaplin, *An Anxious Pursuit: Agricultural Innovation and Modernity in the Lower South, 1730–1815* (Chapel Hill: 1993); Richard Grove, *Green Imperialism: Colonial Expansion, Tropical Island Edens and the Origins of Environmentalism 1600–1860* (Cambridge: 1995); John Gascoigne, *Science in the Service of Empire* (Cambridge: 1998); Marie-Noëlle Bourguet and Christophe Bonneuil, eds., "De L'Inventaire du monde à la mise en valeur du globe: Botanique et colonization," *Revue française d'histoire d'outre-mer* 86 (1999); Lisbet Koerner, *Linnaeus: Nature and Nation* (Cambridge, MA: 1999), pp. 117–23; Londa Schiebinger, *Plants and Empire: Colonial Bioprospecting in the Atlantic World* (Cambridge, MA: 2004); for Scottish tobacco, see National Library of Scotland, MS 11198.

15. Brian Bonnyman, *The Third Duke of Buccleuch and Adam Smith: Estate Management and Improvement in Enlightenment Scotland* (Edinburgh: 2014); Fredrik Albritton Jonsson, *Enlightenment's Frontier: The Scottish Highlands and the Origins of Environmentalism* (New Haven: 2013).

16. Margaret Schabas, *The Natural Origins of Economics* (Chicago: 2006), chap. 5; Wrigley, *Continuity, Change and Chance*, pp. 46–48.

17. Albritton Jonsson, *Enlightenment's Frontier*, chap. 5.

BIBLIOGRAPHIC ESSAY

The debate over the character of the Enlightenment spans a broad range of positions. Recent contributions that stress the unity of the movement include Jonathan Israel, *Radical Enlightenment: Philosophy and the Making of Modernity, 1650–1750* (Oxford: 2001),

Dan Edelstein, *The Enlightenment: A Genealogy* (Chicago: 2010), and John Robertson, *The Case for the Enlightenment: Scotland and Naples, 1680–1760* (Cambridge: 2005). There is also an important literature on the peculiarities of the Scottish national context, most recently, Roger L. Emerson, *An Enlightened Duke: The Life of Archibald Campbell (1682–1761) Earl of Ilay, 3rd Duke of Argyll* (Kilkerran: 2013).

The relation of the Enlightenment to the eighteenth-century economy finds two starkly different interpretations in the works of Joel Mokyr, *The Enlightened Economy: An Economic History of Britain 1700–1850* (New Haven: 2009) and E. A. Wrigley, *Energy and the English Industrial Revolution* (Cambridge: 2011).

Significant texts on Smith and empire include Jennifer Pitts, *A Turn to Empire: The Rise of Imperial Liberalism in Britain and France* (Princeton: 2005) and Emma Rothschild, *The Inner Life of Empires: An Eighteenth-Century History* (Princeton: 2011). Too many scholars have ignored the seminal article on Smith as a bureaucrat by Gary M. Anderson, William F. Shugart, and Robert Tollison, "Adam Smith in the Customhouse," *Journal of Political Economy* 93 (1985), pp. 740–59.

The place of nature and natural knowledge in Smith's thought has stimulated a variety of approaches, from natural philosophy to agricultural improvement and natural history. A few representative titles are Margaret Schabas, *The Natural Origins of Economics* (Chicago: 2006); Brian Bonnyman, *The Third Duke of Buccleuch and Adam Smith: Estate Management and Improvement in Enlightenment Scotland* (Edinburgh: 2014); and Fredrik Albritton Jonsson, *Enlightenment's Frontier: The Scottish Highlands and the Origins of Environmentalism* (New Haven: 2013).

PART V

Smith beyond the Academy

ADAM SMITH: SOME POPULAR USES AND ABUSES

Gavin Kennedy

Adam Smith's name is regularly praised or damned, depending on the author's politics. Unfortunately, partial knowledge of Adam Smith's actual ideas (including his well-hidden politics)[1] is woefully inadequate to praise or blame him. Here I discuss four instances of abuses of Smith's legacy.

1. LAISSEZ-FAIRE AND COMPETITIVE MARKETS

A "most sensible and plain spoken" merchant told Finance Minster Colbert to "laissez nous faire" ("leave us alone"). This became popularized as "laissez-faire" ("leave alone"). Francois Quesnay, a leader of the physiocrats and a man admired by Smith, did not include laissez-faire among his "General Maxims of Government." Like Smith he preferred instead "the full freedom of competition."[2] English speakers since G. Whately in 1774 used the French words, but Smith never mentioned them.[3] How then did he become so strongly associated with laissez-faire? I suggest from an erroneous assumption that "laissez-faire" means general freedom in the interests of consumers rather than mere freedom for employers from state regulations. For example, employers called for laissez-faire when resisting modest safety measures, restrictions on employing child or female labor, and general shorter working hours as proposed in the UK Factory Acts.[4] James Wilson, an avid fan of Adam Smith's and founder of the *Economist* newspaper,[5] supported the Anti-Corn Law League because protectionism by raising farm food prices added to employers' wage costs.

J. B. Say and F. Bastiat argued for laissez-faire linked to Smith's prestigious name, but Smith did not trust merchants and manufacturers on laissez-faire: "People of the same trade seldom meet together, even for merriment and diversion, but the conversation ends in a conspiracy against the public, or in some contrivance to raise prices" (WN I.x.c.27). Laissez-faire was a license for merchants to "fix" their markets against their customers. Employers who secretly combined to lower wages or resist wage rises were hostile to laborers illegally "combining" to resist wage cuts (WN I.viii.12–15).

Smith's teachings of "natural law" did not mean he endorsed laissez-faire. Smith wrote that trying to regulate "the industry and commerce of a great country" as if it was a department of state was doomed to fail because it gave "extraordinary privileges" to "certain branches of industry" while laying upon others "extraordinary restraints." He preferred that "every man . . . pursue his own interest his own way, upon the liberal plan of equality, liberty and justice" (WN IV.ix.3). Laissez-faire for merchants was well short of natural liberty for "every man."

Take away all "preferences" or "restraint," wrote Smith, "the obvious and simple system of natural liberty establishes itself of its own accord." This requires that "every man" who does "not violate the laws of justice is left perfectly free to pursue his own interest in his own way, and to bring both his industry and capital into competition with those of any other men, or order of men." But because state regulation attempts to intervene for which "no human wisdom or knowledge could ever be sufficient," it is better that the superintending of industry is left to "private people" who will direct it "towards the employments most suitable to the interest of the society" (WN IV.ix.51).

When people are exposed to "oppression without a remedy" (WN I.x.c.59), it is the "proper business of law, not to infringe but to support" individuals against "manifest violations" of their "natural liberty." But with this admonition he defended mandatory party walls in buildings that were necessary where the "exertions of the natural liberty of a few individuals" endanger "the security of the whole society." In such circumstances these individuals "are, and ought to be, restrained by the laws of all governments" (WN II.ii.94). Quesnay seemed to have imagined, wrote Smith, that the economy required the "exact regimen of perfect liberty and perfect justice," but, Smith noted, "if a nation could not prosper without the enjoyment of perfect liberty and perfect justice, there is not in the world a nation which could ever have prospered" (WN IV.ix.28).

Smith preferred free competition over central regulation because people were not like the wooden "pieces" on a "chess-board," moved about by the will of their rulers, because "every single" person "has a principle of motion" of his own whatever "legislatures" choose to decree. He did not think "merchants and manufacturers" could be trusted, nor did he think "legislators," who were "very wise" except in their "own conceit" would accept that they did not and could not know enough to micromanage an economy (TMS VI.ii.2.17–18).

2. INVISIBLE HANDS AND REGULATION OF MARKETS

Adam Smith's references to the "invisible hand" in his published works were confined to two occasions only (see below). In both cases, Smith describes the sequential process that begins with the human agents' motivations for the actions they are led to take in support of their intended outcomes and, in turn, their motivated actions lead to the unintended consequences he describes. These unintended consequences could be positive or negative, and hence the "invisible hand" metaphor is neither benign nor malign; it is a metaphoric rhetorical description of human actions, some of which may add positively to market operations (rising GDP and per capita incomes) whereas some may detract negatively from human welfare (environmental destruction, pollution and corruption). In what follows I survey modern misunderstandings among post mid-20th century economists about what Smith meant by innocently using the "invisible hand" metaphor to describe aspects of human behavior long before modern markets came to dominate the more successful economies in the modern world. In short, Smith never said there was a "magical" or "miraculous" "invisible hand" in market exchanges benignly guiding them to a "best of all possible worlds."

Nobel laureate Paul Samuelson authored the world's most successful textbook.[6] He directly influenced millions of students, teachers, researchers, textbook writers, and politicians in his book's nineteen editions. "Adam Smith," Samuelson wrote, "the canny Scot whose monumental book, 'The Wealth of Nations' (1776)" marked "the beginning of modern economics," was "so thrilled by the recognition of an order in the economic system that he proclaimed the mystical principle of the 'invisible hand': that each individual in pursuing only his own selfish good was led, as if by an invisible hand, to achieve the best good of all, so that any interference with free competition by government was almost certain to be injurious."[7] Samuelson also warned that the "invisible hand" as an "unguarded conclusion" had "done almost as much harm as good in the past century and a half" (since 1790). He warned that "too often [the invisible hand] is all that some of our leading citizens remember thirty years later of their college courses in economics." Ironically, he influenced his own readers to make the very same error.

Unsurprisingly, none of Smith's contemporaries mentioned his use of the IH metaphor, and neither did hardly any of his successors until 1875,[8] and then only a dozen or so mentioned it through to the 1930s. A. C. Pigou hints of an oral tradition of Smith's IH metaphor at Cambridge.[9] Contrast this strange absence with the emphatic attention to the *Wealth of Nations* throughout every decade in the nineteenth century by all major economists, yet none of them mentioned Smith's "invisible hand" in an economic role, excepting an occasional theological reference.[10] This absence is in remarkable contrast to the very sharp, sudden increase of secular mentions across all media, academic and popular, after 1942, which continues today. From 1942 to 1974 the average annual mentions of the invisible hand doubled, and doubled again to 1979. Between 1980 and 1989 they were 6.5 times higher than for 1942–74. They increased between 1990 and 1999 again to 8.5 times those of 1942–74, and for 2000–2006 they were 60 percent of the 1990–99 level.[11] While some proportion of the rapid increase of mentions of the invisible hand reflects the growth of popular media, much of it reflected Samuelson's first mover advantage of five million readers, and by the rapid spread of all economics textbooks in all languages, many repeating Samuelson's crude assertions of the role of the invisible hand.[12] After 1948 Smith's metaphoric IH was extended to become the "invisible-hand of markets" in popular discourse.

Mathematical economists working on general equilibrium theory,[13] and Pareto efficiency,[14] claimed credibility for the claim that Adam Smith's IH metaphor referred to markets and that Smith anticipated verbally what their undoubted mathematical competence showed.[15] However, there were skeptical detractors.[16] "Proving" the link to the IH became a litmus test for mainstream tenure-track posts. Dissenting skeptics gradually dropped into heterodox economics despite the fact that claims for Smith's "miraculous" invisible hand are challengeable. Those who claim Smith's authority for their "IH explanations"[17] do not have Smith's authority for their beliefs.

The "invisible hand" was a popular metaphor used by over forty seventeenth- and eighteenth-century theologians and preachers, plus playwrights, novelists, and politicians.[18] Since the 1940s, a "magical" invisible hand showed the need for free markets, absent all regulation, among center-right politicians.[19] Contrawise, it also showed the necessity for extensive "visible" government regulation (the "helping hand") in market economies among center-left rivals.[20]

Senior economists lauded Adam Smith's invisible hand as his "profoundest observation,"[21] even his "most important contribution of economic thought,"[22] and Tobin described it as "one of the great ideas of history."[23] But what exactly did Adam Smith say about the IH metaphor in the eighteenth century to deserve such accolades?

Smith, an authority on rhetoric in English discourse, taught the role of metaphors from 1748 to 1763.[24] So it is unsurprising that Smith's use of the IH metaphor was not commented upon for a hundred years. Smith used the IH metaphor only twice to "describe in a more striking and interesting manner" its rhetorical object (LRBL i.66). In *Moral Sentiments*, the object described by the IH metaphor referred to the absolute and mutual necessary dependence of the "proud and unfeeling landlord" upon his domestic servants, overseers, villeins, serfs, and slaves for his living standards and social "greatness," and the laborers' reciprocal absolute dependence on him for their subsistence and shelter for themselves and their families (TMS IV.1.10). Mutual dependence "led" the landlord to feed his serfs' subsistence from his crops in exchange for their labor and obedience. It had nothing to with his "charity" (nor with markets!). Smith expressed their mutual dependence as leading them to act as they did, which *actions* (not the metaphor!) had important unintended consequences: "They are led by an invisible hand [their mutual dependence] . . . [to] advance the interest of the society, and afford means to the multiplication of the species" (TMS IV.1.10).

The object of Smith's second only metaphoric use of "an invisible hand" is easily identified (WN IV.ii.1–9). This time it was about the "insecurity" felt by some, but not all, merchant traders that led them to prefer to invest in "domestic industry" (mentioned six times), rather than risk their capital abroad (WN, 1776). The outcome of their behavior (not the metaphor!) unintentionally benefitted society by arithmetically adding the insecure merchant's capital to "domestic revenue and employment" (the whole is the sum of its parts). Smith's metaphor for the insecure merchants' motives was that they were "led by an invisible hand"—their insecurity—(WN IV.ii.9) to invest domestically because of the felt insecurity for their capital if they sent it abroad. Many other merchants, who felt more secure, did invest their capital in the "foreign trade of consumption" and "shipping," and Smith considered it well that they did so because when they imported goods that were cheaper than could be manufactured domestically and exported domestic goods that foreign countries could only produce more expensively, foreign trade was mutually beneficial to both parties and was the pathway to general domestic "opulence." Again, in eighteenth-century mercantile trading circumstances, Smith's use of an IH metaphor for the invisible motives of some merchants had visible consequences; but it had absolutely nothing to do with "markets," "supply and demand," the "price system," "equilibrium," "perfect competition," or to any of the post-Samuelson meanings attached to the metaphor.

Smith's third reference to the IH in his posthumous *History of Astronomy* (1795) referred to the Roman god Jupiter, whom credulous Romans believed fired lightning bolts at those who displeased him (HA III.2).[25] This was not a metaphoric use of the IH.

For Smith the popular, mainly theological, seventeenth- to eighteenth-century IH metaphor was a literary figure of speech consistent with English rhetoric. Literary metaphors describe but do not exist, though we can imagine their relation to the object they describe. The invisible hand metaphor "corresponds to nothing in reality," "contributes nothing to knowledge," and, today, is a "distraction and a diversion" in economics.[26] Markets work by visible prices, not by "invisible hands." Believers advise governments to leave recessions to the invisible hand, while skeptics advise governments to intervene with public spending. Such polar positions are political and unconnected to Adam Smith.

Some modern economists extend Smith's use of the "invisible hand" metaphor and apply it to the relationships between intended and unintended consequences by calling them "invisible hand explanations" and analyzing their consequential relationships in an interesting manner.[27] For example, WN IV refers to some (not all) "merchants and manufacturers" whose private motives lead them to execute actions that intentionally lowered their perceived risks from foreign trade. However, just as their motivated actions have intended consequences (security), they also may have unintended consequences, which Smith considered to be of great interest. He used the "invisible hand" metaphor to describe the process in "a more striking and interesting manner" by which the merchant's initial insecurity led him to act to promote "an end" that was no "part of his intention." By investing locally insecure merchants intentionally avoided foreign trade, but in doing so, their intentional actions to achieve their intended consequences (safer investments for themselves) could also have unintended consequences. Specifically by acting in such a manner they add their capital to "domestic revenue and employment," thereby adding, noted Smith, to national wealth creation. This was an unintended consequence of the insecure merchants' initial actions, which were generally, but unintentionally, beneficial to the society. The eventual unintentional outcome had nothing to do with it being caused in some way by the metaphor of an "invisible hand," contrary to the mistaken beliefs of many modern economists, who confuse a descriptive metaphor as an actual invisible force of some undisclosable, possibly theological, description.

There is no actual directing "invisible hand," mysteriously guiding a commercial economy to the benefits of the unintended consequences of the intentional daily multitudinous billions of actions of individuals: the invisible hand is a metaphor describing the consequences of the motives that drive people intentionally to take actions that may have beneficial intended consequences for them. That the intentional consequences of their actions may in turn also cause unintended consequences was a significant observation of several authors before Smith (e.g., Cromwell, Cardinal de Retz, and Adam Ferguson), and the idea is also popularized in the expression that the "road to hell is paved with good intentions." Of importance is that the broad idea of unintended consequences is not confined to economics; it operates in all human activity across all spheres of human endeavor and not just those described by Smith's use of the "invisible hand" metaphor.

It is meaningless, of course, to assert that unintentional consequences are caused intentionally by someone or something! Moreover, the unintended consequences of our actions may be socially benign or calamitous, as the case may be (pollution, overfishing, radiation leaks, tragedies of the commons, etc.). Smith described in TMS how the consequences caused by the initial, motivated actions of "proud and unfeeling landlords," in providing subsistence for the "thousands" whom they employed, and the actions of the "thousands" who labored in his fields for their subsistence, had the unintentional consequence that, in the long run, it led to the "multiplication of the species" (TMS IV.1.10). In contrast, Smith in WN IV also discussed numerous instances of the intentional actions of "merchants and manufacturers," which did not secure "the most efficient and beneficial ends for all." Tariffs, prohibitions, boycotts, trade wars, "jealousies of trade," and such like are seldom beneficial when they intentionally reduce competition and raise prices, or carelessly destroy the earth's resources.

3. SELF-INTERESTS/SELFISHNESS VERSUS MORAL SENTIMENTS

Adam Smith is well known for his focus on the role of self-interest, sometimes presented incorrectly as "selfishness." Smith associated individual self-interest with beneficial economic activity that *could* result in both public and private benefits. He was seldom dogmatic. He reports that not all self-interested activities of individuals necessarily lead to public benefits. Indeed, in the first three books of *Wealth of Nations*, Smith mentions seventy cases of self-interested actions throughout history that caused considerable harm to those affected,[28] to which we could add "tragedy of the commons" concerns.[29] Smith's many strictures on the self-interested, monopolistic behaviors and the clamor for protective tariffs by merchants and manufacturers are clear cases of private self-interests working against public interests.

This subject justifies closer examination because of the alleged different approaches by Adam Smith in his first book, *Moral Sentiments* (1759) and his second, *Wealth of Nations* (1776). It was claimed by several critics, mainly in Germany, but also an Englishman H. T. Buckle,[30] that Smith changed his mind on human motivations between the two books, inevitably still known as "Das Adam Smith Problem." These claims regularly resurface beyond the Academy despite authoritative rebuttals that conclude there was no such "Problem." Critics betray a common misunderstanding of Adam Smith's consistent approach to "sympathy" and to "self-interest." D. D. Raphael and A. L. Macfie's introduction to Smith's 1976 Glasgow Edition of *Moral Sentiments* points to Buckle's error of believing that Smith "ascribed our actions to sympathy" in *Moral Sentiments*; whereas Smith described sympathy as the core of "moral judgment," not of actions, and he also ascribed "a variety of motives" for "action," including "virtuous action," inclusive of "self-interest" or "self-love," which is what comes to the fore in *Wealth of Nations*, whereas Smith's treatment of "selfishness and rapacity" of the "unfeeling landlord" (TMS IV.1.10) remained strictly in a "pejorative sense" as "harm" or "neglect of other people." He also regarded a proper "regard for our own private happiness" (TMS VII.ii.3.15) as a necessary element of virtue. In short, there is no "difference of substance between TMS and WN on self-interest as a motive" for action and there is no "Das Adam Smith Problem."[31]

4. SMITH ON SELF-INTEREST AND BARGAINING

Many passages in *Moral Sentiments* and *Wealth of Nations* capture the dynamics and tensions felt by negotiators as they attempt to conduct their exchanges by seeking agreement on things that are important for their different self-interests. It is from living in society that we judge our own and other people's behaviors, because society mirrors our behavior, providing feedback on what is and what is not acceptable to others. The people we live and interact with show what they think of our behavior, and we notice when others approve and disapprove of our conduct. We learn by experience in the great school of "self-command," starting in the schoolyard.

In the behaviors found in persuasion and bargaining we can see Smith's approach to mediating conflicting self-interests, especially in exchange transactions. We disapprove of the "violent passion" exhibited by those who reject our reasonable proposals, and consider their behavior "extravagant and out of proportion." In contrast, when they exhibit sentiments that "coincide and tally with our own, we necessarily approve of them as proportional and suitable" (TMS I.i.3.9). The tone of the interactions between individuals affects the resolution of disputes, but angry rejections cause us to "become intolerable to one another" (TMS I.i.4.5). Critically, when we anticipate lesser sympathy, we try to "maximize" what little we anticipate by reducing the vehemence of our own passion to a pitch that the other party may be more inclined to go along with. We "flatten," says Smith, "the sharpness" of our "natural tone, in order to reduce it to harmony and concord with the emotions" of others and "though they will never be unisons, they may be concords, and this is all that is wanted or required" (TMS I.i.4.7).

Every man, Smith asserted, is deeply interested in whatever concerns ourselves, but the pursuit of self-love is not a license to violently plunder others or to "disturb [their] happiness" by taking from them what may be "of more use to us" (TMS II.ii.2.1). In the struggle for the place, position, and prizes in life "we must not ruin him" even "to prevent our own ruin" (TMS II.ii.2.1). Disregard for others invites retribution: "In the race for wealth, and honours, and preferments, he may run as hard as he can, and strain every nerve and every muscle, in order to outstrip all his competitors. But if he should justle, or throw down any of them . . . it is a violation of fair play" (TMS II.ii.2.1). People cannot abide foul play. They sympathize with the injured, and the offender suffers the hatred and indignation bursting out from all sides against him. The game of life has rules and norms, and players are expected to abide by them. Therefore "society and conversation" are the most powerful remedies for restoring "the mind to its tranquillity" if it unfortunately loses it, as well as the best preservatives of that "equal and happy temper" so "necessary to self-satisfaction and enjoyment" (TMS I.i.4.10). Therefore, raging self-love does not dominate the social intercourse of mankind, because, paradoxically, no ego can acquire what it wants without the peaceful cooperation of other egos through mutual persuasion, and it is that dependence, effectively total, that safeguards society from self-destruction.

Markets uniquely function in anonymity and the complete interdependence of each on all. This is critical to Smith's theory of the promotion of harmony in society and links directly to the exchange model in *Wealth of Nations* (WN I.ii). Smith writes of "a certain propensity" to "truck, barter, and exchange one thing for another." We all stand "at all times in need of the co-operation and assistance of great multitudes," while our "whole life is scarce sufficient to gain the friendship of a few persons." In practice it is "in vain for him to expect" cooperation and assistance "from their benevolence only." We all have insufficient resources to be benevolent and feed and clothe everybody else. To gain the cooperation of others he must "interest their self-love in his favour" and persuade them that it is for their own advantage to cooperate in an exchange of some kind. We do this by offering an exchange in the mutually conditional format: "give me that which I want, and you shall have this which you want." The conditional offer is how we obtain "the far greater part of those good offices which we stand in need of"; in short, "If you give me this, then I shall give you that." Smith sums the context of the voluntary exchange relationship in the real world: "[I]t is not from the benevolence of the butcher, the brewer, or the baker, that we expect our dinner, but from their regard to their own interest. We address ourselves, not to their humanity but to their self-love, and never talk to them of our own necessities, but of their advantages" (WN I.ii.2).

These passages from both TMS and WN signify the same approach to moral actions between them. It is not selfish to exchange things that we value less for things that we value more with another individual whose valuation is the reverse in his valuing less that which he gives up for something he gets in return from us that he values more. Voluntary exchange is a positive sum game.[32] We achieve such bargains by "never talk[ing] to them of our own necessities, but of their advantages" (WN I.ii.2). We focus on the benefits they will receive and not to "our own necessities"—we are not solely egotistically self-oriented because we can only meet our self-interests by serving theirs.[33] Persuasion and exchange eliminates "Das Adam Smith Problem."[34]

Contrast Smith's approach with how modern economists since the 1930s have formulated the exchange relationship by competitive outcomes not by Smithian processes. They offer versions of "economic warfare,"[35] "coercion,"[36] "optimal rational choice,"[37] "bilateral monopoly,"[38] "valiant mathematics,"[39] and "theories without empirical content."[40] Those who would understand exchange by persuasion and bargaining would do better to start with Adam Smith. Economists would benefit from understanding Adam Smith instead of creating equations without empirical content. Contrast the inadequacy of the economists' approach with recent interdisciplinary work on cooperation and bargaining, which is closer to Adam Smith's ideas.[41]

5. CONCLUDING REMARKS

Space precludes a comprehensive assessment of all the popular abuses and uses of Adam Smith's contributions to philosophy and economics. I have selected only a few examples from many to illustrate something of the extent to which Smith's intellectual legacy has been distorted by generations of academics in the academy and in popular discourse. This is not merely about who was right or wrong. In the course of reading Smith's works to understand what he was actually saying, we can learn a lot about our quite different world from that with which Smith contended. That makes the effort worthwhile and is the least we can do for Smith's reputation.[42]

NOTES

1. D. Winch, *Adam Smith's Politics: An Essay in Historiographic Revision* (New York: 1978); A. Sen, "Uses and Abuses of Adam Smith," *History of Political Economy* 43 (2011), pp. 257–71.

2. W. J. Samuels, "The Physiocratic Theory of Economic Policy," *Quarterly Journal of Economics* 76 (1962), pp. 145–62.

3. G. Whately, *Principles of Trade*, 2nd ed. (London: 1774).

4. Fifteen Factory Acts were passed from 1802 to 1891.

5. R. D. Edwards, *The Pursuit of Reason: The Economist 1843–1993* (London: 1993), p. 6.

6. P. A. Samuelson, *Economics: An Introductory Analysis* (New York: 1948).

7. Ibid., pp. 36.

8. F. W. Maitland, *A Historical Sketch of Liberty and Equality* (Indianapolis: 2000 [1875]).

9. A. C. Pigou, *The Economics of Welfare* (London: 1922), p. 129.

10. T. Chalmers, *On the Power, Wisdom and Goodness of God Manifested in the Adaption of External Nature to the Moral and Intellectual Constitution of Man* (London: 1833), pp. 238, 240.

11. W. J. Samuels, *Erasing the Invisible Hand: Essays on an Elusive and Misused Concept in Economics* (Cambridge: 2011), pp. 118–19.

12. See A. Cairncross, *Introduction to Economics* (London: 1944), p. 400;
G. Myrdal, *American Dilemma: The Negro Problem and Modern Democracy*
(New York: 1944), p. 1055; Samuelson, *Economics*, p. 36; K. E. Boulding,
Economic Analysis, 2nd ed. (London: 1948), pp. 563–64; J. Schumpeter, *History of Economic Analysis* (London: 1954), p. 371; W. Letwin, *The Origin of
Scientific Economics: English Economic Thought 1660–1776* (London: 1963);
H. A. Silverman, *The Substance of Economics: For the Student and the General
Reader* (London: 1922, 1928, 1964), p. 328; R. A. Wyskstra, *Introductory Economics* (New York: 1971), pp. 38, 282–83, 407, 480; J. Lindauer, *Economics:
A Modern View* (Philadelphia: 1977), p. 12; E. V. Bouden, *Economics as the
Science of Common Sense* (Cincinnati: 1974), p. 405; E. Mansfield, *Economics:
Principles, Problems, Decisions* (New York: 1974), pp. 17–18; E. K. Hunt and
H. J. Sherman, *Economics: Introduction to Traditional and Radical Views*, 2nd
ed. (New York: 1975), pp. 11, 48, 55; E. Dolan and D. E. Lindsey, *Basic Economics* (Hinsdale, IL: 1977), p. 328; L. C. Solmon, *Economics* (Reading, MA:
1976), pp. 66, 569–70; J. F. Willis and M. L Primack, *Explorations in Economics*
(Boston: 1977), p. 13; E. Roll, *Use and Abuses of Economics* (London: 1978), pp.
46–57; D. Begg, S. Fischer, and R. Dornbusch, *Economics*, 5th ed. (New York:
1984), pp. 11–12, 326, 333, 402; P. Wonnacot and R. Wonnacot, *Economics*
(New York: 1979), pp. 7, 439; W. J. Baumol and A. S. Blinder, *Economics: Principles and Policy* (New York: 1979), pp. 593–620; R. Caves, "The Structure of
Industry," in *The American Economy in Transition,* ed. Martin Feldstein (Chicago: 1980), p. 502; M. Friedman and R. Friedman, *Free to Choose: A Personal
Statement* (Boston: 1980), p. 25; H. I. Katouzian, *Ideology and Method in Economics* (New York: 1981), p. 28; R. G. Lipsey, *An Introduction to Positive Economics,* 6th ed. (London: 1983), p. 61; Y. S. Bremner, *Capitalism, Competition and
Economic Crisis: Structured Changes in Advanced Industrialized Countries* (Washington, DC: 1984), pp. 99, 153; A. J. Culyer, *Economics* (Oxford: 1985), pp.
183, 185, 212–13, 279; J. Tobin, "The Invisible Hand in Economics," in *Adam
Smith's Legacy: His Place in the Development of Modern Economics,* ed. M. Fry
(London: 1992), p. 115; F. Green and B. Sutcliffe, *The Profit System* (London:
1987), pp. 113, 240; K. Tribe, *The Smith Reception and the Function of Translation*
(Cambridge: 1988), p. 134; B. Ingrao and G. Israel, *The Invisible Hand: Economic Liberalism in the History of Science* (Cambridge: 1990), Preface, pp. 278–
79, 329–32, 324; Luis Perdices de Blas, "*The Wealth of Nations* and Spanish
Economists," in *Adam Smith across Nations: Translations and Receptions of the
Wealth of Nations,* ed. C. Lai (Oxford: 1993), pp. 362, 388, 393, 399; K. Vaughn,
"Can Democratic Society Reform Itself?," in *The Market Process: Essays in
Contemporary Austrian Economics,* ed. P.J.K. Boettke and D. Prychitko (Cheltenham: 1994), p. 240; G. Reisman, *Capitalism: A Treatise on Economics* (Ottawa,
IL: 1996), p. 173; D. M. McCloskey, "The Economics of Choice in Neoclassical
Supply and Demand," in *Economics and the Historian,* ed. T. G. Rawski, S. B. Carter, J. S. Cohen, S. Cullenberg, and R. Sutch (Berkeley: 1996), p. 246; N. G. Mankiw, "Ten Principles of Economics," in *Principles of Economics,* 2nd ed. (Nashville, TN: 1997), p. 11; J. Peil, *Adam Smith and Economic Science: A Methodological
Reinterpretation* (Cheltenham: 1999), pp. xi, 115, 118, 121, 14; B. Caldwell,
Hayek's Challenge: An Intellectual Biography of F. A. Hayek (Chicago: 2004), p.

23; W. Henderson, *Evaluating Adam Smith: Creating the Nation's Wealth* (London: 2006), p. 22; P. Boettke, *Living Economics: Yesterday, Today, and Tomorrow* (Oakland, CA: 2012), pp. 8, 11, cf. 135.

13. G. Debreu, *Theory of Value: An Axiomatic Analysis of Economic Equilibrium* (New Haven: 1959).

14. Pareto optimality: "a perfectly competitive economy is efficient when it cannot increase the economic welfare of anyone without making someone else worse off" (Samuelson and Nordhaus, *Economics* [19th ed. 2010], p. 30).

15. Samuelson, *Economics: An Analytical Introduction* (New York: 1961), p. 598. Samuelson backtracked from his "selfish" assertions about Smith's IH metaphor, by confining the IH to "perfect competition," particularly after Nordhaus became his coauthor from the twelfth edition (1985).

16. R. Lekachman, ed., *Keynes' General Theory: Reports of Three Decades* (New York: 1946), pp. 315–47; Mark Blaug, *Economic Theory in Retrospect*, 5th ed. (Cambridge: 2008), pp. 60–61; J. Cornwall, *Modern Capitalism: Its Growth and Transformation* (Oxford: 1977), preface; Letwin, *Origin of Scientific Economics*, p. 225; Reisman, *Capitalism*, p. 173.

17. For example, R. Nozick, *Anarchy, State, and Utopia* (New York: 1974); N. E. Aydinonat, *The Invisible Hand in Economics: How Economists Explain Unintended Social Consequences* (London: 2008); C. Hillinger, "Adam Smith's Argument of the Existence of 'an Invisible Hand' " (Social Science Research Network working paper, 2012).

18. E. Rothschild, *Economic Sentiments: Adam Smith, Condorcet, and the Enlightenment (*Cambridge, MA: 2001); G. Kennedy, *Adam Smith: A Moral Philosopher and His Political Economy* (London: 2008); P. Harrison, "Adam Smith and the History of the Invisible Hand," *Journal of the History of Ideas* 72 (2011), pp. 29–49.

19. Keith Joseph advised Thatcher's governments on Adam Smith's freer markets and Friedman's monetarism in the 1960s. He gave reading lists on Adam Smith to his senior civil servants in the 1980s. He also influenced Tony Blair, leader of the Labour Party.

20. A popular theme with Prime Minster Gordon Brown (2002–10); see G. Brown, "Forward" in I. Mclean, *Adam Smith, Radical and Egalitarian: An Interpretation for the 21st Century* (Edinburgh: 2006).

21. K. Arrow, "Economic Theory and the Hypothesis of Rationality," in *A Dictionary of Economics*, ed. J. Eatwell, M. Mulgate, and P. Newman (London: 1987).

22. K. Arrow and F. Hahn, *General Competitive Analysis* (San Francisco: 1971).

23. Tobin, "Invisible Hand in Economics."

24. Student notes from the versions of these lectures delivered at Glasgow have been published as LRBL; see also I. Ross, *The Life of Adam Smith*, 2nd ed. (Oxford: 2010).

25. See also G. Vivenza, "A Note on Adam Smith's First Invisible Hand," in *The Adam Smith Review*, vol. 4, ed. V. Brown (New York: 2008).

26. Samuels, *Erasing the Invisible Hand*, p. 146.

27. See again those sources cited in note 17 above.

28. WN Book 1: 40, 43, 52, 71, 77, 78 (2), 79, 80, 83, 84, 91, 100, 106, 112, 115, 135, 136, 139, 140 (2), 141, 142, 143, 144 (2), 145 (3), 146 (3), 151 (3), 152, 153, 154, 157 (2), 158, 160, 171, 174, 267; Book 2: 285, 294, 301(2), 302, 303, 308, 310, 311, 312, 315, 316, 326, 339, 342, 346, 349, 357, 362; Book 3: 378 (2), 380, 382 (2), 384, 385, 386, 387, 390, 393 (3), 397, 398, 402, 406, 415, 418, 419, 422, 427.

29. G. Hardin, "The Tragedy of the Commons," *Science* 162 (1968), pp. 1243–48.

30. H. T. Buckle, *History of Civilisation in England* (London: 1861).

31. D. D. Raphael and A. L. Macfie, "Introduction," in *The Theory of Moral Sentiments,* ed. D. D. Raphael and A. L. Macfie (Oxford: 1976), pp. 21–22.

32. Cf. LJ 390, on mutual "profitability" and "prudence."

33. LJ 352–53.

34. B. Walraevens, "Adam Smith's Economics and the Lectures on Rhetoric and Belles Lettres: The Language of Commerce," *History of Economic Ideas* 18 (2010), pp. 11–32.

35. F. Zeuthen, *Problems of Monopoly and Economic Warfare* (London: 1930)

36. J. Hicks, *The Theory of Wages* (London: 1931).

37. J. Nash, "The Bargaining Problem," *Econometrica* 18 (1950), pp. 155–62.

38. J. Pen, "A General Theory of Bargaining," *American Economic Review* 42 (1952), pp. 24–42.

39. G.L.S. Shackle, "Theories of the Bargaining Process," in *Theory of Wage Determination,* ed. J. T. Dunlop (London: 1964).

40. A. Coddington, *Theories of the Bargaining Process* (London: 1968).

41. H. Gintis, S. Bowles, R. Boyd, and E. Fehr, eds., *Moral Sentiments and Material Interests: The Foundation of Co-operation in Economic Life* (Cambridge: 2005).

42. For regular discussions of the uses and abuses of Adam Smith's works, see www.adamsmithslostlegacy.blogspot.co.uk.

BIBLIOGRAPHIC ESSAY

For the role of metaphors in Smith's published works, see "*Of What Is Called the Tropes and Figures of Speech*," pp. 24–51, in chaps. 6, 7, 8, and 9, in LRBL. For Smith's distinct views on the mediation of self-interests, persuasion, influencing and bargaining exchanges, see pp. 21–24, 81–83, 86, and 154 in TMS; and chap. 2. For Smith's earlier lectures of his ideas about political economy, which appeared later in *Wealth of Nations*, see pp. 347–49, 355, 390 in LJ. For Smith's first use of the "invisible hand" figure of speech, see HA. A close reading of Adam Smith's works reveals the absence of any endorsements, let alone mentions of laissez-faire, as that term is narrowly interpreted by modern economists, and his strictly limited use of the "invisible hand" metaphor (see Smith's HA 49; TMS 184; and WN 456). For the best modern index to all of Adam Smith's works, see K. Haakonssen and A. S. Skinner, *Index to the Works of Adam Smith* (Oxford: 2001).

For an account of Adam Smith's moral philosophy and his political economy, see G. Kennedy, *Adam Smith: His Moral Philosophy and His Political Economy* (London: 2008, 2nd ed. 2010). For the best historical biography of Adam Smith, see Ian Simpson Ross, *The Life of Adam Smith* (Oxford: 1995, 2nd ed. 2010). For a historical survey of Smith's intellectual ideas, see Phillipson, *Adam Smith: An Enlightened Life* (London: 2010). For further analysis of the "uses and abuses" of Smith's authority, see Amartya Sen, "Uses and Abuses of Adam Smith," *History of Political Economy* 43 (2011), pp. 257–71.

ADAM SMITH AND THE LEFT

Samuel Fleischacker

In a widely read essay first published in 1992, Emma Rothschild argued that Adam Smith's politics were at least as much a forerunner of what has come to be known as "the left," as they were of what we now call "the right."[1] Nowadays this point is well known. Many scholars have made a case for left-wing tendencies in Smith.[2]

The case has not gone unchallenged, however. Some Smith scholars have voiced doubts about whether Smith's egalitarianism was as thoroughgoing as the left Smithians suggest.[3] Others stress Smith's fondness for solving problems by way of the private sector, and the absence in his work of major redistributive proposals.

Before the dispute over Adam Smith and the left can be fruitfully explored, we need to address two questions: (1) What exactly do "left" and "right" mean? (2) And to what extent are we concerned with how to read Smith's own writings, and to what extent are we concerned with how Smith can inform or defend a political orientation, or set of policies, today?

1

Strictly speaking, to describe Smith as *either* on the "left" *or* on the "right" is an anachronism. We get those terms from the French Revolution, where they designated who sat where in the National Assembly (those "loyal to religion and the king" on the right of its president, supporters of the revolution on his left).[4] Smith died in 1790, when the Revolution was in its early days, and we do not know what he thought of it.[5] He certainly did not express an opinion, of course, on the elements of the Revolution that occurred after he died: the division between the Girondins and the Jacobins, the execution of the king, the Terror, or the abortive, egalitarian revolution of "Gracchus" Babeuf in 1796. But these events were crucial to the debates between right and left in the nineteenth and twentieth centuries.

Moreover, the terms "right" and "left" have never really achieved a stable, univocal meaning.[6] In the United States today, for instance, being on the right may mean that one opposes government intervention in the economy, but it may also mean that one supports a greater role for religion in government policy. Elsewhere it can take yet other meanings: that one favors a militaristic state, for instance, or the identification of one's state with a particular ethnic group. Correspondingly, those who describe themselves as on the "left" are champions of social democracy in some places and times but elsewhere identify primarily with secularism or pacifism or an opposition to ethnic loyalties.

Such cross-cutting divisions have important implications both for policy and for political alliances. Many opponents of large government are suspicious of religion and of military adventurism, and some ardent advocates of the poor have also been ardent ethnic nationalists. Whether a particular combination of views should be labeled "left" or "right" tends accordingly to depend on the political accidents of a particular place and time. In 1910, the *Encyclopedia Britannica* ranged socialism and free trade together, contrasting them with economic nationalism;[7] a decade later, one presumes, it would not have dreamt of doing that. Today support generally comes from the left for "cap and trade" policies as a way of restraining carbon emissions, but it was originally a proposal made by politicians associated with the right.

Of course one reason for these differences has to do with what problems are salient in a given set of circumstances. In many cases, people who identify with the left share the same set of goals and differ only because, in their contexts, they see different practical obstacles to those goals. Other reasons for such differences are philosophical, however, or arise from different views of human nature. One person may see religion as the greatest barrier to liberty and equality; another may think that a belief in human equality depends on the belief that people are created in the image of God. One person may see liberty and equality as in sharp tension with one another; another may think that they belong together. There are good arguments for and against each side on these issues, and people differ profoundly over them. It is a mistake to assume that even people who, broadly speaking, share the same goals for human life will necessarily agree on how to pursue them.

Bearing these complications in mind, I propose that we understand "left" and "right"—especially when we try to use them across centuries, as we must do when we ask after their application to Smith—as cluster terms, designating views that are often but not always brought together. We have seen a number of elements in the relevant clusters already. Bringing them together, it seems to me that five features generally mark movements associated with the left, in particular:

The first is a confidence that human beings can greatly improve their lot by the use of reason—that we can take deliberate steps to make our future freer, happier, and more peaceful than our past. Those who oppose this view hold that reason is an untrustworthy or dangerous guide to change, and we should rely as much as possible on long-standing traditions instead. Defenders of tradition sometimes see it as underwritten by God or nature, sometimes simply point to the limits of reason, or the hubris of those who want to overturn traditional ways of doing things. This difference marks "left" and "right" more than anything else, and is perhaps the one feature that all uses of these terms have in common: indeed, "progressivist" and "traditionalist" are virtually synonyms for them.

Second, and relatedly, people on the left tend to trust the state over the private sector while people on the right tend to trust the private sector over the state. One of the main functions of the state, according to people on the left, is to curtail private power: to prevent churches, corporations, aristocrats, and wealthy businesspeople from exerting excessive influence over those in the lower ranks of society. People on the right counter either that these loci of informal power are sanctioned by God or tradition, or that they represent "spontaneous orders" that are more likely to help society than government officials can or will. There are, of course, left-wing anarchists and right-wing statists. But even these phenomena fit the pattern I am describing. People on the left favor anarchism if they believe that state power is inevitably allied with, rather than capable of checking, powerful interests in the private sector. People on the right become statists when they hold the same belief; they just think an alliance of the state with powerful private interests is a good thing. We can safely say that only the left values state power *as a way of limiting* private power.

A third mark of the left is a strong egalitarianism, as opposed to an attachment to hierarchies of class, race, religion, or gender. Left-wingers have consistently called for greater political and socioeconomic equality: for the abolition of slavery and for universal male franchise in the eighteenth century; for unions, welfare programs, and other ways of increasing the power of workers in the nineteenth and early twentieth century; for women's rights and laws to ban racial discrimination in the later twentieth century; and for LGBT rights in the twenty-first century.

Fourth, the left is usually secular in orientation, and even proponents of a religious left generally call for a revision of their religion's traditional tenets or practices. To be sure, the right also contains fervently secular elements—Ayn Rand is an example—but an opposition to traditional forms of religion sits especially well with the left's commitment to overturning practices that cannot be readily underwritten by reason.

Finally, the left usually takes itself to be the true standard-bearer for human freedom. Many on the right also treasure that value, of course, but the left tends to think that right-wingers misinterpret freedom. The left champions a kind of freedom that goes with its other commitments: a freedom from religion, or at least from the authority claimed by traditional religions; a freedom to raise questions, more generally, about beliefs and practices passed down by tradition, and to overturn them where they seem unreasonable; and a freedom that is distributed as equally as possible, and goes out in particular to hitherto oppressed groups, rather than being primarily available to a political or economic elite. The right is usually less worried about freedom from religious authority than freedom from government, less interested in a freedom that defies tradition, and more comfortable with freedoms that are used differentially by rich and poor.

This cluster definition of "left" and "right" is meant to stand somewhere between an entirely historicist view by which these terms designate only the precise positions for which they were used in a particular political context and an essentialist view on which they belong with a unified ideology that informs every stance associated with them. The people associated with both left and right are a loose congeries, clustered together by certain common threads running through their views but not holding exactly the same ideology, or emphasizing the same aspects of that ideology in their various circumstances.

2

What can we say, now, about Smith's affinities with the left or progressive end of the political spectrum in his own day?

Well, to begin with, the main issues of his day did not include the most prominent question for progressivists today: whether or not governments should intervene in the economy to redistribute wealth. Only in the wake of the French Revolution did large-scale redistributivist proposals get on the agenda even of radically egalitarian movements.[8] The phrase a "right to welfare" began to be widely used only in the 1790s; Thomas Paine proposed something like social security in 1793, and in this as in much else was a startling innovator; and the first political movement that looks anything like socialism is Babeuf's abortive revolt in 1796.[9] So when Smith died, and certainly when he wrote his major works, there was as yet nothing remotely like a social democratic left with which he might engage. We need to consider his proposals to help the poor in this light, and we need to consider the progressivism, or lack thereof, of his outlook as a whole in a context in which poverty policy was not central to the progressivist/traditionalist divide.

What was? Above all: where one stood on various religious issues —whether one was a traditional Christian, a rational theist, a skeptic or an atheist, and whether one thought governments should promote religion; where one stood on democracy (republicanism) versus monarchy, and whether one favored popular revolution to achieve democracy; whether one favored or opposed aristocracy; and what one thought about slavery. Smith comes out well toward the progressive end on most of these measures, if not wholly so on all of them. His *Theory of Moral Sentiments* (TMS) favors at most a general theism, leaving out its one explicitly Christian passage in its final edition;[10] he also recommends a complete separation of church and state in the *Wealth of Nations* (WN), although he crafts ways for governments to use churches for moral purposes if they cannot achieve complete separation. In his lectures on jurisprudence, and in WN, he makes clear that all governments ought to represent the will of their people, and his suggestion in WN that the American colonists be represented in Parliament, it has been argued, may have in part been an attempt to increase the republicanism of Great Britain.[11] If he also expresses some reservations about republics, that is largely because he was convinced that republics would find it far more difficult than monarchies to outlaw slavery—wealthy slave owners would use their power in legislative assembles to prevent that from happening.[12] (In this, of course, he was prescient.) Smith was a vehement opponent of slavery, and he was one of the sharpest critics of European colonialism of the entire eighteenth century.[13] He also mocked the pretensions of aristocrats and of the wealthy, although he thought that hierarchy of some sort is inevitable in human societies, and has some beneficial effects.[14]

Finally, Smith proposed a number of ways for the state to curtail traditional power sources in the private realm. He praises sovereigns for their role in breaking the power of feudal landowners (WN III.iii.8–12), and looks to them to end slavery. He also says that regulations in favor of workers are "always just and equitable," but are "sometimes otherwise when in favour of . . . masters" (WN I.x.c.61). His sharp critiques of large churches, the East India Company, and the remnants of aristocratic privilege in Britain also fit this pattern. Throughout WN, he favors the disadvantaged over the advantaged, and looks to the state to help the former against the latter.[15]

Together, such views placed Smith firmly in the camp of those who were suspicious of the church, the monarchy, the aristocracy, and the promotion of British glory; his admirers accordingly included such people as Thomas Jefferson and Benjamin Rush in America, the Abbé Siéyès and Marquis de Condorcet in France, and Thomas Paine, John Millar, Mary Wollstonecraft, and William Godwin in Britain. These are, by any reckoning, among the most staunchly progressive figures in the eighteenth century.

3

Smith makes several redistributivist proposals in WN,[16] but what he most bequeathed to other progressivists was a sea change in attitudes toward the poor: an undermining of the reigning views according to which poor people should be kept in their place.[17] Very few people before Smith thought that the world either could or should do without a class of poor people. Until the late eighteenth century, almost all Christian churches taught that God had ordained a hierarchical organization for society, with the truly virtuous people occupying positions of wealth and power at the top, and "the poor and inferior sort" at the bottom.[18] Of course, the people at the top were supposed to help those at the bottom—but not enough to raise them above their proper place. At the same time secular writers, like Bernard Mandeville, offered pragmatic reasons for keeping poor people poor: their innate laziness, lack of self-control, and addiction to various vices would lead them to destroy themselves and their families if they lacked a constant incentive to work hard. Smith was a virulent opponent of both of these ways of justifying social hierarchy; he rejected both religious and secular versions of the idea that the poor are morally or intellectually inferior to the well-off. Over and over again, he pricks the vanity upholding contemptuous pictures of the poor. He presents them as having the same native abilities as everyone else. "The difference of natural talents in different men is, in reality, much less than we are aware of," he says; habit and education make up for most of that supposedly great gap between the philosopher and the common street porter, even though "the vanity of the philosopher is willing to acknowledge scarce any resemblance" between the two (WN I.ii.4). To those who complain that the poor are naturally indolent,[19] Smith declares that, on the contrary, they are "very apt to over-work themselves" (WN I.viii.44). To those—and these were legion, even among defenders of the poor—who saw indulgence in drink as a vice characteristic of poor people,[20] Smith replies that "[m]an is an anxious animal and must have his care swept off by something that can exhilarate the spirits" (LJB 231). To those who wanted to restrain the poor from buying luxury goods,[21] Smith says that it is "but equity" for the lower ranks of society to have a fair share of the food, clothes, and housing they themselves produce (WN I.viii.36)—and that it is "the highest impertinence and presumption, . . . in kings and ministers, to pretend to watch over the economy of private people" (WN II.iii.36)

This is not the end of the list. Smith defends the religious choices of poor people against the contempt and fear of his Enlightenment colleagues, pointing out that the religious sects that they tended to join, while sometimes "disagreeably rigorous and unsocial," provided them with community and moral guidance (WN V.i.g.12). He repeatedly praises the virtues and accomplishments of independent laborers, arguing that it is unnecessary as well as inappropriate to monitor and control their lives (WN I.viii.46–50, II.iii.11–12, III.iv.5–13). He even tries to excuse, if not quite justify, the mob violence characteristic of workers in their struggles with their employers (WN I.viii.13).

Smith thus presents a remarkably dignified picture of the poor, on which they make choices every bit as respectable as those of their social superiors—a picture, therefore, in which there are no true "inferiors" and "superiors" at all. Individual people may be good or bad, but Smith urges his well-off readers to see the average poor person as just like themselves: equal in intelligence, virtue, ambition, and interests with every other human being, hence equal in rights and desert, in dignity. It is this picture of the poor person as equal in dignity to everyone else, and as deserving, therefore, of whatever we would give our friends and neighbors, that sets up the possibility of seeing poverty itself as a harm, as something that no one should have to endure. The possibility that people might have a right not to be poor is one that could open up only once this dignified portrayal of the poor replaced the view, which had reigned unquestioned for centuries, by which poverty went with a difference in kinds of people, not merely a difference in luck. Smith's WN did more than any other writing in his time to effect this replacement;[22] this change in view is one of the book's signal achievements.

4

Two features of Smith's political thought distinguish it from that of his more revolutionary peers. One is an aversion to quick and radical change. Smith is anticlerical and heterodox in his religious beliefs, but inclined to limit rather than to end the power of state churches; and he favors republicanism and dislikes aristocracy, but supports a slow, incremental reform of monarchy and hereditary social hierarchy rather than revolution. In part, Smith's incrementalism in these cases just reflects his understanding of how the problematic institutions in question work. As we have seen, he thought that republics were less likely to end slavery than monarchies, and he also thought that an abrupt end to state support for a church could breed unnecessary turbulence among those who work for or look up to that church (WN V.i.g.19). But Smith also has more general reasons to favor incrementalism. His moral psychology leads him to be more committed than most of his contemporaries to types of political change that ordinary people can easily accept, and to be suspicious of activists and political leaders with schemes for transforming society from the top down.[23] These commitments do not show that Smith was less egalitarian than the revolutionaries he criticized. Indeed, they may display a more thoroughgoing egalitarianism than that of people who think they know better than anyone else how to remake society.

In addition, Smith favors a cool, dispassionate voice in his writing, expressing indignation primarily through irony. Smith's views on rhetoric and sympathy entail that one is most likely to move readers by understating one's sentiments, and projecting the reader into the situation of the oppressed rather than launching an open appeal on their behalf.[24] To persuade people of his dignified picture of the poor, he therefore just presents the details of a life in poverty as they are experienced by the people enduring them. This indirect mode of moral teaching seems however to have had a tremendous impact.[25] So we should not discount the power of Smith's rhetoric for its moderate tone, or underestimate the commitment it reflects to the eradication of poverty.

5

I'd like to close with four conclusions for how we might think about Smith in connection with contemporary left-wing politics.

1. There is nothing in Smith's political economy to bar state intervention on behalf of poor people, and Smith himself speaks for such intervention on several occasions. Smith's free market teachings were meant to fend off state intervention on behalf of *one sector of the economy* as opposed to others (one industry over others, or industry as a whole over agriculture), not to fend off state intervention on behalf of the poor. On the contrary, Smith himself proposes a series of interventions aimed at greater equality of opportunity, and at limiting the power of wealthy or otherwise influential individuals and groups in the private sector. To try to draw from Smith a doctrine along the lines "government aid to the poor only maintains vice or weakness" or "all re-distribution of wealth offends against property rights" or "the private sector helps everyone better than the government can" is a fool's errand. Smith was not Ayn Rand or Robert Nozick or Milton Friedman, and to make it seem as if he were is intellectually irresponsible.

That does not mean that Smith would have identified with today's social democrats or welfare-state liberals. Claiming him for these camps would also be intellectually irresponsible; his approach to policy is far too sensitive to historical circumstance for us to know what he would favor today. Libertarians are also right to point out a strong strain of suspicion of state action in Smith.[26]

That strain might well have kept him from endorsing antipoverty programs that depend on large state bureaucracies. But this leaves room for redistribution via the tax code, state aid to local schools or community groups, and many other ideas.

2. Smith gives us reasons to favor a certain *orientation* to the problems of poverty. We may not be able to say exactly which policies he would favor in the circumstances of the twenty-first century, but he would surely be as suspicious today as he was in his own day of attempts to fashion or defend a government approach to poverty on the basis of the complacent prejudices that well-off people tend to have toward the poor. Without exception, he sees the accusations usually leveled at poor people—of indolence, vice, inherent mental incompetence, and so on—as unjustified, produced by a combination of self-serving dogma and a failure to project oneself into the situation of the poor. He also recognizes the many ways that powerful groups in civil society, and not just the government, can oppress the poor: indeed, he sees the rightful role of government as in part to hold back the oppressive tendencies of these groups, and not just to let private agents do what they will. Whatever one's views on policy, these are teachings that remain of great importance. In response to claims that state action to alleviate poverty will be useless because the poor are innately less intelligent or self-controlled than other people, or because private employers do more for their workers than government measures can ever do, any Smithian should be alert to the likelihood that these claims reveal the speaker's prejudices, and failure to attempt a sympathetic understanding of the people of whom he speaks— failure to project himself into their situation. Achieving such an understanding will not necessarily dictate just one set of policies, but it will guide us more in some directions than others, and prevent us from advocating an approach we would regard as callous or unjust, if we were the ones who had to live under it.

3. A Smithian approach to the suffering or oppression of the poor is unlikely to look like the standard proposals of those who come out of revolutionary traditions on the left. Smith clearly favors policies that do not too quickly alter the institutions under which a society already lives, that work with rather than against

the expectations people have of the social world around them. Ordinary people need to be able to incorporate change with ease and understanding into their daily lives, rather than having to obey official decrees blindly: that is the only way for such change to accommodate itself to liberty and democracy. Once again, what exactly this preference for careful and slow change entails in different historical contexts is hard to say; we can determine that only by a sympathetic understanding of the actual preferences and patterns of life of people in each society at each point in time.

4. Finally, Smithian advocacy works through calm, detailed accounts of facts rather than fiery polemics; this is, for him, both the most effective and the most respectful way of trying to persuade one's moral equals to look differently at a situation, and examine their actions critically. He is, in this regard, sharply different from such writers as Diderot and d'Holbach in his own time, and from Dickens, Engels, Frantz Fanon, and Catharine MacKinnon, later on. But he is not very different stylistically from, say, George Orwell, Barbara Ehrenreich, Jonathan Kozol, or Nicholas Kristoff. Of course he is unlikely to have shared the substantive views of all these people. But they resemble him in their mode of writing: in the way they eschew explicit rancor, and attempt to persuade simply by describing, in detail, the circumstances of poor people.

For some, an approach to politics that is antirevolutionary, rhetorically moderate, and stops short of demanding full socioeconomic equality may not look left-wing at all. This seems arbitrary and dogmatic, however. Many people standardly associated with the left—the New Deal and Great Society Democrats in the United States, certainly—have been gradualists, like Smith, and have stopped short of full-scale egalitarianism. We should recall, again, that "left" and "right" are cluster terms, defined by general aims and orientation rather than specific policies and strategies. And a person who believes that governments can and should take active steps to bring about progress, and who defines progress primarily by way of the freedom and well-being of the disadvantaged, belongs well within the left-wing (progressivist) rather than right-wing (traditionalist) cluster of political views described in section 1. In practice, those in this cluster tend to favor policies that are almost always more liberal than conservative, and sometimes more social democratic than liberal.

Stephen Darwall has called Smith's politics "sympathetic liberalism."[27] That's a good name; "sympathetic progressivism" might be an even better one. One who believes that our sympathy should go out to all members of society, advantaged and disadvantaged alike, will demand of us that we move more slowly on behalf of the disadvantaged, and employ more modest rhetoric in defense of such moves, than some left-wing movements have favored. But Smith also calls on us to work up a deep sympathy for the disadvantaged, and to overhaul any institution that makes their lives miserable. In this respect, his politics belong firmly with the left: those who see overhauling such institutions, even when entrenched by long tradition, as the main goal of politics.

NOTES

1. Rothschild, "Adam Smith and Conservative Economics," *Economic History Review* 45, no. 2 (1992). She has since developed this point in her influential book *Economic Sentiments* (Cambridge, MA: 2001).

2. See the bibliographic essay below.

3. See, for instance, D. D. Raphael, *The Impartial Spectator* (Oxford: 2007), pp. 122–26, or Donald Winch, *Riches and Poverty* (Cambridge: 1996), pp. 166–75.

4. Baron de Gauville, as quoted in Marcel Gauchet, "Right and Left," in *Realms of Memory*, ed. P. Nora, trans. A. Goldhammer (New York: 1992). Gauchet traces the process by which these geographical designations developed in great detail.

5. There has been much speculation that the passage in TMS on "the man of system" (VI.ii.2.13–16) is a comment on the French Revolution. Given that the revisions to TMS were completed by November 18, 1789—a month before the Jacobin Club was formed, and only two weeks after the sermon by Richard Price that so enraged Edmund Burke—I see little reason to believe this. E. Rothschild (*Economic Sentiments: Adam Smith, Condorcet, and the Enlightenment* [Cambridge, MA: 2001], pp. 54–55, and notes thereto) suggests several alternative political events as background to TMS VI.ii.2.13–16.

6. Gauchet argues that they became popular *because* they cover over differences among groups that are trying to hold together: "The terms caught on precisely because there was in reality more than one right and more than one left" (Gauchet, "Right and Left," p. 261; see also 275–76).

7. "Socialism, like free trade, is cosmopolitan in its aims, and is indifferent to patriotism and hostile to militarism. Socialism, like free trade, insists on material

welfare as the primary object to be aimed at in any policy, and like free trade, socialism tests welfare by reference to possibilities of consumption." William Cunningham, "Free Trade," in *Encyclopedia Britannica*, 11th ed. (New York: 1910), vol. 11, p. 92.

8. For more on the historical developments adumbrated in this paragraph, see S. Fleischacker, *Short History of Distributive Justice* (Cambridge, MA: 2004).

9. See ibid., pp. 75–79, and Gareth Stedman Jones, *An End to Poverty?* (London: 2004).

10. I am referring to TMS II.ii.3.12 (note on pp. 91–92), which ended until the sixth edition with an approving reference to the doctrine of Christ's atonement for our sins. For an argument that Smith merely redistributes the content of this passage in the sixth edition—and retained, to a considerable extent, a commitment to Christian ethics—see Ryan Hanley, *Adam Smith and the Character of Virtue* (Cambridge: 2009), pp. 197–98, n. 22.

11. See WN V.iii.90, and Frances Hirst, *Adam Smith* (New York: 1904). It is noteworthy that Smith also recommends union between Britain and Ireland, in the previous paragraph of WN, on the grounds that that would help deliver the Irish people from the power of the aristocrats in their own nation.

12. "In a republican government it will scarcely ever happen that [slavery] should be abolished. The persons who make all the laws in that country are persons who have slaves themselves. These will never make any laws mitigating their usage; whatever laws are made with regard to slaves are intended to strengthen the authority of the masters and reduce the slaves to a more absolute subjection" (LJA iii.101–2; compare WN IV.vii.b.55).

13. See Sankar Muthu, "Adam Smith's Critique of International Trading Companies: Theorizing 'Globalization' in the Age of Enlightenment," *Political Theory* 36, no. 2 (2008).

14. See TMS I.iii.2.5, TMS I.iii.2.11, TMS VI.ii.1.21, WN V.i.b.3–11. Stephen Darwall discusses Smith's lingering fondness for social ranks in "Smith's Ambivalence about Honor," in *The Philosophy of Adam Smith*, ed. V. Brown and S. Fleischacker (London: 2010).

15. See Samuel Fleischacker, *On Adam Smith's* Wealth of Nations: *A Philosophical Companion* (Princeton: 2004), pp. 236–42.

16. The most important of these is his advocacy of public schooling. In addition, he suggests that luxury vehicles pay a higher road toll than freight vehicles, so that "the indolence and vanity of the rich [can be] made to contribute in a[n] . . . easy manner to the relief of the poor" (WN V.i.d.5). And he advocates a tax on house rents, which would fall heaviest on the rich, because it is reasonable to make the rich contribute proportionately more than the poor do to public revenue (WN V.ii.a.19–20).

17. I have discussed this subject extensively elsewhere. What follows relies heavily on my *Short History*, pp. 62–68 and *On Adam Smith's* Wealth of Nations, chap. 10. See also Daniel A. Baugh, "Poverty, Protestantism and Political Economy: English Attitudes toward the Poor, 1660–1800," in *England's Rise to Greatness*, ed. Stephen Baxter (Berkeley: 1983).

18. Walter Trattner, *From Poor Law to Welfare State*, 5th ed. (New York: 1994), p. 18.

19. The lower sort, said Mandeville, "have nothing to stir them up to be serviceable but their Wants, which it is Prudence to relieve but Folly to cure." Mandeville here anticipates Arthur Young, who declared in 1771 that "every one but an ideot knows, that the lower classes must be kept poor, or they will never be industrious" (quotations from Baugh, "Poverty, Protestantism and Political Economy," nn. 53 and 74).

20. Even the radical reformer John Bellers recommended his proposals to help the poor by saying that they may remove "the Profaneness of Swearing, Drunkenness, etc. with the Idleness and Penury of many in the Nation; which evil Qualities of the Poor, are an Objection with some against this Undertaking, though with others a great Reason for it" (George Clarke, ed., *John Bellers: His Life, Times and Writings* [London: 1987], p. 55; see also p. 52).

21. As Neil McKendrick writes, Smith's contemporaries frequently "complained that those becoming marks of distinction between the classes were being obliterated by the extravagance of the lower ranks; that working girls wore inappropriate finery, even silk dresses." McKendrick, "Home Demand and Economic Growth," in *Historical Perspectives: Studies in English Thought and Society*, ed. McKendrick (London: 1974), p. 168.

22. Baugh ("Poverty, Protestantism and Political Economy") argues that WN contributed more than any other eighteenth-century work to a vast change in attitudes toward the poor.

23. On these points, see my *On Adam Smith's* Wealth of Nations, pp. 229–36, 242–46.

24. See my "Bringing Home the Case of the Poor: Adam Smith's Rhetoric in the *Wealth of Nations*" in *The Oxford Handbook of Political Theory and Rhetoric*, ed. Dilip Gaonkar and Keith Topper (Oxford: forthcoming).

25. See again Baugh, "Poverty, Protestantism and Political Economy."

26. See *On Adam Smith's* Wealth of Nations, pp. 229–36.

27. Stephen Darwall, "Sympathetic Liberalism: Recent Work on Adam Smith," *Philosophy and Public Affairs* 28 (1999).

BIBLIOGRAPHIC ESSAY

Recent scholarly writings that bring out Smith's left-wing tendencies include, in addition to Rothschild's *Economic Sentiments*, my own *A Third Concept of Liberty: Judgment and Freedom in Kant and Adam Smith* (Princeton: 1999) and *On Adam Smith's* Wealth of Nations: *A Philosophical Companion* (Princeton: 2004), as well as Amartya Sen's *The Idea of Justice* (Cambridge, MA: 2009), Dennis Rasmussen's *The Problems and Promise of Commercial Society* (University Park, PA: 2008), Gareth Stedman Jones's *An End to Poverty?* (London: 2004), Iain McClean's *Adam Smith, Radi-*

cal and Egalitarian (London: 2006), and Gavin Kennedy's *Adam Smith: A Moral Philosopher and His Political Economy* (London: 2008). Smith's egalitarian tendencies are also discussed in Stephen Darwall, "Equal Dignity in Adam Smith," *Adam Smith Review* 1 (2004), Remy Debes, "Adam Smith on Dignity and Equality," *British Journal for the History of Philosophy* 20, no. 1 (2012), Elizabeth Anderson, "Adam Smith on Equality" (this volume), and Samuel Fleischacker, "Equality," in *The Oxford Handbook of Adam Smith*, ed. Christopher Berry, Maria Paganelli, and Craig Smith (Oxford: 2013).

Doubts about Smith's egalitarianism, and usefulness for the left, are expressed in D. D. Raphael, *The Impartial Spectator* (Oxford: 2007), esp. pp. 122–26, Donald Winch, *Riches and Poverty* (Cambridge: 1996), esp. pp. 166–75, and Craig Smith, "Adam Smith: Left or Right?," *Political Studies* (2012).

ADAM SMITH AND THE RIGHT

James R. Otteson

The reception of Adam Smith's political economy has undergone a sea change.[1] For almost two centuries, Smith was hailed as the founding father of capitalism, with his 1776 *Inquiry into the Nature and Causes of the Wealth of Nations* seen as the definitive case for free trade and free markets.[2] Since the 1970s, however, a succession of commentators has claimed that Smith was not a classical liberal after all but more like a progressive liberal: his concerns for the poor, his worries about the damage that excessive division of labor can do to workers, his criticisms of merchants and monopoly corporations, and his apparent support for progressive taxation all taken as evidence that he was no supporter of laissez-faire.[3] Indeed, some have gone so far as to claim that Smith was a proto-Marxist.[4] So who is the real Adam Smith?

The question of whether Smith should be categorized as on the political right or the political left can risk, however, becoming as futile as recent arguments over whether US President Barack Obama is "socialist" or not. The answer, obviously, depends on what one means by "socialist"—by which, equally obviously, different people mean very different things. Yet perhaps we can make some headway by taking a cue from that contested term "socialism." Like all systems of political economy, socialism comprehends a set of policies in the service of its preferred values—principally fairness, equality, and community (properly defined, of course). Public ownership of the means of production, the traditional definition of socialism, was not an end in itself but instead itself a means, capturing the central method for achieving socialism's goals at a time—the late nineteenth and into the twentieth century—when "means of production" were almost exclusively things like factories and land. Owning them enabled reorganization of society's political economy in the service of socialism's ends. With the advent of the digital age, however, economic production has been utterly transformed; what constitutes "means of production" has now become broad and open-ended. Accordingly, socialism has had to adapt to the times: rather than owning the means of production outright, it now proposes to centrally regulate people's behavior, and to redistribute portions of their productive output, in preferred directions. Whether realizing socialism's moral goals requires owning the means of production depends, then, on historical circumstances, but what will always be required is to *centrally organize political-economic decision making*. Without that, there is no socialism; with it, fairness, equality, and community can, it is hoped, be achieved.

By contrast, socialism's antithesis, capitalism, has at its core *decentralized* political-economic decision making. Its preferred values might be justice, liberty, and individuality (again, properly defined), but it holds that allowing individuals or voluntary groups of individuals to make political-economic decisions for themselves with little state interference is what enables the realization of the values it holds dear. So the former position tends to favor planned patterns of social order, or the correction of unplanned patterns, according to principles and authority centrally derived and administered; while the latter tends to favor unplanned or "spontaneous" patterns of social order that are deferential to what individuals and voluntary groups decide to do and skeptical of what third parties might like to mandate or nudge them to do.

Let us therefore call the two positions *centralist* and *decentralist*, respectively. So defined, they are end states along a continuum, and although they may act as proxies for the political left and right, respectively, there will be good-faith disagreement about where some particular policies or positions fall. But thinking about matters in this way has the benefit of allowing us to avoid some of the partisanship that can vitiate such discussions. In asking, then, whether Smith is on the left or the right, we might rephrase the question and ask whether Smith is a centralist or a decentralist. And here I think we can come to a fairly definite conclusion: Smith is a decentralist.

In what follows I lay out the decentralism I find in Smith, drawing first on his *Theory of Moral Sentiments* (TMS) and then on his *Wealth of Nations* (WN). I then review several reasons for taking the position that Smith is instead a centralist, and I conclude that, despite those reasons, Smith is best understood as a member of the long tradition of classical liberalism now typically associated with the political right.

DECENTRALISM IN TMS

Smith's 1759 *Theory of Moral Sentiments* describes morality as a decentralized evolutionary system, developing according to what I have elsewhere called a "marketplace model."[5] TMS attempts to explain where our moral sentiments come from, how we come to pass the judgments we do, and how we transitioned from amoral infancy to moralized adulthood. Smith's explanation hinges on the pleasure he claims we naturally receive from "mutual sympathy" of sentiments (TMS I.i.2)—that is, the pleasure we receive from realizing that our sentiments are echoed in, or shared by, others. Because all of us have this desire, it acts as a centripetal force drawing us into society with others, as well as a normalizing force inducing us to moderate our sentiments so that they more closely approximate what others would "sympathize" with. According to Smith, shared standards of morality and etiquette are the patterns that emerge from people's localized attempts to achieve mutual sympathy of sentiments. They are subject to change over time, as people's interests, values, and circumstances change, yet because no single person can create or destroy them they enjoy a level of objectivity that transcends individual schedules of value.[6]

Given, however, that human beings have certain unchanging natural features—they desire mutual sympathy of sentiments (see, e.g., TMS I.i.2); their happiness depends in part on loving associations with other people (see TMS I.ii.4.1–2); their love and concern for others is a scarce resource that varies directly with their familiarity with others (see TMS III.3.9 and VI.ii); and so on —then hypothetical moral imperatives follow. If you will not be happy without loving associations with others, if you will not have loving associations with others unless you achieve mutual sympathy of sentiments with them, and if you will not achieve mutual sympathy of sentiments with them unless you moderate your sentiments so that they approximate what others either expect or believe they would themselves have in your position, then to be happy you should cultivate and exercise "self-command"—from which "all the other virtues seem to derive their principal lustre" (TMS VI.iii.11)—so that your behavior and your standards match those of the people about whom you care.

Would that make the standards that arise according to the Smithian evolutionary mechanism *correct?* Like the results of biological evolution, there is no way to say that some developments, varieties, or species are intrinsically better than others—only that they were better adapted. But Smith believes that because these standards depend on their ability to actually serve people's interests (including their desire for mutual sympathy of sentiments), their continued existence over time suggests that they have in fact made people better off. The fit is not perfect, since social inertia, biases, irrationalities, institutionalized superstitions, and so on can all retard and even reverse the "natural" process of development.[7] But Smith seems to have a cautious optimism that in the long run destructive processes will wither and, eventually, die.

In a striking passage from TMS that might initially seem out of place, Smith describes a political type he calls a "man of system," who, Smith says, makes the mistake of thinking that he can arrange the metaphorical pieces of the metaphorical "great 'chessboard' of human society"—that is, people—with the same ease with which the hand arranges the literal pieces on a literal chessboard (TMS VI.ii.2.17). The mistake such a person makes, Smith claims, is to forget that people have "principles of motion" all their own, which the "man of system"—that is, the legislator, regulator, nudger, and so on—can neither control nor anticipate. But this mistake is facilitated by a related cluster of others—chiefly the man of system's inflated view of the scope of his knowledge and his propensity to assume that his own particular schedule of value should hold for others as well—and it often issues in the man of system's resolution to try to mandate, restrain, nudge, or otherwise influence others' behavior so that it more closely coheres with "his own ideal plan of government" (TMS VI.ii.2.17).

Once we understand how Smith's "marketplace of morality" model operates, we can understand why this discussion of the "man of system" would be in TMS. In order for people to develop proper moral sentiments, there must be, as Smith puts it, "free communication of sentiments" (TMS VII.iv.28). Because people's situations, opportunities, preferences, and values change—and the flux is dynamic because people change in response to others' changes as well—no single set of moral sentiments or rules of etiquette, however fitting for a particular place or time, could be appropriate for all people or in all places:

> How is it possible to ascertain by rules the exact point at which, in every case, a delicate sense of justice begins to run into a frivolous and weak scrupulosity of conscience? When is it that secrecy and reserve begin to grow into dissimulation? How far an agreeable irony may be carried, and at what precise point it begins to degenerate into a detestable lie? What is the highest pitch of freedom and ease of behaviour which can be regarded as graceful and unbecoming, and when it is that it first begins to run into a negligent and thoughtless licentiousness? With regard to all such matters, what would hold good in any one case would scarce do so exactly in any other, and what constitutes the propriety and happiness of behaviour varies in every case with the smallest variety of situation. (TMS VII.iv.33)

Having stood the (relative) test of time justifies a set of standards enjoying a default position with presumptive, but not absolute, authority; similarly, the fact that a set of standards prevails in one's community—or in a community (even an imagined one) in which one would like to be a member—is a good reason to train oneself according to it. But it can provide no justification to prevent people who have reached moral maturity from changing their minds, exploring new things, or otherwise entrepreneurially experimenting with other ways of organizing their moral sentiments in efforts to become happy.

The Smithian moral theory tends, then, in the direction of decentralized, rather than centralized, systems of order. Even if Smith knows that people will make mistakes regarding their moral sentiments, he worries far more about the dangers of third-party interposition. The reason is not difficult to understand. Despite the real risks decentralized orders pose of allowing sentiments or behaviors to arise that we dislike or find objectionable, the good news is that decentralism also allows both competition and dissociation. If no single set of sentiments, preferences, values, or behaviors can be cemented into policy, people may choose not to associate with those who adopt sets they do not like.[8] And since everyone may similarly choose, what arises is a competition for the scarce but highly desired resource of mutual sympathy of sentiments.[9] If fewer and fewer people choose to associate with any given person, group, or community, fewer and fewer opportunities for mutual sympathy of sentiments arise; this acts as a natural disincentive for the person, group, or community to maintain its status quo, and as a natural incentive to change. A person's, and a community's, moral standards would retain, then, both the ability to exploit past discovery and at the same time a flexibility to adapt to changing circumstances. Smith's model captures, therefore, both the respect for tradition and the openness to innovation that characterize the most prosperous and humane—what Smith would have called "civilized"—human societies.

DECENTRALISM IN WN

Smith's *Wealth of Nations* employs the "market model" of decentralized decision making extensively, constituting perhaps Smith's most profound legacy to modern social science. Indeed, we find its first hints just three paragraphs into the thousand-page book.

According to Smith, the degree to which any country is "supplied with all the necessaries and conveniences for which it has occasion" depends on "the skill, dexterity, and judgment with which its labour is generally applied; and, secondly, by the proportion between the number of those who are employed in useful labour and that of those who are not so employed," and he claims further that the "abundance or scantiness of this supply too seems to depend more on the former of those circumstances than upon the latter" (WN Intro.2–4). But Smith's argument in the first chapter is that the enormous productive powers of the division of labor are owing to three main factors, one of which is "the invention of a great number of machines which facilitate and abridge labour, and enable one man to do the work of many" (WN I.i.5). This factor captures Smith's discovery that workers who focus on particular tasks will invent methods to economize their efforts—and, crucially, these inventions will not have been discoverable by someone not focusing on those particular tasks. A striking example Smith offers to make this point is that of a boy who discovered a mechanism for automatically opening and shutting a pressure valve on early fire engines; only someone focused on this particular task—but who, as Smith tells us, really wanted to be playing with his friends instead— would have discovered this time-saving technique (WN I.i.8). The increasing productivity that the division of labor enables, therefore, is possible only when individuals are allowed both to specialize and to capitalize on their locally gathered and unique knowledge. Since a community's relative level of prosperity depends on the degree to which division of labor takes place within it, Smith's argument holds that prosperity itself depends on decentralization.

Smith concludes his argument thus: "It is the great multiplication of the productions of all the different arts, in consequence of the division of labour, which occasions, in a well-governed society, that universal opulence which extends itself to the lowest ranks of the people" (WN I.i.10). How have those communities that have raised their estate, including the estate of the least among them, done so? By allowing the division of labor to flower and take its natural course, and by allowing people to exploit and capitalize on their localized skills and knowledge. Smith goes so far as to suggest that this marks the difference indeed between "civilized" and "savage" nations: it is only in the former that "the produce of the whole labour of the society is so great, that all are often abundantly supplied, and a workman, even of the lowest and poorest order, if he is frugal and industrious, may enjoy a greater share of the necessaries and conveniences of life than it is possible for any savage to acquire" (WN Intro.4).

Smith's larger argument in WN rests on three further claims.[10] First is his *Local Knowledge Argument* (LKA): because everyone has unique knowledge of his own "local situation"—including his skills, his schedule of value, and the opportunities available to him—each individual is therefore the person best positioned to make decisions about what courses of action he should take to achieve his goals. "What is the species of domestick industry which his capital can employ, and of which the produce is likely to be of the greatest value, every individual, it is evident, can, in his local situation, judge much better than any statesman or lawgiver can do for him" (WN IV.ii.10).[11] Second is Smith's *Economizer Argument* (EA), which holds that because humans by nature seek to better their own conditions, each of them is naturally led to seek out uses of resources and labor that will maximize their productive output: "The uniform, constant, and uninterrupted effort of every man to better his condition, the principle from which publick and national, as well as private opulence is originally derived, is frequently powerful enough to maintain the natural progress of things toward improvement, in spite both of the extravagance of government, and of the greatest errors of administration" (WN II.iii.31).[12] Finally, third, Smith's *Invisible Hand Argument* (IHA) holds that as each of us strives to better his condition by exploiting his unique reservoirs of knowledge, each of us thereby also, if unintentionally, betters the condition of others:

> As every individual, therefore, endeavours as much as he can . . . to direct [his] industry that its produce may be of the greatest value; every individual necessarily labours to render the annual revenue of the society as great as he can. He generally, indeed, neither intends to promote the public interest, nor knows how much he is promoting it. . . . [H]e intends only his own security; and by directing that industry in such a manner as its produce may be of the greatest value, he intends only his own gain, and he is in this, as in many other cases, led by an invisible hand to promote an end which was no part of his intention. (WN IV.ii.9)[13]

So we seek to achieve our purposes, whatever they are, but because we are economizers we strive to expend the least amount of energy possible while at the same time trying to get the most extensive achievement of our goals possible. When we concentrate our efforts on some small range of tasks or talents, we develop specialized skills and exploit our local knowledge to produce more than we can ourselves consume or use. That means we create a surplus that we can trade or sell away—which, in turn, means that the overall stock of goods and services increases, and their prices thus decrease, for everyone. In addition, as we seek out cooperative labor opportunities, exchanges, forms of contract and trade, and so on that better serve our ends, others may learn from our successes and failures, thereby enabling them to go marginally further in securing their own—and thus, indirectly, others'—ends. According to Smith, then, the "invisible hand" effects a "general plenty," a "universal opulence which extends itself to the lowest ranks of the people" (WN I.i.10). What Smith then describes as "the obvious and simple system of natural liberty" (WN IV.ix.51) is a society-wide allowance of the invisible-hand mechanism to operate:

> All systems either of preference or of restraint, therefore, being thus completely taken away, the obvious and simple system of natural liberty establishes itself of its own accord. Every man, as long as he does not violate the laws of justice, is left perfectly free to pursue his own interest his own way, and to bring both his industry and capital into competition with those of any other man, or order of men. The sovereign is completely discharged from a duty, in the attempting to perform which he must always be exposed to innumerable delusions, and for the proper performance of which no human wisdom or knowledge could ever be sufficient; the duty of superintending the industry of private people, and of directing it towards the employments most suitable to the interest of the society. (WN IV.ix.51)[14]

The LKA, EA, and IHA thus form an integrated foundation for a decentralized Smithian political economy. Smith summarized its policy implications in two key passages. First is his "man of system" passage in TMS, already discussed. The second comes directly after the "invisible hand" passage in WN: "The statesman, who should attempt to direct private people in what manner they ought to employ their capitals, would not only load himself with a most unnecessary attention, but assume an authority which could safely be trusted, not only to no single person, but to no council or senate whatever, and which would nowhere be so dangerous as in the hands of a man who had folly and presumption enough to fancy himself fit to exercise it" (WN IV.ii.10). The statesman's attention is "unnecessary" because, as Smith has demonstrated, people's decentralized strivings to better their conditions are more likely to succeed than centralized attempts because the former exploit local knowledge and natural motivation that the latter cannot. Thus what the statesman would (or should) wish to achieve—bettering people's conditions—is more likely to happen if he does little beyond maintaining a "regular administration of justice" (WN IV.vii.b.2). The "folly and presumption" of the statesman is manifested in his false assumption that he can gather and process all the relevant information of people's changing circumstances, opportunities, schedules of value, and so on required to direct their activities as well as, let alone better than, they themselves can.[15] And this mistaken belief is "dangerous" because, Smith suggests, it often leads statesmen to impose, or attempt to impose, their plan for society coercively—with predictably negative results.

CENTRALISM IN SMITH?

I conclude that Smith's political economy is best understood as decentralist and thus on the political right (so defined). Yet those who see centralism in Smith and thus claim him for the progressive left adduce several reasons in support of their position. These reasons include:

1. Smith is genuinely concerned for the poor in society (WN Intro.4 and passim);
2. Smith is committed not only to a form of moral equality—that is, to viewing each human being as equally deserving of moral

respect (e.g., TMS II.ii.2.1 and TMS III.3.6)—but also to a belief in rough equality of natural human ability (e.g., WN I.ii.4);

3. Smith claims that "it is but equity" that laborers too be "tolerably well fed, cloathed and lodged" (WN I.viii.36);

4. Smith criticizes merchants and businessmen for regularly engaging in conspiracies against the public welfare (e.g., WN I.viii.13 and WN I.x.c.27);

5. Smith argues that if division of labor is allowed to continue to the extremes enabled by markets it will have deleterious effects on workers (WN V.i.f.50), and he suggests public funding for education as a partial remedy (WN V.i.f.55–61);

6. One of the three main duties of government, according to Smith, is to attend to "publick works" that are, while necessary for the good of society, nevertheless not provided by private enterprise (WN IV.ix.51);

7. Smith allows that intruding on people's "natural liberty" is sometimes required for the common good (e.g., WN II.ii.94; cp. TMS II.ii.1.7–8);

8. When discussing tax policy, Smith writes that "[t]he subjects of every state ought to contribute towards the support of the government, as nearly as possible, in proportion to their respective abilities" (WN V.ii.b.3).

Space does not allow a comprehensive discussion of these claims, but a few words about them will indicate why they do not suffice to mark Smith as a left-progressive.

The first three claims above regard, in one way or another, equality, which many consider to be the provenance of the left.[16] Yet concern for the poor, as expressed in claim 1, is of course present among people on both (or all) sides of the political spectrum.[17] Claim 2, moreover, does not suggest a desire for *material* equality, or equality of *resources*, which left-progressivism requires. And the Smithian concern for equal agency that would justify a decentralist political economy is quite consistent with claim 3, insofar as it requires a respect for the agency—as exemplified in the localized decisions and valuations—of everyone equally, including also the laboring class.

Regarding claim 4, Smith argues that the danger arises specifically when merchants and businessmen enlist politicians in their efforts—in other words, when government grants special favors, protections, subsidies, monopolies, charters, and so on to preferred people or firms. The solution, Smith suggests, is not to construct a (centralized) governmental apparatus to counteract the deleterious effects of politically motivated business/state partnerships—since that would fall prey to precisely the baleful rent-seeking dynamics he describes—but, rather, not to allow such partnerships in the first place. Thus he recommends that we forbid government interference in such matters and instead let the (decentralized) free market operate.[18]

The next three claims—5, 6, and 7—are all places Smith suggests that some central authority might be justified in interposing in otherwise decentralized market exchanges or private behavior.[19] Yet in each Smith goes to great lengths to hedge that central authority. When Smith suggests, for example, that "[f]or a very small expence the publick can facilitate, can encourage, and can even impose upon almost the whole body of the people, the necessity of acquiring those most essential parts of education" (WN V.i.f.54), some take this as left-progressive support for public education. But Smith explains that (1) he means educating only to "read, write, and account," which requires only elementary education (not middle or high school, let alone college) (WN V.i.f.54 and passim); (2) to ensure proper alignment of incentives, the public subsidy is to constitute *less than half* of the expense (WN V.i.f.55); and (3) wherever possible, private education is to be preferred to public: "Those parts of education, it is to be observed, for the teaching of which there are no publick institutions, are generally the best taught. . . . The three most essential parts of literary education, to read, write, and account, it still continues to be more common to acquire in private than in publick schools; and it very seldom happens that anybody fails in acquiring them to the degree in which it is necessary to acquire them" (WN V.i.f.16).[20]

Similarly, when Smith suggests that one of the three principal duties of government is that "of erecting and maintaining certain publick works" (WN IV.ix.51), some take this as indicating a perhaps generalized support for public goods,[21] which they associate with left-progressive politics.[22] Yet note the criteria Smith claims are requisite for a "publick work" to warrant state provision: the good must be both (1) "in the highest degree advantageous to a great society"—that is, it must benefit (substantially) everyone in the community, not merely one group at the expense of others; and (2) "of such a nature, that the profit could never repay the expence to any individual or small number of individuals," and therefore would not be provided by private free enterprise (WN V.i.c.1). One might wonder just how many goods would satisfy both those criteria. Given the enormous, and unpredictable, productive powers of commercial society, it might turn out to be few indeed. In any case, Smith goes on to argue that what do qualify as proper "publick works" are "always better maintained by a local or provincial revenue, under the management of a local and provincial administration, than by the general revenue of the state" (WN V.i.d.18; cp. WN V.i.d.1).

That leaves us with claim 8, about taxation. The passage quoted above is the first of Smith's four "maxims with regard to taxes in general" (WN V.ii.b.2). As Smith makes clear in his subsequent discussion, the Smithian government has few (if important) duties, and it therefore requires relatively little revenue from taxation. Moreover, the tax burdens he envisions are not only small but apparently not in the service of charitable activities like poverty relief, old-age pensions, or other redistributive activities typically associated with left-progressivism.[23] There seems, furthermore, no indication in WN that Smith believes taxation should fund government efforts at reducing, or even addressing, material inequality— perhaps the central defining feature of left-progressivism. A recent account of left-progressivism defines "justice" as requiring the state to "guarantee that property is distributed throughout society so that everyone is supplied with a certain level of material means."[24] By contrast, Smith's definition of justice is "negative"—that is, providing only for protection of life, property, and voluntary contract (TMS II.ii.2.2). Since one of Smith's principal concerns is to relieve the misery and suffering of the poor—as suggested, for example, when he claims that "[i]t is but equity, besides, that they who feed, cloath and lodge the whole body of the people, should have such a share of the produce of their own labour as to be themselves tolerably well fed, cloathed and lodged" (WN I.viii.36), he must have intended to address it in a way other than through centralized government transfer or redistribution. The means Smith intends, therefore, is through the prosperity enabled and encouraged by decentralized commercial activity within the confines of markets protected by governments limited primarily to protecting negative justice. This is what Smith has argued, and believes, will lead to the "universal opulence" and "general plenty diffuses itself through all the different ranks of the society" (WN I.i.10). Smith's claim about "equity" can then be seen as an additional reason to favor his "system of natural liberty": the fact that laborers too will enjoy increasing standards of living also matters, since laborers matter too.

Finally, regarding Smith's endorsement of proportional taxation, Smith believes he has demonstrated the "impossibility of taxing the people, in proportion to their revenue, by any capitation" (WN V.ii.k.1). If taxation by capitation is impossible, however, how could we achieve a proportional taxation that tracks the "revenue which [citizens] respectively enjoy under the protection of the state" (WN V.ii.b.3)? There might be several ways, but what is clear is what Smith's argument *disallows*—namely, progressive (or any other) *income* taxation. Thus by "proportional" taxes Smith must mean taxes requiring people who spend more or buy more to pay more taxes. Possible methods of Smithian taxation might include, then, a value-added tax, a sales tax, user fees (which Smith discusses approvingly),[25] or some combination of these. But perhaps the hallmark of left-progressive political policy, the progressive income tax, is disallowed, making even more dubious any attempt to marshal Smith in support of a left-progressive political program.

CONCLUSION: WHO OWNS ADAM SMITH?

I regard Smith's single most important contribution to social science to be his suggestion that complicated and successful systems of social order can arise without any overall designer. He thought this explained the development of moral sentiments, of means of economic production and exchange, and of language. His discovery, moreover, of the implications of the fact that humans have only limited and localized knowledge, and that all humans are roughly equal in their abilities to develop skills and knowledge requisite to their ends (and would do so if allowed),[26] led him to conclude that third parties, including the state, need do little for people other than give them the opportunity to act according to their own lights and to take responsibility for the consequences, positive or negative, of their actions. People's natural desires for mutual sympathy of sentiments and to better their own conditions largely take care of the rest. He is willing to allow that there might be cases in which the state should take on duties beyond those of the night watchman, but the default is against such interventions, and the burden of proof falls on those recommending them to show why an exception should be made. And while Smith is quite skeptical of centralized institutional attempts at improving others' lives, he seems optimistic that under the conditions of "regular administration of justice" people's decentralized pursuits will steadily improve their lives.

How, then, should we categorize Smith? Smith's government is certainly not nonexistent, but by modern standards it is quite small, and it leaves to individuals, rather than to centralized authorities, the freedom and responsibility to direct their lives. I would therefore call Smith a skeptical and empirical *decentralist*, in the tradition of classical, not progressive, liberalism. His project was a serious and open-ended investigation into the moral, economic, political, and cultural institutions that lead to human prosperity. He called himself a "moral philosopher": that seems about right.

NOTES

I thank Ryan Hanley for his many helpful suggestions and criticisms on an earlier draft of this chapter. All remaining mistakes are mine.

1. Smith's discussion of sympathy and fairness, as well as his general position in the "sentimentalist" camp, have inclined some commentators to redefine his place in moral philosophy as well. See, for example, Amartya Sen, *The Idea of Justice* (Cambridge, MA: 2011).

2. See, for example, James M. Buchanan, *The Limits of Liberty* (Indianapolis: 2000 [1975]) and Friedrich A. Hayek, *The Constitution of Liberty* (Chicago: 2011 [1960]).

3. See, for example, Samuel Fleischacker, *A Third Concept of Liberty* (Princeton: 1999), *A Short History of Distributive Justice* (Cambridge, MA: 2005), and *On Adam Smith's* Wealth of Nations: *A Philosophical Companion* (Princeton: 2004); and Emma Rothschild, "Adam Smith and Conservative Economics," *Economic History Review* 16, no. 1 (1992), pp. 74–96, and *Economic Sentiments* (Cambridge, MA: 2002). For general discussion, see Craig Smith, "Adam Smith: Left or Right?," *Political Studies* 61, no. 4 (2013), pp. 784–98.

4. See, for example, Ronald L. Meek, "Smith, Turgot, and the 'Four Stages' Theory," *History of Political Economy* 3, no. 1 (1971), pp. 9–27; and Murray Rothbard, *An Austrian Perspective on the History of Economic Thought,* 2 vols. (Cheltenham: 1995).

5. James R. Otteson, *Adam Smith's Marketplace of Life* (Cambridge: 2002).

6. See Otteson, *Adam Smith* (London: 2013). See also Fonna Forman Barzilai, *Adam Smith and the Circles of Sympathy* (Cambridge: 2011) and Ryan Patrick Hanley, *Adam Smith and the Character of Virtue* (Cambridge: 2009).

7. See Lauren Brubaker, "Why Adam Smith Is Neither a Conservative Nor a Libertarian," *Adam Smith Review* 2 (2006), pp. 197–202. See also Smith on tempering religious enthusiasm, WN V.i.g.8.

8. Many passages in TMS reflect this part of Smith's argument. It is, for example, the implication of his discussion of laughter and joke telling, in which he examines the differing judgments people make about what is an appropriate joke to tell and what not (see, e.g., TMS I.i.2). Another example is when Smith remarks that the "philosopher is company to a philosopher only; the member of a club, to his own little knot of companions" (TMS II.ii.2.6). A third example is Smith's discussion of the fact that "[e]very individual is naturally more attached to his own particular order or society, than to any other" (TMS VI.ii.2.7).

9. Smith's account is actually quite Darwinian—as Darwin himself noticed. See Charles Darwin, *The Descent of Man, and Selection in Relation to Sex* (Princeton: 1981 [1871]), pt. 1, chap. 3. See also Jerry Evensky, *Adam Smith's Moral Philosophy* (Cambridge: 2005).

10. See Otteson, *Adam Smith*, chap. 6.

11. Other statements of the LKA can be found throughout WN. See, for example, WN I.i.8, IV.v.b.16, IV.v.b.25, and IV.ix.51.

12. The EA can be found throughout WN. See, for example, WN I.i.8, I.vii.44, I.x.c.14, II.i.30, II.iii.28, II.iii.31, II.v.37, III.iii.12, IV.ii.4, IV.ii.8, IV.v.b.43, IV.ix.28, and V.i.b.18. See also LJA vi.145.

13. Smith repeats variants of this argument throughout WN as well. See, for example, WN Intro.8, II.intro.4, II.iii.39, IV.ii.4, IV.v.b.25, and IV.vii.c.88. For discussion, see G. Kennedy, *Adam Smith: A Moral Philosopher and His Political Economy* (London: 2008); E. Rothschild, *Economic Sentiments: Adam Smith, Condorcet, and the Enlightenment* (Cambridge, MA: 2001); and C. Smith, *Adam Smith's Political Philosophy: The Invisible Hand and Spontaneous Order* (London: 2006).

14. In his 1793 *Account of the Life and Writings of Adam Smith, LL.D.*, Smith's student Dugald Stewart speaks of a manuscript of Smith's, now unfortunately lost, that Stewart reports as stating, "Little else is requisite to carry a state to the highest degree of opulence from the lowest barbarism, but peace,

easy taxes, and a tolerable administration of justice; all the rest being brought about by the natural course of things. All governments which thwart this natural course, which force things into another channel, or which endeavour to arrest the progress of society at a particular point, are unnatural, and to support themselves are obliged to be oppressive and tyrannical" (Stewart IV.25).

15. Cf. Hayek, *The Fatal Conceit* (Chicago: 1991), chap. 5 and *The Constitution of Liberty*, chaps. 1 and 2. See also Otteson, "Adam Smith and the Great Mind Fallacy," *Social Philosophy and Policy* 27, no. 1 (January 2010), pp. 276–304.

16. See, e.g., Michael Newman, *Socialism: A Very Short Introduction* (Oxford: 2005).

17. As Fleischacker ("Adam Smith on Equality," in *The Oxford Handbook of Adam Smith*, ed. Christopher J. Berry, Maria Pia Paganelli, and Craig Smith [Oxford: 2013], pp. 485–99) and before him Sen (*Inequality Reexamined* [Cambridge, MA: 1992]) have pointed out, a call for equality—of one sort or another—has been a part of much, even most, moral and political theory.

18. See, for example, WN I.vii.26–30, I.x.c.30–31, I.xi.b.5–9, IV.viii.17, IV.vii.c.88–99, IV.ix.17–28, and IV.ix.50–51.

19. See Smith, "Adam Smith: Left or Right?"

20. See also WN V.i.f.4, V.i.f.12, and V.i.g.8.

21. I use "public goods" here not in the technical, modern sense of goods that are both nonexcludable and nonrivalrous, but, rather, in the more common (nontechnical) sense of goods that benefit many people or are generally beneficial to society.

22. Fleischacker speculates that were he alive today Smith might recommend state-mandated pollution standards, mandatory 5 percent of lifetime earnings paid by companies to any of their workers they fire, a mandatory "bicameral form of governance" for corporations "in which one chamber would consist of employee representatives along with representatives of the communities in which firms are located, while the other chamber continue[s] to consist of stockholders" (*On Adam Smith's* Wealth of Nations, pp. 273–79).

23. Smith elsewhere mentions approvingly that private entities have often provided "pensions, scholarships, exhibitions, bursaries, &c." (WN I.x.c.34).

24. Samuel Fleischacker, *A Short History of Distributive Justice* (Cambridge, MA: 2004), p. 4.

25. See, for example, WN V.i.d.3 and V.i.e.3.

26. See David M. Levy and Sandra J. Peart, *The "Vanity of the Philosopher": From Equality to Hierarchy in Post-Classical Economics* (Ann Arbor, MI: 2005).

BIBLIOGRAPHIC ESSAY

How to characterize Smith's political philosophy has been the subject of many treatments for some time. For a classic account, see Jacob Viner, "Adam Smith and Laissez Faire," *Journal of Political Economy* 35 (1927), pp. 198–232. For more recent accounts that question Smith's categorization as a liberal capitalist, see Donald Winch, *Adam Smith's Politics* (Cambridge: 1978) and Ronald L. Meek, "Smith, Turgot, and the 'Four Stages' Theory," *History of Political Economy* 3 (1971), pp. 9–27. Meek goes so far as to consider Smith a proto-Marxist. Samuel Fleischacker's *A Third Concept of Liberty* (Princeton: 1999) and *On Adam Smith's* Wealth of Nations (Princeton: 2005) argue that Smith is a progressive, not classical, liberal; and Emma Rothschild's *Economic Sentiments* (Cambridge, MA: 2001) similarly questions the attempt to claim Smith for the conservative right. On the other side of the ledger, Craig Smith's *Adam Smith's Political Philosophy* (London: 2006) argues that Smith should be seen as an early part of the Hayekian spontaneous-order classical liberal tradition. James R. Otteson's *Actual Ethics* (Cambridge: 2006) attempts to use Smith in partial defense of a classical liberal political economy. Gavin Kennedy's *Adam Smith* (London: 2008) places Smith in his own context and relates him to contemporary debates concerning free trade and globalization. Dennis C. Rasmussen's *The Problems and Promise of Commercial Society* (University Park, PA: 2009) reviews Smith's Rousseauvian worries about the commercial society, and Ryan Patrick Hanley's *Adam Smith and the Character of Virtue* (Cambridge: 2009) examines Smith's concerns about the nature of virtue in capitalist society.

ADAM SMITH IN CHINA: FROM IDEOLOGY TO ACADEMIA

Luo Wei-Dong

The publication of the first Chinese version of WN under the title *Yuan Fu* (The Origin of Wealth) in 1901 brought Adam Smith into China. More than a century has passed since then, during which the status Smith has occupied in the spiritual world of the Chinese has been quite singular. Unlike philosophers such as Kant and Hume, Smith has always been positioned somewhere between two polarities, that is, ideology and academia. In most cases, the interpretations of Smith's thought have been shaped by ideology, with his real message largely neglected until recently.

The very beginning of the introduction of Smith's works into China determined Smith's fortune in China. The first Chinese version of WN titled *Yuan Fu* was translated by the social reformer and great thinker Yan Fu. Yet there are numerous substantive deviations between this Chinese version and the original English version. It would be absurd to attribute such a lack of correspondence to the low-level English proficiency of the translator. A more reasonable explanation is that this translation is based on Yan Fu's own interpretation of WN. To be more specific, *Yuan Fu* is not a translation of WN, but rather a translation mixed with Yan Fu's own commentary. The criterion Yan Fu employed to choose what works should be introduced into China was his personal judgment of the primary demands of the social and political reform of the late Qing dynasty. To him, what the Chinese, especially the intellectuals and the statesmen, needed most was exposure to advanced Western doctrines on society, politics, and economy that would serve to enlighten the masses and empower the country. According to this criterion, the works of Western thinkers such as Montesquieu, Adam Smith, John Stuart Mill, Thomas Henry Huxley, and Herbert Spencer were emphasized, which also reflected Yan Fu's holistic thinking on the future aims of Chinese society. Behind such a practice was the basis of a careful comparison between China and the West, which was an explicit focus of *Yuan Fu*. In retrospect, among all these Western scholars Yan Fu admired, it was only Smith who has been closely intertwined with the continuous political and social transformations of Chinese society. To some extent, the image of Smith in Yan Fu's mind heralds Smith's image in China for the next more than one hundred years. It was through Yan Fu that Smith began his journey in China.

ADAM SMITH AS A PIONEER OF MARXISM

It is well known that the foundation of the PRC on October 1, 1949, brought China a new regime that adopted Marxism for its ideological guidance. This ideological guidance however, went well beyond pure Marxism and in fact presented a fascinating hybrid of refined Marxism (that of the former Soviet Union, with Leninism and Stalinism as its core), and the unique ideology of Chinese revolutionaries, which embraced both a traditional Chinese perception of the relationship between people and government that had gradually evolved over thousands of years, as well as the views on life and social order characteristic of rural Chinese (the lowest level of Chinese society).

In the first years of its foundation, the new regime largely followed the example of the former Soviet Union on issues ranging from economic planning to government organization. At that time, a large number of Russian experts and consultants were sent from the former Soviet Union to provide China with guidance and suggestions until the breakdown in relations between the two countries that occurred in July 1960.

Against this background, Chinese intellectual circles were greatly influenced by the former Soviet Union as well. A great deal of Russian academic literature was translated into Chinese, and the Soviets were employed in educational institutions as lecturers and advisors.

The ensuing consequence was that the first generation of scholars in New China were effectively cultivated by the former Soviet Union. The emergence of these scholars brought several results. First, Stalinized Marxism dominated Chinese academia, and was regarded as the basic academic philosophy and methodology. Second, Russian served as the main foreign language for Chinese scholars to communicate with international intellectual circles, which established an almost complete rupture between Chinese academia and academia in the English-speaking countries. In the same vein, those scholars who were educated in Anglo-American countries and had a good command of the relevant scholarly literature in English found themselves easily marginalized and were even forced to leave academia.

After the deterioration in bilateral relations between China and the former Soviet Union, efforts were made to eliminate Soviet influence. Its basic temperament, shaped by the Soviets, however, did not undergo a complete transformation until the end of the 1970s. Academic studies were still shaped by a strong sense of political ideology with the government authority's ideological education as the primary purpose to observe. Such a situation continued until the launch of the reform and opening up of China at the end of 1978.

During these three decades, how was Adam Smith received in Mainland China? Owing to the influence of the scholars of the former Soviet Union, especially Д.И.Розенберг, the only resource for Chinese scholars to learn Adam Smith's thoughts was from the relevant comments of Karl Marx in his *Theoretical History of Surplus Value*. In this work, and particularly in its chapter on "Adam Smith and the Concept of Productive Labor," Marx spends hundreds of pages citing and commenting on WN. Smith is significant for Marx for two reasons. On the one hand, Smith is the founder of progressive bourgeois classical political economy, which directly inspired David Ricardo's labor theory of value. Marx's "scientific" labor theory, and in particular his theory of surplus value, in turn, was built upon and developed directly from that of Ricardo. In this sense, Smith was regarded as the academic predecessor of Ricardo, which draws positive evaluation from Marx. On the other hand, Smith's doctrine is also regarded as the origin of philistine bourgeois economic theory. This theory was further developed by

Thomas Robert Malthus and Jean Baptiste Say into a full-fledged system to account for and defend the capitalist economic system in general and the economic activities and interests of the bourgeoisie in particular. Marx of course dedicated his life to fighting these errors. In a nutshell, Adam Smith is regarded by Marx as the creator of a controversial economic theory, the "correct" elements of which should be accepted and developed, and the "incorrect" elements of which should be rejected and discarded.

Розенберг's *Theoretical History of Political Economy* could be regarded as a further illustration of Marx's *Theoretical History of Surplus Value*, and its structure and content were adjusted to be suitable to serve as a textbook. Its significance for how Smith was understood in China has not been sufficiently appreciated, however. Розенберг's textbook was so influential on later Chinese textbooks—including the textbook of my college years, *The Theoretical History of Economy*, edited by Lu Youzhang and Li Zongzheng—that they simply followed suit, introducing and commenting on Smith's doctrine merely under the framework constructed by Marx. No significant breakthrough for the study of Adam Smith was achieved during this period.

ADAM SMITH AS AN ECONOMIC LIBERAL

The year 1979 witnessed the unfolding of a new stage in economic development in China. A decision was issued by China's central government to be free of the influence of Marxist fundamentalism (especially the economic and political model of Stalinism) and develop an economic development pattern with Chinese characteristics. This breathed new life and vitality into Chinese society. Academic studies in China began to flourish to an unprecedented extent. Although Marxism was still regarded as the official guiding principle for academic studies, more reflections and criticisms on the old political institution and economic system were voiced. Marxist fundamentalism seemed to be waning.

During this period, the growth of the free market and the decentralization of property rights quickened its pace. This growth looked to theoretical resources other than Marxism for support. Chinese intellectual circles, especially in the field of economics, turned to the revolutionary theories of the former Soviet Union and other socialist countries in Eastern Europe for new insights, owing to the political risks of directly borrowing economic theories from Western countries. As a result, the academic literature of Eastern European scholars such as Ota Sik, Bruce, and Janos Kornai, came to be introduced into China. Kornai, having vainly sought theoretical support from Marxism, created his own economic concepts distinct from those of Marxism, hoping to account for the phenomenon of the coexistence of great surplus and extreme shortage. In the 1980s, Kornai's theory became so prevalent in China that his work *Shortage Economics* was a must-read for economists of the young generation, yet his economic system soon turned out to be just a flash in the pan, possibly because economic theories such as Kornai's were still constructed under the guidance of Marxist ideology, and failed to lend theoretical support to the in-depth reform occurring in China at that time.

The new generation of Chinese economists came to realize that it was impossible to find a theoretical base for competition-oriented socialist economic systems within the Marxist tradition. What the reform in China needed was the theory of price and market competition. As a consequence, a great deal of scholarship on economic libertarianism began to be introduced into China. *Free to Choose: A Personal Statement* by Milton and Rose Friedman was translated into Chinese in 1982, and the next year *Prosperity through Competition* by the German statesman and economist Ludwig Wilhelm Erhard was also published in large circulation by the Commercial Press. *Can Capitalism Survive?* by the famous liberal theorist Benjamin Rogge was also later translated into Chinese. Through these works, Chinese scholars came to understand the theoretical contributions Adam Smith had made to the free market economic system. China was in urgent need of such theoretical support, and Adam Smith, as the founder of economic liberalism, attracted significant attention.

In the first half of the 1990s, many studies were carried out in Chinese intellectual circles on the working principles and institutional framework of the market economy and commercial society. Adam Smith's concept of the invisible hand in WN drew the attention of numerous economists who were enchanted by the notion that the invisible hand or free exchange and competition could coordinate the actions of self-interested people and in effect promote the public welfare of the whole society. Such a proposition was totally foreign to most Chinese scholars, and many simply regarded it as a target for criticism. Chinese scholars turned for further insight on such questions not to Smith himself but to textbooks on neoclassical price theory introduced from English-speaking countries. During this period, Chinese economists came to agree that the price theory of neoclassical economy was the systematic specification of Adam Smith's concept of the invisible hand, both of which are in full consonance with each other. In this sense, economists of the Austrian School (such as Hayek) and the Chicago School could be regarded as the legitimate inheritors of Adam Smith's liberalism.

In this period of time, however, a paradoxical phenomenon was at work: while some scholars were doing academic textual research on Smith's theory of value under the old-patterned Marxist theoretical framework, other public intellectuals more concerned about social reality simply abandoned Smith's texts and employed all available media to illustrate and propagandize the concept of laissez-faire, even though they themselves had not given WN a serious reading. What they cared about was not what Smith actually said or intended to say, but rather how to symbolize and exploit Adam Smith as a father of laissez-faire in order to publicize the concept of the free economy for the benefits of economical development. Of course this was again ideological interpretation, but of a totally different kind.

ADAM SMITH AS AN ETHICIST

Deeply immersed in traditional Confucian political ethics and socialist ideology, the Chinese retain a ubiquitous doubt toward and even a vague fear of the moral framework of market economy.

In the spring of 1992, dissatisfied with the speed of the reform of the Chinese economic system, Deng Xiaoping, already in his advanced years, paid an inspection visit to the southern part of China and made a famous speech calling for even greater reforms. In the wake of this event, the pace of the construction of the free market economic system quickened, including the opening of a stock market that year, as well as price deregulation and release of consumption goods and some important capital goods. The degree of freedom and vitality of the Chinese economy increased, with more private enterprises allowed to enter the public field.

On the other hand, various problems caused by economic liberalization severely undermined the confidence of Chinese society in the free market system, such as the rationalization of certain highly selfish behaviors and the polarization of income distribution. Almost all spheres of Chinese life were influenced by the mechanism of price, including fields like human emotion and various kinds of public affairs, which traditional social ethical norms regarded as immune from such an effect. The specter of free exchange and price adjustment was haunting nearly all the spheres of politics, economics, and medicine. As a result, the traditional ethical system was challenged.

The rise of commercial society has been welcomed by entrepreneurs, but feared by the common people and the intellectuals. It has given rise to a kind of moral anxiety over the whole society. Quite a few people hold that those economic liberals like Smith who introduced the concept of the self-interested rational agent bear an inescapable responsibility for the moral corruption of Chinese society. Fundamentalist free economic liberalism, they argue, should be reexamined and a sound moral basis should be set up in order to promote a healthier free market economic system. Against this background, Chinese academia as well as the central government started to concentrate on the relationship between the market economic system and ethics and behavior. Around 1995, a number of symposia on the construction of the moral framework of the market economy were held in China, mainly by those other than economists. In the field of economics, only a few scholars with humanistic propensities were interested in this topic.

The publication of the Chinese version of TMS in 1997 greatly impacted not only Chinese intellectual circles but also the public. To a certain extent, the publication ushered in a new stage of Chinese scholarship on Smith. During this new stage, the focus of study shifted from WN to TMS. In the decade from 1995 to 2005, Chinese scholars made considerable efforts to explore Smith's moral philosophy and the proper relationship between TMS and WN. Smith's views on human nature, his understanding of economic behavior and ethical requirements, and his moral philosophy have become hot academic topics. A large literature aiming to restore a comprehensive image of Adam Smith in China has emerged.

Another related tendency in academic studies has been to regard Adam Smith as an ethicist, and specifically as one whose theory could meet the psychological demands of various groups within Chinese society. The crucial point is that the image of Adam Smith as an ethicist conforms to the value system of Confucianism. The comparison between Smith's "sympathy" and Chinese ancient Confucianism's *ren* (仁) has been carried out, with the famous Confucian philosopher Du Weiming as the representative. As early as 2005, Zhejiang University held a symposium on "Adam Smith and China" in Hangzhou. One of the topics covered is the intrinsic relationship between Smith's ideas and *ren* theory of Confucianism.

Another example could be invoked here to prove how popular Adam Smith as an ethicist is in China. In the wake of Premier Wen Jiabao's recommendations of Smith's TMS in 2005, the number of Chinese versions of TMS published in recent years in Mainland China reached as high as twenty-four, together with another four simplified versions with either Chinese notes or reading guidance. In addition, there are as many as thirty-seven Chinese versions of WN. They far exceed the number of Chinese versions of even the works of Marx and Kant.

ADAM SMITH AS AN ENLIGHTENMENT THINKER

Market-oriented reforms have resulted in a series of chain reactions, some of which have been quite negative. Severe political, social, and psychological problems have emerged. After thirty years of trial and error, the Chinese have come to regard society as an organic unity with its own history and to think that any attempts to reform it should be part of a comprehensive project. The importance of historical tradition should never be neglected. A unidirectional and one-sided institution design without taking history into consideration could never help a country to fulfill its vision. As a highly complex country with a long historical tradition, China poses a great challenge to scholars of the dual characteristics of social evolution, that is, reform and inheritance, as well as the dynamic interaction between different synchronic factors. French Enlightenment theorists thus cannot provide all the nutrients that the transformation and development of China needs. Adam Smith, as a representative scholar of the Scottish Enlightenment, has thus drawn attention from Chinese scholars in this context as well.

Since 2006, Zhejiang University has been organizing dozens of scholars to study the important works of the Scottish Enlightenment in a systematic fashion, and an annual academic seminar has been held with a relatively specific theme for each seminar. It is hoped that such comprehensive study of the Scottish Enlightenment, and of Adam Smith in particular, will provide further insights into the transformation and development of China from the perspectives of the intellectual history of Western society and through cultural comparisons. In the meantime, Zhejiang University Press has published a series of translations of the works of the towering thinkers of the Scottish Enlightenment, including Francis Hutcheson, David Hume, Thomas Reid, and Adam Ferguson, whose works used to be unduly neglected in China. Some important literature on the research of Adam Smith and the Scottish Enlightenment has been published as well in recent years, including Knud Haakonssen's *The Science of a Legislator: The Natural Jurisprudence of David Hume and Adam Smith* and Istvan Hont and Michael Ignatieff's *Wealth and Virtue: The Shaping of Political Economy in the Scottish Enlightenment*, to name just two. The works of other famous scholars, including Joseph Cropsey, Patricia H. Werhane, Donald Winch, and Emma Rothschild, have also been translated and published by other Chinese publishing houses.

In this academic environment, the richness and profundity of Adam Smith's thoughts have begun to unfold. Adam Smith, as an Enlightenment thinker, is not only an important figure in Western intellectual history, but also an influential one in the transformation of Western society. There are profound and intrinsic connections between Smith's thoughts and the philosophy of late Greece and Rome. His valuable attempts to construct a theoretical framework to grasp the whole structure of society provide modern China with inspiring insights.

To interpret Adam Smith from the perspective of enlightenment could contribute to eradicating the ideological mist shrouding Smith and to establishing a more comprehensive and accurate image of his thought.

ADAM SMITH AS A BEHAVIORAL SCIENTIST

The rise of behavioral economics and experimental economics has given impetus to the development of new research in these fields. Smith made certain claims about human judgment, decision making and behavior in TMS that have aroused the interest of Chinese scientists. In recent years, behavioral scientists have made efforts to prove the important propositions put forward by Smith through laboratory experiments, and to emphasize those parts of his theory that could be made scientific. The experimental study of game strategies done by the Social Science Laboratory of Zhejiang University has drawn great attention at home and abroad, and some experiments on the function of sympathy in moral judgment and moral practice are in full swing. Neuroscience experiments are also being employed to study phenomena described by Smith, including several fMRI empirical studies on the neurological basis of sympathy. These studies may further adjust and consolidate the human nature hypothesis, the cornerstone for the social sciences, and thereby further promote innovation in the social sciences.

That Smith is now being regarded as a behavioral scientist is an indicator of the extent to which Smith scholarship in China has now transcended ideology. Of course, much recent research has also focused on Smith's economic doctrines, including research on top-ics ranging from division of labor, capital, trade, distribution of income, and national revenue to Smith's status in the history of economic thought. Deserving particular mention are the studies carried out by Chinese scholars on Smith's theory of division of labor and its application in China in order to achieve long-term economic growth. The late Yang Xiaokai developed the Smith-Young Theorem from a pure theoretical perspective and founded the Ultra Marginal Economics Analysis School, with the aim of developing a new economic growth theory capable of replacing mainstream neoclassical economic growth theory.

Beyond moral philosophy and economics, scholarship on Smith in China is also being developed in such fields as sociology, govern-ment, education, military studies, jurisprudence, and history. How-ever, compared to studies of Smith in economics and philosophy, these fields are much smaller.

THE WANING OF IDEOLOGICAL COLOR AND THE RISING OF ACADEMIC STUDIES

Smith's entry into China over the course of the past century has been strongly ideologically colored. In recent decades, such ideo-logical color has begun to fade and more exploration of the "facts" from the perspectives of history and careful textual study has been carried out.

Overall, Smith has clearly drawn more and more attention from mainland China in recent years. As mentioned above, by 2013 more than thirty Chinese versions of TMS had been produced. Also the Chinese version of the scholarly edition of TMS will be published very soon. The number of the Chinese versions of WN is even more amazing: in less than ten years since 2006, at least thirty-seven Chinese versions have been published.

Another indicator of Smith's popularity in China is the publica-tion of his biography. As early as 1983, Hu Qilin and his collab-orators translated John Rae's *Life of Adam Smith* into Chinese. Within a month, the Chinese version of Dugald Stewart's *Account of the Life and Writings of Adam Smith* was published. For twenty years these biographies were the main sources for Chinese studies of Smith, though now the Chinese versions of biographies written by D. D. Raphael, James Buchan, and Gavin Kennedy are all available. Chinese scholars have also written their own biographies of Adam Smith to introduce his life experiences and academic achievements, among which the work of Yan Zhijie could be regarded as representative. And in 2013, the latest version of Ian Simpson Ross's *Life of Adam Smith* (2010) was published by Zhejiang University Press, another important event for Smith scholarship in China.

It seems to me that in an age of rising interest on Adam Smith, the collective efforts of intellectuals are still needed to break from the ideological image of Adam Smith and restore an appreciation of his insights.

BIBLIOGRAPHIC ESSAY

Daisun Chen, *From Classic Economics to Marxism* (Shanghai: 1979) offers an important and systematic study of Smith's theory of value. Although Marxist in its orientation, compared to other contemporary Chinese studies it offers a more accurate understanding of the classic theories of Western economics. Zongzheng Li and Lu Youzhang, *A History of Economic Theories* (Shanghai: 1979), widely adopted as a key textbook in China, discusses the influence of Smith on Marxism, especially the labor theory of value, and also offers a critique of the limitations of Smith's thought. It could be regarded as the authoritative evaluation of Adam Smith's economic thoughts from the perspective of the official ideology. Shaowen Zhu, *Classic Economics and Modern Economics* (Beijing: 2000) reinterprets Smith's conceptions of motivation and human behavior, and illustrates the moral nature of Smith's economic thought, and in so doing significantly contributed to the development of a new image of Smith in Chinese academia. More recently, Qiren Chen, *A Study on Adam Smith's Economic Thoughts* (Shanghai: 2012) offers an important study of Smith's economic thought and its influence on Marxist economics, covering both the advantages and disadvantages of Smith's theories from a Marxist standpoint. Finally, Luo Weidong, *Sentiments, Order, Virtue: The Ethics of Adam Smith* (Shanghai: 2006) offers a comprehensive study of the value foundation embedded in Smith's system of social science.

ADAM SMITH AND
SHAREHOLDER CAPITALISM

John C. Bogle

My interest in—indeed, fascination with—Adam Smith goes back to 1948, at the beginning of my sophomore year at Princeton University. In Economics 101, Nobel laureate-to-be Dr. Paul A. Samuelson, in the first edition of his *Economics: An Introductory Analysis*, introduced me to Adam Smith. Over the sixty-five years that followed, my interest in this remarkable Scotsman has not only continued, but grown steadily. Samuelson's magnum opus (now in its nineteenth edition) remains in my library to this day, and its treasured perspective has been honored by time. Consider these excerpts from Samuelson's book, perhaps even more relevant in 2015 than when he wrote them in 1948.

> A competitive system of markets and prices—whatever else it may be, however imperfectly it may function—is not a system of chaos and anarchy. There is in it a certain order and orderliness. It works. It functions. Without intelligence it solves one of the most complex problems imaginable, involving thousands of unknown variables and relations. Nobody designed it. Like Topsy it just grew, and like human nature, it is changing; but at least it meets the first test of any social organization—it is able to survive. . . .
>
> Even Adam Smith, the canny Scot whose monumental book, *The Wealth of Nations* (1776), represents the beginning of modern economics or political economy—even he was so thrilled by the recognition of an order in the economic system that he proclaimed the mystical principle of the "invisible hand": that each individual in pursuing only his own selfish good was led, as if by an invisible hand, to achieve the best good of all, so that any interference with

free competition by government was almost certain to be injurious. This unguarded conclusion has done almost as much harm as good in the past century and a half. . . . [In fact], ours is a mixed system of government and private enterprise; a mixed system of monopoly and competition. It is neither black nor white, but gray and polka-dotted.

A cynic might say of free competition what Bernard Shaw once said of Christianity: the only trouble with it is that it has never been tried. There never was a golden age of free competition, and competition is not now perfect in the economist's sense; probably it is becoming less so every day, in large part because of the fundamental nature of large-scale production and technology, consumer's tastes, and business organization.[1]

So Samuelson begins his book with a salute to Adam Smith's most cited tenet, but ends with profound skepticism about its application. As *New York Times* columnist and 2008 Nobel laureate Paul Krugman observed in his review of David Warsh's fine book, *Knowledge and the Wealth of Nations*, there exists "a struggle between [Adam Smith's] pin factory and the invisible hand. . . . The parable of the pin factory says that there are increasing returns to scale—the bigger the factory, the more specialized its workers . . . the more pins produced per worker. But increasing returns create a tendency toward monopoly [as] bigger firms tend to drive smaller firms out of business until each industry is dominated by just a few players."[2] The logical contradiction between the pin factory and the invisible hand has been resolved—for better or worse—with the dominance of a relatively small number of giant corporations that today control the major share of the world's productive capacity.

In the recent era, that dominance has accelerated markedly. Whether by market power or by merger, the largest firms keep getting bigger. According to the *Economist*, "in the past 15 years the assets of the top 50 American companies have risen from around 70 percent of American GDP to around 130 percent, [and] all of the top ten firms have been involved in at least one large merger or acquisition over the past 25 years."[3] Whether this trend is driven by seeking economies of scale (so often unrealized), maximizing CEO compensation, the accounting manipulations that mergers make possible, or simply empire building, we have come a long way from the pin factories of yore.

The defenders of today's version of capitalism rely on Smith's concept of the invisible hand to validate a laissez-faire system of free, open, and unfettered competition. But the world has changed, and the blind pursuit of self-interest has failed to foster the greater good of society. Joseph E. Stiglitz, another Nobel laureate (2001), puts this contradiction even more starkly than did Samuelson: "It took a long time before the assumptions underlying the [invisible hand] theory—perfect competition, perfect markets, perfect information, etc.—were fully understood. But when information is imperfect, and especially when there are asymmetries of information (that is, different individuals knowing different things), then the economy is essentially never efficient. Sometimes, in other words, the invisible hand is not visible simply because it is simply not there. Markets do not lead to efficient outcomes, let alone outcomes that comport with social justice."[4]

THE CHALLENGE OF PREDICTING THE FUTURE

In a world of steady population growth and increasing productivity, prediction has proven to be far more art (and luck) than science, and much of Adam Smith's analysis into the nature and causes of national wealth is far less relevant to contemporary economic analysis than today's self-styled acolytes of Adam Smith who run the world's big businesses would admit. After all, looking back over history to 1776 when *An Inquiry into the Nature and Causes of the Wealth of Nations* was published, "the Birth of Plenty" that has resulted in the huge wealth in which much of the world basks today was barely beginning.

In his splendid 2004 book, *The Birth of Plenty*, author William J. Bernstein presents a chart showing the rate of growth of the world's production of goods and services (world GDP) over the past two thousand years (figure 31.1).[5] From the beginning of the Christian

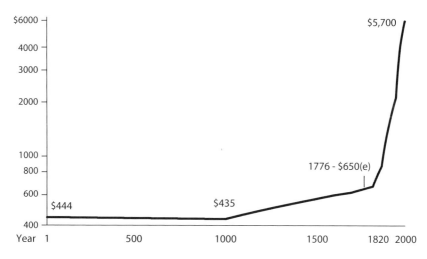

Figure 31.1. "The Birth of Plenty": World GDP per capita.
Source: Angus Maddison, *The World Economy: A Millennial Perspective* (Paris: 2001), p. 264.

Era through AD 1000, world economic growth was essentially zero. Even over the next seven hundred years, it grew at the sluggish annual rate of only 0.05 percent. By 1700, in real (inflation-adjusted) terms, world GDP had risen from an estimated $444 per capita in AD 1 to only $615. By 1776, when *Wealth of Nations* was first published, growth was beginning to accelerate, and by 1820, as the Industrial Revolution took hold, world GDP began to grow at an annual rate that would soon exceed 1 percent. The curve continued to accelerate through the early 1950s ($2,100 GDP per capita) and exploded into the Age of Plenty that we enjoy today. In the post–World War II era, real per capita GDP, growing at 2.5 percent annually, reached an all-time high of $5,700.

This astonishing change reflects, above all, the change in social order of wealth creation from the early days of humanity. In his *Lectures on Jurisprudence* (1762–63), Adam Smith described this development: First, the early Age of Hunters; then the Age of Shepherds; next the Age of Agriculture; and finally the Age of Commerce, then beginning to become the prime force in economic growth. Agriculture would continue as the dominant force until the mid-1800s. While the agricultural economy continues to grow, it is gradually shrinking as a percentage of the US economy, from 37 percent of GDP in 1869,[6] to about 1 percent today.[7]

Commerce, as Smith intuited, became the force that would drive the wheels of economic growth ever since, today accounting for some 80 percent of US production (GDP). But commerce itself has taken multiple forms. First the Age of Manufacturing—revolutionized by the steam engine—created huge economic growth, only to taper off later. For example, manufacturing accounted for 27 percent of the US economy in 1950, but now represents just 11 percent. Today, it is primarily the Age of Services, not goods, that drives our economy. From 26 percent in 1947, our service economy now represents 57 percent of US GDP, and is still rising.[8]

Simply relying on the broad term "service economy" conceals far more than it reveals. In commerce, the Age of Sail (and canals) in the 1650–1820 period was later replaced by the Age of Rail, followed by the Age of Electricity. More recently, driven by soaring stock trading and financial entrepreneurship (not necessarily in the public interest), the Age of Financial Services that began in the 1980s has increased fourfold—from 2 percent of GDP in 1947 to over 8 percent today[9]—diverting a substantial portion of the returns generated in the stock and bond markets from investors to their Wall Street agents.

But the greatest change of all may well be the most powerful single economic force in all human history. In today's Age of Information, which began in the mid-1990s, technology has radically reordered the consumer markets (and continues to do so). This new age revolutionized finance (high-frequency trading in stocks, quantitative investment strategies); transportation in all forms; manufacturing (mass production); distribution ("just-in-time" supply chain management); metallurgy (carbon fibers); and more. So far, the Age of Information shows no sign of abating.

We could hardly expect even a man with the wisdom, intelligence, and logic of Adam Smith to have anticipated in detail these various streams—really rivers—of commerce. But his overarching vision—what one might call the Age of the Consumer—still stands tall today; indeed taller than ever before. As Smith wrote,

"Consumption is the sole end and purpose of all production; and the interest of the producer ought to be attended to, only so far as it may be necessary for promoting that of the consumer. The maxim is so perfectly self-evident, that it would be absurd to attempt to prove it. . . . [T]he interest of the consumer . . . [must be] the ultimate end and object of all industry and commerce" (WN IV.viii.49). This philosophy surely justifies the oft-cited appellation of Smith as "the first consumer advocate."

ANTICIPATING THE PROBLEMS OF AGENCY

But if no one could have possibly foreseen the revolution in commerce that brought us the Age of Information that dominates our society today, Smith's deep concern about the conflicts of interest in corporate conduct and governance seems almost prescient. He articulated the critical problems of agency, but his skepticism has received far too little commentary by his defenders, his critics, or independent academics. In *Wealth of Nations*, Smith pungently expressed his doubts about the corporations of his day.[10]

In Smith's time, most corporations were regulated by the crown, "sort of enlarged monopolies," in his words, largely engaged in foreign trade (for example, the Russia Company, the Hudson Bay Company, and the South Sea Company). But despite their innate advantages, these regulated companies established by either royal charter or act of parliament, "have in the long run proved, universally, either burdensome or useless . . . and mismanaged" (WN V.i.e.5). The other class of corporation of his time was the joint-stock company, with "each member sharing in the common profit or loss . . . [often with] exclusive privileges" (WN V.i.e.6). These joint-stock companies, broadly similar to the publicly held corporations of modern times, differ in several respects not only from regulated companies, but from private copartneries. Here's how Smith described them:

> In a private copartnery, no partner, without the consent of the company, can transfer his share to another person, or introduce a

new member into the company. Each member, however, may, upon proper warning, withdraw from the copartnery, and demand payment from them of his share of the common stock. In a joint stock company, on the contrary, no member can demand payment of his share from the company; but each member can, without their consent, transfer his share to another person, and thereby introduce a new member. The value of a share in a joint stock is always the price which it will bring in the market. . . .

Secondly, in a private copartnery, each partner is bound for the debts contracted by the company to the whole extent of his fortune. In a joint stock company, on the contrary, each partner is bound only to the extent of his share. The trade of a joint stock company is always managed by a court of directors. This court, indeed, is frequently subject, in many respects, to the control of a general court of proprietors. But the greater part of those proprietors seldom pretend to understand anything of the business of the company; and when the spirit of faction happens not to prevail among them, give themselves no trouble about it, but receive contentedly such half yearly or yearly dividend, as the directors think proper to make to them. . . .

This total exemption from trouble and from risk, beyond a limited sum, encourages many people to become adventurers in joint stock companies, who would, upon no account, hazard their fortunes in any private copartnery. (WN V.i.e.18)

Adam Smith then adds this powerful coda:

The directors of such companies, however, being the managers rather of other people's money than of their own, it cannot well be expected, that they should watch over it with the same anxious vigilance with which the partners in a private copartnery frequently watch over their own. Like the stewards of a rich man, they are apt to consider attention to small matters as not for their master's honor, and very easily give themselves a dispensation from having it. Negligence and profusion, therefore, must always prevail, more or less, in the management of the affairs of such a company. (WN V.i.e.18)

Smith's words aptly describe corporate America in the recent era. While looting has been limited (Enron, WorldCom, Tyco, and Bernard Madoff's massive Ponzi scheme are notable exceptions), negligence and profusion have been rife, and too many corporate executives have given themselves, using Smith's word, "dispensations" that would have appalled the thrifty Scot. The malfeasance in our system of modern capitalism has even spread to the very fiscal integrity of our corporate world. These contradictions of managers' capitalism lie beneath many of the failures we've witnessed in our financial markets during the recent era.

It would be difficult to find a better example of this change than the field of US investment banking. The Glass-Steagall Act of 1933 required the separation of investment banking (underwriting of securities) from commercial banking (taking deposits). The investment banks were then controlled by partners, their capital at risk and their liability unlimited, with their balance sheets therefore of high quality. Gradually, most of these firms converted to public ownership, and operated with high leverage (borrowings were often twenty times or more than the firm's capital!), with their balance sheets fraught with risky securities.

Adam Smith got it exactly right: "Though the principles of the banking trade may appear somewhat abstruse, the practice is capable of being reduced to strict rules. To depart upon any occasion from those rules, in consequence of some flattering speculation of extraordinary gain, is almost always extremely dangerous, and frequently fatal to the banking company which attempts it" (WN V.i.e.33). The failure of so many giant investment banks during the 2008–9 financial crisis provides a stark illustration of what can happen when carefully watching over one's own capital is replaced by managing the capital of public investors and throwing caution to the wind.

"THE THEORY OF THE FIRM"

Of course any enterprise that endures must generate profits for its owners. But corporations will do that best when they take into account not only the interests of their stockholders, but the interests of their customers, their employees, their communities, and our society. These are not new ideals for capitalism. All those years ago, Adam Smith expressed them well: "He is certainly not a good citizen who does not wish to promote, by every means of his power, the welfare of the whole society of his fellow citizens" (TMS VI.ii.2.11). To honor Smith's ideal, it is essential that the owners of corporate America—ultimately, our citizenry—speak out and demand that our corporations and our money managers place the interests of their owners and the interests of our society ahead of their own personal interests and counterproductive incentives.

Smith seems to anticipate the risks inherent in today's "corporate/ financial complex" that now dominates the economies of the world's developed nations. In their seminal 1976 article,[11] Michael C. Jensen and William H. Meckling point out, as Adam Smith had two hundred years earlier, that *agents* (managers) were feathering their own nests rather than advancing the interests of their *principals* (shareholders). The article continued,

> Since the relationship between the stockholders and the managers of a corporation fits precisely the definition of a pure agency relationship, it should come as no surprise to discover that the issues associated with the separation of ownership and control in the modern diffused-ownership corporation are intimately associated with the general problem of agency. The problem of inducing an "agent" to behave as if he were maximizing the welfare of the "principal" is quite general. It exists in all organizations at every level of management in firms, in universities, in mutual companies, in cooperatives, in governmental authorities and bureaus, [and] in unions.[12]

It is impossible to deny the logic of the Smith thesis, restated in the Jensen-Meckling thesis, which posits that managers too rarely maximize the interests of the shareholders whom they are duty-bound to serve, and instead too often look out for their own interests. More important, its truth has been confirmed, over and over again, by actual experience in the functioning of today's giant multinational corporations—notably, in recent years, excessive executive compensation and often ill-disclosed corporate political contributions.

THE AGE OF DOUBLE AGENCY

In and of itself, that agency problem would be quite difficult enough to resolve. But during the past half century, a new problem has taken the issue to a far more complex level. The *single* agency system described above—corporate managers versus individual shareholders—has metastasized into a *double* agency system. Too often, corporate manager/agents would, just as Smith said, *give themselves a dispensation*, and *negligence and profusion prevail* at the expense of their shareholder/principals. But today, the vast majority of US corporate shares are held not by individual shareholders, but by their agents—giant financial institutions, investing the assets of mutual fund investors and pension fund beneficiaries. Yes, the Age of Double Agency is now upon us, and with a vengeance.[13] We have, in the memorable words of Leo Strine, now chief justice of the Delaware Supreme Court, "the separation of ownership from ownership."[14]

Today, financial institutions hold some 70 percent of the shares of almost every public corporation in the United States—absolute voting control. Yet too often our institutional agents have failed abjectly to honor their duty to act as gatekeepers that ensure that corporations are managed in the interest of their shareholders, whether directly or indirectly through the ownership of shares in their mutual funds. But our fund manager/agents have so far been passive as owners, conspicuous in their failure to play the governance role which their virtual control of corporate America demands of them.

The failure of so many of our institutional money managers to assume the rights and to honor the responsibilities of corporate governance has become the stuff of legend. As a rule, they make no demand for access to corporate proxies. They vote, sheep-like, for management's slate of directors and executive compensation plans, and largely oppose proposals by corporate minority shareholders. And if *any* large mutual fund manager has *ever* made a proxy proposal that was opposed by management, I'm unaware of it. We could do a lot worse than heeding Adam Smith's warning about the latent harm to investor interests that is wreaked by corporate managers and, now, institutional investors. I reiterate his prescient warning: "the managers of other people's money . . . [fail to] watch over it with the same anxious vigilance . . . with which they watch over their own." The silence of the funds, alas, is deafening.

The mutual fund industry, now holding about 35 percent of all shares of the nation's corporations, offers a clear example of such forbearance. Why? One reason is that it has become more of a "rent-a-stock" industry than an "own-a-stock industry." Renters, to state the obvious, care less about their property than do owners.

Active mutual fund managers, for example, tend to focus on ephemeral short-term stock prices rather than the enduring creation of long-term intrinsic corporate value, and now turn over their portfolios at a record-high annual rate of 140 percent.[15] Rather than fostering capital formation for our businesses and facilitating retirement savings for our citizens, our financial system has taken on the look of a casino. While America's dominant index funds are the consummate long-term investors—buying the shares of our largest corporations and rarely selling them—they seem unwilling to exercise their latent powers.

Another challenge is the potential conflict that exists when managers consider how to vote the proxies of companies for which they are managing pension and thrift plans. It cannot be surprising that they hesitate to offend their clients (to say nothing of their potential clients). And the fact that engaging in governance activism seems to be regarded as a public relations negative in a mutual fund industry that has become focused more on the business of marketing rather than on the profession of investment management simply adds to the funds' reluctance to take a stand on controversial corporate governance issues.

THE IMPARTIAL SPECTATOR

Curiously, Adam Smith recognized this conflict with his own clarion call for us (including, obviously, the leaders of our businesses and political institutions) to heed the better angels of our nature. Smith's "impartial spectator" first appears in his earlier *Theory of Moral Sentiments* (1759). Today, it is almost as universally *un-*

known as his "invisible hand" is *well known*. Yet this impartial spectator uncannily echoes the values that define us as human beings. The impartial spectator, Smith tells us, is the force that arouses in us values that are so often generous and noble. It is the inner man, shaped by the society in which he exists—even the soul—who gives us our highest calling. This impartial spectator, in Smith's words, "is reason, principle, conscience, the inhabitant of the breast, the man within, the great judge and arbiter of our conduct" (TMS III.3.4).

> [The impartial spectator] calls to us, with a voice capable of astonishing the most presumptuous of our passions, that we are but one of the multitude, in no respect better than any other in it; and that when we prefer ourselves so shamefully and so blindly to others, we become the proper objects of resentment, abhorrence, and execration. It is from him only that we learn the real littleness of ourselves. It is this impartial spectator . . . who shows us the propriety of generosity and the deformity of injustice; the propriety of reining the greatest interests of our own, for the yet greater interests of others . . . in order to obtain the greatest benefit to ourselves. It is not the love of our neighbor; it is not the love of mankind, which upon many occasions prompts us to the practice of those divine virtues. It is a stronger love, a more powerful affection, the love of what is honorable and noble, the grandeur, and dignity, and superiority of our own characters. (TMS III.3.4)

> Man was made for action, and to promote by the exertion of his faculties such changes in the external circumstances both of himself and others, as may seem most favorable to the happiness of all. . . . That he may call forth the whole vigor of his soul, and strain every nerve, in order to produce those ends which it is the purpose of his being to advance, Nature has taught him, that neither himself nor mankind can be fully satisfied with his conduct, nor bestow upon it the full measure of applause, unless he has actually produced them. (TMS II.iii.3.3)

Smith's magnificent cadences can hardly help but inspire us citizens of this twenty-first century with the very values that we seem to ignore and are in danger of completely losing. The impartial spectator is the central metaphor that defines those values—the idealistic values that permeated the eighteenth century and the Age of Reason—values that must remain our guiding star, even as we march forward to deal with the challenges of the young new century.

ADAM SMITH'S WISDOM FOR INVESTORS TODAY

While much of Adam Smith's eighteenth-century thinking did not—nay, could not—anticipate the dramatic, even revolutionary changes in the world's economy and in the burgeoning wealth of nations that were just beginning in 1776, his concerns about the role of corporations and his focus on agency issues both seem prescient. Today these issues are even more demanding of both private action and governmental action.

It is time for the establishment of a federal standard of fiduciary duty in the United States, one that demands that investors' interests come first; that managers invest their clients' assets with prudence, with a long-term focus, and at reasonable cost. Such a standard would also mandate assuming the responsibilities of corporate governance, and eliminating the conflicts of interest that are now resolved in favor of the mangers, rather than their clients. Such a standard would also require financial conglomerates to divest their holdings of institutional money managers, a clear conflict of interest, yet the now pervasive structural reality in the world of finance.

I am realistic enough to recognize that this ideal will take years, if not decades, to realize. So I turn to none other than Adam Smith for help, through his concept of the invisible hand. It's worth citing his exact words: "[Every individual] intends only his own security; and by directing his industry in such a manner as to produce its greatest value, he intends only his own gain, and he is in this, as in many other cases, led by an invisible hand to promote an end which was no part of his intention . . . promot[ing] the interests of the society more effectually than when he really intends to promote it" (WN IV.ii.9).

Merely applying this simple principle offers our best hope for ensuring that our citizen/investors will finally get a fair shake in the financial markets. It requires only that *investors themselves* take responsibility for their own security and direct their savings where they will produce their greatest value. If investors act in their own self-interest and move their money to the care of money managers who strive to meet the fiduciary standard, they will necessarily advance the interests of society. Investors must simply "vote with their feet," and choose fund managers who will work solely for their benefit. By acting in their own financial self-interest, investors will force money managers to serve the interests of all of us who invest our hard-earned savings in public corporations.

Adam-Smith-like, then, individual investors need only to look after their own self-interest. They must demand full disclosure, clearer and more pointed than ever. We need a campaign to educate investors about the hard realities of investing, so that they understand not only the magic of compounding long-term returns, but the tyranny of compounding costs, costs that ultimately overwhelm that magic. Investors need to know about sensible asset allocation and the value of diversification; they need to understand the huge gap that exists between the illusion of *nominal* returns and the reality of *real* (after-inflation) returns; they need to recognize that short-term trading—like casino gambling—is ultimately a loser's game; and they need to be aware of the demonstrated costs of the behavioral flaws that plague so many market participants, eager to buy as markets rise toward their highs, frightened into selling as markets tumble.

As Occam's Razor—the rule set by Sir William of Occam in the fourteenth century—suggests, the simplest solution to these multifaceted challenges is for investors to own the entire stock market (and/or the entire bond market), and then hold it forever. By so doing, investors gain the nth degree of diversification, low investment costs, high tax efficiency, and the longest possible time horizon. I have no doubt that the optimal investment strategy for obtaining these advantages is the all-market index fund.

But don't take my word for it. Paul Samuelson enthusiastically endorsed the idea, comparing the creation of the first index mutual fund by Vanguard in 1975 with the invention of the wheel, the alphabet, and Gutenberg printing (as well as wine and cheese!). The index fund also surely matches the philosophy both of Adam Smith's invisible hand and of his impartial spectator, two mighty metaphors.

Ultimately, the future of today's beleaguered financial system will be determined by the actions of enlightened, intelligent investors who demand that their own interests become the highest priority of their money managers. Managers will have to respond to this change and focus on prudence as a central investment strategy, an idea that Adam Smith clearly endorsed:

> The care of . . . the fortune . . . is considered as the proper business of that virtue which is commonly called Prudence. . . . Security, therefore, is the first and the principal object. . . . [Prudence] is rather cautious than enterprising, and more anxious to preserve the advantages which we already possess, than forward to prompt us to the acquisition of still greater advantages. . . . The prudent man always studies seriously and earnestly to understand whatever he professes to understand . . . he is averse to all the quackish arts by which other people so frequently thrust themselves into public notice. (TMS VI.i.6–8)

> In the steadiness of his industry and frugality, in his steadily sacrificing the ease and enjoyment of the present moment for the probable expectation of the still greater ease and enjoyment of a more distant but more lasting period of time, the prudent man is always both supported and rewarded by the entire approbation of the impartial spectator. (TMS VI.i.11)

Finally, it is Adam Smith's principles—especially the invisible hand, the impartial spectator, and prudence—that provide the intellectual underpinning for the triumph of shareholder capitalism.

NOTES

1. Paul A. Samuelson, *Economics: An Introductory Analysis* (New York: 1948), pp. 35–36.

2. Paul Krugman, "The Pin Factory Mystery," *New York Times*, May 7, 2006.

3. "Free Exchange: Land of the Corporate Giants," *Economist*, November 3, 2012, p. 76.

4. Joseph E. Stiglitz, "Evaluating Economic Change," *Daedalus* 133, no. 3 (2004), pp. 18–25.

5. William J. Bernstein, *The Birth of Plenty: How the Prosperity of the Modern World Was Created* (New York: 2004), p. 18.

6. J. M. Alston, M. A. Anderson, J. S. James, and P. G. Pardey, *Persistence Pays: U.S. Agricultural Productivity Growth and the Benefits from Public R&D Spending* (New York: 2010), p. 9.

7. Author's calculations, U.S. Department of Commerce, Bureau of Economic Analysis, U.S. National Income and Product Accounts (NIPA).

8. Ibid.

9. Ibid.

10. For example, I paraphrase Smith's characterizations of the English East India Company: "malicious, miserable; throwing themselves on the mercy of government; [un]fit to govern, the plunderers of India, bad stewards; the pleasure of wasting or the profits of embezzling; unjust, capricious, and negligent."

11. Michael C. Jensen and William H. Meckling, "Theory of the Firm: Managerial Behavior, Agency Costs and Ownership Structure," *Journal of Financial Economics* 3 (1976), pp. 305–60.

12. Ibid., p. 311.

13. I first coined this phase in my 2012 book *The Clash of the Cultures: Investment vs. Speculation* (Hoboken, NJ: 2012).

14. Leo E. Strine, Jr., "Toward Common Sense and Common Ground? Reflections on the Share Interests of Managers and Labor in a More Rational System of Corporate Governance," *Journal of Corporation Law* 33 (2007).

15. Annual purchases and sales of stocks as a percentage of fund stockholdings.

BIBLIOGRAPHIC ESSAY

A comprehensive review of how Adam Smith fits into today's political economy can be found in Patricia H. Werhane's *Adam Smith and His Legacy for Modern Capitalism* (Oxford: 1991). In her text, Werhane describes how Smith essentially created the intellectual discipline of economics. By bringing together and critiquing the views of many noted Adam Smith scholars, as well as her own, she places his theories in the context of contemporary economic thought.

In *Knowledge and the Wealth of Nations: A Story of Economic Discovery* (New York: 1996), journalist David Warsh describes the history of one of the great problems of economics—the problem of increasing returns to scale. Adam Smith described the problem with his analogy of the pin factory. As the size of a firm increases, the division of labor also increases, allowing the firm to reduce costs and increase profitability. As the firm gets bigger and more profitable, it forces smaller competitors out of business, resulting in monopoly power. However, for free market capitalism to function optimally, intense competition is required. Warsh's book describes the history of economic thought and tells the dramatic stories of the contemporary economists who wrestle with this problem.

"Agency Theory and CEO Incentives" (Social Science Research Network working paper, 2012), by Joseph Dunning of Monash University endorses many of my positions on corporate governance, but would be skeptical of the similarity of modern corporations and the joint-stock corporations of Adam Smith's time.

Also of note is Robert L. Heilbroner's essay "The Paradox of Progress: Decline and Decay in *The Wealth of Nations*," *Journal of the History of Ideas* 34 (1973). Heilbroner focuses on the "dark side" of free market capitalism as described by Adam Smith, arguing that Smith provides a "deeply pessimistic prognosis of an evolutionary trend in which both decline and decay attend—material decline awaiting at the terminus of the economic journey, moral decay suffered by society in the course of its journeying."

Three of my ten books, *The Battle for the Soul of Capitalism* (New Haven: 2005), *Don't Count on It!* (New York: 2010), and *The Clash of the Cultures: Investment vs. Speculation* (New York: 2012), include extended discussions of the issues of shareholder capitalism.

ADAM SMITH AND FREE TRADE

Douglas A. Irwin

In terms of his economic policy recommendations, Adam Smith is probably best known for his support for free trade and critique of protectionism. Smith persuasively described the benefits of international commerce and made a strong case for allowing countries to trade freely with one another. He also developed strong arguments against government restrictions on imports or exports. Furthermore, in making this case for free trade, Smith did not merely affirm what everyone already believed; rather he showed intellectual courage and originality in going against the grain of established opinion.[1]

Smith's arguments in favor of free trade were so compelling that almost all subsequent discussions of trade policy, at least at an intellectual level, have taken his views as a starting point. Even today, Adam Smith's name and the arguments he set forth in the *Wealth of Nations* are frequently invoked whenever trade issues are being debated. Partly as a result of his intellectual influence, protectionist trade policies—those that protect domestic producers from foreign competition by imposing barriers on the importation of foreign goods—are largely discredited among economists and policy makers. While the merits of government intervention in trade are still debated, as they always will be, Smith fundamentally changed the terms of the debate.

What were Smith's arguments? And are they still relevant today after nearly two hundred fifty years? This chapter explores Adam Smith's case for free trade, his case against protectionism, and the qualifications that he made to these views. It concludes by discussing the legacy of Smith's work for today.[2]

THE CASE FOR FREE TRADE

As notes from his lectures at Glasgow University in the early 1760s attest, Smith was a convinced advocate of free trade from the very start of his career. Smith held that trade between nations was similar to trade between individuals. Human beings, he noted, have a natural propensity to truck, barter, and exchange goods with one other. If the exchange was voluntary, trade would not take place unless both parties were better off. And just as individuals were better off with trade, so were countries. As he put it, "All commerce that is carried on betwixt any two countries must necessarily be advantageous to both. The very intention of commerce is to exchange your own commodities for others which you think will be more convenient for you. When two men trade between themselves it is undoubtedly for the advantage of both. . . . The case is exactly the same betwixt any two nations" (LJB 261–62).

Smith believed that, as a general matter, individuals should be free to exchange goods with one another without interference and that this presumption did not stop at a country's borders. Given the similarities between an individual and a country, Smith drew a strong policy conclusion: "it appears that Britain should by all means be made a free port, that there should be no interruptions of any kind made to foreign trade." And if there were any other means of raising revenue for the government, all import duties should be abolished and the "free commerce and liberty of exchange should be allowed with all nations and for all things" (LJB 269).[3]

Smith made these arguments at a time when most policy makers and opinion leaders would have dismissed such views as harmful and unrealistic. Yet Smith was not completely alone in championing a liberal view of international trade. In 1752, his fellow Scotsman David Hume published some influential essays that brought an Enlightenment perspective to the issue of international commerce. In "On the Jealousy of Trade," Hume suggested that international trade should not be viewed as a zero-sum game, in which countries were competing with each other as rivals, but rather as a form of mutually beneficial exchange that should be encouraged. Like

Hume, Smith believed that national jealousies and ill will would reduce trade, the division of labor, and the wealth of each country.[4]

However, it was in the *Wealth of Nations* that Smith laid out a systematic case for free trade and against government interference in trade. To understand his case for free trade, one has to begin with his view of the role of commerce in society. Smith starts with the presumption that individuals are motivated by a desire to better their own condition. This deeply ingrained force guides them toward activities that would earn them the greatest reward for their efforts. In his words, individuals "endeavour to employ [their labor and capital] in the support of that industry of which the produce is likely to be of the greatest value, or to exchange for the greatest quantity either of money or of other goods" (WN IV.ii.8). To do so, in a market economy, individuals have to provide goods or services that are demanded by others. In satisfying that demand, they are serving the wants and desires of others. Therefore, as Smith put it, "Every individual is continually exerting himself to find out the most advantageous employment for whatever capital he can command. It is his own advantage, indeed, and not that of the society, which he has in view. But the study of his own advantage naturally, or rather necessarily leads him to prefer that employment which is most advantageous to the society" (WN IV.ii.4).[5] Thus, in a commercial society, individuals seeking to better themselves would have to serve the needs of others. This process relies not on benevolence, but on self-interest, and worked through market transactions, not through central direction. And this process, in his view, works surprisingly well on its own. As a result, Smith did not envision much of a role for government in directing market processes or dictating market outcomes.

That said, Smith was not an advocate of laissez-faire, a term that he never used. He believed that government could and should play an important role in supporting market exchange, by providing certain public goods and establishing a system of law and justice.[6] If it performed those functions well, government could help markets work more effectively. At the same time, Smith generally believed that direct interference in markets by government was unlikely to work out well. There were two reasons for this skepticism. First, government tended to be much less responsive to the needs of the people than self-interested merchants; merchants had more of an incentive (and more information) to attend to the desires of their customers. Second, special interest groups could manipulate governments, leading to policies for their own enrichment rather than the public benefit.

Thus, unlike what some critics would later contend, Smith's case for free trade did not rest upon the case for laissez-faire. Smith did not conflate the two ideas. At the same time, the existence of circumstances in which government could play a productive role did not justify restrictions on trade or necessitate any departure from free trade.

So why was free trade a good idea? In the *Wealth of Nations*, as he had in his Glasgow lectures, Smith drew upon the analogy between an individual (or household) and the nation. Just as a family would never make at home what it would cost more than to buy, the same is true for a country: "What is prudent in the conduct of every private family, can scarce be folly in that of a great kingdom. If a foreign country can supply us with a commodity cheaper than we ourselves can make it, better buy it of them with some part of the produce of our own industry, employed in a way in which we have some advantage" (WN IV.ii.11–12). Just as a household would want to buy goods as cheaply as possible, a country would want to buy imports as cheaply as possible. "The proposition is so very manifest that it seems ridiculous to take any pains to prove it; nor could it ever have been called in question had not the interested sophistry of merchants and manufacturers confounded the common sense of mankind" (WN IV.iii.c.10). The policy recommendation that follows from this conclusion was straightforward. The interest of a country in trading with others was the same as the interest of a merchant, namely, "to buy as cheap and to sell as dear as possible." This was possible, he wrote, only when a country had many potential suppliers of its imports and many possible buyers of its exports. Only free trade would ensure this, he maintained (WN IV.ii.30).

Therefore, Smith advocated "the liberal system of free exportation and free importation." In one of his grandest paragraphs, Smith put it this way:

> All systems either of preference or of restraint, therefore, being thus completely taken away, the obvious and simple system of natural liberty establishes itself of its own accord. Every man, as long as he does not violate the laws of justice, is left perfectly free to pursue his own interest his own way, and to bring both his industry and capital into competition with those of any other man, or order of men. The sovereign is completely discharged from a duty, in the attempting to perform which he must always be exposed to innumerable delusions, and for the proper performance of which no human wisdom or knowledge could ever be sufficient; the duty of superintending the industry of private people, and of directing it towards the employments most suitable to the interest of the society. (WN IV.ix.51)

Adam Smith's case for free trade was richer and deeper than just the simple presumption that trade was beneficial and therefore should be left alone. Smith pointed to two specific benefits that a country would derive from trade. First, countries could exchange their superfluities that "satisfy a part of their wants, and increase their enjoyments." Second, and more important, countries would benefit by increasing their productivity, which would "augment its annual produce to the utmost, and thereby . . . increase the real revenue and wealth of the society" (WN IV.i.31).[7]

In making this second argument, Smith drew on the notion that the division of labor was the key driver of productivity improvements. Increasing productivity allowed more output to be produced from the same amount of capital and labor inputs. Such improvements were the basis for rising living standards. Because the division of labor is limited by the extent of the market, free trade widened the market and therefore permitted a more refined division of labor that improved productivity. In particular, free trade facilitated the exchange of knowledge across countries about new production methods and business practices (WN IV.viii.c.80).

Thus, trade was a mechanism for allowing the benefits of productivity improvements to diffuse to different countries, thereby raising living standards around the world.

Smith made an especially strong plea for free trade in food. Free trade would allow provisions to move from places where they were abundant to places where they were scarce. Merchants would have an incentive—without any central direction—to move food from places where the price was low because supplies were plentiful to places where the price was high because supplies were scarce. This was a desirable outcome, the proper allocation of resources by most standards of justice, and it would occur naturally without government instruction or mandate. Therefore, he concluded, free trade in food was "not only the best palliative of a dearth, but the most effectual preventative of a famine." Furthermore, Smith believed that allowing free imports of inexpensive food would be less disruptive to domestic producers than the importation of manufactured goods; farmers could just switch the crops that they grew on their land, whereas manufactures facing foreign competition would see the value of their invested capital fall and have to retool their production facilities. Yet few countries adopted such a liberal system of agricultural trade even though it could be a matter of life or death: "The freedom of the corn trade is almost every where more or less restrained, and, in many countries, is confined by such absurd regulations as frequently aggravate the unavoidable misfortune of a dearth into the dreadful calamity of a famine" (WN IV.v.b.39).

What did Smith think of bilateral or multilateral trade agreements to reduce trade barriers and expand trade, as is common practice today? He might have supported them provided they opened trade on a nondiscriminatory basis. However, Smith emphatically opposed treaties of commerce (trade agreements) that would give foreign producers preferential access to the domestic market. Such treaties, he wrote, though advantageous to producers in the favored country, would be detrimental to those of the favoring country because it would limit competition in their market (WN IV.vi.2). By giving a foreign country preferential access to its market, an importing country might not get the full benefits of buying from the best source of supply.

To conclude, Smith made an extended argument for the benefits of a free exchange of goods across countries. However, that was only half of his case for free trade.

CASE AGAINST PROTECTIONISM

Smith did not just make a positive case for free trade, he made an equally effective case against government restrictions on trade. Smith attacked what he called mercantilism, which he viewed as the leading approach to economic policy of the day. The "great object" of mercantilism was to promote exports by subsidies and reduce imports by restrictions (WN IV.i.35). Smith proposed to examine the likely effects of export promotion and import restriction on "the annual produce of [a country's] industry," because "according as they tend either to increase or diminish the value of this annual produce, they must evidently tend either to increase or diminish the real wealth and revenue of the country" (WN IV.i.45).

Before discussing Smith's analysis, we should note that this is an interesting standard by which to judge a policy. Prior to Adam Smith, there had been no consensus about what the goals of economic policy should be: To increase the power of the state? To increase a country's manufacturing capability? To increase domestic employment? It was often believed that an import tariff was beneficial simply because employment and output increased in the sector receiving protection from foreign competition. Smith's criterion for evaluating such a policy was different. He argued that one must examine the economy-wide impact of the policy on the real value of a country's national income, or what he called the real annual revenue (or produce) of society.

Smith began with the presumption that a country's resources were fixed at any given point in time. Therefore, increasing output in one sector of the economy could only come at the expense of using resources already employed elsewhere. This had clear and immediate implications for any policy that aimed to promote certain industries or sectors. "No regulation of commerce can increase the quantity of industry in any society beyond what its capital can maintain," Smith argued. Instead, it "can only divert a part of it into a direction into which it might not otherwise have gone" and it is "by no means certain" that this artificial direction would be advantageous to society (WN IV.ii.3). Any government interference with the allocation of resources would divert those resources into industries where they would not naturally have been drawn. By forcing capital into these state-favored activities, government policy would be "subversive of the great purpose which it means to promote" and it would retard, rather than accelerate, economic progress and reduce, rather than increase, the value of economic output (WN IV.ix.50).

For example, consider a government that restricts imports of foreign goods. If domestic goods were cheaper than foreign goods, then such regulations would be "useless." If foreign goods were cheaper than domestic goods, then such regulations "must generally be hurtful." Since the foreign good was cheaper, a country's capital and labor resources naturally would have been turned to producing other goods that could be exchanged for the imports. By restricting imports, the nation's industry is turned toward "a less advantageous employment, and the exchangeable value of its annual produce, instead of being increased, according to the intention of the lawgiver, must necessarily be diminished by every such regulation" (WN IV.ii.11–12). Furthermore, high duties or prohibitions on imports diminished competition in the home market and gave domestic producers a monopoly, enabling them to charge higher prices, leading to sloth and mismanagement. While he agreed that a tariff would increase the output of a domestic industry competing against imports, Smith made a deeper point rarely considered by earlier writers. He conceded that protecting the home market would encourage employment and production in the protected sectors, but "whether it tends either to increase that general industry of the society, or to give it the most advantageous direction, is not, perhaps, altogether so evident (WN IV.ii.2).

In Smith's day, governments often sought to increase exports and reduce imports so that the country would have a trade surplus.

Smith was dismissive of such government attempts to improve the balance of trade. In fact, Smith wrote that nothing could be more absurd than the balance of trade doctrine (WN IV.iii.c.2). If the value of a country's exports exceeded the value of its imports, the country would receive an inflow of gold and bullion from the rest of the world. Smith did not think that this inflow was inherently desirable because it confused money with national wealth. Furthermore, having a trade surplus did not necessarily mean that the economy would flourish, just as having a trade deficit did not necessarily mean that the economy would suffer. Smith argued that there is no country in which "the approaching ruin has not frequently been foretold" by an unfavorable balance of trade. Yet despite all the anxiety and the vain attempts by policy makers to turn the balance of trade in their favor, Smith did not believe that any country had been impoverished because of this cause. Instead, he maintained, "in proportion as they have opened their ports to all nations; instead of being ruined by this free trade, as the principles of the commercial system would lead us to expect, have been enriched by it" (WN IV.ii.c.14).

Smith criticized other rationales for restricting imports as well. In fairly strong terms, he rejected the idea that infant industries should be protected.[8] The idea that developing countries should shield nascent manufacturers from foreign competition so that they could become competitive in world markets was much more acceptable to classical economists in the early nineteenth century, particularly John Stuart Mill, than to Smith. Smith also would have been skeptical of industrial policy, in which government directs resources to certain industries.

Having rejected the case for restricting imports, Smith moved on to reject the case for promoting exports. He scoffed at government efforts to increase exports through artificial methods such as bounties and subsidies, remarking that "trade which cannot be carried on but by means of a bounty" is "necessarily a losing trade" (WN IV.v.a.24). He explained that a country could not force other countries to buy its goods, but it could pay them (through subsidies) to buy them. But without the subsidy, merchants would devote their resources to other activities, and therefore the effect of the subsidy would be to "force the trade of a country into a channel much less advantageous than that in which it would naturally run of its own accord" (WN IV.v.a.1–3).

Smith closed out his analysis of trade policy by explaining that the problem with mercantilism was not its goal of encouraging economic progress, but the means by which that goal was to be achieved. The "laudable motive" of all the mercantilist regulations was to promote one's own manufacturers, but it sought to do this by harming those of other countries and putting an end to competition (WN IV.viii.48).

In Smith's view, the commendable goal of improving the economy became distorted by special interests that influenced governments to intervene on their behalf and to the detriment of national welfare. The architects of the mercantilist system were not consumers, whose interests were neglected, but producers, who were the principal beneficiaries of government policy. But this was wrong because, Smith argued, "consumption is the sole end and purpose of all production" and the government ought to look out for producer interests only to the extent that it was necessary to help consumers. Unfortunately, under the mercantilist system, "the interest of the consumer is almost constantly sacrificed to that of the producer" because that system considers production rather than consumption as the chief objective of commerce and industry. This explains why governments were so willing to restrict the importation of foreign goods to the benefit of producers and the detriment of consumers (WN IV.viii.49–50).

Indeed, Smith was quite cynical about the role of special interests in getting governments to intervene on their behalf. In one letter he wrote that import restrictions and export subsidies were "a complete piece of dupery, by which the interest of the State and the nation is constantly sacrificed to that of some particular class of traders" (CAS 272).

EXCEPTIONS

Smith had strong convictions about the benefits of a liberal system of trade and the costs of government-directed trade. Yet he was not dogmatic or ideological. He was a pragmatic advocate of free trade who conceded two cases in which import duties would be acceptable and made two possible exceptions to his general position.

Smith saw two instances in which import duties were justifiable. The first is when a particular industry is necessary for national defense (WN IV.ii.24). As an example Smith pointed to the Navigation Laws, which gave the British merchant marine a monopoly on the country's foreign trade. The purpose of the laws was to increase the number of British ships and sailors that would be available, if needed, for Britain's defense against foreign invasion or attack. Smith acknowledged that such laws did not encourage commerce and actually reduced the nation's wealth, but he still felt they were justified because, as he put it, defense "is of much more importance than opulence." Consequently, the Navigation Acts were perhaps "the wisest of all the commercial regulations of England" (WN IV.ii.30). This statement implicitly recognizes that national security could be purchased only through the material sacrifice of other desirable goods. By accepting this trade-off, Smith believed that protecting defense-related industries justified protecting them against import competition.[9]

The second exception concerned the equalization of taxes on domestic and foreign goods when domestic goods were subject to taxes not levied on foreign goods. Fairness dictated that equivalent duties be imposed on imports to equalize the tax treatment of domestic and foreign goods. Such duties would not alter the "natural" allocation of resources between domestic and foreign industry and would leave the two on the same footing (WN IV.ii.31).

Smith also discussed two other practical considerations in which a country's policy makers should deliberate about whether to employ import duties. The first concerned the question of whether a country should pursue a policy of free trade when some of its trading partners did not. Smith thought that "revenge in this case naturally dictates retaliation" and that a country should respond by imposing like restrictions on imports from the offending country. But Smith's characteristically practical advice was that retaliation would be a good policy if there was a high likelihood that foreign countries would respond by opening up their market. ("The recovery of a great foreign market will generally more than compensate the transitory inconveniency of paying dearer during a short time for some sorts of goods.") Only politicians, not political econo-mists, could make such a judgment. But Smith advised against re-taliation "when there is no probability that any such repeal can be procured" because "it seems a bad method of compensating the injury done to certain classes of our people, to do another injury ourselves, not only to those classes, but to almost all the other classes of them" (WN IV.ii.39).

Thus, Smith essentially argues that it is hard to establish an un-bending principle about the merits of retaliation against foreign trade restrictions. Smith clearly viewed retaliation as a question of tactics, not of strategy. The fundamental principle was still clear: free trade should be pursued independently of other countries' policies. But if a country can affect the trade policies of its trading partners, a tactical complication is introduced. Economic analysis in itself is of little guidance because it cannot indicate the circumstances under which a given retaliatory action will or will not reduce for-eign trade barriers.

The second "matter of deliberation" concerned the speed with which import duties were reduced in moving toward freer trade. Lower trade barriers would increase imports and harm domestic producers that competed against those goods.[10] To minimize this adjustment problem, Smith recommended that import duties be reduced gradually. As he put it, "Humanity may in this case re-quire that the freedom of trade should be restored only by slow gradations, and with a good deal of reserve and circumspection" (WN IV.ii.40). To reduce the duties all at once might cause im-ports to flood into the market, causing considerable disorder that would deprive many workers of their means of subsistence (WN IV.ii.40)

At the same time, Smith believed that the dislocation of labor and capital as a result of import competition was much less of a problem than commonly imagined. First, he believed that foreign products were imperfect substitutes for domestic goods and there-fore domestic producers were to some extent insulated from for-eign competition. Second, he believed that labor and capital could adjust and find employment elsewhere, pointing to the relatively quick reemployment of a large number of newly unemployed sol-diers after a recent war.

ADAM SMITH'S LEGACY

Smith's goal in writing the *Wealth of Nations* was not simply to provide a systematic treatise on economics but to influence contemporary British policy. Book IV of the *Wealth of Nations* contained what Smith called a "very violent attack . . . upon the whole commercial system of Great Britain" (CAS 251). But he did not believe that his work would have an immediate impact on policy. "To expect, indeed, that the freedom of trade should ever be entirely restored in Great Britain is as absurd as to expect that an Oceana or Utopia should ever be established in it," he wrote. "Not only the prejudices of the public, but what is much more unconquerable, the private interests of many individuals, irresistibly oppose it" (WN IV.ii.43). Still, Smith must have hoped that his ideas would have an impact on British policy makers, as indeed seems to have been the case.[11]

Smith certainly inspired the work of the classical economists in the early nineteenth century, such as David Ricardo and John Stuart Mill, who were as critical of trade restrictions as Smith had been. Smith's work also encouraged political activists such as Richard Cobden, whose Anti–Corn Law League played a major role in shifting public opinion in the 1840s against the restrictions on wheat imports. Indeed, British trade policy underwent far-reaching reforms in the period from 1830 to 1850, including the abolition of the East India Company's monopoly, the elimination of the West Indies sugar preferences, the repeal of the Corn Laws, and the abandonment of the Navigation Acts.

Of course, Smith did not have the final word on trade policy matters. The debate over the costs and benefits of trade restrictions has never ended. In many countries outside Britain, doctrines contrary to Smith's arose and proposed import restrictions as a way of strengthening the economy. Friedrich List, the German author of *The National System of Political Economy* (1841), proved to be Smith's intellectual counterpart in the mid-nineteenth century. He argued that a nation's productive powers, not its ability to consume, were most important and the proper object of government policy. To this end, he concluded, under certain circumstances, import restrictions in support of infant industries and manufactures would be beneficial. For much of the early twentieth century, Smith's ideas were thought to have little relevance either for developing countries (which, it was thought, could not rely on the free market and free trade to foster economic development) or for developed countries (whose governments also play a major role in channeling investment and regulating private enterprise).[12]

Yet disillusionment with the outcome of "import substitution" policies that sought to promote domestic production by restricting imports after World War II led economists to emphasize trade liberalization and export-orientation starting in the 1980s.[13] In particular, the experience of East Asian countries in the 1960s and 1970s demonstrated to most observers that trade expansion is a path to greater prosperity. Yet there remains a serious debate over the pros and cons of "industrial policy," focused not so much on trade restrictions as on indirect government support for domestic industries. Adam Smith still lurks in the background of this debate.

NOTES

1. While not all of his arguments were original, Smith significantly advanced the case for free trade by providing an underlying logic and framework in which the ideas made sense; see Douglas A. Irwin, *Against the Tide: An Intellectual History of Free Trade* (Princeton: 1996). Although "all the important elements in Smith's free-trade doctrine had been presented prior to the Wealth of Nations," Jacob Viner, *Studies in the Theory of International Trade* (New York: 1937), p. 108, rightly notes, "these were often, however, to be found only in isolated passages not wholly consistent with the views expounded in the surrounding text."

2. In focusing on Smith's views on trade policy, this chapter does not examine his views on why countries engage in international trade. On that, see Arthur Bloomfield, "Adam Smith and the Theory of International Trade," in *Essays on Adam Smith*, ed. Andrew Skinner and Thomas Wilson (Oxford: 1975) and H. Myint, "Adam Smith's Theory of International Trade in the Perspective of Economic Development," *Economica* 44 (1977), pp. 231–48.

3. This passage recognizes that a government might have to levy taxes on imports in order to raise revenue.

4. LJA vi.163–66.

5. See also the famous invisible hand statement (WN IV.ii.9). An important caveat is that incentives must be properly aligned to ensure that individual gain comes from serving the public good; see Nathan Rosenberg, "Some Institutional

Aspects of the Wealth of Nations," *Journal of Political Economy* 68 (1960), pp. 557–70, for a penetrating and insightful discussion of this theme in Smith's work.

6. The classic reference is Jacob Viner, "Adam Smith and Laissez Faire," *Journal of Political Economy* 35 (1926), pp. 198–232, but also see Samuel Hollander, "Adam Smith: Market-Failure Pioneer and Champion of 'Natural Liberty,'" in *Essays on Classical and Marxian Political Economy* (New York: 2013).

7. These two passages have been extensively debated; see Bruce Elmslie and Norman Sedgley, "Vent for Surplus: A Case of Mistaken Identity," *Southern Economic Journal* 68 (2002), pp. 712–20.

8. "Were the Americans . . . to stop the importation of European manufactures, and, thus by giving a monopoly to such of their own countrymen as could manufacture the like goods, divert any considerable part of their capital into this employment, they would retard instead of accelerating the further increase in the value of their annual produce, and would obstruct instead of promoting the progress of their country towards real wealth and greatness" (WN II.v.21). Smith is also skeptical of infant industry policies at WN IV.ix.26.

9. "If any particular manufacture was necessary, indeed, for the defence of the society, it might not always be prudent to depend upon our neighbours for the supply; and if such manufacture could not otherwise be supported at home, it might not be unreasonable that all the other branches of industry should be taxed in order to support it. The bounties upon the exportation of British-made sail-cloth and British-made gun-powder may, perhaps, both be vindicated upon this principle" (WN IV.v.a.36).

10. "If the free importation of foreign manufactures were permitted, several of the home manufactures would probably suffer, and some of them, perhaps, go to ruin altogether, and a considerable part of the stock and industry at present employed in them would be forced to find out some other employment" (WN IV.ii.16).

11. James Ashley Morrison, "Before Hegemony: Adam Smith, American Independence, and the Origins of the First Era of Globalization," *International Organization* 66 (2012), pp. 395–428.

12. For a discussion of whether this is the case, see H. Myint, "Adam Smith's Theory of International Trade."

13. Anne O. Krueger, "Trade Policy and Economic Development: How We Learn," *American Economic Review* 87 (1997), pp. 1–22.

BIBLIOGRAPHIC ESSAY

The secondary literature on Adam Smith is enormous, something that is also true regarding the topic of free trade.

What was the intellectual context in which Smith arrived at his views on trade and trade policy? This issue is taken up in Richard Teichgraeber, *Free Trade and Moral Philosophy: Rethinking the*

Sources of Adam Smith's Wealth of Nations (Durham, NC: 1986). On the issue of free trade specifically, see Douglas A. Irwin, *Against the Tide: An Intellectual History of Free Trade* (Princeton: 1996).

Smith's ideas are often believed to have affected the course of trade policy around the world. For a recent article making the case that Smith was indeed influential in British policy circles, see James Ashley Morrison, "Before Hegemony: Adam Smith, American Independence, and the Origins of the First Era of Globalization," *International Organization* 66 (2012), pp. 395–428.

In terms of Smith's theory of international trade, there is no better place to start than Arthur Bloomfield's classic essay "Adam Smith and the Theory of International Trade," in *Essays on Adam Smith*, ed. A. S. Skinner and T. Wilson (Oxford: 1975). Also see Hla Myint, "Adam Smith's Theory of International Trade in the Perspective of Economic Development," *Economica* 44 (1977), pp. 231–48.

On Smith's spirited attack on the mercantilist system, see A. W. Coats, "Adam Smith and the Mercantile System," in Skinner and Wilson, *Essays on Adam Smith*. Also see Gary M. Anderson and Robert D. Tollison, "Sir James Steuart as the Apotheosis of Mercantilism and His Relation to Adam Smith," *Southern Economic Journal* 51 (1984), pp. 456–68. Also see Gary M. Anderson and Robert D. Tollison, "Adam Smith's Analysis of Joint-Stock Companies," *Journal of Political Economy* 90 (1982), pp. 1237–56.

development economics, 281–301; defining, 283; and education, 290–92; and inequality, 298–301; limits of the market and, 287–89; market errors and, 292–94; market theory and, 283–85; and motivation, 295–98; and poverty, 289–90; Smith's analysis of early development and trade, 285–86

Dick, Robert, 5

Dickens, Charles, 220, 489

didactic discourse, 21–22, 26–27, 29

Diderot, Denis, 446, 489

dignity, 188–89, 190n13

discourse, kinds of, 21–23

"A Dissertation on the Origin of Languages," 7

distributive justice, 145, 159–60

division of labor, 68–69, 75, 242, 446–47, 500, 546. *See also* specialization

Dockwra Copper Company, 447

Douglas, David (cousin), 9

Douglas, Janet (cousin), 6, 7, 9

Douglas, Margaret (mother), 4, 6, 7, 9, 106, 305

Drayton, Richard, 449

Drescher, Seymour, 448, 451

Dubos, Jean-Baptiste, 390, 436

duty, 108–10, 176

Du Weiming, 519

Dworkin, Ronald, 371

East India Company, 554

economic development. *See* development economics

economic growth, 241–42, 527–28

economic liberalism, 515–17

economics: moral philosophy in relation to, 282; neoclassical, 517; Smith's place in, 243–44, 423–24. *See also* development economics; experimental economics; modern economics

economization, 500–502

Edelstein, Dan, 443–45

Edinburgh, 4–5, 8–11, 17, 48, 105–6, 110–11, 114–16, 256, 390, 455

education, 84, 217, 290–92, 329, 505

egalitarianism: esteem, 157, 162–66; as feature of political left, 481; moderate, 157–62, 166–69; radical, 157, 168; types of, 157–58

egoism, 192

Ehrenreich, Barbara, 489

Elliot, Gilbert, 41

El Saadawi, Nawal, 367

emotion: and justice/law, 372; in rhetorical theory, 21; role of, in knowledge development, 92–94, 101, 112. *See also* sentiments; *specific emotions*

emotional contagion, 193–95, 199–201, 359, 419n4

empathy, 21, 141, 194, 358

empiricism, 433

Encyclopedists, 436, 446, 447

Engels, Friedrich, 489

enkráteia, 149–51. *See also* self-command

Enlightenment: Chinese study of, 520–21; concept of self in, 340; and empire, 448–53; English, 435–36, 445; French, 436; industrial, 445–48; and the natural environment, 453–55; scholarship on, 443–45, 448–49; science of man as goal of, 105; Smith's place in, 443–55, 520–21. *See also* Scottish Enlightenment

Enron, 532

enthusiasm, 315

environment, natural, 453–55

Epicureans, 143, 147, 430

Epicurus, 430

equality, 44–45, 157–69, 504; commercial society as threat to, 162–66; the market and, 159; policies detrimental to, 159; Smith's moderate egalitarianism, 157–62; types of egalitarianism, 157–58. *See also* inequality

equilibrium economics, 264

equilibrium price, 233

Erhard, Ludwig Wilhelm, 516

Essays on Philosophical Subjects by the Late Adam Smith, LL.D. (Smith), 89–102; on astronomy, 94–97; knowledge development as theme of, 92–97, 100–101; on physics and logic, 97–99; publication and editions of, 10, 89–90, 102n2, 102n3

esteem. *See* praiseworthiness

esteem egalitarianism, 157, 162–66

ethics. *See* feminist ethics; modern ethics; morality

eudaimonism, 188

evolutionary thought, 100, 311, 496–97

exchange. *See* "truck, barter, and exchange"